# Nineteenth-Century Wind Band and Wind Ensemble Repertoire

## Books by David Whitwell

*Philosophic Foundations of Education*
*Foundations of Music Education*
*Music Education of the Future*
*The Sousa Oral History Project*
*The Art of Musical Conducting*
*The Longy Club: 1900–1917*
*A Concise History of the Wind Band*
*Wagner on Bands*
*Berlioz on Bands*
*Chopin: A Self-Portrait*
*La Téléphonie and the Universal Musical Language*
*Extraordinary Women*
*Aesthetics of Music in Ancient Civilizations*
*Aesthetics of Music in the Middle Ages*
*Aesthetics of Music in the Early Renaissance*

## The History and Literature of the Wind Band and Wind Ensemble Series

*Volume 1 The Wind Band and Wind Ensemble Before 1500*
*Volume 2 The Renaissance Wind Band and Wind Ensemble*
*Volume 3 The Baroque Wind Band and Wind Ensemble*
*Volume 4 The Wind Band and Wind Ensemble of the Classical Period (1750–1800)*
*Volume 5 The Nineteenth-Century Wind Band and Wind Ensemble*
*Volume 6 A Catalog of Multi-Part Repertoire for Wind Instruments or for Undesignated Instrumentation before 1600*
*Volume 7 Baroque Wind Band and Wind Ensemble Repertoire*
*Volume 8 Classical Period Wind Band and Wind Ensemble Repertoire*
*Volume 9 Nineteenth-Century Wind Band and Wind Ensemble Repertoire*
*Volume 10 A Supplementary Catalog of Wind Band and Wind Ensemble Repertoire*
*Volume 11 A Catalog of Wind Repertoire before the Twentieth Century for One to Five Players*
*Volume 12 A Second Supplementary Catalog of Early Wind Band and Wind Ensemble Repertoire*
*Volume 13 Name Index, Volumes 1–12, The History and Literature of the Wind Band and Wind Ensemble*

www.whitwellbooks.com

*David Whitwell*

# Nineteenth-Century Wind Band and Wind Ensemble Repertoire

THE HISTORY AND LITERATURE OF THE WIND BAND AND WIND ENSEMBLE, VOLUME 9

EDITED BY CRAIG DABELSTEIN

WHITWELL PUBLISHING • AUSTIN, TEXAS, USA

Whitwell Publishing, Austin 78701
www.whitwellbooks.com

© 1984, 2012 by David Whitwell
All rights reserved. First edition 1984.
Second edition 2012

Printed in the United States of America

PAPERBACK
ISBN-13: 978-1-936512-46-1
ISBN-10: 1936512467

All images used in this book are in the public domain except where otherwise noted.

Composed in Bembo Book

# Contents

|   |   |   |
|---|---|---|
|    | Foreword | vii |
|    | Instrumentation code | ix |
|    | Text abbreviations | ix |
|    | Secondary Sources | x |
|    | Library Abbreviations | xi |
|    | Acknowledgements | xvii |
| 1  | France | 1 |
| 2  | Italy | 115 |
| 3  | Finland | 123 |
| 4  | The Netherlands | 125 |
| 5  | Norway | 127 |
| 6  | Poland | 129 |
| 7  | Spain | 131 |
| 6  | Sweden | 133 |
| 8  | Union of Soviet Socialist Republics | 135 |
| 9  | The United States of America | 137 |
| 10 | Germany | 141 |
| 11 | Austria | 203 |
| 12 | Belgium | 259 |
| 13 | Denmark | 261 |
| 14 | England | 263 |
|    | Index | 283 |
|    | About The Author | 309 |

# Foreword

THIS VOLUME, FIRST PUBLISHED IN 1984, IS THE NINTH, and a companion to the fifth volume, in the series, *The History and Literature of the Wind Band and Wind Ensemble*, comprised of the following volumes:

1. The Wind Band and Wind Ensemble before 1500
2. The Renaissance Wind Band and Wind Ensemble
3. The Baroque Wind Band and Wind Ensemble
4. The Classical Period Wind Band and Wind Ensemble
5. The Nineteenth-Century Wind Band and Wind Ensemble
6. A Catalog of Multi-Part Repertoire for Wind Instruments or for Undesignated Instrumentation before 1600
7. Baroque Wind Band and Wind Ensemble Repertoire
8. Classical Period Wind Band and Wind Ensemble Repertoire
9. Nineteenth-Century Wind Band and Wind Ensemble Repertoire
10. A Supplementary Catalog of Early Band and Wind Ensemble Repertoire
11. A Catalog of Wind Repertoire before the Twentieth Century for One to Five Players
12. A Second Supplementary Catalog of Early Wind Band and Wind Ensemble Repertoire
13. Name Index, Volumes 1–12, The History and Literature of the Wind Band and Wind Ensemble

The present volume presents sources for more than 20,000 manuscripts and early prints for large wind ensemble or band from the nineteenth century. While that is, taken by itself, a significant body of repertoire, it is nevertheless important to remind the reader that this is only a small portion of the extant nineteenth-century wind literature, in particular with regard to the military band.

First, I set out to record only sources for original works, not transcribed band music. However, I did, over the years, write down a few call-numbers of transcriptions which were of interest to me and I have included those. But, I hasten to add that I have seen thousands upon thousands of similar arrangements, both published and manuscript, in European libraries, which I did not bother to record in my notes.

Second, I know of a number of military music collections which the libraries themselves have not yet cataloged. Therefore, since it seems apparent that my lifetime will be too brief to compile a 'complete' catalog of nineteenth-century wind ensemble and military band music, I can only offer the following volume in the hope that others will continue to add to our profession's knowledge of the wind music of this century by expanding upon it.

Where I could not firmly identify the nationality of a composer, I have listed him under the country where his music was published or currently resides in a library. I have left spellings as they are found in library shelf-marks even in cases of apparent errors.

David Whitwell<br>Austin, Texas

# Instrumentation Code

As an abbreviation for wind instrumentation I use a code of 0000-0000, representing: flute, oboe, clarinet, bassoon - trumpet, horn, trombone, tuba.

Thus:

    3000-          means a work for three flutes
    -204           means a work for two trumpets and four trombones
    1-1; 2 cornetts  means bassoon, trumpet, and two cornetts.

# Text Abbreviations

MS    Manuscript
EP    Early print
MP    Modern print

# Secondary Sources

In some cases I have given information on works which I myself have not found in libraries; in these cases the source for my information is represented by abbreviations given in [brackets], the full titles for which are given here.

| | |
|---|---|
| AM | Anton Meysel, *Handbuch der musikalischen Litteratur* ... (1817, supplements to 1827) |
| AMZ | *Allgemeine Musikalische Zeitung* (Leipzig) |
| DJ | Donald Johnson [University of Montana], 'Wind Music List' (Ripon College, Wisconsin) |
| DT | Douglas Townsend, New York City |
| Eitner | Robert Eitner, *Biographish-bibliographisches Quellen-Lexikon* (1900–1904) |
| F | François-Joseph Fétis, *Biographie universelle* (1978–1880) |
| G1, G2 | Ernst Ludwig Gerber, *Historisch biographisches Lexikon der Tonkünstler* (Leipzig, 1790–1792); and *Neues historisch biographisches Lexikon der Tonkünstler* (Leipzig, 1812–1814) |
| Grove | *The New Grove Dictionary of Music and Musicians* (Stanley Sadie, ed., 1980) |
| H | Roger Hellyer, 'Harmoniemusic' (Dissertation, Oxford, 1973) |
| HA | Bruce Haynes, *Catalog of Chamber Music for Oboe* (1980) |
| Jerkowitz | 'Thematische Verzeichniss by Jos Jerkowitz Schasslowitz den 1 July 1832' (now in BRD:Mbs [Mus.Ms.6330]) |
| MAB | *Musica Antiqua Bohemica* (Prague) |
| MGG | *Die Musik in Geschichte und Gegenwart* (Friedrich Blume, ed., 1949-1968) |
| MH | Miroslav Hosek, *Oben Bibliographie* (Wilhelmshaven, 1975) |
| RA | Rudolph Angermüller, *Sigismund Neukomm Werkverzeichnis. Autobiographie, Beziehung zu seinen Zeitgenossen* (Munich, 1977) |
| SJK | S. James Kurtz, 'A Study and Catalog of Ensemble Music ... ca. 1700 to ca. 1825' (Dissertation, University of Iowa, 1971) |
| Veit | Gottfried Veit, *Die Blasmusik* (Innsbruck, 1972) |
| WZ | *Wiener Zeitung* |

# Library Abbreviations for this Catalog

Where the location of a work is known, the library is given in abbreviation according to the following international R.I.S.M. system as was current in 1984. Shelf-marks, or call-numbers, are given immediately after the library abbreviations and contained by (parentheses). I have given many works which are no longer believed to exist for the purpose of expanding the reader's perspective of the wind music of this period.

In the interval since this catalog was first published in 1984 there has been a reunification of Germany with the result that the old R.I.S.M. library symbols have been changed and indeed in many cases the music has been moved to the Staatsbibliothek in Berlin. In this catalog, however, we retain the old R.I.S.M. symbols and shelf-mark because even in those cases where the music has been moved to a new location the old information is necessary for the new library to identify these specific manuscripts for those who may want copies today.

## A: Austria

| | |
|---|---|
| Ee | Eisenstadt, Esterházy-Archiv (secular music now in H:Bn) |
| Gk | Graz, Hochschule für Musik |
| Llm | Linz, Oberösterreichisches Landesmuseum |
| M | Melk an der Donau, Benediktiner-Stift Melk |
| Sca | Salzburg, Museum Carolino Augusteum, Bibliothek |
| Smsb | _____, Mozarteum, Student Bibliothek |
| TU | Tulln, Katholisches Pfarramt Tulln |
| WatSW | Wien, Archiv, Trumpetchors der Stadt |
| Wgm | _____, Gesellschaft der Musikfreunde in Wien |
| Wmi | _____, Musikwissenschaftliches Institut der Universität |
| Wn | _____, Österreichische Nationalbibliothek, Musiksammlung |
| Wn-h | _____, Österreichische Nationalbibliothek, Sammlung Anthony van Hoboken |
| Wph | _____, Wiener Philharmoniker Archiv |
| Wst | _____, Stadtbibliothek, Musiksammlung |

## B: Belgium

| | |
|---|---|
| Bc | Bruxelles, Conservatoire Royal de Musique, Bibliothèque |
| Lc | Liège, Conservatoire Royal de Musique, Bibliothèque |

XII LIBRARY ABBREVIATIONS

## BRD: WEST GERMANY (BUNDESREPUBLIK DEUTSCHLAND)

| | |
|---|---|
| AB | Amorbach, Fürstlich Leiningische Bibliothek |
| AM | Amberg, Staatliche Provinzialbibliothek |
| B | Berlin, Staatsbibliothek, Musiksammlung |
| Bhm | ____, Staatliche Hochschule für Musik |
| BAR | Bartenstein, Fürst zu Hohenlohe-Bartensteinsches Archiv |
| BFb | Burgsteinfurt, Fürstlich Bentheimsche Bibliothek (now in MÜu) |
| BUu | (a few titles were sent me under this code by a correspondent. The library is the same as that given as BRD:BFb.) |
| DO | Donaueschingen, Fürstlich Fürstenbergische Hofbibliothek |
| DS | Darmstadt, Hessische Landes- und Hochschulbibliothek |
| DT | Detmold, Lippische Landesbibliothek |
| DUl | Düsseldorf, Universitätsbibliothek |
| F | Frankfurtl Main, Stadt- und Universitätsbibliothek |
| GSA | Garmisch, Strauss Archiv |
| HL | Haltenbergstetten, Schloss über Niederstetten, Fürst zu Hohenlohe-Jagstberg'sche Bibliothek |
| HR | Harburg, Fürstlich Öttingen-Wallerstein'sche Bibliothek, Schloss Harburg |
| IN | Indersdorf über Dachau (Bayern), Katholisches Pfarramt (Bibliothek des Augustiner- Chorherrenstiftes) |
| Mbs | München, Bayerische Staatsbibliothek, Musiksammlung |
| MGmi | Marburg, Betriebseinheit Musikwissenschaft im Im Fachbereich Geschichtswissenschaften der Philipps-Universität Marburg |
| MÜu | Münster Universitätsbibliothek |
| MZsch | Maiuz, Musikverlag Schott |
| OF | Offenbach, Verlagsarchiv André |
| Rtt | Regensburg, Fürstlich Thurn und Taxissche Hofbibliothek |
| RH | (sometimes, Rheda) Rheda, Fürst zu BentheimTecklenburgische Bibliothek |
| Sl | Stuttgart, Württembergische Landesbibliothek |
| Tmi | Tübingen, Musikwissenschaftliches Institut der Universität |
| Tu | ____, Universitätsbibliothek der Eberhard-Karls-Universität |
| TEG | Benediktbeuern, Pfarrkirche, Bibliothek (formerly BB) |
| TSCH | Tübingen, Musikwissenschaftliches Institut der Eberdhard-Karls-Universitäts (now contains this collection) |
| WERl | Wertheim, Fürstlich Löwenstein'sche Bibliothek |
| WS | Wasserburg, Chorarchiv St. Jakob, Pfarramt |

## CH: Switzerland

| | |
|---|---|
| Bmi | Basel, Bibliothek des Musikwissenschaftlichen Instituts der Universität Basel |
| Bu | ____, Öffentliche Bibliothek der Universität Basel, Musiksammlung |
| E | Einsiedeln, Kloster Einsiedeln, Musikbibliothek |
| SO | Solothurn, Zentralbibliothek, Musiksammlung |
| Zz | Zurich, Zentralbibliothek |

## CS: Czechoslovakia

| | |
|---|---|
| BA | Bakov, Boleslav |
| Bm | Brno, Moravské muzeum, 'Ústav dejin hudby |
| K | Ceský Krumlov, Státní arhív Trebon |
| KRa | Kromeríz Státní zámek a zahrady |
| Kkpm | ____, Kostela p. Marie |
| Ksm | ____, Archiv Collegiate Church of St. Maurice (now in KRa) |
| MH | Mnichovo Hradiste, Mestsk'muzeum |
| Pk | Prag, Konservato' v Praze, hudebni archiv |
| Pnm | ____, Národni muzeum, hudební oddelení |
| Pu | ____, Státní knihovna CSR Universitní knihovna, hudební oddelení |

## DDR: East Germany (Deutsche Demokratische Republik)

| | |
|---|---|
| B | Berlin (used here only with East Berlin private collections) |
| Bds | ____, Deutsche Staatsbibliothek, Musikabteilung |
| Bu | ____, Universitätsbibliothek der HumboldtUniversität |
| Dl(b) | Dresden, Sächsische Landesbibliothek, Musikabteilung |
| Dmb | ____, Musikbibliothek |
| HER | Herrnhut, Archiv der Brüder-Unität |
| RUl | Rudolstadt, Staatsarchiv |
| SWl | Schwerin, Wissenschaftliche Allgemeinbibliothek |
| WRgs | Weimar, Goethe-Schiller-Archiv |
| WRl | ____, Staatsarchiv |

## DK: Denmark

| | |
|---|---|
| A | Arhus, Statsbiblioteket i Arhus |
| Kk | Kobenhavn, Det kongelige Bibliotek |

## E: Spain

Mbmc          Madrid, Biblioteca Musical Circulante

## F: France

Pn            Paris, Bibliothèque nationale

## GB: Great Britain

En            Edinburgh, National Library of Scotland
Lbbc          London, British Broadcasting Corporation, Music Library
Lbm           _____, The British Museum
Lcm           _____, Royal College of Music

## H: Hungary

Bn            Budapest, Országos Szécneny Könyvtár
KE            Keszthely, Helikon Kastélymúzeum

## I: Italy

Baf           Bologna, Archivio dell'Accademia filarmonica
Bc            _____, Civico Museo Bibliografico-Musicale
Bl            _____, Conservatorio di Musica G. B. Martini
Bsf           _____, Archivio del Convento di San Francesco
BGc           Bergamo, Biblioteca Civica 'A. Mai'
BGi           _____, Civico Istituto musicale 'G. Donizetti'
CR            Cremona, Biblioteca statale
Fc            Firenze, Biblioteca del Conservatorio di Musica
Ls            Lucca, Biblioteca del seminario arcivescovile presso la Curia
Mc            Milano, Biblioteca del Conservatorio
MBSF          _____, Biblioteca La Cappella della Basilica di S. Francesco
MOe           Modena, Biblioteca Estense
MZ            Monza, Biblioteca del Duomo
Nc            Napoli, Biblioteca del Conservatorio di Musica
PAc           Parma, Sezione Musicale della Biblioteca Palatina presso il Conservatorio 'Arrigo Boito'
PSas          _____, Archivio di Stato [now in PAc]
PCd           Piacenza, Archivio del Duomo
PLcon         Palermo, Biblioteca del Conservatorio 'V. Bellini'
Vc            Venezia, Biblioteca del Conservatorio 'Benedetto Marcello'

| | |
|---|---|
| Vcr | \_\_\_\_, Pia Casa di Ricovero |
| Vsmc | \_\_\_\_, S. Maria della Consolazione detta 'della Fava' |
| VCdr | \_\_\_\_, (same as Vcr) |
| VLd | \_\_\_\_, Archivio e Bibl. capitolare del Duomo |

## NL: The Netherlands

| | |
|---|---|
| Ura/mZ | Zeist, Archief van de Evangelische Broedergemeente |

## PL: Poland

| | |
|---|---|
| LA | Lancut, Biblioteka, muzyczna zamku w Lancucie |
| Wbu | Warszawa, Biblioteka Uniwersytecka |

## S: Sweden

| | |
|---|---|
| Skma | Stockholm, Kungliga Musikaliska Akademiens Bibliotek |

## US: The United States of America

| | |
|---|---|
| BETm | Bethlehem, Archives of the Moravian Church |
| Bp | Boston, Boston Public Library |
| CDhs | Concord (NH), New Hampshire Historical Society Library |
| DI | Des Moines (Iowa), Iowa State Department of History |
| DT | New York City, private collection, Douglas Townsend |
| DW | Private collection of David Whitwell, now in the Bundesakademie für Musik, Trossingen, Germany |
| HO | Hopkinton (NH), New Hampshire Antiquarian Society |
| MHs | Manchester, New Hampshire Public Library |
| NH | New Haven (Conn), Yale University Library |
| NYp | New York, New York Public Library |
| PHf | Philadelphia, Philadelphia Free Library |
| R | Rochester, Sibley Music Library, Eastman School of Music |
| SA | Salem (Mass), Essex Institute Library |
| Wc | Washington, D.C., Library of Congress |
| WOa | Worcester (Mass), American Antiquarian Society Library |
| WS(Mor) | Winston-Salem, Moravian Music Foundation |

# Acknowledgments

The reader is indebted for the second edition of this book to Mr. Craig Dabelstein of Brisbane, Australia. Without his contribution to design and all things involved as an editor this book would never again have been available.

David Whitwell<br>Austin, 2012

# France

## Collections

*Marches: Danses, et Pas redoublés*
Harmoniemusik
EP (Paris, Schlesinger) [Suites 1–3]

*Journal de Musique militaire*
1042-12, serpent, percussion
EP (Lyon, Leroy) CH:Zz (XIII 3074, a-L)
Contains 37 compositions.

*Journal d'Harmonie* (Compose par une Soc. d'Artistes)
1222-12, serpent
EP (Lyon, Chanel) CH:Zz (XIII 3075, a-L)
Contains 37 compositions.

*Journal d'Harmonie à l'Usage des Musiques militaire*
Harmoniemusik
EP (Paris, Leduc) [in 12 Livraisons]
Contains works by Blasius, Jadin and Bochsa.

*Journal d'Harmonie militaire* (redigé par Louis, Berr et Münchs)
Harmoniemusik
EP (Paris, Pacini) [1ère Année, Liv. 1–41]

*Journal de la Renaissance des Musiques militaires*
Large wind band [pre-saxophone]
EP (Paris, Tournier) [scores] F:Pn (L.3572)

Volume 1 contains 19 original compositions by Narcisse Bousquet (Chevalier de la Légion d'Honneur), Douard (Chef d. M. 51e de Ligne), Frisnais (Chief d. M. 34e de Ligne), J. B. Labric (C. d. M. 23e de Ligne), C. Bonnot (C. d. M. 14e de Ligne), E. Hemet, Victor Gandner, V. Bretonnière, including one of his marches, wild and oriental in character, J. Coll, H. Cousin (C. d. M. 2nd Rég. Da Génie), C. Bru (C. d. M. 8e de Ligne), A. Josneau and Renault.

Volume 2 contains 8 original works by A. Douard, including an overture, Alexandre Artus, T. Pilliard (C. d. M. 3e Rég. d'Inf. le Marine), L. Luce, including an overture, E. Boue (C. d. M. 13e Léger), A. Cappon and L. A. Dessane, including an especially lengthy and interesting overture.

Volume 3 contains 19 original compositions by N. Bousquet [4], including powerful *Marches funèbre et religieux,* Gurtner [4], L. Luce (Chevalier de la Légion d'Honneur), including a fine *Morceau de repos et religieux,* Bonnot, Douart, G. Loustallot, Hte. Niessel (Eléve au Gymnase Musical Militaire), M. Traut, Emile Jonas (Professeur au Conservatoire Impérial), J. Raffara, Léon Chic, including a *Domine Salvum* for TTBB and band, E. Goguelat (C. de M. 56e), and J. Coll (C. de M. 66e de Ligne).

Volume 4 contains 18 original compositions by Sellenik (C. de M. 2e Régiment de Voltigeurs de la Garde Impériale), including a march which appears to be an early band work with saxophone parts, Gurtner [3], including a *Valse* with solo bassoon, Bousquet [3], Bourdeau (C. d. M. 44e de Ligne), Rénault, including a musically interesting march, Lamiable, C. Aubert, including a musical *Polonaise,* G. Loustallot, Raffara (Eléve au Gymnase Musical Militaire), A. de Camas (Capitaine au 2e de Chasseurs à pied), Douard, L. Blanckeman.

Volume '4-bis' contains 7 compositions by:
L. Chic, including an arrangement of '*De La Promise*' with saxophones, including a saxophone solo part. This is followed by a long *Fantaisie* with many solo parts.
L. Luce, including an interesting and technically demanding *Morceau de Repos* and a major work, a *Grande Fantaisie* for solo trombone
Douard, a *Valse* for solo piccolo, and Gurtner (C. d. M. 4e d'Inf. de Ligne).

Volume 5 contains 8 original compositions by Gurtner, A. Guès, L. Chic, J. Viallon (Professeur de composition de l'ex Gymnase-musical-militaire) Douard, Blanckeman, Bousquet, and an anonymous composition, an Octet for six saxophones (petit B♭, soprano E♭, B♭, A♭, tenor in E♭, baritone in B♭), cornet, and snare drum!

Volume 6 contains 41 works, including several national songs, by Bousquet [10], including a *Morceau d'Élévation*, Gurtner [5], Engebert Brépsant (Chevalier de la Légion d'Honneur), Douard, Raffara, Ettling, Camas, Soland, Lamiable, Momigny, Loustallot, E. Jonas, Dumas (C. d. M. a bord du Montebello), G. C. Bru, Blanckeman, and Declerck.

*Fantaisies pour harmonie*
Large wind band
EP (Paris, Gambaro, 1857–1858)
This collection contains 12 original compositions and arrangements by Dallée, Brépsant, Douard [3], including a *Polonaise* for solo E♭ clarinet, Antoni, Gandner [5], and Chic.

*Journal des Fanfares*
Brass band
EP (score) (Paris) F:Pn (Vm.27.3663), containing compositions by:
  Bourgoin (Chef de Musique, 5e Lanciers), a wild solo work for alto saxophone, and an arrangement of an aria from Rossini's *Semiramide*
  Gariel (Chef de Musique, 2e Carabiniers), an arrangement from *Semiramide* for B♭ bugle
  Coqueterre (Chef de Musique, 13e Artillerie), a march, *La Napoleonienne*
  Dieppo, an *Air Varié* for solo trombone
  Buot, a *Valse* for brass band and soli bassoons
  Lacher (Chef de Musique, 9e Cuirassiers a Andrinople), a march
  Godefroid, *Bonheur,* a work for solo quartet (two cornets, baritone horn and alto saxophone) and brass band

## Anonymous

(2) *Pièces [marches] pour Orchestre d'harmonie*
Large wind band, without saxophones
MS [score] F:Pn (D.17294 and D.17295)

*Vivat Rex*, Pas redoublé
Fifteen-part Harmoniemusik
EP (Paris, Janet)

## Abadie

Pas redoublé, *La Favorite*
Large wind band
EP (Paris, 1853) F:Pn (Vm.7.15004)

## Abadie, Egbert

*Pas redoublé*
Brass band
EP (Paris, 1898) F:Pn (Vm.27.48)

## Abadie, Jacques

The following works in F:Pn are all early prints for large wind band, unless otherwise given; all were printed in Paris in 1852–1860.
*Adeste fedeles* (Vm.7.150000)
*Messe Solennelle* [Chorus and 1050-321, ophicleide, bass saxophone, contrabass saxophone, etc.] (Cons.D.1/1)
*Balbao* (Vm.7.15003)
*Overture de Démophon* (Vm.7.15007)
*De profundis* (Cons.D.1/5)
*Domine salvum* (Cons.D.1/2)
*O filii* [motet, arranged for band] (Cons.D.1/4)
*O salutaris* [3 voices with band] (Cons.D.1/9)
*Pas redoublé* (Vm.7.15005)
*Dies Irae* [3 voices with band] (Cons.D.1/18)
*La Reine Hortense, Marche heroique* (Vm.7.15001)
Pas redoublé, *La Revue* (Vm.7.15006)
*Rosate coeli* (Cons.D.1/6)
*Stabat mater* [chorus and band] (Cons.D.1/13 and Vm.1.2991/12)
*Victimae paschali* (Cons.D.1/12 and Vm.1.2591/14)
*Attende Domine* [3 voices with band] (Cons.D.1/3)
*Ave verum* [3 voices with band] (Cons.D.1/8)

## Abbiate, Charles

The following works in F:Pn are all early prints for large wind band; all were printed in Paris in 1881–1886.
March, *Mazeppa* (Vm.7.10.073)
Polka, *Chiffonnette* (Vm.7.10.071)
(2) Mazurkas, *Cousinette* (Vm.7.10.024), *Fomme d'api* (Vm.7.15.011)
*Pas redoublé* (Vm.7.10.072)

## Ackermann ('du 93e Reg. de Ligne')

*Pas redoublé* (Paris, 1855)
Large wind band
MS F:Pn (L.4821)

## Aerts, Felix

The following works in F:Pn are all early prints for large wind band; all were printed in Paris in 1855–1864.
*March religieuse, La Fête Dieu* (Vm.7.15041)
Pas redoublés: *Les Laurieres* (Vm.7.15043), *Le Montrouge* (Vm.7.15042), *L'Age d'or* (Vm.7.15044)
Quadrilles: *Le Repos de minuit* (Vm.7.15067), *Anacréon* (Vm.7.15049), *Le Bien-aime* (Vm.7.15051), *Brindestoc* (Vm.7.15052), *Le Carioleux* (Vm.7.15053)

## Alba, A.

The following works in F:Pn are all early prints for large wind band; all were printed in Paris in 1878–1889.
*Souvenir de 30e de Ligne* (Vm.7.15107)
March, *Concours régional de St. Omer* (Vm.7.15102)
Pas redoublés: *Retour de Camprigne* (Vm.7.15106), *L'Eclatant* (Vm.7.15104), *Le Fa dieze* (Vm.7.15105)
Valses: *Sous la feyillée* (Vm.7.15112), *La Jolie berceuse* (Vm.7.15113)
Polkas: *La Linotte* (Vm.7.15109), *Les Perles d'or* (Vm.7.15110), *Polka des etoiles* [très brillant] (Vm.7.15108), *La Glisseuse* [avec trio pour cornet] (Vm.7.15111)
Mazurka, *La Gondoliere* [avec trio pour cornet] (Vm.7.15113)

## Alberti, D.

The following works in F:Pn are all early prints for large wind band; all were printed in Paris in 1895–1896.
Valses: *Frissons à Amour* (Vm.27.4865), *Les Mines d'or* (Vm.27.4866)
Mazurka, *Sur la glace!* (Vm.27.4867)

## Alday, l'âiné (b. 1763)

*Harmonies*
Harmoniemusik
EP (Paris, Leduc) [Journal Nr. 7]

## Alexandre

The following works in F:Pn are all early prints for large brass band; all were printed in Paris in 1858–1868.
*Constance-Varsoviana* (Vm.27.15)
Quadrilles: *Le Machicadour* (Vm.27.16), *Bock Bier* (Vm.27.13)
Polkas: *Carmen* (Vm.27.14), *Adele* (Vm.27.11), *Asnières* (Vm.27.12)

## Alexandre, E.

Pas redoublé, *Spartacus*
Large wind band
EP (Paris, 1871) F:Pn (Vm.7.10585)

## Alexandre, L.

March, *La Tourangelle*
Large wind band
EP (Paris, 1858) F:Pn (Vm.27.18); reprinted (Paris, 1870) F:Pn (Vm.7.9966bis)

Pas redoublé, *Geep visch*
Large wind band
EP (Paris, 1868) F:Pn (Vm.7.10583)

## Alexandre-Georges

Overture, *L'Artesienne*
Large wind band
EP (Paris, 1885) F:Pn (Vm.7.13120 and Vm.27.1750) [two copies]

## Alkan, Charles [Pseudonym for Morhange] (1813–1888)

*Pas redoublé*
Large wind band
MS [mentioned in Grove]

## Allier, Gabriel

The following works in F:Pn are all early prints for large wind band; all were printed in Paris in 1896–1900.
Overture, *Lugdunum* (Vm.27.4882)
Fantaisie, *Le Réuiel du Soldat* (Vm.27.30)
Allegro, *Le Consciut* (Vm.27.4872)
*Le Joyeux Trompette* (Vm.27.23)

Marches: *Le Magyar* (Vm.27.4883), *Marche des petits piouproies* (Vm.27.24), *Ronde des marcheurs* (Vm.27.4896), *Marche républicaine* (Vm.27.26), *Marche lyonaise* (Vm.27.25)

Pas redoublés: *St. Dié* (Vm.27.4898), *St. Georges* (Vm.27.4899), *Solférino* (Vm.27.4901), *Moscou* (Vm.27.4887)

Polkas: *Jean et Jeaunette* (Vm.27.4879), *Mia Bellina!* (Vm.27.27), *Pick-pocket* (Vm.27.28), *Polka des nachas* (Vm.27.4894)

In F:Pn there are another 50 or so original works from the period 1900–1915 by this composer, together with another 50 or so transcriptions.

### Allmann, H.

Overture, *L'He de la jatte*
Large wind band
EP (Paris, David, 1886) F:Pn (Vm.27.4904)

Pas redoublé, *Le Fuseau d'or*
Large wind band
EP (Paris, David, 1886) F:Pn (Vm.27.4903)

### Alquier, A.-L.

Pas redoublé, *Le Joyeux stenographe*
Large wind band
EP (Ribaute, 1884) F:Pn (Vm.7.9968)

### Altamira, J.

The following works in F:Pn are all early prints for large wind band; all were printed in Paris in 1851–1867.

Marches: *Les Vendanges* (Vm.7.15124), *Asturiana* (Vm.7.15123)

Pas redoublés: *Le Castillan* (Vm.7.15127), *Le 8me Régiment de Ligne* (Vm.7.10582)

### Amat, Jose

March, *Hymne patriotique*
Large wind band
EP (Paris, 1874) F:Pn (Vm.7.15089)

### Amette, Louis

Overture, *La Fée du Vallon*
Large wind band
EP (Paris, late nineteenth century) F:Pn (Vm.27.4905)

### Amourdedieu, Casimir

The following works in F:Pn are all early prints for large wind band; all were printed in Paris in 1864–1896.

Airs Varié: *Sur mer* [solo cornet] (Vm.7.15092), *La Vésave* (Vm.27.4907)

March, *L'Avalanche* (Vm.7.9969)

Pas redoublés: *L'Albertin* (Vm.7.10588), *Le Gange* (Vm.27.34), *Le Kiosque* (Vm.7.15094), *Le Trieux* [brass band] (Vm.27.37)

Polka, *La Perle du Midi* (Vm.27.36)

Mazurka, *Ma Bruyère!* (Vm.27.35)

Bolero, *Alcala* (Vm.27.33)

### Amourdedieu, Pascal

The following works in F:Pn are all early prints for large wind band; all were printed in Paris in 1881–1891.

Fantaisies: *Le Val d'Ajol* (Vm.7.15129), *La Grotte de Calypso* (Vm.7.15130)

March, *Paris* (Vm.27.4906)

Pas redoublé, *Le Cancanier* (Vm.27.4905 bis)

Galop, *La Chasse* (Vm.7.15132)

Valse, *Reves d'orient* (Vm.7.15150)

Polka, *Jolie* (Vm.7.15143)

*Avanèra* (Vm.7.15131)

### André, Ernest

The following works in F:Pn are all early prints for large wind band; all were printed in Paris in 1859–1888.

Overture, *Les Deux journées* (Vm.7.10594)

Marches: *La Rétraite d'Afrique* (Vm.7.9972), *Royal défile* (Vm.7.10591), *La Touraine* (Vm.7.15166), *Défile du 31me Artillerie* (Vm.7.10592)

Redowa, *La Créole* (Vm.27.39)

### André, Paul

The following works in F:Pn are all early prints for large wind band; all were printed in Paris and Lyon in 1894–1912.

*Concert tunisien*, Op. 22 (Vm.27.48)

Ballet, *Le Printemps* (Fol.Vm.15.34)

*Méditation, Rêverie, mystique* (Vm.27.4930)

Overtures: *La Conne Etoile* (Vm.27.4915), *Brunehaut* (Vm.27.43), *Cadet-Rousselle*, Op. 112 (Vm.27.44), *Calme et tempete*, Op. 23

(Vm.27.45), *Le Fils de la Nuit* (Vm.27.4925), *Frédégonde* (Vm.27.4926), *Le Secret del'Olympe* (Vm.27.4931), *Légende rustique* (Vm.27.4928), *Le Secret de Margot*, Op. 110 (Vm.27.54)

Fantaisies: *Bardes et trouveres* (Vm.27.4912), *Le Camp des braves* (Vm.27.4916), *Cassandre* (Fol. Vm.15.488), *Cassiopée* (Vm.27.46), *La Cauchemar de Pierrot* (Vm.27.4918), *Cosmopolis* (Vm.27.49), *Les Echos du Pays* (Vm.27.4024) [reprinted 1910: 40.Vm.15.1070], *La Circassienne* (Vm.27.4922), *La Fee du lac* (Vm.27.50), *La Fee mimoselte* (Fol.Vm.15.40), *La Fête interompue* (Vm.27.51), *Les noces de Ferrette* (Fol. Vm.15.222), *Pendante la Fête* (Vm.27.4929)

Intermezzo, *Caprice de reine* (Vm.27.4917)

Marches: *Les Bayadères* (Vm.27.4913), *Berceuse des anges* (Vm.27.4914), *Le 115me de ligne Défile* (Vm.27.4919) [reprinted in 1899: Vm.27.47], *Le Char d'Isis* [*Cortège triomphal*] (Vm.27.4920), *Cherbourg Défile* (Vm.27.4921), *Gloriosa Spada* [*March Espagnole*] (Fol.Vm.15.490), *Lacrymosa* [*March funèbre*] (Vm.27.4927), *Marche Alsacienne* (Vm.27.53), *Turin* (Vm.27.4933)

Pas redoublés: *Le Coq gaulois* (Vm.27.4023), *Stanislas-le-grand* (Vm.7.15694)

Polka, *Serpentins et confetti* (Vm.27.4932)

*Gavotte des petites Princesses* (Vm.27.52)

*Menuet joli* (Fol.Vm.15.235)

## Antoni

(Collection) *Fantasies pour harmonie*
Large wind band [with saxophones]
EP (Paris, Gambaro, 1857) F:Pn (L.10.655)

The following works in F:Pn are all early prints for large wind band; all were printed in Paris in 1865–1881.

*Fantaisie variée* (Vm.7.15193)

*Marche défile* [*Salut des sociétés musicales au Concours de Reims*] (Vm.7.15194)

*Valse, Eugénie* (Vm.27.55)

*Pas redoublé Barcarolle* (Vm.27.56)

## Apel

*Preussischer Nationallics*
Chorus and military band
MS (autograph) F:Pn (MS 2767 a-d)

## Arban, J. J. (1825–1889)

The following works are for band, printed in London, ca. 1870–1887; shelf-marks given are for GB:Lbm.

Quadrilles: (h.1549, Ser. 37, Nr. 3), (h.1549, Ser. 55), (Nr. 4; h.1544, Nr. 244)

Marches: (f.412.[4]), (f.412.1.[1])

*Galop* (h.1543, Nr. 154)

*Air varié* (f.412.[2]), also found for 'Octett Band,' (f.411.[2])

## Argoin, G.

*Marche militair*
Large wind band
EP (Paris, Rohde, 1862) F:Pn (A.c.p.123)

## Arnaud, C. T.

*Le Territorial défile*
Large wind band
EP (Paris, Cordier, 1883) F:Pn (Vm.7.15.383)

## Arnaud, E.

*Marche*
Large wind band
EP (Paris, Simon, 1887) F:Pn (Vm.7.10036)

## Arnaud, J.

March, *La Melédine*
Large wind band
EP (Paris, Margueritat, 1873) F:Pn (Vm.7.15.386)

Pas redoublé, *Le brillant*
Large wind band
EP (Paris, Festival Artistique, 1899) F:Pn (Vm.27.4910)

## Arnaud, P.-J.

*Neulsyfrotte*
Large wind band
EP (Paris, no date) F:Pn (Vm.7.15.387)

## Arnoldi, Joseph

The following works in F:Pn are all early prints for large wind band; all were printed in Paris in 1875–1878.
Allegro militaire, *Hymne Franco italien* (Vm.7.9975)
March, *La Gallo slave* (Vm.7.9987)
Valse, *La Coquette* (Vm.7.9976)

## Arnould, Eugene

The following works in F:Pn are all early prints for large wind band; all were printed in Paris in 1870–1912.
Airs Varié: *Les Regrets* (Vm.7.15580), *Toinette* [for solo cornet] (Vm.7.15576)
Pas redoublés: *Eugene Etienne* (Fol.Vm.15.489), *Le 2e Tirailleurs* (Vm.7.15574)
Polka, *Pravelotte* (Vm.7.15575)
Mazurka, *Malvina* (Vm.7.15573)

## Arnoux, A.

The following works in F:Pn are all early prints for large wind band; all were printed in Paris in 1882–1913.
Fantaisies: *Les Belles de nuit* (Vm.7.15584), *La Reine des prés fleuris* (Vm.7.15583)
Allegros militaire: *L'Audarieux* (Vm.7.15587), *Le Beau soldat* (Vm.7.15588), *Le Bon comarade* (Vm.7.15590), *Le Chant des héros* (Vm.27.4952), *Les Hommes de cuivre* (Vm.7.15591), *La Marche aux lanterpes* (Vm.7.15582), *Le Roi soleil* (Vm.7.15589), *Le Talisman* (Vm.7.15592), *Tout pour la france* (Vm.7.15593), *Vaillance* (Vm.7.15581), *Le Vaillant* (Vm.7.15594)
*C'est la Fanfare qui passe* (Vm.27.59)
Pas redoublés: *Face defer* (Vm.27.4953), *Le Sans Parcil* (Vm.7.15711) [later edition: 40.Vm.15.3563]
Mazurkas: *L'Amour qui passe* (Vm.27.4951), *Fleurs d'Italie* (Vm.27.60), *Marquise au champagne* (40.Vm.15.3651), *Pour un Baiser!* (Vm.27.4955), *Le Rive de Marguerite* (Vm.7.15586)
Valse, *Fleurs animées* (Vm.27.4954)
Polka, *La Reine Berthe* (Vm.7.15585)

## Arsaut, Gabriel

Pas redoublé, *Libourne*
Large wind band
EP (Paris, Nouvelle france chorale, 1889) F:Pn (Vm.7.15595)

## Artique, P.

Pas redoublé, *Le Bysontin*
Large wind band
EP (Paris, Goumas, 1881) F:Pn (Vm.7.10607)

## Artus, Alexandre

The following works in F:Pn are all early prints for large wind band; all were printed in Paris in 1875–1891.
Marches: *Indieme du Rajah* (Vm.7.15600), *Cleopâtre* (Vm.7.15607)
Pas redoublé, *Les Rendez-vous de chassey* (Vm.7.15.608)
*Hymne russe* (Vm.7.15597)

## Ashton, T.

Pas redoublé, *le petit tambour*
Large wind band
EP (Paris, 1867) F:Pn (Vm.7.15.625)

## Asselin, Th.

Pas redoublé, *Honfleur*
Large wind band
EP (Paris, 1897) F:Pn (Vm.27.4957)

## Astoin

Pas redoublé, *Hasparren*
Large wind band
EP (Paris, 1874) F:Pn (Vm.7.10608)

## Aubert, Aug.

The following works in F:Pn are all early prints for large wind band; all were printed in Paris in 1879–1881.
Overture, *Les Bergers de la claire* (Vm.7.15.634)
March, *Honfleur* (Vm.7.15.635)
Polka, *Minette* [for solo cornet] (Vm.7.15.637)

## Aubert, Charles

The following works in F:Pn are all early prints for large wind band; all were printed in Paris in 1863–1892.
Fantaisie, *Songe doré* (Vm.7.15638)
Marches: *Marche funèbre* (Vm.7.9982), *Mexico defile* (Vm.7.10610)
Pas redoublé, *L'Egyptien* (Vm.27.84)

## Aubréy du Boulley, Prudent-Louis (1796–1870)

(2) *Prière*
Solo oboe, 22-02, 2 'altos'
EP (Paris, Carre, 1868) F:Pn (K.962 and K.963)

*Cantata* (en l'honneur de St. Cecile), Op. 96
SSB, 1042-323, 3 ophicleides, bass drum
EP (Paris, Richault, 1836) F:Pn (Acm 1009)

*Recueil d'harmonie* (composée pour être exécutée aux messes militaires), Op. 68
EP (Paris, Richault) [cited in F]

(60) *Pièces d'harmonie*
Large wind band
EP (Paris, Richault, in ten volumes, Op. 45, 47, 49, 51, 53, 55, 57, 59, 61, and 63) [cited in F]

*Marches: Pas redoublés, et Valses*
Large wind band
EP (Paris, Ebend) [Liv. 1–5]

*Militär musik-Stücke für Nationalgarden 1830–1832*
Large wind band
MS F:Pn [cited in MGG]

*Blechmusik-Stücke für Slosstrupp grenadiere, 1835–1836*
Brass band
MS (?) F:Pn [cited in MGG]

*Stücke für Blechmusik 1858–1859*
Brass band
MS (?) F:Pn [cited in MGG]

*Symphonies, Overtures, Fantaisies for Wind orchestra, 1859–1860*
Large wind band
MS (?) F:Pn [cited in MGG]

The following works in F:Pn are all early prints for large wind band; all were printed in Paris in 1856–1872.
Overture, *Les Echos des Alpes*, Op. 172 (Vm.7.15639)
*Morceau d'Élévation*, Op. 137 (Vm.27.12640)
Marches: *March et pas redoublé* (Vm.7.15702), *Marche funèbre* (Vm.7.15647), *Marche funèbre [pour l'anniversaire du 27 Juillet]* (Vm.7.15703), *Pas de route* (Vm.7.15648)

## Aubin

*Potpourri*
Six-part Harmoniemusik
EP (Paris, Imprimerie mus.)

## Aubry, Abel

Mazurka, *Au bord de la Beumonne*
Large wind band
EP (Paris, 1882) F:Pn (Vm.7.15649)

## Audoir, Barthélemy

*Sultans marsch*
Large wind band
EP (Paris, 1879) F:Pn (Vm.7.15659)

Pas redoublé, *Le Pousse-caillou*
Large wind band
EP (Paris, 1877) F:Pn (Vm.7.10611)

## Augé, Claude

*Lyre de france* (16 morceaux)
Large wind band
EP (Paris, 1896) F:Pn (Vm.7.14533)

## Auzende, Ange-Marie

*Chant Mystique* (à la chapelle Bourron, à Mousieur la Comte de Moretesquiox) [late nineteenth century]
Large wind band
MS (autograph) F:Pn (MS.2920) [score]; (MS.2920a-ee) [parts]

## d'Azémar

Pas redoublé, *Le Chassepot*
Large wind band
EP (Paris, 1867) F:Pn (Vm.7.15692)

## Bachimont, R.

Polka, *L'Annicale*
Large wind band
EP (Paris, 1886) F:Pn (Vm.7.15716)

## Badart, Louis

Fantaisie, *Le Réveil d'une étoile*
Large wind band
EP (Paris, 1889) F:Pn (Vm.7.15748)

## Bagarre, A.

Valse, *Le jolie Patineuse*
Large wind band
EP (Paris, 1895) F:Pn (Vm.27.12648)

### Bagnat

Mazurka, *Abnégation*
Large wind band
EP (Paris, 1889) F:Pn (Vm.7.15780)

### Baille, F.

Mazurka, *Pour vous*
Large wind band
EP (Paris, 1889) F:Pn (Vm.7.10621)

### BailIe, Gabriel

*Marche turque*, Op. 43 bis
Large wind band
EP (Paris, 1881) F:Pn (Vm.27.4975)

### Baille, Martial

The following works in F:Pn are all early prints for large wind band; all were printed in Paris in 1896–1907.
Pas redoublé, *Dévant le Danger* [with ad. lib. chorus] (Vm.27.97)
Polka, *Miga* (Vm.27.4533 and Vm.27.4534) [two copies]
Gavotte, *Lutine* (Vm.27.4532)
Mazurka, *Primevère* (Vm.27.4535)

### Baillon, A.

The following works in F:Pn are all early prints for large wind band; all were printed in Paris in 1886–1892.
Overture, *En Exil!* (Vm.27.4976)
Marches: *La Ligne des patriotes* (Vm.7.10626), *Marche symphonique* (Vm.7.10623)
Pas redoublé, *Fifres et clarions* (Vm.27.99)
Polkas: *Légère* [for solo cornet] (Vm.27.100), *Caprice Polka* [for two solo cornets] (Vm.7.10625) A good, light-hearted piece for modern instruments, with a full score.

### Baillon, Ad. Victor (Chef de Musique au 127e)

The following works in F:Pn are all early prints for large wind band; all were printed in Paris in 1884–1899.
Overture, *La Pierre druidique* (Vm.27.4977)
*Grand air varié* (Vm.7.10624) This is a theme and variations, with virtually every instrument getting one variation. Musical and fun; full score and modern instrumentation.
*Rondo-Polka* [for solo piccolo] (Vm.7.15796)

### Bajus, Z.

The following works in F:Pn are all early prints for large wind band; all were printed in Paris in 1886–1912.
Overtures: *France et russie*, Op. 209 (Vm.7.15798), *Grande Overture dramatique*, Op. 149 (Vm.7.10627)
Fantaisies: *L'Etoile du berger*, Op. 158 (Vm.7.15799), *Palmes et couronnes*, Op. 202 (Vm.7.15803)
*Marche Picarde* (Vm.27.12651)
Pas redoublés: *Le Chasseur* [with trumpet fanfares ad. lib.] (Vm.7.15802), *L'Etendard* (Vm.27.101), *Gambrinus* (Vm.7.15800)
Retraite, *Bonne nuit* (Vm.7.15805)
Quadrilles: *Pandore* (40.vm.15.3135), *Vive la Joie* (Vm.7.15808)
The library has a dozen or so additional works from the twentieth century.

### Balay, Guillaume

*Bruxelles-Ouverture*
Large wind band [10 saxophone parts, 2 Sarrussophone, etc.]
EP (Paris, Buffet, 1938) F:Pn (K.13.078)
This is a brilliant multi-part overture for large band by a former director of the Musique de la Garde Républicaine.

### Baldiani, F.

Pas redoublé, *Gay Troubadour*
Large wind band
EP (Paris, 1863) F:Pn (Vm.27.4981)

### Balocke, E.

Pas redoublé, *Le bon Montidérien*
Large wind band
EP (Paris, 1899) F:Pn (Vm.27.4987)

## Bangratz, A.

Galop, *Ne un'oublie pas!*
Large wind band
EP (Paris, 1869) F:Pn (Vm.27.102)

## Barat, J. Ed.

*Rapsodie sur des airs populaires*
Large wind band
MS F:Pn (K.11.579)

## Barbet, C.

Valse, *Clémencee*
Large wind band
EP (Paris, 1898) F:Pn (Vm.27.103)

Polka, *Ernestine*
Large wind band
EP (Paris, 1882) F:Pn (Vm.27.104)

## Bardin, V.

Mazurka, *Miraila*
Large wind band
EP (Paris, 1887) F:Pn (Vm.7.10631)

## Baron, Eugéne

The following works in F:Pn are all early prints for large wind band; all were printed in Paris in 1860–1882.
Fantaisies: *Qui s'y frotte s'v pigue* (Vm.7.15820), *Soir d'été* (Vm.27.106), *Souvenir de Dieppe* (Vm.27.108).
Allegro, *Le Victorreux* (Vm.27.5001) [reprinted in 1882: Vm.7.109]
*Vallons de l'Helvétie* (Vm.27.5000)
*Paris-Strasbourg et liberte!* (Vm.27.4995)
Pas redoublés: *Le Calyados* (Vm.7.10632), *L'Invincible* (Vm.27.4998) [reprinted: Vm.27.4999]
Valse, *Souvenir d'Etretat* (Vm.27.107)
Polka, *Elmina* (Vm.27.4997)
Quadrilles: *Le Lexavien* (Vm.27.105), *Souventr de Berch* (Vm.27.4996)

## Barraud, E.

March, *Salut à Paris*
Large wind band
EP (Paris, 1868) F:Pn (Vm.27.110)

## Barrès

Pas redoublé, *Le Colonial*
Large wind band
EP (Paris, 1907) F:Pn (Vm.27.5003)

Pas redoublé, *Le Créole*
Large wind band
EP (Paris, 1889) F:Pn (Vm.27.111)

## Barrier, A.

Polka, *La Fontaine de Vaucluse*
Large wind band
EP (Paris, 1880) F:Pn (Vm.27.5004)

## Barthe, C.

Pas redoublé, *Le Bloeus*
Large wind band
EP (Paris, 1877) F:Pn (Vm.7.10638)

Pas redoublé, *Trocadéro*
Large wind band
EP (Paris, 1881) F:Pn (Vm.7.10640)

Under Vm.7.10639 there is an arrangement of Haydn's *Creation* for military band by this man, printed in 1869.

## Bartholomeus, P.

Fantaisie, *L'Eperon d'or*
Large wind band
EP (Paris, 1888) F:Pn (Vm.7.15839 and (Vm.27.12654) [two copies]

March, *Juliette*
Large wind band
EP (Paris, 1890) F:Pn (Vm.7.15838)

## Bary, A.

Overture, *Le Péron*
Large wind band
EP (Paris, 1888) F:Pn (Vm.7.15843)

Pas redoublé, *Partons gaiment*
Large wind band
EP (Paris, 1888) F:Pn (Vm.7.15842)

## Baston, Edm.

The following works in F:Pn are all early prints for large wind band; all were printed in Paris in 1890–1892.

Allegros militaire: *Jupiter II* (Vm.7.15847), *Le Troupier* (Vm.27.113)

Polka, *Souvenir* (Vm.27.112)

## Batiste, Édouard (1820–1876)

*Symphonie militaire* (1845)
1222-121, ophicleide
MS F:Pn (MS.3343)
US:DW (350) [copy of MS.3343]
US:DW (171) [modern copy by Fred Lenk]

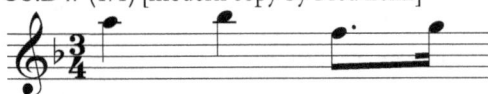

## Baucourt, A.

The following works in F:Pn are all early prints for large wind band; all were printed in Paris in 1862–1881.

Overtures: *Les Adieux!* (Vm.27.4538; Vm.27.5009) [two copies], *Un Jour de fête* (Vm.27.5050)

Fantaisie, *La Reine de Castille* (Vm.27.5044)

Andantes religieux: *La Bienfaisance* (Vm.27.5017), *La Prière* (Vm.27.5039)

Air Varié, *Le Météore* [for solo cornet] (Vm.27.5035)

Marches: *Les Francais au Mexique* (Vm.27.5026), *France et ltalie* (Vm.27.5027), *Honneur et glorie* (Vm.27.5030), *Ismaïl Pacha* (Vm.27.5031), *Le Saint Charlemagne* (Vm.27.116), *Le Soldat francais* (Vm.27.5047), *La Vaillance* (Vm.27.5051), *Villafranca* (Vm.27.5053)

Pas redoublés: *Espérons* (Vm.27.5023), *Le Florentin* (Vm.27.5025), *Marsala* (Vm.27.5034), *La Prise de Palerme* (Vm.27.5042), *Vengeance* (Vm.27.5052)

Polkas: *Blanche* (Vm.27.5018), *La Chinonaise* (Vm.27.5020), *Héloïse* (Vm.27.5029), *La Vivandiere* (vm.27.5054)

Valses: *La Bapaumoise* (Vm.27.5013), *Les belles Ge'orgieunes* (Vm.27.5016), *Clotilde* (Vm.27.5021), *La jolie Flamande* (Vm.27.5032), *Les Jours d'automne* (Vm.27.5033), *Le Printemps* (Vm.27.5041), *Rêves d'amour* (Vm.27.5046), *Les Rêves du jeune age* (Vm.27.115)

Quadrilles: *L'Enfant de troupe* (Vm.27.5022), *Le Charancon* (Vm.27.5019), *Garibaldi* (Vm.27.5028), *Le Pays natal* (Vm.27.5036), *Les Plaisirs de la ville* (Vm.27.5037), *Le Retour en Pologne* (Vm.27.5045)

Schottisches: *L'Aurore!* (Vm.27.5012), *Fleurs de mais* (Vm.27.5024)

Galop, *L'Amazone* (Vm.27.5010)

Boléro, *Barcelone* (Vm.27.5014)

*Le Rabelaisen* (Vm.27.5043)

*Les Souvenirs de Saint-Ouen* (Vm.27.5048)

## Bauderuc, Jouan

The following works in F:Pn are all early prints for large wind band; all were printed in Paris in 1864–1894.

Fantaisie, *Une Sérénade à la mariée* [for two solo oboes] (Vm.27.5056) The solo parts are very easy.

*Air varié* [for solo clarinet] (Vm.7.15878)

Marche funèbre, *Larmes et prière* (Vm.7.15871)

Pas redoublés: *Souvenir de Montaubain* (Vm.7.15872), *Le Départ* (Vm.27.5055)

Suite des Valses: *Les Bords de l'Avde* (Vm.7.15867)

Polkas: *La Gondole Venitienne* (Vm.7.15868), *L'Hirondelle fugitive* (Vm.7.15865)

## Baudin, Henry

Polka, *Ke-za-ko. Lubie* [genre Orientale]
Large wind band
EP (Paris, 1888) F:Pn (Vm.7.13118)

## Baudonck, L.-J.

The following works in F:Pn are all early prints for large wind band; all were printed in Paris in 1883–1892.

Overture, *Perserveranza* (Vm.7.15.884)

Fantaisies: *Les Bergers* (Vm.7.15.881 and Vm.27.5058) [two copies], *Chanson du gondolier* (Vm.7.15.876), *Dans la vallée* (Vm.7.15.886), *Les Emigrants* (Vm.7.15.882), *En traineau* (Vm.7.15.888), *En Vancances* (Vm.7.15.885), *Soirée d'Automne* (Vm.27.5063), *Soirée d'hiver* (Vm.7.15.887), *Voix nationales* (Vm.7.15.875), *Le Roi d'Yuetot* [Opera Comique Fantaisie Nr. 1] (Vm.7.15.874)

*Chanson Bérnaise* (Vm.7.15.889)
Barcarole, *Sur le lac* (Vm.7.15.883)
*Marche solennelle* (Vm.7.15.877)

## de Bauller, A.

The following works in F:Pn are all early prints for large wind band; all were printed in Paris in 1881–1891.
Marches: *Eugénie* (Vm.27.5064), *Pompomette* (Vm.27.5065)
Pas redoublé, *Le Troupier* (Vm.27.119)

## Bazin, Emmanuel Joseph François (1816–1878)

*Melodie* (1840)
Two solo horns, with 1222-
MS F:Pn (MS.3214)

*March Militar* (1856)
Large wind band
MS (autograph) F:Pn (MS.3237)

Pas redoublé *Mirecourt-souvenir*
EP (Paris, 1898) F:Pn (Vm.27.5071)

## Beaucherne, Raphaël

The following works in F:Pn are all early prints for large wind band; all were printed in Paris in 1879–1880.
*Ambroise Pare* (Vm.27.5078)
Marches: *L'Ange gardien* (Vm.27.5079), *Layal* (Vm.27.5081), *St. Cécile* (Vm.27.5082)
Pas redoublés: *Les Courve-feu* (Vm.27.5080), *Le Vaingueur* (Vm.27.5083)

## Beauvarlet-Charpentier, Jacques-Marie (1766–1834)

*Bataille d'Austerliz* [*Journée des trois Empereues*]
Large wind band
MS (autograph score, formerly owned by Napoleon III) F:Pn (D.754); US:DW (393)
This is an arrangement by Gilles Borel (24e Leger) of an original work for piano. The band version is programmatic.

## Bécher, L.

Marche procession, *L'ascension*
Large wind band
EP (Paris, 1864) F:Pn (Vm.27.123)

## Becker, P.

Pas redoublé, *Le Toscan*
Large wind band
EP (Paris, no date) F:Pn (Vm.27.4547)

## Bédard

*Harmonie*, Nr. 2
Harmoniemusik
EP (Paris, Frère) US:Wc

*Marche*, Nr. 1, 2
Harmoniemusik
EP (Paris, David)

*Potpourri*
Eight-part Harmoniemusik
EP (Paris, Janet)

## Bellon, J.

(3) *Quintettes,* Op. 29
Small E♭ bugle or trumpet, cornet, horn, trombone, and ophicleide
EP (Paris, S. Richault, ca. 1850) GB:Lbm (h.2784. aa.[2.])
The titlepages of the first two bear an autograph dedication and the first contains a portrait.

*Quintette,* Op. 29, Nr. 12
Five brass instruments
EP (city unknown, 1881) GB:Lbm (h.1584)

## Belval, E.

The following works in F:Pn are all early prints for large wind band; all were printed in Paris in 1888–1890.
Marche triomphale, *Liberté* (Vm.7.15.934)
Pas redoublé, *Entre choisy et chiais* (Vm.7.15.935)

## Bénard

The following works in F:Pn are all early prints for large wind band; all were printed in Paris in 1871–1873.
*Élévation facile* (Vm.27.5093)
Pas redoublés: *Casse-carreaux* (Vm.27.5092), *Le Roi Carotte mebotte* (Vm.27.5095)

## Bender, V.

*Grand Air Varié*
Large wind band
EP (Paris, 1842) F:Pn (Vm.27.138)

## Benoist, G.

The following works in F:Pn are all early prints for large wind band; all were printed in Paris in 1884–1890.

*Marche triomphale* (Vm.7.15.938) Another copy (K.68730) is found cataloged under 'Benoist, C.'

Valse, *La Vallée d'Ossau* (Vm.27.139)

## Beraud, G.

Pas redoublé, *Le Val d'enfer*
Large wind band
EP (Paris, 1886) F:Pn (Vm.7.15.940)

## Berlioz, Hector (1803–1869)

*Le carnaval romain*
Large wind orchestra, including saxophones
MS (autograph sketches) BRD:B (Mus.Ms.1550)
This signed autograph contains the beginning and final bars only in full instrumentation. Some believe the actual notes were written by Mohr.

*Symphonie Funèbre et Triomphale*
Large wind orchestra, without saxophones
MS (autograph) F:Pn (MS.1.164);
www.whitwellbooks.com [modern edition]

## Bernard, A.

*Cigarette Polka*
Large wind band
EP (Paris, 1873) F:Pn (Vm.27.5107)

## Bernard, Emile (1843–1902)

*Divertissement*, Op. 36
2222-02
MP (Paris, Durand) BRD:Bhm (7358 [score] and 7362 [parts]); US:DW (204)

## Bernier, Antony (Chef de la Musique Municipale de Nantes)

The following works in F:Pn are all early prints for large wind band; all were printed in Paris in 1886–1896.

*Symphonie militaire, Marche du sacre* (Vm.27.154 bis) [parts only] This is a very unusual work, in the form of a march, but slow and very dramatic in character!

Overture, *Le Fête des roses* (Vm.7.15.956 and Vm.27.149) [two copies]

Fantaisies: *Les Bords de la Sévre* (Vm.27.146), *Le Chant des sirénes* (Vm.27.148), *Le Chant du cygne* (Vm.27.5109), *La Fontaine de Bacchus* (Vm.27.150), *La Lyre d'or* (Vm.27.152), *La Reine des prés* (Vm.27.156), *Les Valets de Coeur* (Vm.27.5110)

Marches: *Dernier Salut* [*Marche funèbre*] (Vm.27.12663), *Marche des Janissaires* (Vm.27.153), *Marche des mpmies* (Vm.27.154)

Pas redoublés: *Gargantua* (Vm.27.151 and Vm.7.15953) [two copies], *Le Vert-galant* (Vm.27.157)

*Polka des hussards* (Vm.27.155)

Galop, *Carrousel* (Vm.27.147)

Mazurka, *Gentil Démon* (Vm.27.12664)

## Bernn, Alexandre

Polka, *Girovette*
Large wind band
EP (Paris, 1884) F:Pn (Vm.27.158)

## Berr

*Marche et Pas redoublé*
Harmoniemusik
EP (Paris, Hentz)

*Musique militaire*
Harmoniemusik
EP (Paris, Gambaro) [Liv. 1]

## Bertain, Jules

Polka, *Enchanteresse*
Large wind band
EP (Paris, 1881) F:Pn (Vm.27.5114)

### Berten, Léon

Mazurka, *La Jeune Picarde*
Large wind band
EP (Paris, 1875) F:Pn (Vm.7.10.655)

### Bessières

Pas redoublé, *St. Maixent*
Large wind band
EP (Paris, no date) F:Pn (Vm.27.5120)

### Bignon, Paul

The following works in F:Pn are all early prints for large wind band; all were printed in Paris in 1873.
*Offertoire* (Vm.27.5136)
Polka, *Les Clechettes* (Vm.27.5135)

### Billaut, A.

The following works in F:Pn are all early prints for large wind band; all were printed in Paris in 1885–1892.
Fantaisie, *Les Chants du crépuscule* (Vm.27.169)
*Marche des tirailleurs de la Seine* (Vm.27.170)
Pas redoublés: *Après la Victoire* (Vm.27.5137), *Orléans* (Vm.27.171), *St. James* (Vm.7.16006), *Souvenir de Francouville* (Vm.27.173)
Polkas: *Cécile* [with solo cornet] (Vm.27.168 and Vm.7.16008 [two copies]), *Revéillon* (Vm.7.16007), *Royal Princess* (Vm.27.172)

### Billaut, J.-B.-A.

March, *Lisbonne*
Large wind band
EP (Paris, 1888) F:Pn (Vm.27.174)

### Billaut, Louis

The following works in F:Pn are all early prints for large wind band; all were printed in Paris in 1894–1897.
Fantaisie, *Déruchette* (Vm.27.175)
March, *Parisiana* (Vm.27.176)
Pas redoublé, *Le Camp de César* (Vm.27.4605)
Polka anglaise, *Little Dick* (Vm.27.5138)

### Billot

The following works in F:Pn are all early prints for large wind band; all were printed in Paris ca. 1855.
*Le Berrichon* (Vm.27.178)
Quadrille, *Le Viveur* (Vm.27.4606)

### Biloir, Joseph

The following works in F:Pn are all early prints for large wind band; all were printed in Paris in 1896–1897.
Pas redoublé, *Tombouctou* (Vm.27.5142)
Polka, *La jolie Cantimère* (Vm.27.1897)

### Birk (Birck), Charles

The following works in F:Pn are all early prints for large wind band; all were printed in Paris in 1866–1868.
*Romance* [for solo cornet] (Vm.27.5147)
*Introduction, Andante & Valse* (Vm.7.10.664 and Vm.27.180 bis [two copies])
Marches: *Marche* (Vm.27.5145), *Marche pour procession* (Vm.7.10.665), *Marche pour procession* (Vm.7.10.666)
Polka (Vm.27.5146)
*Fanfare Quadrille* (Vm.27.180)

### Bisch

The following works in F:Pn are all early prints for large wind band; all were printed in Paris in 1881–1897.
Pas redoublés: *Châteaubriand* (Vm.27.5149), *Le Chant du soldat* (Vm.27.182)
Polka, *Petit Rat* (Vm.27.5150)

### Bisch, F.

The following works in F:Pn are all early prints for large wind band; all were printed in Paris in 1877–1891.
*Les Concerts Angevins* (Vm.7.16017) [Nrs. 1, 3, 4, 5, 6, 8, 10, 11, 12 …] This is published (Angers: Metzner Leblanc, 1891) under a series title, 'repertoire de musiques civiles et militaires.'
Pas redoublés: *Duguesclin* (Vm.27.5151), *Fin-guidon* (Vm.7.16018), *Jeanne d'Arc* (Vm.27.183)

## Blanc, P.

Pas redoublé, *Le Rônis*
Large military band
EP (Paris) F:Pn (Vm.27.192)

## Blancheteau

The following works in F:Pn are all early prints for large wind band; all were printed in Paris in 1854–1880.

*L'Escurial Overture espangpole*, Op. 709 (Vm.27.196)

Works for the Church: *Les Adieux aux braves morts en Crimée* [melodie funèbre], Op. 87 (Vm.27.5162), *Andante religieux* [sur un air de Quidron, maitre de musique à Louis XIII], Op. 701 (Vm.7.16025), *Andante religieux*, Nr. 5, Op. 473 (Vm.27.5173), *La Basilique*, Offertoire, Op. 659 (Vm.7.16026), *Le Champ du repos* [Marche funèbre], Op. 96 (Vm.27.5208), *Le Chant des cloches*, Andante religieux [original Schubert], Op. 718 (Vm.7.16027), *Enfant des cieux*, Andante pour Élévation, Op. 308 (Vm.27.5264), *La Fête-Dieu!*, March Procession (Vm.27.5280), *Gloire à Marie*, Andante, Op. 408 (Vm.27.5296), *L'Invocation*, Élévation, Op. 407 (Vm.27.5309), *Invocation à la Vierge*, Andante religieux, Op. 223 (Vm.27.5310), *Kyrie*, Op. 268 (Vm.27.5321), *Marche et Andante* [pour Offertoire], Op. 75 (Vm.27.5336), *Messe facile* [band with organ] (Vm.1.1964), *Notre Dame des Anges*, Fantaisie religieuse, Op. 299 (Vm.27.5363), *Offertoire*, Op. 472 (Vm.27.5366), *Ou pent-on être mieux*, Andante, Op. 108 (Vm.27.5371), *Le Pain bénit*, Offertoire (Vm.27.5374), *St. Gabriel*, Andante religieux, Op. 597 (Vm.7.16040), *Le Tabernacle*, Élévation, Op. 658 (Vm.7.16041), *Mass*, Vm.27.5321 and Vm.1.1964 a full Mass with band and chorus, may be missing a score

Fantaisies: Vm.27.5195, Vm.27.193, Vm.27.194, Vm.27.5258, Vm.27.5275, Vm.27.5304, Vm.27.202, Vm.27.5406, Vm.27.5428, Vm.27.205, Vm.27.5464 [*Le trois Amis*, Op. 269 [soli cornet, alto, and trombone]

Airs varié: *Fleur de rosée* [for solo cornet], Op. 661 (Vm.27.5283, Vm.7.16029 [2 copies]), Vm.27.198, Vm.27.200, Vm.27.5444 The last two are themes with variations, with each variation given to a different instrument.

Marches: Vm.27.5181, Vm.27.5196, Vm.27.5224, Vm.27.5230, Vm.27.5232, Vm.27.5250, Vm.7.10.680, Vm.27.5265, Vm.27.5267, Vm.27.5279, Vm.27.5290, Vm.27.5295, Vm.27.5305, Vm.27.5325, Vm.27.5326, Vm.27.5332, Vm.27.5339, Vm.27.5362, Vm.27.5365, Vm.27.5376, Vm.27.203, Vm.27.5408, Vvm.27.5410, Vm.27.5411, Vm.27.5420, Vm.27.5421, Vm.27.5423, Vm.27.5430, Vm.27.5433, Vm.27.5438, Vm.27.5454, Vm.27.5466, Vm.27.5476

Pas redoublés: Vm.27.5160, Vm.27.5166, Vm.27.5168, Vm.27.5169, Vm.27.5170, Vm.27.5186, Vm.27.5189, Vm.27.5191, Vm.27.5193, Vm.27.5199, Vm.27.5202, Vm.27.5209, Vm.27.5211, Vm.27.5220, Vm.27.5221, Vm.27.5225, Vm.27.5233, Vm.27.5240, Vm.27.5247, Vm.27.5249, Vm.27.5251, Vm.27.5266, Vm.27.5270, Vm.7.10.679, Vm.27.5302, Vm.27.5303, Vm.27.5322, Vm.27.5329, Vm.27.5346, Vm.27.5351, Vm.27.5352, Vm.27.5353, Vm.27.5354, Vm.27.5385, Vm.27.5388, Vm.27.5409, Vm.27.5424, Vm.27.5427, Vm.27.5429, Vm.27.5431, Vm.27.5435, Vm.27.5437, Vm.27.5441, Vm.7.10.674, Vm.7.10.675, Vm.10.676, Vm.27.5446, Vm.27.5455, Vm.27.5456, Vm.27.5459, Vm.27.5461, Vm.27.5467, Vm.7.10.677, Vm.27.5468, Vm.27.5471, Vm.27.5472, Vm.27.5478

Redovvas: Vm.7.10.671, Vm.27.5294, Vm.27.12672, Vm.27.12673

Retraits: Vm.27.5317, Vm.27.5389, Vm.7.16036, Vm.7.16037, Vm.27.5426

Valses: Vm.27.5167, Vm.27.5204, Vm.27.5205, Vm.27.5246, Vm.27.5248, Vm.27.5255, Vm.27.5323, Vm.27.5350, Vm.27.5375

Polkas: Vm.27.5171, Vm.27.5192, Vm.27.5203, Vm.27.5226, Vm.27.5234, Vm.27.195, Vm.27.5316, Vm.27.5377, Vm.27.5390, Vm.27.5396, Vm.27.5400, Vm.27.5432, Vm.27.5463, Vm.7.10.670

Quadrilles: Vm.27.5184, Vm.27.5190, Vm.27.5194, Vm.27.5254, Vm.27.197, Vm.27.5285, Vm.27.5297, Vm.27.5299, Vm.275300 [*Le Grand Albert, Quadrille diabolique*], Vm.27.5348 [*Maximilien*], Vm.27.5387, Vm.27.5392, Vm.27.5413, Vm.27.5442, Vm.27.5460

Schottischs: Vm.27.5187, Vm.27.5210,
Vm.27.5252, Vm.27.5284, Vm.27.5393,
Vm.27.5402
Boleros: Vm.27.5235, Vm.7.16022, Vm.27.5276,
Vm.7.16030, Vm.27.5434, Vm.27.5439
Mazurkas: Vm.27.5217, Vm.27.5263,
Vm.27.5360, Vm.27.5370, Vm.27.5417,
Vm.7.10.672 [two copies]
Galops: Vm.27.5262, Vm.27.5282, Vm.27.5301,
Vm.27.5415
*La Bayadère orientale*, Op. 81 bis (Vm.27.5188)
*Chants nationaux anglais*, Op. 727 (Vm.7.16028)
*Le Charme*, Romance, Op. 406 (Vm.27.5216)
*La Dragonne Vaisoviana*, Op. 109 (Vm.27.5256)
*L'Flandais*, Chant National, Op. 739 (Vm.27.5311)
*Laendler Styrien* (Vm.27.199)
*Le Moulin de la Caille*, Op. 614 bis (Vm.27.5355)
*Une chasse à Nogentet*, Op. 455 (Vm.27.204)
*La Vesuvienne*, Op. 346 (Vm.27.5469)
There are by this composer, in F:Pn, several tutors for individual wind instruments and approximately one hundred transcriptions of orchestral music for band.

## Blanckemann, L.

The following works in F:Pn are all early prints for large wind band; all were printed in Paris in 1851–1867.
Fantaisies: Vm.27.207, Vm.27.208 [for solo basse sarrusophone], Vm.7.10.684 [for solo saxhorn in B♭], Vm.27.209
*Air Varié* [for solo clarinet] (Vm.7.10.683)
*March triomphale* (Vm.7.10.691)
Pas redoublés: Vm.27.206, Vm.7.10.690,
Vm.27.210, Vm.27.213
Quadrilles: Vm.27.5479, Vm.27.211, Vm.7.10.689,
Vm.27.212

## Blangy, Auguste

The following works in F:Pn are all early prints for large wind band; all were printed in Paris in 1867–1876.
Pas redoublés: Vm.27.5480, Vm.27.5481,
Vm.27.5483
Polka-Mazurka, *L'Oriflamme* (Vm.27.5482)

## Blasius, F.

*Harmonie militaire contenant marches, Valses ...*
Harmoniemusik
EP (Paris, Gaveaux aine, no date) F:Pn
(Vm.27.214) [1–4]

*Suite d'harmonie tirée des operas noyeau*
Harmoniemusik
EP (Paris, Imbault, no date) F:Pn (Vm.7.6962) [in three suites], F:Pn (Vm.7.10.530–532) [may be an additional copy]

## Bléger, A.

*Air Varié*
Large wind band [with solo saxophone]
EP (Paris, 1881) F:Pn (vm.7.10.693)

## Bléger, Michel

The following works in F:Pn are all early prints for large wind band; all were printed in Paris in 1867–1902.
Works for the Church: *March funèbre* (Vm.27.216), *March funèbre* (Vm.27.217), *March procession* [La Bénédiction] (Vm.27.5491), *March funèbre* (Vm.27.4618), *Melodie religieuse* ['5 Mai, 1821'] (Vm.27.235), *March funèbre* (Vm.27.250), *March funèbre* (Vm.27.4619), *Fête Dieu!* [Melodie de joie] (Vm.27.5523), *March funèbre* (Vm.27.5529), *Andante* [Les Immortelles] (Vm.27.266), *March funèbre* (Vm.27.279), *Mélodie religieux* (Vm.27.304), *Andante* [pour Offertoire, 'Notre-Dame aulixiatrice'] (Vm.27.280), *Mélodie religieuse* (Vm.7.16048), *Offertoire* (Vm.27.282), *March funèbre* (Vm.27.283), *La Prière des anges* (Vm.27.5558), *March procession* (Vm.27.5559), *Prière* [Les Regrets] (Vm.27.5561), *March funèbre* (Vm.27.5572), *Melodie religieux* (Vm.27.295), *March funèbre* (Vm.27.298), *Mélodie religieux* (Vm.27.301), *Andante* [Chant de Terpsichore] (Vm.27.303)
*Symphonie, Dieu et patrie* (Vm.27.5520)
Overtures: Vm.27.218, Vm.27.226, Vm.27.5507,
Vm.27.236, Vm.27.237, Vm.27.240,
Vm.27.241, Vm.27.5515, Vm.27.243,
Vm.27.5516 [*La Croix de Jerusalem*], Vm.27.245,
Vm.27.246, Vm.27.247, Vm.27.252,

Vm.27.5547, Vm.27.5527, Vm.27 .574 [Hommage à Rossini], Vm.27.274, Vm.27.5545 [Overture à grand effect, Musiciens et Poete], Vm.27.281, Vm.27.12674, Vm.27.5548, Vm.27.287, Vm.27.5557, Vm.27.290, Vm.27.296, Vm.27.307, Vm.27.5579 [Overture pastorale]

Cavatines, Vm.27.5583 [for solo cornet], Vm.27.4634

Fantaisies: Vm.27.219, Vm.27.220, Vm.27.4615, Vm.27.4617, Vm.27.229 [La Caravane Orientale], Vm.27.230, Vm.27.231, Vm.27.5505 [LeChant des Gondoliers], Vm.27.244, Vm.27.5521, Vm.27.262, Vm.27.267, Vm.27.263 [Les Glories de la France], Vm.27.5530, Vm.27.268, Vm.27.269, Vm.27.271, Vm.27.5535, Vm.27.4624, Vm.27.5562, Vm.27.291, Vm.27.294, Vm.27.5573, Vm.27.12675, Vm.27.300, Vm.27.5581, Vm.27.5582, Vm.27.311, Vm.27.313 [Une Fête du solistes], Vm.27.314, Vm.27.317, Vm.7.16049

Marches: Vm.27.215, Vm.27.5490, Vm.27.5487, Vm.27.4614, Vm.27.222, Vm.7.10.697, Vm.27.223, Vm.27.5493, Vm.27.224, Vm.27.5494, Vm.27.4616, Vm.27.5498, Vm.27.5497, Vm.27.5499, Vm.27.5500, Vm.27.5501, Vm.27.5502, Vm.27.5506, Vm.27.233, Vm.27.5509, Vm.27.238, Vm.27.5514, Vm.27.5517, Vm.27.249, Vm.7.16070, Vm.27.253, Vm.27.255, Vm.27.256, Vm.27.258, Vm.27.4620, Vm.27.5524, Vm.7.10698, Vm.27.5525, Vm.27.259, Vm.27.261, Vm.27.5532, Vm.7.16072, Vm.27.4622, Vm.27.272, Vm.27.5537, Vm.27.4623, Vm.27.275, Vm.27.5539, Vm.27.5540, Vm.27.4625, Vm.27.277, Vm.27.278, Vm.27.5542, Vm.27.284, Vm.27.5549, Vm.27.285, Vm.27.5550, Vm.27.4626, Vm.27.5551, Vm.27.5553, Vm.27.5555, Vm.27.4631, Vm.7.16050, Vm.27.5564, Vm.27.5565, Vm.27.292, Vm.27.293, Vm.27.5568, Vm.7.10695, Vm.27.5570, Vm.27.5571, Vm.27.5574, Vm.27.5575, Vm.27.5576, Vm.27.5592, Vm.27.4633, Vm.27.5580, Vm.27.302, Vm.27.305, Vm.27.310, Vm.7.16073, Vm.27.312 [Les Trompettes de la République], Vm.27.5586, Vm.27.315, Vm.27.5588, Vm.27.5589, Vm.27.5590, Vm.27.5591, Vm.27.319, Vm.27.5592

Galops: Vm.27.5486, Vm.27.5488, Vm.27.5511, Vm.27.242, Vm.27.5512, Vm.27.257, Vm.27.5522, Vm.27.273, Vm.27.5538, Vm.27.5560

Valses: Vm.27.5489, Vm.27.5578, Vm.27.227, Vm.27.5569, Vm.27.5504, Vm.27.270, Vm.27.5544, Vm.27.4629, Vm.27.4632, Fol. Vm.15.225

Polkas: Vm.27.221, Vm.27.5495, Vm.27.5496, Vm.27.5510, Vm.27.5518, Vm.27.248, Vm.27.5519, Vm.27.5525, Vm.27.260, Vm.27.276, Vm.27.5543 [Orientale], Vm.27.5546, Vm.27.5552, Vm.27.5554 [solo cornet], Vm.27.289, Vm.27.5566, Vm.27.309, Vm.27.316

Schottischs: Vm.27.5492, Vm.27.232, Vm.27.234, Vm.27.254, Vm.27.265, Vm.27.4621, Vm.27.5584, Vm.27.318, Fol.Vm.15.226;

Mazurkas: Vm.27.225, Vm.27.228, Vm.27.4627, Vm.27.4628, Vm.27.4630, Vm.27.288, Vm.27.5585

Quadrilles: Vm.27.239, Vm.27.251, Vm.27.5533, Vm.27.5534, Vm.27.5541, Vm.27.286, Vm.27.5556, Vm.27.5567, Vm.27.299, Vm.27.306

Boléros: Vm.27.5536, Fol.Vm.15.548, Fol. Vm.15.221, Vm.27.308

*Polonaise,* Vm.27.5513

## Blemant, Louis

The following works in F:Pn are all early prints for large wind band; all were printed in Paris in 1887–1897.

*Overture,* Vm.27.326

Marches: Vm.27.4636, Vm.27.325, Vm.27.5605

*Boléro,* Vm.27.4637

There are another hundred or so works by this composer in F:Pn, dating ca. 1900–1910.

## Blieck, Ad.

*March*
Large wind band
EP (Paris, 1882) F:Pn (Vm.27.5607)

## Bochsa, Karl

*Overture militaire*, Op. 29 (ca. 1820)
2222-221, serpent, percussion
MS BRD:Rtt (Sammelband 14, Nr. 25)
EP (Paris, composer) F:Pn (Vm.27.341 and Vm.7.10.538) [two copies]

(3) *Pot-pouris*, Op. 25
22-02
EP (Paris, composer) F:Pn (Vm.7.10.539)

(3) *Pot-pouris*, Op. 29
22-02
EP (Paris, composer) F:Pn (Vm.27.342)

*Sérénade* à 9, Op. 27
Harmoniemusik
EP (Paris, composer) [cited in AM]

*Harmonie* à 8
Harmoniemusik
EP (Paris, composer) [cited in AM]

## Bochsa, Charles N. (1789–1856)

*Requiem for Louis XVI*
ATB, 2222-441, serpent, bassi, percussion
EP (Paris, Pleyel and Bochsa) F:Pn (D.7418); I:Fc (A.21); US:DW (36)

## Boieldieu, A. (1775–1835)

(6) *Märsche mil. en Harmonie*
Harmoniemusik
EP (Leipzig, Breitkopf & Härtel) [cited in AMZ, 1805]

## Boisdeffre, René de (1838–1906)

*Septet*, Op. 49 (1898)
1111-01, piano, string bass [cited in DJ]

## Bonenfant, F.

*March*
Large wind band
EP (Paris, 1895) F:Pn (Vm.27.415)

## Bonnelle, A.

The following works in F:Pn are all early prints for large wind band; all were printed in Paris in 1864–1890.
Marches: Vm.27.5706, Vm.27.4646 [*pour ceremonies publiques et religieux*), Vm.27.419, Vm.7.11377, Vm.7.11377 bis, Vm.7.11378, Vm.27.5704 (*Marche de procession*), Vm.27.5705 [*avec choeur*]
Valses: Vm.7.11379, Vm.27.418, Vm.7.11376, Vm.7.11383
Polkas: Vm.27.5701, Vm.27.5702, Vm.27.5703
*Mazurka*, Vm.27.5700
*Quadrille*, Vm.7.11382

## Bonnelle, V.

*March*
Large wind band
EP (Paris, 1897) F:Pn (Vm.27.420)

## Bonnisseau

Unless otherwise noted, the following works are in F:Pn and all are early prints for large wind band, printed in Paris in 1859–1870.
Works for the Church: *Funeral March* [London, 1869], Vm.27.5710; *Morceau pour Élévation* [*Prière*], Vm.27.5723; *Andante pour Élévation*, Vm.27.5725; *Andante funèbre*, Vm.27.5728
*Overture*, Vm.27.5711
*Fantaisie* [for solo cornet], Vm.27.5714
*Morceau*, Vm.27.5730
Marches: Vm.27.5712, Vm.27.5713, Vm.27.5715, Vm.27.5716, Vm.27.5717, Vm.27.5718 Vm.27.5720, Vm.27.5721, Vm.27.5722, Vm.27.5724, Vm.27.5726, Vm.27.5729, Vm.27.5732, Vm.27.5733
*Schottsch*, Vm.27.5719
*Polka*, Vm.27.5727 [London, 1868]

## Bonnot, C. (Chef de Musique 14e de Ligne)

The following works in F:Pn are all early prints for large wind band; all were printed in Paris in 1855–1878.
Marches: Vm.27.422, Vm.27.430, Vm.27.426, Vm.7.11396, Vm.27.421, Vm.7.11400, Vm.27.11403, Vm.27.11399

*Galop*, Vm.7.11394 and Vm.7.11395 [two copies]
Valses: Vm.27.424, Vm.7.11391 and Vm.7.11392 [two copies]
*Polka*, Vm.27.428
*Schottisch*, Vm.27.425
*Redova*, Vm.27.431

**Borel, G.**

The following works in F:Pn are all early prints for large wind band; both were printed in Paris in 1867 and 1877.
*Dance havanaise,* Vm.7.11407
*March,* Vm.27.5734

**Borrea, Manuel**

*Valse*
Large wind band
EP (Paris, 1880) F:Pn (Vm.7.11411)

**Borrel, H.**

The following works in F:Pn are all early prints for large wind band; all were printed in Paris in 1890–1899.
Works for the Church: *Andante* (Vm.27.5740), *Andante* (Vm.27.454), *Andante* (Vm.27.5768), *Hymne* [*Avant le Sacre*] (Vm.27 .5739), *Hymne, 'à nos Amis'* [with chorus] (Vm.27 .5737), *Rêverie* (Vm.27.446), *Rêverie* (Vm.27.455)
Overtures: Vm.27.434, Vm.27.5745, Vm.27.441, Vm.27.5751 (*Overture hëroique*), Vm.27.447, Vm.27.5755, Vm.27.5758, Vm.27.12693 (*Overture pastorale*, 1908), Vm.27.5770, Vm.27.5777 (*Overture romantique*), Vm.27.5778, Vm.27.5779
Fantaisies: Vm.27.5738, Vm.27.5744, Vm.27.439, Vm.27.5749, Vm.27.442, Vm.27.5756, Vm.27.5762, Vm.27.453, Vm.27.5767 (*Petit Vovage en mer*), Vm.27.5774, Vm.27.457 (*Soirée intime*), Vm.27.458 (*La Source merveilleuse*), Vm.27.459
Airs varié: Vm.27.435, Vm.27.5772
*Scène champêtre*, Vm.27.5766
*Le Pas de la jouvencelle*, Vm.27.5765
*Aubade,* Vm.27.5748
Marches: Vm.27.5742, Vm.27.5741, Vm.27.5743, Vm.27.436, Vm.27.5752, Vm.27.5753, Vm.27.444, Vm.27.445, Vm.27.448, Vm.27.449, Fol.Vm.15.175, Vm.27.450 (*March solennelle*), Vm.27.451, Vm.27.456, Vm.27.5776

*Mazurka*, Vm.27.438
*Berceuse,* Vm.27.440
*Sérénades* [*Valses*], Vm.27.5757, Vm.27.5759
*Menuet,* Vm.27.5760
*Schottisch,* Vm.27.452
*Gavotte,* Vm.27.5761
*Polka,* Vm.27.5771
There are an additional twenty or thirty orchestral arrangements for band by Borrel in F:Pn.

**Bosch**

The following works in F:Pn are all early prints for large wind band; all were printed in Paris in 1854–1881.
Overtures: Vm.27.5783, Vm.27.472, Vm.7.11412, Vm.7.11413
*Fantaisie,* Vm.27.5782
Marches: Vm.7.11419, Vm.7.11416, Vm.7.11417, Vm.7.11418
Polkas: Vm.7.11414, Vm.7.11415 [solo oboe]

**Boscher, A.**

The following works in F:Pn are all early prints for large wind band; all were printed in Paris in 1870–1882.
Works for the Church: Vm.27.5798 (*Messe mil.*), Vm.27.5803 (*Marche funèbre*)
[Collection of 14 works], *Antiemes,* Vm.27.5795
*Overture,* Vm.27.5791
*Fantaisie,* Vm.27.5784
Marches: Vm.27.5800, Vm.27.5792, Vm.27.5793, Vm.27.5794
*Polka,* Vm.27.5790
*Quadrille,* Vm.27.5804
*Valse,* Vm.27.5806
There are an additional twenty orchestral arrangements by Boscher for band in F:Pn, as well as a *Méthode de le Cor* (L.8.734) which carries the interesting subtitle, '*Extrait de la méthode générale d'ensemble.*'

**Bouchel, J.**

The following works in F:Pn are all early prints for large wind band; all were printed in Paris in 1889–1900.
Overtures: Vm.27.5835, Vm.27.5821 bis

Fantaisies: Vm.27.473, Vm.27.5814 [*Fantaisie romantique*]
Marches: Vm.27.5823, Vm.27.5830, Vm.27.5831
*Polka*, Vm.27.5822
*Schottisch*, Vm.27.5816
There are an additional thirty or so original works from 1900–1910 and more than fifty orchestral transcriptions by Bouchel in F:Pn.

## Boudier, Achille

The following works in F:Pn are all early prints for large wind band; all were printed in Paris in 1855–1856.
Marches: Vm.27.5838, Vm.27.5839, Vm.27.5840
*Quadrille*, Vm.27.5837

## Boué, Ernest (Chef de Musique de 13e Leger)

The following works in F:Pn are all early prints for large wind band; all were printed in Paris in 1859–1886.
Works for the Church: Vm.27.476 and Vm.7.11431 [two copies] (*Marche funèbre*), Vm.27.477 and Vm.7.11423 [two copies] (*Marche funèbre*)
*Variations* (on a theme by Rossini) [solo E♭ clarinet], Vm.7.11427
*Morceau et Variations* (on a theme by Offenbach), Vm.7.11426
Marches: Vm.7.11434, Vm.7.11432 and Vm.7.11433 [two copies], Vm.7.11437 (*Marche comique*), Vm.7.11436, Vm.27.475
Valses: Vm.27.474, Vm.7.11421, Vm.7.11422
Polkas: Vm.7.11429, Vm.7.11428
*Galop*, Vm.27.478 and Vm.7.11425 [two copies]

## Bouffil (clarinet player in Paris, ca. 1820)

*Harmoniemusik*, Op. 6
1022-02
EP (Paris, Gambaro) [cited in H]

## Bougon

*Ordonnance des tambours et fiffres de la garde Impériale*
MS F:Pn (L.9818)

## Bouillon, Paul

The following works in F:Pn are all early prints for large wind band; all were printed in Paris in 1865–1890.
*Overture*, Vm.27.9878
Fantaisies: Vm.27.5870, Vm.27.483 [for solo alto saxophone]
*Galop*, vm.27.5842
Airs varié: Vm.7.11442 [solo trombone and tuba], Vm.27.486, Vm.27.484 [solo alto saxophone], Vm.27.487
Marches: Vm.27.5850, Vm.7.11438, Vm.27.5852, Vm.27.5853, Vm.27.5854, Vm.27.5843, Vm.27.5845, Vm.27.5846, Vm.27.5847, Vm.27.5849, Vm.27.5855, Vm.27.5857, Vm.7.11441 (*Marche funèbre*), Vm.27.5858, Vm.27.5859, Vm.27.5861, Vm.7.11439, Vm.7.11440, Vm.27.5863, Vm.27.5864, Vm.27.5865, Vm.27.5866, Vm.27.5868, Vm.27.5869, Vm.27.5871
Polkas: Vm.27.5856, Vm.27.5841, Vm.27.5867

## Boujut

The following works in F:Pn are all early prints for large wind band; both were printed in Paris without dates.
Marches: Vm.27.488, Vm.7.11443

## Boullard, Marius

*Marche*
Large wind band
EP (Paris, 1880) F:Pn (Vm.27.5873)

## Bourdon, J.

The following works in F:Pn are all early prints for large wind band; all were printed in Paris in 1880–1890.
Overtures: Vm.27.5879, Vm.27.5882
Fantaisies: Vm.27.5880, Vm.27.5881 (*L'Isle d'amour*), Vm.27.5885, Vm.27.5886, Vm.27.5878
Marches: Vm.27.5876, Vm.27.5887
*Quadrille*, Vm.27.5884
Polkas: Vm.27.5877, Vm.27.5883, Vm.27.5888

### Bourgault-Ducoudray

The following works in F:Pn are all early prints for large wind band; both were printed in Paris in 1881 and 1894.
*Hymne à la Patrie* [with chorus], Vm.27.5889
*Au Souvenir de Roland*, Vm.27.495

### Bourgeois, Ed.

*Quadrille*
Large wind band
EP (Paris, 1885) F:Pn (Vm.27.5891)

### Bourgeois, Jules

*Polka*
Large wind band
EP (Paris, 1887) F:Pn (Vm.27.5890)

### Bournigal, Léon

*March*
Large wind band
EP (Paris, 1887) F:Pn (Vm.27.5893)

### Bourrellis, H.-J.

*March*
Large wind band
EP (Clermont, 1877) F:Pn (Vm.27.5894)

*Allegro mil.*
Large wind band
EP (Lyon, 1899) F:Pn (Vm.27.5897)

### Bousquet, N. (Chevalier de la Légion d'Honneur)

The following works in F:Pn are all early prints for large wind band; all were printed in Paris in 1854–1870.
Works for the Church: Vm.7.11461 (*Marche pour procession*), Vm.7.11451 (*Morceau d'Élévation*), Vm.27.511 (*Morceau d'Élévation*), Vm.27.512 (*Morceau d'Élévation*), Vm.27.513 (*Morceau d'Élévation*), Vm.27.510 (*Morceau d'Élévation*), Vm.27.519 (*Morceau d'Élévation*), Vm.7.11452 (*Morceau d'Élévation*), Vm.7.11453 and Vm.7.11454 [two copies], (*Morceau d'Élévation*) Vm.27.520 and Vm.7.11459 (*March funèbre et religieux*)
*Le Bon Goût*, Vm.27.12710
*Le Cri de guerre*, Vm.27.4648
Marches: Vm.27.506, Vm.27.5929, Vm.7.11458, Vm.27.523, Vm.27.524, Vm.7.11445, Vm.27.5942, Vm.27.525, Vm.27.526, Vm.7.11462
Valses: Vm.27.5904, Vm.27.12711, Vm.27.5907, Vm.27.5909, Vm.27.507, Vm.27.508, Vm.27.12712, Vm.7.11447, Vm.27.5931, Vm.27.5936, Vm.27.5939, Vm.27.5944
Polkas: Vm.7.11456, Vm.27.504, Vm.27.505, Vm.27.5911, Vm.27.11432, Vm.27.5919, Vm.7.13435 [solo piccolo], Vm.7.11455, Vm.27.5928, Vm.27.5935, Vm.27.521, Vm.27.5946
Redovas: Vm.27.5905, Vm.27.515, Vm.27.518, Vm.27.5937, Vm.27.5943
Schottischs: Vm.27.5906, Vm.27.5912, Vm.27.5927
Quadrilles: Vm.27.5908, Vm.27.5913, Vm.27.5920, Vm.27.5921
Vm.27.5941 (*Le Triomphe des Trombones*)

### Bousquier, Fréd.

The following works in F:Pn are all early prints for large wind band; all were printed in Paris in 1865–1866.
Marches; Vm.27.5949, Vm.27.5951
*Galop*, Vm.27.527
*Quadrille*, Vm.7.11463

### Bousquier, L.

The following works in F:Pn are all early prints for large wind band; all were printed in Paris in 1863–1877.
Works for the Church: Vm.27.5956 (*Andante religoso*), Vm.27.5990 (*La Fête-Dieu*), Vm.27.6004 (*Morceau d'Élévation*), Vm.27.6002 (*Marche funébre*)
Overtures: Vm.27.5953, Vm.27.5960, Vm.27.5980, Vm.27.5997, Vm.27.536, Vm.27.6006, Vm.27.6007, Vm.27.6026, Vm.27.6035
Fantaisies: Vm.27.5961, Vm.27.5962, Vm.27.5967, Vm.27.5968, Vm.27.5982, Vm.27.5984, Vm.27.531, Vm.27.5985, Vm.27.6003, Vm.27.6010, Vm.27.6018, Vm.27.6024, Vm.27.6029, Vm.27.6030, Vm.27.6033

Marches: Vm.27.5954, Vm.27.5955, Vm.27.5957,
Vm.27.5958, Vm.27.528, Vm.27.5963,
Vm.27.5965, Vm.27.5970, Vm.27.5971,
Vm.27.5972, Vm.27.5973, Vm.27.5975,
Vm.27.5976, Vm.27.5979, Vm.27.5981,
Vm.27.5983, Vm.27.530, Vm.27.531,
Vm.27.5985, Vm.27.535, Vm.27.5993,
Vm.27.5994, Vm.27.5996, Vm.27.5998,
Vm.27.6000, Vm.7.11465, Vm.27.6001,
Vm.27.6005, Vm.27.6011, Vm.27.6017,
Vm.27.6021, Vm.27.5950, Vm.27.6027,
Vm.27.6028, Vm.27.6032
*Galop*, Vm.27.5992
There are an additional twenty or thirty orchestral transcriptions for band in F:Pn by Bousquier.

## Bouthel, L.

The following works in F:Pn are all early prints for large wind band; all were printed in Paris in 1866–1894.
Overtures: Vm.27.543, Vm.27.6063
Fantaisies: Vm.27.6043, Vm.27.542 [solo, Baryton or cornet], Vm.27.345, Vm.7.11471 [solo flute, oboe, and baritone]
*Allegro*, Vm.27.544
Marches: Vm.27.6048, Vm.27.6042, Vm.27.6051,
Vm.27.6052, Vm.27.6053, Vm.7.11472,
Vm.27.6046, Vm.27.6047, Vm.27.541,
Vm.27.6055, Vm.27.6056, Vm.27.6057,
Vm.27.6058, Vm.27.6059 (*March procession*),
Vm.7.11469, Vm.7.11470, Vm.27.6060
*Galop*, Vm.27.6062
*Polka*, [solo cornet] Vm.27.6050

## Bouvier, B.

*March*
Large wind band
EP (Paris, 1889) F:Pn (Vm.27.6066)

## Boyer, Louis

The following works in F:Pn are all early prints for large wind band; all were printed in Paris in 1895–1898.
*Overture*, Vm.27.552
Marches: Vm.27.6068, Vm.27.548

## Boyer, Th.

The following works in F:Pn are all early prints for large wind band; all were printed in Paris in 1887–1894.
*Overture*, Vm.27.559
Fantaisies: Vm.27.553, Vm.27.554
*March*, Vm.27.555
*Polka*, [solo cornet] Vm.27.556 and Vm.27.557 [two copies]
*Mazurka*, Vm.27.558
*Valse*, Vm.7.11474

## Braun

*Pas redoublé* (*sur le Chanson 'C'est Amour'*)
Harmoniemusik
EP (Paris, Pacini)

## Brepsant, Engebert (Chevalier de la Légion d'Honneur)

The following works in F:Pn are all early prints for large wind band; all were printed in Paris in 1855–1885.
Works for the Church: Vm.27.6086 (*Elégie funèbre*), Vm.27.6087 (*March procession*), Vm.27.6076 (*Hymne à S.S. Pie IX*), Vm.27.6089 (*Elégie funèbre*) [*sur Les Martyrs du Japon*], Vm.27.564 (*Mélodie funèbre*), Vm.27.6091 (*Mélodie religieux*)
*Overture, Fantaisie et Theme Varié*, Vm.27.6081
*Réveil de la Pologne*, Vm.27.6099
Fantaisies: Vm.27.6085, Vm.27.566, Vm.27.6092, Vm.27.4650 [*et Theme Varié*]
*6e Air varié*, [solo clarinet] K.1182
Marches: Vm.27.561, Vm.27.6075, Vm.27.4649,
Vm.27.562, Vm.27.6088, Vm.27.565,
Vm.27.6078, Vm.27.6079, Vm.27.6080,
Vm.27.6094, Vm.27.6082, Vm.27.6083,
Vm.27.6095, Vm.27.569, Vm.27.6084,
Vm.27.6096, Vm.27.6097, Vm.27.6098
Collections of Military music, Vm.7.11480 [8 works], Vm.7.11479 [6 works]
*Polka*, Vm.27.563
*Quadrille*, Vm.27.567

### Bretonnière, V. (Professeur de Musique à l'Ambassade turque)

The following works in F:Pn are all early prints for large wind band; all were printed in Paris in 1854–1865.
Marches: Vm.27.576, Vm.9.1677 (*à Abdul Medjid*) [here a flute part only], Vm.12.4086 [here a piano version of a difficult march]

### Bricot, Charles

The following works in F:Pn are all early prints for large wind band; both were printed in Paris in 1855.
*March*, Vm.27.579
*Polonaise*, Vm.27.578

### Brody, A.

*March*
Large wind band
EP (Paris, 1893) F:Pn (Vm.27.581)

### Bru, Jean [Pseud: Bellacour, Jeannette] (Chef de Musique, 8e de Ligne)

The following works in F:Pn are all early prints for large wind band; all were printed in Paris in ca. 1881.
Marches: Vm.27.6111, Vm.27.585, Vm.27.583, Vm.27.584

### Brun, Georges (b. 1878)

*Passacaille*, Op. 25
2121-02, string bass
MP (Paris, Lemoine) [cited in MH]

### Bruyer, Victor

The following works in F:Pn are all early prints for large wind band; all were printed in Paris in 1878–1899.
Overtures: Vm.27.6122, Vm.27.6122 bis (*Overture Symphonique*)
*Concerto* [solo clarinet], Vm.27.609 and Vm.27.610 [two copies]
*Andante et Allegro Pastorale* [solo oboe or soprano saxophone], Vm.27.12719
*Valse*, Vm.7.11524

### Bruyne, E. de

The following works in F:Pn are all early prints for large wind band; both were printed in Paris in 1880.
Marches: Vm.27.6123, Vm.27.6124

### Buhl, Joseph David (b. 1781)

(4) *Fanfares pour Cavallerie*
EP (Paris, Pacini)

(4) *Fanfares*
Nine brass instruments
EP (Paris, Janet) F:Pn (L.9782)

(6) *Fanfares*, Op. 1 (1799).
-4
EP (Paris) F:Pn (L.9.635) [1–13]

*March du Duc de Bordeaux*
Wind instruments
MS F:Pn (MS.13437)

(2) *Marches* and (4) *Pas redoublés* (1812)
-4
MS F:Pn (L.9.634)
EP (Paris) F:Pn (Vm.27.613)

(4) *Marches* (1803–1829)
Wind instruments
EP (Paris) F:Pn (L.9.633)

[Untitled works]
-4
MS F:Pn (L.9781, L.9.628, and L.9781)

*Ordonnances des fifres* (1813)
MS F:Pn (L.9.631)

(16) *Fanfares*
-421
EP (Paris) F:Pn (Vm.27.619)

(3) *Marches*
-421
EP (Paris) F:Pn (Vm.27.614; Vm.27.615; Vm.27.617 and Vm.27.616 [two copies])

### Bulan, Charles

The following works in F:Pn are all early prints for large wind band; both were printed in Paris in 1887 and 1889.
*Fantaisie*, Vm.27.620
*Quadrille*, Vm.27.621

## Buot, Victor (Chef de Musique de l'Artillerie de la Garde)

The following works in F:Pn are all early prints for large wind band; all were printed in Paris in 1858–1887.

Works for the Church: Vm.27.641 (*Marche funèbre*), Vm.27.6138 (*Marche funèbre*), Vm.27.6142 and Vm.27.6143 (*March procession*), Vm.7.11553 and Vm.7.11554 (*March du sacre*), Vm.7.11555 (*March funèbre*), Vm.7.11552 (*Morceau d'Élévation*) [solo alto saxophone], Vm.27.689 (*Overture solennelle*) [*La Prière*] (with chorus), Vm.27.6151 (*Marche solennelle*), Vm.1.1672 (*Stabat Mater*)

Vm.7.11552 is a very interesting full score for large band without double reeds or tuba. Vm.1.1672 is a major work for large band with saxophones, here with both a full score and a piano reduction. The movements of this important work are:

*Stabat mater*

*Quis est Homo* [Baritone (vocal) solo with full band]

*Pro Peccatis svoegentis* [Tenor solo with band]

*Sancta Mater* [a capella]

*Virgo Virginum* [Baritone, Tenor and Bass soli, with band]

*Inflammatus et Accensus* [Bass solo with band]

*Finale* [TTB Chorus and band]

Symphonies: Vm.27.623, Vm.27.630 (*Symphonie imitative*), for large band [here parts only] with virtually every instrument having a very difficult part technically.

Overtures: Vm.27.632, Vm.27.635, Vm.7.11556, Vm.27.642, Vm.27.682, Vm.7.11557, Vm.27.6153 (*Overture symphonique*), Vm.27.683, Vm.27.6159

Fantaisies: Vm.27.656, Vm.7.11534 (*Fantaisie arabe*), Vm.27.669 (*Fantaisie symphonique*), Vm.27.680 (*Fantaisie symphonique*), Vm.7.11545, Vm.27.705, Vm.7.11548, Vm.27.706

Airs varié: Vm.27.625, Vm.7.11542, Vm.7.11551 (*Morceau: tyrolienne varié*)

Marches: Vm.27.622, Vm.27.627, Vm.7.11559, Vm.27.6132, Vm.27.6133, Vm.7.11560, Vm.27.634, Vm.7.11561, Vm.27.636, Vm.27.637, Vm.27.638, Vm.27.6136, Vm.27.6137, Vm.27.645, Vm.27.650, Vm.27.652, Vm.7.11562, Vm.27.6141, Vm.7.11563, Vm.27.660, Vm.27.665, Vm.7.11564, Vm.27.666, Vm.27.667, Vm.7.11565, Vm.27.6147, Vm.27.6148, Vm.27.670, Vm.27.674, Vm.27.675, Vm.27.676 (*March russe*), Vm.27.679, Vm.27.6152, Vm.7.11566, Vm.7.11567, Vm.27.6154, Vm.27.6155, Vm.7.11527, Vm.7.11528, Vm.7.11529, Vm.27.690, Vm.7.11584, Vm.27.691, Vm.7.11532, Vm.27.692, Vm.27.695, Vm.27.697, Vm.7.11569, Vm.7.11568, Vm.27.699, Vm.27.701, Vm.27.702, Vm.27.707, Vm.27.711, Vm.27.712, Vm.7.11570, Vm.27.713, Vm.7.11571, Vm.27.6160

Galops: Vm.27.624, Vm.27.6131 ('tres original'), Vm.27.639, Vm.27.642, Vm.7.11533, Vm.7.11530, Vm.7.11531, Vm.27.6140, Vm.27.663 (solo cornet), Vm.27.644, Vm.27.709 (*Le Vampire*)

Quadrilles: Vm.27.626, Vm.7.11582, Vm.27.673, Vm.7.11583

Polkas: Vm.7.11572, Vm.27.629, Vm.7.11573 [two soli clarinets], Vm.27.6134 [solo cornet], Vm.7.11574 bis, Vm.27.635 bis, Vm.27.6135 [solo cornet], Vm.7.11575, Vm.7.11574, Vm.27.640, Vm.7.11576, Vm.27.644, Vm.27.6139, Vm.27.651, Vm.27.653, Vm.27.655, Vm.27.658, Vm.27.659 [on *Frère Jacques*], Vm.27.661, Vm.7.11578, Vm.7.11579 (*Polka Bavaroise*) ['Liesel und Gretel'], Vm.27.6149, Vm.27.6150 [solo cornet], Vm.27.678, Vm.27.685, Vm.27.686, Vm.7.11580, Vm.27.6157, Vm.27.704, Vm.27.6158, Vm.27.703 [two soli cornets]

Redovas: Vm.27.628, Vm.27.6156

Valses: Vm.7.11586, Vm.7.11587 (*Clair de lune*), Vm.27.6145, Vm.27.6146, Vm.7.11588, Vm.27.700, Vm.27.708

Mazurkas: Vm.27.649, Vm.27.654

Barcarolles: Vm.27.671, Vm.7.11547

Schottischs: Vm.27.681, Vm.7.11585, Vm.27.693

*Souvenir de Bordeaux*, Vm.27.698

[Collection] (1856), Vm.27.3663

There are an additional thirty or so transcriptions for band in F:Pn by Buot.

## Burgmann

The following works in F:Pn are all early prints for large wind band; all were printed in Paris in 1856–1861.
Works for the Church: Vm.27.6163 (*Andante*), Vm.27.6165 (*Andante religieux*) [*L'Angelus*]
Marches: Vm.27.6170, Vm.27.6172, Vm.27.6167
Valses: Vm.27.6171, Vm.27.6164, Vm.27.6169
Polkas: Vm.27.6166, Vm.27.6168

## Cambier, Victor

The following works in F:Pn are all early prints for large wind band; all were printed in Paris in 1853–1864.
Works for the Church: Vm.27.6194 (*Marche funèbre*), Vm.27.6183 (*Andante*)
Fantaisies: Vm.27.6185, Vm.27.6189, Vm.7.13221
Marches: Vm.27.6195, Vm.27.6187, Vm.27.6188, Vm.27.6182, Vm.27.6184
Polkas: Vm.27.6190, Vm.27.6196
Boléros: Vm.27.6186 and Vm.27.6193
*Schottisch*, Vm.27.6192
*Quadrille*, Vm.27.6191
*Grande Chasse*, Vm.27.726

## Camomille, J.

The following works in F:Pn are all early prints for large wind band; both were printed in Paris in 1895 and 1897.
*Overture symphonique*, Vm.27.727
*March du 200e de marche*, Vm.27.730

## Canaple, Henri

The following works in F:Pn are all early prints for large wind band; all were printed in Montdidier in 1854–1855.
Works for the Church: Vm.27.6200 (*Andante religieux*), Vm.27.6202 (*Élévation*)
Marches: Vm.27.6203, Vm.27.6204
*Bolero*, Vm.27.6201

## Canivez, L.

The following works in F:Pn are all early prints for large wind band; all were printed in Paris in 1887–1892.
Works for the Church: Vm.27.6206 (*Andante*), Vm.27.6210 (*Invocation*), Vm.27.6211 (*Marche nuptiale*)
Overtures: Vm.27.6216, Vm.27.6207 and Vm.27.6208 [two copies]
Fantaisies: Vm.27.6215, Vm.27.6212
*Impromptu*, Vm.27.6209
Marches: Vm.27.6214, Vm.27.6205

## Carafa, Michele (1787–1872)

[Collection]
Military Band
MS I:Nc [cited in Grove, III, 769]
According to Grove, this collection of autographs includes a 'Marche funèbre pour la translation des cendres de Napoléon,' as well as works for five solo winds.

*Andante*
Solo horn, 21-, ophicleide
MS (autograph) F:Pn (MS.3945.2); US:DW (311 and 172)

*Allegretto* ('Paris, 1845')
Solo clarinet and 1222-12
MS (autograph) F:Pn (MS.3.929); US:DW (311 and 174)

## Carbon

The following works in F:Pn are all early prints for large wind band; all were printed in Paris in 1852–1856.
Works for the Church: Vm.27.6226 (*March-procession*), Vm.27.6227 (*Marche nuptiale*), Vm.27.6228 (*Offertoire au Morceau d'Élévation*)
Marches: Vm.27.6224, Vm.27.6225

## Carcassone, Georges

The following works in F:Pn are all early prints for large wind band; all were printed in Paris in 1888–1899.

Marches: Vm.27.6236, Vm.27.6237, Vm.27.6242
    (*La Russie et la France*)
*Polka*, Vm.27.6240
*Mazurka*, Vm.27.6243

## Carraut, L.

*Fanfare*
Large wind band
EP (Paris, 1865) F:Pn (Vm.27.6257)

## Carrié, Louis

*Polka*
Large wind band
EP (Paris, 1886) F:Pn (Vm.27.6258)

## Carteron, Alexandre

The following works in F:Pn are all early prints
    for large wind band; all were printed in Paris
    in 1888–1885.
*Overture*, Vm.27.742
*Fantaisie*, Vm.27.743
Marches: Vm.27.6269, Vm.27.6270, Vm.27.6260,
    Vm.27.6263
*Schottisch*, Vm.27.741
*Boléro*, Vm.27.6264
*Galop*, Vm.27.6265
*Polka*, Vm.27.6266

## Casquil

The following works in F:Pn are early prints for
    large wind band printed in Paris in 1885 and in
    Rennes in 1897.
*3e Menuet original*, Vm.27.6274
*Marche solennelle*, vm.27.6272

## Cassard, L.

*Polka*
Large wind band
EP (Paris, 1887) F:Pn (Vm.27.748)

## Castela, A.

*Marche du 79e*
Large wind band
EP (Paris, 1896) F:Pn (Vm.27.6277)

## Castil-Blaze, François (d. 1857)

Pas redoublé, *Vive le Roi*
Harmoniemusik
EP (Paris, Janet)

*Sextet*, Op. 18
22-02
EP (Paris, Aulagnier, 1832) F:Pn (L.1360)

## Cauchie, F.

*March*
Large wind band
EP (Paris, 1887) F:Pn (Vm.27.6279)

## Caudron, L.

*March*
Large wind band
EP (Paris, 1894) F:Pn (Vm.27.775)

## Caussinus, V.

The following works in F:Pn are all early prints
    for large brass band; all were printed in Paris in
    1865–1868.
Works for the Church: Vm.27.6289 (*Grande
    Messe St. Cécile*), Vm.7.13002 (*O Salutaris*),
    Vm.7.13003 (*Sanctus*) ['à grand effet']
Upon submitting the call-number for the *Grande
    Messe*, I received only a march, entitled *Introd:
    Tempo di Marcia*, which I take to be a work
    performed before the Mass.
Marches: Vm.7.13310, Vm.27.777, Vm.27.779
*Sérénade*, Vm.27.780
Quadrilles: Vm.27.778, Vm.7.13308

## Causy

The following works in F:Pn are all early prints
    for large wind band; all were printed in Paris
    in 1899.
Marches: Vm.27.6291, Vm.27.6292, Vm.27.6293,
    Vm.27.6294, Vm.27.6295
*Boléro*, Vm.27.6290
*Valse*, Vm.27.6296
*Schottisch*, Vm.27.6297

### Cavaillé-Massenet, F.

The following works in F:Pn are all early prints for large wind band; all were printed in Paris in 1891–1896.
Allegri militaire: Vm.27.6298, Vm.27.6299
Marches: Vm.27.6302, Vm.27.6303, Vm.27.6304
*Galop,* Vm.27.6301

### Cayron, J.

*Marche du sacre*
Large wind band
EP (Lyon, 1896) F:Pn (Vm.27.6305)

### Cerclier, Jules-H.-L.

(30) *Marches*
-4, timpani
EP (Paris, Hartmann) F:Pn (L.9.004)

### Chambroux, J.

The following works in F:Pn are all early prints for large wind band; all were printed in Paris in 1887–1890.
*March,* Vm.27.795
*Mazurka,* Vm.27.6314
*Schottisch,* Vm.27.793

### Chapelle, Ed.

*March*
Large wind band
EP (Paris, 1899) F:Pn (Vm.27.6323)

### Chargnioux, Marie

The following works in F:Pn are all early prints for large wind band; all were printed in Paris in 1873–1890.
*Overture,* Op. 31, Vm.27.799
*Fantaisie,* Vm.27.802
Marches: Vm.27.800, Vm.27.801

### Charigny, J.-A.-L. de

*March*-
Large wind band
EP (Paris, 1860) F:Pn (Vm.27.6330)

### Charles

The following works in F:Pn are all early prints for large wind band; all were printed in Paris in 1889.
Overtures: Vm.27.6332, Vm.27.6334
Fantaisies: Vm.27.6333, Vm.27.12739

### Chassain, Raoul

The following works in F:Pn are all early prints for large wind band; all were printed in Paris in 1895–1899.
Works for the Church: Vm.27.12740 (*Andante religieux*), Vm.27.6341 (*Andante religieux*), Vm.27.6346 (*Prière à St. Cécile*)
*Fantaisie,* Vm.27.6347
Marches: Vm.27.6338, Vm.27.6350
*Polka,* Vm.27.6344

### Chasseigneau, Paul

*March*
Large wind band
EP (Montevigis, 1895) F:Pn (Vm.27.6352)

### Chassin, A.

The following works in F:Pn are all early prints for large wind band; all were printed in Paris, Pithiviers and Bromeilles in 1866–1884.
*La Prière,* Vm.27.6380
Overtures: Vm.27.6376, Vm.27.6384
*Air Varié,* Vm.27.6385
*Allegro,* Vm.27.6374
Marches: Vm.27.6354, Vm.27.6355, Vm.27.6357, Vm.27.6358, Vm.27.6359, Vm.27.6360, Vm.27.6361, Vm.27.6363, Vm.27.6370, Vm.27.6371, Vm.27.6372, Vm.27.6373, Vm.27.6377, Vm.27.6378, Vm.27.6386
Valses: Vm.27.6353, Vm.27.6387
Polkas: Vm.27.6356, Vm.27.6369, Vm.27.6383
*Schottisch,* Vm.27.6362
*Quadrille,* Vm.27.6382
[Collection] (12 works), Vm.27.12745

## Chaulier, Cyriaque (Chef de Musique au 6md de Ligne)

The following works in F:Pn are all early prints for large wind band; all were printed in Paris and Saintes, Basque in 1882–1895.

Works for the Church: Vm.7.13006 (*March pour procession*), Vm.27.6395 and Vm.27.12746 [two copies] (*Marche funèbre*)

*Overture*, Vm.27.810, This work is for Fanfare, here brass band with saxophones, with a condensed score. The work is a long, multi-sectional.

Fantaisies: Vm.27.6390, Vm.27.811

*March*, Vm.27.6391

*Allegro Militaire*, Vm.27.6397

*Farandole*, Vm.27.808

*Polonise*, Vm.27.6396

## Chausson, Ernest-Amédée (1855–1899)

*Marche Militaire* (1884)
Large wind band [cited in MGG]

*Les Oiseaux*
Wind instruments [according to MGG, incidental music for a play by Aristophanes]

## Chavatte, Henri

The following works in F:Pn are all early prints for large wind band; all were printed in Paris in ca. 1876.

Marches: Vm.27.6402, Vm.27.6403, Vm.27.6399 (*Marche procession*)

*Polka*, Vm.27.6398

*Valse*, Vm.27.6400

*Schottisch*, Vm.27.6401

## Cherubini, Luigi (1760–1842)

Additional original works by Cherubini are found in Volume Eight of this series.

*Marche du Prefet d'Eure-et Loire* (1800)
Band
MS (autograph) DDR:Bds [cited in Grove, IV, 212–213]

*Marche pour le Retour du Prefet*
MS (autograph) DDR:Bds [cited in Grove, IV, 212–213]

*March* (1805, for K. le Baron de Braun)
111-01, string bass
MS (copy) DDR:Bds [cited in Grove, IV, 212–213]

*March* (1808)
Woodwinds
MS (autograph) DDR:Bds [cited in Grove, IV, 212–213]

*March* (July 12, 1809, Chimay)
Woodwinds
MS (autograph) DDR:Bds [cited in Grove, IV, 212–213]

*March* (September 22, 1810, Chimay)
Woodwinds
MS (autograph) DDR:Bds [cited in Grove, IV, 212–213]

*March (for the National Guard*, February 8, 1814)
Band
MS (autograph) DDR:Bds [cited in Grove, IV, 212–213]

*Pas redoublé* (1814)
Band
MS (autograph) DDR:Bds [cited in Grove, IV, 212–213]

(6) *Pas redoublés* and (2) *Marches* (1814, for the Prussian regiment of Col. Witzleben)
-131
MS (autograph) DDR:Bds [cited in Grove, IV, 212–213]
MP (London, 1962) US:DW (397)

*Graduale*
SATB, 22-02, organ, string bass
MS CS:KRa (C33)

## Chevalier, R.

*Valse*
Large wind band
EP (Paris, 1869) F:Pn (Vm.27.6409)

## Chic, Léon

The following works in F:Pn are all early prints for large wind band; all were printed in Paris in 1857–1896.

Works for the Church: Vm.27.837 (*Marche funèbre*) [dedicated to Admiral Courbet], Vm.27.6418 (*March procession*)

*Overture*, Vm.27.855 and Vm.7.12909 [two copies]

Fantaisies: Vm.27.830, Vm.27.841, Vm.7.13040, Vm.7.13283, Vm.7.13233 (*Fantaisie et Variations*) [on a theme of Auber, for solo clarinet], Vm.7.13236, Vm.7.13230 [on a theme of Rossini, for solo E♭ clarinet], Vm.7.13243 [on a theme of Verdi, for solo trombone]

*Intermezzo*, Vm.27.839

*Payane médices*, Vm.27.848

Solos: Vm.7.13288 [solo alto saxophone; under A.5.26 with piano accompaniment], Vm.7.13291 [on a theme by Donizetti, for solo alto saxophone], Vm.7.13290 [on a theme by Rossini, for solo cornet]

*Air varié*, Vm.7.13225 [on a theme by Rossini, for solo baritone]

*Duo*, Vm.7.13026 [on a theme by Rossini, for soli cornet and baritone]

*Sérénade,* Vm.27.6422

Marches: Vm.27.820, Vm.27.831, Vm.27.832, Vm.7.13244, Vm.7.13259, Vm.7.13260, Vm.7.13028, Vm.7.13263, Vm.27.843, Vm.27.6419, Vm.7.13247, Vm.7.13267, Vm.7.13251 (*March espagnol*), Vm.7.13265, Vm.7.13266, Vm.27.854 and Vm.7.13268 [two copies], Vm.7.13269, Vm.27.6421 (*Salut aux Orphéons*)

Polkas: Vm.27.819, Vm.7.13254

Galops: Vm.27.6413 and Vm.27.6414 [two copies], Vm.7.13252, Vm.27.858

*Mazurka*, Vm.27.821

Valses: Vm.7.13297, Vm.7.13300, Vm.7.13301, Vm.27.6423, Vm.7.13299 ['*favorite de la Reine de Prusse*']

*Polonaise,* Vm.27.851

*Quadrille,* Vm.27.849 and Vm.7.13257 [two copies]

[Collection] Vm.7.4990, a full score for large band, containing the following works:
[1] *Air Français (La Reine Hortense)*
[2] *Domine Salvum (Pour Les Cérémonies Religieuses; ad lib solo or choer unison)*
[3] [band version of the above]
[4–6] *Air anglais, Prussien, Sveclois* ['God Save the King']
[7] *Air Russe*
[8] *Austria*
[9] *Belge*
[10] *Hollandais*
[11] *Bavarois*
[12] *Norwegien*
[13] *Danois*
[14] *Swisse*
[15] *Espagnol*
[16] *Hymne de Riego (Espagnol, aprie le Revolution de 1868)*
[17] *Portugais*
[18] *Italien*
[19] *Romain (Marche du Pape)*
[20] *Turc*
[21] *Grec*
[22] *Egyptien*
[23] *Americain*
[24] *Bresilien*
[25] *Air de Buenos Ayres*
[26] *Air de Montevideo*
[27] *Air Chilien*
[28] *Air Peruvien*
[29] *Air Mexicain*
[30] *Air Chinois*

Nr. 23 *Americain*

There are an additional hundred or so transcriptions of orchestral music, including Beethoven symphonie movements, in F:Pn by Chic. There is also found here (Vm.27.6415) Chic's arrangement of Alfred Lair de Beauvais's *Domine salvum fac imperatorem* for military band.

## Chomel, L.

The following works in F:Pn are all early prints for large wind band; all were printed in Paris in 1896–1900.

Marches: Vm.27.6435, Vm.27.6436, Vm.27.6437

*Mazurka*, Vm.27.863

There are an additional twenty-five or so transcriptions in F:Pn by Chomel.

## Choquard, E.

The following works in F:Pn are all early prints for large wind band; all were printed in Paris in 1896–1900.

Marches: Vm.27.6439, Vm.27.6444

Polkas: Vm.27.871, Vm.27.6441 and Vm.27.6442 [two copies]

Mazurkas: Vm.27.870, Vm.27.6443

Gavottes: Vm.27.6438, Vm.27.874

## Clapisson, Louis (1808–1866)

*Sérénade*
-121 [cited in Grove, IV, 426]
Grove also cites many trios for -03, -111 and -021 and mentions that the funeral of Clapisson was conducted on a grand scale with a military band and 'an orchestra of Sax instruments.'

## Clodomir, P.

The following works in F:Pn are all early prints for large wind band; all were printed in Paris in 1866–1884.

Works for the Church: Vm.27.6459 (*March solennelle*), Vm.27.6483 (*Andante funébre*), Vm.21.6489 (*Andante religieux*), Vm.27.6554 (*Andante religieux*), Vm.27.6557 (*Andante religieux*)

Overtures: Vm.27.6465, Vm.21.6474, Vm.27.6486, Vm.27.6513, Vm.27.6536, Vm.21.6570 (*Tour de Babel*), Vm.27.6577, Vm.27.6575

Fantaisies: Vm.27.6551, Vm.27.6576 [solo cornet], Vm.27.6578

*Diament*, Vm.27.6487

*Air Varié*, Vm.27.6544

Marches: Vm.27.6462, Vm.27.6469, Vm.21.6471, Vm.27.6473, Vm.27.6478, Vm.27.6479, Vm.27.6481, Vm.27.6482, Vm.27.6490, Vm.27.6491, Vm.27.6492, Vm.27.6505, Vm.27.6506, Vm.27.6508, Vm.27.6509, Vm.27.6510, Vm.27.6511, Vm.27.6514, Vm.27.6518, Vm.27.6519, Vm.27.6520, Vm.27.6522, Vm.27.6529, Vm.27.6530, Vm.27.6531, Vm.27.6535, Vm.27.6537, Vm.27.6538, Vm.27.6539, Vm.27.6541, Vm.27.6543, Vm.27.6545, Vm.27.6549, Vm.27.6550, Vm.27.6555, Vm.27.6556, Vm.27.6558, Vm.27.6559, Vm.27.6561, Vm.27.6562, Vm.27.6569, Vm.27.6570, Vm.27.6571, Vm.27.6572, Vm.27.6573, Vm.27.6579, Vm.27.6582, Vm.27.6583, Vm.27.6584, Vm.27.6585

Polkas: Vm.27.6464, Vm.27.6477 [solo cornet], Vm.27.6493, Vm.27.6494, Vm.27.6515, Vm.27.6516V, Vm.27.6524, Vm.27.6542, Vm.27.6546, Vm.27.6547

Galops: Vm.27.6467, Vm.27.6512, Vm.27.6580

Boléros: Vm.27.6466, Vm.27.12753

Quadrilles: Vm.27.6476, Vm.27.6484, Vm.27.6485 [two copies], Vm.27.6552 (*Le Roi des jongleurs*)

*Schottisch*, Vm.27.6534

## Coll, Joseph

The following works in F:Pn are early prints for large wind band; both were printed in Paris in the late nineteenth century.

*March*, Vm.27.893

*Schottisch*, Vm.27.894

## Colmier, L.

The following works in F:Pn are all early prints for large wind band; all were printed in Paris in 1891–1894.

Polkas: Vm.27.6591, Vm.27.6594, Vm.27.6597

*Quadrille*, Vm.27.6595

*Pas de quatre independant*, Vm.27.6599

## Comina, W.

*Valse*
Large wind band
EP (Paris, 1898) F:Pn (Vm.27.906)

## Conor, Léon

The following works in F:Pn are all early prints for large wind band; all were printed in Paris in 1861–1900.

Marches: Vm.27.9653, Vm.27.6608, Vm.27.6610, Vm.27.6612, Vm.27.6613

Polkas: Vm.27.6614, Vm.27.6615, Vm.27.6611, Vm.27.4656, Vm.27.913

*Boléro*, Vm.27.6609

*Valse*, Vm.27.912

**Constant, H.**

The following works in F:Pn are all early prints for large wind band; all were printed in Paris in 1855–1889.
Overtures: Vm.27.915, Vm.7.12923
*Fantaisie*, Vm.27.6618
Marches: Vm.27.914, Vm.27.6616, Vm.7.12336, Vm.27.6617, Vm.27.916
*Quadrille*, Vm.7.13315
An arrangement by Constant of Beethoven's Third Symphony for band can be found in F:Pn under Vm.7.10645.

**Conti, A.**

The following works in F:Pn are all early prints for large wind band; all were printed in Paris during the nineteenth century.
*Schottisch*, Vm.27.918
*Quadrille*, Vm.27.919
*Polka*, Vm.27.920

**Coquterre, François**

The following works in F:Pn are all early prints for large wind band; all were printed in Paris in 1858–1878.
Works for the Church: Vm.27.6624 and Vm.7.13050 [two copies] (*Kyrie Eleison*), Vm.27.931 (*Te Deum*) The *Te Deum* is scored for brass band, clarinets, one alto and three tenor saxophones, with TTBB chorus. It consists of one long movement, with very busy wind parts.
Marches: Vm.7.13345, Vm.7.13343, Vm.27.922, Vm.7.13344, Vm.7.13342, Vm.27.6623, Vm.27.4657, Vm.27.13341
Polkas: Vm.7.13339, Vm.27.923, Vm.27.6621, Vm.27.926, Vm.27.927
*Redova*, Vm.27.930
*Valse*, Vm.7.13340
*Mazurka*, Vm.27.932
*Souvenir des enfants du Doubs*, Vm.27.6622

**Coquelet, O.**

The following works in F:Pn are all early prints for large wind band; all were printed in Paris and Pithiviers in 1884–1907.
Overtures: Vm.27.952, Vm.27.955, Vm.27.956, Vm.27.959, Vm.27.961, Vm.27.966 (*La Mission de Jeaune d'Arc*), Vm.27.969, Vm.27.973, Vm.27.977, Vm.27.6630, Vm.27.6631, Vm.27.979, Vm.27.981, Vm.27.982, Vm.27.985
Fantaisies: Vm.27.937, Vm.27.938, Vm.27.940, Vm.27.945, Vm.27.946, Vm.27.950, Vm.27.948, Vm.27.951, Vm.27.4659, Vm.27.4658, Vm.27.4660, Vm.27.4661, Vm.27.965 (*Mars et Venus*), Vm.27.967, Vm.27.971, Vm.27.970 (*Les Noces de Psyché*), Vm.27.4662, Vm.27.984, Vm.27.989, Vm.27.4664, Vm.27.12760, Vm.27.4665, Vm.27.4666
*Cortege de Ballet*, Vm.27.944
Marches: Vm.27.6625, Vm.27.6626, Vm.27.936, Vm.27.939, Vm.27.941, Vm.27.943, Vm.27.6628, Vm.27.954, Vm.27.962 (*Marche funèbre*), Vm.27.964, Vm.7.13054, Vm.27.4663, Vm.27.980, Vm.27.983, Vm.27.986, Vm.27.988
*Polonaise*, Vm.27.987
There are an additional thirty or so original works from 1900–1915 and fifty or more orchestral transcriptions in F:Pn by Coquelet.

**Coquelin, G.**

The following works in F:Pu are early prints for large wind band; both were printed in Paris in 1896–1898.
*Allegro militaire*, Vm.27.992
*Polka*, Vm.27.994

**Corbin, A.**

Works for the Church: Vm.27.4667 (*Rêverie*), Vm.27.1004 (*Marche funèbre*)
*Overture*, Vm.27.1001
*Fantaisie*, Vm.27.1025
Marches: Vm.27.996, Vm.27.1011, Vm.27.1012, Vm.27.1014, Vm.27.1021
Polkas:
Vm.27.995 [solo clarinet], Vm.27.1000, Vm.27.8333, Vm.27.1003, Vm.27.1005, Vm.27.1017, Vm.27.1018, Vm.27.6637, Vm.27.1019, Vm.27.1024

Mazurkas: Vm.27.997, Vm.27.998 [solo oboe], Vm.27.1002, Vm.27.6636 [solo cornet], Vm.27.1020
Valses: Vm.27.999, Vm.27.1022
Galops: Vm.27.1006 (*Furioso*), Vm.27.6638
Quadrilles: Vm.27.1007, Vm.27.1009, Vm.27.1010
Schottisch: Vm.27.1015, Vm.27.3214 and Vm.27.1023 [two copies]

## Correvon de Ribaucourt, Marie-Louise

*March avec Cantate*
TTBB, wind band
EP (Paris, 1896) F:Pn (Vm.7.114764)
Under this number I found only a condensed score with only incipits for the band parts. The works seems to be short but dramatic, with noisy percussion parts.

## Cortazar, M.

The following works in F:Pn are all early prints for large wind band; all were printed in Paris in 1857.
Marches: Vm.27.6643, Vm.27.6645 (*L'Echo*) Vm.27.6646
*Boléro*, Vm.27.6644

## Cotté, E.

The following works in F:Pn are all early prints for large wind band; all were printed in Montereau, Champignolles and Toucy in 1867–1889.
Marches: Vm.27.6649, Vm.27.6648, Vm.27.6651, Vm.27.6652, Vm.27.6654, Vm.27.6655, Vm.27.6656
*Mazurka*, Vm.27.6653
*Quadrille*, Vm.27.6650

## Couleuvrier, A.

The following works in F:Pn are all early prints for large wind band; all were printed in Brivo in 1887.
*Overture*, Vm.27.6668
*Andante*, Vm.27.6664 [solo soprano saxophone with brass band]
Marches; Vm.27.6660, Vm.27.6665, Vm.27.6659

Polkas: Vm.27.6661 [for brass band], Vm.27.6662, Vm.27.6666

## Courtin

(6) *Walses connues*
Seven-part Harmoniemusik
EP (Paris, Janet)

(6) *Nocturnes*
201-01
EP (Paris, Janet) [cited in AM]

## Couthier, E.

The following works in F:Pn are all early prints for large wind band; all were printed in Paris in 1883–1892.
*Overture*, Vm.27.6673
Fantaisies; Vm.27.6677, Vm.27.6678, Vm.27.12763
*Air Varié*, Vm.27.6670
Marches: Vm.27.12766, Vm.27.6680, Vm.27.6672, Vm.27.6681 (*Marche funèbre*)
*Valse suite*, Vm.27.6679
*Polka*, Vm.27.6676
Quadrilles: Vm.27.6671, Vm.27.6674 and Vm.27.6675 [two copies]

## Coyon, Emile

The following works in F:Pn are all early prints for large wind band; all were printed in Paris in 1866–1868.
Marches: Vm.27.1037, Vm.27.6686, Vm.27.4670 (*March procession*)
*Polka*, Vm.7.13348

## Crémont, Pierre (1784–1846)

*Harmonie*
Military band
EP (Paris, Sieber) [Liv. 1–2]
EP (Paris, Gambaro) [cited in F]

*Trois marches funèbres*
Harmonie militaire
EP (Paris, Gambaro) [cited in F]

## Cressonnois, Jules

*Galop*
Large wind band
EP (Paris, 1882) F:Pn (Vm.27.6688)

## Creste, W.

The following works in F:Pn are all early prints for large wind band; all were printed in Montargis in 1886–1894.
*Overture,* Vm.27.6691
Marches: Vm.27.6689, Vm.27.6690, Vm.27.1040

## Crispin, Eugene

The following works in F:Pn are all early prints for large wind band; all were printed in Paris in ca. 1878.
*Valse,* Vm.27.6692
*Mazurka,* Vm.27.6693

## Dagnelies, D.

*March*
Large wind band
EP (Paris, 1880) F:Pn (Vm.27.6700)

## Dallée

The following works in F:Pn are all early prints for large wind band; all were printed in Paris in 1854–1869.
Nocturnes: Vm.7.13356 and Vm.7.13357 [two copies], Vm.7.13355
*Allegro militaire,* Vm.27.6704
Marches: Vm.7.13358, Vm.27.6706, Vm.27.6707, Vm.7.13359, Vm.27.6711 (*Marche funèbre*), Vm.27.6715, Vm.27.6716, Vm.27.6717, Vm.27.6719, Vm.27.6720, Vm.27.6712, Vm.27.6722
*Galop,* Vm.27.6709
*Valse,* Vm.27.6723
*Polka,* Vm.27.6714

## Damian, François

The following works in F:Pn are all early prints for large wind band; all were printed in Paris in 1880–1893.

Overtures: Vm.27.1060, Vm.27.1063, Vm.27.1064, Vm.27.1070
*Andante sonatine,* Vm.27.1061
Fantaisies: Vm.27.1058 and Vm.27.1059 [two copies], Vm.27.6728, Vm.27.1065, Vm.27.1067, Vm.27.1068
Marches: Vm.27.1062, Vm.27.6731, Vm.27.6734, Vm.27.6735, Vm.27.6736, Vm.27.6737 (*Marche funèbre*)
Quadrilles: Vm.27.6727, Vm.27.6729
*Schottisch,* Vm.27.6730
*Valse,* Vm.27.1066
*Mazurka,* Vm.27.6732
*Polka,* Vm.27.6733

## Dasque, Auguste

The following works in F:Pn are all early prints for large wind band; all were printed in Paris and Saintes in 1876–1886.
*Fantaisie,* Vm.27.1077
Marches: Vm.27.6753, Vm.27.6754, Vm.27.6755, Vm.27.6756, Vm.27.6757
*Polka,* Vm.27.6758

## Dassonville

The following works in F:Pn are all early prints for large wind band; all were printed in Paris in 1866–1899.
*Overture,* Vm.27.6762
*Fantaisie,* Vm.27.1081
Marches: Vm.7.13365, Vm.27.6759, Vm.27.6760 (*Marche funèbre*), Vm.27.6761, Vm.27.1080, Vm.7.13366, Vm.27.1084
Polkas: Vm.7.13364, Vm.27.1082 (*Sancta Cecilia*)
*Boléro,* Vm.7.13367

## Daunot, Louis

The following works in F:Pn are all early prints for large wind band; all were printed in Paris in 1883–1896.
Marches: Vm.27.6763, Vm.27.6766, Vm.27.6769, Vm.27.6770, Vm.27.6777, Vm.27.6780, Vm.27.6781, Vm.27.6784, Vm.27.6785
Polkas: Vm.27.6767, Vm.27.6776
*Valse,* Vm.27.6783

There is a large number of additional works by Daunot which date from 1900–1915, including a collection of fifteen compositions under Vm.27.67731.

### Dauprat, Louis François (1781–1868)

*Solo de Cor*
Solo horn, with 21-, ophicleide
MS (autograph) F:Pn (MS.3945.3); US:DW (311) [copy of MS.3945.3], US:DW (173) [modern copy]

*Sextets* [also quartets and trios]
Horns
EP (Paris, author) F:Pn (L.4461), F:Pn (L.4565)

### Davenne, A.

*March*
Large wind band
EP (Paris, 1899) F:Pn (Vm.27.6788)

### Davergne, A.

The following works in F:Pn are all early prints for large wind band; all were printed in Paris in 1855–1867.
Marches: Vm.27.6791, Vm.27.6790, Vm.7.13369 (*Marche religieuse*)
Polkas: Vm.27.6789, Vm.27.1085
*Schottisch*, Vm.7.13368

### David, Édouard

(2) *Polkas*
Large wind band
EP (Paris, 1892) F:Pn (Vm.27.1088; and Vm.27.6792)

### David, Félicien (1810–1876)

(2) *Nonettes*, in 4 movements
Brass instruments
MS F:Pn (MS.1096) [1–2]

*Pieces on Arab Themes* (1835)
Brass instruments [lost, according to Grove, V, 265]

### Debrière

*March*
Large wind band
EP (Paris, late nineteenth century) F:Pn (Vm.27.6802)

### Decq, A.

The following works in F:Pn are all early prints for large wind band; all were printed in Paris in 1876–1877.
Fantaisies: Vm.27.6807, Vm.27.6806
*March*, Vm.27.6805

### Dédé, Eugéne, fils

*Polka*
Large wind band
EP (Paris, 1895) F:Pn (Vm.27.6809)

### Delahaut, Paul

The following works in F:Pn are all early prints for large wind band; all were printed in Paris in 1866–1884.
*Fantaisie*, Vm.27.6820 [soli cornet, bugle, basses]
*Allegro militaire*, Vm.27.6819
*March*, Vm.27.6816
*Polka*, Vm.27.6817 [solo and soli cornets]
*Mazurka*, Vm.27.6818

### Delarue, J.

*March*
Large wind band
EP (Paris) F:Pn (Vm.27.6825 and Vm.27.6826 [two copies])

### Derâtre, Lucien

*March*
Large wind band
EP (Paris, 1867) F:Pn (Vm.27.1099)

### Delattre, A.

The following works in F:Pn are all early prints for large wind band; all were printed in Paris in 1892–1906.
Overtures: Vm.27.6828, Vm.27.6829
*March*, Vm.27.6827

### Delaunay, P.-D.

The following works in F:Pn are all early prints for large wind band; all were printed in Paris in 1856–1857.
Works for the Church: Vm.27.6833 (*Andante offertoire*), Vm.27.6834 (*Morceau religieux*)
Marches: Vm.27.6830, Vm.27.6831, Vm.27.6832, Vm.27.6837
*Valse*, Vm.27.6835
*Schottisch*, Vm.27.6836

### Delaundis, Ad.

The following works in F:Pn are early prints for large wind band; both were printed in Paris in 1891–1893.
Marches: Vm.27.6838, Vm.27.1100

### Delaye, Georges

*Suite concertante* ('*Morceau ayant remporté le premier prix, au Concours de Composition de l'Association des Jures Orphéoniques de Paris, 1907*')
Solo piano with musique d'harmonie
EP (Paris, Evette & Schaeffer, 1908) F:Pn (K.12.454)

### Delbove

The following works in F:Pn are all early prints for large wind band; all were printed in Paris in 1879.
*Berthe*, Vm.27.6841
*Valse*, Vm.27.6842
*Quadrille*, Vm.27.6843

### Delchavalerie, Henri

The following works in F:Pn are all early prints for large wind band; all were printed in Paris in 1895–1898.
Fantaisies: Vm.27.12784 (*Fantaisie pastorale*), Vm.27.12785 (*Scenes champetres*), Vm.27.6845
Marches: Vm.27.6844, Vm.27.6846, Vm.27.6847

### Dellac, H.

The following works in F:Pn are early prints for large wind band; both were printed in Paris in 1880 and 1883.
Marches: Vm.27.6854, Vm.27.6855

### Delsouc, F.

The following works in F:Pn are all early prints for large wind band; all were printed in Paris in 1882–1887.
*Fantaisie*, Vm.27.1107
Marches: Vm.27.6858, Vm.27.6859

### Demance, arranged by Fischer, G.

*Messe*
Small brass band
EP (Paris, 1866) F:Pn (Vm.27.1484)

### Demaré, E.

The following works in F:Pn are all early prints for large wind band; all were printed in Paris in 1866–1897.
Marches: Vm.27.1055, Vm.27.6724, Vm.27.6725, Vm.27.6726 (*March procession*)

### Demersseman, Jules A. E.

*Marche des géants*
For the new Sax instruments: Sax trumpet, 2 Sax trombones, B♭ bass Saxhorn, B♭ contra-bass Saxhorn, E♭ contra-bass Saxhorn and the new instrument 'avec 6 pistons et a tubes independents'
EP (Paris, A. Sax, 1865) F:Pn (K.10.159)
This composer was a friend of Sax and in F:Pn there is a lot of additional solo music, with piano, for the new Sax instruments and a series of compositions for the members of the Saxophone family which appeared as conservatory material in 1866–1867.

### Déo, Louis

The following works in F:Pn are all early prints for large wind band; all were printed in Paris in 1882–1884.
*Overture*, Vm.27.6868
Valses: Vm.27.6870, Vm.27.6872
*March*, Vm.27.6871
(30) *Morceau*, Vm.27.6869
This collection contains mostly polkas, quadrilles, etc., although Number 19 is an overture.

### Déplace, Claude

The following works in F:Pn are all early prints for large wind band; all were printed in Paris in 1855–1873.

Works for the Church: Vm.27.6929 (*1re marche funèbre*), Vm.27.6932 (*Morceau de repos*)

*Overture*, Vm.7.12926 and Vm.27.6919 [two copies]

*Fantaisie*, Vm.27.1120

*Morceau*, Vm.27.6878

*Varsoviana*, Vm.27.6927

Marches: Vm.27.6873, Vm.27.6880, Vm.27.6882, Vm.27.6894, Vm.7.13394 [two copies], Vm.27.6895, Vm.27.6898, Vm.27.6903, Vm.27.6901, Vm.27.6902, Vm.7.13399, Vm.7.13398 [two copies] (soli fifes and piccolo), Vm.27.6907, Vm.27.6908, Vm.27.6910, Vm.7.13396 (*Isabeau de Bayière*), Vm.27.6920, Vm.27.6922, Vm.27.6923, Vm.27.6874 (*Sur des airs nationaux Américains*), Vm.27.6876 (*Sur des airs nationaux Hollandais*), Vm.27.6875 (*Sur des airs nationaux Américains*) [not Vm.27.6874], Vm.27.6930, Vm.27.6931, Vm.7.13397, Vm.27.6933, Vm.7.13395, Vm.27.6934, Vm.27.6936, Vm.27.6937, Vm.27.6938, Vm.27.6939 (*Le Trombone de la Garde*), Vm.27.6942, Vm.27.6943

Redovas: Vm.27.6900, Vm.27.6940

*Schottisch*, Vm.27.6877

*Quadrille*, Vm.27.6897, Vm.27.6896 and Vm.7.13392 [three copies]

*Polonaise*, Vm.27.6906

Polkas: Vm.27.6910, Vm.7.13391, Vm.7.13390, Vm.27.1121, Vm.27.6926, Vm.27.6899

### Deransart, Édouard

The following works in F:Pn are all early prints for large wind band; all were printed in Paris in 1864–1865.

*Overture*, Vm.27.6949

*Polka*, Vm.27.6948

*Valse*, Vm.27.6945

### Dervieux

*March*
Large wind band
EP (Paris, 1894) F:Pn (Vm.27.6956)

### Desailly, L.

The following works in F:Pn are all early prints for large wind band; all were printed in Paris in 1883–1893.

*Air Varié*, Vm.27.1127

Marches: Vm.27.1129, Vm.27.6958, Vm.27.1128, and Vm.7.13083 [three copies]

### Descoins

The following works in F:Pn are all early prints for large wind band; all were printed in Paris in 1865–1883.

*Allegro militaire* [for brass band], Vm.27.1134

Marches: Vm.27.6960, Vm.27.1136

*Valse*, Vm.27.1139

*Mazurka*, Vm.27.1135

### Deserbelles, Claude

The following works in F:Pn are early prints for large wind band; both were printed in Paris in 1891 and 1893.

*Overture*, Vm.27.6961

*March*, Vm.27.6962

### Deshayes

*Harmonie*
Six-part Harmoniemusik
EP (Paris, Schlesinger) F:Pn

### Dessane, L.A.

*France, Angleterre et Sardaigne*
Large wind band
EP (Paris, 1858) F:Pn (Vm.27.1145)

### Destrube

The following works in F:Pn are all early prints for large wind band; all were printed in Paris in 1891–1901.

Overtures: Vm.27.6979, Vm.27.1149, Vm.27.1151, Vm.27.1152

*Fantaisie*, Vm.27.1150

*Ronde provencale*, Vm.27.1155

*March*, Vm.27.1148

*Valse*, Vm.27.1154

*Quadrille*, Vm.27.1153

### Desvignes, Pierre-Louis-Augustin

*De Profundis* (1806)
SATB, 222-023, timpani, bassi
MS (autograph) F:Pn (MS.7209)
This work was performed at Notre Dame during a Mass in honor of the Battle of Austerlitz.

*2e Messe*
SATB, 21-Celli, bassi
MS F:Pn (MS.9330/1)

*4e Messe*
SATB, 21-01, celli, bassi
MS (autograph) F:Pn (MS.9330)

### Dethou, Léon

*Traité d'instrumentation appliqué aux Orchestre à instruments à Vent*
EP (Paris, Collet, 1873) F:Pn (L.9.394)

### De Wailly, L. (b. 1854)

*Octet*
1122-11
EP (Paris, Rouart-Lerolle) [cited in DJ]

### Dias, J.-B.

The following works in F:Pn are all early prints for large wind band; all were printed in Paris in 1866–1886.
*March*, Vm.27.12796
Polkas: Vm.27.7007, Vm.27.7028
Quadrilles: Vm.27.7010, Vm.27.7018
*Suite of Valses:* Vm.27.7011

### Dierolf, H.

The following works in F:Pn are all early prints for large wind band; all were printed in Paris in 1882–1896.
Fantaisies: Vm.27.7038, Vm.27.7037
*Allegro*, Vm.27.7036

### Dietsch, Pierre Louis Philippe (1808–1865)

*XXIIIe Messe*
T, Bar, B Chorus, 2020-22, ATB saxophones, 2 baryton, 4 ophicleide, Bb contre-basse
EP (Paris, Regnier Canaux, 1864) F:Pn (D.3455 and Vm.1.127; [Cot.R.C.22/3/29] in-fol., 140 p.)
This work appeared to me to be a very important score, with independent and lyrical wind parts throughout.

### Divoir, Victor S.

The following works in F:Pn are early prints for large wind band; both were printed in Paris in 1894 and 1895.
*March*, Vm.27.7042
*Valse*, Vm.27.7041 and Vm.27.1164 [two copies]

### Doering

The following works in F:Pn are all early prints for large wind band; all were printed in Paris in 1865–1881.
Work for the Church: Vm.27.1166 and Vm.7.13070 [two copies] *Morceau d'Élévation*
*Overture*, Vm.7.12928
Marches: Vm.7.13401, Vm.7.13402
*Valse*, Vm.7.13403

### Doinelle, A.

The following works in F:Pn are early prints for large wind band; both were printed in Paris in 1886 and 1913.
Marches: Vm.27.7045, Vm.15.3482

### Domerque, Charles, F.

The following works in F:Pn are all early prints for large wind band; all were printed in Paris in 1872–1876.
Work for the Church: Vm.27.7051 *La Patroune de Paris* [*Fantaisie morceau de repos*]
Marches: Vm.27.7049, Vm.27.7050
*Donnez c'est pour la France*, Vm.27.7048

### Domerque, F.

The following works in F:Pn are all early prints for large brass band; all were printed in Paris in 1865–1866.
Marches: Vm.7.13405, Vm.7.13406
*Polka*, Vm.7.13407

## Donjon, Johannes

The following works in F:Pn are early prints for large wind band; both were printed in Paris in 1879 and 1897.

*Petite Marche slave et danse cosaque*, Vm.27.1183
*Cracoline* [soli piccolos], Vm.27.1186

## Dornois

*Polka*
Large wind band
EP (Paris, 1876) F:Pn (Vm.27.11065)

## Douard, A. (Chef de Musique, 51e de Ligne)

The following works in F:Pn are all early prints for large wind band; all were printed in Paris in 1858–1892.

Works for the Church: Vm.27.7059 (*Marche procession*), Vm.7.13432 (*Morceau d'Élévation*) [solo flute and small clarinet]
The work found under Vm.7.13432 is a full score of an Andantino, but in a fast moving and florid style with instrumental solos.
Overtures: Vm.27.4673, Vm.27.4674
Fantaisies: Vm.7.13414, Vm.27.7058, Vm.7.13420 [solo small clarinet], Vm.27.1197, Vm.7.13421 [soli trombone, cornet, and small clarinet], Vm.27.1196 [solo small clarinet], Vm.27.1198 (*Sur airs espagnols*), Vm.27.1200, Vm.7.13429, Vm.7.13433, Vm.27.7060
*Rondo*, Vm.27.1220 [solo piccolo]
*Duo*, Vm.7.13419 [solo flute and clarinet]
Marches: Vm.27.1191, Vm.27.1193, Vm.7.13443, Vm.27.1202, Vm.27.1203, Vm.7.13442, Vm.27.1215
Valses: Vm.27.1190, Vm.27.1194, Vm.27.1217, Vm.7.13412, Vm.27.1204, Vm.27.1206, Vm.27.1219, Vm.27.1209 [solo piccolo], Vm.27.1210, Vm.27.1211 (Suite), Vm.27.1212, Vm.27.1213 (Suite), Vm.27.1214
Galops: Vm.7.13437 and Vm.7.13438 [two copies], Vm.27.1195 and Vm.7.13439 [two copies]
*Polonaise*, Vm.7.13426 [solo small clarinet]
Redovas: Vm.27.1205, Vm.27.1208
*Mazurka*, Vm.27.1221

## Dubois, Charles F.

The following works in F:Pn are all early prints for large wind band; all were printed in Paris in 1874–1899.

Overtures: Vm.27.7075, Vm.27.7087
Fantaisies: Vm.27.7080 (*L'Hiver! Scènes de Noël*), Vm.27.1230, Vm.27.1231 (*Souvenir de Russie*)
Airs varié: Vm.27.7067; and Vm.27.1229
*Andante et Polonaise*, Vm.27.7068 [solo cornet]
*Chant des gaulois*, (with chorus) Vm.27.1235 and Vm.27.7086 [band parts only]
Marches: Vm.27.7073, Vm.27.7076, Vm.27.7085, Vm.27.7079, Vm.27.7081, Vm.27.7071, Vm.27.7082, Vm.27.7070
*Quadrille*, Vm.27.7084
*Polka*, Vm.27.7077
*Mazurka*, Vm.27.7078
*Boléro*, Vm.27.7069

## Dubois, Theodore (1837–1924)

*Au Jardin, Petite Suite*
2121-01
EP (?) GB:Lbbc (Orch.5309)

*I. Suite* (1898)
2122-01
EP (Paris, Heugel) GB:Lbbc (Orch.10291)

*II. Suite* (1898)
2122-01
MP (Paris, Leduc) BRD:Bhm (11567 and 11568)

## Dubreu

*Suite* (2 marches and a polonaise)
Large wind band
EP (Paris, no date) F:Pn (Vm.27.4677)

## Dubreu, F.

*Marche funèbre*
Large wind band
EP (Paris, no date) F:Pn (Vm.27.4678)

## Dubreuil, E.

The following works in F:Pn are all early prints for large wind band; all were printed in Paris in 1890–1897.

Marches: Vm.27.7089, Vm.27.7090, Vm.27.7091, Vm.27.7092, Vm.27.7093, Vm.27.7094, Vm.27.7095

## Duhamel

*Noël, Morceau religieux*, Vm.27.7113
*Fantaisie*, Vm.27.7109
Marches: Vm.27.7107, Vm.27.7108, Vm.27.7114, Vm.27.7111
*Quadrille*, Vm.27.7112
*Polka*, Vm.27.7110

## Dukas, Paul (1865–1935)

'Fanfare,' from *La Peri*
Brass Instruments

## Dumaine, A.

*March*
Large wind band
EP (Paris, 1893 F:Pn (Vm.27.7115)
There are an additional dozen or so works dated 1900–1910 by Dumaine in F:Pn.

## Dumas, Alexandre (Chef de Musique a bord du Montebello)

*March*
Large wind band
EP (Paris, 1853) F:Pn (Vm.27.1247)

## Dupart, Charles

The following works in F:Pn are all early prints for large wind band; all were printed in Paris in 1862–1870.

Works for the Church: Vm.27.1254 (*Andante religieux*) [for soli horn and E♭ Alto], Vm.27.1253 (*Andante religieux*), Vm.27.1295 (*Marche religieuse*), Vm.27.7149 and Vm.27.1305 [two copies] (*4e Andante religioso*), Vm.27.7145 and Vm.27.1294 [two copies] (*Marche funèbre*), Vm.27.7152 and Vm.27.1308 [two copies] (*2e Marche funèbre*), Vm.27.1290 (*Marche religieux*), Vm.27.1296 (*Marche religieux*), Vm.27.7146 (Marche religieux), Vm.27.1297 and Vm.27.7147 [two copies] (*Marche solennelle*)

Under Vm.27.1253 one finds a three-page full score for large instrumentation, although the following instruments are marked 'oblige': 1st clarinet, petit bugle in E♭, 2 B♭ cornets, 2 altos, B♭ baritone, and B♭ bass.

*Overture*, Vm.7.13446 and Vm.27.7132 [two copies]
Fantaisies: Vm.27.7138 and Vm.27.1274 (two copies) [solo cornet], Vm.27.1313, Vm.27.1285
*Air varié*, Vm.7.13445
*Andante*, Vm.27.7127 and Vm.27.1252 (two copies) [soli clarinet, and alto or 'petite soprano E♭' saxophone]
*La Bataille d'In-Kermann*, Vm.27.1255
Marches: Vm.27.7129, Vm.27.1257, Vm.27.1258, Vm.27.7130, Vm.27.1259, Vm.27.1260, Vm.27.1261, Vm.27.1262, Vm.27.1263 (*Le clarinette sentimental*), Vm.27.1270, Vm.27.7135, Vm.27.7136, Vm.27.1272, Vm.27.1277, Vm.27.1278, Vm.27.1279, Vm.27.7142, Vm.27.1281, Vm.27.7143, Vm.27.1282, Vm.27.1283, Vm.27.1289, Vm.27.1288, Vm.27.1291, Vm.27.1292, Vm.27.1293, Vm.27.1303, Vm.27.1309, Vm.27.7153
Valses: Vm.27.1251, Vm.27.7126 (Suite), Vm.27.1248, Vm.27.7131, Vm.27.1269, Vm.27.1280, Vm.27.7151, Vm.27.1306
Polkas: Vm.27.1250, Vm.27.1256, Vm.27.1284, Vm.27.1287, Vm.27.7144, Vm.27.1299, Vm.27.7148, Vm.27.1300, Vm.27.1301, Vm.27.1304
Quadrilles: Vm.27.1264, Vm.27.1265, Vm.27.1286
Schottischs: Vm.27.1266 and 1267 [two copies] Vm.27.1268, Vm.27.7134 [two copies]
[Collection] (a collection of 13 dance movements, Vm.27.7128)
There are an additional fifteen or so transcriptions by Dupart in F:Pn; some, with titles like *Fantaisie on a theme by Bellini*, etc., may be original works.

## Dupiré, A.

*March*
Large wind band
EP (Paris, 1878) F:Pn (Vm.27.7155)

## Dupouy, A.

*March*
Large wind band
EP (Paris, 1897) F:Pn (Vm.27.7157)
There are an additional dozen or so marches dated 1900–1910 by Dupouy in F:Pn.

## Duprato, Jules-Laurent

*Ave Verum*
Three voices, organ, four saxophones
MS F:Pn (MS.10.885 [1–8])

## Duquat

The following works in F:Pn are all early prints for large wind band; all were printed in Paris in 1863–1864.
Work for the Church, Vm.27.7161 (*Morceau de repos*)
*Fantaisie*, Vm.27.7158
Marches: Vm.27.7159, Vm.27.7160, Vm.27.7162

## Dureau, Th.

The following works in F:Pn are all early prints for large wind band; all were printed in Paris in 1865–1893.
Works for the Church: Vm.7.13073 (*Morceau d'Élévation*) [*Prière a la madone*], Vm.7.13476 (*Marche solonnelle*), Vm.7.13474 (*Marche du cortege*)
*Overture*, Vm.7.12954
*Allegro de concert*, Vm.27.7168
Marches: Vm.7.13470, Vm.7.13471, Vm.7.13077, Vm.27.1320, Vm.7.13477, Vm.7.13080, Vm.27.1322, Vm.7.13079
*Galop*, Vm.7.13469
Valses: Vm.7.13463, Vm.27.1321
*Boléro*, Vm.27.7169
Polkas: Vm.7.13467 [original, 'pour la musette'], Vm.7.13468
*Quadrille*, Vm.7.13476
There are many additional orchestral transcriptions by Dureau in F:Pn, including Wagner's 'Ride of the Valkyries' (Vm.7.14511) and music from the *Meistersinger* [*Les Maitres Chanteurs de Nuremberg*] (Vm.7.14508).

## Durrieu, Paul

Overture, *Isaure*
Large wind band
EP (Paris, 1894) F:Pn (Vm.27.1324)

## Durrieu, R.

The following works in F:Pn are all early prints for large wind band; all were printed in Paris in 1890–1896.
*Morceau allegro*, Vm.27.7173
Marches: Vm.27.7171, Vm.27.7172

## Dusautoy

*March*
Large wind band
EP (Paris, 1868) F:Pn (Vm.27.7174)

## Dussap, Dey.

*La Fanfare Marche*
2030-22; bass trumpet, ophlicleide, signal horn, alto cornetta, corno basso, bombardon, percussion
MS (ca. 1870) BRD:B (Mus.Ms.5415)

## Egal, J.

The following works in F:Pn are early prints for large wind band; both were printed in Paris in 1888.
Marches: Vm.27.7182, Vm.27.7184 and Vm.27.7185 [two copies]

## Elwart, Antoine Amable Elie (1808–1877)

*March*
Large wind band
EP (Paris, 1855) [cited in MGG]

## Ernst, Edouard

The following works in F:Pn are all early prints for large wind band; all were printed in Paris in 1851–1866.

Marches: Vm.7.13484, Vm.7.13479
*Boléro,* Vm.27.1342
*Polonaise,* Vm.27.1344
*Valse,* Vm.27.1345
*Quadrille,* Vm.7.13482

## Escudié, H.

The following works in F:Pn are all early prints for large wind band; all were printed in Paris in 1872–1881.

Fantaisies: Vm.27.7196, Vm.27.7199, Vm.27.7206, Vm.27.7221, Vm.27.7226 [solo alto saxophone], Vm.27.7217, Vm.27.7223 [solo soprano B♭ saxophone], Vm.27.7216 (Theme and variations)

Marches: Vm.27.7195, Vm.27.7197, Vm.27.7198, Vm.27.7201, Vm.27.7204, Vm.27.7207, Vm.27.7208, Vm.27.7209, Vm.27.7211, Vm.27.7212 (*La Japonaise*), Vm.27.7214, Vm.27.7218, Vm.27.7219, Vm.27.7220, Vm.27.7224

Polkas: Vm.27.7200, Vm.27.7225
Mazurkas: Vm.27.7202, Vm.27.7215
*Boléro,* Vm.27.7205
*Quadrille,* Vm.27.7210
*Valse,* Vm.27.7213

## Etchepare, H.

The following works in F:Pn are all early prints for large wind band; all were printed in Paris in 1892–1896.
Marches: Vm.27.7228, Vm.27.7230
*Polka,* Vm.27.7229 [solo cornet]

## Ettling, Emile

The following works in F:Pn are all early prints for large wind band; all were printed in Paris in 1872–1876.
*March,* Vm.27.7234
Valses: Vm.27.7233 (Suite), Vm.27.1347 (Suite), Vm.27.7241, Vm.27.1350 [solo cornet] (*La Prima Donna*)
Polkas: Vm.27.7239, Vm.27.7240

## Eustace, Charles

The following works in F:Pn are all early prints for large wind band; all were printed in Paris in 1885–1901.
Work for the Church, Vm.27.7243 (*Andante religieux*)
Overtures: Vm.27.7247, Vm.27.7248, Vm.27.7251 (*Les Janissaires*), Vm.27.7252, Vm.27.7253, Vm.27.1356, Vm.27.7261
Fantaisie, Vm.27.7259, Vm.27.7260
Marches: Vm.27.7249, Vm.27.1354, Vm.27.7254, Vm.27.7255, Vm.27.7256
*Valse espagnole,* Vm.27.1352
*Quadrille,* Vm.27.1353
*Schottisch,* Vm.27.1357

## Eybert

The following works in F:Pn are all early prints for large wind band; all were printed in Paris in 1881–1885.
Marches: Vm.27.7262, Vm.27.7263, Vm.27.7264, Vm.27.7265

## Fabre, Casimir

The following works in F:Pn are all early prints for large wind band; all were printed in Paris in 1869–1889.
Marches: Vm.27.1360, Vm.27.7267, Vm.27.7268, Vm.27.7269, Vm.27.7270, Vm.27.7271, Vm.27.7272, Vm.27.7273, Vm.27.7274, Vm.27.7275, Vm.27.7276, Vm.27.7277

## Fajolle, A.

The following works in F:Pn are all early prints for large wind band; all were printed in Paris in 1885–1889.
Fantaisies: Vm.27.7288, Vm.27.7291
*Marceau,* Vm.27.7290
Marches: Vm.7.13100, Vm.27.7292
*Mazurka,* Vm.27.7289

**Farigoul, J.**

The following works in F:Pn are all early prints for large wind band; all were printed in Paris in 1887–1901.

Overtures: Vm.27.1381, Vm.27.1390, Vm.27.1389 (*Overture symphonique*)

Fantaisies: Vm.27.7293, Vm.27.1382, Vm.27.7302, Vm.27.7303

*Poème Symphonique*, Vm.27.1385

Marches: Vm.27.7294, Vm.27.1381 bis, Vm.27.7295, Vm.27.1384, Vm.27.7301, Vm.27.1391

*Mazurka,* Vm.27.1380

*Valse,* Vm.7.13102

Polkas: Vm.27.12807 [solo piccolo], Vm.21.1386 [solo cornet]

**Farrenc, Jeanne-Louise (1804–1875)**

*Sextet,* Op. 40
Piano, 1111-01
EP (Paris) [cited in Grove, VI, 408]

**Fasquel**

*Chant guerrier*
Harmoniemusik
EP (Paris, Meissonnier)

*La Descente en Angleterre*
Harmoniemusik
EP (Paris, Meissonnier)

**Faurel**

The following works in F:Pn are all early prints for large wind band; all were printed in Paris in 1854–1874.

*March,* Vm.21.1324
*Valse,* Vm.27.7321
*Mazurka,* Vm.21.7322
*Quadrille,* Vm.27.7323

**Favre, E.**

The following works in F:Pn are all early prints for large wind band; all were printed in Paris in 1878–1885.

Fantaisies: Vm.27.7307, Vm.27.1403

Marches: Vm.27.7308, Vm.27.7309, Vm.27.7310, Vm.27.7314, Vm.27.1401, Vm.27.7315 (*Marche de procession*), Vm.21.7317, Vm.27.7318

*Valse,* Vm.27.7306

Polkas: Vm.27.1398, Vm.27.7313

*Boléro,* Vm.27.7311

*Mazurka,* Vm.27.7312

Quadrilles: Vm.27.1402, Vm.27.7316

**Favre, Joanny**

*March*
Large wind band
EP (Paris, 1884) F:Pn (Vm.27.7319)

**Favre-Danne, E.**

*March*
Large wind band
EP (Paris, 1875) F:Pn (Vm.27.7320)

**Feautrier, E.**

The following works in F:Pn are all early prints for large wind band; all were printed in Paris and Montargis in 1879–1895.

Overtures: Vm.27.7328, Vm.27.1410

Fantaisies: Vm.7.13104, Vm.27.1405, Vm.27.1409, Vm.27.1412, Vm.27.1413, Vm.27.1417, Vm.27.1420, Vm.27.1421

*Andante,* Vm.27.1422

Marches: Vm.27.1404, Vm.27.7329, Vm.27.7330 [with chorus], Vm.27.1415, Vm.27.1407, Vm.27.1423, Vm.27.1416, Vm.27.1406, Vm.27.1419, Vm.27.1418, Vm.27.1411, Vm.27.7334 (*March-procession*), Vm.27.1414, Vm.27.1408, Vm.27.7333 (*Marche funèbre*) Vm.7.13488, Vm.7.13489

*Valse,* Vm.27.7331

*Gavotte,* Vm.7.13106

Polkas: Vm.7.13490 [solo cornet], Vm.27.7326

**Feautrier, L.**

*March*
Large wind band
EP (Montargis, 1892) F:Pn (Vm.27.7335)

### Febore, Gustave

The following works in F:Pn are all early prints for large wind band; all were printed in Angers and Charleville in 1873–1881.
*Fantaisie,* Vm.27.7338
Marches: Vm.27.7336, Vm.27.7337, Vm.27.7340
*Polka,* Vm.27.7339

### Fedou, A.

The following works in F:Pn are early prints for large wind band; both were printed in Paris during the late nineteenth century.
*Galop,* Vm.27.4680
*Polka,* Vm.27.4681

### Ferand, Henri

The following works in F:Pn are all early prints for large wind band; all were printed in Paris in 1894–1908.
Overtures: Vm.27.7346, Vm.27.12812, Vm.27.12813, Vm.27.7349
Marches: Vm.27.7347, Vm.27.7348, Vm.27.7344, Vm.27.7345, Vm.27.7350 [with voice ad. lib.]

### Ferranti, L.

*Pas redoublé* [with voice]
Large wind band
EP (Paris, 1896) F:Pn (Vm.27.7351)

### Fessy, Alexandre (Chef de Musique de la 5me Legion de la Garde Nationale de Paris)

The following works in F:Pn are all early prints for large wind band; all were printed in Paris in 1844–1865.
*Fantaisie (pour musique militaire d'infanterie avec des nouveaux instruments iuventes par Ad. Sax et composée expressement pour les concours au Champ de Mars en 1845),* F:Pn (Vm.7.14451) and a copy in the Whitwell Archiv, Trossingen, Germany.
This score was published in Paris in 1845 by A. Sax, plate number 'Ad.S.1'. This is the historic work which began Adolphe Sax's portion of the famous 'battle of the bands' in 1845, which had a great influence on the reorganization of military bands in France. This is a twenty-seven page score for the following instruments (to my knowledge, this is the earliest printed music to use the saxophone):
Petite flute
Petite E♭ clarinet
2 B♭ clarinets
Bass clarinet
B♭ saxophone [Tenor]
2 cornets
2 E♭ trumpets
4 E♭ horns (cylinders)
2 E♭ saxhorns
2 B♭ saxhorns
2 E♭ alto saxhorns
B♭ grave saxhorn, 3 cylinders
B♭ grave saxhorn, 4 cylinders
3 [valve] trombones
Ophicleides in B♭
Contra-basse saxhorn in E♭
Percussion
A companion work on this historic occasion was the *Pas redoublé (pour musique militaire avec les nouveaux instruments iuventes par Ad. Sax, expressement composée pour les concours au Champ de Mars en 1845),* Vm.7.14453

*Deuxième fantaisie (pour musique militaire composée expressement pour les nouveaux instruments d' Adolphe Sax),* Vm.7.14452
Work for the Church, Vm.7.13496 (*Prière anglaise*) ['God Save the King']
Marches: Vm.27.1433, Vm.27.7354, Vm.27.7356, Vm.27.1438, Vm.27.7352, Vm.27.1435, Vm.27.14361, Vm.27.1437, Vm.7.14450 [4 *Pas redoublés* composed for the 'Musique de la Garde imperiale'], Vm.27.7355, Vm.7.13495 (*Les Morchaux de l'Empire*) [*pour defiler avec tambours, compose pour la nouvelle ordonnance des Musiques de la garde imperial*] This last work is for a very large band, including SATB saxophones, saxhorns, saxtromba, etc.
(6) *Fanfares* [*pour la cavalerie*], Vm.27.1439 [1–2]
(6) *Grands Morceaux* [for large brass band], Vm.27.1440 [1-6] Contains:
*Andante et marche*
*Pas redoublé*
*Andante et polonaise*
*Pas redoublé*
*Andante et galop*

*Grande Valse*
*Boléro et fanfare*, F:Pn (Vm.27.1428)
Under this number one finds a simple *Andante et Polonaise*, scored for a very large band, including saxhorns in B♭ alto, A♭, E♭ tenor, low B♭ and contra E♭.
*Valses*: Vm.27.1434
*Choeur d'ensemble et Marche* [for military band], Vm.27.1429

## Fichu, J.

*Quadrille*
Large wind band
EP (Paris, 1888) F:Pn (Vm.27.1443)

## Filiberti

*Marche pour l'Entrée de Charles X*
Harmoniemusik
EP (Paris, ca. 1800–1828)

## Fiquet

The following works in F:Pn are all early prints for large wind band; all were printed in Paris in 1854–1855.
Marches: Vm.27.7362, Vm.27.7363, Vm.27.7377, Vm.27.7378, Vm.27.7368, Vm.27.7372, Vm.27.7371, Vm.27.7370
Polkas: Vm.27.7364, Vm.27.7367
*Polonaise*, Vm.27.7373
*Quadrille*, Vm.27.7374

## [Fiquet], Gabriel

The following works in F:Pn are all early prints for large wind band; all were printed in Paris during the nineteenth century.
Works for the Church: Vm.27.7375 (*La Saint Augustin*) [*Offertoire*], Vm.27.7369 (*Motets au Saint Sacrement, O Salutaris et Ave verum*) This last work seems to have been intended for chorus as well, although no vocal parts are to be found under this number.
*Les Souvenirs de Crecamp*, Vm.27.7376

## Fiquet, [Montididier]

The following works in F:Pn are early prints for large wind band both were printed in Paris ca. 1855.
Marches: Vm.27.7365, Vm.27.7366

## Fischer, Emile

The following works in F:Pn are all early prints for large wind band; all were printed in Paris in 1884–1907.
Marches: Vm.27.1452, Vm.27.7384, Vm.27.1453, Vm.27.7386
*Galop*, Vm.27.7380
*Polka*, Vm.27.7385

## Fischer, G.

The following works in F:Pn are all early prints for large wind band; all were printed in Paris in 1866–1878.
Work for the Church, Vm.27.1459 (*Andante religioso*)
Marches: Vm.27.7388, Vm.27.7401, Vm.27.7391, Vm.27.7397 (*Marche Américaine*) The march given under Vm.7391 indicates that it was composed 'au Festival militaire, 1878,' although no further details are given or known of this festival.
Sets of Variations, Vm.27.1499 (on a theme from Donizetti's *L'Elisire d'Amore*), Vm.27.1501 ('sur un theme irlandais')
*Valse,* Vm.27.7390
Polkas: Vm.27.7389, Vm.27.7405, Vm.27.1492
*Schottisch,* Vm.27.7494 [for small brass band]
*Quadrille,* Vm.27.7399
*Redond* (?), Vm.27.7403
(30) *Fanfares* [pour trompettes de cavalerie], Vm.7.7771
These are fairly lengthy works, in five parts (four parts with bass).
In addition there are many arrangements in F:Pn under the name of G. Fischer.

## Fischlin, E.

The following works in F:Pn are all early prints for large wind band; all were printed in Paris in 1861–1873.

Marches: Vm.27.7408 (*Les Apaches*), Vm.27.7467, Vm.27.7410, Vm.27.7406, Vm.27.7413, Vm.27.7412
*Bolero*, Vm.27.7409

### Flèche, F.

The following works in F:Pn are early prints for large wind band; both were printed in Paris in 1892.
*Polka*, Vm.27.7416
*Redova*, VM.27.12817

### Fleury

*Journal* [Collection]
Harmoniemusik
EP (Paris, Leduc, ca. 1800–1828)

### Fleury, B.

*Allegro militaire*
Large wind band
EP (Paris, 1886) F:Pn (Vm.27.7417)

### Flori,

The following works in F:Pn are all early prints for large wind band; all were printed in Paris in 1858–1859.
Marches: Vm.27.1506, Vm.27.1507, Vm.27.1508

### Foare, Charles

The following works in F:Pn are all early prints for large wind band; all were printed in Paris in 1887–1900.
Overtures: Vm.27.1522, Vm.27.1520
Fantaisies: Vm.27.1521, Vm.27.7422 and Vm.27.7423 [two copies]
*March*, Vm.27.1519
Valses: Vm.7.13108, Vm.27.7421
*Polka*, Vm.27.1524
*Mazurka*, Vm.27.1523

### Fondard, J. T.

*March*
Large wind band
EP (Paris, 1878) F:Pn (Vm.27.7428)

### Fontenelle, Emile

The following works in F:Pn are early prints for large wind band; both were printed in Paris in 1894 and 1899.
Marches: Vm.27.1530, Vm.27.1531

### Fouant, Jolibois

The following works in F:Pn are all early prints for large wind band; all were printed in Paris in 1876–1896.
Fantaisies: Vm.27.1547, Vm.27.7439, Vm.27.7441
Polkas: Vm.27.7443, Vm.27.7442
*Valse*, Vm.27.7438

### Fouque, Octave

*Pas redoublé*
Large wind band
EP (Paris, 1877) F:Pn (Vm.27.7447)

### Fournier, C.

The following works in F:Pn are early prints for large wind band printed in Paris.
Marches: Vm.27.7457, Vm.27.1555, Vm.27.1554, Vm.27.1558, Vm.27.7458, Vm.27.1557 (*Retraite russe*)
Fantaisies: Vm.27.1551, Vm.27.1552 [solo cornet], Vm.27.1556 [solo B♭ clarinet]
*Menuet*, Vm.27.7456

### François

*Pas redoublé*
Large wind band
EP (Paris, 1892) F:Pn (Vm.27.1570)

### François, Emile

*Marche pour procession*
Large wind band
EP (Paris, 1870) F:Pn (Vm.27.7463)

### François, L.

The following works in F:Pn are early prints for large wind band; both were printed in Paris in 1898 and 1900.
*Overture*, Vm.27.1572
*Valse*, Vm.27.1571

### Fré-d'rick, L.

*Pas redoublé*
Large wind band
EP (Paris, 1899) F:Pn (Vm.27.12822)

### Friedheim

*Sextours*, Op. 1
Harmoniemusik
EP (Paris, ca. 1800–1828) [Liv. 1, 2]

### Frier

The following works in F:Pn are early prints for large wind band; both were printed in Paris in 1890–1891.
*March*, Vm.27.7465
*Valse*, Vm.7.13111

### Frion, Eugène

*March*
Large wind band
EP (Paris, 1880) F:Pn (Vm.27.7467)

### Frisnais, ? (Chef de Musique, 34e de Ligne)

The following works in F:Pn are early prints for large wind band; both all were printed in Paris during the nineteenth century.
Marches: Vm.27.1573, Vm.27.1574

### Fritsch, E.

The following works in F:Pn are all early prints for large wind band; all were printed in Paris in 1886–1899.
Marches: Vm.7.13112, Vm.27.7469, Vm.27.1576, Vm.27.1577, Vm.27.1578
Valse suites, Vm.7.13114, Vm.27.1579
*Quadrille*, Vm.27.1575
*Mazurka*, Vm.7.13113

### Fromentin, L.

The following works in F:Pn are early prints for large wind band; both were printed in Paris in 1892 and 1896.
*March*, Vm.27.7470
*Valse*, Vm.27.4685

### Fromont, Célestin

*March*
Large wind band
EP (Paris, 1887) F:Pn (Vm.27.7471)

### Furgeot, J.

The following works in F:Pn are all early prints for large wind band; all were printed in Paris in 1886–1906.
*Symphonia Overture* [1906], Vm.27.7486 and Vm.27.7487 [two copies]
Marches: Vm.27.7488, Vm.27.7472, Vm.27.7475, Vm.7.13117, Vm.27.7473 (*Nimrod*)
*Polka*, Vm.27.1604 [solo cornet]

### Gabriel

*March*
Large wind band
EP (Paris, 1880) F:Pn (Vm.27.9390)

### Gache, F.

*March*
Large wind band
EP (Paris, 1888) F:Pn (Vm.7.13119)

### Gadenne, Henri

The following works in F:Pn are early prints for large wind band; both were printed in Paris in 1895
Marches: Vm.27.7490, Vm.27.7491

### Gaffet, E.

*Allegro militaire*
Large wind band
EP (Paris, 1891) F:Pn (Vm.27.1613)

### Gagne, fils

The following works in F:Pn are early prints for large wind band; both were printed in Paris in 1855
Marches: Vm.27.7494, Vm.27.7495

## Gaillaguet, E.

[March]
Large wind band
EP (Paris, 1898) F:Pn (Vm.27.7496)

## Gaillard, C.

*March*
Large wind band
EP (Paris, 1895) F:Pn (Vm.27.1616)

## Gaittet, J. B.

The following works in F:Pn are all early prints for large wind band; all were printed in Paris in 1851–1878.
Works for the Church: Vm.27.1618 (*Andante pour Élévation*), Vm.27.1617 (*Andante pour Élévation*), Vm.27.7503 (*Prière*) [for brass band], Vm.1.2230 and 40 Vm.1.25 *Messe tres facile* [accompanied by brass band]
*Fantaisie*, Vm.27.7500
*Sérénade*, Vm.27.7506
Romances without Words, Vm.27.7504 [for brass band], Vm.27.7499
Marches: Vm.27.7498, Vm.27.7507, Vm.27.7508
*Polka*, Vm.27.7505
*Quadrille*, Vm.27.7501 [on '*Frère Jacques*']
*Boléro*, Vm.27.7502

## Gambaro, Giovanni Battista (1785–1828)

*Collection de Mus. milit. cont. 12 Morceaux* (Overtures: Valses: Marches: Rondos, etc.)
Harmoniemusik
EP (Paris, Gambaro) [Liv.1–4]

*Vive Henry IV Pas redoublé*
Harmoniemusik
EP (Paris, Ebend)

*Overtures Nr. 1 & 2*
Harmoniemusik
EP (Paris, Gambaro)

*Vive le Roy. Vive la France March*
Harmoniemusik
EP (Paris, Ebend)

*le petit Tambour, Pas redoublé*
Harmoniemusik
EP (Paris, Pacini)

*Harmonie*, Op. 5
Six-part Harmoniemusik
EP (Paris, Gambaro)

## Gambart, A.

*Fantaisie*
Large wind band
EP (Paris, 1895) F:Pn (Vm.27.1626)

## Gand, jeune

The following works in F:Pn are all early prints for large wind band; all were printed in Paris in 1872–1878.
Marches: Vm.27.7511, Vm.27.7513 [for brass band]
*Valse*, Vm.27.7512

## Gandner, Victor

The following works in F:Pn are all early prints for large wind band; all were printed in Paris in 1851–1885.
Works for the Church: Vm.27.1627 (*Morceau religieux à l'Élévation*), Vm.7.13537 (*Marche-procession*), Vm.7.13144 (*Marche funèbre souvenir religieux*), Vm.7.13538 (*March-procession*), Vm.27.1644 (*Marche funèbre*), Vm.7.13520 and Vm.27.1645 [two copies] (*La Prière au camp*), Vm.7.13519 (*Morceau de repos*)
*Fantaisie*, Vm.27.1637
Marches: Vm.7.13536, Vm.7.13535, Vm.27.1629, Vm.7.13534, Vm.7.13530, Vm.7.13529, Vm.7.13524, Vm.27.1631, Vm.27.1632, Vm.7.13532, Vm.7.13527, Vm.7.13528, Vm.7.13528 bis [three copies], Vm.27.1633, Vm.27.1634, Vm.7.13540, Vm.7.13526, Vm.7.13539, Vm.27.1638, Vm.27.1641, Vm.27.1642, Vm.27.1643, Vm.27.1646, Vm.7.13533, Vm.27.1647, Vm.7.13525, Vm.27.1649, Vm.27.1650, Vm.7.13523, Vm.27.1651
Polkas: Vm.27.1628, Vm.27.1635
*Mazurka*, Vm.7.13518
*Schottisch*, Vm.7.13522
*Valse*, Vm.27.1640
Redovas: Vm.7.13531, Vm.27.1636
*Boléro*, Vm.7.13521 and Vm.7.13517 [two copies]
*Quadrille*, Vm.27.1648

## Ganne, Louis

*Fantaisie-Ballet* (Terpschore)
Large wind band
EP (Paris, 1888) F:Pn (Vm.27.1688)

## Gantz, J.

The following works in F:Pn are all early prints for large wind band; all were printed in Paris and Lyon in 1892–1900.
Work for the Church, Vm.27.7525 (*Marche funèbre*)
*Fantaisie*, Vm.27.7524
Marches: Vm.27.7516, Vm.27.7518, Vm.27.7521, Vm.27.1690
Polkas: Vm.27.7519 [two soli cornets], Vm.27.7520 [solo cornet]
Valses: Vm.27.7515, Vm.27.7517
*Schottisch*, Vm.27.7522
*Boléro*, Vm.27.7S24

## Garciau, Ernest

The following works in F:Pn are all early prints for large wind band; all were printed in Paris in 1887–1891.
*Overture*, Vm.27.7530
Marches: Vm.27.7529, Vm.27.1693, Vm.27.7528

## Gariel, J. A. V.

The following works in F:Pn are all early prints for large wind band; all were printed in Paris in 1855–1887.
Overtures: Vm.27.1696, Vm.27.4686
*Air varié*, Vm.27.3663 (Nr. 3, in *Journal des fanfares*) [for solo trombone with brass band]
Marches: Vm.7.13546, Vm.7.13544, Vm.7.13545 (*Marche funèbre*)
*Valse*, Vm.27.1700

## Garnier, Felix

The following works in F:Pn are all early prints for large wind band; all were printed in Paris in 1892–1899.
Overtures: Vm.27.1708, Vm.27.1710
*Fantaisie*, Vm.27.1711
Marches: Vm.27.1707, Vm.27.1709, Vm.27.1712, Vm.27.1713
*Polka*, Vm.27.1706

## Garot, Pierre

The following works in F:Pn are all early prints for large wind band; all were printed in Paris in 1894–1896.
*Prelude et rondo*, Vm.27.1717 [solo piccolo]
Marches: Vm.27.7538, Vm.27.7539

## Garrouste, J.

The following works in F:Pn are all early prints for large wind band; all were printed in Paris in 1855–1858.
Fantaisies: Vm.7.13556 [solo piccolo], Vm.27.1723, Vm.7.13559 [soli E♭ clarinet and piccolo]
Airs varié: Vm.7.13555 [solo cornet], Vm.27.7541, Vm.7.13558 [solo E♭ clarinet or saxophone]
(4) *Morceau*, Vm.7.13557
Marches: Vm.27.7542, Vm.7.13549, Vm.27.7544, Vm.27.754, Vm.7.13550, Vm.7.13551, Vm.7.13552, Vm.27.7548, Vm.27.7547, Vm.27.7549, Vm.27.7551, Vm.7.13548
*Polka*, Vm.7.13547
Quadrilles: Vm.27.7543, Vm.27.7550
Valses: Vm.27.7545, Vm.27.7546, Vm.7.13553 [solo trombone]

## Gasser, Alexandre

*Marche*
Large wind band
EP (Paris, 1879) F:Pn (Vm.27.7552)

## Gasser, Victor

The following works in F:Pn are all early prints for large wind band; all were printed in Paris in 1865–1883.
*Ronde de nuit*, Vm.27.7554 and Vm.27.7555 [two copies]
Marches: Vm.27.7553, Vm.27.7556

## Gattermann, Hubert

The following works in F:Pn are early prints for large wind band; both were printed in Paris in 1884–1886.
Marches: Vm.27.7558, Vm.27.7559, Vm.27.7560

### Gattermann, Philippe

*March*
Large wind band
EP (Paris, 1886) F:Pn (Vm.27.7563)

### Gattermann, Prosper

The following works in F:Pn are all early prints for large wind band; all were printed in Paris in 1894–1895.
Marches: Vm.27.7564 (*Marche funèbre*), Vm.27.7565
*Boléro*, Vm.27.7562

### Gaudefroy, E.

The following works in F:Pn are early prints for large wind band; both were printed in Paris in 1895–1896.
Marches: Vm.27.7566, Vm.27.7567

### Gautier, Léon

The following works in F:Pn are early prints for large wind band; both were printed in Paris in 1883 and 1889.
*Overture*, Vm.27.7569
*Schottisch*, Vm.27.7570

### Gebauer, François René

*Airs favoris variés*
Harmoniemusik
EP (Paris, Sieber)

*Airs favoris variés*
Harmoniemusik
EP (Paris, Beauce) [Liv. 1–3]

*Airs favoris variés*
Harmoniemusik
EP (Paris, Sieber) [Nr. 1–39]

*Airs favoris variés*
Harmoniemusik
EP (Paris, Frey)

(3) *Marches pour l'Entrée de Louis XVIII dans Paris*
Harmoniemusik
EP (Paris, Frey) F:Pn (Vm.27.1741)

(4) *Marches religieuses*
Harmoniemusik
EP (Paris, Sieber)

*Potpourri*
Harmoniemusik
EP (Paris, S. Gaveaux)

*Potpourri*
Six-part Harmoniemusik
EP (Paris, G. Gaveaux)

*la Sentinelle, et Roland, Marche, et Pas redoublé*
Twelve-part Harmoniemusik
EP (Paris, Leduc)

### Gebel, A. François (fl. ca. 1834)

(2) *Harmonies*, Op. 11
Six-part Harmoniemusik
EP (Vienna, Haslinger) [cited in F]

### Gélin, Charles

The following works in F:Pn are all early prints for large wind band; all were printed in Paris in 1868–1898.
*March*, Vm.27.7581
Polkas: Vm.27.12832, Vm.27.7580

### Genard

*Air de Tyroliens et Marche de la Landwehre de Vienne*
-421
EP (Paris, Janet)

(3) *Marches* and (6) *Pas redoublés en Fanfares*
-421
EP (Paris, Ebend)

### Genin, T.

The following works in F:Pn are all early prints for large wind band; all were printed in Paris in 1884–1898.
Marches: Vm.27.7583, Vm.27.7584, Vm.27.7585, Vm.27.7586

### Génisson, Emile

The following works in F:Pn are all early prints for large wind band; all were printed in Paris in 1881–1887.
Overtures: Vm.27.7593, Vm.27.7595, Vm.27.7597
*Allegro militaire*, Vm.27.7598
*Fantaisie*, Vm.27.7600

Marches: Vm.27.7592, Vm.27.7596, Vm.27.7599, Vm.27.7604
Boléros: Vm.27.7587, Vm.27.7590
Quadrilles: Vm.27.7588, Vm.27.7589, Vm.27.7601
*Galop,* Vm.27.7591
*Polonaise,* Vm.27.7594
*Schottisch,* vm.27.7605
Valses: Vm.27.7602, Vm.27.7603

## Gentilt Victor

The following works in F;Pn are all early prints for large wind band; all were printed in Paris in 1874–1902.
*Fantaisie pastorale,* Vm.27.1747
Marches: Vm.27.7607, Vm.27.7608, Vm.27.7609, Vm.27.7610, Vm.27.7611 [for brass band], Vm.27.7613, Vm.27.7616, Vm.27.7618, Vm.27.7625, Vm.27.7632, Vm.27.7636, Vm.27.7631 (Marche-procession), Vm.27.7633, (Marche-procession), Vm.27.7634
Valses: Vm.27.7612, Vm.27.7621, Vm.27.7626, Vm.27.7630, Vm.27.7637
Polkas: Vm.27.7617, Vm.27.7620, Vm.27.7627 [for brass band], Vm.27.7628, Vm.27.7635
Mazurkas: Vm.27.7615, Vm.27.7622
*Quadrille,* Vm.27.7624

## Georges, Jules

The following works in F:Pn are early prints for large wind band; both were printed in Paris in 1876 and 1877.
*March,* Vm.27.7641
*Mazurka,* Vm.27.7640

## Gérard, Marcelin

The following works in F:Pn are all early prints for large wind band; all were printed in Paris in 1882.
Marches: Vm.27.7646, Vm.27.7647, Vm.27.1752

## Gérin, Louis

The following works in F:Pn are early prints for large wind band; both were printed in Lyon in 1894 and 1901.
Marches: Vm.27.7648, Vm.27.7649, Vm.27.7653, Vm.27.7654

## Gerke, Auguste

*Pièces pourHarmonie et musique mil.* Op. 9 and 12
Harmoniemusik
EP (Breitkopf & Härtel) [cited in F]

## Germain, Emile

The following works in F:Pn are all early prints for large wind band; all were printed in Paris in 1867–1887.
*Overture,* Vm.27.1755
*Nocturne,* Vm.27.7659
*Fantaisie,* Vm.27.7656
Marches: Vm.27.7661, Vm.27.7662, Vm.27.7665, Vm.7.13564Vm.27.7660, Vm.27.7663

## Gesus, R.

The following works in F:Pn are early prints for large wind band; both were printed in Paris in 1899.
*Fantaisie,* Vm.27.1760
*March,* Vm.27.1758

## Gibert, Antoine

The following works in F:Pn are all early prints for large wind band; all were printed in Paris in 1866–1880.
*Overture,* Vm.27.7677
Fantaisies: Vm.27.1772, Vm.27.1773
Marches: Vm.27.7674, Vm.27.7672, Vm.27.7675, Vm.27.7676, Vm.27.7678, Vm.27.7683, Vm.27.1774, Vm.27.7689, Vm.27.7691, Vm.27.7692, Vm.27.7693, Vm.27.7697, Vm.27.7698, Vm.27.7701, Vm.27.7703, Vm.27.7704
Valses: Vm.27.1763, Vm.7.13570, Vm.27.7694, Vm.27.1782, Vm.27.7702
Quadrilles: Vm.27.7668, Vm.27.7679
*Carrousel-caprice,* Vm.27.1765
Polkas: Vm.27.7682, Vm.27.7686, Vm.27.7696
In addition there are more than one hundred transcriptions of orchestral music for large wind band in F:Pn by Gibert.

### Gillard, F.

The following works in F:Pn are all early prints for large wind band; all were printed in Paris in 1888–1899.
*Overture*, Vm.27.7708
*Fantaisie*, Vm.27.1789
Marches: Vm.27.1784, Vm.27.1785, Vm.27.1787, Vm.27.1788, Vm.27.1790, Vm.7.13136, Vm.27.1791
*Valse*, Vm.27.13126

### Gillet, F.

*Fantaisie*
Large wind band
EP (Paris, 1870) F:Pn (Vm.27.7714)

### Girard, L.

The following works in F:Pn are all early prints for large wind band; all were printed in Paris in 1865–1869.
Works for the Church: Vm.27.1807 bis (*Andante religioso*) [solo B♭ bugle], Vm.27.1831 [1–15] (*Recueil de Morceau liturgigues*) [for brass band]
Marches: Vm.27.1807, Vm.27.1810 (*Choral et Marche*),Vm.27.7762
Valses: Vm.27.1823, Vm.27.1834 [for brass band]
*Polka*, Vm.7.13591 [for brass band]
Galops: Vm.7.13590, Vm.27.7774 (*Le Sommeil de Polypheme*) [solo E♭ contra-bass saxophone!]
*Variations* (*sur un air allemand*) [soli cornet, alto, baritone, and bass]
In addition there are more than one hundred and fifty transcriptions for band in F:Pn by Girard, together with his instrumentation treatise for (regular) band and brass band (Vm.8.372)

### Giraud, Adolphe

The following works in F:Pn are all early prints for large wind band; all were printed in Paris in 1889–1898.
*Overture de concert*, Vm.27.7789
*Fantaisie*, Vm.27.7793
*Allegro de concert*, Vm.27.7794
Marches: Vm.27.7784, Vm.27.7786, Vm.27.7787, Vm.27.7790, Vm.27.7788 (*Marche procession*), Vm.27.7792 (*Marche procession*)

### Girerd, Edouard

*Polka*
Large wind band
EP (Paris, 1870) F:Pn (Vm.27.1840)

### Girolet

The following works in F:Pn are all early prints for large wind band; all were printed in Paris in 1884–1888.
Overtures: Vm.27.7795, Vm.27.7796 (*La Concorde*), Vm.27.7797, Vm.27.7798 (*Euterpe et Polymnie*), Vm.27.7799
*March*, Vm.27.7800
*Polka*, Vm.27.1841
*Une chasse*, Vm.27.1842

### Givord

The following works in F:Pn are early prints for large wind band; both were printed in Paris in 1868.
*March*, Vm.27.1843
*Polka*, Vm.27.7801

### Gleize, F.

*Fantaisie*
Large wind band
EP (Paris, 1889) F:Pn (Vm.27.12836 and Vm.27.12837) [two copies]

### Godard, Amédée

*March*
Large wind band
EP (Paris, 1872) F:Pn (Vm.27.7810)

### Gostiau, G.

The following works in F:Pn are early prints for large wind band; both were printed in Paris in 1882 and 1900.
Marches: Vm.27.7829, Vm.27.7830

### Gotherot, G.

*Fantaisie*
Large wind band
EP (Paris, 1881) F:Pn (Vm.27.7831)

### Goueytes, R.

The following works in F:Pn are all early prints for large wind band; all were printed in Paris in 1878–1896.

*Fantaisie*, Vm.27.7835

*March*, Vm.27.7838

Polkas: Vm.7.13133 [solo E♭ clarinet or cornet], Vm.7.13596 [solo cornet]

*Valse*, Vm.7.13596

There are also a few transcriptions for band in F:Pn by Goueytes, including one of the second movement of Beethoven's Third Symphony.

### Gouirand, Joseph

The following works in F:Pn are all early prints for large wind band; all were printed in Paris in 1866–1890.

Works for the Church: Vm.27.7849 (*Marche funèbre*), Vm.27.7860 (*Andante religieux*)

Overtures: Vm.27.7850, Vm.27.7865 and Vm.27.7866 [two copies]

*Cavatine*, Vm.27.12843 [solo baritone saxhorn]

Marches: Vm.7.13599, Vm.27.7848, Vm.27.12841, Vm.27.12842

Polkas: Vm.7.7839, Vm.27.7867, Vm.27.12841, Vm.27.12842

Mazurkas: Vm.27.7840, Vm.27.7841, Vm.27.7856, Vm.27.7859

Schottischs: Vm.27.7842, Vm.27.7854, Vm.27.7858, Vm.27.12840

Quadrilles: Vm.27.12839, Vm.27.7861, Vm.27.7862

Valses: Vm.27.7845, Vm.27.7846, Vm.27.7852, Vm.27.7853, Vm.27.7864

### Gouly

*Polka*
Large wind band
EP (Paris, nineteenth century) F:Pn (Vm.27.1880)

### Gounod, Charles François (1818–1893)

*Messe à la mémoire de Jeanne d'Arc*
Chorus, soloists, organ, with a 'Fanfare' band of -803, organ
EP (Paris, Lemoine, 1887) F:Pn (L.11753/1-6)
This is actually for unison brass and is not musically very interesting.

*Marche Fanfare* in E♭ [for the brass band of the 12th Hussars]
EP (Paris, Chaudens, 1878)
EP (Paris) [Piano, 4-hand] F:Pn (Vm.12.11895 and D.4803/3)
Only the piano version seems to survive for this very unusual looking march.

*Hymne à Ste. Cécile*
Solo violin, 2222-24, timpani, harps
EP (Paris, Lebeau, 1865) F:Pn (D .4801/1)
This is a brief Andante; several other versions exist.

*Petite Symphonie*
1222-02
EP (Paris, dedicated to Taffanel)

### Goyer

The following works in F:Pn are early prints for large wind band; both were printed in Paris in 1854 and 1871.

Marches: Vm.27.7882, Vm.27.7883

### Graffeuil, Charles

*Pas redoublé*
Large wind band
EP (Paris, 1889) F:Pn (Vm.27.1929)

### Grangé, Léon

*March*
Large wind band
EP (Paris, 1899 and 1901) F:Pn (Vm.27.7886 and Vm.27.7887) [two copies]

### Grange, Théodore

The following works in F:Pn are all early prints for large wind band; all were printed in Paris in 1887–1889.

Marches: Vm.27.1933, Vm.27.1935 (*Marche de procession*), Vm.27.1934

### Gras, D.-L.

The following works in F:Pn are all early prints for large wind band; all were printed in Paris in 1881.

Quadrille, Vm.27.7890
Polkas: Vm.27.7891, Vm.27.7892

## Grillet, Laurent

The following works in F:Pn are all early prints for large wind band; all were printed in Paris in 1882–1896.
Marches: Vm.27.7902, Vm.27.7900, Vm.27.7901, Vm.27.4691 [three copies]
*Valse*, Vm.27.4690
*Galop*, Vm.27.7899

## Gross, G.

The following works in F:Pn are all early prints for large wind band; all were printed in Paris in 1878–1881.
Marches: Vm.27.7912, Vm.27.7909, Vm.27.7910
*Polka*, Vm.27.7911

## Guéroult, Th.

*March*
Large wind band
EP (Paris, 1896) F:Pn (vm.27.7916)

## Gués, A.

The following works in F:Pn are all early prints for large wind band; all were printed in Paris in ca. 1858.
*Pas redoublé*, Vm.27.1958
*Quadrille*, Vm.27.1957
*Polka*, Vm.27.7919

## Guespereau

The following works in F:Pn are all early prints for large wind band; all were printed in Paris in 1867–1874.
*Fantaisie-Overture*, Vm.27.7926
Marches: Vm.27.7920, Vm.27.7921, Vm.27.7922, Vm.27.7931, Vm.27.7932, Vm.27.7929, Vm.27.7930
*Polka*, Vm.27.7927
*Boléro*, Vm.27.7925

## Guévin, Arthur

The following works in F:Pn are all early prints for large wind band; all were printed in Paris in 1886–1887.
Marches: Vm.27.7938, Vm.27.7941 ('*a grand effet avec tutti de basses*')
Polkas: Vm.27.7940, Vm.27.7936
*Valse*, Vm.27.7939
*Mazurka*, Vm.27.7937
*Quadrille*, Vm.27.7935

## Guilbert

The following works in F:Pn are all early prints for large wind band; all were printed in Paris in 1867–1879.
Fantaisies: Vm.27.7946, Vm.27.7950, Vm.27.7958, Vm.27.7965, Vm.27.7961 (*La Sierra Nevada*) [for brass band], Vm.27.7976, Vm.27.7979, Vm.27.7980
Marches: Vm.27.7945, Vm.27.7848, Vm.27.7951, Vm.27.7952, Vm.27.7953, Vm.27.7954, Vm.27.7956, Vm.27.7957, Vm.27.7960, Vm.27.7961, Vm.27.7962, Vm.27.7963, Vm.27.7964, Vm.27.7966, Vm.27.7967, Vm.27.7970, Vm.27.7971, Vm.27.7973, Vm.27.7974, Vm.27.7975, Vm.27.7977, Vm.27.7978, Vm.27.7981
Polkas: Vm.27.7947, Vm.27.7959, Vm.27.7969
Valses: Vm.27.7949, Vm.27.7983
*Mazurka*, Vm.27.7968
*Quadrille*, Vm.27.7972
*Schottisch*, Vm.27.1962 and Vm.27.7984 [two copies]

## Guille, J.

*Polka*
Large wind band
EP (Paris, 1884) F:Pn (Vm.27.7986)

## Guillement, G.

The following works in F:Pn are all early prints for large wind band; all were printed in Paris in 1887–1892.
Fantaisies: Vm.27.7987, Vm.27.7994

Marches: Vm.27.7989, Vm.27.12857 (*Marche arabe*), Vm.27.7992

There are another twenty or so original works by Guillement dated 1900–1910 in F:Pn.

## Guimbal, A.

The following works in F:Pn are all early prints for large wind band; all were printed in Paris in 1865–1894.
*March religieuse*, Vm.27.8004
*Mosaique des chants nationaux de tous les pays*, Vm.7.13656
*Air varié*, Vm.27.8003
Marches: Vm.27.7997, Vm.27.7998, Vm.27.8001, Vm.27.8002
*Mazurka*, Vm.27.7999
Galops: Vm.27.8005, Vm.27.1972 ('Xylophone')

## Guion, Edmond

*March*
Large wind band
EP (Paris, 1884) F:Pn (Vm.27.1975

## Gurtner (Chef de Musique, 4e de Ligne)

The following works in F:Pn are all early prints for large wind band; all were printed in Paris in 1851–1887.
Works for the Church: Vm.27.2008, Vm.7.13616, Fol.Vm.15.472 [three copies] (*Marche funèbre*), Vm.7.13618 (*Marche funèbre*), Vm.27.2014 (*Marche-procession*), Vm.7.13145 (*Morceau d'Élévation*), Vm.7.13619, Vm.27.2029, Vm.27.2030 [three copies] (*Marche-procession*)
Overtures: Vm.7.12972, Vm.7.12973, Vm.7.12974, Vm.27.2028, Vm.7.12975
*Fantaisie*, Vm.7.13612
Marches: Vm.7.13622, Vm.27.8013, Vm.27.1981, Vm.27.1982, Vm.27.1984, Vm.7.13623, Vm.7.13624, Vm.27.1985, Vm.27.1986, Vm.27.1987, Vm.27.1988, Vm.7.13625, Vm.27.1988, Vm.27.4698, Vm.7.13626, Vm.27.1990, Vm.27.1991, Vm.7.13620, Vm.27.1992, Vm.27.1993, Vm.27.1994, Vm.27.1995, Vm.27.1998, Vm.27.2002, Vm.27.2003, Vm.7.13621, Vm.7.13627, Vm.7.13629, Vm.27.2004, Vm.27.2005, Vm.7.13630, Vm.27.2006, Vm.27.2007, Vm.7.13628, Vm.7.13631, Vm.7.13633, Vm.27.2009, Vm.7.13634, Vm.27.2012, Vm.7.13632, Vm.27.8014, Vm.27.8015, Vm.27.2017, Vm.27.2018, Vm.7.13635, Vm.27.2020, Vm.27.2021, Vm.7.13637, Vm.7.13636, Vm.27.2022, Vm.27.2023, Vm.7.13638, Vm.27.2024, Vm.27.2025, Vm.27.2026, Vm.7.13641, Vm.27.2027, Vm.7.13611, Vm.7.13639, Vm.7.13142, Vm.27.2032, Vm.7.13640, Vm.27.2033, Vm.7.13143, Vm.27.2034, Vm.7.13642, Vm.7.13643, Vm.7.13644, Vm.27.2036, Vm.27.2037, Vm.27.2044, Vm.7.13645, Vm.7.13646, Vm.27.2045, Vm.27.2046
Polkas: Vm.27.1983, Vm.27.1996, Vm.7.13615, Vm.27.1999, Vm.7.13614, Vm.27.2001, Vm.7.13613, Vm.27.2011, Vm.7.13654, Vm.27.2015, Vm.27.2038, Vm.27.2042, Vm.27.2043
Quadrilles: Vm.27.1997, Vm.7.13649, Vm.7.13651
Mazurkas: Vm.7.13653, Vm.7.13652, Vm.27.2040, Vm.27.2041
Valses: Vm.7.13647, Vm.27.2016, Vm.27.2031, Vm.27.2035, Vm.27.2039, Vm.7.13648 (solo ophicleide)

## Hafemeister, Richard

The following works in F:Pn are all early prints for large wind band; all were printed in Paris in 1895–1897.
*March*, Vm.27.8020
*Valse*, Vm.27.8019
*Polka*, Vm.27.12863

## Hainaut, A.

*Allegro*
Large wind band
EP (Paris, 1899) F:Pn (Vm.27.8021)

## Hairaud, Hte.

The following works in F:Pn are early prints for large wind band; both were printed in Paris in 1877 and 1880.
*March*, Vm.27.8023
*Quadrille*, Vm.27.8022

*Valse*
Large wind band
EP (Paris, 1877) F:Pn (Vm.27.8024)

### Halévy, J.-F. Fromental (1799–1862)

*Les cendres de Napoléon*
Large wind band
EP (Mainz, no date) [cited in Grove, VIII, 46]
In F:Pn I could find only a piano version by Ed. Wolff, published by P. Schlessinger under A.40.428, which also speaks of the performance date as December 15, 1840. Judging by this version the original band work was a major work of dramatic nature. The F:Pn catalog also lists another work which may have been used in the same ceremony, *Marche héroique pour les funèrailles de l'Empereur Napoléon*, but when I submitted the call-number (MS.8677), only a vast pile of autograph fragments, mostly operatic in nature, was produced. A piano version of this work can be found under A.40.431.

### Haring, Alfred

The following works in F:Pn are all early prints for large wind band; all were printed in Paris in 1893–1898.
*March*, Vm.27.4705
*Gavotte* (*Noelie*), Vm.27.8029
*Galop*, Vm.27.8027

### Haslinger, J.

The following works in F:Pn are early prints for large wind band; both were printed in Paris in 1869 and 1888.
*Recueil de morceaux* (12 Marches), Vm.27.12864
*Allegro militaire*, Vm.27.8037

### Haslinger, L.-J.

*Concerts harmoniques*
[Collection] for four to six-part brass band
EP (Paris, 1889) F:Pn (Vm.7.5016)

### Hausser, J.

*March*
Large wind band
EP (Paris, 1894) F:Pn (Vm.27.2071)

### Heitz, Alexis

The following works in F:Pn are early prints for large wind band; both were printed in Paris in 1874–1875.
*Fantaisie*, Vm.27.8046
*Boléro*, Vm.27.8047 and Vm.7.13661 [two copies]

### Hellmuth

(2) *Pas redoublés et un Pas de Charge*
Large wind band
EP (Paris, Gambaro, ca. 1800–1828)

### Hemet, E.

The following works in F:Pn are all early prints for large wind band; all were printed in Paris in 1851–1863.
Marches: Vm.27.2082, Vm.7.13662
*Quadrille*, Vm.7.13663

### Hemmerlé, Charles

The following works in F:Pn are all early prints for large wind band; all were printed in Paris in 1860–1895.
*Overture*, Vm.27.12870
Works for the Church: Vm.27.8059 (*Marche funèbre*), Vm.27.8076 (*Méditation, Andante religieux*)
*Fantaisie*, Vm.27.8066
Airs varié: Vm.27.8065, Vm.27.8068, Vm.27.8070
*Solo de Concert* [solo baritone or B♭ bass], Vm.27.8099
Marches: Vm.27.8053, Vm.27.8054, Vm.27.8058, Vm.27.8061, Vm.27.8073, Vm.27.8088, Vm.27.8089, Vm.27.8093, Vm.27.8094, Vm.27.8095, Vm.27.8096
Polkas: Ym.27.8048, Vm.27.8055, Vm.27.8057, Vm.27.8062, Vm.27.8064, Vm.27.8074, Vm.27.8081, Vm.27.8100, Vm.27.8083 [two solo cornets], Vm.27.8087, Vm.27.8092, Vm.27.8101 (*Le Trombone sentimental*)
Valses: Vm.27.8049, Vm.27.8051, Vm.27.8079 (*Mollda*), Vm.27.8082, Vm.27.8084, Vm.27.8085, Vm.27.8098
Mazurkas: Vm.27.8050, Vm.27.8060, Vm.27.8067, Vm.27.8078, Vm.27.8086 [solo alto saxophone]

Quadrilles: Vm.27.8052, Vm.27.12866,
Vm.27.12867, Vm.27.8102, Vm.27.12868 (*Fin de siècle*), Vm.27.12869
*Boléro*, Vm.27.8056
Schottisches: Vm.27.8069, Vm.27.8072, Vm.27.8090, Vm.27.8097, Vm.27.8103
*La Fête de famille* ('16 petites melodies'), Vm.27.8063

### Hemmerlé, J.

The following works in F:Pn are all early prints for large wind band; all were printed in Paris in 1866–1907.

[Collection] (16) *Morceaux de danses*, Vmd.1447
[Collection] (80) *Morceau de danses*, Vm.27.8137 [Part A], Vmd.1448 [Part B], Vm.27.8119 [Part C], and Vm.27.8138 [Part D]
[Collection] (22) [Dance movements], Vm.27.8146
[Collection] (16) *Morceau*, Vm.27.8179 and 17535 [two copies]
[Collection] *L'Orchestre Suite-Bal repertoire* (14 pieces), Vm.27.8222
Overtures: Vm.27.8109, Vm.27.8110, Vm.27.8115, Vm.27.8116, Vm.27.8117, Vm.27.8118, Vm.27.8120, Vm.27.8122, Vm.27.8132, Vm.27.8139, Vm.27.8141, Vm.27.8142, Vm.27.8145, Vm.27.8l54, Vm.27.8155, Vm.27.8161, Vm.27.8162, Vm.27.8163, Vm.27.8165, Vm.27.8166, Vm.27.8168, Vm.27.8171, Vm.27.2088, Vm.27.8177, Vm.27.8181, Vm.27.8190, Vm.27.12889, Vm.27.8206 (*Méphisto*), Vm.27.8212, Vm.27.8215, Vm.27.8221, Vm.27.12890, Vm.27.12891/1-2 *L'Orientale* (1. *à la Mosque*; 2. *au Sérail*), Vm.27.12892, Vm.27.12894, Vm.27.12896, Vm.27.12899, Vm.27.12902, Vm.27.12903, Vm.27.12904, Vm.27.12905, Vm.27.12908, Vm.27.12909
Fantaisies: Vm.27.8108, Vm.27.12871, Vm.27.2085, Vm.27.2086, Vm.27.8136 (*Concert de nuit*), Vm.27.12881, Vm.27.8169, Vm.27.2089, Vm.27.8175, Vm.27.8176, Vm.27.8185, Vm.27.8186, Vm.27.8187, Vm.27.8274 bis, Vm.27.12898, Vm.27.8246, Vm.27.8245, Vm.27.8254, Vm.27.8255 [for brass band], Vm.27.8256, Vm.27.8257, Vm.27.8269, Vm.27.8273
Airs varié: Vm.27.8105 [solo cornet], Vm.27.12878 [solo trumpets], Vm.27.8150, Vm.27.8244, Vm.27.8265, Vm.27.2094 (*Un concours de soli*)
Marches: Vm.27.8104, Vm.27.8106, Vm.27.8107, Vm.7.13664, Vm.27.2084, Vm.27.8121, Vm.27.8127, Vm.27.8129, Vm.27.8130, Vm.27.8131, Vm.27.8135, Vm.27.8140, Vm.27.8143, Vm.27.8147, Vm.27.8151, Vm.27.8164, Vm.27.12888, Vm.27.8182, Vm.27.8183, Vm.27.8188, Vm.27.8189, Vm.27.8207, Vm.27.8208, Vm.27.8210, Vm.27.8214, Vm.27.8218, Vm.27.8219, Vm.27.8224, Vm.27.8226, Vm.27.2092, Vm.27.8230, Vm.27.8235, Vm.27.8237, Vm.27.8238, Vm.27.8241, Vm.27.8242, Vm.27.8249, Vm.27.8250, Vm.27.8253, Vm.27.8258, Vm.27.8263, Vm.27.8264, Vm.27.8270, Vm.27.8271, Vm.27.8272
Quadrilles: Vm.27.8111, Vm.27.8124, Vm.27.8205, Vm.27.8209, Vm.27.2091, Vm.27.8231, Vm.27.8243, Vm.27.8260, Vm.27.8274
Mazurkas: Vm.27.12872, Vm.27.8213, Vm.27.12897, Vm.27.12900, Vm.27.8247, Vm.27.8266
Polkas: Vm.27.8113 [solo cornet], Vm.27.12873, Vm.27.12875, Vm.27.8123, Vm.27.8134 [solo cornet], Vm.27.8144, Vm.27.2087 [solo cornet], Vm.27.8153, Vm.27.8160, Vm.27.8172, Vm.27.8180, Vm.27.8184, Vm.27.8211, Vm.27.8251, Vm.27.8261, Vm.27.8233 [soli two cornets or piccolo and small clarinet], Vm.27.12906
*Gavotte*, Vm.27.12874
Boléros: Vm.27.8128, Vm.27.12885, Vm.27.12887
Schottisches: Vm.27.8133, Vm.27.8149
Galops: Vm.27.12877, Vm.27.8173, Vm.27.8170
Valses: Vm.27.8227, Vm.27.8228, Vm.27.12901, Vm.27.8252, Vm.27.8262 (*La Tour Eiffel*)
*Le Glas funèbre*, Vm.27.8l74
*Les Heures de glorie* [four-part chorus and band], Vm.27.12888 bis
*Phoebus, oules bienfaits du soleif* [voice with band], Vm.27.8229
*Qui vive?*, '*Patroville*' Vm.27.8240

*Souvenir du Camp*, ('*grande manoeuvre dite petite guerre ... Distraction musicale militaire*') Vm.7.13665 and Vm.713666 [later edition]
*Un dernier Hommage*, Vm.27.8267, with Vm.27.8268 and Vm.27.12907 later editions.
In addition there are many transcriptions in F:Pn by Hemmerlé, including some which may be classed as original works, with titles such as *Fantaisie sur Don Juan de Mozart*, and similar works based on Weber, Schumann, etc.]

### Henny, H.

*Marche*
Large wind band
EP (Paris, 1893) F:Pn (Vm.27.8275)

### Hérard, Camille

The following works in F:Pn are all early prints for large wind band; all were printed in Paris in 1884–1898.
Marches: Vm.27.2095, Vm.27.8280, Vm.27.2096
*L'Escorte du Csar*, Vm.27.4711

### Hérbert, Charles

The following works in F:Pn are all early prints for large wind band; all were printed in Paris in 1890–1895.
Marches: Vm.27.1078, Vm.27.2080
*Mazurka de concert*, Vm.27.2079

### Herbuté, E.-N.

*Marche*
Large wind band
EP (Paris, 1893) F:Pn (Vm.27.2097)

### Herzog, Auguste

*Polka*
Large wind band
EP (Paris, 1858) F:Pn (Vm.27.2105)

### Hitz, Franz

The following works in F:Pn are all early prints for large wind band; all were printed in Paris in 1853–1880.
Marches: Vm.27.8291, Vm.27.8292, Vm.27.8293
*Boléro*, Vm.27.8294
*Polka,* Vm.27.12918
*Quadrille*, Vm.27.8296

### Hitzemann, H.

*Polka*
Large wind band
EP (Paris, 1885) F:Pn (Vm.27.8297)

### Hôdier, Romain

The following works in F:Pn are early prints for large wind band; both were printed in Paris in 1867.
Marches: Vm.27.8298 (*Le Saquebute*), Vm.27.8299

### Hofer, Frédéric

The following works in F:Pn are all early prints for large wind band; all were printed in Paris during the nineteenth century.
Marches: Vm.27.2106, Vm.27.2107, Vm.27.2108, Vm.27.2109, Vm.27.2110

### d'Hollandre, Jean (1785–1839)

*Des morceaux d'harmonie pour les instruments a vent* [cited in F]

### Hortense, Reine (1783–1837, Queen of Holland, daughter to Josephine, mother of Napoleon III)

*Marche*
Large wind band
EP (Paris, 1866) F:Pn (Vm.27.8302)

### Hoste, L.

*Marche*
Large wind band
EP (Paris, 1899) F:Pn (Vm.27.4719)

### Hourenaeghel, L.

The following works in F:Pn are all early prints for large wind band; all were printed in Paris in 1894–1898.

Marches: Vm.27.4720, Vm.27.4721 [two copies], Vm.27.4722 (*Pas redoublé de concert*)
*Fantaisie-Boléro*, Vm.27.2113 [solo oboe]

## Houziaux, H. (Chef de Musique, 46e de Ligne)

The following works in F:Pn are all early prints for large wind band; all were printed in Paris in 1875–1901.
*Fantaisie*, Vm.27.2118
Allegri militaire: Vm.27.2115, Vm.7.13671 (*Le Piccolo*)
Marches: Vm.7.13670, Vm.27.8303, Vm.27.4723, Vm.27.8305
Valses: Vm.27.2114, Vm.27.2116, Vm.27.2117
*Galop*, Vm.27.12919

## Hubans, Charles

The following works in F:Pn are all early prints for large wind band; all were printed in Paris in 1868–1899.
Marches: Vm.27.12307, Vm.27.4724, Vm.27.8309, Vm.27.8308
*Polka*, Vm.27.8306
*Valse Suite*, Vm.27.8307

## Huber, Emile

*Marche*
Large wind band
EP (Paris, 1884) F:Pn (Vm.27.8310)

## Hüe, Georges-Adolphe (1858–1948)

*Vox populi* (1891–1904)
Four-part male chorus with Harmoniemusik
EP (Paris, Leduc) [cited in MGG]

## Huyts, C.

*Marche*
Large wind band
EP (Paris, 1862) F:Pn (Vm.27.8322)

## d'Indy, Vincent (1851–1931)

*Chanson et danses*, Op. 50 (1898)
1122-01
EP (Paris) GB:Lbm (f.656.a.[I]); BRD:Bhm (7392) [score]

*Sarabande and Minuet*, Op. 24
1111-01, piano
EP (Paris, Hamelle) [cited by DJ]

*Marche du 76e Regiment d'Infanterie*, Op. 54 (1903)
In F:Pn one can find a piano version of this work under Vm.12.1.1313, published by Durand (transcribed by the composer) and dedicated to 'Colonel Roy'; it is not a strong work.

*Mosaïque sur Feryaal* (1897)
Military band

*La vengeance du mari*, Op. 104/105 (1931)
SATB, 11-01, English horn
MS (autograph, dated July 14, 1931) F:Pn (MS.9232)

## Istres, H.

The following works in F:Pn are early prints for large wind band; both were printed in Paris in 1887 and 1899.
*Overture*, Vm.27.2125
*Quadrille*, Vm.27.8326

## Ithier, Louis

The following works in F:Pn are early prints for large wind band; both were printed in Paris in 1899 and 1903.
Marches: Vm.27.12924, Vm.27.12927

## Jacob

*Marche*
Large wind band
EP (Paris, 1892) F:Pn (Vm.27.4726)

## Jacob, E.

The following works in F:Pn are all early prints for large wind band; all were printed in Paris in 1879–1901.
Marches: Vm.27.8327, Vm.27.8328, Vm.7.13161

## Jacob, Jules

*Marche*
Large wind band
EP (Paris, 1879) F:Pn (Vm.27.2130)

### Jacotin, L.

*Marche*
Large wind band
EP (Paris, 1864) F:Pn (Vm.27.8339)

### Jacque, E.

The following works in F:Pn are early prints for large wind band; both were printed in Paris in 1876 and 1882.
Marches: Vm.27.8341, Vm.27.8340

### Jacquemet, L.

The following works in F:Pn are all early prints for large wind band; all were printed in Paris in 1892–1908.
Overtures: Vm.27.12931, Vm.27.8342
*Valse*, Vm.27.2132 and Vm.27.2133 [two copies]
*Gavotte*, Vm.27.12932 and 12933 [two copies]

### Jacquet, Charles

The following works in F:Pn are all early prints for large wind band; all were printed in Paris in 1868–1885.
Overtures: Vm.27.12936, Vm.27.12938
*Fantaisie*, Vm.27.8345
*Allegro*, Vm.27.8346
Polkas: Vm.27.8347, Vm.27.8344

### Jancières, V.

*Overture*
Large wind band
EP (Paris, 1878) F:Pn (Vm.27.12954)

### Jancourt, E.

The following works in F:Pn are all early prints for large wind band; all were printed in Paris in 1857–1879.
Work for the Church, Vm.27.2140 (*Morceau d'Élévation*)
*Fantaisie*, Vm.27.2138 (*Fantaisie d'après A. Jancourt*)
*Tyrolienne*, Vm.27.8362
Marches: Vm.27.2137, Vm.27.8351, Vm.27.8355, Vm.27.8359
*Galop*, Vm.27.8349
*Mazurka*, Vm.27.8354 and Vm.27.2139 [later edition]
In addition there are a number of transcriptions for wind band by Jancourt in F:Pn, including one of Rossini's *Italian in Algiers*.

### Janin-Jaubert

The following works in F:Pn are early prints for large wind band; both were printed in Paris during the second half of the nineteenth century.
*Overture*, Vm.27.8367
Here one finds the parts for a fast–slow–fast symphony in one movement, scored for a large band with saxophones.
*March*, Vm.27.8366

### Janvier, L.

The following works in F:Pn are all early prints for large wind band; all were printed in Paris in 1893–1900.
Overtures: Vm.27.2143, Vm.27.8368 (Overture pastorale)
Polkas: Vm.27.12947, Vm.27.12949
Mazurkas: Vm.27.12948, Vm.27.12951
*Schottisch*, Vm.27.12950

### Jaubert, J.

*Valse*
Large wind band
EP (Paris, 1889) F:Pn (Vm.27.8369)

### Jauffret

*Marche*
Large wind band
EP (Paris, 1894) F:Pn (Vm.27.4727)

### Jaussaud, C.

The following works in F:Pn are all early prints for large wind band; all were printed in Paris in 1880–1887.
Fantaisies: Vm.27.4728, Vm.27.8371, Vm.27.8373
Marches: Vm.27.8370, Vm.27.8372, Vm.27.8374, Vm.27.8375

## Javault (fl. ca. 1800–1828)

*Marches et Pas redoublés*
Harmoniemusik
EP (Paris, Janet)

*Sextuor*
1112-01
EP (Paris, Gaveaux) [Nr. 1–6]

*Fanfares*
-431
EP (Paris, Ebend) [Liv. 1–2]

*Fantaisie*
Harmoniemusik
EP (Paris, A. Petit)

*Harmonie milit.*
Harmouiemusik
EP (Paris, Janet [Liv. 6–7, and 13–15]; Gaveaux [Liv. 1–12]; and 132; Petit [Liv. 16–20]

## Javelot, Jules

The following works in F:Pn are early prints for large wind band; both were printed in Paris in 1875–1876.
*Marche*, Vm.27.8377
*Galop*, Vm.27.8380

## Jeandel, F.

*Pas redoublé*
Large wind band
EP (Paris, 1886) F:Pn (Vm.27.8384)

## Jeanjean, Camille

The following works in F:Pn are all early prints for large wind band; all were printed in Paris in 1889–1892.
Fantaisies: Vm.27.12952 (*Fantaisie de concours*), Vm.27.12953
Marches: Vm.27.8385, Vm.27.8386

## Jeannin

The following works in F:Pn are early prints for large wind band; both were printed in Paris in 1891 and 1892.
*Pas redoublé*, Vm.27.8388
*Schottisch*, Vm.27.8389

## Jobin, E.

The following works in F:Pn are all early prints for large wind band; all were printed in Paris in 1890–1893.
*Fantaisie*, Vm.27.8393
*Schottisch*, Vm.27.8392

## Jolivet, Jules

*Marche*
Large wind band
EP (Paris, 1883) F:Pn (Vm.27.8394)

## Jonas, Emile (1827–1905)

*Prière*
Four or six saxophones [cited in MGG]

## Jonnet, Henry

Marche, *France-Université*
Large wind band
EP (Paris, 1871) F:Pn (Vm.27.8397)

## Jorelle, J.

*Marche*
Large wind band
EP (Paris, 1884) F:Pn (Vm.27.8399)

## Josneau, Auguste (Chef de Musique du 1er de Ligne)

The following works in F:Pn are all early prints for large wind band; all were printed in Paris in 1858–1885.
Works for the Church: Vm.27.2156 (*Marche funèbre*), Vm.27.13727 (*Marche funèbre*), Vm.27.13728 (Marche funèbre), Vm.27.13729 (*Marche funèbre*), Vm.27.13730 (*Marche funèbre*), Vm.27.2159 (*Morceau de repos*)
*Overture* (*Massilia*), Vm.27.2157
Fantaisies: Vm.27.2166, Vm.7.13696
Marches: Vm.27.2150, Vm.7.13718, Vm.27.2151, Vm.27.2152, Vm.7.13717, Vm.7.13720 and Vm.27.2152 bis [two copies], Vm.7.13719, Vm.27.2153, Vm.7.13716, Vm.7.13715, Vm.7.13714, Vm.7.13712, Vm.7.13711, Vm.27.2155, Vm.7.13710, Vm.7.13713, Vm.7.13709, Vm.7.13731, Vm.7.13708,

Vm.7.13707, Vm.7.13706 and Vm.27.2158 [two copies], Vm.27.2160, Vm.7.13703, Vm.7.13165, Vm.7.13702, Vm.7.13705, Vm.27.2162, Vm.27.2164, Vm.27.2165, Vm.7.13692, Vm.7.13704, Vm.7.13722, Vm.7.13723, Vm.7.13724, Vm.7.13726

*Air de danse*, Vm.27.2749
Valses: Vm.27.2154, Vm.7.13700
Polkas: Vm.27.2163, Vm.7.13721 [solo cornet]

## Jouve (fl. ca. 1800–1828)

*Marches et Pas redoublés*
EP (Paris, Frey)

## Julien

*Polka*
Large wind band
EP (Paris, 1892) F:Pn (Vm.27.12956)

## July

The following works in F:Pn are early prints for large wind band; both were printed in Paris in 1903–1905.
Overtures: Vm.27.8407, Vm.27.8410

## July, Fortune

The following works in F:Pn are all early prints for large wind band; all were printed in Paris in 1891–1905.
Marches: Vm.27.8404 (*Orientale*), Vm.27.8411
*Le Cortége de Satan. Légende fantastique*, Vm.27.1544

## Junod, Laurent

The following works in F:Pn are all early prints for large wind band; all were printed in Paris in 1879–1884.
Marches: Vm.27.8415, Vm.27.8416 (*Marche égyptienne*), Vm.27.8417
*Polka*, Vm.27.8418 [solo cornet]
*Valse*, Vm.27.2175

## Kakosky

The following works in F:Pn are all early prints for large wind band; all were printed in Paris in 1864–1892.
*Fantaisie*, Vm.7.13732
*Marche*, Vm.27.2178
Polkas (some with introductions and/or preludes): Vm.27.8419 [solo clarinet], Vm.27.8420, Vm.27.8421, Vm.27.12957

## Karren, Leon (Chef de Husique a la Division de Brest)

The following works in F:Pn are all early prints for large wind band; all were printed in Paris in 1881–1907.
*Symphonie funèbre*, Vm.7.13733
Here one finds a one-movement work, lyric and dramatic.
Overtures: Vm.7.12980, Vm.7.13171, Vm.27.2201
*Aubade*, Vm.27.12958
*Fantaisie,* Vm.27.2187
*Choral*, Vm.27.8422
*First Concerto* [solo clarinet with band], Vm.7.13168
*Légende* [solo trombone], Vm.27.2192
*Jeanne d'Arc*, Vm.27.2191
*Pour la Patrie!* [Chorus, Tenor solo, band], Vm.7.68341 and Vm.7.117309
*Rapsodie*, Vm.27.2196 bis
Marches: Vm.27.8423, Vm.27.2188, Vm.27.2196, Vm.7.13167, Vm.27.2200
Valses: Vm.27.2199, Vm.27.2190
*Menuet*, Vm.27.2195
*Gavotte* [with chorus!], Vm.27.8424
*Polka*, Vm.7.13169

## Kastner, Jean-Georges (1810–1867)

(10) *Serenades* (1832–1835)
Wind band [cited in Grove]

*Cantate alsacienne* (1859)
TTBB, military band
MS F:Pn (Ac.m4.105) [vocal parts only]

*Le Rive d'Oswald ou les Sirènes*
Large wind band
MS (autograph) F:Pn (MS.17133)

## Katzer, Ignace (b. 1785)

*Pieces d'harmonie* [cited in F]

## Kauffmann

*Mazurka*
Large wind band
EP (Paris, 1869) F:Pn (Vm.27.8426)

## Kelsen (Chef de Musique de l'Ecole d'Artillerie de Bourges)

The following works in F:Pn are all early prints for large wind band; all were printed in Paris in 1886–1906.

Overtures: Vm.27.2211 (*Overture symphonique*), Vm.27.2207, Vm.27.8444, Vm.27.8469, Vm.27.8432, Vm.27.8434

The *Overture*, Vm.27.8432, was written for a contest sponsored by the Orphéon Society and was published by them.

Fantaisies: Vm.27.8446, Vm.27.8461, Vm.27.2205, Vm.27.2216, Vm.27.8430, Vm.27.8431

*Allegro de concert*, Vm.27.8440

*Allegro*, Vm.27.8435

Marches: Vm.27.2210 (*Marche symphonique*), Vm.27.846, Vm.27.8463, Vm.7.13172, Vm.27.2214

*Mazurka*, Vm.7.13173

*Gavotte*, Vm.27.2208

*Ballet-Divertimento*, Vm.27.8447

*Pavane*, Vm.27.2212

*Schottisch*, Vm.27.8456

*Polka*, Vm.27.8458

*Valse*, Vm.27.8460

*Mosaïque*, Vm.27.2206

## Keyser (fl. ca. 1800–1828)

*Marches, Pas redoublés et Valses*
Harmoniemusik
EP (Paris, Richault) [Liv. 1]

*Variations en Harmonie*
Harmoniemusik
EP (Paris, Richault) [Liv. 2]

## Kleitz (fl. ca. 1800–1828)

*Marches et Pas redoublés*
Harmoniemusik
EP (Paris, Beauce)

## Kling, Henri (1842–1918)

The following works in F:Pn are all early prints for large wind band; all were printed in Paris in 1877–1899.

Works for the Church: Vm.27.8474 (*Andante religieux*), Vm.27.2274 (*Andante religieux*)

Overtures: Vm.27.2236, Vm.27.2237, Vm.27.12973, Vm.27.2252, Vm.27.2259, Vm.27.2260, Vm.27.2268, Vm.27.2269, Vm.27.2274

In A:Gk there is an uncataloged copy of Kling's *Ariadne Overture*.

*Poème symphonique* ('*Souvenir de 1792*') Vm.27.8510 and Vm.27.2264 [two copies]

This is one long movement of light battle music, etc. Although the title-page mentions 'full band,' this copy seems to be a form of condensed score, with the parts given for: one clarinet, one cornet, one bugle, three altos, baritone, bass, and percussion.

Esquisse symphoniques, Vm.27.2271 ('*Une Halte Dans Le Jura*'), Vm.27.2258 (*Promenade dans la foret*)

*Polonaise de Concert*, Vm.27.2257

*Romance sans paroles*, Vm.27.12976

*Impromptu espagnol*, Vm.27.2249

Fantaisies: Vm.27.2234, Vm.27.2235, Vm.27.2238, Vm.27.12967, Vm.27.12968, Vm.27.12969, Vm.27.2239 Vm.27.2240, Vm.27.2242, Vm.27.12972 (*Fantaisie classique*), Vm.27.2243, Vm.27.2244 (*Fantaisie romantique*), Vm.27.2245 (*Fantaisie concertante*), Vm.27.8495, Vm.27.12975, Vm.27.2247 (*Fantaisie avec Variations 'Hommage à Haydn'*) [slow movement, 'Surprise' Symphony], Vm.27.2248 and Vm.27.2248 bis [two copies], Vm.27.8498, Vm.27.2253, Vm.27.2254 Vm.27.2255 and Vm.27.12978 [two copies], Vm.27.8506, Vm.27.12980 and Vm.27.12981 [two copies], Vm.27.8508, Vm.27.8509, Vm.27.2261, Vm.27.2262, Vm.27.2263, Vm.27.2267,

Vm.27.2265, Vm.27.2266, Vm.27.2270, Vm.27.12982, Vm.27.12983 (*Fantaisie humoristique*), Vm.27.2272
Marches: Vm.27.2246, Vm.27.8496, Vm.27.8475, Vm.27.8487, Vm.27.8488, Vm.27.8489, Vm.27.8497, Vm.27.8511, Vm.27.2248 (*J. J. Rousseau Marche triomphale*), Vm.27.8499, Vm.27.12977, Vm.27.8502, Vm.27.8507
*Scherzo*, Vm.27.8472
*Galop*, Vm.27.8494
Valses: Vm.27.8477, Vm.27.8478
Polkas: Vm.27.8481, Vm.27.2250, Vm.27.8504
*Menuet*, Vm.27.2251
Mazurkas: Vm.27.8503, Vm.27.8513

### Klosé, Hiacynthe (1808–1880)

The following works in F:Pn are all early prints for large wind band; all were printed in Paris in 1858–1870.
*Overture*, Vm.27.2277
Fantaisie, Vm.7.14469 (on Donizetti's *Lucrezia Borgia*)
*Mélodie*, Vm.27.2276
Marches: Vm.27.8520, Vm.27.2275, Vm.7.13740, Vm.7.13742 and, Vm.7.13743 [two copies], Vm.27.8522, Vm.27.8524, Vm.27.8526 (*Marche funèbre*), Vm.27.2278, Vm.27.8527, Vm.27.8529 and Vm.7.14470 [two copies], Vm.7.13739, Vm.27.8515 and Vm.7.14472 [two copies], Vm.7.13748
The example under Vm.7.13739 is for large band without saxophones. One finds a full score, with rather unusual score order: -343 at the top, with woodwinds below.
Galops: Vm.27.8519, Vm.7.13749
Polkas: Vm.27.8523, Vm.7.13738 [solo small clarinet], Vm.27.8530
An autograph score, dated 1847, of a polka by Klosé can be found under MS.12137.
*Valse espagnole*, Vm.27.8531
*Allegro militaire*, Vm.7.13746 and Vm.7.13747 [two copies]

### Koehler, Benjamin Frederic (b. 1777)

*Jeu de dez d'écossaises à composer*
21-12
EP (Leuckart, 1803) [cited in F]

### Kopff

*Polka*
Large wind band
EP (Paris, 1881) F:Pn (Vm.27.8533)

### Krein, Michel

*Marche*
Large wind band
EP (Paris, 1872) F:Pn (Vm.27.8535)

### Krempel (fl. ca. 1800–1828)

(6) *Morceaux*
-042
EP (Paris, Janet)

(6) *Fanfares*
-532
EP (Paris, Ebend; reprinted Sieber)

### Krempel, Charles

The following works in F:Pn are all early prints for large wind band; all were printed in Paris in 1858–1873.
*Overture*, Vm.27.2285 and Vm.7.12982 [two copies]
This example seems to be the composer's arrangements of his own operetta overture for full band without saxophones.
Marches: Vm.7.13754, Vm.27.2284 and Vm.7.13753 [two copies]
*Galop*, Vm.7.13761

### Krempel, Em. (Chef de Musique au 54e de Ligne)

The following works in F:Pn are all early prints for large wind band; all were printed in Paris in 1873–1876.
*Mélodie sans paroles*, Vm.27.2286
*Les Fiances de la mort* (*Ballade fantastique*), Vm.7.14143
This example, based on melodies of Schubert, is set in six 'scenes,' and is long and programmatic. It was apparently written for the National Guard Band in Paris.
*Marche*, Vm.7.13752

## Krimpel

*Mélodie religieuse*
Large wind band
EP (Paris, 1868) F:Pn (Vm.27.8538)

## Kuhn, F.

*Amité et confiance*
Two solo oboes with military band
EP (Paris, Evette) [cited by MH]

## Labit, Henri (Chef de Musique au 84e de Lignej Directeur de l'Ecole Nationale de Musique de Valenciennes)

The following works in F:Pn are all early prints for large wind band; all were printed in Paris in 1866–1891.

*Prière à St. Cécile*, Vm.27.2294 [soli clarinet and cornet]

*Symphony*, Vm.27.12986 (*Dans la Montagne*)
The catalog indicates this was a three-movement symphony; when I submitted the call-number there was no response.

Overtures: Vm.7.13180, Vm.7.12930, Vm.7.12932

Fantaisies: Vm.7.13179 (*Concertante avec Variations*), Vm.7.13771 [soli trombone, alto, and cornet]

Marches: Vm.27.8539, Vm.7.13182, Vm.7.13773, Vm.7.13774, Vm.7.13767, Vm.7.13776, Vm.27.8541, Vm.7.13181, Vm.7.13775, Vm.27.2293, Vm.7.13765, Vm.7.13777, Vm.7.13778, Vm.7.13779, Vm.7.13782, Vm.27.2296

Polkas: Vm.27.13764 [solo cornet], Vm.27.8540, Vm.27.8542, Vm.27.12987 (solo one or two cornets), Vm.27.8542, Vm.27.8543 (two soli cornets), Vm.27.8544 (*Polka de Concert*) [solo cornet]

*Valse*, Vm.7.13768
*Mazurka*, Vm.7.13770

## Labitzki

*Galop*
Large wind band
EP (Paris, 1859) F:Pn (vm.27.2297 and Vm.7.13772) [two copies]

## Labole, P.-N.

The following works in F:Pn are all early prints for large wind band; all were printed in Paris in 1884–1902.

Works for the Church: Vm.27.8560 (*Andante religieux*) [*par Le Festival Aristique*], Vm.27.12992 (*Andante religieux*), Vm.27.13996 (*Andante religieux*), Vm.27.8619 (*Voix célestes. Rêverie mystique*)

This last example is a brief, slow, and fine work subtitled 'Andantino Religioso.' The publisher is given as '*Le Festival Artistique,*' and this work carries the note, '*Publication musicale de 1er ordre pour Harmonie et Fanfare*' [in Bordeaux].

Overtures: Vm.27.12989, Vm.27.8553 and Vm.27.8561 [two copies], Vm.27.8562, Vm.27.8559, Vm.27.8597 (*La Muse du poéte*), Vm.27.2307, Vm.27.12995

Fantaisies: Vm.27.8551, Vm.27.12991, Vm.27.2303, Vm.27.2304, Vm.27.2305, Vm.27.12993, Vm.27.8586 (*Fantaisie varié*), Vm.27.2302, Vm.27.8615, Vm.27.8590, Vm.27.8613, Vm.27.2306

*Grand Air Varié*, Vm.27.8564 ['*par Le Festival Aristique*']

Marches: Vm.27.8566 ('*par Czar Nicolas II*'), Vm.27.8548, Vm.27.8549, Vm.27.8552, Vm.27.8546, Vm.27.2299, Vm.27.2300, Vm.27.8572, Vm.27.8573, Vm.27.8574, Vm.27.8577, Vm.27.8579, Vm.27.8580, Vm.27.8581, Vm.27.8591, Vm.27.8594, Vm.27.8596, Vm.27.8567, Vm.27.8599, Vm.27.8568, Vm.27.8601, Vm.27.8604, Vm.27.8611, Vm.27.8612, Vm.27.8569, Vm.27.8547, Vm.27.8616, Vm.27.8571, Vm.27.8582

Valses: Vm.27.8585, Vm.27.8610, Vm.27.8588

Mazurkas: Vm.27.2298, Vm.27.8565, Vm.27.8605, Vm.27.8600 (Mazurka de Concert)

Polkas: Vm.27.2301 [two soli cornets], Vm.27.8584 and Vm.27.8584 bis [two copies], Vm.27.8598, Vm.27.8545 [solo cornet or piccolo], Vm.27.8602 [solo cornet], Vm.27.8570

Quadrilles: Vm.27.8583, Vm.27.8617

## Laborde, E.

*Marche*
Large wind band
EP (Paris, 1883) F:Pn (Vm.27.8620)

## Laborde, Léon

The following works in F:Pn are all early prints for large wind band; all were printed in Paris in 1890–1892.
*Polka,* Vm.27.2310 [two soli cornets]
*Valse,* Vm.27.2308
*Mazurka,* Vm.27.2309

## La Bretesche, J. de

*Marche*
Large wind band
EP (Paris, 1849) F:Pn (Vm.27.8621)

## Labric (Chef de Musique du 23e de Ligne)

The following works in F:Pn are all early prints for large wind band; all were printed in Paris in 1855–1881.
*Cantate sur la guerre d'Orient* [with Bass solo, TTBB chorus], Vm.7.13797
Marches: Vm.7.13780, Vm.7.13781, Vm.27.2311

## Lacaire, Thé

[Collection of 14 short works]
Large wind band
EP (Paris, 1885) F:Pn (Vm.27.8622)

## Lacher

*Marche*
Large wind band
EP (Paris, nineteenth century) F:Pn (Vm.27.8623)

## Lacombe, Louis Fr. (1818–1884)

*Cimbres et teutons*
Male chorus, military band [cited in Grove, X, 351]

## Lafille, Charles

The following works in F:Pn are early prints for large wind band; both were printed in Paris during the nineteenth century.
[Collection, 8 short works], Vm.27.2338 [7–8]
*Marche militaire* (performed April 15, 1814), Vm.27.8636

## Lafitte, Jacques

*Polka*
Large wind band
EP (Paris, 1887) F:Pn (Vm.27.8640)

## Lagard, A.

The following works in F:Pn are early prints for large wind band; both were printed in Paris in 1867 and 1889.
*Polka,* Vm.27.9511
*Marche,* Vm.27.8651

## Lagny, A.

The following works in F:Pn are all early prints for large wind band; all were printed in Paris in 1864–1872.
Works for the Church: Vm.27.8657 (*Marche-procession*), Vm.27.8661 (*Marche funèbre*), Vm.27.8664 *Gabrielle. Morceau religieux pouvant servir d'offertoire,* Vm.27.8667 (*Marche-procession*), Vm.27.8674 (*Marche funèbre*), Vm.27.13000 (*Messe facile*), Vm.27.8678 (*Marche-procession*), Vm.27.8679 (*Marche-procession*), Vm.27.8685 (*Morceau religieux*), Vm.27.2351 *Le Saint-Sepulcre Symphonie*
Overtures: Vm.27.8666, Vm.27.8672 (*L'Italienne Fantaisie*), Vm.27.8676, Vm.27.8693, Vm.27.2352
Fantaisies: Vm.27.8658, Vm.27.2342, Vm.27.2353 [solo clarinet]
Airs varié: Vm.7.13788, Vm.27.8656 [solo clarinet or small bugle], Vm.27.2341 [solo cornet], Vm.27.2340
Marches: Vm.27.4731, Vm.27.8660, Vm.27.8662, Vm.27.8663, Vm.27.8665, Vm.27.8675, Vm.27.8680, Vm.7.13789, Vm.27.8687, Vm.27.8688, Vm.27.8689, Vm.27.8690, Vm.27.8691, Vm.21.8698

Quadrilles: Vm.27.8659, Vm.27.8670,
   Vm.27.8677, Vm.27.8683, Vm.27.8694,
   Vm.7.13787
*Valse*, Vm.27.8671
Polkas: Vm.27.2350 (Jupiter), Vm.27.2354
*Polonaise*, Vm.27.8673
*Boléro*, Vm.27.8686 [solo cornet]

### Laigre, Paul

The following works in F:Pn are all early prints for large wind band; all were printed in Paris in 1894.
Marches: Vm.27.8699, Vm.27.8700
*Air varié*, Vm.27.2357
*Polka*, Vm.27.13002

### Lajarte, Théodore-Edouard Dufaure de (1826–1890)

*Messe militaire* (1867)
Chorus and military band [cited by MGG]

*L'Orphéon de l'armee*
Chorus and large band
EP (Paris, Grus, 1869) F:Pn (Cons.D.6616 and Vm.7.8793) [two copies]
   This may be the same work referred to above by MGG.

(6) *Choeurs*
TTBB, brass band
EP (Paris, Grus, 1869) F:Pn (Cons.D.6616—1.6)

The following works in F:Pn are all early prints for large wind band; all were printed in Paris in 1876–1884.
Overture, Vm.27.4824 and Vm.27.13003 [two copies]
Fantaisies: Vm.27.2359, Vm.27.8702
Marches: Vm.27.8705, Vm.27.8710
*Sarabande*, Vm.27.2367
*Quadrille*, Vm.27.8709
*Suite of Valses*: Vm.27.2365

### Lambert, Auguste

The following works in F:Pn are all early prints for large wind band; all were printed in Paris in 1868–1877.

Fantaisies: Vm.27.2384, Vm.27.2381,
   Vm.27.2379, Vm.27.2380, Vm.27.8721
Marches: Vm.27.8715, Vm.27.8716, Vm.7.13791,
   Vm.27.8717, Vm.27.8722, Vm.27.8724,
   Vm.27.8727, Vm.27.2373, Vm.27.4731 bis
*Galop*, Vm.27.2383
Quadrilles: Vm.27.2382, Vm.27.8719,
   Vm.27.8718, Vm.27.2378
*Mazurka*, Vm.27.8714
Polkas: Vm.27.8721 bis, Vm.27.8723,
   Vm.27.8726, Vm.27.8728, Vm.27.2377

### Lambert, E.

The following works in F:Pn are all early prints for large wind band; all were printed in Paris in 1885–1900.
*Overture,* Vm.27.2386
*Scène militaire patriotique* [with chorus], Vm.27.8733
Marches: Vm.27.8732, Vm.27.2385, Vm.27.8735,
   Vm.27.8736
*Mazurka,* Vm.27.8734

### Lamotte, Antony

The following works in F:Pn are all early prints for large wind band; all were printed in Paris in 1853–1895.
*Fantaisie,* Vm.27.8751
*Allegro militaire,* Vm.27.8745
Air variés: ('Jenny Lind') Vm.27.2404,
   Vm.27.2415
*Marche,* Vm.27.2397 and Vm.27.8743 [two copies]
Polkas: Vm.27.8741, Vm.27.8747 (*L'Ophicleide sentimental*), Vm.27.13007, Vm.27.8749
Quadrilles: Vm.27.2396, Vm.27.2408
Valses: Vm.27.2401, Vm.27.2406, Vm.27.2410
   [solo harp], Vm.27.2420, Vm.27.2411
Schottisches: Vm.27.2407, Vm.27.2414,
   Vm.27.2418, Vm.27.2421
*Fleur de Grenade*, Vm.27.2400

### Langlane, Geo.

*Galop caprice*
Large wind band
EP (Paris, 1878) F:Pn (Vm.27.2423)

### Langlois, Jules

The following works in F:Pn are all early prints for large wind band; all were printed in Paris in 1880–1887.
*Overture classique*, Vm.27.2424 and Vm.27.8757 [two copies]
Marches: Vm.27.8756, Vm.27.2425

### Lapara

*Retraite*
Large wind band, with additional clarions, fifes, drums
EP (Paris, 1897) F:Pn (Vm.27.8760)

*Pas redoublé*
Large wind band, with additional ad lib trumpets
EP (Paris, 1897) F:Pn (Vm.27.8759)

### Laporte, Raymond

The following works in F:Pn are early prints for large wind band; both were printed in Paris in 1887 and 1893.
*Pas redoublé*, Vm.27.2428
*Polka*, Vm.27.2427

### Lardenois, Arthur

The following works in F:Pn are all early prints for large wind band; all were printed in Paris in 1886–1897.
Marches: Vm.27.8761, Vm.27.8763, Vm.27.8764
*Polka*, Vm.27.8762
*Mazurka*, Vm.27.8765

### Lardeur, Henri (Chef de Musique a l'École d'Artillerie de Versailles)

The following works in F:Pn are all early prints for large wind band; all were printed in Paris in 1893–1899.
Overture: Vm.27.8769, Vm.27.8770, Vm.27.8772
Fantaisies: Vm.27.8767, Vm.27.13014, Vm.27.8768 (Chanson de Roland), Vm.27.2434, Vm.27.8773, Vm.27.8776, Vm.27.2437, Vm.27.8777, Vm.27.2433
Andantes: Vm.27.8774 (*Rêverie champêtre*), Vm.27.8775 (*Secrète Expérance*)
*Serenade française*, Vm.27.2436
Marches: Vm.27.2435, Vm.27.4734, Vm.27.2432
*Barcarolle*, Vm.27.8766
*Polka*, Vm.7.13793

### Larriu, A.

*Hosanna*, Andante religieux
Brass band, piccolo, and percussion
EP (Paris, 1866) F:Pn (Vm.27.2438)

*Fantaisie*
Large wind band
EP (Paris, 1867) F:Pn (Vm.27.2439)

### Lauga, Pascal

The following works in F:Pn are all early prints for large wind band; all were printed in Paris in 1884–1885.
*Paris-enchanteur*, Vm.27.8785
*Allegro triomphal*, Vm.27.8782
*Mazurka*, Vm.27.8784
*Polka*, Vm.27.8783

### Laurent, E.

The following works in F:Pn are all early prints for large wind band; all were printed in Paris in 1866–1889.
*Méditation*, Vm.27.8807
*Overture*, Vm.27.2447
Marches: Vm.27.2446 [with chorus], Vm.27.8806, Vm.27.8809 (*Le petit trompette*)
*Polka*, Vm.27.8808
*Galop*, Vm.27.8810

### Lautier, F.

The following works in F:Pn are early prints for large wind band; both were printed in Paris in 1882 and 1900.
*Marche*, Vm.27.8812
*Mazurka*, Vm.27.8814

### Lauzun, F.

The following works in F:Pn are all early prints for large wind band; all were printed in Paris in 1864–1867.
Marches: Vm.27.4737 (*Marche religieuse*), Vm.27.2455

Polkas: Vm.27.2449, Vm.27.2453 and Vm.27.8815 [two copies]

### Lazennec, I.

The following works in F:Pn are early prints for large wind band; both were printed in Paris in 1881 and 1898.
Marches: Vm.27.2463, Vm.27.8826 bis (*Marche religieuse*)

### Lazzeri, Sylvio (1857–1944)

*Octour*, Op. 20 (1889, dedicated to Taffnel)
1112-02, English horn
EP (Paris, Evette)

### Lebigre, Auguste

*Marche*
Large wind band
EP (Paris, 1889) F:Pn (Vm.27.2466)

### Leblan, E.

The following works in F:Pn are all early prints for large wind band; all were printed in Paris in 1894–1898.
Marches: Vm.27.2467, Vm.27.2468 (*Marche cortege*)
*Polka,* Vm.27.8828

### Leblanc, L.

*Marche*
Large wind band
EP (Paris, 1892) F:Pn (Vm.27.8829)

### Le Blanc Duvernoy, Paul

*Valse*
Large wind band
EP (Paris, 1870) F:Pn (Vm.27.2469)

### Le Boulch, Jules

*Valse*
Large wind band
EP (Paris, 1893) F:Pn (Vm.27.13017)

### Le Bref, A.

*Pas redoublé*
Large wind band
EP (Paris, 1894) F:Pn (Vm.27.2473)

### Le Breton, H.

The following works in F:Pn are early prints for large wind band; both were printed in Paris in 1890 and 1892
*Marches*: Vm.27.2474, Vm.27.2475

### Lechleitner (Chef de Musique, 14me d'Artillerie)

The following works in F:Pn are early prints for large wind band printed in Paris.
*Une Serenade*, Vm.7.13808
   This is an eight-page full score for brass band, short, slow, and easy in character.
Marches: Vm.27.4738 (*Marche funèbre*), Vm.7.13814, Vm.7.13809, Vm.7.13810, Vm.27.8833, Vm.7.13811, Vm.7.13812, Vm.7.13813, Vm.7.13805
*Boléro*, Vm.27.2480
Polkas: Vm.7.13802, Vm.7.13803, Vm.7.13804
Quadrilles: Vm.7.13806, Vm.7.13807
*Valse*, Vm.27.2481

### Lecoeur, E.

The following works in F:Pn are all early prints for large wind band; all were printed in Paris in 1875–1878.
*Le Concert des anges*, Vm.27.8840
*Chambérg*, Vm.27.8839
Marches: Vm.27.8844, Vm.27.8845, Vm.27.8849
Quadrilles: Vm.27.8841, Vm.27.8842, Vm.27.8848
Polkas: Vm.27.8846, Vm.27.8847, Vm.27.8850

### Lecomte, A.

*Valse*
Large wind band
EP (Paris, 1897) F:Pn (Vm.27.2489)

### Lefabre, A.

The following works in F:Pn are early prints for large wind band; both were printed in Paris in 1884.
Marches: Vm.27.2493, Vm.27.8854

### Lefebvre, Charles (1843–1917)

*II. Suite*, Op. 122
1121-01
MP (Paris, Leduc) [cited by MH]

### Lefebvre, Fortuné

*Marche*
Large wind band
EP (Paris, 1893) F:Pn (Vm.27.8856)

### Lefrancois, F.

Marche, *L'Echo*
Large wind band
EP (Paris, 1888) F:Pn (Vm.27.8860)

### Legendre, Jules

The following works in F:Pn are all early prints for large wind band; all were printed in Paris in 1880–1881.
Marches: Vm.27.8865, Vm.27.8863, Vm.27.8864

### Lelong

The following works in F:Pn are all early prints for large wind band; all were printed in Paris in ca. 1868–1869.
Marches: Vm.27.8872 (*Les Bienfaits de l'éducation*) ['Marche pour marriage'], Vm.27.8878, Vm.27.8879
*Quadrille militaire*, Vm.27.8877

### Lemaigre, A.-T.

The following works in F:Pn are all early prints for large wind band; all were printed in Paris in 1856–1877.
*Laus Deo, Morceau religieux*, Vm.27.8888
*Fantaisie Overture*, Vm.27.8884
Marches: Vm.27.8886, Vm.27.8887, Vm.27.8882, Vm.27.8891, Vm.27.8892 (*Sainte-Cécile*)
*Polka*, Vm.27.8889
*Valse*, Vm.27.8883

### Lemalle, J.

*Marche*
Large wind band
EP (Paris, 1891) F:Pn (Vm.27.8894)

### Lemarié, A.

The following works in F:Pn are all early prints for large wind band; all were printed in Paris in 1893–1898.
*Fantaisie*, Vm.27.2512
Marches: Vm.27.2513, Vm.27.13024

### Lemière de Corvey, Jean F. A. (1770–1832)

*Music for military band* [mentioned in Grove, X, 653]

### Lentz, Frédéric

The following works in F:Pn are all early prints for large wind band; all were printed in Paris in 1884–1897.
*Andante et rondo*, Vm.7.13198
Marches: Vm.27.8921, Vm.27.8922, Vm.7.13192, Vm.7.13195, Vm.27.8923 (*Marche nuptiale*)
*Valse*, Vm.7.13194

### Lépagnole, L.

The following works in F:Pn are all early prints for large wind band; all were printed in Paris in 1884–1905.
Fantaisies: Vm.27.8925, Vm.27.2518, Vm.27.8926, Vm.27.8927, Vm.27.8928, Vm.27.2520, Vm.27.8929, Vm.27.13025, Vm.27.8930, Vm.27.8933
Marches: Vm.27.8924, Vm.27.8931, Vm.27.8932, Vm.27.8934, Vm.27.2521

### Leplat, E.

The following works in F:Pn are early prints for large wind band; both were printed in Paris in 1899 and 1901.
Overture (*Artiste et laboureur*), Vm.27.8935
*Marche*, Vm.27.8941

### Leroux, Charles

The following works in F:Pn are all early prints for large wind band; all were printed in Paris in 1881–1903.
*Fantaisie*, Vm.7.13830
*Marche*, Vm.27.2526
*Mazurka*, Vm.27.8946
*Suite de Valses*: Vm.27.2525

### Leroux, Felix (Chef de Musique, l'Ecole d'Artillerie de Vincennes)

The following works in F:Pn are all early prints for large wind band; all were printed in Paris in ca. 1869–1900.
Works for the Church: Vm.7.13835 (*Fantaisie funèbre*), Vm.27.8960 (*Grande marche funèbre*), Vm.27.2558 (*Pas redoublé de repos*), Vm.27.2570 (*Marche funèbre*), Vm.27.8971 (*Un Baiser d'adieu Morceau pour service funèbre*), Vm.7.13825 *Un dernier adieu* ('... pour les obseques de mon compatriste Huguet Lieutenant au 59e'), Vm.27.8972 (*Une Larme. Andante funèbre*), Vm.7.13215 (*Le 22 Novembre. Fantaisie pour Messe de St. Cecile*), Vm.7.13826 (*Une Pensée lugubre, 2e Marche funèbre*)
Overtures: Vm.27.2563, Vm.7.13204 (*Ouverture de concours*), Vm.7.13210, Vm.27.2553 *Mes Adieux à l'Amérique*
Fantaisies: Vm.27.2564, Vm.27.2528 [soli baritone and cornets], Vm.27.2569, Vm.27.2576 [soli flute and oboe], Vm.7.13831 [solo oboe]
*Air varié*, Vm.27.2530
Cavatines: Vm.7.13833 [solo clarinet], Vm.27.2537 [solo bugle]
*Un Songe. Duo sans paroles*, Vm.27.2575
Marches: Vm.27.2541, Vm.7.13200, Vm.7.13206, Vm.27.2546, Vm.7.13213, Vm.7.13843, Vm.27.2549, Vm.27.2555, Vm.27.2561, Vm.27.2567, Vm.27.2572, Vm.27.8956, Vm.27.2531, Vm.27.2580, Vm.7.13846, Vm.7.13849, Vm.27.2529, Vm.7.13845, Vm.27.2556, Vm.27.2557, Vm.7.13212, Vm.7.13850, Vm.27.2579, Vm.27.2577, Vm.27.2578, Vm.7.13209, Vm.27.2574, Vm.27.8969, Vm.27.8968, Vm.27.2571, Vm.27.2565, Vm.27.2566, Vm.27.2560, Vm.27.8963, Vm.7.13847, Vm.27.8954, Vm.27.2559, Vm.7.13848, Vm.7.13211, Vm.7.13827, Vm.27.2554, Vm.7.13828, Vm.7.13824, Vm.27.2551, Vm.7.13823 (*pour la grande procession de Lille*), Vm.7.13844, Vm.27.2547, Vm.7.13842, Vm.27.2548, Vm.27.8961, Vm.7.13841, Vm.27.2544, Vm.7.13840, Vm.27.8958 Vm.27.2542, Vm.27.2543, Vm.27.2538, Vm.27.2539, Vm.7.13216, Vm.27.2536, Vm.27.2534, Vm.27.2535, Vm.7.13852, Fol.Vm.15.279, Vm.27.2532, Vm.27.2533, Vm.27.8967
Polkas: Vm.7.13820 [solo cornet], Vm.27.2550, Vm.7.13821 [solo cornet], Vm.27.2527
*Galop*, Vm.27.2573
*Mazurka*, Vm.27.8959
Quadrilles: Vm.27.2562, Vm.27.2568
Boléros: Vm.27.2581, Vm.27.2540

### Lesueur, L.

*Pas redoublé*
Large wind band
EP (Paris, 1898) F:Pn (Vm.27.2588)

### Lévêque, Emile

The following works in F:Pn are all early prints for large wind band; all were printed in Paris in ca. 1879–1900.
*Overture*, Vm.27.2594
Marches: Vm.27.2596, Vm.27.2590, Vm.27.2591
*Serenade Valse*, Vm.27.8982
*Berceuse*, Vm.27.8979
*Polka*, Vm.27.2592
Mazurkas: Vm.27.8980, Vm.27.2593

### Lévêque, L.

The following works in F:Pn are early prints for large wind band; both were printed in Paris in 1869.
*Redova*, Vm.27.8984
*Polka*, Vm.27.8985

### Ligner, F.

The following works in F:Pn are all early prints for large wind band; all were printed in Paris in 1878–1905.
*Overture*, Vm.27.8987

*Thême Suisse Varié*, Vm.27.13034
*Cannes-la-jolie. Sélection mélodique*, Vm.27.8990
Marches: Vm.27.13032 (*Marche funèbre*), Vm.27.8997, Vm.27.2602, Vm.27.2603, Vm.27.9005, Vm.27.9007, Vm.27.2598, Vm.27.8993, Vm.27.8989, Vm.27.8988, Vm.27.9014, Vm.27.9008, Vm.27.9001, Vm.27.9000
Polkas: Vm.27.9004 [solo cornet], Vm.27.9003, Vm.27.9011, Vm.27.9015 [solo cornet]
*Valse*, Vm.27.8999
*Quadrille*, Vm.27.9002

### Lilman, V.

The following works in F:Pn are early prints for large wind band; both were printed in Paris in 1880 and 1884.
Marches: Vm.27.9017, Vm.27.9016 (*Marche religieuse*)

### Limnander

*à l'Harmonie* [with chorus]
Brass band
EP (Paris, 1878) F:Pn (Vm.27.9018) [missing choral parts]

### Lindner, Henri

*Recueil de pièces pour la musique militaire*
EP (Breitkopf & Härtel) [cited in F]

### Linglin

*Pas redoublé*
Large wind band
EP (Paris, nineteenth century) F:Pn (Vm.27.9021)

### Logier, Jean Bernard (1780–1846)

*Quelques marches et morceaux pour mus. mil.*
EP (Clementi) [cited in F]

### Lointier, Eugene

The following works in F:Pn are all early prints for large wind band; all were printed in Paris in 1884–1898.

Works for the Church: Vm.27.9039 (*Morceau religieux concertant*), Vm.27.9041 (*Marche funèbre*)
*Overture*, Vm.27.9040
Marches: Vm.27.9037 (*L'Hymen*), Vm.27.9038, Vm.27.13038

### Loubet, A.

The following works in F:Pn are all early prints for large wind band; all were printed in Paris in 1889–1899.
*Overture*, Vm.27.9044
Marches: Vm.27.9046, Vm.27.9043
*Polka*, Vm.27.9045

### Louis

*Journal d'harmonie et de musique militaire*
EP (Paris, Pacini) [12 volumes] F:Pn (Vm.27.2629) [1–12]
Includes works by Berr and Münchs.

*Journal de Musique …*
EP (Paris) F:Pn (Vm.27.2628)
Includes works by Münchs.

*Marches de la Garde royale*
EP (Paris, Gambaro, ca. 1800–1828)

### Loustallot, G. (Chef de Musique de 64me d'Infantrie)

The following works in F:Pn are all early prints for large wind band; all were printed in Paris in ca. 1868.
*Messe basse*, Vm.7.13219
The work one finds under this call-number consists of the following three movements, but contains no vocal parts.
1. 'jusqu'a l'Élévation,' a slow, but very dramatic work with solo baritone saxhorn.
2. 'après l'Élévation,' an Andante for small band, with solo clarinet.
3. 'Sortie,' a brilliant, quasi-fanfare, Allegro for full band.
Marches: Vm.27.2633, Vm.27.2634, Vm.27.2635 bis
*Schottisch*, Vm.27.2635

## Lozes, L.

The following works in F:Pn are all early prints for large wind band; all were printed in Paris in 1883–1886.
*Marche*, Vm.27.9054
Polkas: Vm.27.9051, Vm.27.9052
*Quadrille*, Vm.27.9053

## Luce, E.

The following works in F:Pn are early prints for large wind band; both were printed in Paris during the nineteenth century.
*La Bambo, Divertissement*, Vm.27.2640
*Les Echos de la Victoire*, Vm.27.2642

## Luce, L.

The following works in F:Pn are all early prints for large wind band; all were printed in Paris in 1851–1865.
Works for the Church: Vm.27.2645 bis (*Saint-Pierre! Morceau de repose et religieux*), Vm.7.13857 (*Marche funèbre*), and Vm.27.2644 (*Morceau de repos*)
The first of these is an outstanding looking example, in full score.
Fantaisies: Vm.27.2645, Vm.27.2643 [solo trombone]
*Marche*, Vm.7.13858
*Souvenir d'Afrique*, Vm.27.9058
*L'Odalisque*, Vm.27.9057

## Luigini, Joseph

The following works in F:Pn are all early prints for large wind band; all were printed in Paris in 1864–1880.
Fantaisies: Vm.7.13860, Vm.27.2653, Vm.7.13859
*Grand Fanfare* (from the composer's ballet, *Lore Ley*, arranged by the composer for band), Vm.27.2648

## Luigini, Laurent

The following works in F:Pn are early prints for large wind band; both were printed in Paris in 1884 and 1889.
*Overture*, Vm.27.2657
*Fantaisie de concert*, Vm.27.2655 and Vm.27.2656 [later edition]

## Mabille, H.

*March*
Large wind band
EP (Paris, 1894) F:Pn (Vm.27.9060)

## Mabire, E.

*Pas redoublé*
Large wind band
EP (Paris, 1893) F:Pn (Vm.27.2659)

## Magnan, G.

The following works in F:Pn are all early prints for large wind band; all were printed in Paris in ca. 1893–1900
Marches: Vm.27.9070, Vm.27.2662
*Burlesques*, Vm.27.9069

## Magnan, Louis

The following works in F:Pn are early prints for large wind band; both were printed in Paris in 1883–1901.
*Le Drapeau de Piémont* [with unison chorus], Vm.27.2663
*Polka* [two soli clarinets], Vm.27.9071 and Vm.27.9072 [later edition]

## Magnard, Lucien (1865–1914)

*Quintet*, Op. 8
Piano and winds
EP (Paris, Rouart-Lerolle) [cited by DJ]

## Maguet, H.

The following works in F:Pn are early prints for large wind band; both were printed in Paris in 1896–1897.
Polkas: Vm.27.9138 [solo piccolo], Vm.27.9142

## Maillochaud, J. B.

The following works in F:Pn are all early prints for large wind band; all were printed in Paris in 1873–1906.
Works for the Church: Vm.27.9078 (*Marche nuptiale*), Vm.27.9089 (*Marche religieuse en Procession*), Vm.27.2690 (*Marche religeuse*),

Vm.27.2696 (*Rêverie*), Vm.1.3156 (*Messe in ut*), Vm.27.2702 (*Mélodie religieuse*), Vm.27.9096 (*Andante religieuse*)
The *Messe in Ut* is a full Mass ("Kirie," Gloria, Sanctus, Benedictus, and Agnus Dei) for SATB; the band seems only to double the vocal parts.
Overtures: Vm.27.2692, Vm.27.2685 and Vm.27.9086 [two copies]
Fantaisies: Vm.27.2694, Vm.27.2695, Vm.27.2683, Vm.27.9084, and, Vm.27.9085 [three editions], Vm.27.2684, Vm.27.2700 and Vm.27.2701 [two copies], Vm.27.2709 (*Les Trompettes de Jericho*)
The final example consists of nine programmatic sections, in a light character.
*Un Rêve. Mélodie*, Vm.27.9098
Marches: Vm.27.2693, Vm.27.2682, Vm.27.9080, Vm.27.9082, Vm.27.2686, Vm.27.9087 and Vm.27.9088 [two copies], Vm.27.2688, Vm.27.9093, Vm.27.9099, Vm.27.9100
Quadrilles: Vm.27.9094, Vm.27.13041
Mazurkas: Vm.27.9079 (*Mazurka de Concert*), Vm.27.9090
*Boléro*, Vm.27.9081
*Danse chinoise*, Vm.27.2787
Valses: Vm.27.2697, Vm.27.2703, Vm.27.2710 (*des triangles*)
Polkas: Vm.27.2698, Vm.27.2699, Vm.27.9095, Vm.27.2704
*Gavotte*, Vm.27.2708
*Schottisch*, Vm.27.2707

### Mailly, A.

The following works in F:Pn are all early prints for large wind band; all were printed in Paris and Bordeaux in 1880–1895.
Works for the Church: Vm.27.9108 (*Invocation. Andante*), Vm.27.9111 (*Marche funèbre*), Vm.27.9112 (*Marche funèbre*)
*Fantaisie*, Vm.27.9115
*Grand air varié*, Vm.27.13042
Marches: Vm.7.13868, Vm.27.9105, Vm.27.9103 bis, Vm.27.9014, Vm.27.9109, Vm.27.9113, Vm.27.9101, Vm.27.9114, Vm.27.9102
*Boléro*, Vm.27.9103
*Schottisch*, Vm.27.9107

### Mairetet, E.

[Collection of] *Danses*
Large wind band
EP (Paris, 1900) F:Pn (Vm.27.9116)

### Malézieux, L.

The following works in F:Pn are all early prints for large wind band; all were printed in Paris in 1876–1877.
*Recueil de morceaux divers* … (12 works)
Large wind band
EP (Paris, 1876) F:Pn (Vm.27.9123)

*Recueil de morceaux divers* … (9 works)
Large wind band
EP (Paris, 1876) F:Pn (Vm.27.9120)

*Recueil de morceaux divers* … (11 works)
Large wind band
EP (Paris, 1876) F:Pn (Vm.27.9121)

*Recueil de morceaux divers* … (20 works)
Large wind band
EP (Paris, 1876) F:Pn (Vm.27.9124)
Contains works by Berth, Stager, Alph. Gor, Dufayel, etc. Nr. 13 is a *La Bénédiction* [*Marche, religieuse*] by Malézieux.

*Recueil de morceaux divers* … (12 works)
Large wind band
EP (Paris, 1876) F:Pn (Vm.27.9122)
Contains work by Berth, Stager, a *La Bénédiction* by Malézieux and a *Le Pardon. Prière* by Alph. Gor.

### Mancini, A.

*Overture de concert*
Large wind band
EP (Paris, 1877) F:Pn (Vm.27.2714)

### Mangeant

*Pas redoublé*
Large wind band
EP (Paris, 1859) F:Pn (Vm.27.4755)

## Mansion, P.

The following works in F:Pn are all early prints for large wind band; all were printed in Paris in 1878–1880.
Marches: Vm.27.9129, Vm.27.9130 (*L'Ami des Trombones*), Vm.27.9131, Vm.27.9135
*Quadrille*, Vm.27.9133
*Polka*, Vm.27.9134

## Mansion, Horace

*Andante religioso*
Large wind band
EP (Paris, 1895) F:Pn (Vm.27.2717)

## Marchal

*Harmonie militaire*
EP (Paris, Janet, ca. 1800–1828) [Liv. 1–3]

## Marcus, P.

*Après la Fête*, Allegro
Large wind band
EP (Paris, 1899) F:Pn (Vm.27.9144)

## Marie, E.

The following works in F:Pn are all early prints for large wind band; all were printed in Paris in 1852–1887.
Works for the Church: Vm.27.9158 (*Andante religieux*), Vm.27.9158 (*Morceau religieux*), Vm.27.9243 (*La Fête Dieu*), Vm.27.9282 (*Mater doloros*), Vm.27.9284 (*Mélode funèbre*), Vm.27.9295 (*Notre Dame de Fourvieres*), Vm.27.2746 (*Notre-Dame de Nanteuil. Andante*), Vm.27.9297 (*Notre-Dame de Paris. Andante religieux*), Vm.27.9298 (*Offertoire*), Vm.27.9325 (*Recueillement. Andante*), Vm.27.9341 (*Marche procession*), Vm.27.2749 (*Le Sommeil des Anges*), Vm.27.9342 (*Mélodie pour La Sainte Cécile*), Vm.27.9343 (*Sainte-Philomène. Mélodie religieuse*), Vm.27.9363 (*Sympathie. Morceau religieux*), Vm.27.9373 (*Tumulus. Andante funèbre*), Vm.27.9375 (*Un dernier Hommage. Marche funèbre*), Vm.27.9378 (*Une Prière pour tous! Morceau religieux*)
*Symphonie pastorale* (*Le Réveil de la nature*), Vm.27.9332
Overtures: Vm.27.9154, Vm.27.9164, Vm.27.2738, Vm.27.9302Vm.27.9314, Vm.27.9345, Vm.27.13046
Fantaisies, Vm.27.9377, Vm.27.9357, Vm.27.9340, Vm.27.9274, Vm.27.9210
Airs varié and Variations: Vm.27.9241, Vm.27.9165 (*L'Assaut Musical*), Vm.27.9196 [soli cornet, trombone, alto saxophone], Vm.27.9368 (*Le Tournoi musical*)
Marches: Vm.27.9190, Vm.27.9193, Vm.27.9194, Vm.27.9168Vm.27.9172, Vm.27.9228, Vm.27.9229, Vm.27.9231, Vm.27.9244, Vm.27.9212, Vm.27.9161, Vm.27.9173, Vm.27.9174 (*Le beau trompette*), Vm.27.9175, Vm.27.9176, Vm.27.9177, Vm.27.9183, Vm.27.9184, Vm.27.2736, Vm.27.9186, Vm.27.9198, Vm.27.9201, Vm.27.9217, Vm.27.9218, Vm.27.9225, Vm.27.9227, Vm.7.13872, Vm.27.9254, Vm.27.9255, Vm.27.9276, Vm.27.9285, Vm.27.9286, Vm.27.9290, Vm.27.9291, Vm.27.9306, Vm.27.9305, Vm.27.9304, Vm.27.9329, Vm.27.9331, Vm.27.9346, Vm.27.9351, Vm.27.9353, Vm.27.2750, Vm.27.9362, Vm.27.9365, Vm.27.9379, Vm.27.9380, Vm.27.9382, Vm.27.9275, Vm.27.9372, Vm.27.9312, Vm.27.9313, Vm.27.9337, Vm.27.9326, Vm.27.9338–9339 (two sizes of paper; same edition of *Rule Britannia*), Vm.27.9328, Vm.27.2747, Vm.27.9311, Vm.27.9322, Vm.27.9370, Vm.27.9280, Vm.27.9272, Vm.27.9258, Vm.27.9263
Polkas: Vm.27.9303, Vm.27.9294, Vm.27.2745, Vm.27.9268, Vm.27.9270, Vm.27.9264, Vm.27.9265, Vm.27.9192, Vm.27.9169, Vm.21.9208, Vm.27.9155, Vm.27.9160, Vm.27.9187, Vm.27.9257, Vm.27.9266, Vm.27.9309, Vm.27.9310, Vm.27.9366
Quadrilles: Vm.27.9170, Vm.27.9206, Vm.27.9207, Vm.27.9211, Vm.27.9156, Vm.27.9159 (*Anglais, francais, et turcs*), Vm.27.9202, Vm.27.9315, Vm.27.9318, Vm.27.9334, Vm.27.9383, Vm.27.9371, Vm.27.9376, Vm.27.9367, Vm.27.9358, Vm.27.9330, Vm.27.9308, Vm.27.9281, Vm.27.9267, Vm.27.9247, Vm.27.9273

Valses: Vm.27.9349, Vm.27.9333, Vm.27.9283,
Vm.27.2743, Vm.27.9256, Vm.27.9167,
Vm.27.9248, Vm.27.9189, Vm.27.9200
[soli cornet and baritone], Vm.27.9204,
Vm.27.9216, Vm.27.9387

Boléros: Vm.27.9381, Vm.27.9364, Vm.27.2744,
Vm.27.9191, Vm.27.9182

Galops: Vm.27.9188, Vm.27.2737, Vm.27.2751,
Vm.27.9344, Vm.27.2748, Vm.27.9209,
Vm.27.9199

Barcarolles: Vm.27.9171, Vm.27.9178,
Vm.27.9180, Vm.27.9316

Polonaises: Vm.27.9179, Vm.27.9215, Vm.27.9384

Schottisches: Vm.27.9205, Vm.27.9213,
Vm.27.9348, Vm.27.9388 and Vm.7.13875
[two copies]

*Le Sapeur iptrépide*, Vm.27.9347
*Le Prince impérial des Français 1*, Vm.27.9323
*Les Plaines de Marathon*, Vm.27.9317

## Marin, E.

The following works in F:Pn are all early prints
for large wind band; all were printed in Paris
in 1885–1907.

Marches: Vm.27.2758, Vm.27.2761, Vm.27.2763,
Vm.7.13881, Vm.27.2766 (*Marche Nuptiale*),
Vm.27.4757, Vm.27.2770 (*Marche funèbre*),
Vm.7.13879

Polkas: Vm.27.2759, Vm.27.2760, Vm.27.13047,
Vm.27.2767, Vm.27.2769, Vm.27.2768,
Vm.27.2771

*Quadrille*, Vm.27.2762
Valses: Vm.27.2773, Vm.27.2774
*Galop*, Vm.7.13880
*Mazurka*, Vm.27.2772

## Marion, Claude

*Marche*
Large wind band
EP (Paris, 1889) F:Pn (Vm.27.9391)

## Maron, A.

*Pas redoublé*
Large wind band
EP (Paris, 1866) F:Pn (Vm.27.9393)

## Marsal, E.

The following works in F:Pn are all early prints
for large wind band; all were printed in Paris
in 1886–1901.

Work for the Church, Vm.27.9397 (*Andante
religieux*)

Overtures: Vm.27.2778, Vm.27.9403,
Vm.27.9415, Vm.27.2782

Fantaisies: Vm.27.9400, Vm.27.9408, Vm.27.9410,
Vm.27.13049, Vm.27.9414, Vm.27.2783

Marches: Vm.27.2777, Vm.27.2779, Vm.27.9405,
Vm.27.9409, Vm.27.9411, Vm.27.9412,
Vm.27.9413, Vm.27.9416, Vm.27.2785

*Recueil de morceau de danse* [22 works], Vm.27.9396

Polkas: Vm.27.2781, Vm.27.2775, Vm.27.9399,
Vm.27.2784, Vm.27.9409 [two soli B♭ clarinets], Vm.27.9407

*Schottisch*, Vm.27.9398
Valses: Vm.27.2776, Vm.27.9406
Quadrilles: Vm.27.9402, Vm.27.2780

## Marschalk

*Valse*
Large wind band
EP (Paris, 1880) F:Pn (Vm.7.13884)

## Martin, Camille

The following works in F:Pn are all early prints
for large wind band; all were printed in Paris
in 1881–1897.

Fantaisies: Vm.27.2787, Vm.27.9428 (*Fantaisie pastorale*), Vm.27.9429, Vm.27.9432, Vm.27.9431,
Vm.27.9426, Vm.27.9434 and Vm.27.9435
[two copies], Vm.27.13052

Marches: Vm.27.13051, Vm.27.9430 (*Marche funèbre*), Vm.27.9433 (*Marche funèbre*)

*Polka*, Vm.27.2786
*Valse*, Vm.27.9427

## Martin, Hte.

The following works in F:Pn are early prints for
large wind band; both were printed in Paris in
ca. 1874.

Marches: Vm.7.13885, Vm.27.9441

## Martin, L.

*Marche et Pas redoublé*
Harmoniemusik
EP (Paris, Lemoine, ca. 1800–1828)

## Martin de La Moutte, L.

*Marche*
Large wind band
EP (Paris, 1874) F:Pn (Vm.27.13012)

## Massard, R.

The following works in F:Pn are all early prints for large wind band; all were printed in Paris in 1896–1898.
*Fantaisie*, Vm.27.9454
Marches: Vm.27.9453, Vm.27.9456, Vm.27.9457, Vm.27.9460, Vm.27.9461
*Polka*, Vm.27.9455

## Massat, F.

The following works in F:Pn are all early prints for large wind band; all were printed in Paris in 1871–1874.
*Prière après l'Élévation*, Vm.27.2797
Marches: Vm.27.9462, Vm.7.13892, Vm.7.13893
*Mazurka*, Vm.7.13894

## Masson du Breuil

*Marche*
Large wind band
EP (Paris, 1887) F:Pn (Vm.27.2840)

## Mastio, E.

The following works in F:Pn are all early prints for large wind band; all were printed in Paris in 1877–1908.
*Overture des Noces de Figaro*, Vm.7.12940
Marches: Vm.7.13899, Vm.7.13920, Vm.27.2843, Vm.27.13056, Vm.27.2841, Vm.7.13906

## Matha

The following works in F:Pn are all early prints for large wind band; all were printed in Paris in 1891–1899.

*Mystére, Andante religieux*, Vm.27.9479
Schottisches: Vm.27.9480, Vm.27.9484
Mazurkas: Vm.27.9482, Vm.27.9485
Quadrille: Vm.27.9472, Vm.27.9476
Polkas: Vm.27.9474, Vm.27.9473, Vm.27.9481
*Valse*, Vm.27.9475

## Mauchen, W.

*Valse*
Large wind band
EP (Paris, 1869) F:Pn (Vm.27.2844)

## Mayeur, L.

The following works in F:Pn are all early prints for large wind band; all were printed in Paris in 1863–1893.
*Fantaisie*, Vm.7.13927
*Petit Divertissement* [solo piccolo], Vm.27.2883
Caprices: Vm.27.2851 [solo clarinet], Vm.7.13938 [solo piccolo] and Vm.27.2869 [later edition for solo clarinet or alto saxophone]
Marches: Vm.27.2871, Vm.27.2872, Vm.27.9493, Vm.27.9496, Vm.27.2865
Galops: Vm.27.9499, Vm.27.2856 (*La Dance des Sorcières*)
Polkas: Vm.27.2884, Vm.27.2877, Vm.27.2878, Vm.27.2857 [two soli flutes], Vm.27.2863 [solo piccolo], Vm.27.2868 [with chorus]
Quadrilles: Vm.27.2879, Vm.27.2880
*Gavotte*, Vm.27.2866
*Amore*, Vm.27.2848
*Bonjour*, Vm.27.2849 and Vm.27.2850 [later edition]
*Intermezzo*, Vm.27.2853
*Danse*, Vm.27.2855

## Meister, G.

The following works in F:Pn are all early prints for large wind band; all were printed in Paris in 1887–1891.
Overtures: Vm.27.2907, Vm.27.2908 and Vm.27.2909 [two copies]
*Quadrille*, Vm.27.9512
*Polka*, Vm.27.9513 [solo cornet]
*Mazurka*, Vm.27.9517
There are in addition numerous transcriptions of major works for band by Meister in F:Pn.

## Mennesson, A.

*Marche*
Large wind band
EP (Paris, 1875) F:Pn (Vm.27.9524)

## Mérat, Léon

The following works in F:Pn are all early prints for large wind band; all were printed in Paris in 1875–1892.
Marches: Vm.27.9526, Vm.27.9527, Vm.27.9528, Vm.27.9529, Vm.27.9530, Vm.27.9536, Vm.27.9534, Vm.27.9535
Polkas: Vm.27.13060 [two soli cornets or small or large clarinets], Vm.27.9531, Vm.27.9533 (*Polka de concert avec solo de casse*)
*Quadrille*, Vm.27.9532

## Merciert Roger

The following works in F:Pn are all early prints for large wind band; all were printed in Paris in 1893–1898.
*Overture*, Vm.27.9549
*Marche*, Vm.27.9550 and Vm.27.9551 [later edition]
*Valse*, Vm.27.9552 and Vm.27.13062 [later edition]

## Mercier, V.

*L'Espérance. Marche pour offertoire*
Large wind band
EP (Paris, 1862) F:Pn (Vm.27.9553)

## Mérigeault, Désiré

*Marche*
Large wind band
EP (Paris, 1893) F:Pn (Vm.27.2934)

## Métra, Olivier

The following works in F:Pn are all early prints for large wind band; all were printed in Paris in 1856–1884.
Marches: Vm.27.9559, Vm.27.2940
Quadrilles: Vm.27.9560, Vm.27.9561

## Meunier, Armand

The following works in F:Pn are all early prints for large wind band; all were printed in Paris in 1866–1893.
*L'Indispensable Nouveau repertoire*, Vm.27.9583
Contains 14 short works of no value.
Fantaisies: Vm.27.9574 (*Le Duel des Trombones et Pistons*), Vm.27.9576, Vm.27.9592, Vm.27.9593, Vm.27.9597
*Air varié*, Vm.27.13064 (*Le Duel des Artistes*)
Marches: Vm.27.9565, Vm.27.9570 bis, Vm.27.9579 Vm.27.9571 (*Marche funèbre*), Vm.27.9573, Vm.27.9580, Vm.27.9581, Vm.27.9584, Vm.27.9586, Vm.27.9601, Vm.27.9604, Vm.27.9605
Quadrilles: Vm.27.9578, Vm.27.9588, Vm.27.9590
Polkas: Vm.27.9566, Vm.27.9568, Vm.27.9572 [two solo cornets], Vm.27.8800 [solo cornet], Vm.27.13065, Vm.27.9595, Vm.27.9600
Mazurkas: Vm.27.9570, Vm.27.9587
Schottisches: Vm.27.9582, Vm.27.9598
Valses: Vm.27.9585, Vm.27.9589, Vm.27.9591, Vm.27.9596, Vm.27.9603

## Meurer, Maurice

*Valse*
Large wind band
EP (Paris, 1887) F:Pn (Vm.27.2946)

## Meurgey, L. (Chef de Musique, 2e Reg. de Zouaues; Chevalier de la Legion d'Honneur)

The following works in F:Pn are all early prints for large wind band; all were printed in Paris in 1883–1899.
Fantaisies: Vm.27.13066, Vm.27.9631
Marches: Vm.27.9606, Vm.27.9610, Vm.27.9612, Vm.27.9620
*Polka*, Vm.27.9633
*Valse suite*, Vm.27.9619
In addition there are a large number of original compositions by this composer in F:Pn, dating 1900–1910.

## Meyer

*Marche*
Large wind band
EP (Paris, 1869) F:Pn (Vm.27.9635)

## Meyer, J.

The following works in F:Pn are all early prints for large wind band; all were printed in Paris in 1879–1899.
*Marche*, Vm.7.13951
Polkas: Vm.27.2947 [soli: '*toutes les clarinettes*'], Vm.27.2948

## Michaëli, Jean

The following works in F:Pn are early prints for large wind band; both were printed in Paris in ca. 1875.
*Le Credo republicain* [with chorus], Vm.27.9644
*L'Hymne au trauvail* [with chorus], Vm.27.9645

## Michel

*Pas redoublé*
Large wind band
EP (Paris, 1855) F:Pn (Vm.27.9646)

## Migette, E.

The following works in F:Pn are all early prints for large wind band; all were printed in Paris in 1868–1878.
Works for the Church: Vm.27.9682 (*Marche funèbre*), Vm.27.9676 (*Marche pour Procession*), Vm.27.9677 (*Marche pour Procession*), Vm.27.9678 (*Marche funèbre*), Vm.27.9673 (*Marche pour Procession*), Vm.27.9675 (*Marche pour Procession*), Vm.27.9664 (*Marche pour Procession*), Vm.27.9667 (*Morceau religieux*), Vm.27.9668 (*Offertoire*), Vm.27.9658 (*Marche funèbre*), Vm.27.9662 (*Harmonie e des anges. Morceau religieux*), Vm.27.9657 (*L'Enfant Jésus. Andante pour élévation*)
Fantaisies: Vm.27.9650, Vm.27.13073 and Vm.27.9670 [two copies], Vm.27.9659
Marches: Vm.27.9652 bis, Vm.27.9651, Vm.27.9649, Vm.27.9679, Vm.27.9681, Vm.27.9654, Vm.27.9655, Vm.27.9672, Vm.27.9666, Vm.27.9661, Vm.27.9663

*Galop*, Vm.27.13072
*Quadrille*, Vm.27.9660
*Polka*, Vm.27.9656
*Boléo*, Vm.27.9680

## Mignon, L.

*Fantaisie-Marche*
Large wind band
EP (Paris, 1888) F:Pn (Vm.7.13964)

## Milanscoff, Arman

The following works in F:Pn are early prints for large wind band; both were printed in Paris in 1891 and 1899.
Marches: Vm.27.9685, Vm.27.9686

## Miller

The following works in F:Pn are all early prints for large wind band; all were printed in Paris in 1859–1869.
*Variations*, Vm.27.13075
Marches: Vm.27.9692, Vm.27.9694
*Polonaise*, Vm.27.9690
*Valse*, Vm.27.9691
*Schottisch*, Vm.27.9693
*Polka*, Vm.27.969S

## Millingre

*Marsches* [Nr. 1, 2]
*Valses*
EP (Paris, Sieber, ca. 1800–1828)

## Millescamps, Jules

The following works in F:Pn are all early prints for large wind band; all were printed in Paris in 1863–1887.
Works for the Church: Vm.27.9698 (*Marche religieuse*), Vm.27.9704 (*Marche religieuse*), Vm.27.9709 (*Marche religieuse*), Vm.27.9710 (*Marche religieuse*), Vm.27.9722 (*Marche religieuse*)
Overtures: Vm.27.9701, Vm.27.9718, Vm.27.9728
Fantaisies: Vm.27.2990, Vm.27.2991, Vm.27.9724 [solo cornet], Vm.27.2989, Vm.27.9730

Marches: Vm.27.9699, Vm.27.9700, Vm.27.9703, Vm.27.9696, Vm.27.9706, Vm.27.9708, Vm.27.9711, Vm.27.9717, Vm.27.9720, Vm.27.9721, Vm.27.9723, Vm.27.9725, Vm.27.9726, Vm.27.9729, Vm.27.9731
Polkas: Vm.27.9697, Vm.27.9707
Valses: Vm.27.9705, Vm.27.9713, Vm.27.9712, Vm.27.9715
*Schottisch*, Vm.27.9719
*Quadrille*, Vm.27.9727
In F:Pn there are also a number of trumpet ensemble works, usually three or four parts, of both military and concert nature by Millescamps. For example, under Vm.7.4611, one finds a small book, printed in 1869, containing one hundred trumpet calls in one to four parts.

## Millet, E.

*Allegro militaire*
Large wind band
EP (Paris, 1883) F:Pn (Vm.27.9736)

## Millon, E.

*Allegro militaire*
Large wind band
EP (Paris, 1894) F:Pn (Vm.27.9737)
I suspect this man and the above are the same person.

## Millot, Marius

The following works in F:Pn are all early prints for large wind band; all were printed in Paris in 1896–1908.
*Overture*, Vm.27.13076
Marches: Vm.27.2992, Vm.27.2993, Vm.27.2997, Vm.27.9740, Vm.27.2994, Vm.27.2998, Vm.27.9741
*Mazurka*, Vm.27.2995

## Mimart, Auguste

The following works in F:Pn are all early prints for large wind band; all were printed in Paris in 1859–1876.
*Air varié*, Vm.27.9759 [solo cornet]
Marches: Vm.27.9752, Vm.27.9743, Vm.27.9744, Vm.27.9766, Vm.27.9745 (*Marche slave*), Vm.27.9748, Vm.27.3001, Vm.27.9751, Vm.27.9753, Vm.27.9754, Vm.27.9768, Vm.27.9769, Vm.27.3000, Vm.27.9760, Vm.7.13968, Vm.27.9765
*Schottisch*, Vm.27.9755
Polkas: Vm.27.9750, Vm.27.9757
*Tyrolienne*, Vm.27.9756
*Boléro*, Vm.27.9758
*Galop*, Vm.27.13077
Quadrilles: Vm.27.9761, Vm.27.9762
*Valse*, Vm.27.9764
In addition there are a number of transcriptions by Mimart in F:Pn; including what seems to be most of Beethoven's Sixth Symphony, under Vm.7.10644, Vm.7.13966 and Vm.7.13967.

## Mirambeau, E.

*Marche*
Large wind band
EP (Paris, 1895) F:Pn (Vm.27.9780)

## Mohr

*Marche*
Large wind band
EP (Paris, 1858) F:Pn (Vm.27.9781)

## Mohr, J.

The following works in F:Pn are all early prints for large wind band; all were printed in Paris in 1851–1885.
[Collection] (8) *Morceau*, Vm.7.13981
*Air varié*, Vm.27.9783
Marches: Vm.7.13971, Vm.7.13974 and Vm.7.13975 [two copies], Vm.7.13977, Vm.7.14494 and Vm.7.14495 [two copies]
Galops: Vm.27.13081, Vm.7.13976
*Polonaise*, Vm.7.13973 and Vm.7.13973 bis
Polkas: Vm.7.13980, Vm.27.4788
There is also a great deal of solo horn music by Mohr in F:Pn.

**Momigny, Lysias de ('Ancien Officer de Cavalerie, Organiste de la Cathédrale d'Angouleme')**

The following works in F:Pn are all early prints for large wind band; all were printed in Paris in 1853–1858.

Works for the Church: Vm.27.570 (*Morceau religieux*), Vm.27.3026 and Vm.1.2153 (*3e Messe solennelle*)

This last example, 'composiée expressement pour musique militaire,' is a major work for SATB and full band before saxophones. Here one finds a multi-movement work (95 pages in the published score) dedicated to Napoleon III, in part, 'In the thought which inspired this work, Sir, you will find the echo of one of the greatest thoughts, the consecration of military glory by religious sentiment …'

Marches: Vm.27.3022 and Vm.27.3023 [two copies], Vm.27.9786

*Chant National danois* (arranged in a 'nouvelle ordonnance') Vm.27.3019

*Chant National hollandais* (arranged in a 'nouvelle ordonnance') Vm.27.3020

**Monbarin, E.**

*Marche*
Large wind band
EP (Paris, 1899) F:Pn (Vm.27.3027)

**Moncel, A.**

The following works in F:Pn are early prints for large wind band; both were printed in Paris in 1859.
*Marche*, Vm.27.3030 and Vm.27.3031 [later edition]
*Valse*, vm.27.3028 and Vm.27.3029 [later edition]

**de Monge, Fernandez**

The following works in F:Pn are all early prints for large wind band; all were printed in Paris in 1887–1895.
*Morceau d'élévation*, Vm.27.3035
Marches: Vm.27.9793, Vm.27.3034

**Monicard, G.**

The following works in F:Pn are all early prints for large wind band; all were printed in Lyon in 1898–1899.
*Messieurs, Mentiors! Morceau de lecture à une. Andante*, Vm.27.9796
*Vive le Czar! Allegro de Concert*, Vm.27.9797
*Marche*, Vm.27.9794 and Vm.27.9795 [later edition]

**Monier, F.**

*Schottisch*
Large wind band
EP (Montereau, 1884) F:Pn (Vm.27.9798)

**Monnereau, J.**

*Marche*
Large wind band
EP (Paris, 1894) F:Pn (Vm.27.9800)

**Montalent, R. de**

The following works in F:Pn are early prints for large wind band; both were printed in Paris in 1892 and 1901.
*Overture*, Vm.27.9804
*Marche*, Vm.27.9803

**Moornay, A.**

The following works in F:Pn are early prints for large wind band; both were printed in Paris in 1881 and 1905.
*Overture symphonique*, Vm.27.9847
*Polka*, Vm.7.13994 [solo oboe]

**Morand, G.**

The following works in F:Pn are all early prints for large wind band; all were printed in Paris in 1885–1900.
Works for the Church: Vm.27.3038 (*L'Ange Gabriel. Andante*), Vm.27.3046 (*Marche funèbre*)
*Overture*, Vm.27.3047
*Fantaisie*, Vm.27.9813
Airs varié: Vm.27.9807, Vm.27.3040

Marches: Vm.27.9809, Vm.27.9811, Vm.27.3039,
Vm.27.3041, Vm.27.9816, Vm.27.9820,
Vm.27.9821, Vm.27.9822
Valses: Vm.27.3042, Vm.27.3045, Vm.27.3048
[with chorus], Vm.27.9824
Quadrilles: Vm.27.9810, Vm.27.3043
Polkas: Vm.27.9814, Vm.27.3044
*Mazurka*, Vm.27.3045 bis
In addition there are a large number of original works dated 1900–1915 by Morand in F:Pn.

### Moreau, Charles

The following works in F:Pn are all early prints for large wind band; all were printed in Paris in 1864–1869.
Marches: Vm.27.4789, Vm.27.9838, Vm.7.14215
*Polka*, Vm.27.9839
*Valse suite*, Vm.27.3049

### Moret, Victor

The following works in F:Pn are all early prints for large wind band; all were printed in Paris in 1861–1881.
Marches: Vm.27.3051, Vm.27.3052, Vm.7.13993

### Morhange, Emile

*Mazurka*
Large wind band
EP (Paris, 1896) F:Pn (Vm.27.9841)

### Morillon, F. de

*Ouvertüre* (1867)
Large wind band
MS A:Wn (Sm.17003)
Composed following a visit to Paris by Franz Josef I of Austria.

The following works in F:Pn are early prints for large wind band; both were printed in Paris in 1870 and 1876.
*Andante & Polonaise*, Vm.27.9844
*L'Hommage*, Vm.27.9843

### Mösner

The following works in F:Pn are all early prints for large wind band; all were printed in Paris in 1859–1860.
Marches: Vm.27.9854, Vm.27.9856, Vm.27.9855
*Polka*, Vm.27.9853

### Mougeot, C.

The following works in F:Pn are all early prints for large wind band; all were printed in Paris in 1882–1900.
Fantaisies: Vm.27.9866, Vm.27.9867, Vm.27.9873,
Vm.27.9899, Vm.27.9874 [later edition],
Vm.27.3063
Marches: Vm.27.3056, Vm.27.9860, Vm.27.3057,
Vm.27.3059, Vm.27.9859, Vm.27.9868,
Vm.27.9869, Vm.27.9871, Vm.27.9875,
Vm.27.9877, Vm.27.9879, Vm.27.3061,
Vm.27.3062, Vm.27.9880, Vm.27.13088,
Vm.27.9882, Vm.27.9883, Vm.27.9884,
Vm.27.9890, Vm.27.9892, Vm.27.9895,
Vm.27.9897, Vm.27.9898
Quadrilles: Vm.27.3058, Vm.27.9872
Polkas: Vm.27.9865 [solo cornet], Vm.27.3060,
Vm.27.13087
Valses: Vm.27.9870, Vm.27.13089, Vm.27.9896
*Schottisch*, Vm.27.9887
*Mazurka*, Vm.27.9889

### Mouquet, Jules (b. 1867)

*Suite* (1910)
1122-01
MP (Paris, Lemoine) [cited in DJ]

### Mourque, F.

*Fantaisie*
Large wind band
EP (Paris, 1899) F:Pn (Vm.27.9903)
There are an additional twenty or so original works dating 1900–1910 by Mourque in F:Pn.

### Moussard, A.

The following works in F:Pn are all early prints for large wind band; all were printed in Paris in 1897–1898.

Marches: Vm.27.3073, Vm.27.3074
*Polka*, Vm.27.9912

## Mulder

*Bagatelle*
Large wind band
EP (Paris, 1894) F.Pn (Vm.27.9920)

## Müller

*Polka*
Large wind band
EP (Paris, 1879) F:Pn (Vm.27.5197)

## Müller, J.

The following works in F:Pn are all early prints for large wind band; all were printed in Paris in 1880–1881.
Marches: Vm.27.9927, Vm.27.9928, Vm.27.9929

## Mullot, E.

The following works in F:Pn are all early prints for large wind band; all were printed in Paris in 1870–1898.
Works for the Church: Vm.27.9930 (*Andante religieux*), Vm.27.3133 (*Domine salvum*), Vm.27.3145 (*La Fête-Dieu Marche*), Vm.27.9958 (*Mélodie religieuse*), Vm.27.9972 (*Morceau d'Élévation*), Vm.27.3195 (*Andante*), Vm.27.9988 (*Morceau d'Élévation*), Vm.27.3226 (*Offertoire*), Vm.27.9991 (*Marche funèbre*), Vm.27.3228 (*Andante*), Vm.27.9994 (*Marche funèbre*)
Overtures: Vm.27.3123, Vm.27.3131, Vm.27.3137, Vm.27.3237, Vm.27.13098 [solo alto, cornet or small clarinet], Vm.27.3147, Vm.27.3176, Vm.27.3237
Fantaisies: Vm.27.3097, Vm.27.3098, Vm.27.3099, Vm.27.3103, Vm.27.3105, Vm.27.3110, Vm.27.9942, Vm.27.13096, Vm.27.3118, Vm.27.9943 [soli cornet and baritone], Vm.27.3126, Vm.27.3127, Vm.7.10041, Vm.27.3135, Vm.27.9951 [solo baritone or saxophone and trombone], Vm.27.3139, Vm.27.9953, Vm.27.3140, Vm.27.3141, Vm.27.3146, Vm.27.3148, Vm.27.3161, Vm.27.3164, Vm.27.9965, Vm.27.3175, Vm.27.3180, Vm.27.3181, Vm.27.3183, Vm.27.9980, Vm.27.3201, Vm.27.3203, Vm.27.3204, Vm.27.3209, Vm.27.3210, Vm.27.9987, Vm.27.3216, Vm.27.3219, Vm.27.3227, Vm.27.3236, Vm.27.9995, Vm.27.9996, Vm.27.3240
Airs varié: Vm.27.3125 (*Congrès Artistique*), Vm.27.9949, Vm.27.3132 [solo alto saxophone], Vm.27.3166, Vm.27.3182, Vm.27.3186, Vm.27.3241
Marches: Vm.27.3094, Vm.27.3095, Vm.27.3031, Vm.27.3096, Vm.27.3102, Vm.27.3104, Vm.27.3106, Vm.27.3109, Vm.27.9937, Vm.27.9939, Vm.27.3113, Vm.27.3115, Vm.27.3116, Vm.7.13998, Vm.7.13999, Vm.27.3119, Vm.27.3120, Vm.27.3121, Vm.27.3122, Vm.27.3124, Vm.27.9947, Vm.27.9948, Vm.27.3128, Vm.27.9950, Vm.27.3134, Vm.27.9952, Vm.27.3138, Vm.27.9956, Vm.27.3144, Vm.27.9959, Vm.27.3153, Vm.27.9961, Vm.27.3158, Vm.27.3159, Vm.27.3160, Vm.27.3163, Vm.27.9977, Vm.27.9966 [with chorus and two soli cornets], Vm.27.9968, Vm.27.3168, Vm.27.3169, Vm.27.13099, Vm.21.3171, Vm.27.3172, Vm.21.3173, Vm.27.3174, Vm.27.9969, Vm.27.3177, Vm.27.9973 [with chorus], Vm.27.3187, Vm.27.3188, Vm.21.3189, Vm.27.3190, Vm.27.9975, Vm.27.3192, Vm.7.14000, Vm.27.3196, Vm.27.9979, Vm.27.3197, Vm.27.3198, Vm.27.3199, Vm.27.9981, Vm.27.9982, Vm.27.3206, Vm.7.14003, Vm.27.3212, Vm.27.9986, Vm.27.3213, Vm.27.9989, Vm.27.3215, Vm.27.3218, Vm.27.3231, Vm.27.3233, Vm.27.9993, Vm.27.3235, Vm.27.3242
Mazurkas: Vm.27.9931, Vm.27.3107, Vm.27.3162, Vm.27.3193, Vm.27.9992
Polkas: Vm.27.9932, Vm.27.9933, Vm.27.9935, Vm.27.9936, Vm.27.3111 [two soli cornets], Vm.27.3117, Vm.27.3130, Vm.27.3129 [solo cornet], Vm.27.3136, Vm.27.3191, Vm.27.9957, Vm.27.3149 [solo cornet], Vm.27.3150, Vm.27.3151, Vm.27.9960 [solo cornet], Vm.27.3165, Vm.27.3167, Vm.27.9976 [solo cornet], Vm.7.14002, Vm.27.3221, Vm.27.9990, Vm.27.3230

Quadrilles: Vm.27.9934, Vm.27.9940,
Vm.27.3178, Vm.27.3238, Vm.27.3239,
Vm.27.9999
Valses: Vm.27.3108, Vm.27.3112, Vm.27.3157,
Vm.27.9963, Vm.27.9967, Vm.7.13997,
Vm.27.3200, Vm.27.3220, Vm.27.9984 [soli
cornet and baritone]
Boléros: Vm.27.9938 [soli trombone and cornet],
Vm.27.9970, Vm.27.9974 [soli baritone, two
cornets, and alto], Vm.27.3202
Schottisches: Vm.27.13098, Vm.27.9971,
Vm.27.3208, Vm.27.9985, Vm.27.3211,
Vm.27.3223, Vm.27.3234
Galops: Vm.27.13097, Vm.7.14001
*Serenade*, Vm.27.3217
*Gavotte*. Vm.27.3179
*Cavatine* Vm.27.3100 [solo clarinet]
*Faustina. Solo de Concert*, Vm.27.3143

### Münchs, Conrad

The following works in F:Pn are all early prints
for large wind band; all were printed in Paris
in ca. 1864.
Overtures: Vm.27.10000, Vm.27.3244
*Journal de Musique*, Vm.27.2628 [1re Année]

'*C'est l'Amour,' en Pas redoublé*
EP (Paris, Pacini, ca. 1800–1828)

### Naudin. T.

*Marche*
Large wind band
EP (Paris, 1889) F:Pn (Vm.27.10003)

### Nehr, Emile

The following works in F:Pn are all early prints
for large wind band; all were printed in Paris
in 1860–1872.
Marches: Vm.27.10026, Vm.27.10027,
Vm.27.10028, Vm.27.10029, Vm.27.10024,
Vm.27.10016, Vm.27.10014, Vm.27.10017
(*Innocence. March du procession*)
Polkas: Vm.27.10015, Vm.27.10018, Vm.27.10019,
Vm.27.10020, Vm.27.10023
*Quadrille*, Vm.27.10025

### Neveu, Alban

*Polka Artistique*
Large wind band
EP (Paris, 1890) F:Pn (Vm.27.10035)

### Nicaise, E.

The following works in F:Pn are all early prints
for large wind band; all were printed in Paris
in 1891–1905.
*Fantaisie de concert*, Vm.27.10040
*Pas redoublé*, Vm.27.3256
*Polka*, Vm.27.10041

### Nicolas

The following works in F:Pn are early prints for
large wind band; both were printed in Paris in
1870–1871.
*Fantaisie*, Vm.27.3257
*Marche*, Vm.27.4792

### Nicosias, Charles

The following works in F:Pn are early prints for
large wind band; both were printed in Paris in
1869 and 1885.
Marches: Vm.27.10045, Vm.27.10046

### Nicou, G.

The following works in F:Pn are all early prints
for large wind band; all were printed in Paris
in 1859–1865.
Marches: Vm.27.3261, Vm.27.3262
*Polka*, Vm.7.14009

### Niverd, M.

*Polka*
Large wind band
EP (Paris, 1888) F:Pn (Vm.27.3265)

### Niverd, R.

*Marche*
Large wind band
EP (Paris, 1870) F:Pn (Vm.27.10049)

## Niverd, V.

The following works in F:Pn are early prints for large wind band; both were printed in Paris in 1873–1874.
Marches: Vm.27.10050, Vm.27.10051

## Noël Le Mire, A.

The following works in F:Pn are all early prints for large wind band; all were printed in Paris in 1870–1892.
Fantaisies: Vm.27.8908, Vm.27.8903
Marches: Vm.27.8909, Vm.27.8910, Vm.27.8904, Vm.27.8906, Vm.27.8907, Vm.27.8896, Vm.27.8914, Vm.27.8915, Vm.27.8911, Vm.27.8912, Vm.27.8913, Vm.27.8899, Vm.27.8900, Vm.27.8901
Valses: Vm.27.8905, Vm.27.8897
Polkas: Vm.27.8902, Vm.27.8898

## Norroy, H.

The following works in F:Pn are all early prints for large wind band; all were printed in Paris in 1898–1900.
*Fantaisie choregrahique*, Vm.27.10055
*Pas redoublé*, Vm.27.10056
*Polka*, Vm.27.10053
Mazurkas: Vm.27.10054, Vm.27.10057

## Omer Fort (Chef de Musique au 7e Hussards)

The following works in F:Pn are all early prints for large wind band; all were printed in Paris in 1865–1890.
Works for the Church: Vm.27.4682 (*Marche funèbre*) [for brass band], Vm.27.7434 (*Marche du procession*), Vm.27.4684 (*La Sainte-Anne. Marche religieuse*) [for brass band], Vm.27.7435 (*Sainte—Cécile Marche*)
The first of these examples seems a fine, dramatic composition scored for brass band, including SATB sarrusophones.
Fantaisies: Vm.27.10066, Vm.27.1539 [for brass band]
Marches: Vm.27.7432, Vm.27.12819, Vm.7.13109, Vm.27.7431, Vm.7.13506 ('sur un motif arabé de la tribe des Ouled, Amor'), Vm.27.1535, Vm.27.7433, Vm.7.13508

Valses: Vm.27.7430, Vm.27.1537, Vm.27.1538
Polkas: Vm.27.1541, Vm.27.3288
*Quadrille*, Vm.7.13510
*Schottisch*, Vm.27.1543
*Galop*, Vm.7.13509

## Onslow, Georges (1784–1853)

*Nonet*, Op. 77
EP GB:Lbm (R.H.17.f.9[4])

## Orelly, J. de

The following works in F:Pn are all early prints for large wind band; all were printed in Paris in 1889–1900.
*Fantaisie*, Vm.27.13108
Marches: Vm.27.13109, Vm.27.10067, Vm.27.13110

## Paer, Ferdinand (1771–1816)

*Offertorium*
TTBB, 2222-02 [optional version: 2 violins and bass]
MS CS:Bm (A.19.617)

*Trio* ('Nr 6 … sind im Theater')
STB, 2222-02
MS BRD:Mbs (Mus.Ms.2392)

*Six pièces d'harmonie*
22-02
EP (Offenbach, no date) [cited in Grove, XIV, 84]

*Fantasia*
Two pianos, 2001-02 [cited in DJ]

(4) *Grand Military Marches* [cited in DJ]

(6) *Walzes*
Large wind band [cited in DJ]

### Pagés, Paul

*Pas redoublé*
Large wind band
EP (Paris, 1900) F:Pn (Vm.27.13115)

### Paimparé

The following works in F:Pn are all early prints for large wind band; all were printed in Paris in 1879–1908.
Overtures: Vm.27.13117, Vm.27.3303
Fantaisies: Vm.27.3302, Vm.27.10072
Marches: Vm.27.13116, Vm.27.10074
There is a large number of additional original works dating after 1900 by Paimparé in F:Pn.

### Palausi

The following works in F:Pn are all early prints for large wind band; all were printed in Paris in 1875–1887.
*Allegro militaire*, Vm.27.10084
*Quadrille*, Vm.27.10083
*Valse*, Vm.27.10085

### Paliard, Leon

*Marche*
Large wind band [with chorus]
EP (Paris, 1888) F:Pn (Vm.27.10086)

### Parès, Gabriel (Chef de la Musique de la Garde Républicaine)

The following works in F:Pn are all early prints for large wind band; all were printed in Paris in 1884–1913.
Overtures: Vm.27.3312, Vm.27.3323, Vm.27.3320 Vm.27.3319, Fol.Vm.15.771 [two copies] (*Overture solennelle*), Vm.27.13132, Vm.27.10115, Vm.27.3324, Vm.27.13133 (*Overture dramatique*), Vm.27.10116 and Vm.27.10017 [two copies]
*Pastorale*, Vm.27.3321
*Sérénade*, Vm.27.3326
*Petites scènes romantiques*, Vm.27.10103
*Divertissement*, Vm.27.3313
Fantaisies: Vm.27.10097, Vm.7.14025
Marches: Vm.27.10096, Vm.27.10098, Vm.27.13129, Vm.27.10099 Vm.27.10100, Vm.27.10101, Vm.7.14423, Vm.27.10113, Vm.27.3322, Vm.7.14032, Vm.27.13130, Vm.27.10107, Vm.27.10108, Vm.27.10109, Vm.27.10110, Vm.27.3316, Vm.27.10091, 40.Vm.15.1435, Vm.27.10092, Vm.27.3310, 40.Vm.15.1911, 40.Vm.15.3459, Vm.27.4198
*Danse*, Vm.27.3311
*Polka*, Vm.27.10095
*Tarentelle*, Vm.27.3327
*Rogodon*, Vm.27.3325
*Polonaise de Concert*, Vm.7.14033
*Gavotte*, Vm.7.14029
*Menuet-Caprice*, Vm.27.3317
Mazurkas: Vm.27.3314, Vm.27.3315, Vm.27.3318
*Le Voltigeur*, Vm.27.3328
In addition there approximately one hundred transcriptions for band in F:Pn by Parès.

### Paris, Hte.

The following works in F:Pn are all early prints for large wind band; all were printed in Paris in 1869–1872.
*Overture*, Vm.27.13136
Marches: Vm.27.10140, Vm.27.10141, Vm.27.10135, Vm.27.10132, Vm.27.10128
Polkas: Vm.27.10129, Vm.27.10131, Vm.27.10134, Vm.27.10137
Quadrilles: Vm.27.10139, Vm.27.10138 (*Le Siege de Paris. Quadrille historique*)
*Boléro*, Vm.27.10133

### Paris-Kerjullou, Charles

The following works in F:Pn are all early prints for large wind band; all were printed in Paris in 1858–1874.
*Fantaisie*, Vm.27.10142
Marches: Vm.27.10154 (*Marche funèbre*), Vm.27.10153, Vm.27.10156
Quadrilles: Vm.7.13737, Vm.27.10157
*Polka*, Vm.27.10155

## Pariser, E.

The following works in F:Pn are early prints for large wind band; both were printed in Paris in ca. 1866.
*Pas redoublé*, Vm.27.3335 [for small band]
*Polka*, Vm.7.14037

## Patrie, J.

*Overture*
Large wind band
EP (Paris, nineteenth century) F:Pn (Vm.27.3338)

## Pautrat, Pierre

The following works in F:Pn are all early prints for large wind band; all were printed in Paris in 1895–1900.
*Overture*, Vm.27.10198
Fantaisies: Vm.27.10170, Vm.27.10167
Marches: Vm.27.10164, Vm.27.10166, Vm.27.3341, Vm.27.10169, Vm.27.10177, Vm.27.10178, Vm.27.10191, Vm.27.3343, Vm.27.10194, Vm.27.10185, Vm.27.10184, Vm.27.13139
Mazurkas: Vm.27.10197, Vm.27.10174, Vm.27.10162, Vm.27.10182 (*Mazurka de Concert*), Vm.27.10183 (*Mazurka de Concert*)
Polka: Vm.27.10175, Vm.27.10188 (*Polka des musiciens*)
Schottisches: Vm.27.10190, Vm.27.10186
Valses: Vm.27.10192, Vm.27.10195 (*Valse de Concert*), Vm.27.10163
*Quadrille*, Vm.27.10196

## Payer, Jerome (1787–1845)

*Suites de pièces d'harmonie pour inst. a vent*
EP (Mechetti) [cited in F]

## Peirot, J.

The following works in F:Pn are all early prints for large wind band; all were printed in Paris in 1867–1876.
*Fantaisie*, Vm.27.10201
Marches: Vm.27.10200, Vm.7.14043, Vm.27.10204, Vm.27.10205
*Quadrille*, Vm.27.3344

## Perilhou, Armand (d. 1936)

*Divertissement*
2222-04
MP (Heugel)

*Bourée*
2222-04
MP (Heugel)

## Perin, L.

*Valse*
Large wind band
EP (Paris, 1875) F:Pn (Vm.27.10213)

## Perlat, Lucien

*Overture*
Large wind band
EP (Paris, 1898) F:Pn (Vm.27.10215)

## Perron, Ed.

*Sursum Corda. Offertoire* [solo trombone]
Large wind band
EP (Nancy, 1903) F:Pn (Vm.27.10218)
A brief, but musical example.

## Pessard, Émile

The following works in F:Pn are early prints for large wind band; both were printed in Paris in 1882 and 1896.
*Valse*, Vm.27.3364
*Galop*, Vm.27.1351

## Pessière, Émile

The following works in F:Pn are all early prints for large wind band; all were printed in Paris in 1859–1883.
*Overture*, Vm.27.13155
Fantaisies: Vm.27.10229, Vm.27.10230, Vm.27.10238
Marches: Vm.27.10221, Vm.27.10225, Vm.27.10226, Vm.27.10227, Vm.27.10228, Vm.27.13157, Vm.27.10232 [for brass band], Vm.27.10234, Vm.27.10236, Vm.27.10237
Quadrilles: Vm.27.10235, Vm.27.10239
Polkas: Vm.27.10233, Vm.27.10231

*Schottisch*, Vm.27.10224
*Galop*, Vm.27.13156

## Péter, Sylvestre

The following works in F:Pn are early prints for large wind band; both were printed in Paris in 1889 and 1892.
*Pas redoublé*, Vm.27.10241
*Polka*, Vm.27.10242 [solo cornet or small clarinet]

## Petit, Alexandre

The following works in F:Pn are all early prints for large wind band; all were printed in Paris in 1888–1904.
Fantaisies: Vm.27.10245, Vm.27.10248
Marches: Vm.27.10249, Vm.27.13158
Polkas: Vm.27.10247, Vm.27.10256 [two coli cornets], Vm.27.10259 [solo cornet], Vm.27.10250 [solo cornet]
Mazurkas: Vm.27.10251 (*Fête militaire*) [solo cornet], Vm.27.10246
*Valse*, Vm.27.10244

## Petit, Fernand

The following works in F:Pn are all early prints for large wind band; all were printed in Paris in 1886–1906.
*Rondo Louis XI*, Vm.27.3370 [soli fifes]
Marches: Vm.27.10257, Vm.27.3371, Vm.27.10260, Vm.27.3373, Vm.27.3374
*Polka*, Vm.27.10258 [solo cornet]

## Petit, I.

*Retraite*
Large wind band
EP (Paris, 1883) F:Pn (Vm.27.10261)

## Petit, Oscar

*Pas redoublé*
Large wind band
EP (Paris, 1885) F:Pn (Vm.27.3375)

## Philiberti

*Marche*
Large wind band
EP (Paris, 1855) F:Pn (Vm.27.3378)

## Philippe, Edouard

*Polka*
Large wind band
EP (Paris, 1879) F:Pn (Vm.27.10264)

## Pierné, Gabriel (1863–1937)

*Preludio and Fughetta*, Op. 40
2112-01
MP (New York, International) BRD:Bhm (DA.1002)

*Pastorale*, Op. 14, nr. 1
1111-01
EP (Paris, Leduc, 1887) GB:Lbm (f.244.b.[4])

*Pastorale Variee*
1112-11
EP (Paris, Durand) [cited by DJ]

## Pillevestre, J.

The following works in F:Pn are all early prints for large wind band; all were printed in Paris in 1887–1900.
*Overture*, Vm.27.13165
Fantaisies: Vm.27.3429, Vm.27.3433, Vm.27.3394, Vm.27.3408, Vm.27.3396 [soli oboe and flute], Vm.27.3405, Vm.27.3425 [two soli piccolos]
*Revêrie*, Vm.27.3422 [solo flute]
*Trio comique*, Vm.27.13164 (*Monsieur, Madame et Bébé*) [soli cornet, clarinet and 'trompette d'enfant']
*Idylle bretonne*, Vm.27.3409 [two soli oboes]
*Scène bretonne*, Vm.27.3436 [soli oboes]
Duo concertantes: Vm.27.3410, Vm.27.3402, Vm.27.3386, Vm.27.3399 [soli clarinets], Vm.27.3387 [soli small or large clarinets]
*Duo de concert*, Vm.27.3406 and Vm.27.3407 [later edition]
*Petit poéme pastorale*, Vm.27.3400
*Nocturne*, Vm.27.3424

Marches: Vm.27.3404 (*Marche funèbre*),
Vm.27.3411, Vm.27.3413, Vm.27.3414,
Vm.21.3420 (*Comic Marche*), Vm.27.3390,
Vm.27.3395, Vm.27.3430, Vm.27.3434 [with chorus]
Polkas: Vm.27.3435, Vm.27.3432, Vm.27.3431,
Vm.27.3388, Vm.27.3389, Vm.27.3390,
Vm.27.3391, Vm.27.3426, Vm.27.3401 (*Polka de Concert*) [solo cornet], Vm.27.3423
*Pot-pourri*, Vm.27.3398
*Rondo*, Vm.27.3418
*Tarentelle*, Vm.27.3421
*Gavotte*, Vm.27.3419 (*Le Movement perpetuel*) [*dans le style ancien*]
*Mazurka*, Vm.27.3416
*Chanson*, Vm.27.3415
*Caprice*, Vm.27.3392 [solo cornet]
*Petits Fanfares*, Vm.27.3397
*Villanelle*, Vm.27.3385
*Valse*, Vm.27.3428

## Pinault, V.

The following works in F:Pn are all early prints for large wind band; all were printed in Paris in 1866–1876.
*Mazurka*, Vm.27.10275
Marches: Vm.27.10274, Vm.27.10276, Vm.27.10277

## Pipelart, Maurice

*Souvenir de Cordove*
Large wind band
EP (Paris, 1893) F:Pn (Vm.27.13167)

## Pique, Adolphe

The following works in F:Pn are all early prints for large wind band; all were printed in Paris in 1872–1888.
Marches: Vm.27.10279, Vm.27.10280,
Vm.27.10282, Vm.27.10283, Vm.27.10284,
Vm.27.10287, Vm.27.10288, Vm.27.10289,
Vm.27.10290, Vm.27.10291
Polkas: Vm.27.10281 [two soli cornets], and Vm.27.10285
*Valse*, Vm.27.10286

## Pirouelle

The following works in F:Pn are all early prints for large wind band; all were printed in Paris in 1859–1887.
*Overture*, Vm.27.3442
*Fantaisie*, Vm.27.3453
*Ronde*, Vm.27.10293
*Caprice*, Vm.27.3451
*Cupidon*, Vm.27.10299
Marches: Vm.27.10292, Vm.27.10295,
Vm.27.10296, Vm.7.14054, Vm.7.14053,
Vm.27.10300, Vm.27.10301,
Vm.27.10302, Vm.27.3449, Vm.27.3450,
Vm.27.10310, Vm.27.3452, Vm.27.10311,
Vm.27.10312, Vm.27.10313, Vm.27.10307,
Vm.27.10308 Vm.27.3443 Vm.27.3444
Vm.27.10304, Vm.7.14052, Vm.27.10315,
Vm.27.10309
Polkas: Vm.27.10294, Vm.27.3441, Vm.7.14051 [solo clarinet], Vm.27.10314, Vm.27.3454
Valses: Vm.27.10297, Vm.27.10298, Vm.27.3447,
Vm.27.3448, Vm.27.10303
Mazurkas: Vm.27.10305, Vm.27.3446
Galops: Vm.27.10306, Vm.7.14055
*Boléro*, Vm.27.3445

## Pitot

The following works in F:Pn are early prints for large wind band; both were printed in Paris during the nineteenth century.
*Polka*, Vm.27.3456
*Schottisch*, Vm.27.3455

## Pivet, L.

The following works in F:Pn are all early prints for large wind band; all were printed in Paris in 1877–1900.
*Overture*, Vm.27.3466
Fantaisies: Vm.27.10316, Vm.27.3457,
Vm.27.10322, Vm.27.13169, Vm.27.3464,
Vm.27.3467, Vm.27.10323
Airs varié: Vm.27.10320 (*avec variations par tout les Instruments*), Vm.27.3461, Vm.27.3463, Vm.27.13170
*Nissa Carnaval*, Vm.27.3465

Marches: Vm.27.10318, Vm.27.10319, Vm.27.3460, Vm.7.14058, Vm.7.14062, Vm.27.10327, Vm.27.10329, Vm.27.10325, Vm.7.14061, Vm.27.10330, Vm.27.10331
Polkas: Vm.7.14064, Vm.7.14065, Vm.7.14063, Vm.27.10321, Vm.27.10328, Vm.27.3462, Vm.7.14060
Valses: Vm.27.10317, Vm.27.3459, Vm.7.14059
*Mazurka*, Vm.27.10324

## Plouvier

*La Chasse*
Harmoniemusik
EP (Paris, Richault, ca. 1800–1828)

## Pluchart, H.

The following works in F:Pn are all early prints for large wind band all were printed in Paris in 1875–1877.
Marches: Vm.27.10353, Vm.27.10354, Vm.27.10355
*Polka*, Vm.27.10352

## Pontet, E.

The following works in F:Pn are all early prints for large wind band; all were printed in Paris in 1891–1902.
Works for the Church: Vm.27.13186 (*Andante religieux*), Vm.27.10390 and Vm.27.10391 [later edition] (*Melodie religieuse*)
*Overtures*: Vm.27.10364 and Vm.27.10374
Fantaisies: Vm.27.10376, Vm.27.10383, Vm.27.3494
*Idylle-Gavotte*, Vm.27.10387
Marches: Vm.27.10366, Vm.27.10367, Vm.27.10368, Vm.27.10370, Vm.27.10373, Vm.27.3490, Vm.27.3491, Vm.27.10377, Vm.27.10379, Vm.27.10384, Vm.27.3492, Vm.21.3493, Vm.27.10392, Vm.27.10394, Vm.27.10395
*Mazurka*, Vm.27.10371
*Polkas*: Vm.27.10372, Vm.27.10380, Vm.27.13184
*Schottisch*, Vm.27.10378
There are numerous additional original works by Pontet in F:Pn, dated 1900–1910.

## Préau

The following works in F:Pn are all early prints for large wind band; all were printed in Paris in 1856–1868
Work for the Church, Vm.27.10440 (*La Prière du matin. Morceau religieux*), Vm.27.10436 (*Marche funèbre*)
*Marche*, Vm.27.10441
*Valse*, Vm.27.10431
*Quadrille*, Vm.27.10434
*Polka*, Vm.27.10435
*Schottisch*, Vm.27.10439

## Preisser, M. A.

*Marche funèbre* (*pour Mus.Mil. pour l'Anniversaire des 27. 28. 29 Juillet*)
Harmoniemusik
EP (Paris, Richault, ca. 1800–1828)

## Prèvost, Charles

*Pas redoublé*
Large wind band
EP (Paris, 1874) F:Pn (Vm.27.10444)

## Princiaux, J.

The following works in F:Pn are early prints for large wind band; both were printed in Paris in 1894 and 1897.
*Fantaisie*, Vm.27.10461
*Marche*, Vm.27.10460

## Princiaux, fils

The following works in F:Pn are all early prints for large wind band; all were printed in Paris in 1862–1891.
Fantaisies: Vm.27.10456, Vm.27.10457 (solo cornet), Vm.27.3504, Vm.27.10459
Marches: Vm.27.10448, Vm.27.10450, Vm.27.10451, Vm.27.10452, Vm.27.10454, Vm.27.10458
*Polka*, Vm.27.10449
*Schottisch*, Vm.27.10453
*Mazurka*, Vm.27.10462

## Prost, Jules

The following works in F:Pn are early prints for large wind band; both were printed in Paris in 1857 and 1873.
*Overture*, Vm.27.13195
*Quadrille*, Vm.27.3505

## Provent, C.

The following works in F:Pn are all early prints for large wind band; all were printed in Paris in 1887–1898.
Marches: Vm.27.3506, Vm.27.3508, Vm.27.3509 (*Marche funèbre*)

## Provent

*Polka arabe*
Large wind band
EP (Paris, 1893) F:Pn (Vm.27.3510)

## Prudhomme, Marius

*Mazurka*
Large wind band
EP (Paris, 1890) F:Pn (Vm.27.10472)

## Prunier, Edoward

The following works in F:Pn are all early prints for large wind band; all were printed in Paris in 1866–1884.
*Fantaisie*, Vm.27.10480
Marches: Vm.27.10474, Vm.27.10476, Vm.27.10477, Vm.27.10473, Vm.27.10478, Vm.27.10479
*Schottisch*, Vm.27.10475

## Puchot, L.

The following works in F:Pn are all early prints for large wind band; all were printed in Paris in 1867–1887.
Work for the Church, Vm.27.13197 (*Les Voix célestes. Andante*)
Marches: Vm.27.10481, Vm.7.14074
*Quadrille*, Vm.27.3515
*Polka*, Vm.27.10482

## Pütz, Pierre

The following works in F:Pn are all early prints for large wind band; all were printed in Paris in 1890–1900.
*Overture*, Vm.27.10496
Marches: Vm.27.10492, Vm.27.10495, Vm.27.10499, Vm.27.3520
*Polka*, Vm.27.10493 [solo cornet]
*Valse*, Vm.27.10494

## Puyau, G.

*Marche*
Large wind band
EP (Paris, 1898) F:Pn (Vm.27.3521)

## Quentin, Alfred

The following works in F:Pn are all early prints for large wind band; all were printed in Paris in 1868–1883.
*Les guides au Carrousel*, Vm.27.3523
Marches: Vm.27.3524, Vm.27.3523 bis, Vm.27.1051
*Quadrille*, Vm.27.10503
*Galop*, Vm.27.13206
*Schottisch*, Vm.27.10504
*Polka*, Vm.27.3522

## Raffara, J.

The following works in F:Pn are all early prints for large wind band; all were printed in Paris during the nineteenth century — perhaps ca. 1850 as there are no saxophone parts.
Marches: Vm.27.3528, Vm.27.3529
*Rédova*, Vm.27.3530 [with piano mentioned on the title-page but missing in this copy]

## Ramin

*Harmonie militaire de Cavallerie*
EP (Paris, Pacini, ca. 1800–1828) [Liv. 1- 6]

## Rauchenecker, Georges

*Grand Overture*
Large wind band
EP (Paris, 1867) F:Pn (Vm.27.3535)

Composed for *'l'expositon universelle de 1867 à Paris.'* This is a classical overture for the full modern instrumentation.

### Rauski, Joseph

The following works in F:Pn are all early prints for large wind band; all were printed in Paris in 1878–1889.
*Festival-fantaisie*, Vm.27.10510
*Scène champêtre.* Vm.27.3538
*Madrigal de Francois 1er* [arranged by Rauski], Vm.27.10511

### Raux, Jules

*Galop*
Large wind band
EP (Paris, 1887) F:Pn (Vm.27.13214)

### Ravizza, F.

The following works in F:Pn are early prints for large wind band; both were printed in Paris in 1889.
Galops: Vm.27.13215, Vm.27.13216

### Raynaud

*Marche chinoise*
Large wind band
EP (Paris, 1883) F:Pn (Vm.27.10518)

### Recoux, Charles

The following works in F:Pn are all early prints for large wind band; all were printed in Paris in 1888–1896.
*Andantino*, Vm.27.10521
*Divertissement*, Vm.27.10522
*Fantaisie*, Vm.27.10523
Marches: Vm.27.10524, Vm.27.3544
*Valse*, Vm.27.3541

### Régent, D.

*Marche*
Large wind band
EP (Paris, 1898) F:Pn (Vm.27.10526)

### Reicha, Antoine

*Commemoration Symphony* ('Music for the Celebration of Great Men and Great Events')
666-66; 3 piccolo, 3 contrabassoons, percussion, canons
MS (autograph score) F:Pn (MS.2495, 8425); US:DW (90)

*Choeur dialogue par les instruments à vent*
Chorus, 1111-01, cello, string bass
EP (Paris, author, 1824-1826, in *Traité de haute composition musicale* [i.74]) [cited in Grove, XV, 699]

(6) *Quintets*, Op. 88
1111-01
EP (Paris, Janet; Bonn, Simrock; Mainz, Schott, all before 1828) BRD:MZsch

(6) *Quintets*, Op. 91
1111-01
EP (Paris, Janet; Bonn, Simrock, all before 1828)

(6) *Quintets*, Op. 99
1111-01
EP (Paris, Janet; Bonn, Simrock, all before 1828)

(6) *Quintets*, Op. 100
1111-01
EP (Paris, Zetter; Mainz, Schott, all before 1828) BRD:MZsch

### Renard, Pierre

The following works in F:Pn are early prints for large wind band; both were printed in Paris in 1891 and 1902
*Fantaisie-Overture*, Vm.27.10540
*Polka*, Vm.27.10541

### Requin, L.

The following works in F:Pn are all early prints for large wind band; all were printed in Paris in 1859–1879.
*Elégie (À la Mémoire de mon père et de mère)*, Vm.27.10551

*Fantaisie*, Vm.27.10555
Marches: Vm.27.10552, Vm.27.10553, Vm.27.10554, Vm.27.10556
*Quadrille*, Vm.27.10550

## Reuland, H.

*Marche*
Large wind band
EP (Paris, 1890) F:Pn (Vm.27.10557)

## Reynaud, J.

The following works in F:Pn are all early prints for large wind band; all were printed in Paris in 1876–1888.
*Andante offertoire*, Vm.27.10562
Overtures: Vm.27.13222, Vm.27.13220 and Vm.27.13221 [later edition]
   The latter example is a transcription for band by the composer of his own Overture to his opera, *Jeanne Maillotte*.
Fantaisies: Vm.27.10567, Vm.27.3573 [solo trombone]
*Air varié*, Vm.27.3578
*Jeanne Maillotte*, Vm.7.14099 [solo violin or flute]
   This consists of three long movements: a Mazurka, a slow movement for solo violin or flute, and a Galop. The work is scored for very large instrumentation including the saxophone and bugle families.
Marches: Vm.27.3571, Vm.27.10563, Vm.7.14102, Vm.27.10574, Vm.27.3579, Vm.7.14100, Vm.27.3575, Vm.27.10564, Vm.27.10566
Polkas: Vm.27.3576 [solo cornet], Vm.27.10569, Vm.27.10559, Vm.27.10565 (*Polka de Concert*) [solo cornet]
*Valse*, Vm.27.3577
*Quadrille*, Vm.27.10570

## Reynaud, Louis (Chef de Musique, 74e d'infanterie)

The following works in F:Pn are all early prints for large wind band; all were printed in Paris in 1893–1907.

Overtures: Vm.27.10584 Vm.27.10585, Vm.27.10586, Vm.27.10587, Vm.27.10588, Vm.27.10589 and Vm.27.10590 (*Poém de France. Overture Symphonique*), Vm.27.10592 (*Overture Symphonique*)
   The example under Vm.2710586 looks more like a Valse, slow movement, and Galop.
*Suites épisodiques. 1st Temps hériques*, Vm.27.3582
*Cacilia. Composition Symphopique*, vm.27.10580
Fantaisies: Vm.27.10581, Vm.27.10582, Vm.27.13224, Vm.27.13225
Marches: Vm.27.3581 (*Marche cortege des toréadors. Rhapsodie par harmonie*), Vm.27.10583, Vm.27.10577
Valses: Vm.27.13223, Vm.27.3580
Polkas: Vm.27.10578 [solo cornet], Vm.27.10579 [solo flute]
   The last example has a wildly difficult flute part dedicated to 'Monsieur Leon Fontbonne,' the principal flutist of the Garde Republicaine Band.

## Richard, Charles

The following works in F:Pn are all early prints for large wind band; all were printed in Paris in 1872–1886.
*Offertoire*, Vm.27.10612
Overtures: Vm.27.13228, Vm.27.13229, Vm.27.13231, Vm.27.3588 (*La Sensitive*)
Fantaisies: Vm.27.10596, Vm.27.10604, Vm.27.10606, Vm.27.10607, Vm.27.10601 and Vm.27.10602 [later edition]
Airs varié: Vm.27.3584, Vm.27.13227, Vm.27.10613
Marches: Vm.27.10597, Vm.27.10598, Vm.27.10599, Vm.27.10603 and Vm.27.10604 [later edition], Vm.27.10611
*Polka*, Vm.27.10600
*Quadrille*, Vm.27.3587

## Richard, J.

*Marche*
Large wind band
EP (Paris, 1861) F:Pn (Vm.27.10615)

### Richart, Alfred

The following works in F:Pn are all early prints for large wind band; all were printed in Paris in 1897–1900.
Overtures: Vm.27.3593, Vm.27.3598
*Fantaisie*, Vm.27.3589
Marches: Vm.27.3591, Vm.27.3592, Vm.27.3590
*Polka*, Vm.27.3594 [solo clarinet]

### Richer, H.

The following works in F:Pn are all early prints for large wind band; all were printed in Paris in 1889–1903.
Works for the Church: Vm.27.16621 (*Andante*), Vm.27.3606 (*Marche funèbre*)
*Fête au camp*, Vm.27.3602
*Fantaisie*, Vm.7.1410S
Marches: Vm.27.3604, Vm.27.3605, Vm.7.14104, Vm.27.3608
Mazurkas: Vm.27.3603, Vm.27.3607

### Richoux, L.

The following works in F:Pn are early prints for large wind band; both were printed in Paris in 1883–1894.
*Valse*, Vm.27.3611
*Mazurka*, Vm.27.36l0

### Riedel, A.

The following works in F:Pn are all early prints for large wind band; all were printed in Paris in 1863–1868.
(2) *Marches:* Vm.27.3613
*Polka*, Vm.27.3612

### Rièl, Léon

*Marche*
Large wind band
EP (Paris, 1893) F:Pn (Vm.27.10623)

### Rillé, Laurent de

The following works in F:Pn are all early prints for large wind band; all were printed in Paris in 1882–1888.
Marches: Vm.27.13233, Vm.27.13234
*Marriage du Roi de Bohême*, Vm.27.3615

### Ritiez, B.

The following works in F:Pn are all early prints for large wind band; all were printed in Paris in 1879–1881.
Marches: Vm.27.10627, Vm.27.10628, Vm.27.10629
*Polka*, Vm.27.10630

### Ritz, Jean

*Hymne à la Patrie*
Large wind band [with chorus]
EP (Paris, 1889) F:Pn (Vm.27.3619)

### Rival, L.

The following works in F:Pn are all early prints for large wind band; all were printed in Paris in 1881–1885.
Overtures: Vm.27.13235, Vm.27.13236
*Fantaisie-overture*, Vm.27.10634
*Marche*, Vm.27.10633
*Polka,* Vm.27.10632

### Rivet, H.

The following works in F:Pn are all early prints for large wind band; all were printed in Paris in 1876–1903.
*Fantaisie*, Vm.27.3523
Marches: Vm.27.10638, Vm.27.10639, Vm.27.10637, Vm.27.10640, Vm.27.10641
*Polka,* Vm.27.10636 [solo flute or cornet]

### Rivetti, Giovanni

*Quadrille*
Large wind band
EP (Paris, 1868) F:Pn (Vm.27.3625)

### Riviere, J.

The following works in F:Pn are all early prints for large wind band; all were printed in Paris in 1852–1880.

Marches: Vm.27.10646, Vm.27.10652,
  Vm.27.10648, Vm.27.10657 (*Souvenir de New York*)
*Polka*, Vm.27.10644
*Quadrille*, Vm.27.10650
*Valse*, Vm.27.10647

## Robert, A.

*Marche*
Large wind band
EP (Paris, 1897) F:Pn (Vm.27·.3629)

## Robert, E.

The following works in F:Pn are all early prints for large wind band; all were printed in Paris in 1864–1897.
*Overture*, Vm.27.13239
Fantaisies: Vm.27.10667, Vm.27.10668,
  Vm.27.13240, Vm.27.3633
Marches: Vm.27.10666, Vm.27.10670,
  Vm.27.10672, Vm.27.10674, Vm.27.10669
  (*Marche funèbre*), Vm.27.10677, Vm.21.10678
Polkas: Vm.27.10675, Vm.27.10673
Quadrilles: Vm.27.10663, Vm.27.10664
*Mazurka*, Vm.27.10671

## Roche, Gustave

*Marche*
Large wind band
EP (Paris, 1886) F:Pn (Vm.27.3636)

## Rodes, Oscar

*Pas redoublé*
Large wind band
EP (Lyon, 1883) F:Pn (Vm.7.14109)

## Rodet, Auguste

The following works in F:Pn are all early prints for large wind band; all were printed in Paris in 1881–1888.
*Marche*, Vm.7.14111
Polkas: Vm.27.10683, Vm.7.14112, Vm.7.14110
*Mazurka*, Vm.7.14113

## Rogers

(24) *Divertissement*
Six-part Harmoniemusik
EP (Paris, Pleyel, ca. 1800–1828)

## Rollé, Emile

The following works in F:Pn are all early prints for large wind band; all were printed in Paris in 1874–1891.
Works for the Church: Vm.27.10721 (*Andante. Les Voix célestes. pour Élévation*), Vm.27.10716 (*Offertoire*), Vm.27.10685 (*Andante religieux*), Vm.27.10686 (*Andante religieux*)
Overtures: Vm.27.13241, Vm.27.3646
Fantaisies: Vm.27.3648 [with chorus],
  Vm.27.3645, Vm.27.3644
Airs varié: Vm.27.10700, Vm.27.10720,
  Vm.27.3643
Marches: Vm.27.10718, Vm.27.10702,
  Vm.27.10705, Vm.27.10706, Vm.27.10694,
  Vm.27.10696, Vm.27.10690, Vm.27.10707,
  Vm.27.10708, Vm.27.10709, Vm.27.10710,
  Vm.27.10711, Vm.27.10712, Vm.27.10714,
  Vm.27.10715
*Schottisch*, Vm.27.10717
Polkas: Vm.27.10719, Vm.27.10703, Vm.27.10697,
  Vm.27.10689, Vm.27.10698 [solo clarinet],
  Vm.27.3642
*Galop*, Vm.27.3647
*Quadrille*, Vm.27.10699
There are also a large number of transcriptions for band by Rolle in F:Pn.

## Romain, F.

The following works in F:Pn are all early prints for large wind band; all were printed in Paris and Avernes-le-comte in 1880–1908.
Marches: Vm.27.3650, Vm.27.10732,
  Vm.27.3654, Vm.27.3655
Polkas: Vm.27.3653, Vm.27.3652, Vm.27.13244
  [solo cornet]
*Quadrille*, Vm.27.3649
*Schottisch*, Vm.27.10729
*Valse*, Vm.27.10730

F:Pn has additional works by Romain dating after 1900, as well as his arrangement for solo clarinet and military band of the *3me Solo pour Clarinette* by Klosé (Vm.27.2280 bis).

### Rossini, Gioacchino (1792–1868)

*Marches for the Duc d'Orléans*
Military band
EP (Leipzig, 1837) [cited in Grove, XVI, 248]

*Pas redoublé* in C (Milan, 1853)
Military band [cited in Grove, XVI, 248]

*Passo doppio* (1822)
Military band [Lost, according to Grove, XVI, 248]

*La corona d'Italia* in E♭
Military band
MS (fragment, dated Rome, 1878) [source given as 'Fondazione Rossini,' by Grove, XVI, 248]
EP GB:Lbm (h.1549, Ser. 46, Nr. 2)

*Quartetto da Camera* (à Madame Carmen Aguado)
SATB, piano
EP (Paris, Pacini) US:DW (399)
According to Douglas Townsend, this work was originally for SATB with band.

*Harmonie*
201-02
MS CS:Pnm (XIV.E.115)

### Rouquet, Felix

*Marche*
Large wind band
EP (Paris, 1894) F:Pn (Vm.27.3707)

### Roussel, Albert (1869–1937)

*Divertissement*, Op. 6
Piano with wind instruments
EP (Paris, Rouart-Lerolle) [cited in DJ]

*A Glorious Day*
Band
MP (Philadelphia, Elkan-Vogel)

### Roussel, C.

The following works in F:Pn are all early prints for large wind band; all were printed in Paris in 1890–1903.
*Overture,* Vm.27.3711
*Suite chinoise,* Vm.27.3713 [1–4]
Consists of:
1. *Cortége de fête*
2. *Scènes rustiques*
3. *Patroville chinoise*
4. *Sur le Peï-Ho*

*Madrigal,* Vm.27.3710
*Concerto for Trombone,* Vm.27.13251
*Valses:* Vm.27.10752, Vm.27.3708
*Polka,* Vm.27.3712 [two soli cornets]

### Routier, L.

The following works in F:Pn are all early prints for large wind band; all were printed in Paris in 1888–1889.
*Overture,* Vm.27.13252
Pas redoublés: Vm.27.10755, Vm.27.10756, Vm.27.10757

### Rouveirol, F.

*Pas redoublé*
Large wind band
EP (Paris, 1882) F:Pn (Vm.27.10758)

### Rauveirolis, H.

The following works in F:Pn are all early prints for large wind band; all were printed in Paris in 1884–1906.
*Overture,* Vm.27.3719
Marches: Vm.27.3715, Vm.27.3716, Vm.27.10759, Vm.7.14123
*Valse,* Vm.27.3717
*Polka,* Vm.27.10762
In addition there are numerous transcriptions in F:Pn by Rauveirolis, including a *Selection sur le Walkyrie* (Vm.7.16307), based on Wagner.

### Roux, Emile

The following works in F:Pn are all early prints for large wind band; all were printed in Paris in 1891–1900.
*Overture*, Vm.27.10791
Fantaisies: Vm.27.10792, Vm.27.10786, Vm.27.10773
*Le Leverdel'aurore. Andante*, Vm.27.10779
*Chaise à porteurs. Morceau dans le genre ancien*, 40.Vm.15.1018
Marches: Vm.27.10764 bis, Vm.27.10780, Vm.27.3724, Vm.27.10800, Vm.27.10769, Vm.27.10772
*Polka*, Vm.27.3722
In addition there are in F:Pn another thirty or so original works for band, dating after 1900, as well as numerous transcriptions.

### Roux, Jacques

The following works in F:Pn are all early prints for large wind band; all were printed in Paris in 1894–1899.
Overtures: Vm.27.3725, Vm.27.13260, Vm.27.10817, Vm.27.10824
*Aubade*, Vm.27.3727
*Fantaisie*, Vm.27.10807
Marches: Vm.27.10809, Vm.27.3726, Vm.27.10813, Vm.27.10821, Vm.27.10820
*Mazurka*, Vm.27.10806
Valses: Vm.27.10808, Vm.27.10810
Polkas: Vm.27.10814, Vm.27.3728
In addition there are numerous original band works by Roux, dating 1900–1910 in F:Pn.

### Roÿ, Charles de

*Marche*
Large wind band
EP (Paris, 1893) F:Pn (Vm.27.10825)

### Rozan, Charles de

The following works in F:Pn are all early prints for large wind band; all were printed in Paris in 1893–1894.
Work for the Church, Vm.27.3731 (*Invocation*)
*Fantaisie*, Vm.27.3730
Marches: Vm.27.3729, Vm.27.3732, Vm.27.3733

### Rumler, Jean (b. ca. 1780)

*Quintet*, Op. 6
21-02
EP (Gombart) BRD:B; A:Wgm

### Ryembault

The following works in F:Pn are all early prints for large wind band; all were printed in Paris in 1866–1893.
Marche religieux, Vm.27.10843, Vm.27.10844
*Overture*, Vm.27.3740
Fantaisies: Vm.27.10840, Vm.27.3742, Vm.27.3752, Vm.27.13266 (*Le Papillon métamorphose*)
Marches: Vm.27.10848, Vm.27.3750, Vm.27.10837, Vm.27.3745, Vm.27.10838, Vm.27.3746, Vm.27.3743, Vm.27.10835, Vm.27.10846 (*Les Noces de Ouasimodo*), Vm.27.3744, Vm.27.10836, Vm.7.14127, Vm.27.10830, Vm.27.10831, Vm.27.10832, Vm.27.10833, Vm.27.10834, Vm.27.3747, Vm.27.3749, Vm.27.10841, Vm.27.10842, Vm.27.10847, Vm.27.13264, Vm.27.3739, Vm.27.10828, Vm.7.14128, Vm.27.10845
*Boléro*, Vm.27.13267
Quadrilles: Vm.27.3751, Vm.27.3748, Vm.27.10849
Polkas: Vm.27.10839, Vm.27.10829, Vm.27.3741 [solo cornet]
Valses: Vm.27.13265, Vm.27.10826

### Saint-André, A.

The following works in F:Pn are all early prints for large wind band; all were printed in Paris in 1883–1897.
Fantaisies: Vm.27.10854, Vm.7.14131
Marches: Vm.27.10855, Vm.7.14129, Vm.27.10857, Vm.7.14130
*Galop*, Vm.27.10856

### Saint-Saëns, Charles-Camille (1835–1921)

*Orient & Occident grande marche*
Large military band
EP (Paris, 1881) GB:Lbm (h.1509.i.[5]); US:DW (251) [modern revision, www.whitwellbooks.com]

*Caprice sur de air dapois et russes*
1110-; piano
EP (Paris, Durand) [cited by DJ]

*Feuillet d'Album*, Op. 81 [arr. Paul Taffanel, 1844–1908]
1122-02 [original: four-hand piano]
EP (Paris, Durand) BRD:Bhm (6614); US:DW (250)

*Pas redoublé* (1890) [cited by MGG]
*Vers la Victoire*, Pas redoublé (1918) [cited by MGG]
*Marche interalliée* (1918) [cited by MGG]

## Salis, E.

*Marche*
Large military band
EP (Paris, 1894) F:Pn (Vm.27.10872)

## Salomez, Charles

The following works in F:Pn are all early prints for large wind band; all were printed in Paris in 1892–1897.
*Marche*, Vm.27.3786
Polkas: Vm.27.10873, Vm.27.3787

## Sambin, V.

The following works in F:Pn are all early prints for large wind band; all were printed in Paris in 1868–1896.
*Overture*, Vm.27.13274
*Air varié*, Vm.27.13275
Allegros: Vm.27.10889 [with chorus], Vm.27.10903 [with chorus]
Marches: Vm.27.10876, Vm.27.10877, Vm.27.10896, Vm.27.10898, Vm.27.10899, Vm.27.10900, Vm.27.10902, Vm.27.10883, Vm.27.10886, Vm.27.10887, Vm.27.10891 (*Marche religieux*), Vm.27.10892, Vm.27.10893
Polkas: Vm.27.10875, Vm.27.10879, Vm.27.10897
Quadrilles: Vm.27.10878, Vm.27.10895
*Polonaise*, Vm.27.10882
Valses: Vm.27.10885, Vm.27.13277
Boléros: Vm.27.10890, Vm.27.10894

## Sandra, P. A.

The following works in F:Pn are all early prints for large wind band; all were printed in Paris, Montargis, and places not given between 1878–1881.
Fantaisies: Vm.27.10907, Vm.27.10908, Vm.27.10909
*Valse*, Vm.27.10910

## Sarrè, François

The following works in F:Pn are all early prints for large wind band; all were printed in Paris in 1884–1887.
Fantaisies: Vm.27.3796, Vm.27.3797, Vm.27.3798 and Vm.27.3799 [later edition]

## Sarrus, A.

The following works in F:Pn are early prints for large wind band; both were printed in Paris in 1886 and 1893.
Marches: Vm.27.3800, Vm.27.3801

## Sauvagniac, H.

The following works in F:Pn are all early prints for large wind band; all were printed in Paris in 1876–1888.
Fantaisies: Vm.27.10917, Vm.27.3802, Vm.27.13282, Vm.27.10922, Vm.27.10924
Marches: Vm.27.10918, Vm.27.10921, Vm.27.10923
Boléros: Vm.27.10919, Vm.27.10920
*Polka*, Vm.27.13283 and Vm.27.13284 [later edition]

## Sauvan, F., fils

The following works in F:Pn are all early prints for large wind band; all were printed in Paris in 1870–1874.
*Overture*, Vm.27.13285
Marches: Vm.27.10928, Vm.27.10938, Vm.27.10931
Polkas: Vm.27.10937, Vm.27.10929, Vm.27.10932 [solo trombone], Vm.27.10934 .
Quadrilles: Vm.27.10930, Vm.27.10933

## Savari (Chef de Musique au 34e)

The following works in F:Pn are all early prints for large wind band; all were printed in Paris in 1861–1879.

*Octet,* Vm.22.8 [2S, 2A, 2T, 2 E♭ bass saxophones] This work was published in 1861 by Ad. Sax, under plate number 43.

Marches: Vm.27.10939 (*La belle Américaine*), Vm.27.10940, Vm.27.3803

## Schaffner

*Divertissements militaires*
Twelve-part Harmoniemusik
EP (Paris, Dufant et Dubos, ca. 1800–1828) [Liv. 1–2]

*Boléros Sur un Air de Berton fils*
Harmoniemusik
EP (Paris, A. Petit, ca. 1800–1828)

## Schaller

The following works in F:Pn are all early prints for large wind band; all were printed in Paris in 1863–1875.

Marches: Vm.27.10942, Vm.7.14138, Vm.7.14137, Vm.27.3806, Vm.27.3805, Vm.27.3802 (?) [cataloged as Vm.27.4802], Vm.27.10943

*Galop,* Vm.27.3804
*Valse,* Vm.27.3808
Polkas: Vm.27.3807, Vm.7.14139

## Schaller, J.

The following works in F:Pn are early prints for large wind band; both were printed in Paris in ca. 1867.

*Overture,* Vm.27.3809 and Vm.7.12983 [two copies]
*Marche,* Vm.27.3810

## Schepper, L.-J. de

Overtures: Vm.27.10944 (*Petite Overture symphonique*), Vm.27.10948 (*Petite Overture symphonique*), Vm.27.10946 (*Overture symphonique*)
Fantaisies: Vm.27.3811, Vm.27.13287
Marches: Vm.27.3812, Vm.27.10950

## Schiltz

The following works in F:Pn are all early prints for large wind band; all were printed in Paris in 1858.

Marches: Vm.27.10955, Vm.27.10957 (*Marche funèbre*), Vm.27.10959, Vm.27.10961

## Schmidt, Henri

*Marche*
Large military band
EP (Paris, 1897) F:Pn (Vm.27.10964)

## Schmitt, N.

*Airs italiens*
Harmoniemusik
EP (Paris, Pleyel, ca. 1800–1828)

*Marches et Pas redoublés*
Twelve-part Harmoniemusik
EP (Paris, Pleyel, ca. 1800–1828)

## Schneider, Louis

The following works in F:Pn are all early prints for large wind band; all were printed in Paris in 1862–1867.

Cavatines: Vm.27.10977, Vm.27.10975
*Air varié,* Vm.27.10978
Marches: Vm.27.10968, Vm.27.10969, Vm.27.10970, Vm.27.10973, Vm.27.10971, Vm.27.10979, Vm.27.10980
Polkas: Vm.27.10976, Vm.7.14141
*Valse,* Vm.27.10972

## Schneklud, Ad.

*Gavotte*
Large military band
EP (Paris, 1893) F:Pn (Vm.27.13290)

## Schrammel, J.

*Marche*
Large military band
EP (Paris, 1895) F:Pn (Vm.27.I0982)

### Schubert, Raoul

The following works in F:Pn are early prints for large wind band; both were printed in Paris in 1885 and 1892.
Marches: Vm.27.3820, Vm.27.10983

### Schultz, Th.

The following works in F:Pn are all early prints for large wind band; all were printed in Paris in 1875–1898.
(5) *Movements d'ensemble*, Vm.27.10986 [dance movements]
Marches: Vm.7.14144, Vm.27.3821, Vm.27.10984 [set of ten], Vm.27.10985
*Galop*, Vm.27.13292
*Polka*, Vm.7.14148

### Schwarer, Ph.

*Marche*
Large wind band
EP (Paris, 1872) F:Pn (Vm.27.10992)

### Schwartz

*Marche*
Large wind band with chorus
EP (Paris, 1885) F:Pn (Vm.27.10987)

### Schwartz, Ad.

The following works in F:Pn are all early prints for large wind band; all were printed in Paris in 1877–1895.
Marches: Vm.27.10990, Vm.7.14151
*Fandango*, Vm.7.14153
*Mazurka*, Vm.7.14152

### Schwartz, K.

*Schottisch*
Large wind band
EP (Paris, 1868) F:Pn (Vm.27.3829)

### Schweska, H.

*Polka*
Large wind band
EP (Paris, 1881) F:Pn (Vm.27.10991)

### Sciers, Dominique

The following works in F:Pn are all early prints for large wind band; all were printed in Paris in 1882–1884.
*Fantaisie*, Vm.27.3830
Marches: Vm.27.10994, Vm.27.10995
*Schottisch*, Vm.27.10993
*Polka*, Vm.27.10997
*Mazurka*, Vm.27.10998

### Scrépel, Carlos

*Marche*
Large wind band
EP (Paris, 1862) F:Pn (Vm.21.11008)

### Sega, A.

The following works in F:Pn are early prints for large wind band; both were printed in Paris in 1890 and 1906
*Télégraphe et téléphone. Allegro de concert*, Vm.27.3833
*Polka*, Vm.27.3832

### Seghers, Frédéic

The following works in F:Pn are all early prints for large wind band; all were printed in Paris in 1878–1890.
Marches: Vm.27.11010, Vm.27.3834, Vm.27.11015, Vm.27.11016
Polkas: Vm.27.11011, Vm.27.11014

### Sellenik, Ad. (Chef de Musique 2e Regiment de Voltigeurs de la Garde Imperiale)

The following works in F:Pn are all early prints for large wind band; all were printed in Paris in 1858–1890.
Works for the Church: Vm.27.11035 (*Rêverie*), Vm.7.14186 (*Hamlet. Marche funèbre*), Vm.7.14185 (*Marche funèbre*), Vm.27.3839 (*Ländler. Morceau de repos*), Vm.7.14187 and Vm.27.3842 [later edition] (*Marche funèbre*)
Symphonies: Vm.7.14158 (*Symphonie episodique en trios parties*), Vm.27.11036 (*Symphonie dramatique*)

Under Vm.7.14158 one finds only two of the three movements mentioned in the title. The work seems long, programmatic and very good. The titles of the three parts are:
Pt. I *Scène champêtre*
Pt. II *Rêve et Apparition*
Pt. III *Réalisation du Rêve*
  *Marche Triomphale (Rentrée en France)*
  *Air Espagnol (Fiançailles)*
  *Berceuse (Narssance)*
  *Actions de Grâces*

Under Vm.27.11036 one finds another long programatic work, with the program given in prose form at the beginning of the condensed score.

*Scène de chasse*, Vm.27.3837
*Chant alsacien*, Vm.27.13297 and Vm.27.13298 [two copies]
Fantaisies: Vm.27.3844, Vm.7.14155, Vm.27.3846 and Vm.27.11028 [two copies]
Marches: Vm.27.11029, Vm.27.11030, Vm.7.14233, Vm.7.14189 Vm.7.14165, Vm.7.14188, Vm.27.2859, Vm.27.3854, Vm.27.3855 and Vm.7.14198 [later edition], Vm.27.3856, Vm.7.14162, Vm.7.14161, Vm.7.14176, Vm.7.14179, Vm.27.3853, Vm.7.14178, Vm.7.14180, Vm.7.14181, Vm.27.3848, Vm.7.14191, Vm.7.14170, Vm.27.11027, Vm.27.3841, Vm.7.14168, Vm.7.14172, Vm.7.14194, Vm.7.14197, Vm.27.11031, Vm.27.11032 and Vm.7.14192 [two copies], Vm.7.14166, Vm.27.3838 and Vm.7.14167 [two copies], Vm.27.11026, Vm.7.14193 and Vm.27.11034 [later edition], Vm.7.14195, Vm.7.14174, Vm.7.14175, Vm.27.3857, Vm.7.14182 and Vm.7.14183 [later edition], Vm.27.3858
Valses: Vm.7.14221, Vm.7.14222, Vm.7.14223, Vm.7.1422, Vm.7.14163, Vm.7.14224, Vm.7.14217 [solo oboe], Vm.7.14219
Mazurkas: Vm.7.14201, Vm.7.14200 [solo cornet], Vm.7.14164, Vm.7.14202
Polkas: Vm.7.14211 [solo cornet], Vm.27.3840, Vm.7.14210, Vm.7.14205 (solo piccolo), Vm.7.14207, Vm.27.13300, Vm.7.14214, Vm.7.14216 [soli oboe and piccolo], Vm.7.14203 [solo cornet], Vm.7.14204, Vm.27.11024, Vm.7.14208 [solo cornet], Vm.27.3845 [solo cornet], Vm.7.14209
*Galop*, Vm.27.13299
*Boléro*, Vm.7.14156 [solo horn]

### Selter, H.

*Pas redoublé*
Large wind band
EP (Paris, 1882) F:Pn (Vm.27.11037)

### Senée, Henri

The following works in F:Pn are all early prints for large wind band; all were printed in Paris in 1885–1898.
Fantaisies: Vm.27.3864, Vm.27.11053
*Divertissement*, Vm.27.11040 [solo cornet]
(Introduction, Act IV of) *Le Fils de Porthos*, Vm.27.13301
*Les Gloires de Lyon*, Vm.27.13302
*Coast à l'Alsace*, Vm.27.13305
*Toccata-Polka-Caprice*, Vm.27.11049 [solo cornet]
Marches: Vm.27.11039, Vm.27.11043, Vm.27.11046, Vm.27.11047, Vm.27.11050, Vm.27.11051, Vm.27.11052
*Polka*, Vm.27.11042
*Schottisch*, Vm.27.13304
*Valse*, Vm.27.11048

### Serfert, A.

*Polka*
Large wind band
EP (Paris, 1879) F:Pn (Vm.27.11019)

### Serpette, Gaston

*Marche*
Large wind band
EP (Paris, 1879) F:Pn (Vm.27.11054)

### Sévérény, H.-A.

The following works in F:Pn are early prints for large wind band; both were printed in Paris in 1889 and 1898.
*Marche*, Vm.27.3868
*Polka*, Vm.27.3869 [solo piccolo]

## Sibillot, Charles

The following works in F:Pn are all early prints for large wind band; all were printed in Paris in 1884.
Marches: Vm.27.3871, Vm.27.3872, Vm.7.14235, Vm.27.3874, Vm.7.14236 (*La Marseillaise*)
*Polka*, Vm.27.3875
*Mazurka*, Vm.27.3876
*Quadrille*, Vm.27.3873

## Siégrist

The following works in F:Pn are all early prints for large wind band; all were printed in Paris in 1883–1885.
*Fantaisie*, Vm.27.11062
Marches: Vm.27.11060 and Vm.27.11061 [two copies], Vm.27.11063
*Polka*, Vm.7.14238

## Signard

The following works in F:Pn are all early prints for large wind band; all were printed in Paris in 1873–1896.
(Collection) *Album-Omnibus* [15 short works], Vm.7.17391
Works for the Church: Vm.27.3894 (*Larghetto*), Vm.27.3897 (*Marche funèbre*), Vm.27.3896 (*Marche funèbre*), Vm.7.14256
*Air varié*, Vm.27.11076
*Cavatine*, Vm.27.3884
*Fantaisie*, Vm.27.12781
Marches: Vm.7.14262, Vm.27.3895, Vm.27.11075, Vm.7.14261, Vm.27.3891, Vm.27.11077, Vm.27.11078, Vm.27.3880, Vm.27.3881, Vm.7.14257, Vm.27.3882, Vm.7.14258, Vm.27.3883, Vm.27.3908, Vm.27.3909, Vm.27.11091, Vm.27.11088, Vm.7.14266, Vm.7.14267, Vm.7.14268, Vm.27.3906, Vm.27.3903, Vm.27.3904, Vm.7.14265, Vm.27.13310, Vm.27.3898, Vm.7.14263, Vm.27.3899, Vm.27.3900, Vm.27.3901, Vm.27.11083, Vm.7.14260, Vm.7.14260 bis, Vm.27.11072, Vm.27.11071, Vm.27.3885, Vm.27.3887, Vm.27.3888
Polkas: Vm.27.3892, Vm.27.3886, Vm.27.11092 [soli musette and oboe], Vm.7.14269 [solo musette], Vm.27.11086, Vm.27.3905
Quadrilles: Vm.27.3893, Vm.27.3902
Mazurkas: Vm.27.3907, Vm.27.11074
Valses: Vm.27.11084, Vm.27.13309
*Boléro*, Vm.27.11085

## Signard, P.

*Marche*
Large wind band
EP (Paris, 1900) F:Pn (Vm.27.3889)

## Simiot, André

The following works in F:Pn are all early prints for large wind band; all were printed in Paris in 1868–1882.
Overtures: Vm.27.13311, Vm.27.3910
Marches: Vm.27.11099, Vm.7.14271

## Simon, Anton (b. 1851)

(22) *Ensemble works for winds* [Grove, Fifth Edition, cites 4 Septets, 4 Sextets, 6 Quintets, and 8 Quartets]

## Sinoquet, E.

The following works in F:Pn are all early prints for large wind band; all were printed in Paris in 1861–1885.
Works for the Church: Vm.27.11126 (*Marche funèbre*), Vm.27.11160 (*Messe de Sainte Cécile*)
Overtures: Vm.27.13317, Vm.27.3912, Vm.27.13315, Vm.27.13313, Vm.27.13314
Fantaisies: Vm.27.11117, Vm.27.11121, Vm.27.11135, Vm.27.11148
Airs varié: Vm.27.11173, Vm.27.11176
*Les Clarions de la liberté*, Vm.27.11118
*Le Concert dans les Bois. Duo poetique*, Vm.27.11119 and Vm.27.13312 [later edition]
*Le Départ. Chant National*, Vm.27.11125
Marches: Vm.27.11123, Vm.27.11124, Vm.27.11128, Vm.27.11129, Vm.27.11132, Vm.27.11133, Vm.27.11141 and Vm.27.11142 [later edition], Vm.27.11147, Vm.27.11178

bis, Vm.27.11182, Vm.27.11169, Vm.27.11151,
Vm.27.11156, Vm.27.11157, Vm.27.11103,
Vm.27.11105

Quadrilles: Vm.27.11120, Vm.27.11122,
Vm.27.11112, Vm.27.11113, Vm.27.11114,
Vm.27.11115, Vm.27.11116, Vm.27.11137,
Vm.27.11139, Vm.27.11140, Vm.27.11145,
Vm.27.11149, Vm.27.11150 [two copies],
Vm.27.11174, Vm.27.11178, Vm.27.11180,
Vm.27.11183, Vm.27.11161, Vm.27.11162,
Vm.27.11170, Vm.27.11171, Vm.27.11172,
Vm.27.11152, Vm.27.11155, Vm.27.11101,
Vm.27.11111

Polkas: Vm.27.11127, Vm.27.11104, Vm.27.11138,
Vm.27.11143, Vm.27.11144, Vm.27.11146,
Vm.27.11153, Vm.27.11154, Vm.27.11109

Mazurkas: Vm.27.11131, Vm.27.11134,
Vm.27.11107

Valses: Vm.27.11102, Vm.27.11110, Vm.27.11168,
Vm.27.11177

Schottisches: Vm.27.11136, Vm.27.11106,
Vm.27.11108

In addition there are numerous transcriptions by Sinoquet in F:Pn.

### Sinsoilliez, Adolpbe

(10) *Morceau faciles*
Large wind band
EP (Paris, 1861) F:Pn (Vm.27.3915 [1–10])

### Sohier

The following works in F:Pn are all early prints for large wind band; all were printed in Paris in 1865–1872.
Marches: Vm.7.14294, Vm.7.14295, Vm.7.14296, Vm.7.14297
*Valse*, Ym.27.3919

### Sohier, Henry

The following works in F:Pn are all early prints for large wind band; all were printed in Paris in 1863–1889
*Il y avait une fois*, Vm.27.3924
Fantaisies: Vm.27.3925, Vm.27.3929
Marches: Vm.27.11193, Vm.27.3926, Vm.27.3927, Vm.27.11197, Vm.27.11198
*Polka*, Vm.27.11195

### Solère

*Chant de la Bataille d'Austerlitz*
Thirteen-part Harmoniemusik
EP (Paris, Janet) F:Pn (Vm.27.3931)

*Marche militaire*
Ten-part Harmoniemusik
EP (Paris, Janet, ca. 1800–1828)

*Pas redoublé*
Twelve-part Harmoniemusik
EP (Paris, Janet, ca. 1800–1828)

The following works in F:Pn are early prints for wind band; both were printed in Paris during the nineteenth century
(3) *Marches*: Vm.27.3932 [1–3]
(6) *Marches*: Vm.27.3933 [1–6]

### Sombrun, Alexis

The following works in F:Pn are early prints for large wind band; both were printed in Paris in 1892.
*Marche*, Vm.27.3940
*Polka*, Vm.27.3939

### Souyeux, E.

*Marche*
Large wind band
EP (Paris, 1889) F:Pn (Vm.27.11206)

### Soyer, Adolphe (Chef de Musique, 109e de Ligne)

The following works in F:Pn are all early prints for large wind band; all were printed in Paris in 1885–1900.
*Symphonie brève in Fa mineur*, Vm.27.3969
This is a very interesting one movement work, much of it fugal and contrapuntal in character. It is scored for large band with saxophones.

*Overture*, Vm.27.11225
*Fantaisie*, Vm.27.11213
Marches: Vm.7.14303, Vm.27.3948, Vm.27.3957, Vm.27.11207 bis, Vm.27.11208, Vm.27.3958, Vm.27.13325, Vm.27.3960, Vm.27.11219, Vm.27.3962, Vm.27.3964, Vm.27.11223, Vm.27.3966 (*Marche solennelle*), Vm.27.3967

Polkas: Vm.27.11210 [solo cornet], Vm.27.3970
*Boléro*, Vm.27.13327
*Valse*, Vm.27.11209

### Stappen, A.

The following works in F:Pn are all early prints for large wind band; all were printed in Paris in 1869–1874.
*Marche*, Vm.27.3979
*Galop*, Vm.27.3978
*Polka*, Vm.27.11232

### Sténosse, Ed.

The following works in F:Pn are all early prints for large wind band; all were printed in Paris in 1883–1892.
*Marche*, Vm.27.11242
Polkas: Vm.27.11241, Vm.27.3985 [solo piccolo]

### Stoupan, F.

The following works in F:Pn are all early prints for large wind band; all were printed in Paris in 1895–1899.
*Overture*, Vm.27.3994
Marches: Vm.27.11243, Vm.27.3987, Vm.27.11248, Vm.27.11253, Vm.27.11260, Vm.27.11270, Vm.27.11272
Polkas: Vm.27.11246, Vm.27.3996
Valses: Vm.27.11254, Vm.27.11257, Vm.27.3993
*Galop*, Vm.27.11259
In addition there is in F:Pn an arrangement by Stoupan of the Beethoven *Quintet,* Op. 16, for piano and winds, for full band under Fol. Vm.25.577, together with another forty or so original works dating after 1900.

### Stupfler, Ph.

*Polka*
Large wind band
EP (Paris, 1870) F:Pn (Vm.27.11298)

### Sudessi, P.

The following works in F:Pn are early prints for large wind band; both were printed in Paris in 1894.

*Marche*, Vm.27.11300
*Nuit chantante mandolinata*, Vm.27.13337

### Sudre

The following works in F:Pn are early prints for large wind band; both were printed in Paris in 1883 and 1885.
*Fantaisie*, Vm.27.11301
*Pas redoublé*, Vm.27.11303

### Suzanne, Marius

The following works in F:Pn are all early prints for large wind band; all were printed in Paris in 1883–1893.
Fantaisies: Vm.27.4025, Vm.27.4026
Marches: Vm.27.4029, Vm.27.11306, Vm.27.11307, Vm.7.14311, Vm.27.4030, Vm.27.11308, Vm.27.4031
Polkas: Vm.27.4027, Vm.27.11305, Vm.7.14312, Vm.7.14309, Vm.7.14310

### Teissier, A.

The following works in F:Pn are all early prints for large wind band; all were printed in Paris in 1893–1894.
Fantaisies: Vm.27.4059, Vm.27.4057
Marches: Vm.27.4049, Vm.27.4053, Vm.27.4054, Vm.27.11326
*Schottisch*, Vm.27.4050
Quadrilles: Vm.27.4051, Vm.27.4058
*Valse*, Vm.27.4052
*Polka*, Vm.27.4055
*Mazurka*, Vm.27.4056

### Théret, G.

The following works in F:Pn are all early prints for large wind band; all were printed in Paris in 1892–1897.
*Marche*, Vm.27.4065
Valses: Vm.27.4066, Vm.27.4067

### Thiabot, Victor

The following works in F:Pn are early prints for large wind band; both were printed in Paris in 1892 and 1898.
Marches: Vm.27.11339, Vm.27.4072

## Thomas, J.

*Polka*
Large wind band
EP (Paris, 1876) F:Pn (Vm.27.11351)

## Thomas, P.

*Marche*
Large wind band
EP (Paris, F:Pn (Vm.27.4088 and Vm.27.11353)
[two copies]

## Tilliard, Georges

The following works in F:Pn are all early prints for large wind band; all were printed in Paris in 1862–1900.

Works for the Church: Vm.27.11777 (*Andante*), Vm.27.11825 (*Marche religieuse*), Vm.27.11456 (*Andante*), Vm.27.11855 (*Hymne à Sainte-Cécile*), Vm.27.11564 (*Marche funèbre*), Vm.27.11566 (*Andante. L'Invocation*), Vm.27.11638 (*Mélodie religieuse*), Vm.27.11687 (*Andante pour Élévation*), Vm.27.11905 (*Marche funèbre*), Vm.27.11918 (*Marche solonnelle*)

Overtures: Vm.27.13349, Vm.27.13351, Vm.27.13352, Vm.27.4102, Vm.27.13353, Vm.27.13366, Vm.27.13365, Vm.27.13356, Vm.27.13358, Vm.27.13359, Vm.27.13362, Vm.27.13363, Vm.27.13367, Vm.27.11688, Vm.27.11916, Vm.27.11746, Vm.27.11750, Vm.27.11757

Fantaisies: Vm.27.11769, Vm.27.11361, Vm.27.111364, Vm.27.4101, Vm.27.11372, Vm.27.11378, Vm.27.11389, Vm.27.13350, Vm.27.11787, Vm.27.11796, Vm.27.11797, Vm.27.11819, Vm.27.11528, Vm.27.11832, Vm.27.11452 (*Fantaisie-pastorale*), Vm.27.11804, Vm.27.11807, Vm.27.13354, Vm.27.11467, Vm.27.11836, Vm.27.11838, Vm.27.11852, Vm.27.11571, Vm.27.11574, Vm.27.11575, Vm.27.11581, Vm.27.11598, Vm.27.11599, Vm.27.11870, Vm.27.13361, Vm.27.11876, Vm.27.11607, Vm.27.11887, Vm.27.11651, Vm.27.11892, Vm.27.11893, Vm.27.11663, Vm.27.11683, Vm.27.11686, Vm.21.11906, Vm.27.4106, Vm.27.11696, Vm.27.11708, Vm.21.11714, Vm.27.11922, Vm.27.11923, Vm.27.11724, Vm.27.11737, Vm.27.11937, Vm.27.11942, Vm.27.11759, Vm.21.11767

Airs varié: Vm.27.11135, Vm.27.11362, Vm.27.11442 [solo cornet], Vm.27.11685, Vm.27.11827, Vm.21.11829, Vm.27.11803, Vm.27.11833, Vm.27.11872, Vm.27.11873, Vm.27.11897, Vm.27.11743, Vm.21.11936, Vm.27.11934

Marches: Vm.27.11356, Vm.27.11357, Vm.27.11367, Vm.27.11369, Vm.21.11370, Vm.27.11376, Vm.27.11773, Vm.27.11379, Vm.27.11380, Vm.27.11382, Vm.27.11383, Vm.27.11775, Vm.27.11386, Vm.27.11387, Vm.27.11778, Vm.27.11391, Vm.27.11393, Vm.27.11396, Vm.27.11397, Vm.27.11781, Vm.27.11782, Vm.27.11406, Vm.27.11410, Vm.27.11784, Vm.27.11785, Vm.27.11421, Vm.27.11786, Vm.27.11422, Vm.27.11424, Vm.27.11789, Vm.27.11791, Vm.27.11793, Vm.27.11794, Vm.27.11435, Vm.27.11436, Vm.27.11437, Vm.27.11446, Vm.27.11801, Vm.27.11447, Vm.27.11449, Vm.27.11820, Vm.27.11527, Vm.27.11828, Vm.27.11532, Vm.21.11455, Vm.27.11805, Vm.27.11465, Vm.21.11466, Vm.27.11469, Vm.27.11535, Vm.27.11538, Vm.27.11839, Vm.27.11840, Vm.27.11543, Vm.27.11546, Vm.27.11843, Vm.21.11845, Vm.21.11552, Vm.27.11848, Vm.27.11849, Vm.21.11850, Vm.27.11853, Vm.27.11854, Vm.27.11567, Vm.27.11569, Vm.21.11579, Vm.27.11860, Vm.27.11582, Vm.27.11862, Vm.27.11583, Vm.21.11586, Vm.27.11589, Vm.27.11866, Vm.27.11602, Vm.27.11871, Vm.27.11605, Vm.27.11815, Vm.27.11606, Vm.27.11878, Vm.27.11610, Vm.27.11879, Vm.27.11881, Vm.27.11616, Vm.27.11617, Vm.27.11882, Vm.27.11618, Vm.21.11619, Vm.27.11885, Vm.27.11886 (*Allegro oriental*), Vm.27.11628, Vm.27.11629, Vm.27.11632, Vm.27.4105, Vm.21.11633, Vm.27.11888, Vm.27.11634, Vm.21.11890, Vm.27.11641, Vm.21.1189, Vm.27.11650, Vm.27.11656, Vm.27.11660, Vm.27.11665, Vm.27.11666, Vm.27.11668, Vm.27.11669, Vm.27.11670, Vm.27.11674, Vm.27.11675, Vm.27.11901, Vm.27.11643, Vm.27.11644, Vm.27.11646, Vm.27.11684, Vm.27.11903,

Vm.27.11902, Vm.27.11904, Vm.27.11691,
Vm.27.11692, Vm.27.11908, Vm.27.11910,
Vm.27.11909, Vm.27.11693, Vm.27.11694,
Vm.27.11911, Vm.27.11912, Vm.27.11699,
Vm.27.11917, Vm.27.11705, Vm.27.11919,
Vm.27.11710, Vm.27.11712, Vm.27.11920,
Vm.27.11720, Vm.27.11723, Vm.27.11726,
Vm.27.11728, Vm.27.11927, Vm.27.11928,
Vm.27.11930, Vm.27.11732, Vm.27.11733,
Vm.27.4107, Vm.27.11932, Vm.27.11734,
Vm.27.11938, Vm.27.11739, Vm.27.11939,
Vm.27.11941, Vm.27.11747, Vm.27.11749,
Vm.27.11751, Vm.27.11943, Vm.27.11755,
Vm.27.11758, Vm.27.11760, Vm.27.11945,
Vm.27.11762, Vm.27.11763, Vm.27.11765,
Vm.27.11766

Quadrilles: Vm.27.11768, Vm.27.11368,
Vm.27.11403, Vm.27.11783, Vm.27.11416,
Vm.27.11420, Vm.27.11423, Vm.27.11799,
Vm.27.11802, Vm.27.11806, Vm.27.11462,
Vm.27.11537, Vm.27.11570, Vm.27.11859,
Vm.27.11577, Vm.27.11877, Vm.27.11614,
Vm.27.11615, Vm.27.11676, Vm.27.11903,
Vm.27.11921

Polkas: Vm.27.11770, Vm.27.11772, Vm.27.11774,
Vm.27.11381, Vm.27.11390, Vm.27.11394,
Vm.27.11401, Vm.27.11407, Vm.27.11415,
Vm.27.11417, Vm.27.11790, Vm.27.11426,
Vm.27.11471 [solo cornet], Vm.27.11831,
Vm.27.11541, Vm.27.11544, Vm.27.11844,
Vm.27.11851, Vm.27.11858, Vm.27.11869,
Vm.27.11880, Vm.27.11883, Vm.27.11884,
Vm.27.11626, Vm.27.11657, Vm.27.11894,
Vm.27.11898, Vm.27.11899, Vm.27.11673,
Vm.27.11902, Vm.27.11913, Vm.27.11718,
Vm.27.11933, Vm.27.11935, Vm.27.11944

Schottisches: Vm.27.11377, Vm.27.11780,
Vm.27.11800, Vm.27.11524, Vm.27.11842,
Vm.27.11649, Vm.27.11658, Vm.27.11715,
Vm.27.11926

Valses: Vm.27.11795, Vm.27.11431, Vm.27.11534,
Vm.27.11888, Vm.27.11808, Vm.27.11834,
Vm.27.11542, Vm.27.11847, Vm.27.13360,
Vm.27.11648, Vm.27.11664, Vm.27.11896,
Vm.27.11682, Vm.27.11914, Vm.27.11925,
Vm.27.11725, Vm.27.11929, Vm.27.11931,
Vm.27.11940

Boléros: Vm.27.11439, Vm.27.11440, Vm.27.11526

Galops: Vm.27.13355, Vm.27.13357,
Vm.27.13364, Vm.27.13368
Polonaises: Vm.27.11748, Vm.27.11672
*Mazurka*, Vm.27.11536
*Tyrolieme*, Vm.27.11889
*Une Réunion de solistes*, Vm.27.11738
*La Plage d'Ostende*, Vm.27.11895
There are in addition some 350 arrangements and transcriptions in F:Pn by Tilliard.

### Tinet, Charles

The following works in F:Pn are all early prints for large wind band; all were printed in Paris in 1892–1895.
Marches: Vm.27.11949, Vm.27.11950, Vm.27.13369, Vm.27.11951 (*Marche-orientale, execute au Palais del'Industrie pendant les Expositions de 1894*)

### Tollet, A.-E.

The following works in F:Pn are all early prints for large wind band; all were printed in Paris in 1884–1885.
Marches: Vm.27.11954, Vm.27.11955, Vm.27.11956

### Tollet, Edouard

The following works in F:Pn are all early prints for large wind band; all were printed in Paris in 1852–1889.
Fantaisies: Vm.27.11958, Vm.27.11959
*Air varié*, Vm.27.13370
Marches: Vm.27.11960 (*Marche-funèbre*),
Vm.27.11961, Vm.27.11962, Vm.27.11963,
Vm.27.11964, Vm.27.11965, Vm.27.11969,
Vm.27.4117, Vm.27.11970, Vm.27.11972,
Vm.27.11974, Vm.27.11975, Vm.27.11976,
Vm.27.11978, Vm.27.11981, Vm.27.11980
*Mazurka*, Vm.27.11957
Polkas: Vm.27.13371, Vm.27.11973
*Valse*, Vm.27.11966
*Quadrille*, Vm.27.11971

## Tourey, Charles

The following works in F:Pn are all early prints for large wind band; all were printed in Paris in 1867–1900.
Work for the Church: Vm.27.4118 (*Méditations*)
Grande Fantaisies dramatiques, Vm.27.11983, Vm.27.11986
Marches: Vm.7.14317, Vm.27.11985, Vm.27.11987, Vm.27.11999, Vm.27.4119, Vm.27.11989 and Vm.27.11990 [later edition]

## Tourneur, L.

The following works in F:Pn are all early prints for large wind band; all were printed in Paris in 1878–1899.
*Overture*, Vm.7.14318
Fantaisies: Vm.27.11993, Vm.27.11996, Vm.27.11997
Marches: Vm.7.14319, Vm.27.4121, Vm.27.12004
Polkas: Vm.27.4120, Vm.27.11994 [with chorus], Vm.27.12000, Vm.27.12003 (*Polka comique*)
*Galop,* Vm.27.12001

## Trave, D.

The following works in F:Pn are all early prints for large wind band; all were printed in Paris in 1894–1900.
Marches: Vm.27.12009, Vm.27.12010, Vm.27.4133, Vm.27.4134

## Tréfouel, E.

*Marche*
Large wind band
EP (Paris, 1896) F:Pn (Vm.27.12015)

## Trefz, V.

*Polka*
Large wind band
EP (Paris, 1895) F:Pn (Vm.27.12016)

## Trottier, A.

*Marche*
Large wind band
EP (Paris, 1884) F:Pn (Vm.27.12024)

## Trousseau, Charles

The following works in F:Pn are all early prints for large wind band; both were printed in Paris in 1869.
*Varioviana*, Vm.27.12026
*Valse*, Vm.27.12027

## Truelove, J.

*Marche*
Large wind band
EP (Paris, 1863) F:Pn (Vm.27.12028)

## Trusson, A.

The following works in F:Pn are early prints for large wind band; both were printed in Paris in 1880 and 1882.
*Marche*, Vm.27.12029
*Valse*, Vm.27.12030

## Tual, Théophile

*Marche*
Large wind band
EP (Paris, 1894) F:Pn (Vm.27.12031)

## Tulon

*Fantaisie*
Solo clarinet with Harmonie
EP (Paris, Pacini, ca. 1800–1828)

## Turine, V.

The following works in F:Pn are all early prints for large wind band; all were printed in Paris in 1891–1900.
Overtures: Vm.27.12035, Vm.27.4149
*Fantaisie*, Vm.27.12038
*Marche*, Vm.27.12033
*Bluette*, Vm.27.12040

## Unrath

*Polka*
Large wind band
EP (Paris, 1865) F:Pn (Vm.27.12042)

## Vaillant

*Air suedois avec Variations*
Eight-part Harmoniemusik
EP (Paris, A. Petit, ca. 1800–1828)

*Pas redoublé en Canon sur 3 Marceaux d'Aline*
Military band
EP (Paris, Dufaut et Dubois, ca. 1800–1828)

## Valenti, A.

*Marche*
Large wind band
EP (Paris, 1875) F:Pn (Vm.27.12043)

## Valentin, Léon

The following works in F:Pn are all early prints for large wind band; all were printed in Paris in 1867–1895.
Marches: Vm.27.4157, Vm.27.4158 [later edition], Vm.7.14330, Vm.27.4160, Vm.27.4161 (*Trompettes de Jéricho*)
Polkas: Vm.27.4159, Vm.7.14331, Vm.7.14333
*Galop*, Vm.27.4162
*Mazurka*, Vm.27.4807

## Van Berghe, Carl

The following works in F:Pn are early prints for large wind band; both were printed in Paris in 1898 and 1899.
*Andante religieux*, Vm.27.13389
*Marche*, Vm.27.12053

## Van Buggenhout, Ed.

*Galop*
Large wind band
EP (Paris, late nineteenth century) F:Pn (Vm.27.13390)

## Van Campenhout, François

The following works in F:Pn are early prints for large wind band; both were printed in Paris in ca. 1878.
*Marche*, Vm.27.5198
[Collection], Vm.27.7305[1]
 Here only the first of the works of this collection is extant.

## Vanremoortel

The following works in F:Pn are all early prints for large wind band; all were printed in Paris in 1881–1894.
*Air varié*, Vm.27.4178
Marches: Vm.27.4179, Vm.27.4180 [later edition], Vm.27.4181, Vm.27.4182

## Vanremoortel, A.

*Polka*
Large wind band [solo cornet]
EP (Paris, 1887) F:Pn (Vm.27.4183)

## Vanremoortel, Michel

The following works in F:Pn are early prints for large wind band; both were printed in Paris in 1880.
*Overture*, Vm.27.4185
*Fantaisie*, Vm.27.4184

## Van Wedingen, J.

*Overture*
Large wind band
EP (Paris, nineteenth century) F:Pn (Vm.27.4808)

## Varlet, A.

*Marche*
Large wind band
EP (Paris, 1868) F:Pn (Vm.27.12156)

## Vasseillière, fils

The following works in F:Pn are all early prints for large wind band; all were printed in Paris in 1859–1867.
Works for the Church: Vm.27.12157 (*Andante pour Élévation*), Vm.27.12059 (*Andante pour Élévation*), Vm.27.12060 (*Marche pour offertoire*), Vm.27.12061 (*Marche pour offertoire*), Vm.27.12062 (*Andante religieux*)
Marches: Vm.27.12063, Vm.27.12064, Vm.27.12066, Vm.27.12071, Vm.27.12073
*Quadrille*, Vm.21.12070
*Valse*, Vm.27.12069
*Schottisch*, Vm.27.12065
Polkas: Vm.27 .12067, Vm.27.12068

### Verbregge, Auguste

The following works in F:Pn are all early prints for large wind band; all were printed in Paris in 1894–1899.
*Overture*, Vm.27.4202
Marches: Vm.27.12076, Vm.27.12077, Vm.27.4201

### Verdier, J.

The following works in F:Pn are all early prints for large wind band; all were printed in Paris in 1877–1893.
*Marche*, Vm.27.12082
Polkas: Vm.27.4219, Vm.27.13393 [solo cornet] Vm.27.4220

### Verleye

*Marche*
Large wind band
EP (Paris, 1880) F:Pn (Vm.27.12085)

### Vern

*Nocturne en Harmonie*
Eight and twelve-part Harmoniemusik
EP (Paris, Dufaut et Dubois; Janet; and Leipzig, Breitkopf & Härtel, ca. 1800–1828)

### Vernazobres, C. Z.

*Hymne*
Large wind band [with chorus]
EP (Paris, 1884) F:Pn (Vm.27.13394)

### Vernet, H.

*Polka*
Large wind band
EP (Paris, 1878) F:Pn (Vm.27.12089)

### Viallon, Justinien (Prof. de composition de l'ex-gymnase musical militaire et du college de Vaugirard)

The following works in F:Pn are all early prints for large wind band; all were printed in Paris in 1856–1870.
*Choeur facile a trois yoix*, Vm.7.14338, A work for TTB (and ad. lib. S) chorus, for large band, without saxophones. The text is political in nature.
*Fantaisie*, Vm.7.14339
*Marche*, Vm.27.12092
*Valse*, Vm.7.14340
Vaudevilles: Vm.27.4230, Vm.7.14337 [two copies]
*Quadrille*, Vm.27.12091

### Vidal, H.

The following works in F:Pn are all early prints for large wind band; all were printed in Paris in 1891–1896.
Marches: Vm.27.12095, Vm.27.4239 (*Marche nuptiale*), Vm.27.4240 and Vm.27.4241 [later edition]

### Vidal, Paul

The following works in F:Pn are all early prints for large wind band; all were printed in Paris in 1885–1894.
Marches: Vm.27.4249, Vm.27.4250
*Danse collection* [12 works], Vm.27.13395
*Valse*, Vm.27.12105
*Polka*, Vm.27.4252
*Polonaise de Concert*, Vm.27.4246
In addition there are approximately twenty original works dated after 1900 by Vidal in F:Pn.

### Videix, Paul

*Marche*
Large wind band
EP (Paris, 1895) F:Pn (Vm.27.4254)

### Vié, L.

The following works in F:Pn are all early prints for large wind band; all were printed in Paris in 1864–1868.
Marches: Vm.27.12110, Vm.27.12111, Vm.27.12112, Vm.27.12114, Vm.27.12116, Vm.27.12118, Vm.7.14344 and Vm.7.14345 [two copies]
*Galop*, Vm.27.13397
Polkas: Vm.27.12113, Vm.27.12115

*Valse*, Vm.27.12117
*Le Courounment*, Vm.7.14342
*Hymne russe*, Vm.7.14504
*Le Manteau impérial*, Vm.7.14343
*Rule Britania*, Vm.7.14343 bis

**Villebichot, P. de**

*Marche*
Large wind band
EP (Paris, 1890) F:Pn (Vm.27.1157)

**Vineux, P.-E.**

The following works in F:Pn are all early prints for large wind band; all were printed in Paris in 1887–1891.
*Fantaisie*, Vm.27.12133
Marches: Vm.27.12132, Vm.27.12134

**Vincent, Henri**

The following works in F:Pn are all early prints for large wind band; all were printed in Paris in 1860–1868.
Marches: Vm.7.14351, Vm.27.12774[5], Vm.27.12772[4], Vm.7.14352, Vm.27.12136
*Quadrille*, Vm.27.12135
*Polka*, Vm.27.12771[5]

**Vincent, R.**

*Tarentelle*
Large wind band
EP (Paris, 189S) F:Pn (Vm.7.14349)

**Viney, Victor**

The following works in F:Pn are all early prints for large wind band; all were printed in Paris in 1890–1899.
Fantaisies: Vm.21.4263, Vm.21.4263, Vm.21.4269, Vm.21.4210
Marches: Vm.21.4264, Vm.27.4265, Vm.27.4266, Vm.27.4268
There are an additional twenty or so works dated after 1900 in F:Pn by Viney.

**Violetta, Gregorio**

The following works in F:Pn are all early prints for large wind band; all were printed in Paris in 1872–1884.
Overtures: Vm.27.12144, Vm.21.12158, Vm.21.12160
Fantaisies: Vm.27.12148 [two soli cornets], Vm.27.4272, Vm.27.12149
*Air varié*, Vm.27.13422
Marches: Vm.21.12143, Vm.21.12146, Vm.27.12147, Vm.21.4271, Vm.27.12151, Vm.27.12141, Vm.27.12153, Vm.27.12154, Vm.27.12156 (*Marche religieuse*), Vm.27.12157, Vm.27.12159, Vm.27.4213
Schottisches: Vm.27.12145, Vm.27.12155
Mazurkas: Vm.27.12139, Vm.27.12140
*Polka*, Vm.27.12150
*Un Souvenir d'amour*, Vm.27.4274
*Un Souvenir de Piacenza*, Vm.27.12142

**Violot, Antony**

The following works in F:Pn are early prints for large wind band; both were printed in Paris in 1892 and 1894.
Fantaisies: Vm.27.13423, Vm.27.12169

**Virenque**

The following works in F:Pn are early prints for large wind band; both were printed in Paris in ca. 1869.
*Overture*, Vm.7.12991
*Valse*, Vm.27.4216

**Vivier**

*Allegro Militaire*
Large wind band
EP (Paris, 1897) F:Pn (Vm.27.428l)

**Vivier, A.**

The following works in F:Pn are all early prints for large wind band; all were printed in Paris in 1894–1898.
Marches: Vm.27.12176, Vm.27.12179 (*Marche funèbre*), Vm.27.4284, Vm.27.12180
*Galop*, Vm.27.13426

## Vobaron

*Marches ou Fanfares pour les Troupes à Cheval*, Op. 2
EP (Paris, Richault, ca. 1800–1828)

## Voigt, Marie

*Fantaisie*
Large wind band
EP (Paris, 1876) F:Pn (Vm.27.12186)

## Vogt, Gustave (1781–1870)

*Airs du Ballet de Nina et l'Epreuve villageoise*
Harmoniemusik
EP (Paris, Frey, ca. 1800–1828)

*1ère Sérénade sur un Choix d'Airs d'Opéra*
Harmoniemusik
EP (Paris, Ebend, ca. 1800–1828)

*La Bordelaise*, grande Marche militaie
Military band
EP (Paris, A. Petit, ca. 1800–1828)

## Vos, Camille de

The following works in F:Pn are all early prints for large wind band; all were printed in Paris in 1873–1884.
Overtures: Vm.27.4293, Vm.27.12196
*Fantaisie*, Vm.27.12193 and Vm.27.12194 [later edition]
*Cantabile*, Vm.27.12195
*Cécilia. Hymne*, Vm.27.12197 [missing vocal parts]

## Vulder, J. de

*Boléro*
Large wind band
EP (Paris, 1862) F:Pn (Vm.27.12198)

## Wacker, Charles

The following works in F:Pn are early prints for large wind band; both were printed in Paris in 1867.
*Morceau religieux*, Vm.27.12200
*Marche*, Vm.27.12201

## Waele, Ed. de

The following works in F:Pn are early prints for large wind band; both were printed in Paris in 1897 and 1902.
*Andante pour offertoire*, Vm.27.13435
*Mazurka*, Vm.27.12203
In addition there are some forty more original works dated after 1900 by Waele in F:Pn.

## Wallerstein, F.

*Marche*
Large wind band
EP (Paris, 1863) F:Pn (Vm.27.12222)

## Walrand, J.

*Marche*
Large wind band
EP (Paris, 1899) F:Pn (Vm.27.12223)

## Walter, Albert (d. 1860)

*Valse*
Large wind band
EP (Paris, nineteenth century) F:Pn (Vm.27.4332)

## Waterson, James (Bandmaster 1er Life Guards)

The following works in F:Pn are early prints for large wind band; both were printed in Paris in 1876 and 1881.
*Marche*, Vm.7.14360
*Andante & Polonaise*, Vm.27.4335 [solo E♭ clarinet]

## Watier

The following works in F:Pn are all early prints for large wind band; all were printed in Paris in 1851–1881.
Works for the Church: Vm.27.12233 (*St. Hélène Prière*), Vm.27.12227 (*Élévation*), Vm.27.12230 (*Marche solennelle*), Vm.1.2247 and Vm.1.2883 [parts] (*Messe*)
The last example is for TTBB chorus, a full Mass dedicated to Auber.

Overtures: Vm.27.4345, Vm.27.4339 and
Vm.27.12231 [second edition], Vm.7.4812
(perhaps a catalog error, may be Vm.27.4812),
Vm.27.4342, Vm.27.4338, Vm.27.4343
Fantaisies: Vm.27.4340, Vm.27.4346
Airs varié: Vm.27.4344 [solo E♭ alto saxophone, dedicated to Eugène Gaubert, Prof. Conservertoire de Lille], Vm.27.12226
Marches: Vm.27.4341 (*Marche nuptiale*),
Vm.27.12232, Vm.27.12229, Vm.27.4336,
Vm.7.14361, Vm.27.4337
Valses: Vm.7.14362, Vm.27.12228

### Welter, Louis

The following works in F:Pn are all early prints for large wind band; all were printed in Paris in 1888–1898.

Works for the Church: Vm.27.12247 (*Prière et invocation pour service religieux*), Vm.27.13451 (*Prière et invocation pour service religieux*), Vm.27.12242 (2 *Andantes*), Vm.27.13448 (*Marche Esperance*), Vm.27.13449 (*Procession Marche*), Vm.27.12243 (2 *Marches solennelles*), Vm.27.12244 (2 *Marches solennelles*), Vm.27.12248 (*Marche funèbre*), Vm.27.13450 (*Messe solennelle*)

The last example, five separate works for military band without chorus, provides, perhaps, an insight into how these many church works were employed in the actual service. The separate parts here are:

1. *Entree* (Tempo di Marcia)
2. *Offertoire* (Maestoso)
3. *Élévation* (Andante
4. *Communion* (Moderato)
5. *Sortie* (Allegretto)

*Fantaisie*, Vm.27.13447
(2) *Marches*: Vm.27.12245
*Le Souvenir français*, Vm.27.12249

### Wettge, Gustave (Chef de Musique de la Garde Républicaine)

The following works in F:Pn are all early prints for large wind band; all were printed in Paris in 1876–1895.

Overtures: Vm.7.14367, Vm.7.12994,
Vm.27.21394, Vm.7.14387, Vm.27.4395,
Vm.7.14396, Vm.27.12285, Vm.7.14371,
Vm.27.12271, Vm.27.3288
Fantaisies: Vm.27.4386, Vm.27.12283,
Vm.27.12274
*Concerto*, Vm.7.14369 [solo clarinet]
This example is a full score, reading for 'Petites et Grandes clarinettes' in unison, or for one B♭ clarinet.
*Air varié*, Vm.27.12270
*Fête*, Vm.27.4387
*Divertissement*, Vm.27.12279
*Hymne Nationale Japonais*, Vm.7.14375
*Air Nationale Roumain*, Vm.27.12364
*Hymne Nationale Siamois*, Vm.7.14375 bis
Marches: Vm.27.12264, Vm.27.12265,
Vm.27.12266, Vm.27.4385, Vm.7.14370,
Vm.27.12268, Vm.27.13455 (*Marche funèbre*),
Vm.27.12269, Vm.27.13456, Vm.27.12284,
Vm.27.12286, Vm.7.14402, Vm.7.14516,
Vm.7.14381, Vm.27.12277, Vm.27.12289
Polkas: Vm.7.14366 [solo piccolo], Vm.7.14394,
Vm.27.4396, Vm.7.14400 [solo cornet],
Vm.27.4391, Vm.7.14377 [solo piccolo]
*Mazurka*, Vm.7.14393
Gavottes: Vm.27.4389, Vm.27.4390

### Wettge, Léon (Chef de Musique du génie en retraite, Chevalier de la légion d'Honneur)

The following works in F:Pn are all early prints for large wind band; all were printed in Paris in 1868–1890.

Overtures: Vm.27.13457 and Vm.27.12290 [later edition] (*Overture symphonique*), Vm.7.12993, Vm.27.12293 and Vm.27.12294 [later edition], Vm.27.12295, Vm.27.4399
*Air varié*, Vm.27.12296
Marches: Vm.7.14403, Vm.7.14404
Polkas: Vm.27.12291, Vm.27.12292, Vm.7.14395 [solo cornet]

### Widor, Charles-Marie (1845–1937)

*Salvum Fac Populum Tuum*, Op. 84
-303, timpani, organ
EP (Paris, Heugel) [cited in DJ]

## Wittmann

The following works in F:Pn are all early prints for large wind band; all were printed in Paris in 1868–1872.

Works for the Church: Vm.27.12312 (*Le Conducteur d'omnibus*) [a march], Vm.27.12313 (*La Contrition. Entèe de Messe*) [a march], Vm.27.12325 (*Fantaisie-religieuse*), Vm.27.12326 (*Petite Fantaisie religieuse*), Vm.27.12327 (*Petite Fantaisie religieuse*), Vm.27.12328 (*Petite Fantaisie religieuse*), Vm.27.12329 (*Petite Fantaisie religieuse*), Vm.27.12333 (*Morceau religieus*)

*Fantaisie*, Vm.27.4405

Marches: Vm.27.12314, Vm.27.12315, Vm.27.4406, Vm.27.12318, Vm.27.12334, Vm.27.12336, Vm.27.12338, Vm.27.12346, Vm.27.12347

*Boléro*, Vm.27.12301

*Mazurka*, Vm.27.12303

Polkas: Vm.27.12305, Vm.27.4408

Schottisches: Vm.27.12320, Vm.27.12493

Valses: Vm.27.12302, Vm.27.12337

*Quadrille*, Vm.27.12324

*Galop*, Vm.27.13458

## Wittmann, G. [fils]

The following works in F:Pn are all early prints for large wind band; all were printed in Paris in 1865–1900.

Overtures: Vm.27.4420, Vm.27.12395, Vm.27.4478

Fantaisies: Vm.27.12348, Vm.27.4419

*Air varié*, Vm.27.4411 [two soli cornets]

Marches: Vm.27.4412, Vm.27.12361, Vm.27.12350, Vm.27.12389, Vm.27.12391, Vm.27.4440, Vm.27.4448, Vm.27.4449, Vm.27.12372, Vm.27.12371, Vm.27.4454, Vm.27.12375, Vm.27.4457, Vm.27.12354, Vm.27.4477, Vm.27.12385, Vm.27.12387

Gavottes: Vm.27.4413, Vm.27.4436

Valses: Vm.27.4415, Vm.27.12390, Vm.27.4438, Vm.27.4460, Vm.27.4470, Vm.27.4480, Vm.27.4484

*Schottisch*, Vm.27.12360

Quadrilles: Vm.27.12362, Vm.27.4417, Vm.27.4422, Vm.27.4439, Vm.27.4471

Polkas: Vm.27.4418, Vm.27.4427, Vm.27.4428, Vm.27.4430, Vm.27.4455 [solo cornet], Vm.27.4458, Vm.27.4467, Vm.27.4468 Vm.27.4472 [solo cornet, with variations], Vm.27.12394 and Vm.27.12381 [later edition], Vm.27.4474 [solo flute] Vm.27.4479

Galops: Vm.27.12364, Vm.27.4424, Vm.27.13459, Vm.27.4446, Vm.27.4489

Mazurkas: Vm.27.4426, Vm.27.4432, Vm.27.4459, Vm.27.4481, Vm.27.4485

*Gigue*, Vm.27.4461

*Boléro*, Vm.27.4463

*Menuet*, Vm.27.4476

*Tarentelle*, Vm.27.4483

*Farandole*, Vm.27.4486

*Arrangements* for 3, 4, 5, 6, 7, and 8 saxophones, Vm.10.h.9

In addition there are several hundred arrangements and transcriptions in F:Pn by G. Wittmann.

## Wittmann, J.-B.

The following works in F:Pn are all early prints for large wind band; all were printed in Paris in 1863–1891.

*Overture*, Vm.27.12408

*Fantaisie*, Vm.27.4490

Marches: Vm.27.12398, Vm.27.12403, Vm.27.12405, Vm.27.12406, Vm.27.12407, Vm.27.12409, Vm.27.12410, Vm.27.4491, Vm.7.14407, Vm.27.12413, Vm.27.12414, Vm.27.12416

*Valse*, Vm.27.12404

## Wormser, Andre (1851–1926)

*Les Lupercales* [Symphonic Poem]
Brass ensemble
EP (Buffet-Crampon) [cited by DJ]

## Ziegler (Officer Chef de Musique, 1er Hussards)

The following works in F:Pn are all early prints for large wind band; all were printed in Paris in 1853–1887.

Works for the Church: Vm.27.12426 (*Andante religioso*), Vm.27.12432 (*Offertoire*), Vm.27.12441 (*Morceau religieux*), Vm.27.12446 (*Marche procession*), Vm.27.12440 and Vm.27.4496 [two copies] (*Morceau d'offertoire*), Vm.27.12452 (*Marche religieuse*), Vm.27.12465 (*Marche religieuse*), Vm.27.12482 (*Marche-funèbre*), Vm.27.12526 (*Marche procession*), Vm.27.12492 (*Andante pour offertoire*), Vm.27.12544 (*Andante*), Vm.27.12532 (*Andante pour offertoire*), Vm.27.12545 (*Andante*), Vm.27.12534 (*Marche funèbre*), Vm.27.12543 (*Marche religieuse*), Vm.27.13465 (*Morceau religieux*), Vm.27.12562 (*Andante religieux*)

Overtures: Vm.27.4497, Vm.27.12458 and Vm.27.4498 [two copies], Vm.27.12459, Vm.27.4499, Vm.27.4500, Vm.27.12499, Vm.27.12520, Vm.27.4505, Vm.27.12569 and Vm.7.12995 [two copies], Vm.27.12571, Vm.27.12591, Vm.27.12602, Vm.27.12608

Fantaisies: Vm.27.12449, Vm.27.12475, Vm.27.12476, Vm.27.4501, Vm.27.12493, Vm.27.4503 and Vm.27.13464 [two copies], Vm.27.12510, Vm.27.12531, Vm.27.12536, Vm.27.4506, Vm.7.14415 [solo trombone], Vm.27.12559, Vm.27.12563, Vm.27.12567 [soli baritone and cornet], Vm.27.12570, Vm.27.4509 Vm.27.4510 [soli trombone and cornet], Vm.27.12583, Vm.27.4511, Vm.27.4512

Airs varié: Vm.27.12495 [solo cornet], Vm.27.4513

Marches: Vm.27.12427, Vm.27.12429, Vm.27.12430, Vm.27.12433, Vm.27.12434, Vm.27.12435, Vm.27.12436, Vm.27.12439, Vm.27.12442, Vm.27.12443 and Vm.7.14418 [two copies], Vm.7.14317, Vm.27.12444, Vm.27.12445, Vm.27 .12447, Vm.27.12448, Vm.27.12450, Vm.27.12451, Vm.27.12454, Vm.27.12455, Vm.27.12457, Vm.27.12460, Vm.27.12461, Vm.27.12463, Vm.27.12464, Vm.27.12467, Vm.27.12468, Vm.27.12469, Vm.27.12472, Vm.27.12473, Vm.27.12483, Vm.27.12484, Vm.27.12489, Vm.27.12494, Vm.27.12496, Vm.7.14419, Vm.27.12497, Vm.27.12498, Vm.27.12611, Vm.27.12500, Vm.27.4502, Vm.27.12504, Vm.27.12509, Vm.27.12511, Vm.27.12512, Vm.27.12513, Vm.27.12519, Vm.27.12521, Vm.27.12523, Vm.27.4504, Vm.27.12528, Vm.27.12530, Vm.27.12535, Vm.27.12538, Vm.27.12539, Vm.27.12541, Vm.27.12542, Vm.27.12548, Vm.27.12552, Vm.27.12553, Vm.27.12556, Vm.27.12558 and Vm.7.14413, Vm.27.12560, Vm.27.12561, Vm.27.12563, Vm.27.12566, Vm.27.4507, Vm.27.12573, Vm.27.12574, Vm.27.12575, Vm.27.4508, Vm.27.12576, Vm.27.12577, Vm.27.12578, Vm.27.12580, Vm.27.12477, Vm.27.12584, Vm.27.12586, Vm.27.12588, Vm.27.12589, Vm.27.12590, Vm.27.12596, Vm.27.12597, Vm.27.12599, Vm.27.12605, Vm.27.12606

Barcarolles: Vm.27.12428, Vm.27.12453, Vm.27.12516, Vm.27.12540

Galops: Vm.27.13460, Vm.27.13461, Vm.27.14363, Vm.27.13462, Vm.7.14414

Valses: Vm.27.12456, Vm.27.12462, Vm.17.12503, Vm.27.12506, Vm.27.12572, Vm.27.12581, Vm.27.12592, Vm.27.12604, Vm.27.12609

Quadrilles: Vm.27.12479 and Vm.7.14416 [two copies], Vm.27.12485, Vm.27.12487, Vm.27.12490, Vm.27.12501, Vm.27.12522 and Vm.27.12763 [later edition], Vm.27.12529, Vm.27.12565, Vm.27.12594, Vm.27.12595, Vm.27.12601, Vm.27.12610, Vm.27.12612

Polkas: Vm.27.12488 [soli flute and cornet], Vm.27.12508, Vm.27.12507, Vm.27.12514, Vm.27.12524 and Vm.27.12525, Vm.27.12546, Vm.27.12555, Vm.27.12557, Vm.27.12613

Schottisches: Vm.27.12491, Vm.27.12553, Vm.27.12568

*Boléros:* Vm.27.12517, Vm.27.12518, Vm.27.12579, Vm.27.12587, Vm.27.12603

*Épisode symphonique* (*Un Jour de Bataille* [*Épisode de Crimée*]. *Symphonie Héroique*), Vm.27.12600

*Morceau carnavalesque*, Vm.27.12470

## Zimmermann

*Walses*
Hamoniemusik
EP (Paris, Momigny, ca. 1800–1828)

## Representative Arrangements

Unless otherwise indicated, the following transcriptions in F:Pn are late nineteenth century prints, published in Paris, for large wind band.

### Adam, H. C. (arr. H. Klosé)

*Messe de St. Cecile*
Chorus and band
EP (Paris, Lebel, 1852) F:Pn (D.6380)

### Beauplan (arr. Louis)

*Chansonette, 'l'Enfant du Regiment'*
Hamoniemusik
EP (Paris, A. Petit, ca. 1800–1828)

### Beethoven

*Egmont Overture*, Vm.27.8996 [arr. Ligner]; Vm.27.1486 [arr. Fischer]
'March,' from *Egmont*, Vm.27.4554 [arr. Fischer]
*Leonore Overture*, Vm.27.1489 [arr. Fischer]
*Marche Turque* (*Ruines d'Athénes*), Vm.27.7398 [arr. Fischer]
'Adagio,' *Sonata Pathetique*, Vm.7.13501 [arr. Fischer]
'Allegretto,' *Sonate in Ut# Minor*, Vm.27.8703 [arr. Lajarte]
'Andante,' *Symphonie Nr. 5*, Vm.27.1949 [arr. Grillet]
'Allegro,' *Symphopie Nr. 6*, Vm.7.13502 [arr. Fischer]
'Allegretto,' *Symnhonie Nr. 8*, Vm.27.1454 [arr. Fischer]

### Beffroy de Reigny, Louis Abel (arr. F. Devienne)

*Le Club des bonnes gens*
Two flutes or two oboes, 22-22, serpent, percussion
EP (Paris, Gaveaux, Hr. 38) BRD:AB

### Gaveaux, Pierre (arr. F. Devienne)

Overture and six morceaux from *Amour Filial*
Two flutes or two oboes, 22-22, serpent, percussion
EP (Paris, author, Hr. 36) BRD:AB

### Handel (arr. Fischer)

'Alleluia,' du *Messie*, Vm.27.7387; and Vm.27.1455 [brass band]

### Haydn

'Adagio,' *Surprise Symphony* Vm.7.13587 [arr. Gibert]
*Symphony, 'la Reine,'* Vm.27.2075 [arr. Gibert]
*Symphonie*, Vm.27.7982 [arr. Gibert]
*Symphonie Militaire*, Vm.27.2076 [arr. Gibert]

*Die Schöpfung* (10 movements)
2042-221, serpent
EP (Paris, Pleyel) CR:Zz (XIII 1091/2 a-o)

### Le Sueur, Jean-François (arr. Louis)

*Paul et Virginie*
Twelve-part military band
EP (Paris, Henry) S:Skma

### Mozart (arr. Fischer)

*Ave verum*
-3232, baritone
F:Pn (Vm.7.13500)

### Rossini

Introduction, *Barbier de Seville*, Vm.27.1483 [arr. Fischer]
Overture, *La Cenerentola*, Vm.27.1488 [arr. Fischer]
'Preghiera,' *Il Mose in Egitto* [arr. Bleyle, in Verona, 1850]
MS A:Wn (Sm.20621)

### Schubert (arr. Fischer)

*La Sérénade* [solo cornet], Vm.27.1495

### Wagner

[Prelude to] *Lohengrin*, Vm.27.9012 [arr. Ligner]
*Fantaisie sur Lohengrin* [Act I], Vm.27.8998 [arr. Ligner]
*Marche de Rienzi*, Vm.27.4810 bis [arr. Fischer]

**Weber (arr. Brod)**

*Mélange ou Choix de Morceaux de l'Opéra: der Freischütz*
Grande Harmonie militaire
EP (Paris, A. Petit, ca. 1800–1828)

# Italy

**Anonymous**

[Collection of 20 Italian] *Märsche*
Military band
MS BRD:Mbs (Mus.Ms.8740)

*Credo* in B♭
Three voices [three-part choir is assumed], winds, organ
MS I:Vsmc

(4) *Gloria*
Three voices, winds, organ
MS I:Vsmc

*Kyrie & Gloria*
Three voices, six winds
MS I:Vsmc

*Gloria*
TTB, 201-02, organ
MS I:Vcr (Busta II N. 25)

*Qui Tollis*
Baritone voice, 201-02, organ
MS I:Vcr (Busta III N. 37)

*Tantum ergo*
Baritone voice, 21-02, organ
MS I:Vcr (Busta X N. 161)

**Acerbi, Domenico**

*Gloria* (1859)
Three voices, seven winds, organ
MS I:Vsmc

*Laudate pueri* (1871)
Four voices, seven winds, organ
MS I:Vsmc

(2) *Tantum Ergo*
Three voices, winds
MS I:Vsmc [missing winds]

**Altafulla, Ubaldo Antonio**

*Messa*
TTB, winds
MS I:Bsf (M.A.VII-13)

**Amadei, Amedeo (1866–1935)**

According to MGG, Amadei was a composer of military music for the 73rd Inf. Reg. in Alba

**Antonio, Grotto (1753–1831)**

*Kyrie & Gloria* (1803)
SATB, 101-021, 2 organs, string bass
MS I:Vld (Mazzo I, N. 1)

**Asioli, Bonifazio (1769–1832)**

*Sextet*
Wind instruments [cited in MGG]

[Untitled work]
Wind instruments
MS I:MOe (Mus.F.1742)

*Gloria*
Three voices, eight winds, organ
MS I:Vsmc

**Belli, Sandre M.**

*Tantum ergo*, Op. 22
Tenor, three voice choir, seven winds, organ
MS I:Vsmc

**Bernini, Frediano**

*Gloria in excelsis* (1880)
SATB, 1000-42, organ
MS I:Ls (B.310)

*Kyrie* (1899)
SATB, 1111-4, organ
MS I:Ls (B.321)

**Bimboni, Gioacchino (celebrated trombonist, b. ca. 1810 in Florence, arr.)**

*Sinfonia della Muta di Portici*
Banda
MS (46 page score) I:Baf

## Boara, Giovanni

*Credo*
Two voices, six winds, organ
MS I:Vsmc

*Credo* (1836)
Three voices, ten winds, organ
MS I:Vsmc

*Domine Deus*
Baritone solo, six winds, organ
MS I:Vsmc

*Gloria* (1835)
Three voices, nine winds, organ
MS I:Vsmc

*Gloria*
Two voices, eight winds, organ
MS I:Vsmc

*Haee tua Virgo* ('Inno di S. Caterina da Siena')
Three voices, eight winds, organ
MS I:Vsmc

*Kyrie* (1835)
Three voices, thirteen winds, organ
MS I:Vsmc

*Marcia* (1857)
Seven-part wind band
MS I:Vsmc

*Marcia*
Winds, organ
MS I:Vsmc

## Bolzoni, Giovanni (1841–1919)

*Sextet*
122-01 [cited in MGG]

## Brambilla

*Tantum ergo*
Bass solo, three voice choir, seven winds, organ
MS I:Vsmc

## Buzzolla, Antonio (1815–1871)

*Marcia*
Winds, organ
MS I:Vsmc

## Cagliero, Giovanni (1838–1926)

*Credo*
Three voices, eight winds, organ
MS I:Vsmc

*Dixit*
Three voices, six winds, organ
MS I:Vsmc

*Domine ad adjuvandum*
Three voices, eight winds, organ

*Gloria*
Three voices, eight winds, organ
MS I:Vsmc

*Kyrie*
Three voices, eight winds, organ
MS I:Vsmc

## Califf

*Sanctus e Agnus Dei*
Three voices, eight winds, organ
MS I:Vsmc

## Carulli, Benedetto (1797–1877)

*Divertimento*
Solo trombone and winds
MS I:Bsf (M.C.VII-15)

## Cianchi, Emilio

*Nonetto*
222-02, contrabassoon
EP (Firenze, Paoletti, 1868) I:Bc

## Cimoso, Domenico (1780–1850)

*Tantum ergo* ('Festa di S. Giuseppe Caiasanzio in S. Pantaleone')
Two voices, six winds, organ
MS I:Vsmc

## Coccon, Nicolo (Venice, 1826–1903)

*Credo*
Two Voices, fifteen winds, organ
MS I:Vsmc

*Gloria* (1847)
Two Voices, nine winds, organ
MS I:Vsmc

*Gloria* (1850)
Two Voices, eight winds, organ
MS I:Vsmc

*Kyrie*
Three voices, ten winds, organ
MS I:Vsmc

*Laetatus sum*
Three voices, eight winds, organ
MS I:Vsmc

*Laudate*
Two voices, nine winds, organ
MS I:Vsmc

## Codivilla, Filippo (b. 1841)

*Ottetto* in E♭
1111-121
MP (Pizzi) [cited by MH]

## Constantini, Francesco (1789–1854)

*O lingua benedicta*
TTBB, 200-221 [bassoon given as option for trombone]
MS I:MBSF (Mss.N.253/3)

## Dal Vasco, Agostino

*Tantum ergo* (1855)
Two voices, nine winds, organ
MS I:Vsmc

## Deola, Paolo

*Beatus Vir* (1845)
Three voices, eight winds, organ
MS I:Vsmc

*Confitebor* (1851)
Two voices, seven winds, organ
MS I:Vsmc

*Gloria* (1847)
Three voices, eight winds, organ
MS I:Vsmc

*Kyrie* (1847)
Three voices, six winds, organ
MS I:Vsmc

*Laudate Dominum omnes gentes* (1845)
Three voices, seven winds, organ
MS I:Vsmc

*Marcia*
Winds, organ
MS I:Vsmc

*Regina Coeli* (1852)
Three solo voices, -44, organ
MS I:Vsmc

*Regina sine labe* (1855)
Three voices, eight winds, organ
MS I:Vsmc

*Salve Regina*
Three solo voices, six winds, organ
MS I:Vsmc

*Salve Regina* (1845)
Three voices, eight winds, winds
MS I:Vsmc

*Sanctus & Agnus Dei* (1851)
Two voices, nine winds, organ
MS I:Vsmc

## Desiro

*Gloria*
Three voices, seven winds, organ
MS I:Vsmc

*Kyrie*
Three voices, seven winds, organ
MS I:Vsmc

## Devasini, Giuseppe (1822–1878)

*Sextett*
1121-01
MP (Ricordi) [cited in MH]

## Donizetti, Gaetano (1797–1848)

*Kyrie*
STB, 200-02, organ
MS I:BGi

*Salve regina*
STB, winds, cello, string bass
MS F:Pn [cited by Grove, V, 567]

*Tantum ergo*
Tenor, winds, string bass
MS I:BGi

*Sinfonia* in G minor
1222-02
MS I:BGi; US:DW (373)

*Luge Qui Legis* (1842) [funeral march]
Winds
MP (Recordi) [cited by DJ]

*Domine ad adjuvandum*
STB, winds
MS F:Pn

(3) *Marches* (for the Sultan Abdul Medjid)
Wind band
One is by Donizetti and two are by his brother, Giuseppe Donizetti.

### Fanucchi, Domenico

*Cantata*, 'Se dell'or la wete avara' (1839)
AATB, 1021-221, contrabassoon
MS I:Ls (B.41)

*Aria con cori*
SAB, 110-02
MS I:Ls (B.41)

*Il figlio reconosciuto* (1822)
Voices, 2121-02, contrabassoon
MS I:Ls (B.41)

### Ferri, Angelo

*Gloria*
Three voices, eleven winds, organ
MS I:Vsmc

*Tantum ergo*
Three voices, seven winds, organ
MS I:Vsmc

### Fontebasso, Pietro

*Tantum ergo*
Three voices, nine winds, organ
MS I:Vsmc

### Galli, Amintore (1845–1919)

*Fantaisien*
Military band [cited in MGG]

### Gasparini, Giovanni Batta.

*Marcia*
Twelve winds, string bass
MS I:Vsmc

*Salve Regina* (1850)
Bass solo, winds, organ
MS I:Vsmc

### Generali, Pietro (1773–1832)

*Litanie*
Three voices, seven winds, organ
MS I:Vsmc

*Tantum ergo*
Three voices, seven winds, organ
MS I:Vsmc

### Giorza, Paul

(3) *Marchs*
Winds
EP (Milano, 1860) F:Pn (Vm.7.14459, Vm.7.14456, and Vm.7.14458)

### Lamperini

*Kyrie*
Three voices, seven winds, organ
MS I:Vsmc

### Lipawsky, Giuseppe

*Cantata*, 'La liberazione d'Italia'
Wind instruments
MS I:Fc (A.189)

### Mabellini, Teodulo (1817–1897)

(6) *Walzes*
Wind instruments [cited in Grove, XI, 409]

*Sinfonia*
1222-02, contrabassoon
EP (Firenze, Paoletti, 1868) I:Bc

### Manfrin, Giuseppe

*Tantum ergo*
Three voices, seven winds, organ
MS I:Vsmc

## Mandanici, Placido (1798–1852)

*Gloria*
Three voices, eight winds, organ
MS I:Vsmc

*Credo*
Three voices, seven winds, organ
MS I:Vsmc

## Manina, Fortunato

*Tantum ergo*
Three voices, seven winds, organ
MS I:Vsmc

## Marchesi, Tommaso (1773–1852)

*Sinfonia*
Wind instruments [cited in MGG]

## Marra, Vincenzo (Naples band conductor)

*Passo doppio*
Banda
MS (25-page score) I:Baf

## Marsano, Luigi (1769–1841)

*Inno per la Festivilà della Reliquie*
Three voices, six winds, organ
MS I:Vsmc

## Marulli, Angelo

*Stabat Mater*
Three voices, fifteen winds, organ
MS I:Vsmc

## Mayr, Simone (1763–1845)

(12) *Bagatellen*
Flute, clarinet, basset horn or bassoon
MS (autograph) I:Mc; BRD:Mbs (Mus. Ms.App.2033) [xerox of above]

*Sonata*
21-02, 2 basset horns, viola (?)
MS I:BGc

*Sextetto*, Op. 9, nr. 1
202-02
MS BRD:HR (III.4.1/2.40.96)
EP (Augsburg, Gombart) [advertised in AMZ in 1805]; H:Bn; BRD:Tu; DDR:SWl

*Sextetto*, Op. 9, nr. 2
202-02
MS BRD:HR (III.4.1/2.40.97)
EP (Augsburg, Gombart) [advertized in AMZ in 1805]; H:Bn; BRD:Tu; DDR:SWl

*Motet*, 'O salutaris hostia'
SSSS, -243, serpent, organ
MS BRD:Mbs (Mus.Ms.A353)

## Mazzorin, Michele

*Credo* (1848)
Three voices, ten winds, organ
MS I:Vsmc

*Gloria*
Three voices, ten winds, organ
MS I:Vsmc

*Kyrie*
Three voices, ten winds, organ
MS I:Vsmc

*Lauda Jerusalem*
Three voices, eight winds, organ
MS I:Vsmc

*Salve Regina*
Three voices, six winds, organ
MS I:Vsmc

## Mercadante, Saverio (1795–1870)

*Sinfonia marcia* (performed by twelve regimental bands for the birth of the Prince of Naples in 1869)
Military band
MS I:Nc [cited by Grove, XII, 175]

*Gloria*
Three voices, thirty winds, organ
MS I:Vsmc

*Tantum ergo*
Three voices, seven winds, organ
MS I:Vsmc

### Morandi, Giovanni (1777–1856)

(32) *Militärmärsche* (1852)
Organ
MS (autograph) [in private hands]

### Moretti, Niccolo

*Quoniam*
Two bass voices, 2201-02, organ
MS I:VCdr (Busta X.N.143)

*Credo*
Three voices, eight winds, organ
MS I:Vsmc

*Gloria*
Three voices, nine winds, organ
MS I:Vsmc

*Kyrie* (1823)
Three voices, eight winds, organ
MS I:Vsmc

### Nava, Gaetano (Milan, 1802–1875)

*Tantum ergo*
Bass solo, three voices, eight winds, organ
MS I:Vsmc

### Nocentino, Domenico (1848–1924)

*Symphonia* in B♭
1222-, string bass
MS I:Fc

### Pacini, Giovanni (1796–1867)

*Gran concertone ridotto per Banda*
MS I:Ls (B.118)

### Pellarin, Giuseppe (Venice, 1815–1865)

*Beatus vir*
Three voices, ten winds, organ
MS I:Vsmc

*Dixit*
Three voices, nine winds, organ
MS I:Vsmc

*Kyxie*
Three voices, seven winds, organ
MS I:Vsmc

*Laudate Pueri*
Three voices, nine winds, organ
MS I:Vsmc

*Requiem*
Three voices, eleven winds, organ
MS I:Vsmc

### Petrali, Giuliano

*Quoniam*
Bass solo, eight winds, organ
MS I:Vsmc

### Poli, Giovanni Batta.

*Kyrie* (1861)
Two voices, six winds, organ
MS I:Vsmc

### Ponchielli, Amilcare (1834–1886)

*Fantasia militaire*
Band
EP (Milan, Ricordi, 1863)

*March*, '*Principe Umberto*'
Band
MS (autograph) I:CR

*Divertimento*, '*Il convegno*'
Two solo clarinets, band
MS I:Ria

*Marcia funebre* (1869) (for the funeral of F. Lucca)
Band
MS I:CR

*March*, '*Funerali di Alessandro Manzoni*' (1874)
Band

*Elegia funebre* (1873, for Manzoni)
Band

*Marcia funebre* (1874)
Band

*Elegia funebre* (1881)
Band
MS I:CR

*Elegia, 'Sulla tomba di Garibaldi'* (1886)
Band
EP (unknown) US:DW (254)

*Quintet*
Piano, 1110-, E♭ clarinet
MP (Ricordi) [cited by DJ]

## Puccini, Giacomo (1858–1924)

*March, Scossa elettrica* (1896)
Band (?) [cited without instrumentation in Grove, XV, 439]

## Quilici, Domenico

*Miserere*
TTB, 1111-02
MS I:PAc

*Stabat Mater* (1805)
TTB, 1111-02
MS I:PAc

*O Lingua*
SATB, -12, bassi
MS I:PAc

*Sequenza a 4 voci Di S. Antonio de Padova* (1815)
SATB, -22, bassi
MS I:PAc

*Stabat Mater* (1805)
TTB, 1111-01
MS I:PHas

## Quirici, Giovanni

*Credo*
Three voices, eight winds, organ
MS I:Vsmc

*Kyrie*
Three voices, eight winds, organ
MS I:Vsmc

## Rova, Giovanni Batt.

*Credo* (1830)
Three voices, six winds, organ
MS I:Vsmc

*Kyrie* (1832)
Three voices, six winds, organ
MS I:Vsmc

*Messa*
Three voices, seven winds, organ
MS I:Vsmc

*Tantum ergo* (1832)
Tenor solo, three-part chorus, eleven winds, organ
MS I:Vsmc

*Veni Creator*
Three voices, six winds, organ
MS I:Vsmc

## Scontrino, Antonio (1850–1922)

*Adagio*
Violin and winds
MS I:PLcon

## Setaccioli, Giacomo (1868–1925)

*Nonett*
Wind instruments [cited in MGG]

## Strepponi, Feliciano (1767–1832)

*Gloria in Excelsis*
SATB, 1221-22, percussion, organ
MS I:MZ (MS.87)

*Dixit. Introduzione e Finale*
SATB, 1221-22, percussion, bassi
MS I:MZ (MS.99)

## Tebaldini, Giovanni (1864–1952)

*Vexilla*
TB, -6441, 2 alto horns
MS I:PCd

## Wachs, Paul

*Madrilena*
Band
MS I:Bsf (FC.W.X.8)

## Zifra, Antonio

*Marcia, Nr. 2* (1827)
Six winds, organ
MS I:Vsmc

*Marcia*, Nr. IV (1835)
Winds and organ
MS I:Vsmc

*Marcia funebre*
-122, organ
MS I:Vsmc

*Suonata,* Nr. 9 (1855)
Ten winds, organ
MS I:Vsmc

## REPRESENTATIVE ARRANGEMENTS

### Anonymous

*Passo doppio nel ballot 'Catarina Cornaro'*
Arranged by Agostino Guida (Banda del L.
 di Linea)
MS DDR:SWl [cited by Eitner]

### Bellini

'Aria,' from *La Sonnambula*
Arranged by Agostino Belloli (Maestro nel IR
 Conservatorio di Musica, Milano)
Band
MS A:Wn (Sm 2425)
 Belloli has also arranged one number from the
 ballet, *Didone*, by Salvatore Vigano for band.

### Cimarosa

*Armonia* (on themes of Cimarosa) (1826)
2222-221
MS I:Bc
 In addition this library has similar works based
 on Paer and Paisiello.

### Fioravanti (1764–1837)

*Duetto*
Arranged by Gennaro Cozzo
42-02, percussion
MS CH:SO [missing clarinet 2 and bassoon 1]

### Wagner

'March,' from *Tannhäuser*
Arranger unknown
MS I:Bsf (FC.W.X.9)

# *Finland*

**Sibelius, Jan (b. 1865)**

*Song of the Athenians*, Op. 31a (1899)
Boys and male chorus, -07, percussion
MS [cited in Grove, Fifth Edition]

*Suite*
Small brass band with clarinet
MS [location unknown] US:DW (52)

*Tiera*
Brass band
MS [location unknown] US:DW (51)

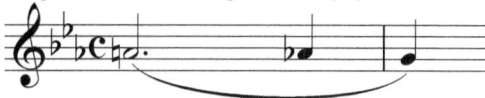

# The Netherlands

**Berlyn, Aron Wolff (1817–1870)**

*Nonett*
Eight winds, string bass [cited in MGG]

**Brandts Buys, R. F. R. (b. 1850)**

*Serenade* (1879), Op. 6
Male chorus, brass
EP (Amsterdam, Roothaan)

*Marche*
Band
MS [location unknown]

*Quintet*
Piano, winds
MS [location unknown]

**Bekker, Johannes (b. 1826)**

*Feesttonen*
Band [original version for strings]
MS [location unknown]

**Dunkler, Franz (1779–1861)**

*Une l'arme sur la tombe Elegie et marche funèbre*
Military band
MS DDR:Bds (MS.5340) [cited by Eitner]

**Hol, Richard (b. 1825)**

*Holland's Glorie*, Op. 24
Male chorus, brass
EP (Rotterdam, Lichtenauer)

*Concert-Overture*, Op. 110
Military band
EP (Tillburg, Kessels)

*De Oranjevaan*
Male chorus, brass
EP (Deierkauf)

**Hutschenruyter, Wouter (1859–1943, founder of the band of the Rotterdam Municipal Guard)**

*Festmarsche*
Military band
MS [location unknown] US:DW (419)
EP (Paris, 1885) F:Pn (Vm.27.4494)

**Nicolai, Willem, (b. 1829–1896)**

*Prinses Wilhelmina Cantata*
Children's chorus and band
MS [location unknown]

**Röntgen, Julius (b. 1829)**

*Serenade*, Op. 14
Seven winds
EP (Leipzig: Breitkopf & Härtel) BRD:Bhm
 (3898; 3899); US:DW (211)

**Sylvani van [a student of Mozart, according to Eitner]**

*Harmonie,* Op. 5
22-02
EP (Paris, Pleyel; Paris, Leduc, ca. 1800–1828)

**Verhulst, Johannes J. H. (1816–1891)**

*Requiem*, Op. 51
Male chorus, brass
EP (Den Haag, 1854) [cited in MGG]

*Vlaggelied,* Op. 35
Male chorus, brass
EP (Den Haag, 1850) [cited in MGG]

# Norway

**Grieg, Edvard (1843–1907)**
> *Funeral March* (*Sörgemarsch* over Rikard Nordraak, Op. 6b)
> Brass band
> Bergen: Offenlige Bibliotek

**Olsen, Ole (1850–1927)**
> According to Grove, XIII, 537, Olsen wrote many marches based on Norwegian folk tunes while director of the Akershus 2nd Brigade band.

**Selmer, Johan Peter (1844–1910)**
> *Hilsen til Nidaros* (1883)
> Tenor solo, male chorus, military band [cited in MGG]

# Poland

**Anonymous**

*Harmonie* (ca. 1800–1868)
22-02
MS PL:LA (2289)

*Collection* of 71 works without titles (ca. 1800–1868)
222-02
MS PL:LA (2323-2393)

*Collection* of 9 works, apparently arrangements of arias (ca. 1800–1868)
222-02
MS PL:LA (2394-2402)

*Aria* in B♭ (ca. 1800–1868)
222-02
MS PL:LA (2403)

*Aria Calmica & Ballo Calmuca* (ca. 1800–1868)
222-02
MS PL:LA (2404)

*Ariette*, in C minor (ca. 1800–1868)
222-02
MS PL:LA (2405)

*Ballo & Menuetto* (ca. 1800–1868)
222-02
MS PL:LA (2406)

*La Chasse* (ca. 1800–1868)
222-02
MS PL:LA (2407)

*Ciacone* (ca. 1800–1868)
222-02
MS PL:LA (2408)

*Duetto* in B♭ (ca. 1800–1868)
222-02
MS PL:LA (2409)

*Duetto* in B♭ (ca. 1800–1868)
222-02
MS PL:LA (2410)

*Finale* in B♭ (ca. 1800–1868)
222-02
MS PL:LA (2411)

*Kantata. Allegro maestoso. Andante Polonoises Chor* (ca. 1800–1868)
222-02
MS PL:LA (2412)

*Kantata. Allegro assai. Andantino moderato. Polonosso* (ca. 1800–1868)
222-02
MS PL:LA (2413)

*Marche* in B♭ (ca. 1800–1868)
222-02
MS PL:LA (2414)

*Marche* in B♭ (ca. 1800–1868)
222-02
MS PL:LA (2415)

*Menuetto* in E♭ (ca. 1800–1868)
222-02
MS PL:LA (2416)

*Menuetto* in B♭ (ca. 1800–1868)
222-02
MS PL:LA (2417)

*Tempo Menuetto* in E♭ (ca. 1800–1868)
222-02
MS PL:LA (2418)

*Opera comic* in C minor (ca. 1800–1868)
222-02
MS PL:LA (2419)

*Ouvertura* in E♭ (ca. 1800–1868)
222-02
MS PL:LA (2420)

*Overtura* in B♭ (ca. 1800–1868)
222-02
MS PL:LA (2421)

*Overtura* in E♭ (ca. 1800–1868)
222-02
MS PL:LA (2422)

*Overtura* in F minor (ca. 1800–1868)
222-02
MS PL:LA (2423)

*Overtura alia opera seria* in E♭ (ca. 1800–1868)
222-02
MS PL:LA (2424)

*Polonoises* (ca. 1800–1868)
222-02
MS PL:LA (2425-2434)

(5) *Quartets* (ca. 1800–1868)
222-02
MS PL:LA (2435-2439)

(2) *Romances* (ca. 1800–1868)
222-02
MS PL:LA (2440-2441)

(5) *Rondos* (ca. 1800–1868)
222-02
MS PL:LA (2442–2446)

*Sinfonia Opera Fivei* in B♭ (ca. 1800–1868)
222-02
MS PL:LA (2447)

*Sinfonia* in B♭ (ca. 1800–1868)
222-02
MS PL:LA (2448)

*Suita* (*Polonoises, Maldaviena, Quadrila en militaire, & Allemande*) (ca. 1800–1868)
222-02
MS PL:LA (2449)

*Zingara Russa* (ca. 1800–1868)
222-02
MS PL:LA (2450)

### Kleczinsky, Jan (d. 1828)

*Partie*
Seven-part Harmoniemusik
MS BRD:DO [lost]

### Kozlowski, Józef (1757–1831)

*Adagio & Largo* (ca. 1800–1816)
222-02
MS PL:LA (2458)

*Polonoises* (ca. 1800–1816)
222-02
MS PL:LA (2459)

*Terzetto* (ca. 1800–1816)
222-02
MS PL:LA (2460)

### Karlowicz, Mieczyslaw (1876–1909)

*Largo: marcia funèbre* (1899)
Winds
MS [cited in MGG]

### Lessel, Franciszek (1780–1835)

*Parthia* in E♭
22-02
MS CS:Pnm (XLI.B.162)

*Parthia* Nr. 3
22-02
MS CS:Pnm (XLI.B.164)

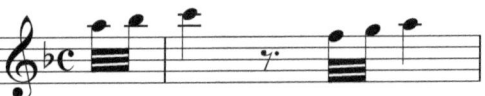

*Parthia* Nr. 4
22-02
MS CS:Pnm (XLI.B.163)

*Partita*
22-02
MS A:Wgm (VIII 5226)

## Representative Arrangement

### Meyerbeer

*Die Hügenotten & Robert der Teufel*
Arranged by Josef Dawid (Kapellmeister, Wadowice) in 1856
Military band
MS A:Wn (Sm 20729)

# Spain

**Carnicer, Ramon (1789–1855)**

*Military marches* [cited in Grove, III, 801]

**Gavaldá José (Spanish bandmaster, 1818–1890)**

*Mass*
Six-part chorus, military band [cited in Grove, VIII, 196]
Grove adds that in 1856 Gavaldá began a highly successful magazine for bandmasters, *El eco de Marte*, which he sold, together with his compositions, to the firm of Romero Andia in 1867.

**Soler, Francisco**

*Marcha Real Religiosa*
For both, or either, orchestra and band
EP [unknown publisher] F:Pn (K.12.866)

**Sor, Joseph Fernando (1778–1839)**

*March*
Band
MS [lost, cited by Grove, XVII, 534]

# Sweden

### Berwald, Franz (1796–1868)

*Soldatenlied*, 'Schwed' (1845)
Chorus, wind orchestra
MS [cited by MGG, without location; try S:Skma]

*Kantata, Gustaf Adolph den stores seger och död vid Lützen* (1845)
SATB, wind orchestra
MS [cited by MGG, without location; try S:Skma]

*Nordiska fantasibilder* (1846)
Male chorus, winds, organ
MS [cited by MGG, without location; try S:Skma]

*Tongemälde* (1849)
Male chorus, winds, organ
MS [cited by MGG, without location; try S:Skma]

*Musik till industrieerpositionens* (1866)
Male chorus, winds
MS [cited by MGG, without location; try S:Skma]

*Allegro con spirito*
SATB, winds
MS [cited by MGG, without location; try S:Skma]

### Henneberg, Richard (1853–1925)

*Serenade*
1122-02
MP (Musikaliska konstfördeningen, 1916)

# Union of Soviet Socialist Republics

**Liadov (1855–1914)**

*Valse Badinago*, Op. 32
2030-, piccolo, harp, bells
EP (Belaiev) [cited by DJ]

*The Music Box*, Op. 32
2030-, piccolo, harp, bells
EP (Belaiev) [cited by DJ]

**Heinrich IV (of Russia)**

*Geschwind-Marsch*
Kavalleriemusik
MS DDR:Bds (Hausbibliothek) [lost]

**Tanejew, Alexander Sergejewitsch (1850–1915)**

*Andante*
2222-02
MP (Leeds; McGinnis & Marx) [cited by MH]

**Tschaikowsky, Peter (1840–1893)**

*Adagio*
2220-, English horn, bass clarinet
MS (autograph) USSR:KTSCHM; US:DW (236)
   [with Tschaikowsky Horn *Quartet*]

*Marche militaire* (for the 98th Inf.)
Military band
EP (Moscow, Jorgenson, 1894)

Overture, from *Yolande*
Winds [of the orchestra]
EP (Moscow, Jorgenson, 1891)

# United States of America

**Collections**

*Brass Band Journal*
EP (New York, 1854)
US:Wc (M1200.B82; MIC.no.Music-1496)
Contains 24 works for twelve-part brass band.

*25th Massachusetts Regiment Band Books*
Eighteen-part military band
MS US:WOa (Mss.boxes 'Mil')
Contains approximately 70 works, ca. 1861–1865.

*3rd New Hampshire Infantry Band Books*, ca. 1861
Military band
MS US:Wc (M1200.C7 no. 1 case; MIC. no.Music-654) [Set I]; US:CDhs [Sets II, III]; US:HO [Set III]
Includes 50 works in Set I; 50 works in Set II; and 36 works in Set III.

*Collection of Dances, Marches, and other Music*, ca. 1862
Brass band
MS US:NYp (Mus.Res.-Amer.*MV)
Contains 65 full scores for ten- or twelve-part brass band with percussion.

*Collection*, 11th U.S. Infantry, 1862
Military band
MS US:NYp (Mus.Res.-Amer.*MV) [E♭ cornet only]
Contains 50 works by Gilmore, Dodworth, Halloway, Downing, Baton, etc.

*26th Regimental Band. North Carolina Troops. C.S.A.*
Brass band
MS US:WS
Six sets of part-books, each containing several works, ca. 1862–1865.

*Stratton Military Band Journal*
Brass band, E♭ clarinet, percussion
EP (New York, 1866–1871)
US:Wc (M1200.M64s; MIC.no.Music-1981)
Contains 150 works [of an original 300].

**Bechler, Johann Christian (1784–1857)**

*Parthia* in E♭
21-12
MS US:WS

**Collauf**

*Parthia*
222-02
MS US:WS [missing clarinet 1]

**Dignam, Walter**

[Collection]
Brass band
MS US:Mhs (Dignam Collection)
Contains approximately 165 works, cl 1849–1864.

**Dodworth, Allen**

*Dodworth's Brass Band School*
EP (New York, 1853)
US:Wc (MT733.D64B5; MIC.no.Music-1978)
Part IV contains full scores.

**Eaton, E. K.**

(12) *Pieces of Harmony*
Brass band
EP (New York, 1846) US:Wc (M1.A13E; Mic. no.Music-1983)
Contains works for seventeen-part brass band.

*Eaton's Series of National & Popular Songs*
Small brass band
EP (Boston, 1852) US:Wc (Uncataloged)
Contains 12 works in five to twelve parts.

*Eaton's Series of National & Popular Songs*
Small brass band
EP (Boston, 1853) US:Wc (M1200.E; MIC. no.Music-1983)

## Fanciulli, Francesco

[Collection]
Military band
MS NYp (*MMZ-Amer.)
Contains works for band, ca. 1870–1915.

## Gilmore, Patrick S.

*P. S. Gilmore's Brass Band Music*
EP (Boston, 1859) US:Wc (M1200.G) [Set I, E♭ cornet only]
Contains 12 works. Gilmore's original library was sold to E. A. Courturier of Easton, Penna, in 1897, and then possibly to Carl Fischer, New York.

## Goodale, Ezekiel

*The Instrumental Director*
Large military band
EP (Hallowell, 1829) US:Wc (ML30.4 no.156 case)

## Heinrich, Anthony Philip (1781–1861, in the US after 1850)

*Marcia funebre for the Heroes* (ca. 1850–1854)
Brass band with percussion
MS [cited in Grove, VIII, 443]

*Marcia funerale* (after 1850)
Brass band, percussion
MS [cited in Grove, VIII, 443]

## Herbert, Victor (1859–1924)

*McKinley Inauguration March*
Band
EP (New York, 1897) [cited in MGG]

*The President's March*
Band
EP [cited in MGG]

*March of the 22nd Regiment, New York*
Band
EP [cited in MGG]

## Hitchcock, E. A., General

[Collection]
Military band
MS US:Wc (M1200.H65)
Contains several works, ca. 1825.

## Howe, Elias, Jr.

*Musicians's Companion*
Six to eight-part brass band
EP (Boston, 1844) US:Wc (M177.H85; MIC. no.Music-1979)
Contains some 300 works.

## Kyle, Alexander

[Collection of Manuscripts, 1820–1843]
MS US:Wc (M196.K97 case; M1.Ai218; M1.A13K [and T] case)
Contains one work for 2021-12, bass.

## Michael, David Moritz

*Parthie* I
21-02
MS US:WS

*Parthie* II
21-02
MS US:WS

(14) *Partitas*
    I: 21-11
    II: 1021-01
    III, VI, X–XII: 22-01
    IV, V: 22-02
    VII–IX: 21-02
    XII, XIV: 21-01
MS US:BETm, US:WS [Nrs. I, II, IV, V, and these are incomplete]

*Parthia* ('bestimmt zu einer Wasserfahrt auf der Lecha')
22-02
MS US:BETm, US:WS

*Parthia* ('bey einer Quelle zu Blasen')
21-02
MS US:BETm, US:WS

## Missud, Jean M.

[Collection]
Military band
EP US:SA (Missud Collection)
Contains some 65 works dating from ca. 1840.

## United States of America

**Morse, Samuel**
>[Collection]
>21-02 and larger
>MS US:Wc (M177.M88 case; and Mic. no.Music-1993)
>Contains one work for 21-02, *Pandean Waltz*, 'as arranged for King George's Band.' The collection dates from ca. 1811.

**Peters' [Publisher]**
>*Peters' Saxhorn Journal*
>Brass band
>EP (Cincinnati, 1859) US:Wc (Uncataloged)
>Contains 13 works.

**Phile**
>*Harmonymusik*
>122-02
>MS [cited by Hellyer]

**Reeves, D. W.**
>*Rienzi Marsch*
>Military band
>EP (Unknown) US:DW (410)

**Prendiville, Hayyr**
>*Pirates of the Savate*
>Military band
>EP (Boston, 1881) F:Pn (Vm.27.10442)

**Scala, Francis**
>[Collection]
>Military Band
>MS US:Wc (Uncataloged)
>Contains approximately 600 items associated with this leader of the US Marine Band, 1855–1871.

**Shipman, W. H.**
>[Collection]
>Military band
>MS US:DI (Vault 11)
>Contains approximately 158 works, ca. 1885–1890.

**Sousa, John Philip**
>The Sousa manuscripts which date from before 1900 are found primarily in three locations:
>Band Building
>School of Music
>The University of Illinois
>Urbana, Illinois
>
>Military Music Collection
>U.S. Marine Corps Museum
>Washington, D. C.
>
>J. Sterling Morton High School
>Cicero, Illinois

**Webb, William**
>*Grand Military Divertimentos*
>Military band
>EP (Philadelphia, ca. 1816–1820)
>Contains 24 works.

# Germany

## Collections

*Sammlung von Märschen für vollstandige türkische Musik, zum bestimmten Gebrauch der Königlich Preussischen Armée*
EP (Berlin, Schlesinger [in score]; Paris, Ebend [individual compositions]) A:Wn [first ten volumes]

Volume 1   13 *Geschwindmärsche*
1a. *Dessuer Marsch*
1b. von Sazenhofer
2–6. von Klopow
7–9. von Boieldieu
10. von Stackelberg
11. aus dem Ballet: *les Amours de Vénus*
12. von Cavos

Volume 2   12 *langsame Märsche*
1–3. von Dörffeld
4. aus dem Ballet: *les Amours de Vénus*
5–6. von Dörffeld
7. des ersten Garde-Bataillons
8. von Vogel
9. des Herzogs von Braunschweig
10. des Prinz August
11–12. von G. A. Schneider

Volume 3   12 *Geschwindmärsche*
13. von Cavos
14. des siberischen Grenadier Regiments
15. von Dörffeld
16. aus dem Ballet: *les Amours de Vénus*
17. aus Cherubini's *les 2 Journées*
18. von Cavos
19. des Königs von Preussen
20–22. von Dörffeld
23. des Fanagoriskischen Regiments
24. von Nicolo

Volume 4   12 *Geschwindmärsche*
25. des Königs v. Preussen, arr. von Cavos
26–27. von Dörffeld
28. *Pariser Einzugsmarsch 1815*
29. von Boieldieu
30. von Devienne
31. von Steibelt
32. der Reserve-Artillerie
33. von Dörffeld
34. von Paer
35. von Dörffeld
36. aus Spontini's *Vestalin*

Volume 5   12 *langsame Märsche*
13. von Koslowsky
14. von Titoff
15–16. der Jasmaulaschen Garde
17. aus Mozart's *Titus*
18. des Archangel-Gorodizkischen Regiments
19–20. von Cavos
21. des Königs Friedrich II
22–23. à la Turque
24. *alter russischer Marsch* von Gluck

Volume 6   12 *langsame Märsche*
25–27. des Prinzen von Coburg
28. von Dörffeld
29–31. aus Mozart's *Zauberflöte*
32. von Dörffeld
33. von Zingarelli
34. aus Spontini's *Vestalin*
35. aus Mozart's *Figaro*
36. von Dörffeld

Volume 7   12 *langsame Märsche*
37. des Wjatkaschen Regiments
38. *Pariser Marsch, 1815*
39. von Gloger, 1815
40. aus Spontini's *Cortez*
41. des Polokischen Regiments
42. des Regiments Erbach Eger, 1815
43. Triumphmarsch aus Spontini's *Vestalin*
44. aus *Alfred*
45. aus Spontini's *Lalla Rúkh*
46–48. aus *Calto und Colama*

Volume 8   12 *Geschwindmärsche*
37. von Beethoven
38. *Pariser Einzugsmarsch*, 1814
39. aus Spontini's *Vestalin*
40. aus Spontini's *Cortez*

41. *Wiener Marsch*
42. des Collardo
43–44. aus *Flore und Zephire*
45. polnischer Marsch
46. aus Spontini's *Cortez*
47. aus den *vier Freiern*
48. *la Castiglione*

Volume 9    12 *Geschindmärsche*
49–50. des Grossfürsten Nicolaus
51–52. der hannöverischen Grenadiere
53. aus Schweden
54. aus Spontini's *Vestalin*
55–56. aus Neapel
57–58. aus Rossini's *Moses*
59. der Volhynischen Jäger
60. von Seelicke

Volume 10    3 *langsame Märsche*
49–50. von Naue
51. von C. Eckard

Volume 11    6 *Geschindmärsche*
61. aus Spontini's *Alcidor*
62. des Regiments Semenowsky
63. *Pratermarsch*
64. des Regiments Ismailowsky
65. aus dem Ballet: *la Festa di Terpsichore*
66. von Naue

*Sammlung von Märschen, auf allerhöchsten Befehl Sr. Majestät, des Köngis, zum bestimmten Gebrauche der Königl. Press. Infanterie. Für vollständige türkische Musik*
67. *Marche du Ballet: Malle Cadella*, arrangée par Neithardt
68. *Marsche* (Warschau), arr. par Hasse
69. *Marsche* de Posen
70. *Marsche* de *Alcidor* de Spontini, arr. p. Neithardt
71. *Marsche* des Grénadiers hongroises
72. *Marsche* tirée de *La Dame blanche* de Boieldieu

Volume 12    12 *Geschwind-Märsche*
73. Marche rapportée de S. A. R. le Prince héréditaire de l'Italie 1829, arr. p. A. Neithardt
74. Marsche de l'Opéra: *La Muette de Portici* d'Auber, arr. par Schick
75. Marsche napolitaine, rapportée de l'Italie p. S. A. R. le Prince héréditaire
76. Marche Cavalleggiero della Guardia, rapportée de l'Italie p. S. A. R. le Prince héréditaire
77. Marsche dal 3 Regimento Svizzero, rapportee de l'Italie p. S. A. R. le Prince héréditaire
78. Marsche de S. A. R. le Prince Frédéric de Prusse
79. Marsche de S. A. R. le Prince Frédéric de Prusse
80. Marsche de C. Merz
81. Marsche de l'Opéra: *Le Siège de Corinthe* de Rossini, des Grénadiers du Grand-Duc de Bade
82. Marsche des Chansonniers des Alpes, arr. par N. Neithardt
83. Pasta-Marsche, arr. p. A. Neithardt
84. Marsche rapport'e du Hague, arr. p. A. Neithardt

Volume 13   *Geschwind-Märsche*
85. Marsche de la Garde russe, arr. p. Engelhardt
86. Marsche de la Garde russe, Bat. De Sapeurs, arr. par Engelhardt
87. Marsche de Weller
88. Marsche de Weller
89. Schweizermarsch
90. Marsch aus den *Kreuzrittern*, v. Meyerbeer
91. Marsch des K. K. Regiments, Herzog Wellington
92. Marsch des K. K. Regiments, Prinz Wasa
93. Marsch aus Petersburg, arr. v. Engelhardt
94. Marsch nach Steyerischen Alpenliedern, von Neithardt

*Sammlung von Märschen und Fanfaren für Trompeten-Musik zum Gebrauche der preussischen Cavallerie*
EP (Berlin, Schlesinger)
Volume 1    12 *Märsche*
1. von Krause
2. von Hayn
3. von Magner
4. von Spontini
5. von Krause
6. von Hayn
7. von Dörffeld
8. von Wintzler
9. aus der *Schweizer Milchmädchen*

10. von Hayn
11. aus Aline
12. aus Kiaking

Volume 2  6 *Märsche*
13. aus *der Fee aus Frankreich*
14. aus *der Fee und der Ritter*
15. von Neithardt
16. von Krause
17–18. Redowatschka
19. Marche à Pas redoublé de *Guillaume Tell* ou *Andreas Hofer* de Rossini, arr. par Liess

*Journal für Mil. musik*
EP (Leipzig, Hofmeister, ca. 1800–1828)
[Heft 1–5]
Contained works or arrangements by Hummel, Marschner, Rothe, and Theuss.

*Märsche für türk. Musik*
EP (Offenbach, André, ca. 1800–1828) [Heft 1–3]

(6) *Märsche*
121-22
MS BRD:DS (Mus.Ms.1223/19)
Contains:
1. Prinzess Amalie v. Prussen
2. Alte Dessauer
3. *Bataillonsmarsch* v. Ludwig IX, 1/1/1764
4. Aus *Julius Caesar* f. Reg. d'Alsasc
5. *Bataillonsmarsch* comp. 1759 v. Hesse
6. *March*, comp. Ludwig IX für sein französ Reg. Royal Hesse Darmstadt

## Anonymous (Collections)

*Tänze und Märsche*
Instrumentation unknown
MS BRD:B (Mus.Ms.3445)

100 *Märsche*
MS DDR:Bds (Mus.Ms.Anon.38214)
A volume containing the melody only.

(6) *Quick Marsche*
221-12
MS DDR:Bds (Mus.Ms.Anon.1217)

(4) *Märsche f. Inf. Reg. Nr. 60*
Blas. Orchestra
MS DDR:Bds (Mus.Ms.Anon.1236)

(5) *Märsche*
(One is for SATB, 2-22)
MS DDR:Bds (Mus.Ms.Anon.1231)

(6) *Neue Märsche*
120-1
MS DDR:Bds (Mus.Ms.Anon.1232)

(12) *Russiche Märsche f. Harmonie musik*
223-02
MS DDR:Bds (Mus.Ms.Anon.38026–38027)

(20) *Stücke* (ca. 1800–1820)
200-12, string bass
MS BRD:DS (Mus.Ms.1188/a-f)

(23) *Militarmärsche*
MS BRD:F (Mus.Hs.2184)
Includes works by Wieprecht and Frederick II.

*Pas de Manoeuvre* [a large collection]
Military band
MS BRD:F (Mus.Hs.1799)

(6) *Pieces pour Bugle-Music*
-222, 7 bugles
MS BRD:F (Mus.Hs.1178); US:DW (338)

*Echo & 6 Ländler* (ca. 1820)
2032-221, serpent
MS BRD:Rtt (Inc.IVb/9)

(35) *Stücke* (ca. 1810)
41-02
MS BRD:Rtt (Inc.IVa/28)

(225) *Stücke* (ca. 1810)
1-01, basset horn, viola (?)
MS BRD:Rtt (Inc.IVa/22)

(9) *Harmonien zur Trauer* Musik (early nineteenth century)
2021-12
MS BRD:TSCH (Gg.98)

(5) *Marches* (early nineteenth century)
-24
MS BRD:TSCH (Z.34)

(12) *Stücke* (early nineteenth century)
Harmoniemusik
MS BRD:TSCH (Z.136)

(2) *Stücke* (early nineteenth century)
-261
MS BRD:TSCH (Z.33)

(70) *Stücke* (early nineteenth century)
242-22, serpent, tamburo
MS BRD:TSCH (G.35)

(12) *Harmonie Stücke* (early nineteenth century)
3032-22, percussion
MS BRD:TSCH (Gg.99a)

(4) *Dances* (early nineteenth century)
1-14, post horn
MS BRD:TSCH (Z.36)

(7) *Marches and Dances* (early nineteenth century)
-14 (horn parts are in duplicate)
MS BRD:TSCH (Z.38)

(43) *Marches and Dances* (early nineteenth century)
-04
MS BRD:TSCH (Z.35)

(6) *Marches and Dances* (early nineteenth century)
-532
MS BRD:TSCH (Z.37)

**Anonymous (Single Titles)**

[Untitled]
21-02
MS DDR:Bds (Mus.M8.Anon.952)

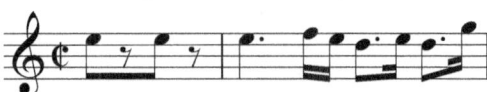

*Adagio* (early nineteenth century)
1222-032, piano
MS CH:E (Th.60,12)

*Andantino* (early nineteenth century)
1222-02, 2 viola (?), string bass
MS BRD:Rtt (Sammelband 32, Nr. 4)

*Echo-Walzer* ('Dessau, 1810')
1122-02
MS DDR:SWl (600/4) [cited by SJK]

*General Bertrand's Abschied* (early nineteenth century)
21-02
MS F:Pn (D.17240[2])

*Kriegslied*, 'Krieger auf!'
Large military band
EP (Breslau, Grass, ca. 1800–1828)

*Hoch Mecklenburg*, Parademarsch (for the military music of Johann Albrecht of Mecklenburg-Schwerin)
MS DDR:SWl (Mus.1406a)

*Militär-Marsch*
MS DDR:SWl (Mus.610)

*Marcia* in E♭
Wind orchestra
MS DDR:Bds (Mus.Ms.Anon.1213)

*Marsch*
1043-432
MS DDR:Bds (Mus.Ms.Anon.1237)

*Marsche der Kais. Russ. Chevalie-Garde*
1232-343, serpent, 2 basset horns, percussion
MS DDR:Bds (Mus.Ms.Anon.38007)

*Parademarsch*
Thirteen winds, 2 trommeln
MS BRD:TSCH (Z.26)

*Dubel Marsch*
-14
MS BRD:TSCH (Z.27)

*Marche, Der Rheinstrohmer* (ca. 1820)
122-1
MS BRD:DS (Mus.Ms.1223/14)

*Marsch*
1000-7, 2 tenorhorns, baritone, bassi, timpani
MS DDR:SWl (C.h.42)

*Marsch* (ca. 1830)
2020-26, timpani, bass
MS BRD:BB (Ms.282)

*Märsche* (from library of Ludwig I)
2062-221, serpent, percussion
MS BRD:Mbs (Mus.Ms.2816)

*Kunstreiter-Tanz* (for Grossherzog Friedrich Franz I Jäger-Bataillon Nr. 14)
1000-4222, 2 tenorhorns
MS DDR:SWl (C.h.51)

*Music for the Riding School* (1831), 9 movements
1052-641, serpent, 2 violins, basso, percussion, contrabassoon
MS BRD:Rtt (Inc.IVa/29)

*Music Zur Toden-Feyer du Frau Herzogin Amalia*
 (April 20, 1807)
1222-022, contrabassoon
MS DDR:WRl (Hofmarschallamt 3820)

(2) *Polonaise* (early nineteenth century)
1032-12, serpent, bass drum
MS BRD:TSCH (Z.28)

(3) *Polonaise* (early nineteenth century)
32-02
MS BRD:TSCH (Z.29)

*Pottpouri*
Ten winds
MS BRD:TSCH (243)

*Septett*
Solo horn, with -141
MS BRD:TSCH (223) [solo part only]

*Still und Heilig* (Funeral music [July 1, 1824] for Fräulein Josepha von Menz, königl. Landrichters Tochter, in Wasserburg.)
SATB, 1020-021
MS BRD:WS (Ms.779)

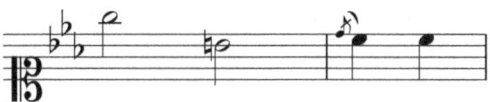

*Tanz Musik* (ca. 1815)
20-02, string bass
MS BRD:Mbs (Mus.Ms.7615)

## Abt, Franz (1819–1885)

*Pas redoublé, 'Chant de la Garde mobile'*
Military band
EP (Paris, Gautrol, 1870) F:Pn (Vm.21.1392)

### Albert, Johann Joseph (1832–1915)

*100th Psalm* (1881)
Male chorus with wind orchestra
MS [cited in MGG]

### Almenraeder, Karl (1786–1843)

*Fantaisie*
111-01, basset horn
MS [cited in F]

### Ambroz, Anton (Kapellemeister, K.K.Östereich 57. Linien-Inf. Reg., Grossherzog von Mecklenburg-Schwerin)

*Verlobungs-Fest-Marsch*
1000-02, 2 Flügelhorn, bassi
MS DDR:SWl (Ambroz, A. 2.)

### Amon, Johann Andreas (1763–1825, after 1817 in Wallerstein)

(6) *Pièces pour Musique turque*, Op. 40
EP (Offenbach, André, Nr. 2233, [1806])
  BRD:MÜu; H:KE
(7) *Pièces pour musique turque*, Op. 57
EP (Offenbach, André, Nr. 3170 [before 1828])
A:Wgm [four pieces only]; BRD:MÜu, BRD:AM

*Musik für Harmonie* (ca. 1820)
1122-02
MS BRD:HR (111.4.1/2.20.364)

*De profondis*
SATB, 20-32, organ
MS BRD:HR (111.4.1/2.20.213)

### André, Johann Anton (1775–1842)

*Ouverture militaire*, Op. 24
EP (Offenbach, composer)
CH:Bu [cited by SJK]

### Anschüz, G.

*Fest-Hymne* 'Hohenzollern Hoch!'
TTBB Male chorus, military band
MS DDR:Bds (Hausbibliothek) [lost]

### Anschütz, Johann Andreas (1772–1856)

*Marche de Francs-Macons*
Thirteen-part Harmoniemusik
EP (Bonn, Simrock, ca. 1800–1828)

### Anton, C.

*The Royal Lancers Galopp*
Military band
MS BRD:DS (Mus.1481)

*Polka* (1857)
Wind orchestra
MS BRD:DS (Mus.1478)

*Geschwind Marsch & Parade Marsch* (1853)
Military band
MS BRD:DS (Mus.1476)
In addition this library has under Mus.1394: Nr.2 *Huldignungs Walzer* and Nr.3 *Trauermarsch*, which may be for band as well.

### Apel

*Kronprinz-Marsch*, Op. 27
MS DDR:Bds (Hausbibliothek) [lost]

### Apell, David August [Pseudonym=Capelli] (1754–1832)

*Notturni*
Wind instruments [cited in MGG]

*Marsche für hess. garde*
Military band [cited in MGG]

### Appel, K.

*Märsch (mit der Melodie des Liedes von 'Anhalt')*
Military band
MS DDR:Bds (Hausbibliothek) [lost]

## Arndt, C.

*Berliner Pferde-Eisenbahn Galop*, Op. 13
Military band
EP (London, Boosé's *Military Journal*, ser. 43, Nr. 4) GB:Lbm (h.1549)

## Arnold, F. W.

*Sie sollen ihn nicht haben*
Male chorus with military band
MS DDR:Bds (Hausbibliothek) [lost]

## Asche, W. (Kapellemeister, 1st Hanseatischen Regiment, Hamburg)

*Deutschland Hoch!* Marsch (1870)
1242-5232, 2 tenorhorn, euphonium, contrabassoon, percussion
MS BRD:B (Mus.Ms.800)

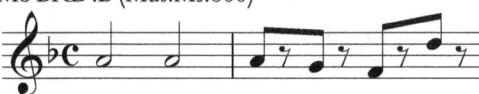

## Aufsess. B. von

*Sie sollen ihn nicht haben*
Brass instruments
MS DDR:Bds (Hausbibliothek, Thouret Nr. 288)

## Azereta

*Variations pour petite Clar. princ. et Musiq. turque*
EP (Hamburg, Böhme, ca. 1800–1828)

## Bach, Chr.

*Jubel-Overture*, Op. 66
Military band
EP (Dresden, Bellmann) A:Gk [uncataloged]

## Bach, Pierre

*Variations pour Musique milit.*, Nr. 2
EP (Bonn, Simrock, ca. 1800–1828)

## Bach, Wilhebn Friedrich Ernst (1759–1845) [Grandson to J. S. Bach]

*Parthia* in B♭
222-02
MS GB:Lbm (Add.32316); US:DW (336)

*Parthia*
Two oboes or two flutes, 22-02
MS GB:Lbm (Add.32.040); US:DW (81)

(2) *Märsche*
222-1
MS DDR:Bds (Hausbibliothek) [lost]

(5) *Konzertstücke*
22-02
MS DDR:Bds (Hausbibliothek) [lost]

## Bagge, Selmar (1823–1896)

*Weihegeschenk* (1896)
SATB, winds
MS CH:Bu [cited in MGG]

## Ballmüller, E.

*Grosser Siegesmarsch*
3262-5432, euphonium, contrabassoon, percussion
MS BRD:B (Mus.Ms.1075)
This is an autograph score fifty pages in length.

## Barth, Friederick Aug. Wilh. (b. 1813 in Leipzig)

*Cantata. 'Sey gesegnet stille Morgensone'*, Op. 54 (1839)
Bass solo, three-part mixed chorus, wind orchestra
MS [in private bands, cited by MGG]

## Barthel, K.

(5) *Altpreussische Armee-Märsche und drei Trios. Mit untergelegten Texten*
MS DDR:Bds (Hausbibliothek) [lost]

## Bassus, Jean M.

*Sextet* (ca. 1800)
Flute solo, with 20-02, viola (?)
MS BRD:Mbs (Mus.Ms.5506)

*Sextet*
20-02, viola (?), bass
MS BRD:Mbs (Mus.Ms.5507)

## Beck, Peter

(12) *Märsche* (1872)
Military band
EP (München) DDR:SWl (Beck, P.2.)

*Schweriner-Parade Marsch* (1874)
Military band
EP (München) DDR:SWl (Beck, P.3.)

## Becker, Heinrich

*Mecklenburgische Volkshymne*, Op. 16 (dedicated to 'Grossherzog Friedrich Franz II')
TTBB, -2431, Flügelhorn, ophicleide
MS DDR:SWl (Becker, H.1)

## Becker, Vincenz Ernst

*Trauermarsch* (1896)
Wind orchestra
MS DDR:Bds (Mus.Ms.Auto.DMS.58667/8)

*Trauermarsch*
Wind orchestra
MS DDR:Bds (Mus.Ms.Auto.DMS.58666)

*Dem Andenken Kaiser Friedrich's. Trauer-Marsch*, Op. 136
Military band
EP (Leipzig, Forberg, 1888) GB:Lbm (f.245.i.[1])

*Das Deutsche Lied*
Male chorus with brass and percussion or piano
EP (Leipzig, 1888) GB:Lbm (E.308.k.[5])

## Behr, Franz (1837–1898)

*Andantino*, 'La Légère,' Op. 406
Band
EP (London, 1884) GB:Lbm (h.1544, Nr. 330)

*Kaiser-Fanfare*
Band
EP (London, 1904) GB:Lbm (h.1549, Ser. 117, Nr. 2)

## Belcke, Friedrich August (1795–1874)

(6) *Märsche*
Large military band
MS DDR:Bds (Hausbibliothek) [lost]

## Berger, Ludwig (1777–1839)

*Marcia* in E♭
Wind instruments
MS DDR:Bds (Mus.Ms.Auto.L.Berger 25)

*Marsche pour les armées anglaises-espanoles dan les Pyrenees*, Op. 1
Wind instruments
MS DDR:Bds (Mus.Ms.Auto.L.Berger 23)

*Triumphal Marsch* (of the Prussian Army, 1814)
Harmonie-orchestra
MS DDR:Bds (Mus.Ms.Auto.L.Berger 47)

(3) *Marches militaires*, Op. 16
Large Harmoniemusik
EP (Leipzig, Hofmeister, ca. 1814–1828)

(3) *Märsche für der Infanterie für Militair-Musik*, Op. 21
EP (Paris, Ebend, ca. 1814–1828)

## Berner, Friedrich Wilhelm (1780–1827)

*Der Herr ist Gott*
TTBB, winds
EP (Breslau, Leuckart) DDR:Bds [cited in Eitner]

## Berr, Friedrich (1794–1838, famous Mannheim clarinetist)

*5ème Air varié*
Solo clarinet with Harmoniemusik
EP (Mainz, Schott) BRD:HZsch

In F:Pn one can find this work with piano accompaniment under K.1209, as well as three similar works under K.1208 [*6th Air varié*], K.1207 [*7th Air varié*], and K. 1206 [*8th Air varié*]. The F:Pn catalog indicates that there were four such works with band accompaniment published in Paris by Lemoine.

*Grande Harmonie*
EP (Paris, Ebend) [Nr. 1–2]
EP (Mainz, Schott) [2 Suites] BRD:MZsch

*Musique militaire*
Twelve-part Harmoniemusik
EP (Paris, Ebend) [Cah. 1–6]
EP (Mainz, Schott) [6 Suites] BRD:MZsch

[Unfinished score, dated 'Paris, Jan. 6, 1837']
Military band
MS F:Pn (W.24.55)

*March*
Instrumentation unknown
MS BRD:TSCH (Z.136, Nr. 6)

*Marche du couronnement de Charles X*
Instrumentation unknown
MS BRD:TSCH (Z.136)

*Pas redoublé* (based on the 'Barcarole' from *Marino Falieri* of Rossini)
EP (Paris, Pacini)

(3) *Pièces*
Military band
EP (Mainz, Schott) BRD:MZsch
Contains an Overture, Andante and Menuetto.

*La Réunion*
Military band
EP (Bonn, Simrock)
Contains:
  1. *Marche* de Rossini
  2. *La Clochette* de Paganini
  3. *Le Sabbat*. Pas redoublé de Niedermeyer
  4. *Pas redoublé, le petit Blanc* de Panseron
  5. *Le petit Porteur d'Eau* de Panseron
  6. *La Favorite*. Valse allemande

*Valse et Pas redoublé, sur la dernière Pensée de C.M. de Weber*
Military band [arranged?]
EP (Mainz, Schott) BRD:MZsch

### Berthold

*Parade-Marsch*
Kavalleriemusik
MS DDR:Bds (Hausbibliothek) [lost]

### Billert, Karl Fr. Aug. (1821–1875)

*Marcia funèbre* (ca. 1850)
Cavallerie musik [here: small cornet, cornets, 2 tenorhorn, baritone, 4 trumpets, bass, percussion]
MS BRD:B (Mus.Ms.1840)

*Kronplungen Marsch* (Berlin, 1856)
TTBB, band
MS F:Pn (MS.3540)

### Bilse, Benjamin (1811–1902)

*Jubel-Fest-Marsch* (ca. 1880)
2252-6431, 2 alto clarinets, alto horn, tenorhorn, baritone, percussion
MS BRD:B (Mus.Ms.1845)

*Polka*, Op. 35
Military band
EP (Berlin, Bote & Bock) DDR:SWl (Bilse, B.1)

### Birnbach

*Volkslied am Geburtsfeste des Königs*
Apparently for military band
MS DDR:Bds (Hausbibliothek) [lost]

### Bitterman, Carl Friedrich

*Marche pour corps de Janitchare* (dedicated to Prince
 Eugene Napoleon)
Military band
MS BRD:Mbs (Mus.Ms.3052)

### von Blon, Franz (1861–1945)

*Marche*, Unterm Siegshanner
Military band
MS BRD:Mbs (Mus.Ms.11559)

*Marche*, 'Die Freundschafts-Flagge'
Military band
MS BRD:Mbs (Mus.Ms.11598)

### Blumenfeldt, Aron Wolff (b. ca. 1825)

*Deutscher Triumph Marsch*
Brass band with timpani
MS BRD:B (Mus.Ms.1989/5)

*Die heimkekrenden Sieger*
Brass band with timpani
MS BRD:B (Mus.Ms.1989)

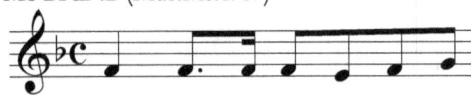

### Blummer, Martin (1827–1901)

*Hymne* ('zur Enthullung des Lessing-Denkmals')
Chorus and brass [cited in MGG]

### Boh, Alb. Ludwig

'Die Jagd,' *Tongemäde*
Wind orchestra
EP (Braunschweig, Bauer Nr. 638.139.0)
 A:Gk [uncataloged]

### Böhner, Johann Ludwig (1787–1860)

*Motetta*, 'Preise Jerusalem den Herrn'
SATB, 120-223, timpani
MS DDR:Bds (Mus.Ms.2100)

(3) *Harmoniemärsche*
EP (Augsburg, Gombart, 1811) [cited in MGG]

### Bonasegla, Carl Philipp (b. 1779)

*Walzer et Eccors* (ca. 1810)
2022-2
MS BRD:BFb (B-on 40)

*Gesang*, 'Recois de notre amour'
1121-12, contra basso
MS US:DW (337)

*Walzer*
2022-12
MS BRD:BÜu (13-ou-10)

### Bonvin, Ludwig (1850–1939)

*Romanze*, Op. 19a
1122-02
MP (Breitkopf & Härtel) [cited in MH]

*Melodie*
1222-02
MP (Breitkopf & Härtel) [cited in MH]

### Bost (Rost?)

*Adagio* (early nineteenth century)
32-12
MS BRD:TSCH (Gg.130)

### Bothe, Gustav

*Deutscher Kaiser-Marsch* (ca. 1900)
Large military band
MS BRD:B (Mus.Ms.2310)

## Brahms, Johannes (1833–1897)

*Begräbnisgesang*, Op. 13
SATB, 2222-243, timpani
MP (Evanston, 1970) US:DW

*Ellens Zweite Gesang*
Soprano, SS chorus, 2-04
MP (Evanston, 1970) US:DW

## Bratfisch, A.

*Jubel-Marsch* ('zur Erinnerungs-Feier an den Tag der Vereinigung des ehemaligen Pommerns und Rügens mit der Krone Preussen, 1865')
MS DDR:Bds (Hausbibliothek) [lost]

## Braun, C.

*Heilig ist der Herr*, Op. 31
SATB, brass instruments (or organ)
EP (Stuttgart, ca. 1885) GB:Lbm (F.1171.q.[1])

## Büchler, Ferd. (1817–1891)

*Marcia funèbre* (1846)
1122-021
MS BRD:DS (Mus.156)

## Buchholz

*Prelude & Fugue* (for the 100th birthday of Queen Louise of Prussia, March 10, 1876)
Military band
MS A:Gk [uncataloged]

## Bülow, Hans von (1830–1894)

*Bayrische Volkshymne*
Nine-part wind music
EP (München, Aibl, 1880 and 1885) [cited in MGG]

## Bürg, R.

'Hat ibm schon' ('Erinnerung an die Schlacht bei Wörth ... für Crown Prince Fried. Wilh. v Prussia') [1870]
Large military band
MS BRD:B (Mus.Ms.2625/2)

## Burmeister, Paul

*Der Gratulant Geschwind-Marsch*
Military band
MS DDR:SWl (Burmeister, P.3.)

*Soldatenlust Marsch*
Military band
MS DDR:SWl (Burmeister, P.5.)

## Buskies, Rudolph

*Augusta Marsch* (1862)
Large military band
MS BRD:B (Mus.Ms.2651)

*Wilhelms Marsch*
Large military band
MS BRD:B (Mus.Ms.2650)

## Carl, Carl (1830–1898)

*March*, 'Die Hochlander'
Military band
MS BRD:Mbs (Mus.Ms.7865)

*Military Band Collection*
Large military band
MS BRD:Mbs
This is a collection of music of the '4-Feld Artillerie-Regiment-König,' donated by Carl, who was the Kapellmeister. The dates range from 1884 to 1890. Most, if not all, of these works seem to be incomplete; following are the call-numbers, number of titles under this number, and the surviving parts:
Mus.Ms.11713, 196 titles. Here only Flügelhorn 2, alto horn, tenorhorn, 2 alto tromba, 3 E♭ tromba, 3 basso tromba, trombone 2 and 3, baritone, bombard
Mus.Ms.11714, 145 titles. Here only Flügelhorn 2, alto horn, alto tromba, 4 basso tromba, 3 E♭ tromba, trombones 2 and 3

Mus.Ms.11717, 139 titles. Here only 3 Flügelhorns, alto horn, alto tromba, 2 B♭ tromba, E♭ tromba, 2 bass tromba, 3 trombones, baritone, bombard

Mus.Ms.11715, 225 titles. Here only Flügelhorn 2 and 3, tromba alto 1, 3 E♭ tromba, 3 bass tromba, tenorhorn, baritone, trombones 2 and 3

Mus.Ms.11716, 215 titles. Here only 3 Flügelhorns, 3 E♭ tromba, 2 B♭ tromba, 3 bass tromba, alto horn, tenorhorn, baritone, 3 trombones

Mus.Ms.11718, 136 titles. Here only Flügelhorn, alto tromba, 2 F tromba, 2 bass tromba, bombard

Mus.Ms.11719, 95 titles. Here only Flügelhorn 1

Mus.Ms.11720, 77 titles. Here only Flügelhorn 2

Mus.Ms.11721, 88 titles. Here only Flügelhorn 3

Mus.Ms.11722, 128 titles. Here only Alto horn

Mus.Ms.11723, 107 titles. Here only Tromba alto 1

Mus.Ms.11724, 121 titles. Here only Tromba alto 2

Mus.Ms.11725, 106 titles. Here only Eb tromba 1

Mus.Ms.11726, 95 titles. Here only Eb tromba 2

Mus.Ms.11727, 96 titles. Here only Eb tromba 3

Mus.Ms.11728, 103 titles. Here only Tromba basso 1

Mus.Ms.11729, 106 titles. Here only Tromba basso 2

Mus.Ms.11730, 93 titles. Here only Tromba basso 4

Mus.Ms.11731, 105 titles. Here only Trombone 1

Mus.Ms.11732, 110 titles. Here only Trombone 2

Mus.Ms.11733, 81 titles. Here only Trombone 3

Mus.Ms.11734, 88 titles. Here only Baritone

Mus.Ms.11735, 316 titles. Here only percussion parts

Mus.Ms.11736, 191 titles. Here only 3 Flügelhorns, alto horn, tenorhorn, 2 tromba, 4 tromba basso, 3 trombones, bariston, bombard

## Carl, Gustav Adolf

*Kaiser Wilhelm Siegmarsch* (ca. 1875)
Large military band
MS BRD:B (Mus.Ms.3125)

## Charlotte von Preussen

*Marsch* (March 22, 1848)
Military band
MS DDR:Bds (Hausbibliothek, Thouret, 28)

## Chelard, Hippolyte Andie (1789-1861)

(36) *Marches & Dances* (ca. 1830)
Wind orchestra
MS BRD:B (Mus.Ms.3445/28)

*Cycle Symphonique*, Nr. 6, 'Elégie'
1000-303, ophicleide, 2 harps, percussion, 4 celli, string bass
MS BRD:B (Mus.Ms.3445)

## Cohen, Karl Hubert (1851–1938)

*Requiem*, Op. 2
Four-part chorus, winds
EP (Regensburg, Pustet) [cited in MGG]

*Te Deum*
Five-part chorus, winds, organ
EP (Regensburg, Pustet) [cited in MGG]

## Commer, Franz (1813–1887)

*Abendlied* and *Die drei Sterne*
TTBB, 22-02
MS DDR:Bds (Mus.Ma.Auto.F.Cammer 55)

## Conradi-Carlshall, W.

*Grand Marcia funèbre* (for Wilhelm I, June 19, 1864)
Large military band
MS BRD:B (Mus.Ms.4065)
A fifty page score!

## Cossart, Leland (b. 1877)

*Suite*, Op. 19
2222-02, harp
MP (Hinrichshofen) [cited by MH]

### Curschmann, Karl Friedrich (1805–1841)

*Motette*, 'Barmherzig und gnadig'
Four-part chorus, brass instruments
MS [cited in MGG]

### Czibulka, Alphons (1842–1894)

*Kronprinz Friedrich Wilhelm Defilir March*
Large military band
MS BRD:B (Mus.Ms.4366)

### Dickhut

(6) *Stücke*
-543, 2 Klappenflügelhorner, posthorn, 2 bass trumpets
EP (Mainz, Schott, ca. 1800–1828) BRD:MZsch

### Donderer, Benedick (second half, nineteenth century)

*Plaenkler Marsch*
MS BRD:Mbs (Mus.Ms.5606)

### Dornaus, Jr.

(6) *Petites pièces*, Op. 2
21-02
EP (Offenbach, André, ca. 1800–1828)

### Dornheckter, Robert (1839–1890)

*Jubel-Marsch* (for Wilh. I, June 8, 1865)
1000-6, Flügelhorn, 2 tenorhorns, baritone
MS BRD:B (Mus.Ms.5160)

### Dunkler, Franc. (1816–1878)

*Une l'arme sur sa Tombe. Elégie et Marche funèbre* ('comp. pour Musique Militaire et Executee a l'Enterrement Solennel du Sa Majeste la Reine Mère des Pays-Bas')
Large military band
MS BRD:B (Mus.Ms.5340)

### Dreher, Jos Anton

*Harmonie* (early nineteenth century), 4 movements
1021-021
MS BRD:TSCH (Gg.158)

### Drobisch, Karl Ludwig (1803–1854)

*Erntefest*, Op. 47 (Nr. 5 of *Die Festzeiten Sammlung yon Kirchen Cantaten*)
SATB, -023, cello, bass
EP (Leipzig, Hofmeister, ca. 1850) F:Pn (K.18496)

### Ebers, Charles Frederic (1770–1836)

(12) Petites pieces, Op. 5
2-02, 2 basset horns
EP (Hummel) [advertized in AMZ, 1804]

(6) *Marches*, Op. 18
Eleven-part Harmoniemusik
EP (Leipzig, Peters, ca. 1800–1828)

### Eberwein, Traugott (1775–1831)

*Musique d'harmonie*
2112-02
MS BRD:DS [cited by Eitner]

### Egwolf, Joseph

*Marsch Sieg bei Orleans* [Sept. 29, 1870] ('für Stabshoboists K. Bayer. 6 Inf. Reg.')
Large military band
MS BRD:B (Mus.Ms.5555)

### Eichhorn, A.

*Kronprinz Friedrich Wilhelm Marsch*
MS DDR:Bds (Hausbibliothek) [lost]

### Eilhardt, Friedrich Christian Carl

*Sieges Triumph Festmarsch* (1866)
Two military bands (Infantrie & Cavalerie)
MS BRD:B (Mus.Ms.5560)
This work is scored for:
  Orch. I: 1242-4432, E♭ piccolo, 2 E♭ clarinets, 2 tenorhorns, contrabassoon, small and large drum
  Orch. II: E♭ piccolo, 2 E♭ cornets, 2 B♭ cornets, Flügelhorn, 2 tenorhorns, 4 E♭ trumpets, baritone, 2 tubas

### Emmerig, Joseph

*Theodolindens Traumgeschicht* (for the birthday of the Queen of Bavaria, 1827)
TTBB, 1021-22
MS A:Sca (Hs.734)

### Enckhausen

*Militärmusik*, Op. 1
EP (Hanover, Bachmann, ca. 1800–1828)

### Endres, Franz Andreas

*Serenade* in C (ca. 1805)
200-12, timpani, string bass
MS BRD:Hbs (Mus.Ms.10467) [formerly in BRD:HL]

(2) *Marches* and a *Waltz* (ca. 1810)
21-02, string bass
MS BRD:BAR

### Enzinger, Ludwig

*Die Abend-Glocke Märche*
MS BRD:Mbs (Mus.Ms.7868)

### Esterl

*Melodin-Chronick 'Potpourri'* (1898)
Brass and percussion
MS BRD:Mbs (Mus.Ms.11548)

### Ett, Casper

Lied, *'Singt Brüder im Jauthzensen Tone'*
Two singers, -331, timpani
MS (autograph) BRD:Mbs (Mus.Ms.3694)

*'Hymn windet Rosenketten', Hochzeitsgesang* (1822)
Four singers, 1122-02
MS [cited in MGG]

### Fackler, M.

*Huldigungsmarsch* (1840)
Large military band
MS DDR:Bds (Hausbibliothek) [lost]

### Faisst, Immanuel Gottlob (1823–1895)

*Den Herrn mit. Willkürl.*
Voices, brass, timpani
EP (Kranzl) [cited in MGG]

(4) *Kriegs- und Siegeslieder*, Op. 28
Voices and brass
EP (Leipzig, Forberg) [cited in MGG]

*Siegesps.*, Op. 29
Voices and brass
EP (Stuttgart, Ebner) [cited in MGG]

*Cantata, Sängers Wiederkehr*, Op. 30
Singers, brass, timpani, string bass
EP (Stuttgart, Ebner) [cited in MGG]

*Schillerkantate*, Op. 31
Voices and brass
EP (Stuttgart, Ebner) [cited in MGG]

### Febvre, F.

*Grande marche militaire* (1867)
MS DDR:Bds (Hausbibliothek) [lost]

### Fesca, Alexander Ernst (1820–1849)

*Serenade*
Large military band
MS [cited in Grove, VI, 500]

## Fiedler

*Marsch* in C
22-12
EP (Hamburg, Böhme, ca. 1800–1828)

## Fischer, C.

*Recueil de Musique Militaire*
EP (Mainz, Schott, ca. 1800–1828)
BRD:MZsch [Suites 1-3]

*Potpourri brillant à grande Harmonie milit.*, Op. 5
EP (Offenbach, André, ca. 1800–1828)

*Harmonie*
Nine-part brass ensemble
EP (Bonn, Simrock, ca. 1800–1828)

*Musique militaire pour Cavallerie*, Op. 11
Two 'Cors de Signal à Clefs,' 2 E♭ trumpets, 2 B♭ trumpets, 1 A♭ trumpet 2 'Principales,' and 3 trombones
EP (Mainz, Schott) BRD:MZsch

*Introduction et Polonaise d'après des Themes de Kalkbrenner et Kalliyoda*, Op. 13
Large military band
EP (Paris, Ebend)

## Fischer, Heinrich Wilhelm (fl. ca. 1815, Braunschweig)

*Trauer-Marsch* (December 14, 1815)
222-02
MS DDR:SWl (Fischer, W.1.)

## Fischer, Hermann

*Hymnus*
TTBB, wind orchestra
MS DDR:SWl (Ms.1869)

## Fischer, J. G. C.

*Militarmuik*
EP (Hanover, Bachmann, ca. 1800–1828)

## Florschutz, Eucharius (b. 1757)

*Ave Maria* (1829)
SATB, 1022-, continuo
MS DDR:SWl (Florschutz, E.1.)

## Frank, Ernst (1847–1889)

*Fanfare* (on a subject from Handel's *Alexander's Feast*)
Twelve trumpets and 2 timpani
MS (autograph) BRD:Mbs (Mus.Ms.6679)

## Franke, F. C. (late nineteenth century)

*Defilir-Marsch*
Large military band
MS DDR:Bds (Mus.Ms.6595)

## Fränzel (Frantzl)

*Echo für die Harmony*, 2 movements
22-02
MS CS:KRa (IV.B.25)

*Concerto* for Violin
'türkischer musik,' accompaniment
MS [heard in a concert in Munich, as reported in AMZ, January 26, 1803 (p. 307)]

## Frese, C.

*Altpreussiche militär-Märsche* (edited for 'grosser Orchester Infanterie-musik, Cavallerie-, Jäger- und Pioniermusik')
EP (Leipzig, Breitkopf & Härtel, no date)
F:Pn (Vm.7.7888)

## Friedemann, F.

*Die 2. Compagnie. Defilir-Marsch*
MS DDR:Bds (Hausbibliothek) [lost]

## Friedrich II (King)

*Overture*
Large military band
MS A:Gk [uncataloged]

## Friedrich Wilh. III (King)

(4) *Preussischer Armée-Marsch*
MS DDR:Bds (Hausbibliothek) [lost]

[fragment] *Marsch*
MS DDR:Bds (Hausbibliothek, Thouret, Nr. 23)

*Pfeifenmarsche*
MS (autograph) DDR:Bds (Hausbibliothek, Thouret, Nr. 248)

*Alte Pfeifenmarsche*
MS (autograph) DDR:Bds (Hausbibliothek, Thouret, Nr. 249)

### Friedrich Wilh. IV

*Geschwind-Marsch*
Large military band
MS DDR:Bds (Hausbibliothek) [lost]

### Fröhlich (first half, nineteenth century)

*Harmonie*
1022-01
MS BRD:DO (Mus.Ms.475/2)

### Fuchs, Julius

*Hymne* (1867)
TTBB, large military band
MS DDR:Bds (Mus.Ms.6140)

### Gabrielli, Graf Nicolaus (1814–1891)

*Marsch* (dedicated to General Guzman Blanco of Venezuela)
Brass, percussion, 'Kanonen-schlage'
EP (Paris, Rouvayre et Leblont, 1883) [cited in MGG]

### Gebaur, Franz Xavier (1784–1822)

*Overture Pastorale* (ca. 1803–1816)
1222-02
MS BRD:AB (S.32)

### Gentsch, E. (Stabshautboist, Kgl. Preuss., 2. Westpf. Inf. Reg. Nr. 15)

*Fest-Overture* (1863)
MS DDR:Bds (Mus.Ms.7361)

*Prinz-Friedrich-Marsch* (1863)
MS DDR:Bds (Mus.Ms.7361/1)

### Gerke, A.

(2) *Pièces pour Mus. turque* ('tirées du Requiem de Rzewuski'), Op. 9
EP (Leipzig, Breitkopf & Härtel, ca. 1800–1828)

(6) *Pièces*, Op. 12
Mus. turque
EP (Paris, Ebend, ca. 1800–1828)

### Göpfert, Carl Andreas

(12) *Pièces*, Op. 26
21-02
EP (Offenbach, André, Nr. 3129, ca. 1800–1828) [Liv. 1-2] BRD:OF; DK:A

(18) *Pièces*
Oboe or flute, 21-02, serpent
EP (Paris, Ebend, ca. 1800–1828) BRD:OF [for 121-12, serpent]

*Allegrino alla Turca* (ca. 1820)
2222-221, serpent, percussion
MS BRD:Rtt (Sammelband 14, Nr. 70)

(4) *Grosse Parthien*
1222-22, contrabassoon [cited in AMZ, 1818]

### Golde, J.

(4) *Märsche uber Kriegslieder* (1813–1815)
MS DDR:Bds (Hausbibliothek) [lost]

### Gouvy, Louis Theodore (1819–1898)

*Octet*, Op. 71
1122-02
EP (Leipzig, Kistner) A:Wgm (VIII 28213); BRD:Bhm (4809); GB:Lbm (e.705); US:Wc (M857G718)

*Petite Suite Gauloise*, Op. 90
1222-02
EP (München, Aibl) A:Wgm (VIII 30079; GB:Lbm (g.1123.d.[8]); US:Wc (M957G75)

## Grawert, E.

*Letzlinger-Rüden-Signal-Marsch*
Large military band
MS DDR:Bds (Hausbibliothek) [lost]

## Grell, Eduard (1800–1886)

*Cantata.* 'Labet ihr Völker' (1830)
SATB, winds
MS DDR:Bds (Mus.Ms.Auto.E.Grell 322)

(2) Chöre (*'Herr Gott, dich loben wir,'* and *'Komm heiliger Geist'*
SATB, winds
MS DDR:Bds (Mus.Ms.Auto.E.Grell 237)

[Chöre], *'Saepins yentis agitator'* (1832)
TTBB, wind orchestra
MS DDR:Bds (Mus.Ms.Auto.E.Grell 471)

*Lateinische Festgesänge* (1830)
TTBB, wind orchestra
MS DDR:Bds (Mus.Ms.Auto.E.Grell 470)

[Chöre], *'Hic dies vere miki festus'* (1831)
TTBB, wind orchestra
MS DDR:Bds (Mus.Ms.Auto.E.Grell 469)

[Chöre], *Gesang bei der Epthüllung von Hegels Denkmal* (October 17, 1870)
TTBB, brass
MS DDR:Bds (Mus.Ms.Auto.E.Grell 504)

[Chöre], *'Non sic excubiae non circumstantial'* (1831)
TTBB, wind orchestra
MS DDR:Bds (Mus.Ms.Auto.E.Grell 468)

*Cantata Hymnus, 'Ich rede von deinen Zeugnissen vor Königen'*
SATB, winds, organ
MS DDR:Bds (Mus.Ms.Auto.E.Grell 317)

## Grimm

(19) *Harmonie stücke* (ca. 1810)
-12
MS BRD:Rtt (Grim 2)

## Grimm, Julius Otto (1827–1903)

*Zum Geburtstage des Kaisers*, Op. 27
Male chorus, wind orchestra
EP (Munster, 1899) [cited in MGG]

*An Kaiser Wilhelm II*, Op. 28
Male chorus, wind orchestra
EP (Munster, 1901)

## Grote, A. R.

*Militar-Marsch und Hymne* (1886)
MS DDR:Bds (Hausbibliothek) [lost]

## Grund, Eduard (1802–1871)

*Oktett*
Piano and winds [cited in MGG]

## Guerra, E.

*Deutsch-italienischer Marsch* (1888)
MS DDR:Bds (Hausbibliothek) [lost]

## Günther, Karl Fried

(12) *Märsche* (for the 'K. Prussia & Elector' of the Saxony army)
222-22, serpent
EP (Torgau, author) [Advertized in AMZ, 1802]

## Habert, Johannes (1833–1896)

*Scherzo*, Op. 107
1112-02
MP (Breitkopf & Härtel) [cited in MH]

## Hacker, Benedikt (1769–1829)

*'Juvayiens Gruss bei der ... Ankunft ... Furst-Erzbischofs Augustin Gruber'* (1824)
TTBB, 22-02
MS A:Wn (Sm.9773); A:Sca (Ms.1858)

## Hagmann

*Harmonie*
Nine-part Harmoniemusik with Klappentrompete
EP (Frankfurt, Fischer, ca. 1800–1828)

## Hallager, A.

*Reminiscenzen aus den letzten Tagen auf St. Helena* (Tone Poem in three parts)
Large military band
MS DDR:Bds (Hausbibliothek, Thouret Nr. 371)

### Hamm, Johann Valentin (1811–1875)

(2) *Polkas, Marsch,* and *Trumpeten Polonaise* (ca. 1850)
Large military band
MS BRD:Mbs (Mus.Ms.2278)

### Hammer, August ('1st Hautbois chez le 7 Reg. s. Hollande')

*Fantaisie*
Solo oboe and 1042-243, serpent, percussion
MS DDR:SWl (MS.2286)

### Hammerl, Cornelius (1769–1839, 1st clarinet, Hofkapelle, Schwerin)

(3) *Parties*
223-12, serpent,
MS DDR:SWl (MS.2288)
Contained here are 4 original movements by Hammerl, together with arrangements of the music of Haydn, Winter, and others.

*Suite* (December 25, 1802)
222-12
MS DDR:SWl (MS.2288/1) [missing oboe II]

*Pollonaisse*
222-12, serpent
MS DDR:SWl (MS.2288/2)

*Andante & Pollaca*
222-12, serpent
MS DDR:SWl (MS.2288/3)

### Hansel, A.

*Militair-Musik*, Op. 31 (Reveille, Parade, Ordinair, Geschwindmarsch, and Retraite)
Seven or Fifteen-part Harmoniemusik
EP (Dresden, Meser, ca. 1800–1828)

*Divertissement. Introduction. Variationen u. Polonaise nach bel. Opern-Motiven*
Fifteen or Seventeen-part Harmoniemusik
EP (Paris, Ebend, ca. 1800–1828)

(6) *Märsche fur Militair-Musik*
Six or thirteen-part Harmoniemusik
EP (Paris, Ebend. ca. 1800–1828)

### Hasse, A. G.

*Serenade*, Op. 6
2000-02, harp, bass [cited in G2]

### Hassloch, Carl (1769–1829)

(3) *Marches* (ca. 1810 or earlier)
2222-22, percussion
MS BRD:DS (Mus.Ms.234)
Contains:
1. Marche de Sauvages
2. Trauermarsch
3. Quickmarsch

*Marche to Ubal, Pastorale & Andantino*
2222-02, bass [last movement with SATB chorus]
MS (autograph) BRD:DS (Mus.1214)

### Haunreiter, Peter

*Feldschritt für Mil. Musik* (1877)
MS (autograph) BRD:Mbs (Mus.Ms.7888)

### Hauptmann, Moritz (1792–1868)

*Motet*, 'Ehre sei Gott in der Höhel' (ca. 1873)
Male chorus and winds
MS BRD:Mbs (Mus.Ms.11504)

### Hause, Carl

*Concert Overture*
Military band
EP (Hannover, Oertel) A:Gk (uncataloged)

### Heine, Gotthelf Sigismund (Kapellmeister, Sebnitz in Sachsen)

*Te Deum*
Voices, 22-223, timpani
EP (Meissen, Klinkicht, 1805) A:Wn, A:Wgm;
   DDR:Bu [cited by Eitner]

### Heine, Samuel Friedrich (member of Hofkapelle in Ludwigslust)

*Auferstehn, ja Auferstehn* (1804)
SSATB, 22-04, serpent, 2 violas (?), bass
MS DDR:SWl (Heine.S.1.)

*Salve Regina*
Soprano, 22-02, bassi
MS DDR:SWl (Heine.S.2.)

### Hennig, Karl (1819–1873)

*Der Königspsalm* (1849)
Chorus, brass, flute, 4 harps [cited in MGG]

### Hennig, T. (civic music director in Gustrow)

(3) *Märsche für das Gardehautboisten-Corps des 89 Reg.*
MS DDR:SWl (Hennig, T.1.)

### Hepworth, George

(3) *Marches* (for Friedrich Franz II)
Large military band
MS DDR:SWl (Hepworth, G.1.)

### Herfurth, R.

*Fantasia, Auf den Alpen*
Band
EP (London, 1879) GB:Lbm (h.1549, Ser. 61, Nr. 4)

### Herold, A.

'Krieger's Heimkehr,' *Defilirmarsch*
Military band
MS DDR:Bds (Hausbibliothek) [lost]

### Herweg, Georg

*Rheinland als Feldschriff*
One vocal part and Harmonie, for soldiers
MS DDR:Bds (Mus.Ms.10555/50)

### Heuschkel, Johann Peter (1773–1853)

*Pièces d'harmonie*
1022-02
EP (Mainz, Schott, ca. 1800–1828) BRD:MZsch

### Heyn, Catharina, Frau

*Der Sieben-Brüder-Marsch*
Instrumentation unknown
MS DDR:Bds (Mus.Ms.10,575)

### Hiebesch, Johann (1766–1820)

*Partita* in D (1813)
1222-12, string bass
MS BRD:HR (111.4.1/2.20.606)

*Partita* in F
2222-03, string bass
MS BRD:HR (111.4.1/2.20.609)

*Partita* in F
2222-03, string bass
MS BRD:HR (111.4.1/2.20.607)

*Partita* in D (ca. 1800)
2222-02, string bass
MS BRD:HR (111.4.1/2.40.99)

### Hiller, Ferdinand (1811–1885)

*Bundeslied*, Op. 174
Male chorus and winds
EP (Leipzig) [cited in MGG]

## Hoffmann, Ernst T. (1776–1822, important German literary figure)

*Türkische Musik*
MS DDR:Bu (under 'ZeIter') [cited by Eichner]

## Hofmann, Heinrich Karl Johann (1842–1902)

*Hymnus an Kaiser Wilhelm II* ('zur Eröffnung der Berliner International Kunstausstellung, 1891')
Male chorus and large military band
EP (Leipzig, Breitkopf & Härtel, 1891) DDR:Bds (Hausbibliothek) [lost]

## Horn, Karl Friedrich (1762–1830)

(12) *Divertissements*
Wind band [F, according to Grove, VIII, 715]

## Hübschmann, J.

*Harmonie* (ca. 1803–1816)
222-02
MS BRD:AB (S.41)
EP (Bonn, Simrock, ca. 1800–1828)

## Jadassohn, Saloman (1831–1902)

*Serenade*, Op. 104c (1890)
2222-02
EP (Leipzig and Boston, A. Schmidt) GB:Lbm (f.244.ww.2); US:DW (249) [sc]

## Jaeger, Will.

*Kriegsmarsch*
Wind orchestra
MS (autograph) DDR:Bds (Mus.Ms.Auto.W.Jaeger 1)

## Jannopulos, Anastas

*Gebel* (for King Otto I of Greece, 1847)
Military band
MS BRD:Mbs (Mus.Ms.3524)

## Jenette, Adolf

*Jubeleums-Marsch* (1870, for the 25th year of the Reign of the King of Bavaria)
MS (autograph) BRD:Mbs (Mus.Ms.7896)

## Jochum, Otto

*Liebesspiegel,* Op. 38
2022-
EP (Augsburg: Böhm) BRD:Bhm (27200)

## Joerg, N.

(12) *Piecen für Harmoniemusik*
EP (Mainz, Schott, ca. 1800–1828) BRD:MZsch

## Kalliwoda, Johann Wenzel (1801–1866)

(6) *Pièces d'Harmonie*, Op. 202
Large military band
EP (Leipzig, Peters) GB:Lbm (h.1570.[1–2]); US:DW (252) [part I only]
Contains a Polka, Marche solennelle, Overture, Mazurka, Choeur de Soldat (with chorus), and Marche funèbre (with chorus).

*Galopp* in E♭
1022-02
MS BRD:DO [cited by SJK]

*Harmonie*
1022-02
MS BRD:DO [cited by SJK]

*Harmoniemusik für Heil Comunion*
22-02
MS BRD:DO [cited by SJK]

## Kanka, Johann N. (1772–1865)

(4) *Märsche*
Woodwinds and 2 horns [cited in MGG]

*Marcia*
Winds, serpent [cited in MGG]

## Kattner, Otto

*Hurrah! Duke Fried. Franz III*
Military band
MS DDR:SWl (MS.3092)

## Katzer, Ignaz

(12) *Veränderungen* (French dances, ca. 1820, for
   Fürsten Eugen zu Bentheim-Bentheim)
1022-12, contrabassoon
MS BRD:BFb (K-at 90b)

## Kempter, Friedrich (b. 1810)

*Militär-Messe* (1898), 5 movements
Large brass band
MS BRD:Mbs (Mus.Ms.11584) [apparently missing choral parts]

## Kempter, Karl (1819–1871)

*Il Tantum ergo* (ca. 1860)
SATB, 1020-521, bombard, timpani
MS BRD:BB (MS.207)

## Kern, Max Josef

*Prinzregent Luitpold-Hymne*
Singer, winds
MS BRD:Mbs (Mus.Ms.7645)

## Kessels, Joseph

*Jungfrau v. Orleans*
Military band
EP (Hannover, Oertel) [reprint of an earlier Tilburg, Kessels print] A:Gk (Uncataloged)

## Kewitsch, Th.

*Volks-Festgesang*
Military band
MS DDR:Bds (Hausbibliothek) [lost]

## Kistler, Cyrill (1848–1907)

*Festmarsch* (Augsburg, 1886, dedicated to Wagner)
MS (autograph) BRD:Mbs (Mus.Ms.7899)

## Klee, L.

*Marsch*
MS DDR:Bds (Hausbibliothek) [lost]

## Kleiber, Leonhard (b. 1863)

*Wittelsbacher Ruhm. Marsch* (ca. 1900)
MS BRD:Mbs (Mus.Ms.7643)

## Klein (?), Bernhard (1793–1832)

(2) *Divertimenti*
Solo clarinet, with 222-02
MS A:Wn [lost]

## Kleinheinz, Franz Xaver (1765–1832)

*Der Huldigungsfeier*
Eight winds
MS [cited in MGG]

*Okett*
Winds
MS [cited in MGG]

*Quintet*
Winds
MS [lost, according to MGG]

## Klughardt, August (1847–1902)

*Nonett*, Op. 36 (1876)
Wind instruments
MS [cited in MGG]

## Kniess, Fr. (b. ca. 1800)

*Der Landsknecht im Frieden* (ca. 1850, 'Feldschritt ...
   [from the collection of] Luitpold v. Bayern')
Wind orchestra
MS (autograph) BRD:Mbs (Mus.Ms.7630)

## Knipfer, F.

*Volkslied*
Large military band
MS DDR:Bds (Hausbibliothek, Thouret Nr. 307a)

## Koch, A.

*Vogesenwacht*
Large military band
MS DDR:Bds (Hausbibliothek, Thouret Nr. 297)

### Kohler, Ernst

*Chor* (1831)
Chorus with Harmoniemusik
MS (autograph) F:Pn (MS.7311)

### Körnlein, Justus (d. 1866)

*Introduction, Waltz, & Galopp* (1841)
1011-121
MS BRD:DO (Mus.Ms.1083)

### Kosleck

*Deutsche Kaiser-Hymne* (1889)
Trumpets and timpani
MS DDR:Bds (Hausbibliothek) [lost]

*Erinnerung an Peterhof Marsch*
Kavalleriemusik
MS DDR:Bds (Hausbibliothek) [lost]

### Kösporer, Johann (second half, nineteenth century)

*Saengers Gebet*
Voice and piano or brass instruments
MS BRD:BB (MS.211) [here piano only]

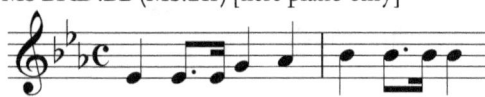

### Kraknest, Herrmann

*Bei der Heimkekr 1871*, Triumphmarsch und Finale
EP (39 page full score) (Berlin, Preuss)
MS (parts) A:Gk (Uncataloged)

### Kraus, Joseph

*Högtidsmarsch*
Wind orchestra
MS BRD:Mbs (Mus.Ms.5170)

### Krause, J. H.

*Arméemärsche fur Trompetmusik*
EP (Berlin, Schlesinger) [Nr. 1–14]
DDR:Bds (Hausbibliothek) [Nr. 1, lost]

(6) *Galanteriestücke*
Trompetenmusik
EP (Leipzig, Breitkopf & Härtel)

*Baierischer Galoppwalzer*
Trompetenmusik
EP (Berlin, Schlesinger)

(2) *Geschwindmärsche*
Militair-Horn-Musik
EP (Paris, Ebend)

*Fackeltanz* (Nov. 29, 1823)
Trompetenmusik
MS DDR:Bds (Hausbibliothek, Thouret, Nr. 321)

### Kreutzer, Konradin (1780–1849)

*Baiersches Volkslied*
Military band
EP (Augsburg, Schlosser, ca. 1800–1828)

### Krug, Diederich (1821–1880)

*Hymne an Germania*, Op. 79
Several versions, including large military band and brass band
EP (Leipzig, Kistner) [cited in MGG]

### Küffner, Jos. (1776–1856)

*Pièces d'Harmpnie*, Op. 40
1021-01
EP (Mainz, Schott) BRD:HZsch [Nr. 1, 2]
EP (Mainz, Schott; Paris, Ebend) BRD:MZsch [Nr. 3, for 1011-1, basset horn]

(3) *Duplier-Märsche*, Op. 51
Large military band
EP (Mainz, Schott) BRD:DS
EP (Paris, Ebend) [as 3 *Pas redoublés*]

(6) *Duplirmarsche*, Op. 60
Military band
EP (Paris, Ebend)

*Harmonie*, Op. 92
1021-01
EP (Mainz, Schott, Nr. 1537) BRD:HR [missing the flute]
EP (Paris, Ebend) [for 21-02]

*3ème Potpourri*, Op. 101
Musique militaire
EP (Paris, Ebend)
Three of these 'Potpourris' can be found in B:Bc; at least one is a manuscript.

*4ème Potpourri*, Op. 102
Musique militaire
EP (Paris, Ebend)

*Overture*, Op. 108
Musique turque
EP (Paris, Ebend)

(2) *Potpourri,* Op. 109
Musique turque
EP (Paris, Ebend)

*5ème Potpourri*, Op. 110
Musique militaire
EP (Paris, Ebend)

*6stes Potpourri & Jägerchor* [from *Der Freischütz*]
Türkische Musik
EP (Paris, Ebend)

*Türkische Musik*, Op. 115
EP (Offenbach, André)

*Türkische Musik*, Op. 116
EP (Offenbach, André)

*7ème Poutpourri*, Op. 126
Musique militaire
EP (Mainz, Schott) BRD:KZsch

*8ème Potpourri*, Op. 132 (based on *Der Freischütz*)
Musique militaire
EP (Paris, Ebend)

*9ème Potpourri*, Op. 134 (based on *Der Freischütz*)
Musique militaire
EP (Paris, Ebend)

*Pièces d'Harmonie*, Op. 138 (based on *Otello* and *Preciosa*)
1022-02
EP (Mainz and Paris, Schott) BRD:MZsch; A:Wgm [cited by Eitner]
EP (Paris, Richault)

*Musique turque*, Op. 146 (March and Dance collection)
EP (Mainz, Schott) BRD:MZsch

*10ème Potpourri*, Op. 153 (based on *Euryanthe*)
Musique militaire
EP (Paris, Ebend)

*Ouverture* in F, Op. 160
Musique militaire
MS B:Bc [cited by Eitner]
EP (Mainz and Paris, Schott) BRD:MZsch

*Ouverture* in E♭, Op. 161
Musique militaire
MS B:Bc [cited by Eitner]
EP (Mainz and Paris, Schott) BRD:MZsch

*Sinfonie*, Op. 163
Musique militaire
EP (Mainz, Schott) BRD:MZsch

*Musique Militaire* [Potpourri, Nr. 11], Op. 169
52-542, serpent, percussion
EP (Mainz, Schott, 1826) BRD:MZsch; BRD:B (DMS.85.393)

*Musique Militaire* ('*Walses et Danses bavaroises*'), Op. 170
52-542, serpent, percussion
EP (Mainz. Schott, 1826) BRD:MZsch; BRD:B (DMS.85.394)
EP (Offenbach. André) [as 'Potpourri pour Musique militaire']

*Potpourri*, Op. 182 (on Auber's *le concert à la Cour*)
1022-02
EP (Mainz, Schott) BRD:MZsch; BRD:B (DMS.85.368)

*Potpourri,* Op. 183 (on Rossini's *Corradino et Moïsé*)
1022-02
EP (Mainz, Schott) BRD:MZsch; BRD:B (DMS.85.369)

(3) *Marches* and (4) *Pas redoublés*
52-542, serpent, percussion
EP (Mainz, Schott) BRD:MZsch; BRD:B (DKS.85.397)

(6) *Pièces d'harmonie*, Op. 205
1022-02
EP (Mainz, Schott) BRD:MZsch; F:Pn (vm.27.2288); A:Wgm (VIII 9148)

(3) *Grande Marches*, Op. 207
Military band
EP (Mainz, Schott) BRD:MZsch
EP (Offenbach, André)

(2) *Parade-* & (2) *Geschwindmärsche*
Turkische Musik
EP (Offenbach, André)

*Overture & Airs d'Fiorella* (Auber), Op. 208
1022-02
EP (Mainz, Schott) BRD:MZsch; BRD:B (DMS.85.363)

*Boléro*, Op. 219 (from Auber's *Portici*)
Military band
EP (Mainz, Schott) BRD:MZsch;
   BRD:B (DMS.85.399)

*Grande Valse*, Op. 232 (quotes 'La Marseillaise' and
   'La Parisienne')
Military band
EP (Mainz, Schott) BRD:MZsch

(3) *Polonaises*, Op. 235
Nineteen-part military band
EP (Paris, Ebend)

(3) *Polonaise*, Op. 237 (including one by Général
   Uminsky), *Valse*, and (5) *Galopades*
1052-322, serpent, percussion
EP (Mainz, Schott) BRD:MZsch
EP (Paris, Ebend)

*Musique turque*
EP (Offenbach, André) [Vols. 1–8, 11, 12, 14, 15]
   BRD:DS [cited by Eitner]
EP (Mainz, Schott) [Vols. 9, 10, 13] BRD:MZsch
MS DDR:Bds (22065) [Pas redoublé from
   'Musique turque,' scored for 21-1, pic-
   colo, serpent]

(10) *Trompetenaufzuge*
Twelve trumpets
EP (Paris, Ebend)

*Harmonie*
Seven or ten-part Harmoniemusik
EP (Paris, Gambaro)

*Fantaisie*
Türkische Musik
EP (Offenbach, André)

(12) *Märsche*
Four trumpets or four 'Halbemondhörner,'
   with trombone
MS CH:E (TH.54, 27)
EP (Offenbach, André)

*Ouverture aus Johann yon Wieselburg*
Türkische Musik
EP (Mainz, Schott) BRD:MZsch

*Quintet*
1011-1, basset horn
MS CS:Pnm (V.C.427)

[Untitled], 11 movements
1042-221, serpent, percussion
MS BRD:TSCH (Z.85)

In addition, MGG gives the sources for '20 volumes' of six-, eight-, nine-, and twelve-part
   Harmoniemusik, including marches, overtures,
   fantaisies, and variations, as DDR:SWl, Dlb,
   and Bds; and BRD:Mbs.

### Kunerth, Johann

*Die 4 Evangelien Zur Fronleichnamsfeier*
SATB, 20-3, Flügelhorn, bombard
MS CS:Kkpm

*Die 4 Evangelien Zur Fronleichnamsfeier* (1854)
SATB 1020-2, 2 Flügelhorns, bombard
MS CS:Kkpm

### Kunheim, W. L.

*Andante, Lied ohue Worte*, Op. 8
Kavalleriemusik
EP (no name or city) A:Gk (Uncataloged)

### Kuntze, Carl

*Vom Fels zum Meer*
Tenor, male chorus, military band
MS DDR:Bds (Hausbibliothek) [lost]

*Herr, bleib 'bei uns ...*, Op. 300
Male chorus, 1020-2211, 2 tenorhorns, piano
EP (unknown) BRD:DS (Mus.1627)

### Kunz, Konrad (1812–1875)

*Reiterlied* (1868)
Unison male chorus, nine-part wind
   band, percussion
MS BRD:Mbs (St.Th.643)

**Kupler**

    Galop, *'All'heil! deutscher Radfahrer'*
    Band
    EP (London, 1894) GB:Lbm (h.1549, Ser. 96, Nr. 6)

**Lachner, Franz (1803–1890)**

    *Auf Grüner* (1836)
    Male chorus, brass
    MS BRD:Mbs (Mus.Ms.6076)

    *Brüder auf!* (fragment, 1844)
    Male chorus, brass
    MS BRD:Mbs (Mus.Ms.6059)

    *Bundeslied* (1859)
    Male chorus, winds
    MS BRD:Mbs (Mus.Ms.5956)

    *Die Elementenweihe* (1827)
    TTBB, -04
    MS BRD:Mbs (Mus.Ms.6058)

    *Frühlingsgruss an das Vaterland* (1873)
    Male chorus, winds, piano
    MS BRD:Mbs (Mus.Ms.11504)

    (3) *Gedichte*, Op. 93 (1848)
    Male chorus, winds
    MS BRD:Mbs (Mus.Ms.6096-8)

    *Hornesklänge* (1876)
    Male chorus, 2-14
    MS BRD:Mbs (Mus.Ms.6073)

    *Lass uns treten in den Kreis* (1866)
    Male chorus, brass
    EP (Maiuz, Schott)
    MS (autograph) BBD:Mbs

    (2) *Chöre* (1840)
    Male chorus, brass
    MS BBD:Mbs (Mus.Ms.6055)

    *Welch'Herr steht auf der grünen aven.* (1844)
    Male chorus with 'Willk.' brass
    MS BBD:Mbs (Mus.Ms.5954)

    *Septet*
    -043
    MS A:Wgm (VIII. 8111)

    *Octet*
    1122-02
    EP (Kistner) BRD:Bhm (56 92)
    MP (Musica Rara) US:DW (369)

    *Nonett*
    -243
    MS A:Wgm (VIII. 8113)

    *Andante* (1833)
    1243-
    MS (autograph) BBD:Mbs (Mus.Ms.5776)

    (3) *Quintets*
    1111-01
    MS (autograph) BBD:Mbs (Mus.Ms.5783, 5796, 5797)

    *Festmarsch*, Op. 24
    Military band
    EP (Wien, Pennauer, 1828) [cited in MGG]

    *Festmarsch*, Op. 143
    EP (Mainz, Schott, 1866) [cited in MGG] BRD:Mzsch
    MS (autograph) BRD:Mbs (Mus.Ms.5940)

**Lampe, Walther**

    *Serenade*, Op. 7
    2202-04, contrabassoon, English horn, bass clarinet
    EP (Berlin, Simrock) A:Wgm (VIII 30768)

**Lange, Gustav**

    *Nonett* in F
    1222-02
    MP (Dresden, Seeling) BRD:Bhm (6606 [score]; 6606/7305 [parts]) [under Friedrich Lange]; A:Wgm (VIII 28210); GB:Lbbc (Cm363) [score]

    *Defilir-Marsch*
    Kavalleriemusik
    MS DDR:Bds (Hausbibliothek) [lost]

**Lasalle, E.**

    *Marsch*
    1022-12, contrabassoon, 2 basset horns
    MS BRD:F (Mus.Hs.1174)

## Lasek

*Geschwindmarsch der Dresdener Communalgarde*
Harmoniemusik
EP (Dresden, Meser, ca. 1800–1828)

## Latann, C.

*Konzert-Overtüre ('über d. Thüringer Volkslied')*
Military band
EP (Hannover, Lehne) A:Gk (Uncataloged)

## Legrand (LeGrand), William (first half, nineteenth century)

(551) *Pièces d'Harmonie*
222-02
MS BRD:Mbs (Mus.Ms.2316)
This, the largest collection of Harmoniemusik under a single call-number in Europe, consists of leather bound part-books, containing in some cases multi-movement works under one number. There seem to be original works, works for solo oboe accompanied by 222-02, and opera transcriptions of the music of Rossini, Auber, etc.

(6) *Pièces d'Harmonie*
1022-02
EP (Leipzig, Breitkopf & Härtel; Paris, P. Petit) [Liv. 1]
Contains transcriptions of music by Meyerbeer and Nicolini.

(6) *Pièces d'Harmonie*
1022-02
EP (Leipzig, Breitkopf & Härtel; Paris, P. Petit) [Liv. 2]
Contains transcriptions of music by Rossini, Nicolini, and Pacini.

## Lehmann, Friedrich Adolph von

(6) *Marches (qui peuvent s'exécuter aussi bien en entre-acts à plein orchestre qu'en harmonie par les instruments à vent.)*
Eighteen-part Harmoniemusik
EP (Leipzig, Hoffmeister & Kühnel, Nr. 328) A:Wgm

## Leibl, Karl (1784–1870)

*Festkantate* (for the laying of the cornerstone of the Köln Cathedral, 1842)
TTBB, 3-143, timpani, string bass
MS CS:Pnm (XXXI.E.235)

## Lennert, V.

*Altpreussische Militar-Märsche*
MS (copied from BRD:DS) DDR:Bds (Hausbibliothek) [lost]

## Lindner

*Musique Militar* (ca. 1820)
2222-221, serpent, percussion
MS BRD:Rtt (Sammelband 14, Nr. 64–69)

## Lindner, H.

*Musique Militaire*
EP (Leipzig, Breitkopf & Härtel, ca. 1800–1828)

## Lindpaintner, Peter Jos. Von (1791–1856)

*Die Fahnen*
Wind orchestra
MS DDR:Bds (Mus.Ms.13031)

## Link, Joseph (1783–1837)

(6) *Neue Original Märsche*
Large brass band
MS DDR:Bds (Mus.Ms.13055)

## Loewe, Johann Carl (1796–1869)

(2) Ballades (Nr. 1 is '*Prinz Eugen der elde Ritter*')
Military band
EP (Hannover, Oertel) A:Gk (Uncataloged)

## Lortzing, Albert (1801–1851)

*Fest-Overture*
Military band
EP (Hannover, Oertel) A:Gk (Uncataloged)

## Löw, Jos.

(2) *Hungarian Dances*
Military band
EP (Hannover, Kibatyek) A:Gk (Uncataloged)

## Ludwig, F.

*Marsch*
Military band
MS DDR:Bds (Hausbibliothek) [lost]

## Malchow, F.

*Rubenow's Festmarsch*
Military band
MS DDR:Bds (Hausbibliothek) [lost]

## Mangold, Wilhelm (1796–1875)

*Harmoniemusik* (1832)
1122-12, contrabassoon
MS (autograph score) BRD:DS (Mus.Ms.733)
MS (autograph parts) BRD:DS (Mus.Ms.733/2);
   US:DW (195) [score and parts]

[illegible title] (1854)
Military band
MS (autograph) BRD:DS (Mus.Ms.753)

*Harmoniemusik* (for a festival day, 1832)
1122-12, contrabassoon
MS (autograph) BRD:DS (Mus.Ms.733/1);
   US:DW (196) [score and parts]

(3) *Orchestersätze* (1827)
Nr.1 22-22, timpani
Nr.2 1112-02, cello, string bass
Nr.3 22-041
MS (autograph) BRD:DS (Mus.Ms.704); US:DW
   (194) [score and parts]

*Harmonie* in B♭ (for '29 June, 1835 *Johannis Fest.*')
122-12, contrabassoon, timpani
MS (autograph) BRD:DS (Mus.Ms.730)

*Festmarsch*
Wind orchestra
MS (autograph) BRD:DS (Mus.Ms.734)

(4) *Movements* (1844–1861)
1-04
MS (autograph) BRD:DS (Mus.Ms. 874)

(4) *Movements* (1845)
1-04
MS (autograph) BRD:DS (Mus.Ms.783)

*Quintet* (1833)
1111-01
MS (autograph) BRD:DS (Mus.Ms.782)

*Trio* (1854)
111-
MB (autograph) BRD:DS (Mus.Ms.720)

*Trauerkantate* (1830)
Male chorus, Harmonie orchestra
MS (autograph) BRD:DS (Mus.Ms.739)

[Music from the Schauspiel] *Herman und Dorothea*
1222-02
MS (autograph) BRD:DS (Mus.Ms.754)

[illegible title]
SATB, 2002-02
MS (autograph) BRD:DS (Mus.Ms.758)

*Hymne*
Male chorus, -243
MS (autograph) BRD:DS (Mus.Ms.736)

[Chorus from *Hamlet*], '*Tempo di Marchia funebre*'
SSATTBB, 22-023
MS (autograph) BRD:DS (Mus.Ms.708)
Possibly another portion from *Hamlet* for similar
   instrumentation can be found under Mus.
   Ms.751.

## Mankels

*Divertissement*, Nr. 1
22-02
EP (Hamburg, Böhme, ca. 1800–1828)

## Marteau, Henri (1874–1934)

*Serenade*, Op. 22
2222-, 2 bass clarinets
MP (Steingräber) [cited by MII]

## Mattiozzi, Rudolphe

*Ladowa Marsch*
Musique militaire
MS DDR:Bds (Mus.Ms.14010)

## Maurer, Ludwig (1789–1878)

*Variations sur un Air russe*, Op. 38
1022-02
EP (Leipzig, Hofmeister, ca. 1800–1828)

## Mayer

*March, 'Erinnerung an deinen Kamerad'*
  (ca. 1870–1880)
Military band
MS BRD:Mbs (Mus.Ms.7912)

## Meier

*Recordare* (1899)
SATB, brass band
MS BRD:IN (Ms.118)

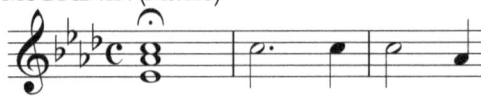

## Meinhardt, F.

(3) *Märsche*
Military band
MS DDR:Bds (Mus.Ms.14182)

## Meissner, F. W.

*Pièces d'Harmonie*, Nr. 1
222-02
EP (Leipzig, Breitkopf & Härtel) A:Wgm (VIII
  17359); US:DW (124)

*Pièces d'Harmonie*
222-02
EP (Leipzig, Breitkopf & Härtel) A:Wgm (VIII
  17360); US:DW (125)

## Mejo, W.

*Variations* (on 'Gaudeamus igitur')
1042-033, serpent
EP (Leipzig, Breitkopf & Härtel, ca. 1800–1828)
MP www.whitwellbooks.com

*Variations*, Nr. 2
Fourteen-part Harmoniemusik
EP (Paris, Ebend, ca. 1800–1828)

*Variations*, Nr. 3
Ten or eleven-part Harmoniemusik
EP (Paris, Ebend, ca. 1800–1828)

*Variations*, Op. 5
1222-021, serpent, basse
EP (Leipzig, Breitkopf & Härtel) A:Wgm
  (VIII 5340)

## Mendelssohn, Arnold (1855–1933)

*Suite,* Op. 6
Winds and percussion
EP (Leuckart) [cited in DJ]

## Mendelssohn, Felix (1809–1847)

[Little funeral march from *Pyramus and Thisbe*]
101-, timpani [cited in Grove, IX, 61]

*Festgesang, 'Baeghet mit heil'gem Lobgesang'*
TTBB, -666, ophicleide, 2 timpani players
US:DW (235)
  For the opening of the Festival in honor of
  Printing, St. Thomas Church, Leipzig, June
  25, 1840. The second movement is the original
  music used for the English Christmas carol,
  'Hark the Herald Angels Sing.'

*Festlied zur Enthullung der Statue des Königs Friedrich
  August v. Sachsen* (1843)
Two male choirs, brass
MS DDR:Bds [lost during WWII]
  For the uncovering of the statue of Friedrich
  August the Just, at Dresden, on June 9, 1842.

*Begrüssung* (for the 'Naturforscher-Versammlung,' Berlin, 1827) 7 movements
TTBB, 20-22, timpani, celli, bass
MP (Leipzig, Breitkopf & Härtel, 1930) A:Wgm (III 42334); US:DW (256)
    For a festival given in the Hall of the Royal Theater in Berlin by Alexander von Humboldt. Words by Rellstab.

*Trauer-Marsch*, Op. 103
Military band

*Notturno*
1222-12, corno basso
MS BRD:DÜl; US:DW (192 [modern MS]; US:DW 271, copy of the autograph)
    This is the original version of the *Overture for Band*, composed for the band of the Dobberan Baths.

*Overture*, Op. 24
Large military band
EP (Gesamtausgabe)

*Ave Maria*
SSAATTBB, 202-, organ
EP (London, Novello, no date) I:Bc; US:DW (212)

*Festgesang*, 'An die Künstler', Op. 68 (*'nach Schiller's Gedicht'*)
TTBB, -4441
EP (Bonn, Simrock, 1846) GB:Lbm (fol.H.1096.i)
EP (Leipzig, Breitkopf & Härtel, 1875) BRD:Mbs (Mus.pr.2/2643/118-120); US:DW (244)
    A Cantata composed for the first German-Flemish Vocal Festival at Köln.

*Andante und Allegro*
Winds [lost according to Grove, Fifth Edition]

*Todeslied der Bojeren*, from Immermann's *Tragedy of Alexis*.
Unison male chorus and wnd instruments.
    First published as a contribution to the fourth volume of Immermann's works [Dusseldorf: Schalub].

*Marches* for small bands, composed for use in the Church processions at Dusseldorf in 1833. Lost

## Merz, Karl (1836–1890)

*Fackeltanz*
Wind orchestra
MS DDR:Bds (Mus.Ms.38221)

(2) *Geschwind-Märsche* (1825)
Trompeten-Harmonie
MS DDR:Bda (Hausbibliothek, Thouret, Nr. 234)

(3) *Geschwind Märsche*
Militarmusik
EP (Berlin, Schlesinger, ca. 1800–1828)

## Mettenleiter, Johann Georg (1812–1858)

*Hymnus Crux fidelis*
Two mixed choirs, and winds
EP (Brixen, Weger, 1868) [cited in MGG]

## Metzdorff, F. G.

*Braunschweiger-Hussaren Marsch* (1894)
Large military band
MS (autograph) DDR:Bds (Mus.Ms.Auto.F.G.Metzdorff 1)

*Erinnerung* ('an das 5et Kügl Preussiche Inf. Reg., 1894')
Large military band
MS (autograph) DDR:Bds (Mus. Ma.Auto.F.G.Metzdorff 2)

*Leichte Cavallerie Märsche* (1895)
MS (autograph) DDR:Bds (Mus. Ms.Auto.F.G.Metzdorff 3)
In addition there are in DDR:Bds another fourteen similar marches, which can be found under Mus.Ms.Auto.F.G.Metzdorff 4-17.

## Metzdorff, Richard

The following are the composer's own arrangements for large military band of his own compositions:
'Overture' and 'Frauen Chor' from *Rosamunde*
MS (autograph, ca. 1895) DDR:Bds (Mus. Ms.Auto.R.Metzdorff 3)

'Ballet' from *Rosamunde*
MS (autograph, ca. 1895) DDR:Bds (Mus. Ms.Auto.R.Metzdorff 4)

'Chor' from *Rosamunde*
MS (autograph, ca. 1895) DDR:Bds (Mus. Ms.Auto.R.Metzdorff 6)

'Chor' from *Rosamunde*
MS (autograph, ca. 1895) DDR:Bds (Mus. Ms.Auto.R.Hetzdorff 8)

'Adagio' from *Violin Concerto*, Op. 49
MS (autograph, ca. 1899) DDR:Bds (Mus. Ms.Auto.R.Hetzdorff 56, 1)

## Meyer, Carl Heinrich [Charles Henri] (b. 1772)

*Partita* (c. 1821)
222-12
MS BRD:Rtt (Meyer 1)
EP (Peters) [according to AM]
(Kühnel) [according to G2]
(Paris, Ebend, ca. 1800–1828)

*Journal d'Harmonie*, Op. 15 (12 compositions)
1032-121, E♭ clarinet, serpent, percussion
EP (Leipzig, Hofmeister) [Liv. 1–2]

*Musique militaire*
EP (Leipzig, Peters, ca. 1800–1828)

*Ouverture*
Musique militaire
EP (Paris, Ebend, ca. 1800–1828)

## Meyerbeer, Giacomo (1791–1864)

The following four *Fackeltänze* by Meyerbeer are assumed by Grove (XII, 255) to be original works for wind band. Following are the original materials which were extant in DDR:Bds up until the Second World War. The librarians of both the East and West Berlin depositories of the old Prussian collection have told me that all autograph Meyerbeer materials were lost during that war. I suspect they may be in private hands.

*Fackeltanz* [Nr. 1] (for the marriage of 'Princesse Marie de Prusse & Prince de Baviere,' August 29, 1842)
MS (autograph, 4 pages) DDR:Bds (Mus.Ms.Auto. Meyerbeer.1027)
MS (autograph, 16 pages, for brass band) DDR:Bds (Mus.Ms.Auto.Meyerbeer.1028)

*Fackeltanz* [Nr. 2] (for the marriage of 'Princesse Charlotte de Saxe & Le Prince de Saxe-Meiningen,' May 1850)
MS (autograph, 3 pages) DDR:Bds (Mus.Ms.Auto. Meyerbeer.1025)
MS (autograph, 20 pages, for wind orchestra) DDR:Bds (Mus.Ms.Auto.Meyerbeer.1026)
EP (Berlin, Bote & Bock) US:DW (253)
This print, for large band, is given as an arrangement by Wieprecht. Perhaps this refers more to his instrumentation which includes no fewer than five separate parts for his new tuba!

*Danse aux flambeaux* [Fackeltanz Nr. 3] (for the marriage of 'Anne de Prusse & Frédéric de Hesse,' 1856)
MS (in Wieprecht's hand, for large military band) DDR:Bds (Mus.Ms.Auto.Meyerbeer.1029)

MP A portion of this score is given at the end of Vessella's famous history, *La Banda*.
MS DDR:Bds (Mus.Ms.Auto.Meyerbeer.1030) [*Marche aux flambeaux pour mus. mil*, arranged for orchestra]

*Fackeltanz* [Nr. 4] (for the marriage of 'Princesse Royale d'Angleterre & Prince Frédéric Guillaume de Prusse,' Feb. 12, 1858)
MS (in Wieprecht's hand, for wind orchestra) DDR:Bds (Mus.Ms.Auto.Meyerbeer.1024)
MS (autograph, 2 pages, piano score) DDR:Bds (Mus.Ms.Auto.Meyerbeer.1022)
MS (autograph, 2 pages, sketches) DDR:Bds (Mus.Ms.Auto.Meyerbeer.1023)

*Quatre Marches* ('aux flambeau composes pour musique militaire arranges pour Orchester Ordinaire par Wieprecht')
EP (Paris, Branduset & Dufouz, 1865) F:Pn (Vm.26.716[2])
EP (Firenze:Guidi, 1865) I:Bc

*Fackeltanz* [identity unknown]
Brass
MS GB:Lbm (R.M.21.d.10.Nr.2)

*Fackeltanz*
Large military band
MS A:Gk (Uncataloged)

*Fackeltanz* [identity unknown]
2242-6431, contrabassoon, tenorhorn, serpent, percussion
EP (Leipzig, Peters) GB:Lbm (h.1570)

*Reveille*
Wind orchestra
MS DDR:Bds (Mus.Ms.38104)

*Festmarsch* (1843)
Wind orchestra
MS (autograph) DDR:Bds (Mus.Ms.Auto.Meyerbeer.841)

*Märsche* ('26 Dec.,' [no year given])
122-12
MS (autograph) DDR:Bds (Mus.Ms.Auto.Meyerbeer.1198)

*Marcia*
122-12
MS (autograph) DDR:Bds (Mus.Ms.Auto.Meyerbeer.1183)

*Marsch für die Nationalgarde v. Berlin*
Instrumentation unknown
MS (autograph) DDR:Bds (Mus.Ms.Auto.Meyerbeer.1195)

*Das Hoffest in Ferrara* (for the arrival of court persons from Ferrara)
-443, timpani
MS (autograph) DDR:Bds (Mus.Ms.Auto.Meyerbeer.993a)

*Königslied* (December 28, 1813)
TTBB, 1222-
MS (autograph) DDR:Bds (Mus.Ms.Auto.Meyerbeer.1008

*Preussiche Kronnungsmarsch*
Symphony orchestra and Cavallerie band
MS (autograph) DDR:Bds (Mus.Ms.Auto.Meyerbeer.1020b)

*Coronation March*, for Wilhelm I
EP BRD:B, arr. Wieprecht for large Infantry band and off-stage Cavalry band
MP www.whitwellbooks.com

*La stella del Nord*
Band
MS I:Bc

*Der Bayerische Schützenmarsch* (January, 1814)
TTBB, 4-454, serpent, contrabassoon, percussion
MS BRD:Mbs (Mus.Ms.ST.Th.405); US: DW

*Das Jägers Lied*
Bass voice with horns [cited in Grove, Fifth Edition]

## Miltitz

*Preussische Marschlied*
Türk.Musik
EP (Berlin, Schlesinger, ca. 1800–1828)

## Mischke, L.

*Psalmodie* and *Jubel-Hymnus*
Seven-part Trompetenmusik
MS DDR:Bds (Hausbibliothek) [lost]

## Mohr, Andreas

*Der Einzug des Prinzen Carneval Bureske*
Large wind band
MS (autograph) DDR:Bds (Mus. Ms.Auto.A.Mohr 16)

*Elegie*
Wind orchestra
MS (autograph) DDR:Bds (Mus. Ms.Auto.A.Mohr.18)

*Feenmärchen*
Wind orchestra
MS (autograph) DDR:Bds (Mus. Ms.Auto.A.Mohr.49)

(3) *Festmarsch*
Large wind band
MS (autograph) DDR:Bds (Mus. Ms.Auto.A.Mohr.39)
In addition there are many march manuscripts by Mohr in DDR:Bds dating from 1900–1914.

## Möller, M.

*Zwei Freunde. Konzert-Polka*
Two oboes, brass band
EP (Hannover, Oertel) [cited by MH]

## Mühling

*Nocturne*, Op. 29
Grande Harmonie
EP (Leipzig, Probst, ca. 1800–1828)

## Müller, C. F.

(12) *Originalmarsche*, Op. 55
Large military band
EP (Berlin, author, ca. 1800–1828) DDR:Bds (Hausbibliothek) [lost]

*Festgesang* (November 29, 1823)
Chorus and military band
MS DDR:Bds (Hausbibliothek) [lost]

(5) *Märsches*
Large military band
MS DDR:Bds (Mus.Ms.15, 671)
One of these is for two bands, 'Doppel-Cavallerie Musik.'

## Müller, Christian Gottlich

*Morgengruss*
Wind orchestra
MS DDR:Bds (Mus.Ms.15679/35)

*Singt dem Herrn*
SATB, 21-02
MS DDR:Bds (Mus.Ms.Auto.C.G.Muller.60)

*Potpourii über Deutsche Volkslieder*
Military band
MS DDR:Bds (Mus.Ms.Auto.C.G.Muller.99)

*Overture*, Op. 4
Military band
EP (Leipzig, Breitkopf & Härtel, ca. 1800–1828)

## Müller, Frederic (1786–1871)

*Pièces d'Harmonie*, Op. 28
1222-22, serpent
EP (Leipzig, Breitkopf & Härtel) [Liv.1–2] A:Wgm

*Musique Militaire*
Eighteen-part military band
EP (Leipzig, Hofmeister, ca. 1800–1828)

*Grand Musique militaire*
Large wind band
MS A:Gk (Uncataloged); US:DW

## Müller, F. D.

*Siegesmarsch*
Military band
MS DDR:Bds (Mus.Ms.15, 698)

## Münchs, A.

*Grande Harmonie*
1222-122, serpent
EP (Mainz, Schott, ca. 1800–1828) [Three Suites] BRD:MZseh

*Musique Militaire*
1032-121, serpent, percussion
EP (Mainz, Schott, ca. 1800–1828) [Five Suites] BRD:MZsch

## Naue, J. F.

*Preussischer Armée-Marsch*. Nr. 48
Large military band
MS DDR:Bds (Hausbibliothek) [lost]

*Te Deum*
Male chorus with Janitscharenmusik
MS DDR:Bds (Hausbibliothek) [lost]

*Triumphrnersch* ('zum Empfang Ihrer Kgl. Hoheit der Prinzessin Elise von Bayern, aufgefürt bei der Durchreise durch Halle')
Voices with military band
MS DDR:Bds (Hausbibliothek) [lost]

*Triumph-Marsch* ('uber "Des Preussen Losung ist die Drei"')
Voices with large military band
MS DDR:Bds (Hausbibliothek) [lost]

## Necke, Herman

*Deutsche Kaiser-Overture*, Op. 151
Chorus with military band
EP (Hannover, Oertel) A:Gk (Uncataloged)

## Neithardt, August Heinrich (1793–1861, Musikdirector, Kaiser Franz Grenadier Regiment, Berlin)

(3) *Märsche*, Op. 58
Military band
MS A:Wn (Sm.11358)
EP (Berlin, Laue; Berlin, Schlesinger; Leipzig, Hofmeister, ca. 1800–1828)

(3) *Märsche*, Op. 88
Military band
EP (Wagenfuhr)

(8) *Märsche*, Op. 92
Military band
MS DDR:Bds (Hausbibliothek) [lost]

(8) *Märsche*, Op. 102
Military band
EP (Berlin, Schlesinger) DDR:Bds (Hausbibliothek) [lost]

(8) *Märsche* (together with those by F. Weller)
Military band
MS DDR:Bds (Hausbibliothek) [lost]

*Geschwind Marsch*
Ten trumpets, 2 trombones
EP (Berlin, Schlesinger); US:DW (438)

*Festgesang* (1832)
Male chorus, 2232-143, serpent, basset horn, percussion
MS A:Wn (Sm.10198)

*Variations*, Op. 80 ('sur l'air tyrolien de l'opera *La Fiancée* d'Auber')
Military band
EP (Leipzig, Breitkopf & Härtel)

*Hymnus*, 'Wo ist, soweit die Schöpfung reicht?' Op. 98
TTBB, piano, organ or winds
EP (Trautwein)

*Cantata*, 'Das Band der Weihe' (for the 'grossen Festmahle der Stadt Berlin am 17 Oct. 1840')
Tenor solo, TTBB, wind orchestra
MS [location unknown]

## Neukäufler, F. (b. 1780–d. after 1843)

(6) *Märchen*
Military band
MS [cited without source by Eitner]

*Quartet zum Fest Johann des Evangelisten*
Voices with 4 horns [cited by Eitner]

## Neumann, H.

*Eine Phantasie, Die Rheinfahrt Sr. Kgl. Hoheit des Kronprinzen von Preussen*, Op. 31 (October 30, 1833)
Military band
MS DDR:Bds (Hausbibliothek) [lost]

## Nitzchke, C.

*Kronprinz Friedrich Wilhelm Marsch*
Military band
MS DDR:Bds (Hausbibliothek) [lost]

## Nosvadba, J. (1824–1876)

Paraphrase, 'Loreley'
Large military Orchestra
MS BRD:DS (Mus.Ms.837)

*March* in E♭
Wind instruments
MS BRD:DS (Mus.Ms.839)

## Ochernal

(5) *Marches et* (1) *Angl.*
Eleven-part Harmoniemusik
EP (Leipzig, Breitkopf & Härtel, ca. 1800–1828)

## Ostreich, Carl

*Sextet*
1000-031, basset horn
MS BRD:F (Mus.Hs.749)

*Sextet*
22-02
MS BRD:F (Mus.Hs.674)

*Octet* (1831)
1022-12
MS BRD:F (Mus.Hs.716); US:DW (334)

*Blasermusik* [Collection]
Five and six winds
MS BRD:F (Mus.Hs.750)

*Andante*
Solo horn, with 1011-02, piano
MS BRD:F (Mus.Hs.775)

(12) *Works* [marches, dances, etc.]
Military band
MS BRD:F (Mus.Hs.712)

*Trauermarsch*
Wind instruments
MS BRD:F (Mus.Hs.713); US:DW (339)

*Simphonia* (Dresden, 1831)
Wind orchestra
MS BRD:F (Mus.Hs.686); US:DW (157)

*Fantasie*
Wind orchestra
MS BRD:F (Mus.Hs.708); US:DW (351, 156)

## Payer, Hyr.

(7) *Wälzer* (ca. 1810)
32-22, contrabassoon
MS BRD:DO (Mus.Ms.1533/1)

## Pearsall, Robert (1795–1856, Swiss)

*March* in C
*Introitus* in D
Organ and winds
MS CH:E [cited in Grove, XIV, 321]

## Pfeffel

*Das Hallelujah*
SATB, 22-021
MS [Owned by a rare materials dealer, Reeves, in London in 1882, according to Eitner]

## Pfisterer, K. L.

[Untitled work]
Chorus, -241
MS BRD:F (Mus.Hs.462)

## Piefke, Gottfried

*Königgratzer Marsch*
EP (Berlin, Bote & Bock)
DDR:SWl (Piefke, G. 1)

*Galop, Feldpost relais*
Band
EP (London, 1880) GB:Lbm (h.1549, Ser. 39, Nr. 4)

## Poissl, Johann Hepomuk (1783–1865)

(10) *Harmoniestücke* ('für die Harmonie der Königl [Ludwig I] Tafelmusik')
1122-02
MS BRD:Mbs (Mus.Ms.2438)
Contains arrangements of Donizetti, Auber, Lachner, with perhaps four original movements.

## Proksch, Robert Ludwig

*Fest Overture*, Op. 32
Military band
EP (Dresden, Bellmann) A:Gk (Uncataloged)

## Raff, Joseph Joachim (1822–1882)

*Sinfonietta*, Op. 188
Wind instruments
MP (Eullenberg)

## Rastrelli, Joseph (1799–1842)

(3) *Marches triomphales*
Grand Orch. Militaire
MS DDR:Dlb (Nr. 4905)

## Ratzenberger, Th.

*Trauermarsch* ('auf Tod Sr. Maj. des Kaisers Wilhelm's I')
Large military band
MS DDR:Bds (Hausbibliothek) [lost]

## Reckling, August (1843–1900)

*Anastasia Marsch* (ca. 1890–1900)
Military band
MS BRD:Mbs (Mus.Ms.7924)

*Hubertus Overture*
Military band
EP (Hannover, Oertel) A:Gk (Uncataloged)

## Reh, Hermann

*Marsch,* 'Der Gute Onkel' (ca. 1860)
Military band
MS BRD:Mbs (Mus.Ms.7925)

## Reill, Josef (1793–1865)

(3) *Grablieder* (ca. 1840)
SATB, 1022-121
MS BRD:WS (MS.544)

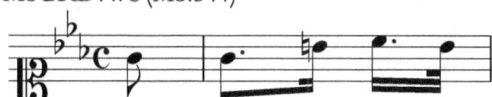

## Reinecke, Carl Heinrich (1824–1910)

*Sextet*, Op. 271
Winds
EP (Publisher unknown) US:R

*Oktett*, Op. 216
1122-02
EP (Kistner) BRD:Bbm (6602 and 6603)

## Reinhardt, C., Jr.

*Waldegruüsse*
Two solo trumpets, band
EP (Hannover, Oertel) A:Gk (Uncataloged)

## Reissinger, Carl G. (1798–1859)

(2 Songs) *Wiedersehn* and *Pilgrim und Wiederhall*
Voice and winds
MS [in private hands]

## Reuss, August (1871–1935)

*Octet*, Op. 37
222-02
EP (Munich, Zierfuss) BRD:Bhm (32242)

## Rheinberger, Josef (1839–1901)

*Sextet,* Op. 191b
Piano, 1111-01
EP (Leuckart) [cited by DJ]

*Mass*, Op. 172
Male chorus, 2222-22, timpani, string bass
MS (autograph) BRD:Mbs (Mus.Ms.4642)
EP (Leipzig, Leuckart, 1897) US:DW (127)

*Die Rosen v. Hildesheim*, Op. 143
TTBB, -2331, timpani
MS (autograph) BRD:Mbs (Mus.Ms.4613)

## Rieger, Gottfried (1764–1855)

*Variations*
Harmoniemusik [cited in MGG]

*Stücke*
Wind music [cited in MGG]

## Ries, Ferdinand (1784–1838)

(2) *Nocturnes* (1834 and 1836)
1022-01
MS US:DT

*Nun Lasset uns den Leib begraben*
STTBB, 2-02, 2 viola, cello, bass
MS CS:Bm (A.19.783)

March, *The Return of the Troops*, Op. 53, Nr. 2
Military band
MS (autograph) DDR:Bds (Mus.Ms.Auto.F.Ries.51)

March
Military band
MS (autograph) DDR:Bds (Mus.Ms.Auto.F.Ries.52)

## Riess

[Collection of 12 works]
2232-22
MS NL:Ura [cited in HA]

## Rinck, Johann Christian Heinrich (1770–1846)

*Cantata, 'Stimmt auf in Chören'* (1832)
SSTB, 1022-22, timpani, contrabassoon
MS US:NH (MS.32/4405)

*Cantata, 'Jubelwonne Tag'* (1834)
SATB, 1022-02, timpani
MS US:NH (MS.33/4406)

*Cantata, 'Anbetung Dir'*
SATB, 2022-22, timpani, contrabassoon
MS US:NH (MS.34/4432)

*Cantata, 'Die Freundschaft ist des Himmelsbild'* (1833)
SATB, 1022-22, timpani, contrabassoon
MS US:NH (MS.37/4434)

*Cantata, 'Unsre Lebenzeit Verschwindet'* (1808)
SSTB, 22-22
MS US:NH (MS.39/4436)

*Cantata, 'Allmächtiger'* (1829)
SATB, 2022-22, timpani, contrabassoon
MS US:NH (MS.49/4489)

'Dich von Ewiger Preissen wir' (1812)
SSTB, 2022-22, timpani, organ
MS US:NH (MS.27/4400)

'Heilig, Heilig'
SATB, 1022-22, timpani, contrabassoon
MS US:NH (MS.36/4433b)

*Preis Gottes* (1830)
SATB, 1022-22, timpani, contrabassoon
MS US:NH (MS.40/4437)

*Lob, Preis und Dank* (1830)
SATB, 1022-22, timpani, contrabassoon
MS US:NH (MS.40/4437)

*Osterlied*
SSTB, 2022-22, timpani, organ
MS US:NH (MS.41/4439)

'Gross ist der Herr' (1831)
SATB, 1022-22, timpani, contrabassoon
MS US:NH (MS.42/4440)

*Psalm, 'Singet dem Herrn'*
SATB, 1022-22, timpani, contrabassoon
MS US:NH (MS.43/4440b)

'Wie gross ist der Allmächtiger'
SATB, 1022-02, contrabassoon
MS US:NH (MS.44/4441)

*Choral, 'Herr Gott, Dich Loben Wir'*
202-224, organ
MS US:NH (MS.53/4454)

*Choral, 'Nun Danket Alle Gott'*
202-223, timpani
MS US:NH (MS.56/4458)

The following are secular works
*Cantata, 'Der Frühling'* (1833)
SATB, 1022-22, timpani, contrabassoon
MS US:NH (MS.31/4404)

'Zur Begräbnissfeuer des Capellmeisters Wagners' (1822)
2122-023, contrabassoon
MS US:NH (MS.29/4402)

'Aufmunterung zum Gesang'
SATB, 1022-02, contrabassoon
MS US:NH (MS.32/4405)

'An die Freundschaft'
SATB, 1022-02, contrabassoon
MS US:NH (MS.32/4405)

'Vaterlandslied'
SATB, 1022-02, timpani, contrabassoon
MS US:NH (MS.32/4405)

'Mailied von Hölty'
SATB, 1022-02, contrabassoon
MS US:NH (MS.35/4433)

'Menschenliebe' (1833)
SATB, 1022-02, contrabassoon
MS US:NH (MS.37/4434)

'Sammelt Euch, Freunde' (1830)
SATB, 1022-02, contrabassoon
MS US:NH (MS.40/4437)

Duettino, 'Bänder' (1830)
SA, 1022-02, contrabassoon
MS US:NH (MS.40/4437)

'Das Vaterland-rundgesang' (1830)
SATB, 1022-02, contrabassoon
MS US:NH (MS.40/4437)

'Auf und Singt!' (1831)
SA, 1022-02, contrabassoon
MS US:NH (MS.42/4440)

'Wie Schön Leuchtet der Morgenstern'
22-223, timpani
MS US:NH (MS.56/4558)

Gebet, 'Leise, Leise, Fromme, Weise' [Weber]
STB, 1022-02, contrabassoon
MS US:NH (MS.44/4441)

'Dem Höchsten Regierer sich Jubelgesang' [Mozart]
SATB, 1022-02, contrabassoon
MS US:NH (MS.44/4441)

Arie ('aus der Zauberflöte of Mozart')
Bass voice, 1022-02, contrabassoon
MS US:NH

Andante
TBB [without text], 1022-02, contrabassoon
MS US:NH (MS.36/4433)

Trio
-03
MS US:NH (MS.46/4443)

### Rohner

Harmonie concertante, Op. 5
22-12 [Advertized in AMZ, 1810]

### Rose, G.

Triumphmarsch, 'Mit Gott für Kaiser und Reich'
Trompotenmusik
MS DDR:Bds (Hausbibliothek) [lost]

### Rosenkranz, Fr. (Kapellmeister, 27th Inf. Reg.)

Overture Militaire (on the 100th anniversary of the birth of Schiller)
MS DDR:Bds (Mus.Ms.18878)

### Rossberg, G.

Gedenkblatt ('zur Feier des 25 jähr. Bestehens des 4. Garde-Regiments zu Fuss, 2.7.1885')
MS DDR:Bds (Hausbibliothek) [lost]

(5) Märsche
MS DDR:Bds (Hausbibliothek) [lost]

### Rothe

Pièces d'Harmonie
EP (Leipzig, Hofmeister, ca. 1800–1828)

Andante & Allegro scherzando
222-22, 'Serbano'
MS DDR:Dlb [cited by Eitner]

### Ruhl, Hans H.

Hermann Cantate
TTBB, military band
MS DDR:Bds (Mus.Ms.19085)

### Rumler

Quintet, Op. 6
21-02
EP (Augsburg, Gombart, ca. 1800–1828)

### Rummel, Christian (1787–1849)

Concertino, Op. 58
Solo B♭ clarinet with strings; or 1202-22, timpani; or piano
EP (Mainz, Schott) BRD:MZsch; I:Bc [piano version only]

*Variations*, Op. 40 ('*Romance de Joseph*')
222-02, contrabassoon
EP (Mainz, Schott) BRD:MZsch

*2 Grandes Pièces*, Op. 52 ('*d'après des Motifs de Kalkbrenner et Dussek, et l'Ouverture jubilaire de C. M. de Weber*')
Nine-part Harmoniemusik
EP (Paris, Ebend)

*Musique militaire*
EP (Paris, Ebend) [Cah.1–6]

*Quintetto*, Op. 41
1011, basset horn, English horn
EP (Paris, Ebend)

*Quintetto*, Op. 42
1011, basset horn, English horn
EP (Paris, Ebend)

### Ruppert

*Parthie*
2201-02
EP (Vollmer) [Advertized in AMZ, 1806]

### Ruscheweyh, E.

*Vor Sedan* (a 24-movement, programmatic, battle piece, in memory of September 1, 1870)
Band
EP (Hannover, Lehne) A:Gk (Uncataloged)

### Sabel, Carl

*Fest Marsch*
Military band
MS BRD:Mbs (Mus.Ms.2791) [formerly library of Ludwig I]

### Sachse, C.

*Fest-Marsch*
MS DDR:Bds (Hausbibliothek) [lost]

### Santner, Karl

*Das ganze Deutschland soll es sein!*
TTBB, wind orchestra
EP (Wien, Kranzl) A:Llm (III/11)

### Sartorius, G.

*Marsch*, 'Hochfürstl. Hessen-Darmstadtischen Leibregiments'
MS DDR:Bds (Hausbibliothek, Tbouret, Nr. 402)

### Sauer

*Blankenstein Hussar Marsch* (ca. 1870)
Military band
MS BRD:Mbs (Mus.Ms.7931)

### Scherrer, H. (b. 1865)

*Old French Dances*, Op. 11
1121-01
MP (Schmitt) [cited in DJ]

### Scherzer

(12) *Deutsche Tänze*
Harmoniemusik
MS BRD:DO [lost]

### Scherzer, A. P.

(6) *Märsche* (1805)
222-12
MS DDR:Bds (Hausbibliothek, Thouret, Nr. 136)

### Schilling, Hans (b. 1869)

*Sancta Barbara March* (ca. 1890)
Military band
MS BRD:Mbs (Mus.Ms.7932)

### Schillings, Max von (1868–1933)

*Weihechor* (1900)
Female voices, 2222-02, harp
MS BRD:Mbs (Mus.Ms.10074)

### Schletterer, Hans Michael (1824–1893)

*Türmerlied*, Op. 4
Male chorus, wind orchestra
EP (Leipzig, Rieter) [cited in MGG]

## Schmacht, F. (Stabshornist, Füsilier-Bataillion de Duke de Braunsweig lnf. Reg. Nr. 92)

*Reveille*
Military band
MS DDR:Bds (Mus.Ms.19846)

*Koenigs-Marsch*
Military band
MS DDR:Bds (Mus.Ms.19845)

## Schmid, Josef (b. 1868)

*Serenata*, Op. 42 (1904)
2222-02, contrabassoon
MS (autograph) BRD:Mbs (Mus.Ms.7173); US:DW (258)

## Schmidt, E.

*Fest Marsch* ('über ein Volkslied')
Cavallerie Musik
MS DDR:Bds (Mus.Ms.19870)

## Schmiedecke, A.

*Marsch*, 'Zur Erinnerung an das Kaiser' (1891)
Wind orchestra
MS DDR:Bds (Mus.Ms.19965/5)

## Schmitt, A.

*Scherzo* (*Puppenspiel*)
1022-02
EP (Offenbach, André, ca. 1800–1828)

## Schmitt, Alois

*Trauer-Cantate* (1892, for the duke's mother, Alexandrine)
Voices, 222-223, organ, timpani
MS DDR:SWl (MS.4893/1)

## Schnabel, Joseph Ignaz (1767–1831)

*Missa Quadragesimlis*
SATB, 22-023, organ, bass
MS CS:Bm (A.20.102)

*Missa*
SATB, 2-023, 2 basset horns, organ
EP (Breslau, Leuchart) A:Wgm (I 5315)

*Stationen*
SATB, 2222-22, timpani
MS DDR:Bds (Mus.Ms.20010)

(8) *Pieces*
-132
EP (Breslau, Förster, ca. 1800–1828)

*Marsch*
-8
EP (Breslau, Förster, ca. 1800–1828)

(5) *Stücke*
-7, timpani
EP (Breslau, Förster, ca. 1800–1828)

## Schneider

(21) *Partitien*, Op. 6
222-02
MS PL:Wbu (Ka.16)

*Partita* in C
1-02, 2 English horns
MS BRD:HR (III.4.1/2.40.723)

## Schneider, Anton

*Harmonie* (1822), 9 movements
1211-01 [flute doubles on basset horn]
MS (autograph) BRD:Rtt (Schneider 1)

Following are extensive Schneider collections of wind music both original and arranged.
BRD:Rtt (*Sammelband 12*)
1222-121, 2 viola (?), string bass
Contains 45 arrangements dated 1826. The first four works constitute a complete Haydn *Symphony* [Hob. I, 63]

BRD:Rtt (*Sammelband 13*)
2222-121, serpent, string bass
Contains 59 works dated 1820:
| | |
|---|---|
| 1–11 | Mozart, *Clemenza di Tito* |
| 12–27 | Boieldieu, *Jean de Paris* |

| | |
|---|---|
| 28–37 | Rossini, *Tancredi* |
| 38 | Spontini (arr. Vogt), *Fernand Cortez* |
| 39–46 | *Suite Harmonie Italienne* (7 songs and a march) |
| 47–50 | *Sinfonie* B♭ |
| 51–52 | *Allemande-Andante* for 1222-02, string bass |
| 53 | Overture, *Roi et la ligue* by Baehr (arr. Bochsa) |
| 54–56 | Rossini, *L'inganno felice* |
| 57–59 | Rossini, *La Gazza ladra* |

BRD:Rtt (*Sammelband 14*)
2222-221, serpent, percussion
Contains 93 works dated ca. 1820:

| | |
|---|---|
| 1 | Spontini, *Ferdnand Cortez* |
| 2–5 | Paer, *Angnese* |
| 6–24 | Walch |
| 25 | Bochsa, père, *Overture Militar*, Op. 29 |
| 26–33 | Isouard, *Aschenbrodel*, for nine-part Harmoniemusik |
| 34 | Bethoffen, *Eggmunt Simponie* |
| 35–48 | Spontini, *Vesttalien* |
| 49–55 | Spontini, *Cortez* |
| 56–59 | Pleyel, *Serenade* in F |
| 60–63 | [Suite of opera movements] |
| 64–69 | Lindner, *Musique Militar* |
| 70 | Goepfert, *Allegrini alla Turca* |
| 71–79 | Neukomm [various marches and dances] |
| 80–90 | Beethoven, *Fidelio* |
| 92–93 | Neukomm, (2) *Marches* |

BRD:Rtt (*Sammelband 15*)
1222-221, serpent, string bass
Contains 64 works dated before 1821 (when it was advertized for sale). Includes dance movements and opera aria transcriptions from Méhul, *La jeune Henri*; Rossini, *La gazza Ladra*; Hummel, *Gude nachricht*; and Kreutzer, *Lodoiska;* with apparent original *Notturni* by Vern and Spohr and a set of *Pièces* by Meissner.

BRD:Rtt (*Sammelband 16)*
1242-121, serpent
Contains 150 works dated 1822. Includes numerous original movements by Schneider, as well as the following:

| | |
|---|---|
| 1–4 | Stumpf, *Harmonie* |
| 19–24 | (6) *Eccossaisen* |
| 25–32 | (8) *Waltzes* |
| 33 | Kreuzer, *A la chasse col Echo* |
| 39–40 | Weber, *Freischütz* |
| 41–76 | Mozart, *Don-Juan* |

BRD:Rtt (*Sammelband 17*)
1242-121, serpent
Contains 86 works dated ca. 1813, which are apparently a continuation of the materials under Sammelband 16. Contents include many dance movements, as well as the following:

| | |
|---|---|
| 151–154 | Haydn, *Symphony* [Hob. I, 94] |
| 217–219 | Schneider, *Schlacht Sinfonie* |

BRD:Rtt (*Sammelband 18*)
1242-121, serpent, 2 violas (?)
Contains 90 works dated 1823, including arrangements [Nrs. 71-90] of five Haydn *Symphonies* [Hob. I, 93, 99, 101, 103, 104] and four original works by H. de Croes.

BRD:Rtt (*Sammelband 21*)
1242-121, string bass [trumpet doubles as horn 3]
Contains 19 works dated 1823, including:

| | |
|---|---|
| 5 | Weber, *'Lutzow's wilde Jagd'* |
| 6–9 | Steinacker, *Polonoise* |

BRD:Rtt (*Sammelband 23*)
1242-121, string bass
Contains 40 works dated ca. 1823, including:

| | |
|---|---|
| 1–11 | Gretry, *Blaubarth* |
| 14–15 | Schneider, (2) Original *Variations* [for solo horn and solo flute] |
| 23–26 | Cotischau, *Kantata* |
| 37–40 | Weber, *Symphonie* in C |

BRD:Rtt (*Sammelband 25*)
1222-121, 2 violas (?), string bass
Contains 51 works dated 1824, including:

| | |
|---|---|
| 3 | Schneider, *Adagio* |
| 36 | *'Hail Britania'* |
| 37–51 | Rossini, *Türk in Italy* |

BRD:Rtt (*Sammelband 26)*
1222-121, 2 violas (?), string bass
Contains an undetermined number of works dated 1825, including mostly opera arias, but also 10 original works by Sommer.

BRD:Rtt (*Sammelband 27*)
1222-121, 2 violas (?), string bass
Contains an undetermined number of works dated 1826.

BRD:Rtt (*Sammelband 28*)
1222-121, 2 violas (?), string bass
Contains 83 works dated 1827, including 50 waltzes by minor composers; 16 movements of Rossini *Barbier v. Sevilla*; and the following original works by Schneider:
2   *Andantino & Polonoise*
3   *Adagio & Andante* [with 6 variationsl
11  *Andante* [with 6 variations]
12  *Adagio & Allegretto* [with 10 variations]

BRD:Rtt (*Sammelband 29*)
1222-121, 2 violas (?), string bass
Contains 46 works dated 1827, including a dozen dance movements by Schneider; a *Quartet* by Rossini; and an original *Adagio* [Nr. 21] by Schneider.

BRD:Rtt (*Sammelband 30*)
1242-121, string bass
Contains 31 works dated 1823, including:
1–22 Mozart, *Zauberflute*
24   Schneider, *Cantabile & Polonoise*

BRD:Rtt (*Sammelband 32*)
1222-02, 2 violas (?), string bass
Contains 3 arrangements by Schneider, an *Andantino-Allegro* by Croes, and an Anonymous *Andantino*, all dated ca. 1820.

## Schneider, Friedrich (1786–1853)

*Fest-Marsch* (1833)
Military band
MS GB:Lbm (R.M.21.g.30/31)

*Fest-Overture* ('Heil Dir im Siegerkranz')
Military band
EP (Hannover, Oertel) A:Gk (Uncataloged)

*Hymne, 'Jehovah, dir frohlocket der König',* Op. 94 (1834)
TTTTBBBB, brass, timpani, bassi
EP (Berlin, Trautwein) DDR:SWl (Schneider, F.2.)

## Schneider, Georg Abraham (1770–1839)

(6) *Pièces d'Harmonie*, Op. 8
22-02
EP (Augsburg, Gombart) A:Wgm; BRD:B
In the issue of March 25, 1801, AMZ advertised these pieces, noting, 'As many Oboisten from the military and other musical societies play (schmieren) now partitas.' These works were described as, 'pleasant, smooth singing melodic movements. Other outstanding characteristics are successful imitation and good taste.'

(7) *Quintetten*
Winds
MS BRD:B [cited by SJK]

*Partitta*
1-02, 2 English horns
MS BRD:HR [cited by SJK]

(12) *Harmonien*
2022-02
MS DDR:Bds (Mus.Ms.Auto.G.A.Schneider 47)

*Harmonie*
2022-02
MS DDR:Bds (Mus.Ms.Auto.G.A.Schneider 48)

*Harmonie*
222-22, serpent
MS DDR:Bds (Mus.Ms.Auto.G.A.Schneider 46)

*Harmonie*
2022-02
MS DDR:Bds (Mus.Ms.Auto.G.A.Schneider 109)

*Terpodium Concert*
202-02
MS DDR:Bds (Mus.Ms.Auto.G.A.Schneider 84)

*Sextett*
2-02, 2 basset horns, string bass [cited in G2]
In addition, for this composer Eitner cites 'Mehrere Overtüren f. Harmonie-Musik' in DDR:Bds; Concerti for one to three horns in BRD:DS; and 18 Trios for horns in DDR:SWl.

## Schneider, Hermann J. (b. 1862)

*Bienenhaus Marsch*, Op. 124
Military band
MS BRD:Mbs (Mus.Ms.7935)

### Schneider, Julius

*Festgesang, 'Borussia's fünfzehnter October'*
Four-part male chorus, military band
MS DDR:Bds (Hausbibliothek) [lost]

### Scholl, W.

*Racouzy Marsch ('componist von W. Scholl, KM des Löbl:K:K Fürst Esterhazy, 32. Linnien Inf. Reg.')*
1251-221, serpent, contrabassoon, timpani
MS BRD:TSCH (Z.123)

### Scholz, Bernhard (1835–1916)

*Serenade*
1111-02
MS DDR:Bds (Mus.Ms.20167/7)

### Schönemann

*Militairmusik*
EP (Braunschweig, Spehr, ca. 1800–1828) [Heft 1]
EP (Braunschweig, Meyer, ca. 1800–1828) [Heft 2]

### Schreck, Gustav (1849–1918)

*Nonett*, Op. 40
2122-02
EP (Breitkopf & Härtel, 1905) BRD:Bhm (9984/9985); US:Wc (M.957S37)

### Schreck, P.

*Trauer-Marsch ('zur Todtenfeier Ihrer Majestat der Königin Therese von Bayern')*
Military band
MS DDR:Bds (Hausbibliothek, Thouret, Nr. 369)

### Schreiner, Adolf

*Slavische Fantasie*
Military band
EP (Hamburg, Benjamin) A:Gk (Uncataloged)

*Paraphrase über 'Gaudeamus igitur'*
Military band
EP (Hannover, Oertel) A:Gk (Uncataloged)

### Schröder, F.

*Mazurka ('zur goldenen Hochzeit Sr. M. Kaiser Wilhelm's I')*
Military band
MS DDR:Bds (Hausbibliothek) [lost]

### Schroll, Ludwig

*Fest-Fanfare* (1902)
Brass
MS BRD:Mbs (Mus.Ms.7654)

*Marsch, 'Heimkekr vom Manöverfeld'* (1902)
Military band
MS BRD:Mbs (Mus.Ms.7655) [library of Prince Luitpold v Bayern]

### Schultz (fl. Mecklenburg-Schwerin)

*Triumphmarsch*
Military band
MS DDR:Bds (Mus.Ms.20380)

### Schulz, Christian (1773–1827)

*Salvum fac regem* (1818)
SATB, -143, timpani
MS DDR:SWI (Schulz, C.1.)

### Schumann, Robert (1810–1856)

*Beim Abschied zu singen*, Op. 84
SATB, 2222-02
EP (Leipzig, Breitkopf & Härtel) US:DW (94)

### Schwarz, A. (fl. Mecklenburg-Schwerin)

*Festmarsch*
Military band
MS DDR:SWl (Schwarz, A.1.a.)

### Schwencke, Christian Friedrich Gottlieb (1767–1822)

[Collection of marches and dances]
Six or seven-part Harmoniemusik
EP (Hamburg, Böhme, ca. 1800–1828) [Liv. 1]

## Seidel, Arthur

(2) *Gavottes*
EP (Hannover, Oertel) [reprint of Rotterdam, Lichtenauer] A:Gk (Uncataloged)

## Seifer, R.

*Marsch und Lied*, Op. 3 (*'für die Communalgarde'*)
Seven-part Harmoniemusik
EP (Dresden, Friese, ca. 1800–1828)

## Seiff, J.

(6) *Aufzüge*
-4, timpani
EP (München, Falter, ca. 1800–1828)

*Harmoniestücke*
1021-22
EP (Paris, Ebend, ca. 1800–1828)
EP (München, Falter, ca. 1800–1828) [according to H]

*Militair-Musik*
Fifteen-part winds, with percussion
EP (Paris, Ebend, ca. 1800–1828)

(6) *Pièces d'Harmonie* ('tirées des Opéras favoris: La Muette de Portici, Macbeth, Comte Ory et les 2 Nuits')
21-02
EP (Paris, Ebend, ca. 1800–1828)
EP (München, Falter, ca. 1800–1828) [according to H)
EP (Mainz, Schott) [Liv. 1] (advertized in AMZ, 1817) BRD:MZsch; DK:Kk

(6) *Pièces d'Harmonie* ('tirées des Opéras favoris: Macbeth, Siège de Corinthe, Vampyr, la Muette de Portici, Comte Ory et Guill. Tell')
21-02
EP (Paris, Ebend, ca. 1800–1828)
EP (Mainz, Schott) [Liv. 2] BRD:MZsch

## Seiller, Franz

*Marsch*, 'Zum Neuer Jahr 1844' (for Otto & Queen Amalia of 'Greischenland')
Military band
MS BRD:Mbs (Mus.Ms.3535)

## Selmair, Franz X. (d. 1888)

*Grosser Gott, vir loben dich* (1881)
Voices, brass band
MS (autograph) BRD:DS (MS.621c)

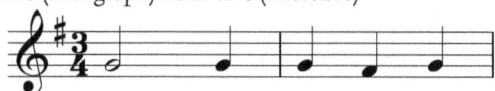

## Siebert, E.

*Bayerischer Militar-Marsch*
Military band
MS DDR:Bds (Hausbibliothek, Thouret, Nr. 316)

## Siegbert, S.

*Deutsche Messe* (ca. 1870)
Chorus, -711, bombard
MS BRD:BB (MS.278)

## Sowinski, A. (arr. Berr)

*Marche heroique des Parisiens*, Op. 24 ('dediée au Général Lafayette')
Harmoniemusik
EP (Bonn, Simrock; Leipzig, Peters, ca. 1800–1828)

## Späth, André (1790–1876)

*Potpourri*, 'Die Heuernte-Landliche Scene,' Op. 52
222-02
EP (Offenbach, André) A:Wgm (VIII 5144)

*Sérénade*, Op. 54
Harmoniemusik with Guitarre
EP (Paris, Ebend)

*Scène pastorale suisse*, Op. 93
222-02
EP (Offenbach, André) A:Wgm (VIII 5143)
EP (Paris, Ebend)

*Drei Psalmen* (dedicated to the Duchess of Kent)
TTBB, winds
MS GB:Lbm (R.M.18.a.21)

*Deutsche Militarische Te Deum*, Op. 210
TTBB, Janisarmusik
MS DDR:Bds (Mus.Ms.20930)

*Deutsche Militar Messe*
TTBB, band
MS A:Wn (Sm 15542)

*Six Fantaisies*
3242-343, ophicleide, percussion
MS (autograph) GB:Lbm (R.M.21.g.36);
    US:DW (101–106)
    Consists of six independent works:
    Nr. 1    Greetings from Afar
    Nr. 2    Evening Calm
    Nr. 3    The Serenade
    Nr. 4    Greetings to your Brother
    Nr. 5    The Beggar
    Nr. 6    My Farewell

## Spohr, Ludwig (1784–1859)

*Notturno*, Op. 34 (composed ca. 1815–1820 and dedicated to Günther Friedrich Carl, Prince of Schwarzenburg)
222-221, piccolo, contrabassoon, percussion
MS BRD:Rtt (Sammelband 15, Nr. 64) [for 1222-22, contrabassoon]
MS DDR:SWl [parts]
EP (Leipzig, Peters, 1853) GB:Lbm (h.1099.C.[4]) [score], GB:Lbm (h.1570.[4]) [parts]
MP (Broude)

*Quintet*
Piano, 1011-01
EP (Paris, 1830) GB:Lbm (h.2784/6)

## Spontini, Gasparo Luigi (1774–1851, in Berlin from 1820)

*Ballo marziale*
2241-143, basset horn, bass horn, contrabassoon, percussion
MS I:Mc [cited by Eitner] US:DT
    Consists of:
    *Evoluzioni militari*
    *Preludio ai combattimenti ed alla vittoria sul campo di Marte*

*Borussia*
Military band
MS DDR:Bds (Hausbibliothek, Thouret, Nr. 283)

*Prussischer Krieggesang* (1840)
Instrumentation unknown
MS (autograph) DDR:Bds (Mus.Ms.Auto.G.Spontini 4)

*Grande Bacchanale*
Harmonie militaire
EP (unknown) DDR:Bds [cited by Eitner]

*Les Dieux rivaux* (1816) [arr. E. Gebauer]
Harmoniemusik
EP (Paris, Erard) DDR:Bds [cited by Eitner]

*Grosser Sieges- und Festmarsch*
Large military band
EP (Berlin) DDR:Bds; A:Wgm; US:DW (60)

*Fackeltanz* (November 29, 1823)
Trompetenmusik
MS DDR:Bds (Bausbibliothek, Thouret, Nr. 324)

*Fackeltanz* ('zur Vermählung I.I.K.K.H.H. des Friedrich der Niederlande und der Prinzessin Louise, 21.5.1828')
Instrumentation unknown
MS DDR:Bds (Hausbibliothek) [lost]

*Fackeltanz* ('zur Vermählung I.I.K.K.H.H. des Wilhelm von Pr. und der Prinzessin Auguste von Saxe-Weimar, 11.6.1829')
Instrumentation unknown
MS DDR:Bds (Hausbibliothek) [lost]

## Steffens, Fr.

*Marsch, 'Erinnerung an Friedrich den Grossen'*
Large military band
MS DDR:Bds (Hausbibliothek) [lost]

*Triumph-Marsch*
Large military band
MS DDR:Bds (Hausbibliothek) [lost]

## Stich, Josef

*March, 'Bayeru Heil'* (ca. 1890)
Wind orchestra
MS BRD:Mbs (Mus.Ms.7628)

## Stock, Christoph Reinrich (b. 1862)

*Festmarsch 1821–1901* (for the 80th birthday of Prince Luitpold v. Bayern)
Kavalleriemusik
MS BRD:Mbs (Mus.Ms.7629)

## Storch, Anton

*Weidmanns Lust* (1838)
TTBB, -241
MS (autograph) DDR:Bds (Mus. Ms.Auto.A.M.Storch 2)

## Storck

(9) *Pièces d'Harmonie*
1021-02
EP (München, Falter) [cited by H]

## Stössel

*Militair-musik*
Harmoniemusik
EP (Mainz, Schott, ca. 1800–1828) BRD:MZsch

## Strauss, Richard (1864–1949)

*Suite* in B♭, Op. 4 (1884)
2222-04, contrabassoon
EP (Leuckart) US:DW (93)

*Serenade*, Op. 7
2222-0401
MS (autograph) A:WUE; US:DW (375)

*Feierlicher Einzug Der Ritter des Johanniter-Ordens* (1909)
Fifteen trumpets, -0442, timpani
MS (autograph) BRD:GSA

*Wiener Philharmoniker Fanfare* (1924)
-6862, 2 timpani
MS (autograph) A:Wph
EP (Boosey)

*Fanfare Zur Eröffnung der Musikwoche der Stadt Wien* (1924)
-6862, 2 timpani
MS (autograph) US:Samuel Wachtell, NY
MP (Boosey) US:DW (407)

*Festmarsch der Stadt Wien* (1943)
Ten trumpets, -0072, 5 timpani
MS (autograph) BRD:GSA;
    US:DW (Uncataloged)
MS (autograph) A:WatSW (MS.259) [shorter version for trumpets only]
MP (Boosey)

*Sonatine,* in F (1943)
2232-04, contrabassoon, basset horn, bass clarinet
MS (autograph) BRD:GSA
MP (Boosey) US:DW (313)

*Symphonie* in E♭ (1944–1945)
2232-04, contrabassoon, bass clarinet, basset horn
MS (autograph) CH:Wsr
MP (Boosey)

## Streck, Peter

*Collection* of 15 opera arrangements
1032-02
MS BRD:Mbs (Mus.Ms.2570)
Includes works by Weber (*Oberon*), Lanner, Strauss, and Fahrbach.

*Collection* of 7 opera arrangements
1022-02
MS BRD:Mbs (Mus.Ms.2569)
Includes Rossini, *Wm. Tell*.

(12) *Neue Märsche* (1833, for King Otto I of Grieschenland)
Large military band
MS BRD:Mbs (Mus.Ms.3536)

(9) *Pièces d'Harmonie*
1021-02
EP (München, Falter; Mainz, Schott, 1828) BRD:MZsch

(6) *Militärische Alpen Märsche* (dedicated to King Léopold I)
Large military band
MS B:Bc (W.13,411)

## Streicher, Nanette (born Stein)

*Marche*
222-02
EP (Bonn, Simrock, ca. 1800–1828)

## Stumpf, Johann Christian

*Harmonie* (arr. in 1822 by Schneider)
1242-121, serpent
MS BRD:Rtt (Sammelband 16, Nr. 1–4)

*Pièces d'Harmonie*
2002-02, percussion
EP (Offenbach, André) [Liv. 3] BRD:RH (may be incomplete?)

## Stuntz, Joseph Hartmann (1793–1859)

*Aufruf*
TTBB, brass
MS (autograph) BRD:Mbs (Mus.Ms.4039/5)

*Am Grabe*
TTBB, brass
MS (autograph) BRD:Mbs (Mus.Ms.4038/2)

*Der bayerische Schützenmarsch* (1850)
TTBB, -44
MS (autograph) BRD:Mbs (Mus.Ms.8320)

*Bankett Lied* (1840, for an Artist's masked carnival)
TTBB, -541, ophicledie
MS (autograph) BRD:Mbs (Mus.Ms.4039/6)

*Die Burgfrau* (1842, *Fesgesang* for Crownprincess Marie von Bayern)
TTBB, -051, ophicleide
MS (autograph) BRD:Mbs (Mus.Ms.4034 and Mus.Ms. 4035)

*Chorgesang* (October 19, 1842, for the laying of a corner stone for a *Befreuingshalle*, dedicated to Ludwig I of Bayern)
TTBB, large military band
MS (autograph) BRD:Mbs (Mus.Ms.4073)

*Das Dampfschiff* (1851, Festgesang to launch a new ship on the Stamberger See)
TTBB, brass
MS (autograph) BRD:Mbs (Mus.Ms.4040/6)

*Der deutsche Landstrum* (1848)
TTBB, brass
MS (autograph) BRD:Mbs (Mus.Ms.4039/11)
MS (autograph) BRD:Mbs (Mus.Ms.4035/3) [for large military band]

*Festgesang* (for the unveiling of Gluck memorial)
TTBB, wind orchestra
MS (autograph) BRD:Mbs (Mus.Ms.4038/6)

*Festlied* (June 24, 1840, for the Frankfurt Gutenberg Fest)
TTBB, large wind orchestra
MS (autograph) BRD:Mbs (Mus.Ms.4075/6)

*Heldengesang in Walhalla*
TTBB, brass
MS (autograph) BRD:Mbs (Mus.Ms.4070-4072)

*Grablied*
SATB, -043
MS (autograph) BRD:Mbs (Mus.Ms.4039/3)

*Husaren Lied*
TTBB, -151
MS (autograph) BRD:Mbs (Mus.Ms.4039)

*Offertorum-Mottetto*, 'Jubilate Deo'
Five voice chorus, -44, bombard, timpani
MS (autograph) BRD:Mbs (Mus.Ms.4045/10)

*Der Landsknecht*
TTBB, fifes, percussion
MS (autograph) BRD:Mbs (Mus.Ms.4038/4 and 4039/10)

*Der Landstrum*
TTBB, brass
MS (autograph) BRD:Mbs (Mus.Ms.4039/12)

*Marche*
Wind orchestra
MS (autograph) BRD:Mbs (Mus.Ms.4024)

*Marche* (for the 1st Reg. Inf.)
Military band
MS (autograph) BRD:Mbs (Mus.Ms.4024/3)

*Marches Militaires* (for Prince Charles of Baviere)
MS (autograph) BRD:Mbs (Mus.Ms.4021)

(3) *Marches* (for the 1st Reg. Inf.)
MS (autograph) BRD:Mbs (Mus.Ms.4024/2)

*Hymn*, 'Pange Lingua'
SATB, -123, bombard
MS (autograph) BRD:Mbs (Mus.Ms.4041)

*Sänger Festlied*
TTBB, brass
MS (autograph) BRD:Mbs (Mus.Ms.4035/6)

*Marche Triomphale* ('a l'occasion de la premiere paix faite par Bonnaparte, executée par la Musique der Cannoniers ... Strasbourg, 5 de la Republique')
MS (autograph) BRD:Mbs (Mus.Ms.4024/1)

*Schützenmarsch*
Male chorus and two wind orchestras [I: 2062-041, ophicleide, bombard, percussion; II: -541. ophicleide, bombard]
MS (autograph) BBD:Mbs (Mus.Ms.4068–4069)
EP (unknown) [choral parts only] BBD:Mbs (20. Mus.Pr.3794)

*Tafellied*
TTBB, wind orchestra
MS (autograph) BBD:Mbs (Mus.Ms.4039/17)

*Teutscher Gruss*
TTBB, large brass band
MS (autograph) BBD:Mbs (Mus.Ms.4033)

*Die Teutsche Kunst* ('den Künstler Gesellschaften Stubenvoll v. New England')
TTBB, large brass band
MS (autograph) BRD:Mbs (Mus.Ms.4035)

*Walhalla Lied* (1839, for the unveiling of a statue of Maximilian I)
TTBB, 2244-463, ophicleide, percussion, timpani
MS (autograph) BRD:Mbs (Mus.Ms.4040/10 and Mus.Ms.8766)

*Hymn* (for a similar occasion in 1835)
SATB, wind orchestra
MS (autograph) BRD:Mbs (Mus.Ms.4040/11)

*Willkommen* (1831)
Double male chorus, wind orchestra
MS (autograph) BRD:Mbs (Mus.Ms.4039/4)

*Festgesang* (1853, for the return of Maxilian II from Italy)
TTBB, wind orchestra
MS (autograph) BRD:Mbs (Mus.M8.4040/9)

## Tag, Christian Traugott (1777–1839)

*Gloria*
Chorus, eleven winds, timpani and organ [cited in MGG]

## Teike, Carl (1864–1922)

*Unter Waffengefährten* (ca. 1900)
Brass band
MS BBD:Mbs (Mus.Ms.11664)

## Theuse

(12) *Pièces*, Op. 43
Cor de Signal, with -231
EP (Leipzig, Hofmeister, ca. 1800–1828)

*Sérénade*, Op. 21
1011-02
EP (Augsburg, Gombart, ca. 1800–1828)

*Potpourri milit. des Chansons et Danses russes*, Op. 41
EP (Leipzig, Hofmeister, ca. 1800–1828)

### Thomas, P. J. von

*Vaterländische Kriegslieder*
Piano, wind instruments
MS DDR:Bds (Hausbibliothek) [lost]

### Titl, Anton Emil (1809–1882)

*Militarmärsche* [cited in MGG]

### Tschirch, Ernst

*Rastlose Liebe*
Male chorus, 202-02, piano, harp
MS DDR:Bds (Mus.Ms.Auto.E.Tschirch 22)

### Tschirch, Rudolf

(2) *Märsche* (1868)
MS DDR:Bds (Mus.Ms.Auto.R.Tschirch 3)

*Jägd-Quadrille* (1859)
Wind orchestra
MS DDR:Bds (Mus.Ms.Auto.R.Tschirch 5)

*Musicalische Humoresken* (1856)
Kavalleriemusik
MS DDR:Bds (Mus.Ms.Auto.R.Tschirch 4)

*Defilir Marsch* (1854, Jäger Bat.)
MS DDR:Bds (Mus.Ms.Auto.R.Tschirch 6)

*Tonepoem*, 'Die St. Hubertus-Jagd,' Op. 6
Brass
EP (Berlin, Bote & Bock)

### Tuch, Heinrich Agatius Gottlob (1766–1821)

*Sonata*, Op. 22
222-02
EP (Leipzig, Kollmann, ca. 1800–1828)

*Harmonia*, Op. 35
22-121, E♭ clarinet, 2 E♭ flutes, serpent, percussion
EP (Paris, Ebend, ca. 1800–1828)
EP (Dessau-Leipzig, Musik-Comptoir) A:Wmi

*Serenata*, Op. 42 (1816, dedicated to Fürst Friedrich Leopold v. Anhalt-Dessau)
22-02
EP (unknown) DDR:RUh

(3) *Geschwindmärsche*
Türkische Musik
EP (Paris, Ebend, ca. 1800–1828) [Nr. 1–3]
MS DDR:Bds [according to Eitner]

*Trauermarsch* ('auf den Heldentod des Herzogs von Braunschweig, im Jahr 1815')
Ten-part Harmoniemusik
EP (Paris, Ebend, ca. 1800–1828)
MS DDR:Bds [according to Eitner]

*Menuet*
Seven or nine-part Harmoniemusik
EP (Paris, Ebend, ca. 1800–1828)

### Ulrich, E.

*Overture*
Harmoniemusik
EP (Leipzig, Breitkopf & Härtel, ca. 1800–1828)

### Vern, Auguste

*Notturne* in F
1122-121, serpent
MS BRD:Rtt (Sammelband 15, Nr. 62)

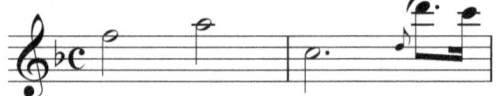

### Volke

*Musique mil.*
EP (Mainz, Schott) [Cah. 1] BRD:MZsch

### Vollstedt, Robert (1854–1919)

*Die Trompeter des Keisers*, Op. 61 ('Characterstuck das Vorbeidefiliren der Kerserl. Leibgarde characteresirent.')
Large brass band
MS (autograph) BRD:Mbs (Mus.Ms.7957)

GERMANY 189

**Wagner**

*Militairmusik* in F
EP (Mainz, Schott, ca. 1800–1828) [Liv. 1] BRD:MZsch

**Wagner, F. A.**

(4) *Märsche* and (3) *Polonaisen*
-903, 2 Kenthorns
MS DDR:Bds (Hausbibliothek) [lost]

**Wagner, Richard (1813–1883)**

(3) *Fanfares* (dedicated to the 'K.Bayr. 6. ChevaulegersRegiment')
Four Signal Trumpets, timpani
MP (1933) BRD:Mbs (20.Mus.Pr.9120); GB:Lbm (h.356.s.[6].pag.2,3); US:DW (272)
MS DDR:Bds (Hausbibliothek) [lost] (score, for -403)
MP www.whitwellbooks.com

*Gruss* (1844)
TTBB, 4282-4661
MS (partial autograph) BRD:Mbs (Mus.Mss. App.2028, xerox); US:DW (208)

*Weihegruss* (1843)
TTBB, -4431
MS BRD:?; US:DW (207)

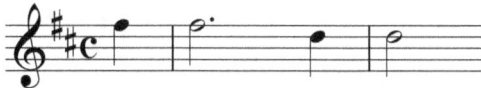

*Huldigungsmarsch*
Large wind orchestra
MS BRD:B
EP (Schott, 1871) US:DW (161)
MP www.whitwellbooks.com

*Trauermusik*
Large wind orchestra
MS (autograph) DDR:Bds (Mus.Ms.Auto.Richard Wagner 3)
MS BRD:Mwg (xerox of autograph)
MS (autograph) BRD:Bayreuth (Wagner Archiv, Wahnfried) [original piano draft, now perhaps moved to BRD:B or Mwg]; US:DW
MP www.whitwellbooks.com

**Walch, Johann Heinrich**

*Pièces d'Harmonie*
Military band
EP (Leipzig, Peters) [Liv. 1–9, 13]
Volume 13 contained arrangements of the music of Hummel and Weber.

*Pièces d'Harmonie* [Liv. 12]
EP (Paris and Mainz, Schott) BRD:MZsch; F:Pn (Vm.27.4311)
Contained here are 12 short pieces for 42-223, piccolo, serpent, and percussion.

*Pièces d'Harmonie* [Liv. 14-19]
EP (Paris, Ebend)
The instrumentation in Volume 15 calls for 1032-322, E♭ clarinet, sepent, and percussion. Volume 16 contained *Variations* on an aria from *Leonore* and 4 '*Pièces d'Harmonie.*' Volume 19, for eighteen-part military band contained arrangements of Rossini's *Le Comte Ory* and 4 '*Pièces d'Harmonie.*'

*Pièces d'Harmonie* [Liv. 29]
EP (London, Wessel & Stapleton, ca. 1845) GB:Lbm (h.1555.[3]); US:DW (751)
Contained here are 12 pieces for 1142-423, serpent, percussion.

*Pièces d'Harmonie*
MS BRD:Rtt (Walch 1)
This manuscript for 1242-121, serpent, and signal horn was composed for the Elector of Hesse, ca. 1830.

(21) *Märsche & Tänze*
1110-001, triangle [apparently incomplete]
MS DDR:Bds (Mus.Ms.22518)

*Collection*, 18 movements
2222-221, serpent, percussion
MS BRD:Rtt (Sammelband 14, Nrs. 6–24)

## Wangemann

*Musique Militaire*
EP (Mainz, Schott, ca. 1800–1828) [Cah. 1]

*Pièces d'Harmonie*, Op. 3 (1822)
1201-02, basset horn
MS BRD:Rtt (Wangemann 1) [perhaps incomplete]
EP (Mainz, Schott) BRD:MZsch

## Warmuth, C.

*Jubilaums-Marsch*
Large military band
MS DDR:Bds (Hausbibliothek) [lost]

## Weber, Bernhard (1766–1821)

*Marsch*
Wind orchestra
MS DDR:Bds (Mus.Ms.Auto.B.A.Weber)

*Trauerspiel Klÿtemnestra*
2-043
MS A:Wn (Sm 2065)

*Sie Welken hin*
Soprano, 2002-02
MS DDR:Bds (Mus.Ms.Auto.B.A.Weber 15)

## Weber, Carl Maria von (1786–1826)

*Grablied*, 'Leis wandeln mir, wie Geisterhauch', J. 37 (1803)
STTB, 222-021
MS (autograph) [lost]
MS (autograph) [last known in the private collection of Adolf Henselt, St. Petersburg, an alternate version for SATB, 1022-023, with a new text, '*Zerrissen had des Todes Hand.*']
EP (Berlin, Schlesinger)

*Tusch*, J. 47A (1806)
Twenty trumpets
MS (autograph) DDR: (Leipzig, private collection of G. M. Clauss)
EP (Complete print in Jähn, *Weber Verzeichnis*)

*Trauer-Musik*, 'Hörst du der Klage dumpfen Schall', J. 116 (1811)
SATB, 1022-023
MS (autograph) [last known in the private collection of Adolf Henselt, St. Petersburg]

*Kriegs-Eid*, ‚Wir stehn vor Gott,' J. 139
Unison male chorus, 1-231
MS (autograph) [last known in the private collection of Jähns]

*Walzer*, 'Maienblümlein,' J. 149 (1812)
MS (autograph) [last known in the private collection of Jähns]

*Lebe wohl, mein süsses Leben*, J. 151 (for the birthday of the Herzog von Gotha, November 17, 1812)
1022-02
MS (autograph) [last known in the private collection of Jähn]

*Die verliebte Schäferin*, J. 152 (for the birthday of the Herzog von Gotha, November 17, 1812)
1022-02
MS (autograph) [last known in the private collection of Jähn]

*Beim kindlichen Strahl des erwachendan Phoibos*, J 153 (for the birthday of the Herzog von Gotha, November 17, 1812)
1022-12
MS (autograph) [last known in the private collection of Jähn]

*Musik zu König Yngurd*, J. 214 (1817)
MS (autograph) [last known in the private collection of Jähn]
Contained 10 numbers in varying combinations of -643, percussion.

*Chorus, 'Heil dir, Sappho!,'* J. 240 (1818)
2222-223, timpani
MS DDR:Dlb

*Du hoher Rautenzweig*, J. 271 (1819)
SATB, 2022-
MS (autograph) DDR:Dlb

*Agnus Dei*, J. 273 (1820)
SSA, 2022-02
MS (autograph) [last known in the private collection of Jähn]
Composed for the Trauerspiele, *Carlo*.

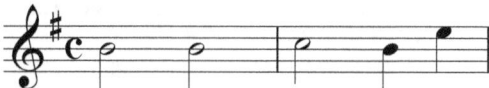

'Fröhliche Musik,' from *Preciosa*, J. 279
2022-02, percussion

*Marcia vivace*, J. 288 (1822)
Ten trumpets
MS (autograph) [last known in the private collection of Jähn]
This was found together with the score of *Euryanthe*, bearing the note, 'für Königl: Preuss: Leib Regiment. Schwarze Husaren. July 29, 1822.'

'Hunting Chorus,' from *Euryanthe*
TTBB, -041

'Warum musst du schlafen,' from *Oberon*
Singer, 22 01, guitar

'Nr. 6,' from *Oberon*
222-, percussion [off-stage band]

'Nr. 14,' from *Oberon*
2020-01

*Marsch*, J. 307 (1826) (for the Royal Society of Musicians, London)
1222-221
EP (Leipzig, Bureau de Musique-Peters) US:DW (372)
This work appeared later in a version for SATTB, orchestra.

*Concertino*, J.Anh.II, 39
1022-121, string bass
ME BRD: (private collection) US:DW (396)
I believe this is the work mentioned by Weber in his diary for November 10, 1811, an *Adagio* he wrote for the oboist, Anton Flad.

*Adagio & Rondo*
22-02
ME (autograph) DDR:Bds (Mus.Ms.Auto.F.299)
MS F:Pn [according to H]
MP (Musica Rara) US:DW (391)

*Harmonie* in B♭, J.Anh.II, 31
Mentioned in Weber's printed *Verzeichnis* of 1808. Jähn suggests it may be one of a series of anonymous manuscripts ('Nr. 88, 92, 94, 107, 121 [which share an incipit with J. 64 and J. 94], 126, 128, 145/3, or 145/9') in BRD:Sl.

## Weber, Jacob Gottfried (1779–1839)

*Triumphmarsch*, Op. 20
Large wind band
EP (Mainz, Schott, ca. 1800–1828) BRD:MZsch

## Weiss, Heinrich

*Festgruss an Deutschlands Kaiser*
Military band
MS DDR:Bds (Mus.Ms.23005)

## Weller, F.

(8) *Märsche für Infanterie* [with A. Neithardt]
Military band
EP (Berlin, Schlesinger, ca. 1800–1828) DDR:Bds (Hausbibliothek) [lost]

*Erinnerung vergnugter Stunden im Lager bei Teltow*, 1832
Military band
MS DDR:Bds (Hausbibliothek) [lost]

## Wenzel, Edovard

*Fantaisie Militaire*
Military band
MS GB:Lbm (R.M.18.a.17)
Based on a theme by the King of Hannover, dedicated to Queen Victoria.

## Werkmeister, Rudolf (of Oranienburg)

*Journal de Musique Militaire*
222-12
MS CS:KRa (IV.B.I93) [Vol. 1, with 5 works; Vol. 2, with 4 works]
The AMZ advertized, in December, 1804, a similar work, *Journal militairischer Musik*, for *Hautboisten* in six, seven, and eight-parts, by Werkmeister and Herrn v. Sydow.

## Weschke, Paul

[Untitled work]
TB chorus, wind orchestra
MS (autograph) DDR:Bds (Mus.Ms.Auto. VII, 1–18)

## Wieprecht, Wilhelm (1802–1872)

*Festmarsch uber Themen aus Beethoyens Konz. Es* Op. 73
Military band
EP BRD:B
MP www.whitwellbooks.com
Based on the themes of the E♭ piano concerto.

*Siegesmarsch*
Military band (?)
EP (Berlin, Heinrichshofen, 1871) [cited in MGG]

*Triumphmarsch*
Military band (?)
EP (Berlin, Heinrichshofen, 1871) [cited in MGG]

*Grosse Völkerschlacht bei Leipzig*
MS BRD:B (Mus.Ms.23104) scores for bands 2 and 3, complete parts
MP Full score, US:DW

Sometime during the 1840s Wieprecht organized an outdoor performance in Berlin of the trumpet signals from Part I of Beethoven's *Wellington's Victory* for massed trumpets and actual cannons. The performance created a great sensation. This led to a much more ambitious work in memory of the Battle of Leipzig called *Remembrance 1813–1815* composed for Albrecht von Prussen. This score was published between 1852–1859 by Breslau: Koenig & Co. A score of this work exists today in BRD:B (Alte Deutsche Musiksammlung, Mus. 7821) under the title *Musikalische Erinnerungen*. In 1987 Keating Johnson, at my suggestion, made a trip to Berlin to study the various Wieprecht materials and he reported the following scheme of the *Erinnerung*.

| | | |
|---|---|---|
| *Introduzione* | 18 bars | 4/4 |
| Marsch *Der Hohenfriedberger* | 25 bars | 4/4 |
| Interade. Marsch Tempo | 19 bars | 4/4 |
| Marsch. *Frisch auf Kameraden* | | |
| *Sehr munter* | 29 bars | 4/4 |
| Andante con moto. *Der Ritter muss zum blat'gen Kampf hinaus* | 25 bars | 4/4 |
| Variation. Andante | 21 bars | 4/4 |
| *Gebet vor der Schlacht*. Adagio | 16 bars | 3/4 |
| *Lutzow's Freicorps nahet heran* | 4 bars | 6/8 |
| *Jubelruf der Kriegerschaar* | 5 bars | 4/4 |
| *Fortsetzung der Schlacht* | 98 bars | 6/8 |
| *Siegesruf*. Allegro | 53 bars | 4/4 |
| *Domine* with male choir | 20 bars | 4/4 |
| *Die in der Schlacht gefallenen Bruder*. Largo | 32 bars | 3/4 |
| *Die Schaaren sichen. Buvouaqs* | 26 bars | 4/4 |
| Buvouaq. *Harmonische Retraite* | | |
| Erste Post. | 21 bars | 4/4 and 2/4 |
| 2te Post | 10 bars | 4/4 and 2/4 |
| 3te Post | 13 bars | 4/4 and 2/4 |
| Largo. *Amen* | 6 bars | 4/4 |
| *Finale … für gott & Vaterland* | 51 bars | 2/4 |
| *Die Landwehr* | 16 bars | 4/4 |
| Ankunf der Colonnen den … *Monarchen* | 21 bars | 2/4 |
| *Das Yorksche Korps* [with chorus] | 78 bars | 2/4 |
| *Der Friede*. Maestoso ['God save the King'] | 17 bars | 3/4 |

Finally, in 1863, for the 50th anniversary of the Battle of Leipzig, Wieprecht organized a great public outdoor performance of an even more extensive composition, his Tone Poem, the *Battle of Leipzig* for three bands, a work of some 40 minutes in duration. This work was scored for a very large Prussian Infantry Band, a Prussian Cavalry Band and a French Infantry Band, with separate ensembles of (natural) signal trumpets in G, E, E♭, D♭, C, and B (with separate conductor), a separate ensemble of natural signal horns, a separate Tambour Corp (with separate conductor), directions for cannons accompanying bands 2 and 3 and a score for fireworks cues.

Each of the three bands has some original music of its own and on several occasions they play together in different meters. While the large Infantry band is the principal one, bands 2 and 3 are not used as mere 'echo' effects but do on occasion function in *concertato* style. Subtitles appear frequently to identify music of specific regiments and of specific music actually used in the battle of 1813.

The composition is, of course, programmatic and is divided into three parts. Part One (18 October 1813) begins with a dark and somber introduction called 'Daybreak,' followed by music appropriate to the arrival of the various international armies. These include the Russians represented by the well-known *Alexander March* and the arrival of the Austrians playing the Austrian national anthem, also known as 'Haydn's Hymn.'

Now comes military signals, cannons, rifle fire and an extensive and detailed musical representation of the battle of this first day. As we near the end of Part One, and of October 18, there is music for the various national troops to retire for the night, a performance of '*Eine fest Burg ist unser gott*' (with fireworks!), an Adagio called 'Lamentations of the People over the Pain of the Wounded' and finally drinking music.

Part Two (19 October 1813) begins with a very interesting series, a competition really, of fanfares representing the various nations. There is a resumption of the battle, now with music to represent important turning points in the battle. The French are defeated on this day and therefore toward the end of this part and in the following Part Three the French band is heard no more. At the close of Part Two we hear a beautiful setting of 'Now Thank we all our God,' with this slow chorale interrupted by Ives-like brief, loud fanfares.

Part Three represents the victorious entry of the allied troops into Leipzig with traditional music representing nine regiments. Finally we hear 'God Save the King' (every nation's national anthem except Austria), cannons and fireworks.

*Marsch*, 'Vorwarts' (June 22, 1862)
MS DDR:Bds (Mus.Ms.Auto.W.F.Wieprecht 2), a 14 page score

*Notturno*, Op. 8
Harmonie Orchestra
MS DDR:Bds (Mus.Ms.23104/1), parts only
MS DW, score

*Die Königskugel*, 'War einst ein alter könig'
Unison male chorus, 121-1131, percussion
MS DDR:Bds (Mus.Ms.Auto.W.F.Wieprecht 3), a 7-page score

*Postillion Marsch* and *Grande-Pas Redoublé*
MS DDR:Bds (Mus.Ms.Auto.W.F.Wieprecht 4), 46 pages of music and 2 pages of instructions and history by Wieprecht.

(6) *Märsche*
Kavallerie-Musik
MS DDR:Bds (Bausbibliothek, Thouret Nr. 237) Some of these can also be found in BRD:F

*Marsch sinfonique* for 3 bands [Infantry, Cavalry and Jäger]
MS DDR:Bds (Mus.Ms.23103)

*Trompeten Musik* (1860)
MS DDR:Bds (Mus.Ms.23105)

*Trauermarsch*
EP BRD:B
MP www.whitwellbooks.com
  'The concert ended with a very fine and well-written funeral march, composed by Wieprecht, and played with only one rehearsal!!' [Berlioz, 1843]

*Die Schlacht*
MS BRD:B (Alte Deutsche Musiksammlung Mus.7820) (for piano, probably intended for scoring for band)

*Friedrich Wilhelm & Victoria*
MS BRD:B (Alte Deutsche Musiksammlung Mus.7822) (for piano, probably intended for scoring for band)

3 *Marches*
MS BRD:B (Alte Deutsche Musiksammlung Mus.7823) (for piano, probably intended for scoring for band)

A complete list of the original band compositions and arrangements of Wieprecht (most of which are lost) is given in Volume Five of this series.

## Wilk von

*Trompeters Signals* ('für die Magdeburgische Cavallerie Inspection, 3.3.1803')
MS DDR:Bds (Mus.Ms.23009/10)

## Winkelmayer

*Serenade*
-221
EP (Mainz, Schott, ca. 1800–1828) BRD:MZsch

## Witt

*Pièces d'Harmonie*
Harmoniemusik
EP (Mainz, Schott, ca. 1800–1828) BRD:MZsch

(2) *Parthien*
Ten winds
MS US:DT

## Witzleben von

(2) *Festmarsche* ('zur Vermählung des Kronprinzen von Preussen') [Friedrich Wilhelm IV]
Trumpets
MS DDR:Bds (Hausbibliothek, Thouret, Hr. 238)

## Wohlmuth, Andreas Mich. (1809–1884)

*Festgesang zur Primitz-Feier*
TTBB, winds
MS [xerox of 1833 autograph] BRD:Mbs (Mus. Ms.App.1245)

## Wöhning, S. C.

*Harmonie*, Op. 3
Cavallerie-Musik
EP (Dusseldorf, Beyer, ca. 1800–1828) [Liv. 1]

## Wüllner, Franz (1832–1902)

*Serenade*
TTBB, wind orchestra
MS DDR:Bds (Mus.Ms.23359/13)

*Serenade*
TTBB, wind orchestra
MS DDR:Bds (Mus.Ms.Auto.F.Wallner 40)

## Wurst, M. L. F.

Tone Poem, *Die Schlacht* (1824)
Chorus, large military band
MS DDR:Bds (Hausbibliothek, Thouret, Nr. 314)

## Zaininger, Benedikt

(2) *Libra* (ca. 1840)
SATB, large brass ensemble
MS BRD:BB (MS.311)

*Libra*
SATB, -321
MS A:Wn (Sm 22632 Sbd 23)

*Libra*
SATB, woodwinds
EP (München, Falter) A:Wgm (I 44365)

## Zimmermann, Carl

*Geistliche Gesänge für den militärgottesdenst*
EP (Basel, 1847)
CH:Bmi (mil.Dc.38)

## Zetterquist, L. J.

*Festmarsch*
Military band
MS DDR:Bds (Hausbibliothek) [lost]

## Zichy, Graf Geza (1849–1924)

*Liszt-Marsch*
Military band
MS [cited in MGG]

## Zulehner, Georg Carl (1770–1841)

*Freimaurercantate*
Male chorus, winds
MS (Mainz, Schott) BRD:MZsch

## Zweckstetter, Christoph (1772–1836)

*Salve Regina* (ca. 1810)
SSA, 1021-02
MS (autograph) BRD:WS (MS.721)

*Veni Sancte Spiritus* ('eigens für die Secundiz Feyer des Herrn Phillip Blum am 10 June, 1820')
SATB, -801, timpani
MS BRD:WS (MS.724)

## Representative Arrangements

### Anonymous

*Stücke für Harmoniemusk* (ca. 1850)
1020-241, timpani
MS BRD:BB (MS.336)
> Contains three original anonymous pieces; 6 *Viennese Walzes* by Ph. Fahrbach (the elder), and arrangements of Rossini (*Tancredi*, and *L'Italiana in Algeri*), Weber (*Preziosa*), Lindpainter and Nicolini.

'Bacchus' Blessings Chorus,' from *Alexander's Feast* (ca. 1840)
TTBB, -041
MS BRD:Mbs (Mus.Ms.9221)

*Die Hermannschlacht* (ca. 1850)
Arranged by H. A. Chelard
1052-243, serpent, percussion
MS BRD:B (Mus.Ms.3435/11)

*Hymne a Orphée*
Arranged by H. A. Chelard
2022-04, ophicleide
MS BRD:B (Mus.Ms.3442/5)

### Auber

'La Guarache,' from *la Muette de Portici*
Arranged by Küffner
Military band
EP (Mainz, Schott) BRD:MZsch

### Beethoven

*Egmont*
Arranged by Starke
'Harmonie und türkische Musik'
MS (autograph) DDR:Bds (Mus.Ms.Auto.F.Starke 1)

*Eggsmunt Simphonie* (ca. 1820)
Arranged by Schneider
2222-221, serpent, percussion
MS BRD:Rtt (Sammelband 14, Nr. 34)

*Fidelio* (ca. 1820)
Arranged by Schneider
2222-221, serpent, percussion
MS BRD:Rtt (Sammelband 14, Nr. 80–90)

'Adagio cantabile,' from *Septet*, Op. 20
Large military band
EP (Hannover, Oertel) A:Gk (Uncataloged)

*Pottpourri*
1042-243, percussion
MS BRD:TSCH (Z.24)
> Based on the music of 'Bethofen' & Auber.

> A review by Hans von Bülow speaks of Wieprecht's arrangements of the complete Fifth and Seventh Symphonies, now apparently lost.

### Benda

*March aus Medea* (ca. 1810)
1132-021
MS BRD:Rtt (G.Benda 2/IV)

### Berlioz

Overture, *Roman Carnaval*
Arranged by R. Lehmann
Military band
MS A:Gk (Uncataloged)

### Boieldieu

[16 movements from] *Jean de Paris*
Arranged by Schneider
2222-121, serpent, string bass
MS BRD:Rtt (Sammelband 13, Nr. 12–27)

### Catel

'Air,' from *Africains*
Arranged by Schmitt
2232-24, serpent, timpani
MS BRD:AB (N.1/8)

### Cherubini

Overture, from *Der Wassertrager*
Arranged by Geo. Schmitt
2262-231, serpent, timpani
MS BRD:AB (S.27)
MS BRD:AB (N.1/9) [here for 2232-24, serpent, timpani]

Overture, from *Demophon*
Arranged by S. J. Weber
2242-221, serpent, percussion
MS BRD:AB (T.4)

Overture, from *Lodoiska*
Arranged by Schmitt
2232-24, serpent, timpani
MS BRD:AB (N.1/7)

## Dalayrac

Overture, from *Adolphe et Clara*
Arranged by Schmitt (ca. 1810)
2242-221, serpent
MS BRD:AB (S.26)

*Nacht im Walde*
Arranged by Schmitt
3232-24, 2 basset horns, contrabassoon, percussion
MS BRD:AB (T.13)

*Maison a Vendre*
Arranged by Schmitt
3242-021, serpent
MS BRD:AB (S.55)

## Deschalumeaux

Overture, from *Monsieur des Chalumeaux*
Arranged by Schmitt (ca. 1810)
1222-201, serpent, percussion
MS BRD:AB (S.29)

## Fahrbach, Philipp (1815–1885)

[Title unknown]
Arranged by Krokowitsch
Large military band
MS BRD:B (Mus.Ms.5767)

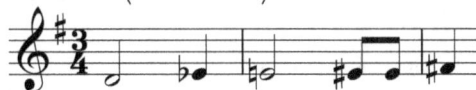

## Grétry

[11 movements from] *Blaubarth*
Arranged by Schneider (ca. 1823)
1242-121, string bass
MS BRD:Rtt (Sammelband 23, Nrs. 1–11)

## Haydn

'Lieblings' *Symphony*
Arranged by Schneider (ca. 1826)
1222-121, 2 violas (?), string bass
MS BRD:Rtt (Sammelband 12, Nr. 1–4)

*Symphony* [I, 93]
Arranged by Schneider (1823)
1242-121, serpent, 2 violas (?)
MS BRD:Rtt (Sammelband 18)

*Symphony* [I, 94]
Arranged by Schneider (ca. 1813)
1242-121, serpent
MS BRD:Rtt (Sammelband 17, Nrs. 151–154)

*Symphony* [I, 99]
Arranged by Schneider (1823)
1242-121, serpent, 2 violas (?)
MS BRD:Rtt (Sammelband 18)

*Symphony* [I, 101]
Arranged by Schneider (1823)
1242-121, serpent, 2 violas (?)
MS BRD:Rtt (Sammelband 18)

*Symphony* [I, 103]
Arranged by Schneider (1823)
1242-121, serpent, 2 violas (?)
MS BRD:Rtt (Sammelband 18)

*Symphony* [I, 104]
Arranged by Schneider (1823)
1242-121, serpent, 2 violas (?)
MS BRD:Rtt (Sammelband 18)

## Hummel

*Notturno*. Op. 99
Arranged by J. D. Rose
1042-121
EP (Leipzig, Hofmeister, ca. 1800–1828)

## Isouard

Overture, from *Medecin Turc*
Arranged by Schmitt (*Fürstlich Leiningische Musik, Nr. 6*)
3242-24, serpent
MS BRD:AB (T.8)

*Aschenbroedel*
Arranged by Schneider
Nine-part Harmoniemusik (ca. 1820)
MS BRD:Rtt (Sammelband 14, Nr. 26–33)

## Körnlein

*Kegeltanz*
Arranged by Pirnsler (1847)
1121-121
MS BRD:DO (Mus.Ms.1084)

## Kreutzer

(14) *Lieder*
Arranged by Schneider (ca. 1822)
1242-121, serpent
MS BRD:Rtt (Sammelband 16, Nr. 35, 83–95)

Overture, from *Paul et Virginie*
Arranged by Schmitt
1242-242, serpent
MS BRD:AB (S.25)

Finale, from *Paul et Virginie*
Arranged by Schmitt
1242-242, serpent
MS BRD:AB (S.54)

'Chor der Negres,' from *Paul et Virginie*
Arranged by Schmitt
2242-02, contrabassoon
MS BRD:AB (S.61)

[Untitled excerpt] from *Paul et Virginie*
Arranged by Schmitt
3242-221, contrabassoon, percussion
MS BRD:AB (T.9)

## Leoncavallo

*Der Bajazzo* [Faust]
Arranged by Seidel
Military band
EP BRD:Bhm (29510)

## Leontieff

*Polonaise*
Arranged by L. Schneider
1202-02, serpent
MS BRD:AB (S.40)

## Lobe, J. C.

Overture, from *Les Flibustiers*
Arranged by Hinkel
Military band
EP (Leipzig, Breitkopf & Härtel, ca. 1800–1828)

## Mendelssohn

*Ein Sommernachtstraum*
Arranged by F. L. Schubert [brother to Franz Schubert]
Harmoniemusik
EP (Leipzig, Breitkopf & Härtel)

'Wedding Marsch,' from *Ein Sommernachtstraum*
Arranged by Nosvadba
Winds
MS (score) BRD:DS (MS.810)
  According to Viet, Wieprecht rearranged the *Overture,* Op. 24 (for band) while Mendelssohn was still alive.

## Meyerbeer

*Meyerbeeriana*
Arranged by Seidel
Large military band
EP (Hannover, Oertel) A:Gk (Uncataloged)

## Mozart

[36 movements from] *Don Juan*
Arranged by Schneider (1822)
1242-121, serpent
MS BRD:Rtt (Sammelband 16, Nr. 41–76)

Overture, from *Idomeneo*
Arranged by Schmitt
4242-221, serpent
MS BRD:AB (S.23)

Finale, from *Idomeneo*
Arranged by Schmitt
3242-221, serpent
MS BRD:AB (S.43)

'Libera,' from the *Requiem*
Arranged by Seyfried
Male chorus, 1-103, basset horns, string bass, timpani
EP DDR:SWl; DDR:Bds; A:Wgm
  Arranged for and performed at the funeral of Beethoven in Vienna.

Overture, from *Clemenza di Tito*
Arranged by Schmitt
2232-24, serpent, timpani
MS BRD:AB (N.1/4)

Overture, *La Clemenza di Tito*
'Par Hr. W. A. Mozart'
22-12, piccolo, E♭ clarinet, serpent, percussion
EP (Berlin and Amsterdam, Hummel, Nr. 1151) BRD:Tmi

[11 movements from] *Clemenza di Tito*
Arranged by Schneider
2222-121, serpent, string bass
MS BRD:Rtt (Sammelband 13, Nr. 1–11)

*Zauberflöte*
Arranged by Satorus
3222-22, serpent, percussion
MS BRD:DS (Mus.Ms.820)

[22 movements from] *Zauberflöte*
Arranged by Schneider (1823)
1242-121, string bass
MS BRD:Rtt (Sammelband 30, Nr. 1–22)

## Müller

[4 movements from] *Das neue Sonntagskind*
Arranged by Schmitt
2242-42, serpent, percussion
MS BRD:AB (S.48 and N.1/3)

## Paer

Overture, from *Der Lustige Schuster*
Arranged by Schmitt
2232-24, serpent, timpani
MS BRD:AB (N.1/2)

Overture, from *Achilles*
Arranged by Schmitt
2242-221, serpent
MS BRD:AB (S.30)

Marsch, from *Achilles*
222-22, piccolo, serpent, percussion
MS DDR:Bds (Hausbibliothek) [lost]

Marsch, from *Sargino*
222-22, piccolo, sepent, percussion
MS DDR:Bds (Hausbibliothek, Thouret, Nr. 121)

*Angnese*
Arranged by Schneider (ca. 1820)
2222-221, serpent, percussion
MS BRD:Rtt (Sammelband 14, Nr. 2–5)

## Ries, F.

*Grande Overture et Marche triomphale*, Op. 172 ('pour la Fête Musicale de Cologne')
Arranged by Küffner
EP (Mainz, Schott, ca. 1800–1828) BRD:MZsch

## Righini

Overture, from *Ariadne*
Arranged by F. Weller
Military band
EP (Berlin, Schlesinger, ca. 1800–1828)

## Rossini

'Airs' from *Cenerentola*
Arranged by Berr
EP (Mainz, Schott, ca. 1800–1828) BRD:MZsch

Overture from *Guillume Tell*
Arranged by Berr
EP (Mainz, Schott, ca. 1800–1828) BRD:MZsch

Overture, from *Guillaume Tell*
Arranged by Küffner
EP (Leipzig, Hofmeister, ca. 1800–1828)

[3 movements from] *L'inganno felice*
Arranged by Schneider (ca. 1820)
2222-121, serpent, string bass
MS BRD:Rtt (Sammelband 13, Nr. 54–56)

[3 movements from] *La Gazza ladra*
Arranged by Schneider (ca. 1820)
2222-121, serpent, string bass
MS BRD:Rtt (Sammelband 13, Nr. 57–59)

'aus' *La gazza ladra*
Instrumentation unknown
MS (8 page score) BRD:TSCH (Z.117)

Sinfonia, from *La Gazza Ladra*
Grosse harmonie
MS BRD:BUu (R-os-117/2)

[10 movements from] *Tancredi*
Arranged by Schneider (ca. 1820)
2222-121, serpent, string bass
MS BRD:Rtt (Sammelband 13, Nr. 28–37)

[15 movements from] *Türk in Italy*
Arranged by Schneider (ca. 1824)
1222-121, 2 violas (1), string bass
MS BRD:Rtt (Sammelband 25, Nr. 37–51)

## Salieri

Overture, to *Palmyra*
Arranged by Schmitt
2232-24, serpent, timpani
MS BRD:AB (N.1/10)

## Schmitt (arranger)

[Collection]
Arranged by Schmitt
2232-24, serpent, timpani
MS BRD:AB (N.1/1)
Contains 12 arrangements of the music of Winter, Mozart, Paer, Muller, Catel, Cherubini, Weigl, and Fioravanti.

## Spontini

*Cortez*
Arranged by Schneider (ca. 1820)
2222-221, serpent, percussion
MS BRD:Rtt (Sammelband 14, Nr. 49–55)

Marcia dell' *La Vestale*
2222-22, basso
MS DDR:Dlb [cited by Eitner]

*Vesttalien*
Arranged by Schneider (ca. 1820)
2222-221, serpent, percussion
MS BRD:Rtt (Sammelband 14, Nr. 35–48)

## Wagner

*Faust Overture*
Arranged by Godfrey
MP (London, Chappell) US:DW (213)

*Der Fliegende Holländer*
Arranged by Seidel
EP (Berlin, Fürstner) BRD:Bbm (29508); A:Gk (Uncataloged)

*Grand Fantasie über Götterdämmerung*
Arranged by Seidel
Large wind band
EP (Schott, Mainz, ca. 1890) [score] BRD:MZsch; BRD:Mbs (2.Mus.Pr.4199); US:DW (220)
MS BRD:MZsch; US:DW (212)

Siegfried's Funeral Music from *Götterdämmerung*
Arranged by Godfrey
MP (London, Chappell) US:DW (215)

'Introduction, Act III,' *Lohengrin*
Arranged by Nosvadba
Large wind band
MS BRD:DS (Mus.Ms.835)

Overture, from *Die Meistersinger*
Arranged by Th. Grawert
Wind orchestra
EP (Mainz, Schott, Nr. 28380) A:Gk (Uncataloged)

Overture, from *Die Meistersinger*
Arranged by A. Abbas
Large wind band
EP (unknown) GB:Lbm (h.1582.a.[14])

'Good Friday Music,' from *Parsifal*
Arranged by Godfrey
MP (London, Chappell) US:DW (214)

*Rheingold*
Arranged by G. F. Schmidt-Kothen
Military band
EP (Hannover, Oertel) A:Gk (Uncataloged)

*Fantasie über Siegfried*
Arranged by Seidel (ca. 1880)
EP (Mainz, Schott) BRD:MZsch; US:DW (210, 211)

'Brünhilden Erwachen,' from *Siegfried*
Arranged by Seidel, under Wagner's 'Aufsicht'
Large wind band
EP (Hannover, Oertel) A:Gk (Uncataloged)

Overture, from *Tannhäuser*
Arranged by Nosvadba
Large wind band
MS BRD:DS (Mus.Ms.836)

*Fantasie über Walküre*
Arranged by Seidel
Large wind band
EP (Hannover, Oertel, 'Im Einverständniss mit Schott') A:Gk (Uncataloged)
MS BRD:Mbs (Mus.Ms.11638) [Seidel's arrangement, arranged for brass band by V. Leilbert, ca. 1900]

## Weber

*Fantasie, Nachruf an Weber*
Arranged by E. Bach
Large wind band
EP (Hannover, Oertel) A:Gk (Uncataloged)

*Euryanthe*
Military band
EP (Paris, Richault)

Overture, from *Der Freischütz*
Arranged by Weller
EP (Berlin, Schlesinger; London, Boosey; Paris, Richault)

'Arias,' from *Der Freischütz*
Arranged by Weller
EP (Leipzig, Hofmeister)

*Jubel-Overture*
Arranged by Rummel
Nine-part military band
EP (Mainz, Schott) BRD:MZsch

*Jubel-Overture*
Arranged by V. Bousquet
Large Wind Band
EP (Paris, Ebend)

[Multi-movement arrangement from] *Oberon*
Arranged by Weller
Large wind band
EP (Berlin, Schlesinger); A:Wgm (VIII 44025); US:DW (357
EP (Paris, Richault)

Overture, from *Preciosa*
Arranged by Weller
Large wind band
EP (Paris, Richault)

'Arias,' from Preciosa
Arranged by Weller
Large wind band
EP (Berlin, Schlesinger)

## Weigl, Josef

Overture, from *Schweitzer Familie*
Arranged by Schmitt
2242-24, serpent, timpani
MS BRD:AB (N.1/11)

Overture, from *Vestales*
Arranged by Schmitt
4242-221, serpent, percussion
MS BRD:AB (T.6)

# Austria

**Anonymous**

(3) *Adagios* & (1) *Polones* (ca. 1817)
222-02
MS CS:Bm (A.33.264)

*Adagio*
31-43
MS CS:Pnm (XL.F.155)

*Allegro* in G
Large wind band
MS CS:Bm (Inv.43.095/A.31137)

*Andante and Trio*
222-02
MS A:Wn [lost]

*Alpenhorn & Zwicker Marsch*
20-321, basso, percussion
MS A:Wn (Sm.355)

*Aufzüge*
20-2, timpani, '*tuccatto*'
MS A:Wn (Sm.21792)

*Aufzüge*
2022-02, timpani
MS A:Wn (Sm.349.ch.XIX.9 fol)

*Aufzüge*
2-22
MS A:Wn (Sm.350)

*Aufzüge*
2-3, timpani
MS A:Wn (Sm.3026)

*Baccanalia* (ca. 1820)
222-22, contrabassoon
MS CS:Bm (A.36.849)

*Cantus Festivus* (ca. 1840)
Soprano. SATB, 2222-02, timpani, contrabassoon
MS CS:BA (68/22-164)

*Cantus funeralis*
SATB, 21-02
MS CS:Pnm (XLVI.F.19)

*Cantus funeralis*
SATB, 21-02
MS CS:Pnm (XLVI.F.66)

*Carroussel Musik für Türkische Musik*
3032-23, percussion
EP (Wien, K.K.priv.chem.Druckerei, Nr. 1620)
CS:Pnm (XLII.F.772)

*Chyálozpey Kavatému* (ca. 1840)
SATB, 21-32, timpani
MS CS:BA (97/109-251)

*Divertimento* (1827)
222-22, contrabassoon
MS CS:Bm (A.37.322)

*Ecce Panis*
SATB, 2041-12, timpani
MS CS:Pnm (XL.F.85)

*Eccossaise et Walzer* (ca. 1825)
Military band
MS CS:Bm (A.37.323) [parts missing]

(5) *Ecossa a Harmonie* (before 1830)
1222-22, contrabassoon
MS CS:Bm (A.35.263)

(4) *Stücke* ('*Zum- Frohnleichnams Umgange*')
Ten-part Harmoniemusik
MS A:M (1204)

*Graduale*
Five Voices, 1021-02
MS CS:Pnm (XVII.B.140)

*Griechisches Lied*
Band
MS A:Wn (Sm.20753)

*Harmonie* (ca. 1830)
222-02, contrabassoon
MS CS:Bm (A.36.852) [parts missing]

*Die Heerschau*
2010-421, basso, bombard, percussion
Ms CS:Pnm (II.D.171)

*Hongroises* (1817)
Winds
MS CS:Bm (A.35.265)

*Intrade*
12-22
MS A:Wn (Sm.409)

*Ländler* (ca. 1830)
222-22, contrabassoon
MS CS:Bm (A.37.324)

(4) *Ländler mit Trio* (ca. 1820)
Türk.musik
MS CS:Bm (A.18.773)

*Libera*
SATB, 22-02
MS A:Wn (Sm.670)
The cover bears the name, 'Frz. Gilg.'

(3) *Marcie* (ca. 1820)
222-02
MS CS:Bm (A.35.926) [parts missing]

(36) *Märsche* (ca. 1867)
MS A:Wn (Sm.20836)

(7) *Märsche* (ca. 1862)
MS A:Wn (Sm.20817)

(5) *Märsche* (ca. 1862)
MS A:Wn (Sm.20818)

(6) *Märsche*
MS A:Wn (Sm.20970)

(5) *Märsche*
Large brass band
MS A:Wn (Sm.716.ch.XIX.98 fo1)

*Marcia*
222-321, Flügelhorns
MS A:Wn (Sm.351.ch.XIX.17 fol)

(6) *Märsche*
Brass band
MS A:Wn, (Sm.20837)

(13) *Märsche*
MS A:Wn (Sm.20878)

(12) *Märsche*
MS A:Wn (Sm.23811)

*Trauer Marsch*
Large wind band
MS A:Wn (Sm.20834)

*Todten Marsch*
43-02
MS A:Wn (Sm.345.ch.XIX.10 fol)

*Marsch*
MS A:Wn (Sm.20970)

*Ritirata*
Military band
MS A:Wn (Sm.20773)

*Marsch*
Military band
MS A:Wn (Sm.13835)

*Marsch & Ecossaise*
Military band
MS A:Wn (Sm.21972)

*beliebter Marsch*
Eight-part Harmoniemusik
EP (Wien, Haslinger ca. 1800–1828)

(2) *Märsche* ('*Der Alexander*' and '*Blöde*')
32-32, serpent, percussion
EP E:Mbmc (K.846)

*Alexander Marsch* (1816)
Türk.musik
MS CS:Bm (A.35.256) [parts missing]

*Favoritmarsch des Kaisers Alexander*
Harmoniemusik
EP (Wien, Haslinger ca. 1800–1828)

*Ungarischer Krönungsmarsch*
Harmoniemusik
EP (Wien, Pennauer, ca. 1800–1828)

*March* ('Ecouse') in F
1022-12
MS CS:Pnm (XLII.F.128)

(2) *Marcia la Turcc*
221-02
MS CS:Pnm (XLII.E.38)

*Marcia* (ca. 1820)
3020-12, percussion
MS CS:Pnm (XLII.F.198)

*Marsch* (1862)
-301
MS CS:Pnm (XL.E.337)

(14) *Marches & Dances*
2041-
MS CS:Pnm (XLII.A.334)

*La Marseillaise Marsch* ('Ludwig und Louise auf den Theater')
221-12
MS A:Wn (Sm.2092); US:DW (37)

(2) *Mazurkas*
Harmoniemusik
MS A:Wn (Sm.20900)

(33) *Menuetts & trios*
22-02
MS A:Wn (Sm.3028)

*Missa Ceská* (ca. 1830)
SAB, 21-02, organ
MS CS:MH (Hu.32)

*Deutsche Messe* (1820)
SATB, 22-02
MS CS:Pnm (XLIX.F.232)

*Deutsche a Harmonie*, 10 movements (before 1830)
1222-22, contrabassoon
MS CS:Bm (A.35.262)

*Deutsche*, 8 movements (ca. 1830)
222-22, contrabassoon
MS CS:Bm (A.25.261)

*Deutsche*, 6 movements
Türk.musik
MS CS:Bm (A.35.260)

*Deutsche Messe* in D
SATB, 1042-02, bombard, organ
MS A:Wn (Sm.21451 sbd.17) [missing choral parts]

*Messe* in E♭
SATB, 1142-221, optional keyboard or two additional bassoons
MS A:Wn (Sm.26 90)

*Motetto Funebralis* (ca. 1810)
ATB, 1-02
MS CS:BA (81/59-201)

*Pange lingua*
SATB, 20-22, bonbard, timpani
MS CS:Pnm (XLVI.F.157)

*Pange lingua*
SATB, 22-02
MS CS:Pnm (XL.E.278)

*Pange lingua*
SATB, 22-02
MS CS:Pnm (XL.E.277)

*Pange lingua*
SAABB, 2-21-02, timpani
MS CS:Pnm (XL.F.38)

*Pange lingua*
SA, 201-02
MS CS:Pnm (L.C.173)

*Pange lingua* (ca. 1840)
SATB, 2021-12, timpani
MS CS:BA (160/41-512)

*Pange lingua*
SATB, 2021-02
MS CS:BA (158/38-509)

*Parthia*
2022-22
MS CS:BA (188/45-599)

*Parthia*
22-02
MS CS:Pnm (XLII.F.36, Nr. 11)

*Parthia*
22-02
MS CS:Pnm (XLII.F.36, Nr. 13)

*Partia* in E♭
21-02
MS CS:Pnm (XIII.A.214)

*Parthia* in C
2020-02
MS CS:Pnm (XLII.F.150)

*Písen* (ca. 1845)
SAB, 2000-02, continuo [two clarinets given as an option for the two flutes]
MS CS:BA (177/19-573)

*Herz Dame Polka* and *Wanderlust, Polka française* (1880)
Military band
MS A:Wn (Sm.20880)

(5) *Polkas*
Military band
MS A:Wn (Sm.20958)

(13) *Polkas*
Military band
MS A:Wn (Sm.20894)

(2) *Polkas*
Military band
MS A:Wn (Sm.20899)

*Polonaise*
Türk.musik
MS CS:Bm (A.36.854)

*Pot Pourri, Nr. 2*
Türk.musik
MS CS:Bm (A.35.268)

*Redout Deutsche*, 8 movements
Türk.musik
MS CS:Bm (A.35.924) [parts missing]

*Rumänische Ardeliana*
Military band
MS A:Wn (Sm.21010)

*Russischer Zapfenstreich*
Military band
MS A:Wn (Sm.20877)

*Salve Regina* in E♭ (ca. 1810)
SA, 21-02
MS CS:BA (147/78-427)

*Spanische Hymne*
Military band
MS A:Wn (Sm.20751)

*Stationes*
SATB, 2021-42, timpani
MS CS:Pnm (XL.E.269) [missing most wind parts]

*Te Deum*
SATB, 2201-12, organ
MS CS:Pnm (XXXVIII.B.268)

*Theme et 5 Variations*
Türk.musik
MS CS:Bm (A.37.326)

*Todenmarsch*
2021-321
MS CS:Pnm (XLVI.F.17)

*Todenmarsch*
2222-221, timpani
MS CS:Pnm (XLVI.F.63 and XLVI.F.68)

*Todesfeyer*
SSAATB, 2221-021
MS CS:Pnm (XLVI.F.64)

*Variations* (on 'God save the King')
222-02
MS A:Wn [lost]

*Wälzer*
Türk.musik
MS CS:Bm (A.37.329)

(6) *Fayorit-Wälzer*
Türk.musik
MS CS:Bm (A.37.328) [parts missing]

*Wälzer*
Türk.musik
MS CS:Bm (A.36.855)

(4) *Wälzer à Harmonie*
Harmoniemusik
MS CS:Bm (A.35.271)

(5) *Wälzer à Harmonie*
Harmoniem.usik
MS CS:Bm (A.35.270)

### Achleitner, Rudolf

*Oberst graf-giouanelli Marsch*
Military band
MS CS:Pnm (II.B.4)

*Roschaff-Marsch*
Military band
MS CS:Pnm (II.B.5)

### Albrechtsberger, Johann Georg (1736–1809)

*Serenata* a 5 in B♭ (1806)
211-01
MS H:Bn [cited by SJK]

### Anacker, M.

(8) *Märsche* (October 10, 1824, for the Russian horn band)
MS CS:Pnm (XX.F.51)

### Austrian military

*Abrichtungs-Reglement für die kaiserl. königl. Kavallerie 1863*
EP (Wien, 1863) GB:Lbm (M.L.d.124)
Includes trumpet signals.

*Abrichtungs-Reglement für die kaiserlich-königlichen Fuss-Truppen*
EP (Wien, 1862) GB:Lbm (M.L.d.125)
Includes horn signals and '*Trommelstreiche.*'

*Abrichtungs-Reglement für die k. k. Linien- und Grenz-Infanterie*
EP (Wien, 1851) GB:Lbm (M.L.d.137)

### Bach, Otto

*Trauer Marsch* (1861)
Military band
MS A:Wn (Sm.9293)

*Nachtwachter Lied*
TTBB, 2222-04
MS A:Wn (Sm.9371)

## Bachmayer

(36) *Ländler*
Six-part Harmoniemusik
EP (Wien, Haslinger, ca. 1800–1828)

## Batka, Edvard

(2) *Märche* (for Franz Josef I)
Military band
MS A:Wn (Sm.18607)

## Beethoven

*Bundeslied*
SSS, 22-02
MS (autograph) BBD:Mbs (Mus.Ms.2760)

*Ecossaise* in D, WoO 22 (Baden, 1810)
222-12, piccolo, contrabassoon, percussion
MS (autograph) Wilderswil, Maria Wach

*Ecossaise* in G, WoO 23 (ca. 1810)
MS (autograph) [lost]

*Marsch* in F, Nr. 1, WoO 18 (ca. 1809)
2032-22, piccolo, contrabassoon, percussion
MS (autograph) Wien: Zentralarchiv des Deutschen Ritterordens
MS [copies] A:Wgm, A:Wn (Sm.19594); F:Pn
EP (Berlin, Schlesingerschen, Nr. 37) GB:Lbm (h.400.4.[3]; and h.400.mm) [two copies]

*Marsch* in F, Nr. 2, WoO 19 (1810)
2022-22, piccolo, contrabassoon, percussion
MS (autograph) A:Wien, Zentralarchiv des Deutschen Ritterordens
MS [copies] A:Wgm; DDR:Bds (Artaria Sammlung); A:Wn (Skm.19595)

*Marsch* in C, WoO 20 (1809–1810)
222-22, piccolo, contrabassoon, percussion
MS (autograph) [lost]

*Marsch* in D, WoO 24 (1816)
252-862, serpent, 2 piccolos, contrabassoon, percussion
MS (autograph) DDR:Bds (Artaria Sammlung)

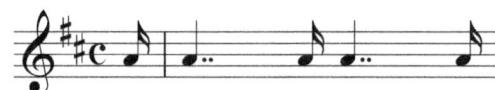

*Marsch*, WoO 29
22-02
MS (autograph) DDR:Bds (Nachlass Grasnick)

*Octett*, Op. 103
222-02
MS (autograph) DDR:Bds (Artaria Sammlung)
EP (Wien, 1830) GB:Lbm (Hirsch iv.362.a.)

*Polonaise* in D, WoO 21 (Baden, 1810)
222-12, piccolo, contrabassoon, percussion
MS (autograph) F:Pn (Sammlung Malherbe)

*Rondo. Andante*
222-02
MS (autograph) BRD:BNba
EP (Wien, Diabelli, 1830) GB:Lbm (h.3213.h.[2])

*Siegessinfonie*
4452-223, piccolo, orgelbass, percussion
MS (autograph) [presentation copy, autograph cover and corrections]
DDR:LEdb (Ort 181)
After WWII this score has been returned to Berlin.
MP www.whitwellbooks.com

*Sextett*
22-02
MS (autograph) [lost]
MS (autograph, 'Menuetto quasi allegretto') GB:Lbm (f.104b)
EP (Leipzig, Breitkopf & Härtel, 1810) GB:Lbm (h.383.dd)

*Sextetto*
1111-02
MS (autograph, sketch) GB:Lbm (f.45b)

### Benz, D.

*Offertorium*
SATB, 20-22, organ
MS CS:Ksm (C.9)

### Berka, Frantilek

*Ariete*
Brass band
MS CS:Pnm (XXIX.D.287)

### Beseda

[Untitled]
1020-22, bass horn, bombard
MS CS:Pnm (II.D.175)

### Bibl, Rudolf (1832–1902)

*Gloria et Honore* (1898, for the 50th year of the reign of Franz Joseph I)
Chorus, woodwinds, timpani
MS A:Wn (Sm.3109)

### Bláha, Filip

*Klagenfurster Lieder Marsch*
Military band
MS CS:Pnm (II.E.96)

### Blumenthal, C.

*Harmonie* (ca. 1819)
222-22
MS CS:Bm (A.35.153)

### Blumenthal, Leopold von

(2) *Marches*
232-22
EP (unknown) E:Mbmc (K.846)

### Bocchorone, R.

*Overture* (1839)
222-22, contrabassoon
MS CS:Bm (A.36.850) [parts missing]

### Bohm

(12) *Deutsche Tänze*
22-02
EP (Wien, Steiner, Nr. 873)

### Bolardt, Thomas

*Trauermarsch* (1846)
20-221, Flügelhorn
MS (autograph) CS:Pnm (XXII.F.294)

## Borovansky

*Polka Mazur*
Military band
MS A:Wn (Sm.22160)

## Bruckner, Anton (1824–1896)

*Germanenzug*
Male chorus, large wind band
EP (Wien, 1892) GB:Lbm (G.517.9[10]);
    US:DW (243)

*Mass* in E minor (1866)
SSAATTBB, 222-243
MP (Wien, 1959) US:DW

*Kantata*, 'Auf. Brüder auf'
Soli male quartet, male chorus, SATB,
202-233
EP (Gollerich) US:DW (238)

*Kantata*, 'Auf. Brüder auf'
SATTBB, -231
EP (Göllerich) US:DW (241)

*Kantata*, 'Preiset den Herrn'
Male chorus, 2242-2431
EP (facsimile) US:DW (239)

*'Lasst Jubeltöne laut erklingen'*
Male chorus, -224
EP (Göllerich) US:DW (240)

*Das deutsche Lied*
Male chorus, -3431
EP (Wien, Universal Edition) GB:Lbm
    (G.111.3.[1]); US:DW (242)

*Apollo-Marsch*
EP (Göllerich) [for piano] US:DW (237)

*Marsch* in E♭
EP (Göllerich, facsimile) US:DW (237)

*Aeguale*
-003
EP (Göllerich) US:DW (237)

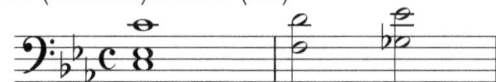

## Dolezálek, Jan (1780–1858)

(12) *Ecossaisen*
Harmoniemusik
EP (Wien, 1813)

## Dorfner, Felise

*Fröhlich-March*
Military band
MS CS:Pnm (II.F.33a)

*Lieschen Polka*
Military band
MS CS:Pnm (II.F.34a)

*Oberst Latschen-Marsch*
Military band
MS CS:Pnm (II.F.35a)

### Doubravsky, Franticsk

*Stationes* (1860)
SATB, 1020-221, timpani, Flügelhorn
MS CS:Pnm (VIII.D.133)

*Pisen*
SATB, 1021-22
MS CS:Pnm (XII.E.318)

*Stabat Mater* (1834)
SATB, 21-2, timpani
MS (autograph) CS:Pnm (VIII.D.137)

### Dubez

*Marsch* ('from Franz Josef I to the King of Hungary, 1867')
Military band
MS A:Wn (Sm.15521)

### Dvořák, Antonín (1841–1904)

*Serenade*, Op. 44
222-03, celli, string bass, contrabassoon
MP (Simrock, Benjamin, Musica Rara, IMC)

### Dwurzek, Josef

*Offertorium*, 'Lauda, Jerusalem' (for the Cathedral in Bruno, 1852)
TTTBBB, small brass band
MS CS:Ksm (C.71)

### Eckhardt, Josef

*Ungarischer Marsch* (1861)
Military band
MS A:Wn (Sm.20812)

### Eckschlager, R.

(2) *Waltzes* and (3) *Polkas* (1868)
Military band
MS A:Wn (Sm.23979)

### Eder, Philipp

*Leichengesang*
SATB, 22-02
MS A:Wn (Sm.21727)

### Eitzenberger, Joseph

*Fest Cantata* (1845, for the Schwarzenberg Court)
TTBB, 1000-221, keyboard
MS A:Sca (Hs.655)

### Emmert, Adam

*Kirchenlied*
SATB, winds
EP (Salzburg, 1800) A:Sca

*Harmonieen*
22-02
EP (Salzburg, 1800) A:Sca; BRD:Rtt; CH:E; CS:Pnm

*Harmonieen*
2002-02
MS BRD:Rtt
EP (Salzburg, 1804) A:Sca (Hs.20709); A:Smsb [cited by SJK]

*Harmonieen*
22-12
EP (Salzburg, 1807) A:Sca (Hs.20219); CS:Pnm (XLI.B.109); US:DW (86)

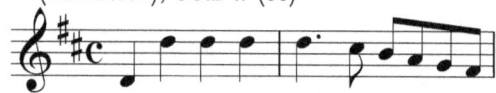

### Eppinger

*Marsch*
Harmoniemusik
EP (Wien, Chemischen Druckerey, 1810)

*Marsch*
222-02, contrabassoon
EP (Wien, Steiner, Nr. 413)

*Marsch der Wiener Bürger*
Ten-part Harmoniemusik
EP (Wien, Haslinger, ca. 1800–1828)

### Erkel, Ferenc (1810–1893)

*Hunyady March*
Brass band
MS H:Bn (Mus.Ms.1299)

### Ernst, Heinrich Wilhelm (Moravian, 1814–1865)

*Polka*
Military band
EP (Paris, 1866) F:Pn (Vm.27.7194)

### Ernesti, Titus

*Defilier Marsch* (ca. 1850)
Military band
MS CS :Pnm (XXXIV.D.109)

### Eybler, Joseph (Wien, 1765–1846)

*Variations*
22-02
MS CS:KRa (IV.B.24)

*Ecce quomodo* (1830)
SATB, 201-2
MS A:Wn (Sm.13040)

*Libera*
SSAATTBB, 222-, contrabassoon
MS CS:Pnm (III.B.131) [missing oboe 1]

### Fahrbach, Anton

*Marsch, Nr. 6*
Military band
MS A:Wst (MH 9791/6)

### Fahrbach, J.

*Erinnerung an Baden* (ca. 1840)
1222-02
MS CS:Bm (A.35.165)

### Fahrbach Philipp, Sen.

*Militar-Conzertstück* (1856)
Military band
MS (autograph) A:Wn; US:DW (185)

*Dobraunoc-Polka*
Military band
MS DDR:Bds (Hausbibliothek, Thouret, Nr. 437)

The following works are for band and were printed in London ca. 1860–1872; shelf-marks given are for GB:Lbm.
(2) *Marches*, h.1562, Hr. 86; and h.1562, Nr. 71
(1) *Quadrille*, h.1544, Nr. 186
*Kärtner Volkslieder*, h.1544, Nr. 198

### Fahrbach, Philipp Jr.

*Zum Kaiser-Jubiläum* (1889)
Military band
MS A:Wst (MH 10622/c)

*Wiener Corso* (1894)
Military band
MS A:Wst (MH 10625/c)

*Miniatur-Ball* (1893)
Military band
MS A:Wst (MH 10624/c)

*Musikalisches Panorama*
Military band
MS A:Wst (MH 10617)

*Retraite & Sapfenstreich* (1880)
Military band
MS A:Wst (MU 10615/c)

*Bruder lustig Marsch*
Military band
MS A:Wst (MU 29972/c)

*Im Mondenlicht Walzer*, Op. 260
Military band
MS A:Wst (MU 29337/c)

*Sturmangriff Marsch*, Op. 161
Military band
MS A:Wst (MH 30229/c)

*Die nachtliche Heerschau*
Military band
MS A:Wst (MH 429)

*Grazer Marsch*
Military band
MS A:Wst (MH 6190/c)

*Militarparade Musik*
Military band
MS A:Wst (MH 2681/c)

In A:Wst one can also find Fahrbach's arrangement of Strauss, Jr., *Overture Prinz Methusalem* (MH 9708/c) and of some music of Mendelssohn (MH 1979/c).

The following Fahrbach works are for band and were printed in London ca. 1881–1900; shelfmarks given are for GB:Lbm.

*Valses*: h.1544, Nr. 425; h.1549, Ser. 95, Nr. 4; h.1549, Ser. 88, Nr. 3; h.1544, Nr. 337; h.1544, Nr. 99; h.1549, Ser. 96, Nr. 6; h.1549, Ser. 77, Nr. 2; e.372.c.[5]; h.1544, Nr. 348; h.1549, Ser. 86. Nr. 6; h.1544. Nr. 342; h.1544, Nr. 359; h.1549, Ser. 83, Nr. 3; h.1549, Ser. 85, Nr. 2; h.1549, Ser. 50, Nr. 4

*Polkas*: h.1549, Ser. 80, Nr. 1; f.412.m.[10]; h.1549. Ser. 82, Nr. 1; e.372.c.[10]; h.1544, Nr. 431; f.414.a.[22]; e.372.c.[9]; h.1549, Ser. 79, Nr. 1; h.1549, Ser. 76, Nr. 1; f.414.b.[6]; h.1544, Nr. 333; h.1549, Ser. 84, Nr. 5; f.401.0.[2]

*Galops*: f.4l3.f.[6] (for brass band); e.372.c.[6]; f.414.b.[4]; h.1549, Ser. 85. Nr. 2; f.412.m.[9]

*Quadrille*, h.1549, Ser. 95, Nr. 2

*Gavotte*, h.1549, Ser. 100, Nr. 6

*March*, e.372.c.[7]

### Faltis, Josef

(4) *Stationes*
SATB, 21-22, timpani
MS CS:Pnm (IX.A.53)

*Stationen für das hohe Frohenleichnams-Fest*
SATS, 2022-32, timpani
MS CS:Pnm (IX.A.52)

### Fanst, Karl

(2) *Märsche* ('Städtische Musikkapelle' and 'St. Pölten,' ca. 1872)
Military band
MS A:Wn (Sm.20814)

### Fendt, A.

*Harmonie-Stücke* (ca. 1812, for the Kaiser's Guard)
1032-221
MS A:Sca (Hs.75)

*Türkische-Musik* (ca. 1812)
1032-121, timpani, percussion
MS A:Sca (Hs.76)

*Harmoniestücke* (ca. 1812)
2042-02, contrabassoon
MS A:Sca (Hs.260)

### Fiala, Alois

*Libera*
SATB, -201, bass Flügelhorn
MS CS:Pnm (XXXVII.F.176)

### Fiala, Anton

*Grussfüsscht für Constantin von Russland* (1867)
Military band
MS A:Wn (Sm.15113)

### Fibiger, Jan

*Salve Regina*
SATB, 21-02
MS CS:Pnm (XII.E.310)

### Fraulich, Joseph

*Giselle Marsch*, Op. 72
Military band
MS (autograph) A:Wn (Sm.21957); US:DW (98)

### Fried, Gotther

(4) *Märsche*
1022-42, contrabassoon, percussion
EP (Wien, Haslinger, ca. 1800–1828)
    E:Mbmc (K.846)

### Frohmann, C.

*Adastra Trauermarsch*, Op. 25 (Prag, 1894)
Military band
MS CS:Pnm (II.F.31)

### Fucik, Julius

*The Mississippi March*
Piano
MS CS:Pnm (I.C.353)
In CS:Pnm there are also a large number of trios for 21-, including a *Fantasie* (VII.D.117) and a *Symphonie Scandaleuse* (V.F.159).

### Führer, Robert

*Graduale, Offertorium, Tantum ergo*, Op. 188
SATB, military band
MS CS:Pnm (XLIII.A.34)

*Te Deum*
TTBB, 20-221, timpani
MS CS:Pnm (XLIII.C.29)

(2) *Veni Sancte Spiritus*
SATB, 1020-22, timpani, organ
MS CS:Pnm (XLVII.E.276)

*Choral Requiem*
SATB, 1021-01, organ
MS CS:Pnm (XLVII.E.263)

(6) *O Salutaris hostia*
SAB, 20-021, organ
MS CS:Pnm (XLIII.D.93)

(4) *Stationen, Frohnleichnamsmusik*, Op. 263
SATB, 20-211
MS CS:Pnm (IX.D.122)

*Harmonie Messe* in E♭
SATB, military band
MS CS:Pnm (XXIX.D.305)

### Gänsbacher, Johann Baptist (1778–1844)

*Jagd-Marsch (für k.k. Jäger Regiment Kaiser)*
50 trumpets
EP (Innsbruck, Kunstanstalt) [for piano]
EP (Sykora, 1880)
MP (Anton Bernhauer, 1930) [cited in MGG]

*Marsch* ('für das Bürgerl. Schützen-Corps, Innsbruck, 1819')
[cited in MGG]

*Alpenlied* ('lnnsbruck, Oct. 5, 1822')
SSAATTBB, 2022-02, contrabassoon
MS A:Llm (Autographensammlung I)

### Gebel

(2) *Harmonies*, Op. 11
Six-part Harmoniemusik
EP (Wien, Haslinger, ca. 1800–1828)

### Geisler, Victor

*Ecce quo modo moritur justus*
SATB, 1022-22
MS (autograph) CS:Pnm (IX.D.200)

### Gellert

*Deutsche Messe* (ca. 1835)
SSAATTBB, 2021-02, 2 organs
MS CS:Pnm (XXXII.D.116)

### Godard, Charles

*Pioa-Pioa-Marsch Joyeuse*
Military band
MS A:Wn (Sm.20816)

## Goldmark, Carl (1830–1915)

*Frühlingsnetz*
Male voices, -04, piano

*Meerstille & glückliche Fahrt*
Male voices, horns

## Götz, Francesco

*Collection of 9 Marches and Dances*
2022-42, percussion
MS CS:KRa (IV.B.33)

## Grimm, Anton

(2) *Pastorale-Graduale*
STB, 1001-02, organ, string bass
MS CS:Pnm (IX.E.166)

## Groh, A.

*Marian Marsch & Polka*
Military band
MS CS:Pnm (II.F.42, a, b)

## Groh, Josef

*Veni sancte*
TTBB, -03, basso
MS CS:Pnm (IX.E.197)

[Untitled]
SATTTTBBBB, -022
EP (Prag, Hoffmann) CS:Pnm (IX.E.170)

*De Sante Caecilia*
TTBB, -022
MS CS:Ksm (C.144)

## Gruber, Felix

*Prozeesionshymus* (1878)
SATB, wind orchestra
MS A:Sca (Hs. 750)

## Gruber, Johann Georg

*Marsch*
21-121
MS A:Wn (Sm.5645)

*Deutscher*
-5
MS A:Wn (Sm.5644)

## Gruber, Josef

(9) *Fronleichnamsgesänge*, Op. 178
SATB, brass band, organ
MS CS:Pnm (XLIII.A.166)

*Te Deum*, Op. 296
SATB, 30-221, timpani, organ
MS CS:Pnm (XLIII.A.165)

## Gueringe

*Serenade* (1818)
1222-02
MS CS:Bm (A.18.854)

## Gung'l, Jozsef (1810–1889)

The following works are for band and were printed in London ca. 1866-1893; shelf-marks given are for GB:Lbm.

Marches: f.401.p.[13]; f.401.t.[17]; f.401.r.[11]; f.412.b.[26]; h.1545, Nr. 4; h.941.[16]; h.1562, Nr. 107; f.413.a.[21]; f.413.a.[23]; h.1562, Nr. 71

Valses: h.1549, Ser. 38, Nr. 2; h.1549, Ser. 50, Nr. 6; h.1544, Nr. 333; h.1549, Ser. 36, Nr. 6; f.411.a.[13]; h.1544, Nr. 244; h.1549, Ser. 95, Nr. 2; h.1549, Ser. 79, Nr. 6; h.1544, Nr. 350; h.1544, Nr. 255; h.1549, Ser. 57, Nr. 6; h.1544, Nr. 265; h.1544, Nr. 217; f.411.a.[19]; h.1549, Ser. 35, Nr. 6; h.1549, Ser. 48, Nr. 4; h.1549, Ser. 70, Nr. 2; h.1544, Nr. 268; h.1544, Nr. 225; h.1549, Ser. 43, Nr. 5; h.1544, Nr. 208; f.411.a.[21]; h.1549, Ser. 47, Nr. 4; h.1549, Ser. 67, Nr. 1; h.1549, Ser. 49, Nr. 1; h.1549, Ser. 15, Nr. 2; f.401.e.[5]; f.411.a.[23]; h.1549, Ser. 51, Nr. 2; h.1549, Ser. 52, Nr. 2; h.1544, Nr. 226; h.1544, Nr. 222; h.1544, Nr. 241; f.416.[2]; h.1549, Ser. 54, Nr. 2; h.1549, Ser. 40, Nr. 2; h.1549, Ser. 60, Nr. 2; h.1549, Ser. 48, Nr. 1; h.1549, Ser. 93, Nr. 4; h.1544, Nr. 248; h.1544, Nr. 320; h.1549, Ser. 43, Nr. 2; f.417.[1]; h.1544, Nr. 209; f.411.a.[25]; h.1549, Ser. 65, Nr. 5; h.1549, Ser. 98, Nr. 4; h.1544, Nr. 232; h.1549, Ser. 57, Nr. 2; h.1549, Ser. 10, Nr. 6; f.411.a.[20]; h.1549, Ser. 42, Nr. 1; h.1549, Ser. 62, Nr. 3; h.1549, Ser. 41, Nr. 3; f.411.a.[22]; h.1549, Ser. 64, Nr. 3

*Polkas*: h.1544, Nr. 237; h.1544, Nr. 214; h.1544, Nr. 291; h.1549, Ser. 9, Nr. 3; h.1544, Nr. 210; h.1544, Nr. 316; h.1544, Nr. 207; h.1544, Nr. 213; h.1544, Nr. 262

*Galops*: h.1544, Nr. 284; h.1549, Ser. 49, Nr. 3

*Polonaise*, h.1549, Ser. 72, Nr. 2

*Mazurka*, h.1549, Ser. 61, Nr. 3

*Sammlung von äarschen für Militar Musik*
Band
EP (Berlin, ca. 1850) GB:Lba (h.1509.o.[4])
This set contains only Nrs. 5, 8, 9, and 11.

*Sammlung von Märschen für Militair Musik*
Band
EP (Berlin, 1854) GB:Lbm (h.3212.[2])
This set contains only Nrs. 23–25.

## Hájek, Josef

*Andante*
-522
MS CS:Pnm (II.F.111)

## Haller, Michael

*Das Deutsche Amt*
SSATB, 2200-02, organ
MS A:Wn (Sm.22986)

## Hallmayr, Victtorin

*Overture*, Nr. 2
Military band
MS (autograph) A:Wn (Sm.20688); US:DW (166)

*Overture*, Nr. 3
Military band
MS (autograph) A:Wn (Sm.20689); US:DW (162)

## Handl, Johann

(13) *Polonoisen*
222-02
MS A:Wn [lost]

## Haslinger

*Europa's Siegesfeier*
Türk.musik
EP (Wien, Haslinger, ca. 1800–1828)

## Hausser, Josef

*Waltz, Heimveh* (1867)
Military band
MS A:Wn (Sm.20789)

## Havel

*Echo*
201-02
MS CS:KRa (IV.B.165)
This is the fifth movement of a set of works of which the first four are arrangements of an opera by Weigl.

## Heidenreich

*Tandum Ergo*
SATB, 22-, contrabassoon
MS CS:Bm (A.20.671)

## Heinrich, Carl

*Carnawall*
Military band
MS A:Wn (Sm.22839)

## Hejtmanek

*Salve Regina*
SATB, 21-02
MS CS:Pnm (X.D.11)

## Henneberg, Johann Baptist (1768–1822)

*Une grande pièce par musique militaire*
[cited in F]

## Herbeck, Johann Ritter von (1831–1877)

The following works are all cited in MGG:

*Zum Walde*, Op. 8
Voices, -04
EP (Breslau, 1859; Leipzig, Leuckart)

*Zur Enthüllung des Erzherzog Karl-Monuments* (1860)
Voices and wind orchestra

*Festgesang zur Enthüllung des Maria Theresien-Monuments* (1862)
Voices and wind orchestra

*Festgesang zur Enthüllung des Schwarzenberg-Monuments* (1867)
Voices and wind orchestra

*Festgesang zur Grundsteinlegung der neuen Univ. in Wien* (1868)
Voices and wind orchestra

*Messe* in F (1863)
Voices and winds

*Libera* (1854)
Voices and -004
EP (Augsburg, Bobm)

*Te Deum* (1856)
Male chorus and winds

*Psalm 26, 'Der Herr ist mein Licht'* (1856)
Male chorus and winds

*Hallelujah* (1859)
Mixed chorus and winds

*Welcher Mensch wird da nicht weinen*
Mixed chorus, 11-

## Herzogenberg, Heinrich (1843–1900)

*Begräbnisgesang, 'Der Herr gab dir den Schmerz zu tragen,'* Op. 88 (1896)
Chorus, -0431 [cited in MGG]

## Hnojil, J.

(6) *Deutsche* (ca. 1820)
Türk.musik.
MS CS:Bm (A.18.911)

(4) *Deutsche*
Türk.musik.
MS CS:Bm (A.35.927)

*Proba Marsch* (ca. 1820)
Türk.musik.
MS CS:Bm (A.18.910)

## Hoch

*Erinnerung an Prag, Fantasic Hongriose*
2122-223
MS H:Bn (Mus.Ms.480)

## Hotis, Jan

*Salve Regina*
SATB, 21-02
MS CS:Pnm (X.E.105)

## Höppler

(4) *Stationes*
SATB, 2022-32, timpani, string bass
MS CS:Pnm (XXXVIII.B.137)

## Hottisch

*Cantate mit Türkische musik*
2031-22
MS CS:Pnm (XLII.F.725) [missing choral parts]

## Hradecky

*VI Variations & Coda*
22-02
MS CS:KRa (IV.B.56)

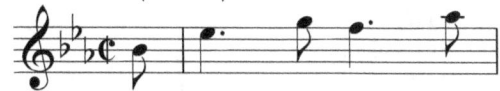

## Hummel, Johann Nepomuk (1778–1837)

(3) *Grandes Marches Militaires* (for 'Grand Duc Nicolas de Russia')
2221-02, basset horns, percussion
MS (autograph) GB:Lbm (Add.32217)

*Parthia* in E♭ (1803)
222-02
MS (autograph) GB:Lbm (Add.32226); US:DW (87)

*Leichen Gesang*
SATTB, 22-22, timpani
MS A:Wn (Sm.2734)

Overture, *Johann von Finland*
Harmoniemusik [1222-02] and symphony orchestra
MS GB:Lbm (Add.32216); US:DW (314)

### Hummel, Joseph Friedrich

*Hymne* ('von Richard Ritter von Strele-Bärwangen') (1901)
SATB, wind orchestra
MS A:Sca (Hs.576)

### Jedlüczka

*Österreicher Brigade March* (1860)
Military band
MS BRD:Mbs (Mus.Ms.7895)

### Jell, J.

*Variationen*
Wind
MS (autograph) A:Wgm [cited by SJK]

### Kanne

*Marsch für die k.k. Österreich Armée*
222-02, contrabassoon
EP (Wien, Steiner, Nr. 732)

*Marsch*
Harmoniemusik
EP (Wien, Chemischen Druckerey, 1810)

### Kathaliery

*Parthia*, 5 movements
22-02
MS CS:KRa (IV.B.58)

*Parthia*, 5 movements
22-02
MS CS:KRa (IV.B.59)

### Katschthaler, Philipp

*Marsch* (ca. 1863)
Military band
MS A:Wn (Sm.0088)

### Kaulich, Josef

*Grosse Motette* (1896)
TTBB, -204, timpani
MS A:Wn (Sm.2576)

### Kélér, Béla (1820-1882, Hungarian)

(26) *Marches* (ca. 1858–1880)
Military band
MS H:Bn (Ms.Mus. 520, 522, 524, 526, 529, 530-536, 538, 540, 572-574, 576, 578-580, 583, 586, 588, 699, and 670)

*'Preussens Aar' Jubelmarsch* ('zur Feier der silbernen Hochzeit I.I.K.K.H.H. des Prinzen und der Prinzessin von Preussen 1854')
Military band
MS DDR:Bds (Hausbibliothek) [lost]

*Prinz Friedrich Karl-Marsch* ('zur Feier der Vermählung Sr. Kgl. Hochzeit des Prinzen Friedrich Karl von Preussen')
Large military band
MS DDR:Bds (Hausbibliothek) [lost]

The following works are for band and were printed in London ca. 1870–1880; shelf-marks given are for GB:Lbm.
*Valse*, h.1549, Ser. 53, Nr. 5
Overtures: h.1549, Ser. 80., Nr. 1; h.1549, Ser. 79, Nr. 1

### Kittl, Jan Bedrich (1809–1868)

*Grand septuor* in E♭, Op. 25
Piano and winds
EP (Leipzig, ca. 1832) [cited in Grove, X, 91]

### Klaus, Josef

(3) *Cantatas*
SATB, 22-02
MS A:Wn (Sm.5727)

## Knofl, G.

*Retraite*
Military band
MS A:Wn (Sm.20777)

## Kodrin

*Conzert-Variationen* (1886)
Solo E♭ clarinet, with band
MS A:Wn (Sm.20800)

## von Kölb

*Marsch* (ca. 1835)
1030-62, string bass
MS CS:BA (186/39-592)

## Kolovrátek, Tomás

*Cantus funebris*
SATB, 222-02, timpani
MS (autograph) CS:Pnm (XI.D.75)

*Parthia pastoralis*
Solo flute, 22-02
MS CS:Pnm (XI.D.93)

*Pjsen*
SATB, 22-02
MS CS:Pnm (XI.D.89)

*Stationes Theophorices* (1812)
SATB, 22-02
MS (autograph) CS:Pnm (XI.D.92)

## Komzak, Karl

*Neues Leben Valse*, Op. 210
Band
EP (London, 1896) GB:Lbm. (h.1544, Nr. 398)

## Koubek

(4) *Rastaveni*
SATB, 1022-22, timpani
MS CS:Pnm (XI.D.155)

## Kovacs, Josef

*Polka*
Military band
MS A:Wn (Sm.20884)

(4) *Märsche*
Military band
MS A:Wn (Sm.20820)

(2) *Märsche*
Military band
MS A:Wn (Sm.20821)

## Kral, Johann Nep.

(2) *Märsche* ('für k.k. Infr. Regmt. v. Hess, Nr. 49')
Military band
MS A:Wn (Sm.20822)

## Krasa

*Missa* in B♭
SATB, 222-22, timpani
MS CS:Pu (59-R-1624)

## Krenn, Franz (1839–1890)

*Marsch*
1021-22
MS A:Wn (Sm.24410)

## Kreutzer

(6) *Wälzer und trio*
22-02
EP (Wien, Steiner, Nr. 1093)

## Krickel

*Missa Bohemica*
SATB, 22-021, organ
MS CS:Pnm (XI.E.210)

## Kroh

*Grosse Retraite* (1859)
Military band
MS A:Wn (Sm.20774)

**Krommer, Franz (1759–1831)**

*Partita* in B♭, Op. 45, Nr. 1
222-12, contrabassoon
MS BRD:Rtt (Krommer 7/1); F:Pn (L3.123, Nr. 2) [for 222-121]; US:DW (358); CS:KRa (IV.B.68) [for 22-12, as 'Parthia Nr. 3,' arr. by Havel]
EP (Wien, Bureau des arts et d'industrie, Nr. 99) A:Wgm (VIII 1291); US:DW (50); A:Wn (MS.9242); DDR:RUl

*Partita* in E♭, Op. 45, Nr. 2
222-12, contrabassoon
MS F:Pn (L.3.123, Nr. 1) [for 222-121]; US:DW (315); US:DW (168) [parts]; (363) [early MS parts]; (316) [score by Middlehoven]; (366) [score by Schwebel])
EP (Wien, Bureau des arts et d'industrie, Nr. 99) A:Wn (MS.9242); BRD:DT, BRD:Rtt; CS:Pnm (XX.F.5); DDR:RUl; H:KE
EP (Paris, Dufont et Dubois) I:Bc
EP (Leipzig, Breitkopf & Härtel) [advertized in AMZ in 1804]

*Partita* in B♭, Op. 45, Nr. 3
222-12, contrabassoon
MS BRD:Rtt (Krommer 7/11) F:Pn (L3.123, Nr. 3) [for 222-121]; US:DW (359); CS:KRa (IV.B.67) [for 22-12, as 'Parthia Nr. 2,' arr. by Havel]; CS:Pum (XI.E.244)
EP (Wien, Bureau des arts et d'industrie, Nr. 99) A:Wn (MS.9242); US:DW (167); BRD:DT; CS:Pnm (XX.F.4); DDR:Bds
EP (Paris, Dufont et Dubois) I:Bc; US:DW (367)

*Harmonie* in F, Op. 57
222-02, contrabassoon
MS BRD:Rtt (Krommer 8) F:Pn (L3.123, Nr. 4) [for 222-121]; US:DW (360); CS:KRa (IV.B.66) [for 22-12, as 'Parthia Nr. 1,' arr. by Havel]; DDR:RUl (RB-K.110)
EP (Wien, Chemische Druckerei, Nr. 600) A:Wgn (VIII 17357); US:DW (11); A:Wn (MS. 9243); BRD:AB; BRD:B (DMS.197.107); BRD:MGmi; H:Bn; H:KE; I:Bl; I:Mc
EP (Paris, Dufont et Dubois) I:Bc

*Harmonie* in B♭, Op. 67
222-02, contrabassoon
MS F:Pn (L.3.123, Hr. 5) [for 222-121]; US:DW (361); CS:KRa (IV.B.70) [for 22-12, as 'Parthia Nr. V.' arr. by Havel]
EP (Wien, Chemische Druckerei, Hr. 775) [as Op. 61]; BRD:HGmi
EP (Wien, Chemische Druckerei, Nr. 775, 1808) [as Op. 67] A:Wgm (VIII 17358); US:DW (12); A:Wn (MS. 9243); BRD:AB; BRD:DT; CS:Bm (A.35.173); H:KE; I:Mc; S:Skma

*Harmonie* in E♭, Op. 69
222-02, contrabassoon
MS BRD:Rtt (Krommer 9) F:Pn (L3.123, Nr. 6) [for 1222-02, contrabassoon]; US:DW (362); CS:KRa (IV.B.69) [for 22-12, as 'Parthia Nr. IV,' arr. by Havel]
EP (Wien, Chemische Drukerei, Nr. 877) A:Wn (MS. 9243); BRD:B (DMS.197.108); BRD:A.B; BRD:DT; H:Bn; S:Skma
EP (Wien, Steiner, Nr. 877, 1808) A:Wgm (VIII 17352); US:DW (3); I:Nc; CS :Bm (A.35.17 9)
EP (Wien, Steiner, Nr. 1381) I:Mc

AUSTRIA 221

*Harmonie* in E♭, Op. 71
222-02, contrabassoon
MS (autograph) I:PAc (F-V-7) US:DW (59); A:Wn (Sm.3711); F:Pn (L3.123, Nr. 7) [for 1222-02, contrabassoon]; DDR:RUl (RH.K.108); I:Mc
EP (Wien, Chemische Drukerei, Nr. 999) A:M; BRD:AB; BRD:B (DMS.197.109); BRD:DT; BRD:MGmi; BRD:Rtt; CS :Bm (A.35.180); H:Bn; I:Vc; S:Skma
EP (Wien, Haslinger) CS:KRa (IV.B.77)

*Harmonie* in F, Op. 73
222-02, contrabassoon
MS (autograph) F:Pn (MS.6579); A:Wn (Sm.3711); US:DW (364); F:Pn (MS.6579) [score]
EP (Wien, Chemische Druckerei, Nr. 1092) BRD:AB; BRD:DT; H:Bn; S:Skma; I:Vc
EP (Wien, Steiner, Nr. 1092) A:Wgm (VIII 17355); US:DW (61)

*Harmonie* in C, Op. 76
222-02, contrabassoon
MS A:Wn (Sm.3711); CS:Pum (XX.F.3) [missing clarinets]
EP (Wien, Chemische Druckerei, Nr. 1187, ca. 1810); I:Vc; S:Skma
EP (Wien, Steiner, Nr. 1187) A:Wgm (VIII 17354); US:DW (63); CS:Bm (A.35.175) [missing horn I]; CS:KRa (IV.B.78); I:Nc

*Harmonie* in F, Op. 77
222-02, contrabassoon
MS CS:Bm (A.35.177)
EP (Wien, Chemische Druckerei, Nr. 1380) A:Wn (MS.8237); BRD:Rtt; S:Skma
EP (Wien, Steiner, Nr. 1380, ca. 1809) A:Wgm (VIII 17351); US:DW (65); I:Nc; I:Vc

*Harmonie* in B♭, Op. 78
222-02, contrabassoon
MS CS:Bm (A.35.174); CS:Bm (Ham.A.6574) [1831, for 222-02]
EP (Wien, Steiner, Nr. 877, ca. 1809) I:Mc
EP (Wien, Chemische Druckerei, Nr. 1381) A:Wn (MS.8237); BRD:Rtt; CS:KRa (IV.B.79); I:Vc; S:Skma
EP (Wien, Steiner, Nr. 1381) A:Wgm (VIII 1598); US:DW (68); I:Nc

*Harmonie* in E♭, Op. 79
222-02, contrabassoon
MS BRD:Rtt (Krommer 11); DDR:HER (Mus.C.21=2)
EP (Wien, Chemische Druckerei, Nr. 1382, ca. 1809) A:Wn (MS.8237); US:DW (70); CS:Bm (A.35.178); CS:Pnm (XX.F.2); I:Vc; S:Skma
EP (Wien, Steiner, Nr. 1382) I:Mc; I:Nc
MP (Hofmeister)

*Harmonie* in F, Op. 83
222-12
MS BRD:Rtt (Krommer 12); CS:Bm (A.35.189)
EP (Wien, Chemische Druckerei, Nr. 1509) CS:Bm (A.35.181); S:Skma
EP (Wien, Steiner, Nr. 1509, ca. 1810) A:Wgm (VIII 17356); US:DW (72); I:Mc

*Partita* in E♭
222-02
MS BRD:DO (Mus.Ms.1159); BRD:Rtt (Krommer 13/11, Nr. 8); CS:KRa (IV.B.72) [for 22-02, as 'Parthia Nr. 1,' arr. by Havel, 1808]; CS:Pnm (XX.F.6); US:DW (88)

*Partita* in E♭
Two solo borus, 222-, contrabassoon
MS BRD:Rtt (Krommer 15); US:DW (99)

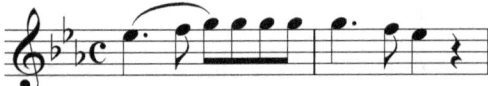

*Partita* in E♭ ('La Chasse')
222-02
MS BRD:DO (Mus.Ms.1165); BRD:Rtt (Krommer 13/III); BRD:DO [for 211-, arr. by Rosiniack]; CS:Pnm (XX.F.9)

*Partita* in E♭
222-02
MS A:M; BRD:Rtt (Krommer 14/I); BRD:DO [for 211-, arr. by Rosiniack]

*Partita* in E♭
222-02
MS BRD:DO (MS. 1529); BRD:Rtt (Krommer 13/IV, as Nr. 11); CS:Pnm

*Partita* in E♭
222-02
MS BRD:DO (Mus.Ms.1162); BRD:DO [for 211-, arr. by Rosiniack]; CS:Bm (A.35.178); CS:Pnm (XX.F.8) [for 22-02, missing bassoon 2]; CS:Pnm (XL1.B.143) [for 22-02]

*Partita* in E♭
222-02
MS BRD:DO (Mus.Ms.1160); CS:KRa (IV.B.73) Las 'Parthia Nr. IV,' arr. Havel]

*Partita* in E♭
222-02
MS BRD:DO (Mus.Ms.1161); BRD:DO [for 211-, arr. by Rosiniack]
[a lost version for 22-02 was cited by Jerkowitz]

*Partita* in B♭
222-02
MS BRD:Rtt (Krommer 14/III); CS:Pnm (XX.F.10) [for 22-02]; CS:Pnm (XL1.B.145) [for 22-02]

*Partita* in B♭
222-02, contrabassoon
MS BRD:Rtt (Krommer 10) [incorrectly identified as Op. 73]

*Partita* in B♭
MS BRD:DO (Mus.Ms.1164); BRD:Rtt (Krommer 14/II)

*Partita* in B♭
222-02
MS BRD:DO (Mus.Ms.1163); BRD:Rtt (Krommer 13/I); CS:KRa (IV.B.74) [for 22-02, as 'Parthia Nr. 2,' arr. by Havel, 1808]

*Partita*
22-02, 2 basset horns, 2 violas (?)
MS BRD:Rtt (Krommer 17/I, Nr. 1)

*Partita*
22-02, 2 basset horns, 2 violas (?)
MS BRD:Rtt (Krommer 17/I, Nr. 2)

*Partita*
22-02, 2 basset horns, 2 violas (?)
MS BRD:Rtt (Krommer 17/I, Nr. 3)

*Partita*
22-02, 2 basset horns, 2 violas (?)
MS BRD:Rtt (Krommer 17/I, Nr. 4)

*Partita*
22-02, 2 basset horns, 2 violas (?)
MS BRD:Rtt (Krommer 17/I, Nr. 5)

*Partita*
22-02, 2 basset horns, 2 violas (?)
MS BRD:Rtt (Krommer 17/I, Nr. 6)

*Partita*
22-02, 2 basset horns, 2 violas (?)
MS BRD:Rtt (Krommer 17/I, Nr. 7)

*Parthia*
Clarinet concertanto, 12-02
MS CS:KRa (IV.B.75)

*Partita*
22-02
MS DDR:HER (Mus.C.21=1)

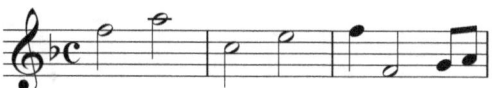

*Partita* in B♭ ('De Lucile')
22-02, 2 basset horns, 2 violas (?)
MS BRD:Rtt (Krommer 17/II, Nr. 7)

*Partitta* in C minor
22-02
MS [lost version cited by Jerkowitz]; CS:KRa (IV.B.71) [for 22-02, as 'Parthia Nr.6,' arr. Havel]

*Partitta* in C minor
22-02
MS [lost version cited by Jerkowitz] CS:Pnm (XLII.F.36) [as 'Parthie Nr. 3']; CS:Pnm (XLI.B.144) (as 'Parthia C moll')
EP (MAB) US:DW (379)

*Partitta* in A♭
22-02
MS [lost version cited by Jerkowitz]

*Parthia* ('Nr. 10')
22-02
MS CS:Pnm (XLII.F.36)

*Partitha* in E♭
222-12, contrabassoon
MS CS:Pnm (XX.F.7) [missing bassoon 2]

The following are partitas for which possible correspondence with those above has not been established.

*Partita*, Nr. 1
222-12, contrabassoon
MS CS:Pk (4866)

*Partita*, Nr. 2
222-12, contrabassoon
MS CS:Pk (4866)

*Parthia*, Nr. 1
122-12, contrabassoon
MS CS:Pk (4913)

*Harmonie*, Nr. 2
222-02, contrabassoon
MS CS:Pk (4913)

*Parthia* in F
2022-02
MS CS:Bm (HAM.A.6575)

'Eine gestochene Partie'
BRD:DO [lost]

*Parthia*
22-02
EP (Hofmeister)

*Partita* in B♭ ('Allegro/Menuetto/Romance/Rondo')
222-02
MS BRD:DO (Mus.Ms.1530); BRD:DO [for 211-, arr. by Rosiniack]; CS:Bm [for 22-02]

*Harmonie* in C
222-021
EP (Paris, Bochsa père, Nr. 141) [2e suite]; BRD:Rtt

*Harmonie* in C
222-021
EP (Paris, Dufaut et Dubois) I:Bc

*Partita* in E♭
22-02
EP (Leipzig, Peters, Nr. 1341) [Advertized in AMZ in 1817] BRD:Rtt; BRD:WERl; DDR:Dmb; I:Mc; S:Skma
MP (Hofmeister, 1956)

*Partita* in E♭
22-02
MS DDR:Dlb [cited by SJK]

(2) *Partitas*
MS CS:Bm (A.35.176; A.35.178)

(3) *Parthien*
MS A:Ee

*Parthia* in B♭
22-02
MS PL:LA (2294)

(2) *Sextets*
MS I:Mc [cited by Eitner]

*Partita*
Military band, arr. Reznicek
MS A:Wn (Sm.2280); US:DW (57)

*Harmonie Stücke für des Frohnleichnams Umgange* (1829)
222-22, contrabassoon
MS A:M (V.1189)

*Volkslied* ('Gott erhalte Franz den Kaiser')
Large military band
MS A:Wgm (XVI 1331)
EP (Wien, Haslinger, Nr. 4951) [as Op. 100] A:Wgm

(3) *Märsche*, Op. 6
222-12, contrabassoon
EP (unknown) E:Mbmc (K.846)

*Märsche für die Türkischemusik*, Op. 9
242-44, serpent, percussion
EP (unknown) E:Mbmc (K.846)

(6) *neue Regiments Harmonie-Märsche nach dem geschwinden Tempo*
222-12, contrabassoon
EP (Wien, Chemische Druckerei, Nr. 2860) A:Wgm

(6) *Märsche*, Op. 31
222-12, contrabassoon
EP (Wien, bureau des arts et d'industrie, Nr. 175) A:Wgm (XVI 1292); BRD:B (DMS.197.106); H:Bn; H:KE
EP (Wien, Steiner, Nr. 286) [for 222-02, contrabassoon]
EP (Offenbach, André, Nr. 3135) BRD:OF

(3) *Märche*, Op. 60
222-12, contrabassoon
EP (Wien, Chemische Druckerei, Nr. 1262) H:Bn; I:Nc; I:Mol
EP (Wien, Steiner, Nr. 1262) [for 222-02, contrabassoon]

March, Op. 82
222-12
EP (unknown) E:Mbmc (K.846)

(6) *Märsche*, Op. 98
242-54, serpent, percussion
EP (Wien, Chemie Druckerey) CS:Bm (A.19.289); E:Mbmc (K.846)

(2) *Märche*, Op. 99
232-44, serpent, percussion
EP (unknown) E:Mbmc (K.846)

*Marsch für türkische Musik*, Op. 100
232-44, contrabassoon, percussion
EP (Wien, Chemische Druckerei, Nr. 2810) A:Wgm; E:Mbmc (K.846)

(6) *Märsche*
222-12
MS BRD:Rtt (Krommer 16)

(12) *Märsche*
222-02, contrabassoon
MS CS:KRa (IV.B.76)

(3) *Marcia*
222-02
MS PL:LA (2608–2610)

## Kubicek, V.

(7) *Deutsche*
Türk.musik
MS CS:Bm (A.35.182)

(7) *Ländler*
Türk.musik
MS CS:Bm (A.19.294)

*Partita*
Harmoniemusik
MS CS:Bm (A.20.825) [incomplete]

*Redout Deutsche*
Türk.musik
MS CS:Bm (A.35.273) [missing parts]

*Polonese*
Türk.musik
MS CS:Bm (A.19.296)

## Kunerth, J. Leopold (Stadt Kremsierer Turnermeister)

(50) *Quartellen*
-3, bass Flügelhorn
MS CS:KRa (I.D.7/a-l)

*Gloria in excelsis*
Tenor, SATB, 20-022, 2 Flügelhorns, cello, organ
MS CS:Ksm (C.701)

(4) *Stationen*
SATB, 21-22
MS CS:Kkpm

### Kussy, Franz

(3) *Märsche* (ca. 1848)
Military band
MS A:Wn (Sm.20967)

### Kwiatkowski

*Srbské-kolo*
Military band
MS CS:Pu (59-R-247)

### Lábler, Frantiscek

(4) *Stationes*
SATB, 22-22, timpani
MS CS:Pnm (XI.F.183)

### Laforest, Thiard Josef

*Cantate*, 'zum Tempelweihfeste …'
SATB, 222-02
MS H:Bn (Ms.Mus.309)

### Landa, W.

*Giuramento-Marsch*
Military band
MS I:Bsf (M.L.1-4)

### Lanner, Joseph (1801–1843)

(6) *Amoretten Walzer* (ca. 1830–1840)
Türk.musik
MS CS:Bm (A.35.233b)

*Nixen-Tänze*
Türk.musik
MS CS:Bm (A.37.336)

(6) *Märche*, Op. 130 and 157 (for the 2nd Wiener Bürger Regiment)
EP (Leipzig, 1889–1890) [keyboard only]

*Marien-Walzer*
222-221, contrabassoon
MS CS:Bm (A.37.335)

### Lanz, Engelbert

*Franz Josef Lied* (1887) [Birthday song]
Male chorus and winds
MS A:Wn (Sm.21832)

*Er naht im leichten Tanz der Horen*
TTBB, 22-02
MS A:Sca (Hs.693)

### Lattenberg, Felix

*Marsch* in C (1815)
Harmoniemusik
MS CS:Pu (V=59-R-749)

*Jägermarsch*, Op. 6
Harmoniemusik
MS CS:Pu (V=59-R-746)

### Leidersdorf, Franz (arr. Oscar Kolbe?)

*Fest Overture* ('bei Gelegenheit der Feyerlichen Krönung Ihrer Majestat Carolina Kaiserin von Österreich zur Königin von Ungarn') (1837)
222-02
MS H:Bn (Ms.Mus.1837)

### Leonhardt, Andreas

*Caroussel, Einzugs, Auszugs, Marsch* (ca. 1809)
Military band
MS A:Wn (Sm.17937)

*Vermählungs Marsch* (1861)
Military band
MS A:Wn (Sm.17938)
Contains the Austrian and German national hymns.

*Die Englische, Preusische & Sächsische Volks Hymne.* 'Heil unserem König Heil!'
Military band
MS A:Wn (Sm.20747)

(3) *Märsche* (ca. 1809)
Military band
MS A:Wn (Sm.26829)

(5) *Märsche*
Military band
MS A:Wn (Sm.19114)

## Lickl, Johann (1769–1843)

(2) *Harmonies*
22-02
EP (Wien, Haslinger, ca. 1800–1828) [Nr. 1, 2]
EP (Wien, Steiner) [as Op. 11]

*Quintetto*, Op. 21
21-02
MS PL:LA (2276)
EP (Wien, Magasin della Caes. Real priv.)
   CS:KRa (IV.B.80)
EP (Wien, Steiner)

*Quintetto concertante* in F
1111-01
MS BRD:Rtt; A:M [missing]
EP (Wien, Magasin de l'imprimerie) A:Wgm
MP (Kneusslin, 1966)

(2) *Suites*
Six-part Harmoniemusik
EP (Wien, Haslinger) [lost]

## Linek, Yiri

*Vidi aguam*
SATB, 2020-3, timpani
MS CS:Pnm (XIX.F.267)

## Liszt, Franz (1811–1886)

*An den heiligen Franziskus von Paula*
TTBB, -003, timpani
EP (Leipzig, Breitkopf & Härtel, *Complete Works*
   V/16, 117ff) US:DW (231)

*Domine salvum fac regem*
TTBB, 222-2431, timpani
EP (Leipzig, Breitkopf & Härtel, *Complete Works*
   V/15, 109ff) US:DW (230)
'Instrumented' by Joachim Raff.

*Göthe-Feier-Weimar*
TTBB, -02
EP (Hamburg, Schuberth, Nr. 2385a)
   US:DW (228)

*Der Herr bewahret die Seelen*
SATB, -2031, timpani
EP (Leipzig, Breitkopf & Härtel, *Complete Works*
   V/34, 46ff) US:DW (233)

*In domun Domini ibimus*
SATB, -202, timpani
EP (Leipzig, Breitkopf & Härtel, *Complete Works*
   V/18, 139ff) US:DW (232)

*Karl August weilt mit uns*
TTBB, brass, percussion, organ
EP (Licht, 1887)
   Grove, XI, 55, gives the title as *Festgesang zur
   Enthüllung des Carl-August-Denkmals in Weimar*,
   and dates the work September 3, 1875.

*Licht, mehr Licht!*
Male chorus, -203
EP (Hamburg, Schuberth, Nr. 2385b, 1860)
   GB:Lbm (E.1644.d.[1]); US:DW (227)
   Composed for a secular celebration of
   Goethe's birthday.

*Nun danket alle Gott*
SATB, brass, percussion
EP (Leipzig, 1884, *Complete Works*, V/7, 190)

*Psalm 118*
TTBB, 222-2431, timpani
EP (Westmead [England], 1972) BRD:Mbs (Mus.
   Pr.5291 [40-57]); US:DW (257)

*Requiem*
TTBB, -202. timpani, organ
EP (Leipzig, Breitkopf & Härtel, *Complete Works*
   V/5, 63ff) US:DW (229)

*Soldatenlied aus Goethes Faust* (July 6, 1844)
Male chorus, trumpets, timpani
EP (1861, Nr. 7 of '*12 Songs*') [cited in Grove,
   XI, 55]

*Te Deum I*
SATB, brass, organ
EP (Leipzig, Breitkopf & Härtel, *Complete Works*
   V/7, 161ff)

*Weimars Volkslied* (1857)
Male chorus, winds
MS DDR:WRgs; DDR:B [private collection, L. Landshoff, 1871; cited in Grove, XI, 54]

## Livorka (arr. Honig)

*Walzer* (ca. 1818)
222-22, contrabassoon
MS CS:Bm (A.37.338)

## Maschek, Albin (1804–1878, son to Vincenc Maschek)

*Salve Regina*
Mixed chorus, -003
EP (Prag, without year) [cited in MGG]

(2) *Jagdstücken*
-04 [cited in MGG]

## Maschek, Paul (1761–1826)

*Die Schlacht bei Leipzig*
3232-121, serpent, contrabassoon, percussion
MS (autograph) A:Wn (Sm.11384); US:DW (58)
 An early source mentions this title by Maschek as having been a Cantata, sung in Vienna in December, 1813. No such performance or no such materials can be presently documented in Vienna. The present version, with the following two parts, is in the hand of the composer and the cover indicates his desire to sell copies of the work in this form at his home ('the Prince's Henhouse'). This epic cycle of original pieces for band is programmatic and follows the entire campaign of 1813–1814 to Leipzig, to Paris, and home to Vienna. Part I consists of 8 movements:
 I The Imperial Royal Austrian and Imperial Russian Armies, under the command of His Grace, Lord Fieldmarshal Karl, Prince of Schwarzenberg, march out to meet the enemy.
 II The approach of the French troops, marching in double-time is heard.
 III The Russians approach from all sides!
 IV The cannons call to battle.
 V The battle ... the French are defeated ... the victory march is heard.
 VI The victorious armies receive their praise.
 VII The Monarchs give thanks to God.
 VIII General rejoicing because of the victory.

*Die Besitznahme von Paris durch die Hohen Verbundeten Siegreichen Truppen den 30 April 1814*
3232-121, serpent, contrabassoon, percussion
MS A:Wn (Sm.11387); US:DW (89)
 Part II of the above cycle consists of 12 original pieces for band:
 I After the Battle of Champenoise, the victorious army pursues the enemy with resounding noise.
 II The Battle of Paris ...
 III The great Allies appear before Paris under the leadership of His Royal Highness, the Crown Prince of Württemberg.
 IV Jubilation of the Allied troops at the sight of a city which believed itself invincible.
 V Napoleon's sorrowful retreat to Fontainbleau ... more Allied troops are still arriving.
 VI Officials of Paris arrive at the headquarters of the Allies to plead for surrender ...
 VII The entry march of their Majesties, the Czar of Russia, the King of Prussia, Crown Prince of Württemberg and Fieldmarshal Prince of Schwarzenberg with their respective troops into Paris.
 VIII The Hunter's Batalione enters Paris.
 IX General rejoicing of the French, having been freed from a terrible ruler.
 X The Allied troops spread out during the night and are well taken care of [!]
 XI Everywhere the Allies are received by the inhabitants with respect and cordiality.
 XII Solemn thanks of the freed population to the Allied Monarchs.

*Österreichs Triumph oder die Rückkunft*
3232-101, contrabassoon, percussion
MS A:Wu (Sm.11385); US:DW (92)
MS A:Wu (Sm.11386) [under *Heil dir Europa!!*, for 222-02, with some additional movements]
EP (Wien, Eder, 1814) A:Wst (M.14013) [for piano]
 Part III of the above cycle consists of 9 original pieces for band:
 I The longing of the subjects for their adored monarch.

II The travels of his Majesty through the lands of his inheritance to the rejoicing of the people.
III The military, the home guard, ride out to meet His Majesty.
IV The Magistrate welcomes His Majesty.
V Even the Youth honor him!
VI Procession of his Majesty through the triumphal arch toward St. Stefan's.
VII The clergy receives His Majesty.
VIII Prayer with cannons roaring.
IX General rejoicing.

## Maschek, Vincenc (1755–1831)

*Concertino*
Solo four-hand piano, 2022-02
EP (Leipzig, 1801) DDR:Bu [cited by Eitner]; CS:Pnm (XIII.F.375); CS:Pnm (II.C.19)

*Concertino per due Piano Forti*
Two soli pianos, 22-02
MS CS:Pnm (XXXVIII.C.281); US:DW (187; 420); DDR:Bds (Mus.Ms.13795/3)

*Concerto* in D
Three clavicembalos, 221-02
MS DDR:Bds (Mus.Ms.13795)

*Duet*, 'Adorare'
SA, 22-02
MS CS:Pnm (XII.E.90)

*Köngismarsch*
-3, timpani
[cited in MGG]

*Leichenlied*
SATB, 1021-02, contrabassoon
MS CS:Pnm (XXXVIII.F.300)

*Il Marcia per il giorno della Festa dei tre Re*
-301, timpani
[cited in MGG]

*Notturno*
22-02, 2 ,violas (?)
EP (Leipzig, Breitkopf & Härtel) [Catalog of 1785–1787]

*Notturno* in F
202-02
MS CS:Bm
MP (MAB, Nr. 35) US:DW (392)

*Pange lingua*
SATB, 2021-02, timpani
MS CS:Pnm (XII.E.109)

*Partitta* in C
202-02
MS CS:Pnm (XXII.D.247)

*Partitta* in C
202-02
MS CS:Pnm (XXII.D.248)

*Partitta* in C
22-02
MS CS:Pnm (XXII.D.230)

*Partitta* in C
22-02
MS CS:Pnm (XXII.D.229)

*Partitta* in C
22-02
MS CS:Pnm (XXII.D.228)

*Partitta* in C
201-02
MS CS:Pnm (XXXII.B.32)
Oboe 1 and bassoon are marked 'a.2'

*Partitta* in C
201-02
MS CS:Pnm (XXXII.B.31)
Oboes and bassoon are marked 'a.2'

*Partitta* in C
202-02
MS CS:Pnm (XXII.D.237)

*Partitta* in C
202-02
MS CS:Pnm (XXII.D.234)

*Parthia vel Variatione*
22-02
[cited in Jerkowitz]

*Partitta* in D
201-02
MS CS:Pnm (XXXII.B.33)
Bassoon marked 'a.2'

*Partitta* in D
202-02
MS CS:Pnm (XXII.D.243)

*Partitta* in D
201-02
MS CS:Pnm (XXXII.B.29)

*Partitta* in D
202-02
MS CS:Pnm (XXII.D.241)

*Partitta* in D
202-02
MS CS:Pnm (XXII.D.242)

*Partita* in E♭
MS BRD:Rtt (Masek 4)

*Partitta* in E♭
1121-12. contrabassoon
MS CS:Pnm (XX.F.14)

*Partitta* in E♭
202-02
MS CS:Pnm (XXII.D.249)

AUSTRIA 231

*Partitta* in E♭
202-02
MS CS:Pnm (XXII.D.245)

*Partita* in F
1112-, basset horn
MS CS:Bibl.Radio Prag

*Partitta* in F
202-02
MS CS:Pnm (XXII.D.246)

*Partitta* in F
1112-12, basset horn, contrabassoon
MS CS:Pnm (XX.F.13)

*Partitta* in F
202-02
MS CS:Pnm (XXII.D.250)

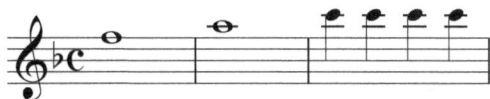

*Partitta* in F
201-02
CS:Pnm (XXXII.C.46); CS:Pnm (XXXII.B.27)
Oboes and bassoon marked 'a.2'

*Partitta* in F
202-02
MS CS:Pnm (XXII.D.233)

*Partitta* in F
202-02
MS CS:Pnm (XXII.D.232)

*Partia* in F
202-02
MS CS:Pnm (XXII.D.231)

*Partitta* in F
202-02
MS CS:Pnm (XXII.D.239)

*Partitta* in G
202-02
MS CS:Pnm (XXXII.D.244)

*Partitta* in G
201-02
MS CS:Pnm (XXXII.B.28)
Oboes and bassoon marked 'a .2'

*Partitta* in A
202-02
MS CS:Pnm (XXII.D.240)

*Parthia* in B♭
22-02
MS CS:Pnm (XXX.C.112)

*Partitta* in B♭
202-02
MS CS:Pnm (XXII.D.235)

*Partitta* in B♭
202-02
MS CS:Pnm (XXII.D.236)

*Partitta* in B♭
202-02
MS CS:Pnm (XXII.D.238)

*Partitta* in B♭
22-02
MS CS:Pnm (XXII.D.252)

*Partita* in B♭
222-02
MS BRD:DO (Mus.Ms.1597, Nr. 4)

(3) *Parthia*
-02, 3 basset horns
MS PL:LA (2277–2279)

*Serenata* in F
222-04
MS CS:Pnm (XXII.D.251)

(2) *Serenaden*
222-02
MS CS:Pnm (XX.F.15)

*Stationes*
SATB, -3, timpani, organ
MS CS:Pnm (XLVI.F.678)

*Stationes*
SATB, 2022-52, timpani
MS CS:Pnm (XL.A.72)

*Todten Marsch*
22-12
MS CS:Pnm (XII.F.318)

*Todten Marsch*
22-22
MS CS:Pnm (XII.E.119)

*Variatione*
22-02
MS CS:KRa (IV.B.83)

*Variatione*
22-02
MS CS:KRa (IV.B.84)

*Variatione*
22-02
MS CS:KRa (IV.B.82)

*Parthia vel Variatione*
22-02
[cited by Jerkowitz]

*Allegretto con Variationi*
Solo clarinet [or flute or oboe], with 11-02
MS A:Wn (Sm.5855); US:DW (33)

## Massak, Franz

(4) *Märsche*
Military band
MS A:Wn (Sm.10823)

## Matous

*Parthia* in E♭
21-02
MS CS:Pnm (IX.C.12)

## Melusin, Rudolf

(2) *Märsche*
Military band
MS A:Wn (Sm.20824)

## Michalicka

*Mose Ceska* (1818)
SATB, 21-02
MS (autograph) CS:Pnm (XII.F.78)

*Pisen*
SATB, 22-22, timpani, organ
MS CS:Pnm (XII.F.100)

*Pisen*
SATB, 2021-22, timpani
MS CS:Pnm (XII.F.101)

*Cantus funebris*
SATB, 22-02
MS (autograph) CS:Pnm (XII.F.102)

*Homo guidam* (for 'Corporis Christe')
SATB, 2021-02
MS (autograph) CS:Pnm (XII.F.82)

*Libra*
SATB, 21-02
MS (autograph) CS:Pnm (XII.F.97)

## Moser, Franz (1880–1939)

*Serenade*, Op. 35
2333-04
MP (Universal Edition)

## Mrkvicka, Josef

*Trauer Marsche*
22-22, timpani
MS CS:Pnm (XIII.B.53)

## Muck, Beda

*Halleluja* (1833)
SATB, 2021-02, timpani [trumpets given as optional for horns]
MS (autograph) CS:Pnm (XLIX.D.518)

*Halleluja* (1836)
SATB, 2021-02, timpani
MS (autograph) CS:Pnm (XLIX.F.40)

## Müller

*Offertorium*
STBB, 22-02, organ
MS CS:Ksm (C.345)

## Nagiller, Mathaus

*Missa* in F
SATB, 1020-221, timpani
MS A:Wn (Sm.20290); US:DW (uncataloged)

## Nanke, Senior

*Offertorium* in B♭
TT, 21-02
MS CS:Ksm

## Navratil, Fran.

*Parthia*, 5 movements
21-02
MS CS:KRa (IV.B.102)

## Neukomm, Sigismund (1778–1858)

*L'Adoration du Saint Sepulcre*, NV.170 ('fantaisie pour des instrum. a vent, pour le Vendredi Saint Rio de Janeiro 17 March 1819')
MS [NV cites 'Volume 4']

*Anthem*, NV.487 ('Hyeres, 14 April 1835')
Two choruses, brass, organ
MS [NY cites 'Volume 52']

*Anthem*, NV.552 [119th Psalm] ('London 8 July 1837')
Chorus, -223, organ, double percussion
MS [in private hands]

*Ave verum Corpus*, NV.660 ('Paris 13 March, 1840')
SS, 2022-02

*Awake, & Grand Chorus*, NV.485 ('Hyeres 27 March 1835')
Chorus, brass band, organ, double percussion
MS [NV cites 'Volume 27']

*Grand Choeur*, NV.664 ('pour l'inauguration des monument de Guttenberg, a l'occasion de ... celebré à Strassbourg. Toutes les voix à l'unisson et à l'octave. Accomp. d'orchestre militaire')

*Grand Chorus*, NV.488 ('Hyeres, 18 April 1835')
Chorus, brass band, organ

*Der Deutsche Rhein*, NV.680 ('Berne 8 Nov. 1840')
TTBB, military band [another version for TTBB and symphony orchestra]
MS [NY cites 'Volume 47']
EP (Mainz, Schott) BRD:MZsch; DDR:Bds (Hausbibliothek, Thouret, Nr. 289)

*Divertimento*, NV.469 ('London, 31 Oct. 1834')
Solo trumpet, with -023, ophicleide
MS [NV cites 'Volume 37']

*Domine Salvum*, NV.1186 ('Trouville 15 Sept. 1855')
Unison chorus, large military band
EP (Paris, 1868) F:Pn (Vm.27.10030)

*Fantaisie Concertante*, NV.399 ('London, 1832')
1111-11, string bass
MS [NV cites 'Volume 30']

*Hymne a Jeanne hachette*, NV.1024 (1851, for the inauguration of a statue in Beauvis)
Unison chorus, large military band

*Hymne de la nuit*, NV.432 ('London 14 June, 1833')
Chorus, brass, organ

*Hymne martial*, NV.151 ('Rio de Janeiro 25, April 1817')
Chorus, military band
MS [NV cites 'Volume 4']

*Military Hymn* and *March*, NV.807 ('Oakhill, 10 April 1844')
Chorus and military band

(2) *Marches* (ca. 1820)
2222-221, serpent, percussion
MS BRD:Rtt (Sammelband Nr. 14, Nr. 92–93)

*Collection of Marches and Dances*, ca. 1820
2222-221, serpent, percussion
MS BRD:Rtt (Sammelband Nr. 14, Nr. 71–79)

(12) *Marches* ('für kriegerische Instrumente, seiner Majestiät dem Könige Friedrich Wil. III')
EP (Bonn and Cöln, Simock, Nr. 1697) NL:Ura/mZ (M.A.Zcm.116) [here only a 'Gebet' and 2 marches, *Der Kronprinz* and *Der König* for 2230-, percussion]

*Marche funèbre militaire*, NV.122 ('Paris 12 Dec. 1813,' for the funeral of General Walter)
MS [NY cites 'Vol. 55–67']

*Marche funèbre*, NV.124 ('Paris, 30 Dec. 1813')
Two brass choirs, timpani
MS [NV cites 'Vol. 55']

*Marche funèbre*, NV.153 ('sur la mort du Cte da Barca pour Inst. à vent. Rio de Janeiro 22 June 1817')
MS [NV cites 'Vol. 4; 36–72']

*Marche funèbre*, NV.571 ('Paris 25 March 1838')
-143, ophicleide

*Marsche*, NV.158 ('pour la fete de S.A.R. Rio de Janeiro 19 Jan. 1818')
MS [NV cites 'Vol. 4–36']

*March*, NV.416 ('Derbyshire, 1832')
Brass band
MS [NV cites 'Vol. 37']

*Marche triomphale*
Military band
MS B:Bc [cited by Eitner]

*Marche triomphale*, NV.142 bis ('Rio de Janeiro, 27 September 1816')
Large military band
MS [NV cites 'Vol. 53']
EP (Wien, Machette)

*Marche triomphale* ('Rio de Janeiro Dec. 6, 1816')
Large military band
MS (autograph) DDR:Bds (Mus. Ms.Auto.S.Neukomm 12)

*Triumphmarsch*, Op. 20 (1816)
Military band
EP (Leipzig, Breitkopf & Härtel)
[in private hands]

*Marche triomphale de Constantine*, NV.568 ('Paris Jan., 1838')
Large military band

*March*, NV.445 ('Hyeres 8 Dec. 1833/ A.R. le Duc d'Orleans')

*March & Gallop*, NV.496 ('Birmingham 1 Sept. 1835')
Brass band
MS [NV cites 'Vol. 30']

*Marche*, NV.600 ('Quebmiller 30 Jan. 1839')
Brass

*Marche*, NV.610 ('Wesserling 22 Feb. 1839')
Large military band

*Marche*, NV.623 ('Paris 28 April 1839')
Large military band

*Trauermarsch* for the Trauerspiel, *Hanno*, NV.11 ('St.Petersburg, Oct., 1804')
Wind instruments
MS [NV cites 'Vol. 70']

*Messe* ['*precede d'une Introductionen forme de marche*'] ('Rio de Janeiro 16 Aug., 1818')
TTBB, large military band
MS [NV cites 'Vol. 10']

*Missa pro defunctis manibus parentum Praeceptorumque suorum Mich. et Jos. Haydn*
Large wind orchestra
MS A:Wgm (I 2081; Q.413); A:Wn (Sm.15750) [cited by Eitner]; DDR:Bu
Eitner mentions that the introductory march was for the *Viennese Weidingersche Inventions-Trompete* and -043.

*Missa St.Hieronvini*, NV.55 (1809)
Voices and winds
MS [NV cites 'Vol. 55']
   This is a reworking of a Mass originally composed by Michael Haydn at the request of Archbishop Kolloredo of Salzburg. In his autobiography, Neukomm writes,
   I had some six years earlier asked my teacher, Michael Haydn, for a copy of his Mass for wind instruments but he answered that he wanted to first make some changes, using the new clarinets and flutes. He had

in fact began, writing three score pages. Since this masterwork is little known, I have finished it in the name of the widow.

Another little known Mass by Michael Haydn, the *Missa Pro Defuncto Archiepiscopo Sigismundo*, bares an extremely familiar relationship with the Mozart *Requiem*.

*Messe 'St. Louis Philippi.'* NV.582 [dedicated to the King of France] ('Quebmiller, 12 Deco, 1838')
Unison chorus with wind instruments
MS [NV cites 'Vol. 26']
EP (Maiuz, Schott) BRD:MZsch

In his autobiography, Neukomm says, 'I have composed this messe in two days.' In another place he describes a performance (June 24, 1840) in the Place de Guttenberg, Mainz, with a chorus of two thousand accompanied by military bands.

*Messe militaire*, NV. 783 [29th Messe] ('St. Ferdinand Messe/Paris 21 July 1843')
Unison chorus, wind instruments

In his autobiography, Neukomm writes of a performance of this Mass in June 1845, in Beauvais, by five hundred voices and a wind band of 'proportional size.' The following month the work was performed in the Church of Madeleine in Rouen.

*Messe Episcopale*, NV.849 [32nd Messe] ('St. Cecile, Oakdale, 25 Nov., 1845')
Unison Chorus, wind instruments, cello, string bass

*Messe solennelle* [33rd Messe]
TTBB, 2020-22[3], timpani, cello, string bass
EP (Paris, 1858) F:Pn (Vm.1.2159) [missing trombones]
A full length Mass, '*Sous le Titre distinctif de St.-Frederic et de Notre-Dame de Rouen*')

*Messe solennelle* ('St. Joseph')
Voices and winds
EP (Paris, ca. 1858) F:Pn (Vm.1.2158)

(13) *Morceaux*, NV.166 ('*Rio de Janeiro, Feb., 1819, pour S.M. le Roi de Prusse.*')
Large military band
MS [NV cites 'Vol. 111']
EP (Bonn)
Consists of a work in religious character, followed by 12 marches.

*Ottetto*, NV.421 ('Derbyshire, 24 Dec., 1832')
1111-11, cello, string bass
MS [NV cites 'Vol. 37'] US:Bp

*Oratorio*, 'The last day,' NV.449 ('Rome, 27 Feb., 1834')
TB soli, chorus, brass band, percussion
MS [NV cites 'Vol. 68']

*Pange lingua*, NV.542 ('Quebmiller, 26 Dec., 1836')
Chorus and brass
MS [NV cites 'Vol. 56']

*Preludes and Marche funèbre*, NV.136 ('*pour mon Requieml Vienna 26 Nov., 1814*')
-143

*Requiem*, NV.544 [14th Messe] ('Montbeliard, 12 Jan., 1837')
Large unison chorus with wind instruments
EP (Paris)
In his autobiography, Neukomm mentions a performance of this work in St. Peters', Salzburg, on September 11, 1838.

*Requiem et Kyrie,* NV.791
Large unison chorus wind wind instruments
EP (unknown)

> In his autobiography, Neukomm says he mislaid the score for the *Requiem,* NV.544 and in the course of making a new one from the parts, he began rewriting the work in the present form.

*Requiem* (for Franz I)
SATB, 3232-223, 2 ophicleides, timpani, optional celli
MS A:Wn (Sm.3220) [here are found three autograph versions: 1) .with organ, 2) with band, and 3) with small orchestra]

*Messe de Requiem,* NV.971 [35th Messe] ('Salzburg, 16 Nov., 1849')
Large two-part chorus, large military
EP (unknown)

*Septetto,* NV.458 ('Cherbourg, 21 Aug.')
1111-11, string bass
MS [NV cites 'Vol. 37']
EP (in England) [for two pianos]

*Septetto,* Nr. 3, NV.517 ('London, 28 March, 1836')
1111-11, string bass
MS [Nv cites 'Vol. 37']

*Military Te Deum,* NV.440 ('to be performed at a grand review or on the battlefield, for a very large band of Military Instruments and Chorus of Mens voices/ Paris 12, Oct., 1833')
MS [NV cites 'Vol. 52']

This volume also contains a score [NV.443] dated November 1833 with additional instruments for this work, 'if performed at a festival.' In his autobiography, Neukomm mentions two performances he gave with this work, the first on August 14, 1837 by a chorus of 1300 and a military band of 200, made up of three regimental bands and additional winds from the local theater and nearby towns. The band at this performance included 40 tambour and during the Sanctus the cannons fired three times! In Frieberg, on July 16, 1842 he performed the work with 1200 singers.

*Te Deum,* NV.933 ('Manchester, 5 August, 1848')
TTBB, organ, -223, cello

> NV.934 is an arrangement of the above organ part for 'grand militaire orchestre.'

*Te Dewn,* NV.1070 ('London, 6 March, 1853')
TTBB, large wind orchestra

*Waltz,* 'La Blosseville'
1031-11, bass drum
MS F:Pn (MS.6653)

> In his autobiography, Neukomm speaks of composing various 'morceaux' for the military band on board the frigate Hermione during his voyage to Rio de Janeiro. Luiz de Azevedo, 'Sigismund Neukomm,' in *Musical Quarterly* [1959], 475, identifies this work as one composed on ship.

## Nicola, Georg

*Marsch* ('nach einer amerikanischen melodie')
Military band
MS A:Wn (Sm.20826)

(2) *Märsche*
Military band
MS A:Wn (Sm.20826)

*Retraite*
Military band
MS A:Wn (Sm.20780)

## Novácek, Rudolf (1860–1929)

*Sinfonietta*, Op. 48 (1905)
1122-02
EP (Leipzig, Breitkopf & Härtel) BRD:Bbm (17988); GB:Lbm (h.2785.1.[3]); US:PHf (2387)

*Defilier Marsch* (1886)
Military band
MS CS:Pnm (II.C.75)

*Juristenball Polka*
Military band
MS CS:Pnm (II.F.66a)

*Castaldo March*
Band
EP (London, 1895) F:Pn (Vm.27.10061)

## Novotni

(4) *Stationen*
SATB, 20-32, 2 Flügelhorns, timpani, basso
MS CS:Pnm (XLIII.D.207)

## Nudra, J.

*Parthia* in E♭
22-02
[cited by Jerkowitz]

## Obersteiner, Johann

*Harmonie Fest Messe*, Op. 237
SATB, 1020-422, euphonium 2 bombardons, timpani, organ
MS A:Wn (Sm.23272)

*Pange lingua* ('für Procession')
SATB, brass band
MS A:Wn (Sm.13885) [incomplete]

## Osswald, A.

(5) *Allegmannes* (ca. 1827)
222-22, contrabassoon
MS CS:Bm (A.35.198)

(5) *Deutsche*
222-22, contrabassoon
MS CS:Bm (A.35.197)

## Pacak, Frantisek

(4) *Statio*
SATB, 1021-22, timpani
MS CS:Pnm (XIII.E.163)

## Panizza, Giacomo

*Sestetto*
1021-02
EP (Wien, Artaria, Nr. 2672, 1822)

## Parízek, Alexius

*Marcia militaire* (1808)
222-02
MS CS:Pnm (XL.C.378)

*Nocturno* in B♭
222-02
MS CS:Pnm (XL.C.379)

*Pater noster*
SATB, 22-02, organ
MS CS:Pnm (XLVII.E.14)

## Parlow, Albert

*Napoleon Marsch*
Military band
MS A:Wn (Sm.20827)

## Paulmann, S. A.

*Franz Joseph Parade Marsch*
Military band
MS A:Wn (Sm.16715)

## Pawlikowski, Franz

*Rheinlandsfanfare*
-4431
MS A:Wn (Sm.22967)

*Schober Fanfare*
-633
MS A:Wn (Sm.22968)

*Post-fanfare*
-443
MS A:Wn (Sm.22969)

*Fanfare* in E♭
-333
MS A:Wn (Sm.22970)

*Fanfare* in E♭
-333
MS A:Wn (Sm.22971)

## Payer, Hieronymus

*Eichenkränze* [Collection, ca. 1819]
Military band
EP (Wien, Mechetti) [Vol. 1 in D; Vol. 2 in C]

*Andante & Rondo* (c. 1819)
Twenty-four-part military band
EP (Wien, Mechetti, Nr. 702, 703)
   A:Wgm (X.1293)

## Pechacek [Pechatschek, Pethaczek] Franz (1793–1840)

(12) *Ländler*
21-02
EP (Straubing, 1801) BRD:Hbs [cited by Eitner]

(6) *Märsche*
Türk.musik
EP (Wien, Haslinger, ca. 1800–1828)

*Variatione*
222-22
MS CS:KRa (IV.B.112)

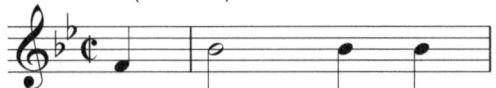

## Pejrinovsky, Martin

*Cantate* (1844)
SATB, 1032-221. timpani
MS (autograph) CS:Pnm (XXXVIII.B.308)

## Pertl, Vincez

*Waltz*, 'Aus dem Hochwald' (1872)
Military band
MS A:Wn (Sm.20922)

## Proch, Heinrich (1809–1878)

*Lied*, 'Die Täuberln'
Voice, 1021-01
MS A:Wn (Sm.14618)

*Motette*
SATB, 22-02, organ
MS (autograph) A:Wgm (III 53298 and Q.987)

## Purebl, Joseph (1768–1838)

(4) *Märsche*
222-02, contrabassoon
EP (Wien. Steiner, Nr. 1003; Paris. Ebend)

(6) *Märsche*
Ten-part Harmoniemusik
EP (Wien, Steiner, Nr. 1496; Paris, Ebend)

(5) *Türkische Stücke* in C
Harmoniemusik
EP (Wien, Steiner, Nr. 1006; Paris, Ebend)

(5) *Türkische Stücke* in F
Harmoniemusik
EP (Wien, Steiner, Nr. 1018; Paris, Ebend)

(6) *Eccosaises mit trios* ('oder militarische Reise Märsche
   fü Türkische Musik')
EP (Wien, Steiner, Nr. 1006; Paris, Ebend)

(4) *Stücke aus ballet Figaro*
Türk.musik
EP (Wien, Steiner, Nr. 1483; Paris, Ebend)

(2) *Märsche aus Die Bachanten und Bachus und Ariadne*
Türk.musik
EP (Wien, Steiner, Nr. 1502)

(4) *Stücke aus Paul und Virginia*
Türk.musik
EP (Wien, Steiner, Nr. 1503; Paris, Ebend)

(2) *Märsche*
Türk.musik
EP (Paris, Ebend)

(6) *Märsche*
Ten-part Harmoniemusik
EP (Paris, Ebend)

*Rundtanz aus Ballet Figaro*
Eight-part Harmoniemusik
EP (Paris, Ebend)

*Türtkische Stücke*
Solo E♭ clarinet with 1022-12
MS A:Wn (Sm.608); US:DW (8)

*Thürcishe Music*, 5 movements
2022-22, serpent, percussion
MS CS:Bm (A.19.719)

*Türkische Stücke*, 5 movements
3042-22, contrabassoon, percussion
MS CS:Bm (A.19.717)

*Türkische Stücke*, 5 movements
MS CS:Bm (A.19.716)

(2) *neue türkische Märsche*
22-22, percussion
EP (Wien, Eder) [advertized in WZ, 1824]

(3) *neue Harmoniemärsche der N.Ö.Landwehre*
EP (Wien, Eder) [advertized in WZ, 1808]

*Marcia turca*
3021-221, bass drum
MS BRD:TSCB (Z.113)

(6) *Märsche*
Harmoniemusik
EP (Wien, Chemischen Druckerey) [advertized in 1810]

(4) *Märsche*
3022-22, small drum
EP (Wien, k.k.priv.chem.Druckerein, Nr. 1896)
    CS:Pnm (XLII.F.155)

*Türkischer Zapfenstreich, 'Der Nachtwachter'*
Janitscharmusik
MS DDR:Bds (Hausbibliothek, Thouret, Nr. 334, under 'Burebl')

## Rafael, Fr.

*Nocturne sans paroles*
Military band
MS CS:Pnm (XXXVII.F.473)

## Randhartinger, Benedict (1802–1893)

*Messe* (1858)
TTBB, 1222-023
MS A:Wn (Sm.0145)

## Richter, Pius

*Frohnleichnamsfeste* (ca. 1880), 4 movements
SATB, 1022-22, bombard, timpani
MS A:Wn (Sm.2192)

## Rieger, Gottfried

*Harmonie*, 6 movements
222-22, contrabassoon
MS CS:Bm (A.36.887) [missing horn 2, both bassoons]

## Rikl, Vaclav

*Requiem ex meis Wenceslai*
SATB, 22-02
MS CS:Pnm (XIV.D.141)

## Röder, Georg Vincent

*Deutsche Messe*
SATB, 2010-02, organ
MS CS:Pnm (XXXVIII.F.203)

*Regina coeli*
SATB, 20-32, timpani, organ
MS CS:Pnm (XIV.F.36)

## Rosenkranz, Anton

*Märsche* ('Feldpromenade' & 'Soldatenfreund')
(ca. 1880)
Military band
MS A:Wn (Sm.20828)

## Rosulek, Antonin

(4) *Stationes*
SATB, 1020-222, timpani, organ
MS CS:Pnm (XIV.E.139)

## Ruzitska, Georg

*Pater noster* (1837)
SATB, six winds
MS H:Bn (Ms.Mus.221)

## Ruzni (Rugni)

*Deutsche Marche*
222-22, contrabassoon
MS CS:Bm (A.36.893)

*Journal* [with three original works]
222-22
MS CS:Bm (A.35.252)

## Santner, Karl

*Trinklied vor der Schlacht*
Male chorus, -341
EP (Wien, Glöggl) A:Llm (III/12)

## Schandl, Franz

(7) *Aufzüge*
-601, timpani
MS A:Wn (Sm.21791)

## Sauer (Saver), Ignaz

*Trauergesang* (9 July, 1825)
SATB, fourteen-part Harmoniemusik
EP (Wien, author, Nr. 185)

*Festgesang, 'Wo ist das Land, wo Milch und Honig fliesst?'* (4 November, 1824)
SATB, Harmoniemusik
EP (Wien, author, Nr. 184) A:Wgm (1.8434)

*Festgesang* (5 Feb., 1824)
SATB, Harmoniemusik
EP (Wien, author, Nr. 182) A:Wgm (1.3117)

*Fest-Gesang* [Nr. 2] (19 April, 1824)
SATB, twelve-part Harmoniemusik
EP (Wien, author, Nr. 183) A:Wgm (1.3118)

*Kriegslied*
TTBB, Harmoniemusik
EP (Wien, author) CS:Pn (Sg.Kacina, VI.1073)

## Scheibl, Johann

*Missa*
SATB, -002, cornetto
MS CS:Bm (A.20.051)

*Missa*
MS CS:Bm (A.20.052)

## Schenk, Johann Baptist (1753–1836)

(7) *Nocturns*
Four voices, winds
MS (autograph) A:Wgm [cited in Grove, XVI, 626]

*Das Veilchen* (1832)
Voice, 21-02
MS (autograph) [cited without source by Eitner]

*Denkspruch, Schweig. meid* (1819)
SSAA, 220-
MS (autograph) [cited without source by Eitner]

## Schiedermayr, Johann Baptist

*Deutsche Messe*, Nr. 53 (1815)
SATB, 2-02, 2 basset horns, organ
MS A:Llm (VI/3)

(4) *Evangelien* (1827)
SSAATB, 22-02
MS A:Wn (Sm.27151)
EP (Wien, Haslinger) A:Wgm (1.5326)

(4) *Evangelien*, Op. 71
SATB, 22-02
EP (Wien, Haslinger) CS:Pnm (XLIII.A.109)

*Aria*
Soprano, flute solo, with 2-02
MS A:Wn (Sm.21659)

*Pange lingua*, Op. 70
SATB, 22-02
MS CS:Pnm (XLVII.B.284)
EP (Wien, Haslinger) A:Wgm (1.3156);
   CS:Pnm (XLIII.A.112)

(4) *Stationes* (1856)
SATB, 1020-221
MS CS:Pnm (XLVII.D.223)

*Deux Harmonies*, Nr. 2
222-12
EP (Wien, Magasin de l'impr.chem.)
   CS:Bm (A.20.144)

(6) *Märsche für Harmonie*
222-02, contrabassoon
EP (Wien, Chemischen Druckerey and Steiner,
   Nr. 1294, ca. 1810) E:Mbmc (K.846)

*March der Landwehr im Erzherzogthum Öst.*
22-12
EP (Linz, Eurich, ca. 1805) A:Wgm (XVI.5105)

(8) *Neue Türkische Stücke*, Op. 2
2022-22, contrabassoon, 2 piccolos, percussion
EP (Linz, Eurich, ca. 1805) A:Wgm (XVI.5I05)

## Schindlocker, M.

(12) *Aufzüge*
-5, timpani [alternate version: -6]
EP (Wien, Haslinger, ca. 1800–1828)

## Schlier, Johann

*Libera* (1835)
SATB, 22-222, contrabassoon
MS A:Sca (Hs.573)

## Schubert, Franz (1797–1828)

*Eine kleine Trauermusik*
22-022, contrabassoon
MP (*Neue ausgabe sämtlicher Werke*, i, 25)

*Hymne,* Op. 154
TTBB or SATB, 222-223
EP (Wien, Diabelli) US:DW (95)

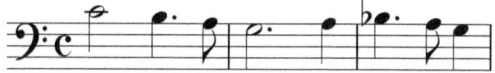

(6) *Minuets*
222-12
MS A:Wgm
MP (Neue (Schubert MS.D) I–III are in a full
   autograph score; IV–VI in an autograph draft
   for piano.
MP (*Neue ausgabe sämtlicher Werke*, ix)

*Nachtgesange im Walde*
TTBB, -04
EP (Leipzig, 1884) US:DW (117)

*Octet*
222-02
MP (*Neue ausgabe sämtlicher Werke*, i, 3)

*Allegro* [unfinished]
222-02
MP (*Neue ausgabe sämtlicher Werke*, i, 151)

## Schubert, Ferdinand (1794–1859, brother to Franz Schubert)

*Laudate Dominum*
SATB, winds and brass
MS US:DT

*Salve Regina*
SATB, 202-222, timpani
EP (Wien, Diabelli) A:Wgm (1.3621)
    Ferdinand also scored a *Salve Regina* by his brother Franz Schubert for winds. These wind parts may be found in his hand in GB:Lbm (Add.50253).

*Veni sancte Spiritus* (1849)
SATB, Harmoniemusik
EP (Wien, Glöggl) A:Wgm (1.22030)

*Lied* (1844)
SATB, 202-
MS A:Wgm (1.42257)

## Schwarz, M.

(6) *Märsche*
3232-22, contrabassoon, percussion
EP (Wien, Haslinger, ca. 1800–1828)
    E:Mbmc (K.846)

(6) *Märsche* (with Posthorn trio)
Türk.musik
EP (Wien, Haslinger)

## Seidel

*Salve Regina*
Bass voice, 21-02
MS CS:Pnm (XL111.A.315)

## Seiffert

(6) *Wälzer* (ca. 1830)
31-22, contrabassoon
MS CS:Bm (A.35.933)

## Sellner, Josef

*Allegro*
222-22
MS (autograph) A:Wn (Sm.3772); US:DW (123)

*Divertimento*
Solo horn, 222-22, contrabassoon
MS A:Wn (Sm.3771); US:DW (30)

*Pièce pour la Harmonie*
222-22
MS (autograph) A:Wn (Sm.3373); US:DW (122)

*Variations* (1834)
Solo clarinet, 212-22, contrabassoon
MS (autograph) A:Wn (Sm.3770); US:DW 75)

*Variations* (1835)
Solo clarinet, 212-02, contrabassoon
MS A:Wn (Sm.3769); US:DW (74)

## Seyfried, Ignaz von

*Equale*
-003
MS (autograph) DDR:Bds (Mus. Ms.Auto.R.v.Seyfried 3)

*Motette, Psalm 23*
Chorus and winds
MS DDR:SWl (Seyfried, I.R.8)

*Libera*
SATB, 2-203, 2 basset horns, timpani, organ
MS BRD:BB (Ms.173)
EP (Wien, Haslinger) A:Wn (MS.39910)
This was intended as an additional movement for the Mozart Requiem.

'Allegretto non molto,' from [his] *Julius Caesar*
1222-02, percussion
MS (autograph) BRD:DS (Mus.Ms.1016, Nr. 2)

'Larghetto,' from his *Julius Caesar*
Female chorus, 2222-223, timpani, percussion
MS (autograph) BRD:DS (Mus.Ms.1016, Nr. 5)

The following five works represent a huge cycle, performed in Vienna for the Emperor's birthday, in October, 1805:

*March* (on a theme by Grétry)
444-04, 2 contrabassoons
MS A:Wn (Sm.11105, Nr. 1); US:DW (55)

*Echo Divertimento*
444-04, 2 contrabassoons
MS A:Wn (Sm.11105, Nr. 2); US:DW (2)

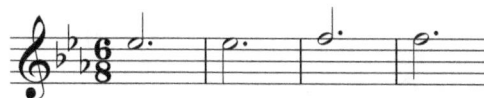

*Cantatina*, 3 movements
SATB, 444-04, 2 contrabassoons
MS A:Wn (Sm.11105, Nr. 3); US:DW (54)

*Quodlibet*, 24 movements
444-04, 2 contrabassoons
MS A:Wn (Sm.11105, Nr. 4); US:DW (53)

*March* (on a theme of Cherubini)
444-04, 2 contrabassoons
MS A:Wn (Sm.11105, Nr. 5); US:DW (56)

## Seyler, Josef

*Missa Solemnis*
SATB, 202-22, timpani, organ
MS A:Wgm (I.8419)

## Skroup, Jan (1811–1892)

(4) *Stationen*
SATB, -4, timpani
MS CS:HX (394/H.266)

*Te Deum*
SATB, -33, timpani
EP (Prag, Medau, 1854) A:Wgm (I.22874)

## Sonneleiter, Antonius

*Parthia*, 5 movements
21-02
MS CS:KRa (IV.B.137)

## Splichal, Jan

(4) *Stationes pro Festo Corporis Christi*
SATB, 21-3, timpani
MS CS:Pu (59-R-1534)

(4) *Stationes pro Festo Corporis Christi*, Nr. 5
SATB, 21-3, timpani
MS CS:Pu (59-R-1534)

(4) *Stationes pro Festo Corporis Christi*
SATB, 1021-32, timpani
MS CS:Pu (59-R-1601)

(2) *Salve Regina* in E♭ (1830)
SATB, 21-02
MS CS:Pu (59-R-1535)

## Springer

*Wachtparade*
Türk.musik
EP (Wien, Haslinger, ca. 1800–1828)

## Stadler, Maximilian [Abbé] (1748–1833)

*Hoch du mein Osterreich* (1818)
Voices, winds [cited in Grove, XVIII, 47]

## Stadler, J.

(12) *deutsche Tänze*
Six-part Harmoniemusik
EP (Wien, Haslinger, ca. 1800–1828)

## Starke, Friedrich (1774–1835)

(6) *neue lebhafte Militarmärsche*, Op. 14
222-22
EP (Wien, Artaria, Nr. 1830) [advertized in WZ, 1806]

(6) *Märsche fur Türkische Musik*, Op. 48
EP (Wien, Haslinger)

(6) *neue Cavallerie Parade-Stücke*, Op. 113
Ten trumpets, with -023
EP (Wien, author) A:Wgm (XVI.2412)

(3) *Märche du Oestreicher Truppen* (ca. 1820)
1022-22
MS CS:Pnm (XLII.F.152)

*Marsch*
1042-23, percussion
MS CS:Pnm (XLII.F.149)

*Alexanders Favoritmarsch und dessen Paradermarsch*
Türk.musik
EP (Paris, Ebend)

*Wiener Potpourri*, Nr. 4
Jägerchor
EP (Wien, Eder) [advertized in WZ, 1822]

*Trauermarsch*
Trompeten-musik
EP (Wien, Eder) [advertized in WZ, 1822]

*Journal militairischer Musik* ('in monatlichen Lieferungen')
EP (Wien, author, before 1828) CS:Bm (A.35.252); A:Wgm (XVI.7459) [*Pièce Joyeuse*, III. *Jahrgang Heft* 25]

*Variations* (on Mozart's '*O dolce Concento*')
222-02
MS CS:Bm (A.40.170)

*Variations* (on Paisiello's '*Nel cor piu non mi sento*')
222-02
MS CS:Bm (A.40.170)

*Variationen* (on '*ich bin liederlich*')
222-02
MS A:Ee

*Serenata*
222-02
MS A:Ee

## Steiner, Ernst

*Österreich Hurra!*
Male chorus, brass
MS A:Wn (Sm.3318)

## Streck, P.

(6) *neue Difilir-Märsche*
Large military band
EP (unknown) A:Wn (S.A.67.C.65)

# AUSTRIA

### Stechi, Antonine

*Marche triomphale* ('composée a l'ocasion du couronnement de Sa Majesti Apostolique Comme Roi d'Hongrie')
Large military band
MS A:Wn (Sm.0087)

### Strauss, E.

*Valse, Hochzeitslieder*, Op. 290
Band
EP (London, 1897) GB:Lbm (h.1549, Ser. 103, Nr. 2)

### Strauss, Johann, Sr. (1804–1848)

*Märsche* for Harmoniemusik
EP (Breitkopf & Härtel) [cited in MGG]

### Strauss, Josef (1827–1870) [son to the above]

(2) *Mazurkas*
Large band
MS A:Wn (Sm.20908)

### Strobe, Heinrich

*Serbischer Tanz* (1870)
Large band
MS A:Wn (Sm.20809)

### Suppé, Franz von (1819–1895)

*Trauer Chor*
Voices and wind orchestra
MS A:Wn (Sm.5377)

*Trauer Chor* (1845)
TTBB, trombones
MS A:Wn (Sm.5335)

March, *Boccaccio*
Band
EP (London, 1882) GB:Lbm (h.1549, Ser. 72, Nr. 6)

### Swoboda

*Infanterie Marsch*
Military band
EP (Wien, Beck, ca. 1800–1828)

### Theny, Jan

*Missa* in E♭
SAB, 20-02, organ
MS CS:Bm (A.20.169)

### Thiele, Eduard

*Festgruss* (for the wedding of Prince Wilh. v. Schaumburg-Lippe)
Male chorus and winds
MS (autograph) CS:Pnm (XXVIII.B.9)

### Tomásek, Vaclav (1774–1850)

*Karl ist wieder de*
22-02
MS (autograph) CS:Pnm (III.E.112)

*Doppel-Marsch*
Wind orchestra
MS DDR:Bds (Mus.Ms.21945/20)

*Marcia funebre*
222-12, contrabassoon
MS (autograph) CS:Pnm (III.E.107)

### Tost, Frantisek

(6) *Parthie*
22-02
MS CS:Pnm (XLI.B.174) [missing clarinet I and horn 2]

### Trautzl, Jacob

*Parthia*
3-, string bass [bassoons marked 'a.3']
MS CS:Pnm (XXXII.C.85)
   There is another Parthia by Trautzl [the instrumentation of which may be similar] under XXXII.C.86.

*Cantata Funebris* (1805)
SATB, 21-02
MS (autograph) CS:Pnm (XXXIV.A.77)

*Cantata Funebris*, Nr. 2 (1811)
SATB, 22-02
MS (autograph) CS:Pnm (XXXIV.A.23)

## Triebensee, Joseph

The greater part of Triebensee's contribution lies in his numerous opera and ballet transcriptions, contained in his various collections called '*Miscellannies de Musique,*' and which have been listed in Volume Eight of this series. Given here are only the original works for wind ensemble in his hand.

*Marche Douplée*
222-02
MS A:Wn (Sm.3739, Jg. I, Oevre 3, Nr. 5); US:DW (79; 325)

*Marsch*
222-02
MS A:Wn (Sm.3739, Jg. I, Oevre 3, Nr. 9); US:DW 79; 326)

[Original] *Trio* (for a march by Gluck)
222-02
MS A:Wn (Sm.3739, Jg. I, Oevre 7, Nr. 5); BRD:Kbs (Mus.Ms.2583); CS:KRa (IV.B.146) [for 222-12, contrabassoon]

*Collection* of 16 pieces
222-02
MS A:Wn (Sm.3739, Jg. I, Oevre 9, Nr. 1-16); US:DW (346)

**1. Allegro**
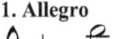

**2. Menuetto**

**3. Presto**

**4. Andantino**

**16. Menuetto**

*March*
222-02
MS A:Wn (Sm.3739, Jg. I, Oevre 10, Nr. 11);
   US:DW (79; 323)

*Variations* (on an original theme)
222-02
MS A:Wn (Sm.3739, Jg. I, Oevre 12, Nr. 2);
   US:DW (62)

*Menuet* in E♭ (with 2 trios)
222-02
MS A:Wn (Sm.3739, Jg. I, Oevre 12, Nr. 3);
   US:DW (347)

*Ländler* in B♭
222-02
MS A:Wn (Sm.3739, Jg. I, Oevre 12, Nr. 4);
   US:DW (347)

*Trauer Marsch* (for the funeral of Prince
   Alois Liechtenstein)
222-02
A:Wn (8m.3739, Jg. I, Oevre 12, Nr. 5)

*Allegretto* in B♭
222-02
MS A:Wn (Sm.3739, Jg. I, Oevre 12, Nr. 6);
   US:DW (347)

*Andante Cantible* in F
222-02
MS A:Wn (Sm.3739, Jg. I, Oevre 12, Nr. 7);
   US:DW (347)

*Allegretto* in E♭
222-02
MS A:Wn (Sm.3739, Jg. I, Oevre 12, Nr. 8) [missing page 2, bassoon 1]; US:DW (347)

*March* (based on Haydn's 'Austrian Hymn')
222-02
MS A:Wn (Sm.3739, Jg. II, Oevre 6, Nr. 11);
   US:DW (79; 321); A:Wgm (VIII 47729)

*Echostücke*
222-02
MS A:Wn (Sm.3739, Jg. II, Oevre 8, Nr. 8–10);
   US:DW (60)

*Marsch*
222-02
MS A:Wn (Sm.3739, Jg. II, Oevre 12, Nr. 11);
   US:DW (79; 322)

*Marsch*
222-02
MS A:Wn (Sm.3739, Jg. III, Oevre 4, Nr. 8);
   US:DW (79; 324)

*Variations* (on a theme by Gyrowetz)
222-02
MS A:Wn (Sm.3739, Jg. III, Oevre 4, Nr. 9);
   US:DW (64)

*Ländler*
222-02
MS A:Wn (Sm.3739, Jg. III, Oevre 4, Nr. 10);
   US:DW (320)

*Marsch*
222-02
MS CS:KRa (IV.B.40 [Nr. 11])

*Variations* (on a theme of Mozart)
222-02
MS A:Wn (Sm.3792, Nr. 38); US:DW (32)

*Variations* (on a theme from *Der Champagner*)
222-02
MS A:Wn (Wm. 3792, Nr. 39); US:DW (69)

*Variations* (on an original march)
222-02
MS A:Wn (Sm.3792, Nr. 40); US:DW (31)

*Variations* (on a Zapfenstreich)
222-02
MS A:Wn (Sm.3792, Nr. 41); US:DW (71)

*Variations* (on a theme by Haydn)
222-02
MS A:Wn (Sm.3792, Nr. 43); US:DW (29)

*Variations* (on 'Ach! du Lieber Augenstein')
222-02
MS A:Wn (Sm.3792, Nr. 44); US:DW (73)

*Andante & Variations* (on a theme by Haydn)
222-02
MS A:Wn (Sm.3792, Nr. 46); US:DW (66)

*Partitta* in E♭
222-02, contrabassoon
MS A:Wgm (VIII 39986); US:DW (85); CS:K
  (Nr. 146.K.II); CS:Bm (A.35.240)

*Partitta*
222-02, contrabassoon
MS CS:K (Nr.145.K.II)

*Parthia* in B♭ ('Nr. 3')
222-02
MS A:Wgm (VIII 39987); US:DW (100)

*Parthie* in B♭
222-12, contrabassoon
MS A:Wn (Sm.3739, Jg. II, Oeuvre 4, Nr. 7–11);
  US:DW (83)

*Echo Partitta*
221-02 with 111-02 'echo'
MS A:Wgm (VIII 38669); US:DW (28)

(9) *Partiten*
2-02, 2 English horns
MS A:Wgm (VIII 8541)

*Parthia* in E♭
22-02
MS PL:LA (2297)

3) *Parthien*
222-02
MS A:Ee

*Concertino*
Clavicembalo, 222-02
MS A:Wn (Sm.11077); US:DW (3)

*Grand Quintet*
Piano, 11-, English horn, basset horn
EP (Wien, Magasin de l'imprimiere)
  A:Wgm (XI.10905)

## Tucek, Vincenc

*Pange lingua*
SATB, 2022-02
MS CS:Pnm (XVII.A.126)

*Pange lingua*
SAB, 21-02, organ
MS CS:Pnm (L.C.151)

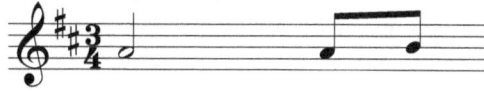

## Valenta, Bedrich (d. 1934)

*Prostna dorostencu*
Piano with wind orchestra
MS A:Wn (Sm.22825)

## Veselý [Wessely], Thad

Pisen pokreny
SATB, 1022-02
MS CS :Pnm (XVIII.F.12)

## Vitisek [Witasek], Jan M. N. A (1770–1839)

*Cantate* (1839)
SATB, 1022-022, timpani
MS CS:Pu (59-R-935)

*Graduale* in B♭
SATB, 1020-121
MS CS:Pu (59-R-1659)

(2) *Aufzüge Märsche*
Winds and percussion
MS DDR:Bds (Mus.Ms.23209)

*Marcia in F für Hörnermarsch*
MS DDR:Bds (Mus.Ms.23204)

*Marsch and Allegro*
Military band
EP (Hofmeister) [cited in DJ]

*Partita* (1813)
21-02 [cited in Grove, XX, 21]

*Pisen na Weliký*
SATB, 22-22
MS CS:Pnm (XVIII.C.27)

*Pisen*
SATB, 22-22, timpani, organ
MS CS:Pnm (XVII.B.77)

*Terzetto*
STB, 1022-02
MS CS:Pnm (XVII.B.78)

## Vojacek, H.

*An die Zukunft* (ca. 1843–1845)
Türk.musik
MS CS:Bm (A.20.286)

*Ein Jux*
Türk.musik
MS CS:Bm (A.20.283)

*Uvitani vesny*
Türk.musik
MS CS:Bm (A.20.277)

## Volkert, František

*Echo und Rusische Arie*
22-02
MS CS:KRa (IV.B.151)

*Pastorella*
22-0101
MS CS:KRa (IV.B.149)

*Statio pro Festo Corporis Christi*
SATB, 21-02
MS CS:Pu (59-R-1689)

*Variation*
22-02
MS CS:KRa (IV.B.148)

*Variationen*
22-02
MS CS:KRa (IV.B.150)

### Wagner, Franz Josef

(54) *Marches* (ca. 1876–1890)
Military band
MS A:Wn (Sm.20838–20869, 20871, 20971, 20973, 20979–20985, 20987, 20989, 20990, 20992, 20993, 20995-21000, and 21032)

*Nächtlicher Gruss*
Four Flügelhorns and bombardon
MS A:Wn (Sm.20764)

(9) *Polkas*
Military band
MS A:Wn (Sm.20895–20897, 20960–20963, 20965, and 23810)

(10) *Polkas*
Military band
MS A:Wn (Sm.20943–20951, and 21033)

### Waldeck, Karl

*Christmas Offertorium, 'Laetentur coeli'* (1874)
SATB, 1022-02
MS A:Llm (Automss. 1/4)

### Wanisek, Otto

*Wien Tanzmarsch*
Military band
MS A:Wn (Sm.5817, Bd. II)

### Weber, Friedrich Dionys (1766–1842)

(6) *Marches*
1202-12, piccolo, contrabassoon [as given in MGG]
EP (Leipzig, Breitkopf & Härtel) BRD:DS [cited by Eitner, who describes the instrumentation as '2 clarinettes, 2 Hautb. etc.,']

(3) *Sextetti*
-06
MS [cited in MGG]

(3) *Quatuors*
-04
EP (Prag, Berra) [cited in MGG]

### Weber, Wilhelm

(2) *Leichenlied*
Male voices, 21-02
MS A:Wn (Sm.21692-21693)

### Weigl, J.

*Variationen sur l'air, 'Wer hörte wohl jemals'* (1818)
Türk.musik
MS CS:Bm (A.35.248)

*Journal*
222-02, contrabassoon
EP (?) CS:Bm (A.20.232)

### Wenusch, Stanislaus

(18) *Stücke*
-5, timpani
MS A:Wn (Sm.21798)

(13) *Leichen Arias*
SATB, with combinations of flutes, clarinets, horns, bassoon, and bombardons
MS A:Wn (Sm.21759–21761, 21763–21768, and 21770–21773)

### Wiedemann, Josef

*La vie parisieune* (1867)
Military band
MS A:Wn (Sm.20918)

### Winkler, Johann

(8) *Trauer Arien*
SATB, with combinations of clarinets, horns, and trombones
MS A:Wn (Sm.3065)

### Winkler, Martin

(11) *Ländler*
22-22
MS A:Wn (Sm.23971)

### Wittassek, August

*Ave Maria*, 1842–1843
SATTBB, 22-02
MS A:TU (401)

### Witte, Johann
*Aus Nah und Fern* (1872)
Military band
MS A:Wn (Sm.20745)

### Wolf, Josef
*Jubel-Marsch* (for Franz Josef I)
Military band
MS A:Wn (Sm.17906)

*Hymn*, 'Pange lingua', Op. 48
SATB, -121, organ
EP (Wien, Hammer, Nr. 207)
   CS:Pn (XXXIII.C.194)

### Wolf, Cyrill
*Tantum Ergo* (1848)
SATB, 22-02
MS A:Wn (Sm.22748)

### Wölfl, Joseph (1773–1812)
(6) *Sonatas* (dedicated to 'Rauschgat in Hallein')
202-02
MS A:Sca

### Wranitzky, Anton, Jr.
(12) *deutsche Tänze*
Piano and Türkischer Musik
EP (Wien, Hoftheater, Op. 157 [Nr. 157])
   A:Wgm (XV.4555)

### Zangl, Josef Gregor
*Bethstunde* ('am Schlusse Bochnia')
Harmoniemusik
MS A:Wn (Sm.20772)

### Zavertal, Josef (1819–1893)
[Marches, Quadrilles, and Polkas for band, cited in Grove, XX, 654]

### Zavertal, Ladislao (1849–1942)
*Fulget Sabaudiae virtus*
SATB, military band
EP (Milar, 1901) [cited in Grove, XX, 655]

### Zavertal, Vaclav
'*God Save the King*'
Band
MS (autograph) GB:Lbm (Add.45102.Q)

### Ziehrer, Carl Michael
(8) *Wien. Lieder & Tänze*
Military band
MS A:Wn (Sm.21003)

(6) *Märsche* ('Im Schwarzwalde')
Military band
MS A:Wn (Sm.20970)

### Zitek
*Pange lingua*
SAB, 2020-32, timpani, organ
MS CS:Pnm (XLIII.C.19)

### Zumsteeg, Jan
*Ritter Toggenburg Ballade*
Voice, 1111-02
MS CS:Pu (59-R-29)

## Representative Arrangements
### Collections

MS CS:Bm (A.36.366)
Contains works by Kubicek, Birnbaum, and Anonymous, arranged ca. 1830 for Türk. musik.

MS CS:Bm (A.35.235)
Contains works by Kubicek and J. Strauss, arranged in 1831 for Türk.musik. [missing parts]

MS CS:Bm (A.36.660)
Contains works by Adam and Donizetti, arranged in 1844 for Türk.musik.

MS (?) CS:Bm (A.20.038)
Contains works by Walter, Haydn, and Blasius, arranged ca. 1800 for Türk.musik.

MS CS:Pnm (VII.B.1)
Contains 49 opera arias by Bellini, Busek, Donizetti, Gabetti, etc., arranged in 1852 for large (?) military band. [very incomplete parts]

## Adam, Charles Adolphe (1803–1856)

*Conversations-Stücke*, from *Regine*
Arranger unknown
Türk.musik
MS (1844) CS:Bm (A.36.659)

## Auber

*Fra Diavolo*
Türk.musik
MS (1831) CS:Bm (A.35.148)

## Beethoven

Overture to *Egmont,* Op. 84
Arranged by Starke
Twenty-part military band
EP (Wien, Steiner; Haslinger; and Paris, Ebend)

*Equale* [original for trombones}
Arranged by Seyfried [for Beethoven's Funeral in Vienna]
TTBB, -004
EP (Wien, Baslinger) A:Wst (M24597/C); US:DW (116)

Overture to *Fidelio*
Arranged by J. F. Wagner
Military band
MS A:Gk (uncataloged)

First Movement, *Sonata,* Op. 27
Arranged by Franze Hulbe (1867–1876)
Military band
MS A:Wn (Sm.20786)

*Türkischer Marsch*
Arranger unknown (1847)
Türk.musik
MS CS:Bm (A.37.334)

*Wellingtons-Sieg oder: die Schlacht bey Vittoria,* Op. 91
Arranger unknown
Twenty-seven part military band
EP (Wien, Steiner, Nr. 2368) A:Wn (MS.14550); GB:Lbm (Hirsch iv.345) [incomplete]

## Bellini

*Adagio*
Arranged by Selva
1020-401, Flügelhorn
MS CS:Pnm (VIII.C.104)

'Cavatina' from *Montechi e Capuleti*
Arranger unknown
Military band
MS CS:Pnm (VI.B.64)

Overture to *Norma*
Arranged by Franz Massak (1850)
Military band
MS A:Wn (Sm.20487)

Overture to *Norma*
Arranger unknown
Military band
MS CS:Pnm (VI.B.63)

Overture to *Norma*
Arranger unknown
Military band
MS CS:Pnm (VI.B.67)

Overture to *Norma*
Arranger unknown
Military band
MS (1835) CS:Bm (A.35.150)

'Duetto' from *I Puritani di Scozia*
Arranged by H. Vojacek (1844)
Türk.musik
MS CS:Bm (A.20.284)

## Berlioz

'Fuge über das motiv in Branders Lied' from *Damnation of Faust*
Arranged by G. A. Kinast (1886)
Military band
MS A:Wn (Sm.15316)

## Boieldieu

*Jean de Paris*, 5 movements
Arranger unknown
Türk.musik
MS (1819) CS:Bm (A.35.154) [incomplete]

## Diabelli

*Overture*
Arranged by Vojacek (1844)
Türk.musik
MS CS:Bm (A.20.282)

## Dalayrac

Marsch from *Der Dichter und Tonsetzer*
Arranger unknown
Türk.musik
MS (1828) CS:Bm (A.35.159)

## Donizetti

'Cavatina' from *Belisar*
Arranger unknown
Türk.musik
MS (ca. 1840) CS:Bm (A.36.865)

'Cavatina' from *Esula di Roma*
Arranged by Franz Egger
1022-12, keyed trumpet
MS A:Wn (Sm.23968)

'Cavatina' from *Faust*
Arranged by Anton Fiala (1867)
Military band
MS A:Wn (Sm.15113)

[Arias] from *La Favorita*
Arranged by Johann Witte (1866)
Military band
MS A:Wn (Sm.10506)

'Aria' from *Fernando e Bianca*
Arranger unknown (1844)
Türk.musik
MS CS:Bm (A.35.161)

*Potpourri aus dem Liebestrank*
Arranged by Vojacek (1844)
Türk.musik
MS CS:Bm (A.20.292)

'Duetto' from *Linda di Chamonix*
Arranger unknown (1844)
Türk.musik
MS CS:Bm (A.35.163)

'Introduction & Cavatina' from *Lucia di Lammermoor*
Arranger unknown (1843)
Military band
MS A:Wn (Sm.2425)

'Finale' from *Lugretia*
Arranger unknown (Linz, 1841)
Military band
MS A:Wn (Sm.20517)

'Aria' from *Lucrezia Borgia*
Arranged by Valentin (1844)
Türk.musik
MS CS:Bm (A.35.164)

Walzer & Polonaise from *Maria de Rudenza*
Arranger unknown (1844)
Türk.musik
MS CS:Bm (A.37.327)

'Harmonie-Musik' from *Maria de Rudenza*
Arranger unknown (1844)
Türk.musik
MS CS:Bm (A.35.162)

'Marziale' from *Maria de Rudenza*
Arranged by Vojacek (1844)
Türk.musik
MS CS:Bm (A.20.293)

## Gomez, Carlos

Ballet music from *Il Guarany*
Arranged by Johann Witte (1866)
Military band
MS A:Wn (Sm.20538)

## Gounod

[Music] from *Faust*
Arranged by Johann Paulis, Director, Military Music Club, Prague
Military band
MS A:Wn (Sm.20540–20542)

## Herold

Overture to *Zampa*
Arranger unknown (ca. 1832)
Türk.musik
MS CS:Bm (A.35.297) [incomplete]

## Marschner

'Marcia' from *Der Templer und die Jüdin*
Arranger unknown (1844)
Türk.musik
MS CS:Bm (A.19.378)

### Meyerbeer

'Cavatine' from *Huguenotten*
Arranged by Vojacek (1834)
Türk.musik
MS CS:Bm (A.20.930)

*Die Kreuzfahrt in Egypten*
Arranger unknown (1824)
Türk.musik
MS CS:Bm (A.35.190)

*Robert Walzer*
Arranger unknown (1834)
Türk.musik
MS CS:Bm (A.37.340)

### Mozart

(2) 'Arias' from *Don Juan*
Arranged by A. Nowotny (1845-1847)
Türk.musik
MS CS:Bm (A.36.866 and A.37.342)

*Symphony*, Nr. 11 [K.319]
Arranged by Adalbert Buresch
Military band
MS A:Wn (Sm.21004)

*Symphony*, Nr. 12 [actually by Leopold Mozart]
Arranged by Adalbert Buresch
Military band
MS A:Wn (Sm.21005)

*Symphony*, Nr. 14 [K.162b]
Arranged by Adalbert Buresch
Military band
MS A:Wn (Sm.21006)

*Symphony*, Nr. 15 [K.161a]
Arranged by Adalbert Buresch
Military band
MS A:Wn (Sm.20801)

### Müller, W.

'Quartetto' from *Schlagenfest*
Arranged by Riegel
Türk.musik
MS CS:Bm (A.36.663)

Overture from *Tivoli*
Arranger unknown (1835)
Türk.musik
MS CS:Bm (A.35.194)

### Pacini, G.

(2) 'Piècen' from *Alexander von Indien*
Arranger unknown (ca. 1830)
Türk.musik
MS CS:Bm (A.35.201)

### Paer

*Duetto*
Arranger unknown (ca. 1829)
Türk.musik
MS CS:Bm (A.20.880)

### Purebl, J. (1768–1838) [as arranger and composer?]

'3 Pièces de Ballet *Figaro*, pour la Musique Militaro, du Sieur Jos: Purebl, Musicien de la cour'
2032-22, percussion
MS BRD:TSCH (Z.114)

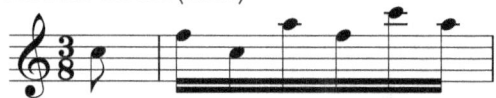

### Rossini

*Armida,* 7 movements
Arranger unknown (ca. 1830)
Türk.musik
MS CS:Bm (A.37.345)

Overture from *Elisabeth Königin von England*
Arranger unknown (1824)
3042-641, contrabassoon, percussion
MS CS:Bm (A.35.213)

### Schiedermayer

*Deutsche*
Arranged by Osswald
Türk.musik
MS CS:Bm (A.35.229) [incomplete]

### Strauss

*Astrea Tänze*
Arranged by Weinlich (1845)
Türk.musik
MS CS:Bm (A.37.349)

*Erinnerung an Pesth*
Arranged by Hladky (after 1830)
Türk.musik
MS CS:Bm (A.37.350)

*Der Frohsinn mein Ziel*
Arranger unknown (ca. 1835)
Türk.musik
MS CS:Bm (A.35.233a)

*Das Leben ein Tanz*
Arranger unknown (ca. 1830)
Türk.musik
MS CS:Bm (A.35.236)

*Mode Quadrille*
Arranger unknown (1843)
Türk.musik
MS CS:Bm (A.35.238)

*Tivoli Walzer*
Arranger unknown (after 1830)
Tük.musik
MS CS:Bm (A.35.239) [incomplete]

*Walzer Mittelgegen der Schlaf*
Arranger unknown (after 1832)
Türk.musik
MS CS:Bm (A.35.237)

*Die Berggeister-Walzer*
Arranger unknown (1840)
Türk.musik
MS CS:Bm (A.35.231) [incomplete]

*Haute Volée-Quadrille*
Arranger unknown (1843)
Türk.musik
MS CS:Bm (A.35.234)

*Musen Quadrille*
Arranged by Beyerbach (after 1850)
Türk.musik
MS CS:Bm (A.35.340)

### Strauss, Johann

Blaue Donau
Arranged by Franz Kaschte
Military band
MS A:Wn (Sm.30939)

### Suppé, Franz von

*Poet and Peasant*
Arranged by Kinast (1874)
Military band
MS A:Wn (Sm.15174)

### Sykora, Franz

*Jagd-Marsch* (1816)
Arranged by Gänsbacher
Military band
MS A:Wn (Sm.3482)

### Titl, A. E.

Overture from *Der Todtentanz*
Arranged by Vojacek
Türk.musik
MS CS:Bm (A.20.928) [incomplete]

Potpourri *Der Zauberschleier*
Arranged by Vojacek
Türk.musik
MS CS:Bm (A.20.929) [incomplete]

### Verdi

Overture from *Giovanna d'Arco*
Arranged by Buresch (1865)
Military band
MS A:Wn (Sm.20708)

Overture from *Lombardi*
Arranged by Kaschte (1864)
Military band
MS A:Wn (Sm.20650)

'Arias' from *Il' Lombardi*
Arranged by F. W. Weyr (1857)
Military band
MS A:Wn (Sm.20655)

'Arias' from *Oberto*
Arranged by Belloli (ca. 1840–1850)
Military band
MS A:Wn (Sm.20665)

Overture from *Traviata*
Arranged by Francesco Török (1858)
Military band
MS A:Wn (Sm.20688)

Overture from *Traviata*
Arranged by W. Landa (1862)
Military band
MS A:Wn (Sm.20712)

**Wagner**

Overture from *Lohengrin*
Arranged by C. Riefenstahl (1858)
Military band
MS A:Wn (Sm.23289)

'Zug der Frauen' from *Lohengrin*
Arranged by Riefenstahl (1858)
Military band
MS A:Wn (Sm.23289)

Overture from *Tannhäuser*
Arranged by Riefenstahl (1856)
Military band
MS A:Wn (Sm.23291)

**Winter**

*Le sacrifice interrompu*, 8 movements
Arranger unknown (after 1796)
Türk.musik
MS CS:Bm (A.20.035)

**Zincarelli**

*Quinto Fabio*
Arranger unknown
4222-241, percussion
MS CS:KRa (IV.B.190)

# Belgium

**Ancot, Jean (1779–1848)**

The following are given in MGG, quoting Fétis, without sources:
(2) *Overturen*
Fifteen winds

(2) *Fantasien*
Fifteen winds

*Air varié* (1832)
Fifteen winds

(8) *Pas redoublés*
Wind orchestra

*Walzer & Marches*

**Ansiaux, Hubert**

*Boléro* (1825)
222-02
MS B:Lc (Ms.291-2.L.VI)

**Benoit, Petrus (1834–1901)**

*Treur- en Trionfzang* (1896)
Mixed choir with winds [cited in MGG]

**Burbure de Wesembeek, Chevalier Leon (1812–1889)**

(15) *Compositions* for Wind Orchestra [cited in MGG]

**Campenhaut, François Van (1779–1848)**

(29) *Morceaux de differents characteres*
Harmoniemusik [cited by F]

**Fauconier, B. C.**

(4) *Marches*
Military band
EP (Malines) F:Pn (Vm.27.7305, Nrs. 6, 7, 8, 11)

**Fétis, François Joseph (1784–1871)**

*Messe de Requiem* (1850, for *Marie-Louise d'Orléans, le Reine des Belges*)
SATB, large brass band, organ, percussion
MS B:Bc (Wotquenne 126) US:DW (395)

*Walses*
Harmoniemusik
EP (Paris, Lemoine, ca. 1800–1828)

**Gilson, Paul (1865–1942)**

*Fackelzug* (1899)
Brass and percussion
MS B:Bc (Wotquenne 7344)

*Gavotte*
Military band
EP (Paris, 1898) F:Pn (Vm.27.7715)

*Morceau*
Brass band
MS B:Bc (Wotquenne 7343)

*Scherzo*
Brass and percussion
MS B:Bc (Wotquenne 7345)

**Hanssens, Charles-Louis (1802–1871)**

[Band music] (cited in Grove, VIII, 154)

**Henchenne, Laurent**

*Marche des Liégeois*
Large military band
EP (Liege, Gout et Terry) B:Lc (332-2.L-VII)

**Lekeu, Guillaume (1870–1894)**

*Introduction et Adagio* (1891)
Wind orchestra
MS [cited in MGG]

### Mees, Joseph-Henri (1777–1858)

*Chant National*
TTB, wind band
EP (Brussels) [cited in Grove, XII, 60]

### Mengal, Martin Joseph (1784–1851)

(12) *Fantaisies*
Wind instruments [cited in MGG]

*Harmonie militaire*
Harmoniemusik
EP (Paris, Dufaut et Dubois, ca. 1800–1828)

*Morceaux d'harmonie*
MS [cited in F]

### Samuel, Adolphe-Abraham (1824–1898)

*L'Union fait la force*, Op. 27 (1855)
Male chorus, brass [cited in MGG]

*Cantate nationale*, Op. 29 (1859)
Two choirs with wind orchestra [cited in MGG]

*Léopold Ier*, Op. 40 (1880)
Male chorus, brass [cited in MGG]

### Snel, Joseph François (1793–1861, conductor of the Société Royale de la Grande-harmonie in 1831)

According to Grove, XVII, 427, the following are to be found in Manuscript in B:Bc:
*Caprice et Variations brilliantes*
Band

*Grandes marches funèbres*
Band

*Fantaisies* [on opera themes]
Band

### Tuerlinckx, Corneille Jean (1783–1850, founded and directed several wind band societies in Mechlin)

According to Grove, XIX, 250, Tuerlinckx 'wrote mainly for wind band: operatic potpourris, overtures, fantaisies, military symphonies, sets of variations, etc.'

### Zerezo, Isidore

*Grand Marche*
Military band
MS B:Bc (Wotquenne 12, 643)

# Denmark

**Hartmann, Emil (1836–1898)**

    *Serenade*, Op. 43
    1122-02, cello, string bass
    MP (Ries & Erler) [cited by MH]

**Hartmann, Johann Ernst (1805–1900)**

    *Skanderberg Festmarsch*, Op. 42 (1845)
    Wind orchestra [cited in MGG]

    *Thoryaldsen's Funeral March* (1844)
    Winds and organ [cited in MGG]

    *Indledningsmusik ved Univ. Jubelfest i Vor Frue Kirke* (1879)
    Winds and organ [cited in MGG]

# England

**[Collection]**
MS GB:Lbm (R.M.21.e.4, Nrs. 5, 9, and 10)
Military band
Contains 2 marches, by Voight and Anonymous, and a 'Welcome to France,' by Miguel, all dedicated to Queen Victoria.

**Anonymous**
*The Grand Neapolitan March*
Band
EP (London, Cahusac, ca. 1800)
  GB:Lbm (H.1568.b/12)

**Ackermann**
The following works are all for band and were printed in London, ca. 1883–1893; shelf-marks given are for GB:Lbm.
*Divertimento* [on ancient Scotch melodies] h.1544, Nr. 322
Marches: h.1544, Nr. 383; h.1549, Ser. 93, Nr. 6
In GB:Lbm, (h.1544, Nrs. 169–444) represents C. Boosé's *Supplemental military Journal* [London, 1858–1903]; and (h.1549, Nrs. Ser. 1-74) represents C. Boosé's military *Journal* [London, 1846–1883]. These sets are incomplete in GB:Lbm.

**Adams, Thomas (1785–1858)**
*Grand March and Quick Step* (ca. 1808)
Military band
EP (London) [cited in Grove]

**Aigrette [Pseud.]**
Polka, *Fun of the Fair*
Band
EP (London, 1893) GB:Lbm (h.1549, Ser. 95, Nr. 4)

**Allen, William**
*The Criterion Polka*
'Octett band'
EP (London, 1877) GB:Lbm (f.411.[1])

**Amillon, Édouard**
The following works are for band and were printed in London, ca. 1886–1888; shelf-marks given are for GB:Lbm.
*Air de ballet*, h.1544, Nr. 350
*March*, h.1549, Ser. 85, Nr. 4
Gavottes: h.1544, Nr. 338; h.1549, Ser. 82, Nr. 6

**Andreozzi, Gaetano (Italian in England, 1775–1826)**
*The Celebrated March*
Wind instruments
EP (London, Dale, ca. 1810) GB:Lbm (g.1780.q.[8])

**Andrew, Enos**
Valse Suite, *Noisette*
Band
EP (London, 1885) GB:Lbm (f.412.0.[2])

**Aniebas, J.**
The following works are for band and were printed in London, ca. 1897–1898; shelf-marks given are for GB:Lbm.
*Polka*, h.1549, Ser. 103, Nr. 2
*Mazurka*, h.1544, Nr. 410

**Ansel, M.**
*March, Hibernia*
Band
EP (London, 1885) GB:Lbm (a.237.[1])

**Applin, W. T.**
*Pas seul, Claire*
Band
EP (London, 1899) GB:Lbm (h.1549, Ser. 107, Nr. 5)

### Arbuckle, John

The following works are for band and were printed in London, ca. 1887; shelf-marks given are for GB:Lbm.
*March,* 3.372.b.[1]
*Polka,* f.401.dd.[2]

### d'Archambeau

*The Emchantress*
Band
EP (London, 1866) GB:Lbm (h.1544, Nr. 220)

### Arscott, Julius

March, *Albuhera*
Band
EP (London, 1885) GB:Lbm (f.412.o.[5])

### Asch, Georg

The following works are for band and were printed in London, ca. 1883–1894; shelf-marks given are for GB:Lbm.
*Gavotte,* h.1549, Ser. 96, Nr. 2
*March,* f.412.o.6
*Polka,* f.800.[30]

### Ascher, Joseph (Dutch, 1829–1869)

The following works are for band and were printed in London, ca. 1885–1897; shelf-marks given are for GB:Lbm.
*Fanfare militaire,* Op. 40, h.1544, Nr. 404
*Galop,* h.1544, Nr. 336

### Balfe, Michael William (Irish, 1808–1870)

March, *Riflemen Form*
1232-443, percussion, bassi
EP (London, *Boosey's Military Journal* of 1859) US:DW (758)

### Ball, S.

*The Ipswich Volunteers* (Slow & Quick Marches, with a Funeral March)
Band
EP (London, 1808) GB:Lbm (H.1895.[18])

### Banner, John

*The Loyal London Volunteers' March*
Band
EP (London, ca. 1805) GB:Lbm (g.271.h.[1])

### Banta, Frank P.

March, *Wheelmen's Patrol*
Band
EP (London, 1896) GB:Lbm (h.1549, Ser. 101, Nr. 6)

### Barrett, Emmeline

Gavotte, *Daisy*
Band
EP (London, 1898) GB:Lbm (h.1544, Nr. 383)

### Barrett, R.

The following works are for band and were printed in London, ca. 1894–1896; shelf-marks given are for GB:Lbm.
Marches: f.800.[60], f.800.[62]
*Polka,* f.800.[63]

### Barthmann, Charles

The following works are all for band and were printed in London, ca. 1883–1893; shelf-marks given are for GB:Lbm.
Marches: f.412.[7], f.401.j.[1] (Funeral March), f.412.[9], f.401.j.[2]

### Bartholomeus

*Parade March*
Band
EP (London, *Boosey's Military Journal,* Ser. 66, Nr. 6, 1880) GB:Lbm (h.1549, Ser. 66, Nr. 6)

### Basquit, Heinrich

The following works are all for band ud were printed in London, ca. 1868–1879; shelf-marks given are for GB:Lbm.
Fantasias: h.1549, Ser. 45, Nr. 3 (on Irish songs); f.412.[11], f.402.[2]
Waltzes: h.1544, Nr. 230, h.1549, Ser. 41, Nr. 5
*March,* h.1549, Ser. 10, Nr. 6

### Beer, Alfred

*Parade March*
Band
EP (London, 1900) GB:Lbm (h.1549, Ser. 109, Nr. 5)

### Belville, Edward

March, *The Highland Patrol*
Fife and drum band
EP (London, 1885) GB:Lbm (f.414.a.[6])

### Becker

*Marche aux flambeaux*
Band
EP (London, 1884) GB:Lbm (h.1549, Ser. 76, Nr. 4)

### Benedict, Sir Julius

The following works are all for band and were printed in London, ca. 1877–1883; shelf-marks given are for GB:Lbm.
*Overture*, h.1544, Nr. 196
Marches: f.412.[13], h.1549, Ser. 56, Nr. 4, h.1549, Ser. 74, Nr. 6
*Jig*, h.1549, Ser. 75, Nr. 6

### Bennet, C. W.

The following works are all for band and were printed in London, ca. 1894–1900; shelf-marks given are for GB:Lbm.
*Overture*, f.800.[101] (with solo cornet)
Marches: f.800.[94] (with solo cornet), f.800.[104] (with solo cornet), f.800.[106] (with solo cornet), f.800.[124] (with solo cornet), f.800.[128] (with solo cornet), f.800.[128] (with solo cornet)
GB:Lbm has an additional eleven band works by Bennet, dating ca. 1900–1906.

### Bergmann, Eduard

The following works are for band and were printed in London, ca. 1854; shelf-marks given are for GB:Lbm.
*Waltz*, h.1545, Nr. 8
*Galop*, h.1545, Nr. 2

### Bergson, M.

*Air de concert*
Band
EP (London, 1894) GB:Lbm (h.1549, Ser. 97, Nr. 3)

### Bidgood, Thomas

Pas redouble, *The Mountaineer*
Band
EP (London, 1887) GB:Lbm (e.372.b.[7])
GB:Lbm also has several works for band by Bidgood, dated ca. 1900–1905.

### Billema

*Polka*
Band
EP (London, 1875) GB:Lbm (h.1549, Ser. 21, Nr. 3)

### Bishop, Henry (1786–1855)

*Funeral March* (for the Duke of Wellington, 1852)
2242-443, bass saxophone, serpent, ophicleide, percussion
MS GB:Lbm; US:DW (760)

*Marches*
1221-221, serpent
MS (autograph) GB:Lbm (Add.34725); US:DW (766)

*Grand National Hymn*
SATB, band, organ
GB:Lbm (R.M.21.d.1.[1])

*Marcia*
2222-22
MS (autograph) GB:Lbm; US:DW (769)

### Blake, Charles Dupee

March, *Ivanhoe*
Band
EP (London, 1898) GB:Lbm (f.800 [140])

### Blancheteau

The following works are for band and were printed in London, ca. 1873–1881; shelf-marks given are for GB:Lbm.
*Varsoviana*, f.414.a.[8] (for fife and drums)

*Fantasia*, f.412.1.[4] (solo cornet)
*Barcarolle*, f.403.[7] (for fife and drums)
*March*, f.403.[6] (for fife and drums)

### Bogaerde, F. L. van den

The following works are for band and were printed in London, ca. 1885–1887; shelf-marks given are for GB:Lbm.
Marches: e.372.b.[8], f.412.[17]
*Valse*, f.402.e.[4]
*Concertino*, f.800.[156] (for solo clarinet, on a theme from Bellini's *Norma*)

### Boggetti, Edwin

The following works are for band and were printed in London, ca. 1889–1895; shelf-marks given are for GB:Lbm.
Dances: h.1549, Ser. 86, Nr. 1; h.1549, Ser. 85, Nr. 4; h.1549, .97, Nr. 6
*March*, h.1549, Ser. 99, Nr. 5
*Gavotte*, h.1544, Nr. 359

### Bonnisseau

The following works are for band and were printed in London, ca. 1873–1881; shelf-marks given are for GB:Lbm.
*Overture*, f.411.[21] (for 'Octett band')
*Cambria, Welsh medley*, f.411.[22] (for 'Octett band')
*Funeral Andante*, f.413.[25] (for brass band)
Marches: f.403.c.[3] (for fife and drums); f.412.[16]; f.413.[5] (for brass band); f.412.[19]; f.402.[9] (for brass band); f.401.p.[5]; f.413.f.[3] (for brass band); f.412.i.[4]; f.412.[21]; f.403.d.[4] (for fife and drums); f.412.i.[5]; f.413.[8] (for brass band); f.412.i.[6]; f.412.a.[1]; f.412.m.[3]; f.412.a.[2]; f.412.a.[3]; f.412.[18]; f.412.a.[6]; f.402.[13] (for brass band); f.412.i.[7]; f.412.a.[7]; f.412.a.[8]; f.413.[9] (for brass band); f.413.[10] (for brass band); f.402.[6] (for brass band); f.412.a.[10]; f.412.a.[11]; f.402.[7] (for brass band); f.402.[17] (for brass band); f.402.[14] (for brass band); f.412.i.[8]; f.401.i.[3]; f.412.i.[9]; f.401.p.[6]; f.411.[24] (for 'Octett band'); f.401.[4] (for fife and drums); f.403.[5] (for fife and drums); f.413.[11] (for brass band); f.412.a.[12]; f.413.[12] (for brass band); f.412.1.[6]; f.401.1.[6]; f.402.[8] (for brass band); f.413.[13] (for brass band); f.412.i.[10]; f.402.[16]; (for brass band); f.412.a.[15]; f.402.[15] (for brass band); f.412.a.[13]
Polkas: f.412.[20]; f.401.q.[4] (for solo piccolo); f.412.[22]; f.402.[10] (for brass band); f.401.q.[3] (for two soli cornets)
Themes varsoviana: f.402.[12]; f.412.a.[14] (for brass band)
Schottisches: f.402.[11] (for brass band); f.412.a.[9]
*Quadrille*, f.412.[24]
*Set of Valses*, f.412.[25]
Galop, e.372.b.[9]

### Bosisio

March. *Queen Jane*
Fife and drums
EP (London. 1887) GB:Lbm (f.403.g.[2])

### Boulcourt, Alfred

*Trombone Polka*
EP (London, 1877) GB:Lbm (f.413.[17]), for brass band; GB:Lbm (f.415.c.[13], for 'Octett band')

### Bousquet, Narcisse

The following works are for band and were printed in London, ca. 1873–1881; shelf-marks given are for GB:Lbm.
Marches: f.412.a.[2]; f. 412.a.[21]; f.412.a.[22]; f.401.0.[1]; f.402.[23]; f.412.a.[23]; f.402.f.[4]
Polkas: f.414.[5] (for fife and drums); f.414.[6] (for fife and drums); f.402.[20] (for brass band); f.402.[24] (for brass band); f.411.[28] (for 'Octett band'. with solo piccolo'); f.411.[30] (for 'Octett band' with solo piccolo'); f.411.[31] (for 'Octett band'); f .403. [2] (for fife and drums); f.403.c.[8] (for fife and drums); f.403.g.[3] (for fife and drums)
*Bolero*, f.412.m.[4]
Valses: f.415.[19] (for 'Octett band'); h.1549, Ser. 61, Nr. 5
Varsovianas: f.402.[22] (for brass band) [same work for fife and drums under f.403.c.[6] and a later edition of the latter under f414.[7]); f.402.[19] (for brass band)

Redovas: f.401.[6]; f.412.1.[7]; f.401.i.[5]
Schottisches: f.401.[5]; f.414.[8] (for fife and drums)
*Quadrille*, f.401.1.[7]
*Fandango* (with variations), h.1543, Nr. 159
GB:Lbm (h.1543, Nrs. 1-160) represent *Jullien's Military Journal*, mostly edited by Charles Godfrey, Senior.

### Braham, Charles

March, *England*
Band
EP (London, 1877) GB:Lbm (f.412.i.[11])

### Brepsant, Engebert

The following works are for band and were printed in London, ca. 1877–1887; shelf-marks given are for GB:Lbm.
Marches: f.411.a.[1] (for 'Octett band'); f.412.a.[25]; f.412.a.[16] (the same for 'Octett band' under f.411.a.[2]); f.412.a.[27]; f.412.a.[28]; f.401.j.[4]; f.403.[3] (for fife and drums); e.372.b.[12]; f.412.a.[29]; f.413.[23] (for brass band)
*Air varie*, f.401.z.[3]

### Brewer, Josiah

Polka, *The Deep Blue Sea*
Band, with solo piccolo
EP (London, 1892) GB:Lbm (h.1549, Ser. 93, Nr. 1)

### Brewer, Mark A.

Concert Polka, *Lilliputian*
Band, with solo piccolo
EP (London, 1895) GB:Lbm (h.1549, Ser. 98, Nr. 4)

### Bridge, Sir John F.

Jubilee Anthem, 'Blessed be the Lord thy God'
Band
EP (London, 1887) GB:Lbm (h.1549, Ser. 82, Nr. 5)

### Briffaux, J. B.

The following works are for bsnd and were printed in London, ca. 1885–1887; shelf-marks given are for GB:Lbm.
*Pas redouble*, e.372.b.[13]
*Valse*, f.414.a.[9]

### Briggs, E. C.

Pas redouble, *Light Dragoons*
Band
EP (London, 1877) GB:Lbm (f.412.a.[30])

### Brooks, C.

'American Quick March,' *Sgnotters*
Band
EP (London, 1884) GB:Lbm (f.401.z.[4])

### Brooks, E.

The following works are for band and were printed in London, ca. 1881–1884; shelf-marks given are for GB:Lbm.
Marches: f.412.m.[6]; f.402.e.[6] (for brass band); f.401.r.[3]; f.412.m.[5]

### Brunet, L.

The following works are for band and were printed in London, ca. 1877; shelf-marks given are for GB:Lbm.
Marches: f.412.a.[32], f.412.e.[33], f.412.a.[34], f.412.a.[35], f.412.a.[36]

### Brunette

Waltz, *Galatea*
Band
EP (London, 1871) GB:Lbm (h.1549, Ser. 45, Nr. 4)

### Bucalossi, Ernest

The following works are for band and were printed in London, ca. 1886–1898; shelf-marks given are for GB:Lbm.
Valses: h.1549, Ser. 85, Nr. 4; h.1549, Ser. 89, Nr. 5; h.1549, Ser. 81, Nr. 1; h.1544, Nr. 346; h.1549, Ser. 86, Nr. 5

Polkas: h.1549, Ser. 86, Nr. 2; h.1549, Ser. 79, Nr. 4; f.800.[215] (for fife and drums)
*March*, h.1549, Ser. 83, Nr. 4

## Bucalossi, Procida

The following works are for band and were printed in London, ca. 1883–1898; shelf-marks given are for GB:Lbm.
Valses: h.1544, Nr. 391; h.1549, Ser. 89, Nr. 5; f.412.o.[11]
*Galop*, f.403.e.[12]
*Song*, h.1544, Nr. 354
*Eastern Patrol*, f.800.[220] (for fife and drums)

## Burald

*Gavotte*
Band
EP (London, 1885) GB:Lbm (h.1549, Ser. 79, Nr. 6)

## Burckhardt

The following works are for band and were printed in London, ca. 1863–1864; shelf-marks given are for GB:Lbm.
Quadrilles: h.1544, Nr. 198 and 204
*Galop*, h.1544, Nr. 198

## Burns, Felix, Sen.

Polka, *Khedive*
Band
EP (London, 1887) GB:Lbm (f.403.g.[4])

## Calcott, J. W.

*Queen of the Valley*
Band
EP (London, 1877) GB:Lbm (f.413.[25])

## Cambier, Victor

The following works are for band and were printed in London, ca. 1873–1877; shelf-marks given are for GB:Lbm.
*March*, f.401.i.[6]
*Schottische*, f.401.[8]

## Capati, R. D.

Valse, *Night Breeze*
Brass band
EP (London, 1873) GB:Lbm (f.402.[27])

## Carbon

*Redowa du Casino*
Fife and drum band
EP (London, 1873) GB:Lbm (f.403.[9])

## Cardew, Phil.

Polka, *The Whirlwind*
Band
EP (London, 1858) GB:Lbm (h.3211.b)

## Carter, Henry

*March*
Band
EP (London, 1868) F:Pn (Vm.27.6259)

## Cavallini, P.

*Scotch Medley*
Band
EP (London, 1866) GB:Lbm (h.1544, Nr. 219)

## Cellier, Alfred

Valse, *A Summer Night in Munich*
Band
EP (London, 1889) GB:Lbm (h.1549, Ser. 86, Nr. 2)

## Clement, J.

Concert Polka, *The Village Festival*
Band
EP (London, 1887) GB:Lbm (h.1544, Nr. 348)

## Clendon, Hugh

The following works are for band and were printed in London, ca. 1883–1895; shelf-marks given are for GB:Lbm.
Dances: h.1544, Nr. 396; h.1544, Nr. 320
*Gavotte*, f.800.[284] (with solo cornet)

## Colline, Victor

*Quadrille*
Band
EP (London, 1865) GB:Lbm (h.1544, Nr. 213)

## Conradi, A.

The following works are for band and were printed in London, ca. 1860–1874; shelf-marks given are for GB:Lbm.
*Quadrille*, h.1544, Nr. 183
*Sing Vogelein*, h.1544, Nr. 267

## Conterno, G. E.

*Aria e coro*
Band
EP (London, 1894) GB:Lbm (h.1549, Ser. 96, Nr. 6)

## Cook, H. J.

March, *Victoria*
Band
EP (London, 1892) GB:Lbm (h.1544, Nr. 378)

## Cooke, Grattan

*Russian Carriage Song*
Band
EP (London, 1854) GB:Lbm (h.1545, Nr. 4)

## Coote, Charles, Sen.

The following works are for band and were printed in London, ca. 1877–1880; shelf-marks given are for GB:Lbm.
Valse sets: f.414.[17] (for fife and drums); h.1549, Ser. 36, Nr. 3
Quadrilles: h.1549, Ser. 36, Nr. 6; h.1544, Nr. 265

## Coote, Charles, Jr.

The following works are for band and were printed in London, ca. 1876–1894; shelf-marks given are for GB:Lbm.
Quadrilles: f.401.d.[10]; h.1544, Nr. 352; h.1549, Ser.35, Nr. 6; h.1549, Ser. 62, Nr. 3; h.1549, Ser. 71, Nr. 5; h.1549, Ser. 76, Nr. 4; h.1549, Ser. 80, Nr. 4; h.1549, Ser. 86, Nr. 6; h.1549, Ser. 60, Nr. 2; f.414.a.[14] (for fife and drums); h.1549, Ser. 67, Nr. 5
Valses: h.1549, Ser. 91, Nr. 4; f.413.a.[8] (for brass band); f.413.a.[9] (for brass band); f.401.d.[11]; h.1549, Ser. 90, Nr. 4; h.1549, Ser. 97, Nr. 3; h.1544, Nr. 204; h.1549, Ser. 76, Nr. 6; h.1549, Ser. 75, Nr. 3; f.413.f.[5] (for brass band); h.1544, Nr. 340; h.1549, Ser. 71, Nr. 1; h.1549, Ser. 66, Nr. 2; h.1544, Nr. 229; h.1549, Ser. 85, Nr. 6; h.1544, Nr. 206
Polkas: h.1549, Ser. 63, Nr. 2; f.403.g.[6] (for fife and drums); f.414.a.[13] (for fife and drums); h.1562, Nr. 141; h.1549, Ser. 70, Nr. 2; f.402.e.[9] (for brass band; the same for band under h.1544, Nr. 321)
Galops: f.402.[301 (for brass band); f.401.d.[12]
*Echoes of London Lancers*, h.1549, Ser. 40, Nr. 4
In GB:Lbm (h.1562) represents the S. A. Chappell *Army Journal*

## Couldery, Claudius Herbert

*Fantasia for Trumpet*
Band
EP (London, 1899) GB:Lbm (h.1544, Nr. 418)

## Cowen, Sir Frederic Hymen

The following works are for band and were printed in London, ca. 1871–1896; shelf-marks given are for GB:Lbm.
*March*, h.1544, Nr. 250
*Song*, h.1549, Ser. 101, Nr. 4 (with solo cornet)

## Croft, Frederick

March, *The Warriors*
Band
EP (London, 1886) GB:Lbm (h.1544, Nr. 342)

## Croisez

*Quadrille*
Band
EP (London, 1871) GB:Lbm (h.1549, Ser. 43, Nr. 2)

## Crowe, Alfred Gwyllym

Valse, *Hebe*
Band
EP (London, 1868) GB:Lbm (h.1562, Nr. 61)

## Czibulka

Quadrille, *Vis-à-vis*
Band
EP (London, 1875) GB:Lbm (h.1544, Nr. 275)

## Czibulka, Alphons W.

The following works are for band and were printed in London, ca. 1874–1894; shelf-marks given are for GB:Lbm.
*Galop*, h.1544, Nr. 267
*Gavotte*, h.1544, Nr. 386

## Deacon, Charles E.

The following works are for band and were printed in London, ca. 1885–1892; shelf-marks given are for GB:Lbm.
Valses: f.800.[324] (with solo cornet); h.1544, Nr. 378

## Desblins, A.

The following works are for band and were printed in London, ca. 1877; shelf-marks given are for GB:Lbm.
*Valse*, f.414.a.[16] (for fife and drums)
*Polka*, f.402.e.[10] (for brass band)

## Dodwell, Samuel

The following works are for band and were printed in London, ca. 1884–1885; shelf-marks given are for GB:Lbm.
*Gavotte*, f.800.[350] (with solo cornet)
*Schottische*, f.403.e.[17] (for fife and drums)

## Dust, Charles

The following works are for band and were printed in London, ca. 1873–1885; shelf-marks given are for GB:Lbm.
Marches, f.401.j.[11]; f.402.[38] (for brass band); a.237.a.[4]
*Galop*, f.401.1.[12]

## Dyke, Robert

The following works are for band and were printed in London, ca. 1877–1892; shelf-marks given are for GB:Lbm.
Polkas: f.403.d.[18] (for fife and drums, with variations); f.403.e.[20] (for fife and drums); f.403.g.[11] (for fife and drums)
Quadrilles: f.403.e.[29] (for fife and drums); f.403.g.[9] (for fife and drums); f.403.d.[20] (for fife and drums); f.403.g.[12] (for fife and drums); f.403.g.[21] (for fife and drums)
Marches: f.403.d.[9] (for fife and drums); f.401.dd.[9]; f.403.d.[10] (for fife and drums); f.403.c.[13] (for fife and drums); f.403.e.[19] (for fife and drums); f.403.c.[14] (for fife and drums); f.403.g.[8] (for fife and drums); f.401.dd.[11]; f.403.e.[23] (for fife and drums); f.403.e.[24] (for fife and drums); f.403.e.[38] (for fife and drums); f.414.b.[3] (for fife and drums); f.403.e.[40] ('Sunday March,' for fife and drums); f.403.e.[25] (for fife and drums); f.401.z.[9] (the same for fife and drums, under f.403.g.[14]); f.403.d.[12] ('Sunday March,' for fife and drums); f.403.e.[26] (for fife and drums); f.403.d.[13] (for fife and drums); f.403.g.[7] (for fife and drums); f.403.c.[16] (for fife and drums); f.403.g.[20] (for fife and drums); f.403.d.[14] (for fife and drums); f.40l.z.[10]; f.403.g.[15] (for fife and drums); f.403.e.[35] (for fife and drums); f.401.z.[8]; f.403.e.[43] (for fife and drums); f.403.e.[36] (for fife and drums); f.403.g.[13] (for fife and drums); f.403.e.[34] (for fife and drums); f.403.e.[37] (for fife and drums); f.403.d.[15] (for fife and drums); f.403.e.[45] (for fife and drums); f.403.e.[46] (for fife and drums); f.403.d.[17] (for fife and drums); f.403.f.[47] (for fife and drums); f.403.f.[2] (for fife and drums); f.403.f.[3] (for fife and drums); f.403.g.[23] (for fife and drums); f.403.c.[18] (for fife and drums); f.403.f.[4] (for fife and drums); f.403.d.[19] (for fife and drums); f.403.c.[19] (for fife and drums); f.403.d.[20] (for fife and drums); f.401.z.[11]; f.403.f.[7] (for fife and drums); f.403.d.[22] (for fife and drums); f.403.f.[9] (for fife and drums); f.403.g.[19] (for fife and drums); f.403.f.[8] (for fife and drums); f.403.f.[6] (for fife and drums); f.401.dd.[12]

Schottisches: f.403.c.[15] (for fife and drums); f.403.d.[11] (for fife and drums); f.403.e.[27] (for fife and drums); f.403.f.[5] (for fife and drums)
Valses: f.403.g.[10] (for fife and drums); f.403.e.[30] (for fife and drums); f.403.d.[21] (for fife and drums)
*Fantasia*, f.403.f.[1] (for fife and drums)
*Galop*, f.403.g.[17] (for fife and drums)

## Eaton, William George

Quadrille, *Homeward Bound*
Fife and drum band
EP (London, 1885) GB:Lbm (f.414.a.[20])

## Eilenberg, Richard

Idylle, *The Forest Ranger's Courtship*
Band
EP (London, 1899) GB:Lbm (h.1549, Ser. 106, Nr. 5

## Elliot, Stanislaus

*Intermezzo*
Band
EP (London, 1895) GB:Lbm (h.1549, Ser. 98, Nr. 4)

## Elrington, William

*The Austrian Retreat*
Band
EP (London, ca. 1795) GB:Lbm (g.272.n.[6])
EP (London, ca. 1800) GB:Lbm (g.443.aa.[9])

## Embury

*Military Overture*
Band
EP (London, 1866) GB:Lbm (h.1544, Nr. 220)

## Ercilla, B. de

Schottische, *Mascarita, me conoces?*
Band
EP (London, 1898) GB:Lbm (h.1549, Ser. 104, Nr. 6)

## Evans, Charles

*March*
Band
EP (London, 1804) GB:Lbm (h.109.[33])

## Fare, Florence (pseud., for Rawlings, Alfred William)

The following works are for band and were printed in London, ca. 1891–1893; shelf-marks given are for GB:Lbm.
Valses: h.1549, Ser. 91, Nr. 1; h.1549, Ser. 93, Nr. 2; h.1549, Ser. 92, Nr. 3
*Schottische*, h.1549, Ser. 95, Nr. 6

## Farrell, James

The following works are for band and were printed in London, ca. 1889–1896; shelf-marks given are for GB:Lbm.
Polkas: h.1544, N. 355 (with cornet solo); h.1544, Nr. 398; h.1549, Ser. 96, Nr. 6 (with cornet solo); h.1549, Ser. 89, Nr. 5 (with cornet solo)

## Faust, C.

The following works are for band and were printed in London, ca. 1864–1883; shelf-marks given are for GB:Lbm.
Galops: h.1549, Ser. 64, Nr. 3; h.1544, Nr. 230; h.1549, Ser. 40, Nr. 4; h.1549, Ser. 55, Nr. 4
Polkas: h.1549, Ser. 77, Nr. 6; h.1544, Nr. 206
Mazurkas: h.1549, Ser. 75, Nr. 3; h.1544, Nr. 340
*Quadrille*, h.1549, Ser. 61, Nr. 3

## Fechner, A. M.

The following works are for band and were printed in London, ca. 1894; shelf-marks given are for GB:Lbm.
Marches: f.800.[426] (for fife and drums); f.800.[421] (for fife and drums)

## Fetras, Oscar

The following works are for band and were printed in London, ca. 1896–1899; shelf-marks given are for GB:Lbm.
Valses: h.1549, Ser. 102, Nr. 5; h.1544, Nr. 404; h.1549, Ser. 106, Nr. 1; h.1549, Ser. 100, Nr. 5; h.1544, Nr. 422; h.1549, Ser. 100, Nr. 4; h.1549, Ser.104, Nr. 6
Marches: h.1544, Nr. 404; h.1544, Nr. 400
Polkas: h.1549, Ser. 101, Nr. 5; h.1549, Ser. 103, Nr. 5

*Quadrille*, h.1549, Ser. 106, Nr. 5
*Gavotte*, h.1549, Ser. 105, Nr. 6

### Fiehrer

March, *Giskra*
Band
EP (London, 1870) GB:Lbm (h.1562, Nr.78)

### Field, Alfred L.

The following works are for band and were printed in London, ca. 1883–1892; shelf-marks given are for GB:Lbm.
Marches: f.403.f.[14] (for fife and drums); f.403.f.[12] (for fife and drums); f.403.f. [13] (for fife and drums); f.800.[430] (for fife and drums); f.403.f.[16] (for fife and drums); f.403.f.[15] (for fife and drums); f.800.[431] (for fife and drums); f.800.[433] (for fife and drums)
*Galop*, f.800.[432] (for fife and drums)

### Foster, D.

March, *New York*
Band
EP (London, 1881) GB:Lbm (f.401.r.[8])

### Franke, Theodor

The following works are for band and were printed in London, ca. 1896–1899; shelf-marks given are for GB:Lbm.
*Polka*, h.1544, Nr. 418
*Intermezzo*, h.1549, Ser. 101, Hr. 6

### Fredhe

Polka, *Roderich*
Band
EP (London, 1880) GB:Lbm (h.1549, Ser. 39, Nr. 4)

### Frewin, Edward

The following works are for band and were printed in London, ca. 1878; shelf-marks given are for GB:Lbm.
*Polka*, f.412.b.[14]

Quadrille, f.412.k.[4]

### Fricke, C.

Galop, *The Planters*
Band
EP (London, 1880) GB:Lbm (h.1549, Ser. 85, Nr. 6)

### Gassner, G.

The following works are for band and were printed in London, ca. 1880-1887; shelf-marks given are for GB:Lbm.
*Overture*, h.1549, Ser. 82, Nr. 1
*Fantasias*: h.1549, Ser. 68, Nr. 5; h.1544, Nr. 339
*Cavatina*, h.1549, Ser. 77, Nr. 6 (for solo clarinet)
Marches: h.1549, Ser. 70, Nr. 5; f.402.a.[2] (for brass band)
*Valse*, h.1549, Ser. 72, Nr. 1

### Glover, Charles W.

*Divertimento* (on Chinese melodies)
Band
EP (London, 1897) GB:Lbm (h.1549, Ser. 103, Nr. 5)

### Godfrey, Adolphus Frederick

The following works are for band and were printed in London, ca. 1861–1881; shelf-marks given are for GB:Lbm.
Marches: h.1562, Nr. 44; h.1562, Nr. 74; h.1562, Nr. 54; h.1570.[6]; h.1562, Nr. 78 (two marches); h.1562, Nr. 96 (six marches); h.1562, Nr. 102; h.1562, Nr. 19 (two marches); f.414.a. [26]
Galops: h.1562, Nr. 56; h.1562, Nr. 40; h.1562, Nr. 93; h.1562, Nr. 74
Waltzes: h.1562, Nr. 56; h.1562, Nr. 93; h.1562, Nr. 68
*Polka*, h.1562, Nr. 29
Quadrilles: h.1562, Nr. 68; h.1562, Nr. 41
Russian Dance, *Pas des Patineurs*, h.1562, Nr. 110
Bassoon solo, *Lucy long*, h.1544.a
*Reminiscences of all Nations*, h.1562, Nr. 139
*Reminiscences of Ireland*, h.1562, Nr. 115
*Reminiscences of Scotland*, h.1562, Nr. 109
*Reminiscences of Wales*, h.1562, Nr. 121

### Godfrey, Arthur Eugene

The following works are for band and were printed in London, ca. 1892–1893; shelf-marks given are for GB:Lbm.

*Polka*, h.1549, Ser. 93, Nr. 6

*March*, f.800.[485] (with solo clarinet and ad lib. vocal trio)

*Wedding hymn*, 'God bless the royal Pair,' f.800.[486]

### Godfrey, Charles, Sen.

*Sardinian national Airs*
Band
EP (London, 1856) GB:Lbm (h.1543, Nr. 145)

### Godfrey, Charles, Jun.

The following works are for band and were printed in London, ca. 1870–1887; shelf-marks given are for GB:Lbm.

Marches: f.414.b.[10] (for fife and drums); f.401.q.[10]; f.40l.o.[4]; f.402.b.[8] (for brass band); f.402.b.[10] (for, brass band); f.403.[20] (for fife and drums); f.401.[14]; f.401.t.[13]; f.401.ee.[5]; f.402.b.[1] (for brass band); h.1544.a; f.401.t.[12] (the same for fife and drums, under f.403.f.[19]); f.403.f.[19] (for fife and drums); f.402.a.[13] (for brass band); f.401.aa.[2]; f.401.q.[8] (the same for fife and drums, under f.403.f.[20]); f.401.z.[15]; f.402.a.[17] (for brass band); f.401.[15]; h.1548, Nr. 31; f.403.[19] (for fife and drums); h.1562; f.401.t.[16]; f.402.a.[29] (for brass band); f.40l.e.[2]; f.402.a.[30] (for brass band); f.401.a.[4]; f.404.[121 (on Welsh melodies, for brass band; the same for fife and drums under f.403.c.[21]), f.402.a.[9] (for brass band); h.1562, Nr. 37; f.402.a.[8] (for brass band); f.401.t.[15]; f.402.b.[2] (for brass band)

Valses: h.1548, Nr. 48; h.1562, Nr. 187; f.402.a.[11] (for brass band); h.1548, Nr. 12; f.402.a.[19] (for brass band, the same for fife and drums, under f.403.[22]); h.1549, Ser. 46, Nr. 4; f.402.b.[3] (for brass band); h.1548, Nr. 30 ('Masonic Valse'); f.402.a.[24] (for brass band); f.402.a.[6] (for brass band); f.402.a.[20] (for brass band, the same for fife and drums, under f.403.[21]); f.402.a.[21] (the same for fife and drums, under f.403.b.[20]); f.402.b.[5] (for brass band); f.401.[17]; h.1548, Nr. 5; h.1562, Nr. 11; h.1548, Nr. 40

Galops: f.402.b.[7] (for brass band); f.401.a.[6]; f.401.a.[5] (the same for fife and drums, under f.403.[24]); f.401.a.[3]; f.402.a.[28] (the same for fife and drums, under f.403.[23])

Polkas: f.401.[13]; h.1548, Nr. 31 (the same for fife and drums, under f.414.a.[24]); h.1548, Nr. 7 (another edition under f.401.p.[11]

Quadrilles: f.402.a.[15] (for brass band); f.402.a.[25] (for brass band); f.401.a.[1]; f.402.a.[14] (for brass band); f.402.b.[6] (for brass band)

*Schottische*, f.401.a.[2]

Fantasias: h.1548, Nr. 45; h.1562, Nr. 201

Popular Selection, *Coster Songs*, h.1562, Nr. 207

*Grand selection on Austrian melodies*, h.1584, Nr. 26

### Godfrey, Daniel

The following works are for band and were printed in London, ca. 1854–1865; shelf-marks given are for GB:Lbm.

Waltzes: h.1562, Nr. 103; h.1562, Nr. 36; h.1562, Nr. 64; h.1562, Nr. 48; f.402.e.[14]

Marches: h.1543, Nr. 128; f.413.a.[20] (for brass band); h.2932.a.[19]; h.1543, Nr. 152; h.1562, Nr. 102; h.1543, Nr. 124

Quadrilles: h.1562, Nr. 33 (on Danish melodies); h.1543, Nr. 143

Polkas: f.414.a.[25] (for fife and drums); f.402.b.[12] (for brass band)

*National Airs*, h.1543

### Godfrey, Sir Daniel Eyers

The following works are for band and were printed in London, ca. 1888–1897; shelf-marks given are for GB:Lbm.

*Polka*, h.1549, Ser. 85, Nr. 2

*Six Hymn Tunes* ('for the Commemorations of the Queen's Reign'), f.800.[496]

**Graves, W. T.**

The following works are for band and were printed in London, ca. 1873–1877; shelf-marks given are for GB:Lbm.

Polkas: f.402.b.[13] (for brass band); f.411.a.[15] (for 'Octett Band')

**Gurtner, Jean**

The following works are for band and were printed in London, ca. 1876–1880; shelf-marks given are for GB:Lbm.

Marches: f.412.b.[27]; f.401.p.[14]; f.401.n.[6]; f.413.a.[24] (for brass band); f.412.b.[28]; f.412.b.[29]; f.412.b.[30]; f.413.a.[25] (for brass band); f.4011m.[1]; f.401.m.[2]; f.401.n.[7]; f.413.a.[26] (for brass band); e.372.c.[16]; f.401.p.[15]; f.412.b.[32]

**Guest, George (1771–1831)**

*Wisbech Volunteer Troop* (1815)
2022-02, bugle, serpent, percussion
EP (London, author) GB:Lbm (H.129.[4]); US:DW (737)

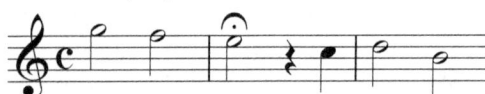

*A Third Grand Bugle Horn Troop* (1815)
2022-02, bugle, serpent, percussion
EP (London, Preston) GB:Lbm (H.129.[7]); US:DW (738)

*A Fourth Troop* (1815)
2022-12, serpent, percussion
EP (London, Preston) GB:Lbm (H.129.[8]); US:DW (739)

*A Fifth Troop* (1815)
2022-12, serpent, percussion
EP (London, Preston) GB:Lbm (H.129.[9]); US:DW (740)

*A Sixth Troop* (1815)
2022-12, bugle, serpent, percussion
EP (London, Preston) GB:Lbm; US:DW (741)

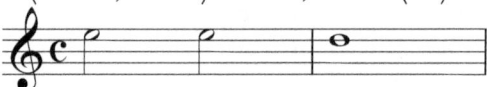

**Hare, Edwin C. F.**

The following works are for band and were printed in London, ca. 1873–1887; shelf-marks given are for GB:Lbm.

Marches: f.403.d.[30] (for fife and drums); f.402.b.[32] (for brass band); f.401.q.[11] (the same for fife and drums, under f.403.d.[31]); f.401.m.[6] (the same for fife and drums, under f.403.d.[32]); f.401.o.[9] (the same for fife and drums, under f.403.d.[33]); f.401.a.[8] (the same for fife and drums, under f.403.[32]); f.403.[30] (for fife and drums); f.403.[31] (for fife and drums) f.401.u.[8]; f.414.b.[12] (for fife and drums); f.304.d.[35] (for fife and drums); f.403.c.[24] (for fife and drums); f.401.0.[10]; f.403.[37] (for fife and drums); f.401.0.[7]; e.372.d.[5]; f.403.a.[10] (for fife and drums); e.372.d.[1] ('Elijah. Sunday March'); f.403.a.[7] (for fife and drums); f.401.u.[10] (the same for fife and drums, under f.403.f.[23]); e.372.d.[3]; f.401.o.[8] (the same for fife and drums, under f.403.d.[39]); (the same for brass band, under f.402.f.[10]); f.401.i.[16] (the same for fife and drums, under f.403.d.[40]); f.401.m.[8]; f.401.u.[9] (the same for fife and drums, under f.403.f.[24]); f.403.a.[2] (for fife and drums); f.401.j.[20] (the same for fife and drums, under f.403.0.[27]); f.403.a.[12] (for fife and drums); f.403.a.[5] (for fife and drums); f.403.c.[28] (for fife and drums); f.404.[7] (for brass band); f.403.a.[4] (for fife and drums); f.403.a.[11] (for fife and drums); f.401.j.[19]; f.412.m.[19];

f.401.a.[13]; f.401.e.[6] (the same for fife and drums, under f.403.c.[31]); f.402.b.[29] (for brass band); f.403.a.[3] (for fife and drums); f.403.a.[17] (for fife and drums); f.404.[8]; f.401.c.[2] (the same for fife and drums, under f.403.c.[43]); f.403.b.[20] (for brass band); f.401.i.[17]; f.403.a.[14] (for fife and drums); f.412.l.[9]; f.403.c.[35] (for fife and drums; a later edition, under f.403.d.[44]); f.401.e.[10] (the same for fife and drums, under f.403.[37]); f.401.u.[11] (the same for fife and drums, under f.403.f.[26]); f.402.b.[31] (for brass band); f.403.c.[41] (for fife and drums); f.401.j.[22] ('Sunday March' on 'Onward Christian Soldier'); f.401.e.[8] (the same for fife and drums, under f.403.c.[38]); f.401.e.[7] (the same for fife and drums, under f.403.c.[39]); f.403.c.[40] (for fife and drums); f.402.b.[161 (for brass band); f.403.a.[13] (for fife and drums); f.402.b.[23] (for brass band)

*Christmas Carol*, f.402.b.[26] (for brass band)

Country dances: f.403.d.[28] (for fife and drums); f.403.d.[371 [three dances]; f.401.n.[9] (for fife and drums) [four dances]

Galops: f.403.a.[16] (for fife and drums) [a later edition under f.403.c.[25]; f.403.[33]; f.401.u.[7]

*Mazurka*, f.402.b.[25] (for brass band) (the same for fife and drums, under f.403.d.[43])

Quadrille, f.403.a.[8]

Fantasias: e.372.d.[4]; f.401.q.[12] (the same for fife and drums, under f.403.f.[25]

2nd Series of *Quintetts*, h.2915.|31| (for wind instruments)

Grand selection, *Sea-Side*, f.401.a.[12]

Selection, *National melodies*, f.403.c.[36] (for fife and drums)

## Harper

Galop, *Down the Road*
Band
EP (London, 1875) GB:Lbm (h.1544, Nr. 275)

## Hartner, H.

March, *Black Diamond*
Military band
EP (London, 1868) F:Pn (Vm.27.8033)

March, *Quicksilver*
Military band
EP (London, 1869) F:Pn (Vm.27.8034)

Galop, *The Storming*
Military band
EP (London, 1869) F:Pn (Vm.27.8035)

*3rd Troop*
Military band
EP (London, 1868) F:Pn (Vm.27.8036)

## Hawkes, W.

Pas redoublé, *Billy Patterson*
Military band
EP (London, 1863) F:Pn (Vm.27.8042)

Pas redoublé, *Caledonian*
Military band
EP (London, 1861) F:Pn (Vm.27.8043)

## Heinsdorff

The following works are for band and were printed in London, ca. 1867–1880; shelf-marks given are for GB:Lbm.
*Galop*, h.1549, Ser. 65, Nr. 1
Polkas: h.1544, Nr. 226; h.1549, Ser. 47, Nr. 4

## Hinchliff, W. S.

*Ave Maria*
Band
EP (London, 1899) GB:Lbm (h.1549, Ser.107, Nr. 5)

## Hoby, C.

Intermezzo, *Phryne*
Band
EP (London, 1890) GB:Lbm (h.1544, Nr. 366)

## Holden, A. Jr.

Gavotte, *Dame Margery*
Band
EP (London, 1896) GB:Lbm (h.1549, Ser. 101, Nr. 6)

**Jones, J. G.**

*Nightingale Waltz*
*Good Night Polka*
1040-443, alto horn, tenor horn, 'Clavicor,' Opheclyde
EP (London, *Jones' Military Journal*, Nr. 2, ca. 1852) GB:Lbm (h.1550, Nr. 2); US:DW (756)

**Jones, Sidney**

March, *Loyalty*
Band
EP (London, 1890) GB:Lbm (h.1544, Nr. 366)

**Jouve, J.**

*The Austrian Retreat* (1815)
2022-12, serpent, percussion
EP (London, Goulding) GB:Lbm (H.1480.x.[15]); US:DW (742)

**Jullien**

*The Nobility Balls Polka*
*The Drawing Room Polka*
1042-443, serpent, ophicleide, percussion
EP (London, *Jullien's Journal*, Nr. 11, ca. 1850) GB:Lbm; US:DW (755)

**Kappey, Jacob A.**

The following works are for band and were printed in London, ca. 1877–1887; shelf-marks given are for GB:Lbm.
*Serenade*, h.1549, Ser. 83, Nr. 4
Marches: h.1544, Nr. 285; h.1549, Ser. 65, Nr. 5
*Gavotte*, h.1549, Ser. 93, Nr. 4

**Koenig, H. L.**

Polka, *Rosebud*
Band
EP (London, 1854) GB:Lbm (h.1543, Nr. 124)

**Kuecken, F. W.**

Arie, *Der Pratendent*
Band
EP (London, 1880) GB:Lbm (h.1549, Ser. 66, Nr. 6)

**Kühner**

The following works are for band and were printed in London, ca. 1863–1864; shelf-marks given are for GB:Lbm.
Polkas: h.1544, Nr. 306; h.1549. Ser. 55, Nr. 4; h.1544. Nr. 360
Galops: h.1544, Nr. 196; h.1544, Nr. 217
*Redowa*, h.1544, Nr. 225
*March*, h.1549, Ser. 65, Nr. 5

**Laurent, H.**

*Valse*
Band
EP (London, 1856) GB:Lbm (h.1544, Nr. 186)

*The Malakof Galop*
*The Egyptian Polka*
1252-443, alto horn, bassi, percussion
EP (London, *Boosey's Military Journal*, Nr. 20, 1856) GB:Lbm; US:DW (757)

**Lange, G.**

The following works are for band and were printed in London, ca. 1878–1882; shelf-marks given are for GB:Lbm.
*Songs without Words*: h.1544, Nr. 316; h.1549, Ser. 63, Nr. 2; h.1549, Ser. 72, Nr. 2

**Leslie, Steward**

*Danse des Zauyes*
Band (with solo piccolo)
EP (London, 1899) GB:Lbm (h.1549, Ser. 107, Nr. 5)

**Liddell, John**

*Valse*
Band
EP (London, 1886) GB:Lbm (h.1549, Ser. 80, Nr. 4)

**Lincke. P.**

*Valse*
Band
EP (London, 1899) GB:Lbm (h.1544, Nr. 418)

**Loetz, Paul de**
> Intermezzo, *On the Road to Moscow*
> Band
> EP (London, 1892) GB:Lbm (h.1549, Ser. 92, Nr. 3)

**Lortzing, G. A.**
> *Fest-Ouverture*
> Band
> EP (London, 1894) GB:Lbm (h.1549, Ser. 96, Nr. 2)

**Lucas, Charles (1808–1869)**
> *Septett*
> 1122-01
> MS GB:Lbm (RM.21.d.6.Nr. 6); US:DW (114)

**Luschwitz, H.**
> *March*
> Band
> EP (London, 1888) GB:Lbm (h.1549, Ser. 85, Nr. 4)

**Lutz, Meyer**
> *Polka*
> Band
> EP (London, 1883) GB:Lbm (h.1549, Ser. 75, Nr. 3)

**Maanen, J. C. van**
> The following works are for band and were printed in London, ca. 1865–1875; shelf-marks giveu are for GB:Lbm.
> Valses: h.1544, Nr. 210; h.1549, Ser. 37, Nr. 3

**Mackenzie, Alexander (1847–1935)**
> *Funeral March*
> Band [cited in Grove, Fifth Edition]

**Maillart, L. A.**
> Overture, *Les Dragons de Villars*
> Band
> EP (London, 1879) GB:Lbm (h.1549, Ser. 41, Nr. 5)

**Marliani, M. A.**
> Aria, *Stanca di piu combattere*
> Band
> EP (London, 1862) GB:Lbm (h.1544, Nr. 192)

**Mazzinghi, Joseph (1765–1844)**
> (67) *Military Airs or Divertimenti*, Op. 31, 33, 40, 44
> EP [cited in Grove, XI, 868]

**Meissler, J. [Pseud.]**
> *Belle amie*
> Band
> EP (London, 1893) GB:Lbm (h.1544, Nr. 383)

**Michaelis**
> *Galop*
> Band
> EP (London, 1870) GB:Lbm (h.1544, Nr. 244)

**Michiels**
> *Polka*
> Band
> EP (London, 1895) GB:Lbm (h.1544, Nr. 391)

**Molloy, J. L.**
> Song, *Love's old sweet Song*
> Band
> EP (London, 1890) GB:Lbm (h.1549, Ser. 88, Nr. 3)

**Morten, F.**
> Valse. Wiener Chic
> Military band
> EP (London, *Boosey's Military Journal*, ser. 109, Nr. 5, 1900) GB:Lbm (h.1549)

**Moths**
> *Nachfalter*
> Band
> EP (London, 1899) GB:Lbm (h.1544, Nr. 418)

**Muth, A.**
> *Polka*
> Band
> EP (London, 1891) GB:Lbm (h.1549, Ser. 91, Nr. 4)

**Napravnik**
> *March*
> Band
> EP (London, 1896) GB:Lbm (h.1549, Ser. 100, Nr. 5)

### Neumann

*Galop*
Band
EP (London, 1868) GB:Lbm (h.1544, Nr. 232)

### Oelschlegel, Alfred

*March*
Band
EP (London, 1900) GB:Lbm (h.1549, Ser. 105, Nr. 6)

### Oldenburg, P. G.

*Polonaise*
Band
EP (London, 1865) GB:Lbm (h.1544, Nr. 209)

### Parry, C. H. H. (1848–1918)

*Nonet*
1122-02, Eng. horn
MS GB:Lcm; US:DW (432)

### Parry, John (1776–1851)

[Series of *'Walisischer Airs für Militärmusk,'* 1804]
MS [cited in MGG]

*The Barouche Ouick Step* (1805)
2022-02, bugle horns [with second version for piccolo, 2 fifes, 2 bugles]
EP (London, Power) GB:Lbm; US:DW (736)

### Peplow

*Galop*
Band
EP (London, 1876) GB:Lbm (h.1549, Ser. 48, Nr. 1)

### Pick, Henry ('of Her Majesty's [Queen Charlotte] Band')

(20) *Harmonie*
2042-12, serpent
EP (London, Astor) GB:Lbm; US:DW (749)

[Collection of Part-books]
202-02, serpent, 2 basset horns
EP GB:Lbm (R.M.21.C.32. and 21.d.2)
Contains an *Andantino* by Sir Wm. Herschel and 2 chorales, 'Ewigkeit du Donnerwort' and 'Nun ruhen alle Walder.'

[Collection of 11 works, perhaps 4 marches and a Divertimento] (ca. 1800)
2042-221, serpent, percussion
MS (autograph) GB:Lbm (21.b.16); US:DW (765)

(37) Military *Divertimentos*
22-12, serpent
EP (Böhme) [cited by H]

### Posse

*Galop*
Band
EP (London, 1867) GB:Lbm (h.1544, Nr. 225)

### Potter, Samuel

*New Slow Marches* (ca. 1800)
Band
EP (London, author) GB:Lbm (B.60[6])

### Pritchard

*Galop*
Band
EP (London, 1892) GB:Lbm (h.1549, Ser. 93, Nr. 2)

### Prout, Edwin H.

The following works are for band and were printed in London, ca. 1881–1895; shelf-marks given are for GB:Lbm.
Valses: h.1549, Ser. 99, Nr. 5; h.1549, Ser. 70, Nr. 5; h.1549, Ser. 82, Nr. 6

### Reissigler, G. G.

*Yelva*
Band
EP (London, 1896) GB:Lbm (h.1544, Nr. 400)

### Relle, H.

*Quadrille*
Band
EP (London, 1873) GB:Lbm (h.1549, Ser. 48, Nr. 4)

### Reyloff, Ed.

[Slow movement]
Band (with solo cornet or euphonium)
EP (Loudon, 1871) F:Pn (Vm.27.10558)

## Riche, J. B.

*Galop*
Band
EP (London, 1868) GB:Lbm (h.1544, Nr. 229)

## Robertson, G. P.

*Reveil d'amour*
Band (with solo cornet)
EP (London, 1898) GB:Lbm (h.1549, Ser. 104, Nr. 6)

## Roedeberk

*Galop*
Band
EP (London, 1867) GB:Lbm (h.1544, Nr. 226)

## Roeder, O.

The following works are for band and were printed in London, ca. 1888–1892; shelf-marks given are for GB:Lbm.
*Polka*, h.1549, Ser. 85, Nr. 4
*The Sultan of Mocha*, h.1549, Ser. 93, Nr. 6

## Rosenstein, T.

*Romance*
Band
EP (London, 1896) GB:Lbm (h.1549, Ser. 101, Nr. 6)

## Royle, Thomas P.

*Valse*
Band
EP (London, 1894) GB:Lbm (h.1549, Ser. 96, Nr. 3)

## Schallehn

Galop, Death or Glory
Band
EP (London) GB:Lbm (h.1545, Nr. 5)

## Schmidt, G.

Quartet and Chorus, *Die Weibertreue*
Band
EP (London, 1871) GB:Lbm (h.1549, Ser. 40, Nr. 2)

## Seifert, Anton

*Quadrille*
Band
EP (London, 1876) GB:Lbm (h.1549, Ser. 57, Nr. 2)

## Seydel, Oscar

*March*
Band
EP (London, 1893) GB:Lbm (h.1549, Ser. 95, Nr. 6)

## St. Leger, W. N.

*Balaclava March*
1252-443, alto horn, bassi, percussion
EP (London, *Boosey's Military Journal*, Nr. 20, 1856) GB:Lbm; US:DW (757)

## Standhaft, R. F.

*Galop*
Band
EP (London, 1878) GB:Lbm (h.1544, Nr. 291)

## Stanford, Charles (1852–1924)

*Installation March*, Op. 108 (for the Chancellor of Cambridge University, 1892)
Band [cited in Grove, Fifth Edition]

(3) *Military Marches*, Op. 109, ca. 1892
Band [cited in Grove, Fifth Edition]

## Stasny

*Polka*
Band
EP (London, 1879) GB:Lbm (h.1549, Ser. 65, Nr. 5)

## Thomas, C. S.

*Funeral March*, 'In memoriam' (for the military funeral of Friedrich III)
Military band
MS DDR:Bds (Hausbibliothek) [lost]

## Tinney, F. G.

*Avalance Galop*
2252-453, percussion, bassi
EP (London, *Coote's Military Band Journal*, Nr. 7, ca. 1845) GB:Lbm; US:DW (753)

## Vasseur, J.

*Conti*
Band
EP (London, 1885) GB:Lbm (h.1544, Nr. 333)

## Vivian, L.

*Hampton Court Quick-Step*
Band
EP (London, 1867) F:Pn (Vm.27.12175)

## Vogler, C.

*Polka*
Band
EP (London, 1854) GB:Lbm (h.1543, Nr. 128)

## Waddell, James

*Fackeltanz*
4252-443, tenor clarinet, 2 tenor horn. bassi, percussion
MS (autograph) GB:Lbm (R.M.21.e.2); US:DW (767)

## Waldteufel, E.

The following works are for band and were printed in London, ca. 1879–1894; shelf-marks given are for GB:Lbm.
Valses: h.1549, Ser. 71, Nr. 4; h.1549, Ser. 69, Nr. 4; h.1549, Ser. 59, Nr. 1; h.1549, Ser. 83, Nr. 6; h.1544, Nr. 322
*Gouttes de rosee*, h.1544, Nr. 357
*La Plus belle*, h.1544, Nr. 301
*Declaration*, h.1544, Nr. 386
*La Source*, h.1544, Nr. 321
*Recits d'amour*, h.1549, Ser. 75, Nr. 6

## Waley, Simon W.

*Marche des guides*
Band
EP (London, 1856) GB:Lbm (h.1543, Nr. 154)

## Watson, William H.

The following works are for band and were printed in London, ca. 1886–1895; shelf-marks given are for GB:Lbm.
*March*, h.1544, Nr. 338
*Morris Dance*, h.1544, Nr. 396

## Webb, William

*Isle of Wight Slow March*
42-12
EP (London, Preston, ca. 1810) GB:En (Glen 347-16); US:DW (773)

## Weilland

*Harmonie*
222-02
EP (London, Broderip & Wilkinson, ca. 1800) GB:Lbm (H.125/20)

## Weill, Karl (First flute, band of George III)

(8) *Märsche*
1052-641, percussion
MS A:Wn (Sm.2291)

## West, Alfred H.

*March*
Band
EP (London, 1888) GB:Lbm (h.1544, Nr. 352)

## Williams, Warwick

The following works are for band and were printed in London, ca. 1883–1896; shelf-marks given are for GB:Lbm.
*Air varie*, h.1549, Ser. 74, Nr. 6
*Quadrille*, h.1549, Ser. 83, Nr. 3
*March*, h.1549, Ser. 100, Nr. 4
*Overture*, h.1549, Ser. 83, Nr. 1
*Cavatina*, h.1549, Ser. 101, Nr. 4
[Untitled], f.800.[284] (for solo cornet)
*Round-about*, h.1544, Nr. 320
*Merry England*, h.1544, Nr. 336

## Wood, James
*March*
Band
EP (London, 1890) GB:Lbm (h.1549, Ser. 88, Nr. 5)

## Ziehrer
*Galop*
Band
EP (London, 1869) GB:Lbm (h.1544, Nr. 236)

## Zikoff
*Mazurka*
Band
EP (London, 1879) GB:Lbm (h.1549, Ser. 54, Nr. 3)

# Index

# Index of Names

## A

Abadie, ?, 19th century French composer, 2
Abadie, Egbert, 19th century French composer, 2
Abadie, Jacques, 19th century French composer, 2
Abbiate, Charles, 19th century French composer, 2
Abdul Medjid, 19th century Turkish Sultan, 22
Abt, Franz, 1819–1885, German composer, 145
Acerbi, Domenico, 19th century Italian composer, 115
Achleitner, Rudolf, 19th century Austrian composer, 207
Ackermann, 19th century French composer, conductor 93e de Ligne, 3, 263
Adam, Charles Adolphe, 1803–1856, arranged for band, 253, 254
Adam, H. C., work arranged for band, 113
Adams, Thomas, 1785–1858, English composer, 263
Aerts, Felix, 19th century French composer, 3
Aibl, 19th century publisher in Munich, 151, 156
Aigrette (Pseud.), (1808), English composer, 263
Alba, A., 19th century French composer, 3
Albert, Johann, 1832–1915, German composer, 146
Alberti, D., 19th century French composer, 3
Albrechtsberger, Johann, 1736–1809, 207
Alday, l'âiné, b. 1763., 19th century French composer, 3
Alexandre, 19th century French composer, 3
Alexandre, E., 19th century French composer, 3
Alexandre, L., 19th century French composer, 3
Alexandre-Georges, ?, 19th century French composer, 3
Alfred, ?, German composer, 141
Alkan, Charles [Pseud. for Morhange], 1813–1888, French composer, 3
Allen, William, 19th century English composer, 263
Allier, Gabriel, 19th century French composer, 3
Allmann, H., 19th century French composer, 4
Almenraeder, Karl, 1786–1843, German composer, 146
Alquier, A.-L., 19th century French composer, 4
Altafulla, Ubaldo, 19th century Italian composer, 115
Altamira, J., 19th century French composer, 4
Amalie v. Prussen, as composer, 143
Amat, José, 19th century French composer, 4
Ambroz, Anton, 19th century German composer, conductor for K. K. Österreich 57. Linien-Inf. Reg. Grossherzog von Mecklenburg-Schwerin, 146
Amette, Louis, 19th century French composer, 4
Amillon, Édouard, 19th century English composer, 263
Amon, Johann, 1763–1825, German composer, 146
Amourdedieu, Casimir, 19th century French composer, 4
Amourdedieu, Pascal, 19th century French composer, 4ff

Anacker, M., 19th century Austrian composer, 207
Ancot, Jean, 1779–1848, Belgium composer, 259
André Johann, 1775–1842, German, as composer, 146
André, Johann, 19th century publisher in Offenbach, 153, 155, 156, 163, 164, 183
André, Ernest, 19th century French composer, 4
André, Paul, 19th century French composer, 4ff
Andreozzi, Gaetano, 19th century Italian composer, 263
Andrew, Enos, 19th century English composer, 263
Aniebas, J., 19th century English composer, 263
Anne of Prussia, 170
Anonymous, 275 Austrian works for band or Harmoniemusik, 203ff
Anonymous, 643 German works for band or Harmoniemusik, 143ff
Anschütz, Johann, 1772–1856, German composer, 146
Anschüz, G., German composer, 146
Ansel, M., 19th century English composer, 263
Ansiaux, Hubert (1825), Belgium composer, 259
Anton, C., 19th century German composer, 146
Antoni, ?, 19th century French composer, 2, 5
Antonio, Grotto, 1753–1831, Italian composer, 115
Apel, ?, 19th century composer, 5, 146
Apell, David (pseudo. Capelli), 1754–1832, German composer, 146
Appel, K., 19th century German composer, 146
Applin, W. T., 19th century English composer, 263
Arban, J. J., 1825–1889, 19th century French composer, 5
Arbuckle, John, 19th century English composer, 264
Archambeau, 19th century English composer, 264
Argoin, G., 19th century French composer, 5
Aristophanes, ancient Greek playwright, 27
Arnaud, C. T., 19th century French composer, 5
Arnaud, J., 19th century French composer, 115
Arnaud, P.-J., 19th century French composer, 5
Arnaud. E., 19th century French composer, 5
Arndt, C., 19th century German composer, 147
Arnold, F. W., 19th century German composer, band, 147
Arnoldi, Joseph, 19th century French composer, 6
Arnould, Eugene, 19th century French composer 6
Arnoux, A., 19th century French composer 6
Arsaut, Gabriel, 19th century French composer, 6
Arscott, Julius, 19th century English composer, 264
Artaria, 19th century publisher in Vienna, 246
Artique, P., 19th century French composer, 6
Artus, Alexandre, 19th century French composer, 1, 6

Asch, Georg, 19th century English composer, 264
Asche, W., 19th century German composer, conductor 1st Hanseatischen Regiment, Hamburg, 147
Ascher, Joseph, 1829–1869, English composer, 264
Ashton, T., 19th century French composer, 6
Asioli, Bonifazio, 1769–1832, Italian composer, 115
Asselin, Th., 19th century French composer, 6
Astoin, ?, 19th century French composer, 6
Auber, Daniel, 1782–1871, French composer, 28, 142, 163, 166, 173, 174, 196, 254
Aubert, Aug., 19th century French composer, 6
Aubert, Charles, 19th century French composer, 1, 6
Aubin, ?, 19th century French composer, 7
Aubréy du Boulley, Prudent, 1796–1870, French composer, 7
Aubry, Abel, 19th century French composer, 7
Audoir, Barthélemy, 19th century French composer, 7
Aufsess., B., 19th century German composer, 147
Augé, Claudo, 19th century French composer, 7
August, Prince, composer, 141
Aulagnier, 19th century publisher in Paris, 25
Auzende, Ange-Marie, 19th century French composer 7
Azémar, ?, 19th century French composer, 7
Azerets, ?, 19th century German composer, 147

## B

Bach, Chr., 19th century German composer, 147
Bach, Otto, 19th century Austrian composer, 207
Bach, Pierre, fl. 1800–1828, German composer, 147
Bach, Wilhelm Friedrich, German composer, 147
Bachimont, H., 19th century French composer, 7
Bachmann, 19th century publisher in Hannover, 155
Bachmayer, ?, 19th century Austrian composer, 208
Badart, Louis, 19th century French composer, 7
Baehr, 19th century German composer, 180
Bagarre, A., 19th century French composer, 7
Bagge, Selmar, 1823–1896, German composer, 147
Bagnat, ?, 19th century French composer 8
Baille, F., 19th century French composer, 8
Baille, Gabriel, 19th century French composer, 8
Baille, Martial, 19th century French composer 8
Baillon, Ad. Victor, 19th century French composer, conductor Musique au 127e, 8
Bajus, Z., 19th century French composer, 8
Balay, Guillaume, 19th century French composer, conductor, Garde Républicaine Band, 8
Baldiani, F., 19th century French composer, 8
Balfe, Michael, 1808–1870, Irish composer, 264
Ball, S., 19th century English composer, 264
Ballmüller, E., 19th century German composer, 147
Balocke, E., 19th century French composer, 8
Bangratz, A., 19th century French composer, 9
Banner, John, English composer, 264

Banta, Frank, 19th century English composer, 264
Barat, J. Ed., 19th century French composer, 9
Barbet, C., 19th century French composer 9
Bardin, V., 19th century French composer, 9
Baron, Eugéne, 19th century French composer, 9
Barraud, E., 19th century French composer, 9
Barrés, ?, 19th century French composer, 9
Barrett, Emmeline, 19th century English composer, 264
Barrett, R., 19th century English composer, 264
Barrier, A., 19th century French composer, 9
Barth, Freiderick, b. 1813, German composer, 147
Barthe, C., 19th century French composer, arranger, 9
Barthel, K., 19th century German composer, 148
Barthmann, Charles, 19th century English composer, 264
Bartholomeus, ?, 19th century English composer, 264
Bartholomeus, P., 19th century French composer, 9
Bary, A., 19th century French composer, 21
Basquit, Heinrich, 19th century English composer, 264
Bassus, Jean, 19th century German composer, 148
Baston, Edm., 19th century French composer 10
Batiste, Édouard, 1820–1876, composer, 10
Baucourt, A., 19th century French composer 10
Bauderuc, Jouan, 19th century French composer, 10
Baudin, Henry, 19th century French composer, 10
Bauller, A., de, 19th century French composer, 11
Bazin, Emmanuel, 1816–1878, French composer, 11
Beauce, 19th century publisher in Paris, 48, 61
Beaucherne, Raphaël, 19th century French composer, 11
Beaudonck, L.-J., 19th century French composer, 10
Beauvarlet-Charpentier, Jacques, 1766–1834, composer, 11
Bécher, L., 19th century French composer, 11
Bechler, Johann, 1784–1857, American composer, 137
Beck, Peter, 19th century German composer, 148
Beck, 19th century publisher in Vienna, 247
Becker, ?, 19th century English composer, 265
Becker, Heinrich, 19th century German composer, , 148
Becker, P., 19th century French composer, 11
Becker, Vincenz, 19th century German composer, 148
Bédard, ?, 19th century French composer, 11
Beer, Alfred, 19th century English composer, 265
Beethoven, Ludwig, van, 19th century German composer, arranged for band, 28, 30 51, 78, 102, 113, 141, 180, 208ff, 254,
Behr, Franz, 1837–1898, German composer, 148
Bekker, Johannes, b. 1826, Dutch composer, 125
Belcke, Friedrich, 1795–1874, German composer, 148
Belli, Sandre, Italian composer, 115
Bellini, Vincenzo, 1801–1835, Italian composer, arranged for band, 38, 122, 253, 254, 266
Bellmann, 19th century publisher in Dresden, 147, 175
Belloli, ca. 1840–1850, as arranger, 257
Belloli, Maestro nel IR Conservatorio di Musica, Milano, as arranger, 122

Bellon, J., 19th century French composer, 11
Bellroy de Reigny, work arranged for band, 113
Belval, E., 19th century French composer, 11
Belville, Edward, 19th century English composer, 265
Bénard, ?, 19th century French composer, 11
Bender, V., 19th century French composer, 12
Benedict, Sir Julius, 19th century English composer, 265
Benjamin, 19th century publisher in Hamburg, 182
Bennet, C. W., 19th century English composer, 265
Benoist, G(C), 19th century French composer, 12
Benoit, Petrus, 1834–1901, Belgium composer, 259
Benz, D., 19th century Austrian composer, 209
Beraud, G., 19th century French composer, 12
Berger, Ludwig, 1777–1839, German composer, 148
Bergmann, Eduard, 19th century English composer, 265
Bergson, M., 19th century English composer, 265
Berka, Frantisek, 19th century Austrian composer, 209
Berlioz, Hector, French composer, *Symphonie Funèbre et Triomphale* for band, 12
Berlioz, arranged for band, 196, 254
Berlyn, Aron, 1817–1870, Dutch composer, 125
Bernard, A., 19th century French composer, 12
Bernard, Emile, 1843–1902, French composer, 12
Berner, Friedrich, 1780–1827, German composer, 148
Bernier, Antony, 19th century French composer, conductor, la Musique Municipale de Nantes, 12
Bernini, Frediano, 19th century Italian composer, 115
Bernn, Alexandre, 19th century French composer, 12
Berr, ?, 19th century French composer, arranger, 1, 12, 70, 183
Berr, Friedrich, 1794–1838, famous clarinetist, 148
Bertain, Jules, 19th century French composer, 12
Berten, Léon, 19th century French composer, 13
Berth, ?, 19th century French composer, 72
Berthold, ?, 19th century German composer, 149
Berwald, Franz, 1796–1868, Swedish composer, 133
Beseda, ?, 19th century Austrian composer, 209
Bessière, ?, 19th century French composer, 13
Beyerbach, ?, as arranger, 256, 257
Bibl, Rudolf, 1832–1902, Austrian composer, 209
Bidgood, Thomas, 19th century English composer, 265
Bignon, Paul, 19th century French composer, 13
Billaut, A., 19th century French composer, 13
Billaut, J.-B.-A., 19th century French composer, 13
Billaut, Louis, 19th century French composer, 13
Billema, ?, 19th century English composer, 265
Billert, Karl, 1821–1875, German composer, 149
Billot, ?, 19th century French composer, 13
Biloir, Joseph, 19th century French composer, 13
Bilse, Benjamin, 1811–1902, German composer, 149
Bimboni, Gioacchino, 19th century Italian arr., 115
Birk (Birck), Charles, 19th century French composer, 13
Birnbach, ?, 19th century German composer, 149

Birnbaum, ?, German composer, 253
Bisch, F., 19th century French composer, 13
Bishop, Henry, 1786–1855, English composer, 265
Bitterman, Carl, 19th century German composer, 150
Bláha, Filip, 19th century Austrian composer, 209
Blake, Charles, 19th century English composer, 265
Blanc, P., 19th century French composer, 14
Blancheteau, ?, 19th century French composer 14, 265
Blanckeman, L., 19th century French composer, 1, 15
Blangy, Auguste, 19th century French composer, 15
Blasius. F., 19th century French composer, 1, 15, 253
Bléger, A., 19th century French composer 15
Bléger, Michel, 19th century French composer, 15ff
Blemant, Louis, 19th century French composer, 16
Blieck, Ad., 19th century French composer, 16
Blon, Franz von, 1861–1945, German composer, 150
Blumenfeldt, Aron, b. ca. 1827, German composer, 150
Blumenthal, C., 19th century Austrian composer, 209
Blumenthal, Leopold, 19th century Austrian composer, 209
Blummer, Martin, 1827–1901, German composer, 150
Boara, Giovanni, 19th century Italian composer, 116
Bocchorone, R., (1839) Austrian composer, 209
Bochsa, 19th century French composer, 1
Bochsa, 19th century publisher in Paris, 17
Bochsa, Charles, 1789–1856, French composer, arranger, 17, 180
Bochsa, Karl, Ad., 19th century French composer, 17, 180
Bogaerde, F. L., 19th century English composer, 266
Boggetti, Edwin, 19th century English composer, 266
Boh, Alb., 19th century German composer, 150
Bohm, ?, 19th century Austrian composer, 209
Böhm, 19th century publisher in Augsburg, 160, 217
Böhme, 19th century publisher in Hamburg, 147, 167, 182
Böhner, Johann, 1787–1860, German composer, , 150
Boieldieu, A., 1775–1835, French composer, arranger for band, 17, 141, 179, 254
Boisdeffre, René, 1838–1906, French composer, 17
Bolardt, Thomas, 19th century Austrian composer, 209
Bolzoni, Giovanni, 1841–1919, Italian composer, 116
Bonasegla, Carl, b. 1779, German composer, 150
Bonenfant, F., ? 19th century French composer, 17
Bonnelle, A., 19th century French composer, 17
Bonnelle, V., 19th century French composer, 17
Bonnisseau, ?, 19th century French composer, 17, 266
Bonnot, 19th century French composer, 1
Bonnot, C., 19th century French composer, conductor, 14e de Ligne, 1, 17
Bonvin, Ludwig, 1850–1939, German composer, , 150
*Boosey's Military Jounal*, London, 264
Borel, G., 19th century French composer, 18
Borovansky, ?, 19th century Austrian composer, 210
Borrea, Manuel, 19th century French composer, 18
Borrel, H., 19th century French composer, 18

Bosch, ?, 19th century French composer, 18
Boscher, A., 19th century French composer, 18
Bosisio, ?, 19th century English composer, 266
Bost (Rost), ?, 19th century German composer, 150
Bote & Bock, 19th century publisher in Berlin, 174, 188
Bothe, Gustav, 19th century German composer, 150
Bouchel, J., 19th century French composer, 18
Boudier, Achille, 19th century French composer, 19
Boué, Ernest, 19th century French composer, conductor Musique de 13e Leger, 1, 19
Bouffil, clarinetist in Paris, ca. 1820, 19
Bougon, ?, 19th century French composer, 19
Bouillon, Paul, 19th century French composer, 19
Boujut, ?, 19th century French composer, 19
Boulcourt, Alfred, 19th century English composer, 266
Boullard, Marius, 19th century French composer, 19
Bourdeau, 19th century French composer, conductor 44e de Ligne, 1
Bourdon, J. 19th century French composer, 19
Bourgault-Ducoudray, 19th century French composer, 20
Bourgeois, Ed., 19th century French composer, 20
Bourgeois, Jules, 19th century French composer, 20
Bourgoin, 19th century French composer, conductor 5e Lanciers, 2
Bournigal, Léon, 19th century French composer, 20
Bourquier, Fréd., 19th century French composer, 20
Bourrellis, H.-J., 19th century French composer, 20
Bousquet, Narcisse, 19th century French composer, 1, 20, 266
Bousquier, L., 19th century French composer, 20ff
Bouthel, L., 19th century French composer, 21
Bouvier, B., 19th century French composer, 21
Boyer, Louis, 19th century French composer, 21
Boyer, Th., 19th century French composer, 21
Braham, Charles, 19th century English composer, 267
Brahms, Johannes, 1833–1897, 151
Brambilla, ?, 19th century Italian composer, 116
Brandts Buys, H. F. R., b. 1850, Dutch composer, 125
Bratfisch, A., (1865) German composer, 151
Braun, ?, 19th century French composer, 21
Braun, C., (ca. 1885) German composer, 151
Braunschweig, Duke, composer, 141
Breitkopf & Härtel, 19th century publisher in Leipzig, 17, 49, 70, 107, 150, 155, 156, 157, 162, 166, 168, 172, 173, 174, 182, 188, 209, 220, 227, 229, 236, 239, 247, 252,
Brépsant, Engbert, 19th century French composer, 2, 21, 267
Bretonnière, V., 19th century French composer, professor of music for the Turkish ambassador in Paris, 1, 22
Brewer, Josiah, 19th century English composer, 267
Brewer, Mark, 19th century English composer, 267
Bridge, Sir John, 19th century English composer, 267
Briffaux, J. B., 19th century composer, 267
Briggs, E. C., 19th century English composer, 267

Briscot, Charles, 19th century French composer, 22
Brody, A., 19th century French composer, 22
Brooks, C., 19th century English composer, 267
Brooks, E., 19th century English composer, 267
Bru, C., 19th century French composer, military conductor, 8e de Ligne, 1
Bru, G. C., 19th century French composer, 2
Bru, Jean (Pseud: Bellacour, Jeannette), 19th century French, 22
Bruckner, Anton, 1824–1896, 210
Brun, Georges, b. 1878, French composer, 22
Brunet, L., 19th century composer, 267
Brunette, ?, 19th century English composer, 267
Bruyer, Victor, 19th century French composer, 22
Bruyne, E. de, 19th century French composer, 22
Bucalossi, Ernest, 19th century English composer, 267
Bucalossi, Procida, 19th century English composer, 268
Buchholz, ?, (1876) German composer, 151
Büchler Ferd., 1817–1891, German composer, 151
Buffet, 19th century publisher in Paris, 8
Buffet-Crampon, early 20th century publisher in Paris, 111
Buhl, Joseph, b. 1781, French composer, 22
Bulan, Charles, 19th century French composer, 22
Bülow, Hans von, 1830–1894, German composer, 151
Buot, Victor, 19th century French composer, conductor, Musique de l'Artillerie de la Garde, 2, 23
Burald, ?, 19th century English composer, 268
Burbure de Wesembeek, 1812–1889 Belgium composer, 259
Burckhardt, ?, 19th century English composer, 268
Bureau des arts et d'industrie, 19th century publisher in Vienna, 220
Buresch, Adalbert, as arr., 256
Bürg, R., 19th century German composer, 151
Burgmann, ?., French composer, 24
Burmeister, Paul, 19th century German composer, 151
Burns, Felix, Sr., 19th century English composer, 268
Buskies, Rudolph, 19th century German composer, 151
Buzzolla, Antonio, 1815–1871, Italian composer, 116

## C

Cagliero, Giovanni, 1838–1926, Italian composer, 116
Calcott, J. W., 19th century English composer, 268
Califf, ?, 19th century Italian composer, 116
Camas, A. de, 19th century French composer, Capitaine au 2e de Chasseurs à pied, 1
Cambart, A., 19th century French composer, 46
Cambier, Victor, 19th century French composer, 24, 268
Camomille, J., 19th century French composer, 24
Campenhaut, François, 1779–1848, Belgium composer, 259
Canaple, Henri, 19th century French composer, 24
Canivez, L., 19th century French composer of works, 24
Capati, R. D., 19th century English composer, 268
Capelli, ?, [see Apell, David]

Cappon, A., 19th century French composer, 1
Carafa, Michele, 1787–1872, French composer, 24
Carbon, ?, 19th century English composer, 268
Carcassone, Georges, 19th century French composer, 24
Cardew, Phil., 19th century English composer, 268
Carl August of Weimar, 227
Carl, Carl, 1830–1898, German composer, 151ff
Carl, Günther Friedrich, Prince of Schwarzenburg, 184
Carl, Gustav, (1875) German composer, 152
Carnicer, Ramon, 1789–1855, Spanish composer, 131
Carolina, empress of Austria [1837], 226
Carraut, L., 19th century French composer, 25
Carre, 19th century publisher in Paris, 7
Carrié, Louis, 19th century French composer, 25
Carter, Henry, 19th century English composer, 268
Carteron, Alexandre, 19th century French composer, 25
Carulli, Benedetto, 1797–1877, Italian composer, 116
Casquil, ?, 19th century French composer, 25
Cassard, L., 19th century French composer, 25
Castela, A., 19th century French composer, 25
Castil-Blaze, François, d. 1857, French composer, 25
Cauchie, F., 19th century French composer, 25
Caudron, L., 19th century French composer, 25
Caussinus, V., 19th century French composer, 25
Causy, ?, 19th century French composer, 25
Cavailini, P., 19th century English composer, 268
Cavaillé-Massenet, F., 19th century French composer, 26
Cavos, 19th century German composer, 141
Cayron, J., 19th century French composer, 26
Cellier, Alfred, 19th century English composer, 268
Cerclier, Jules-H.-L., 19th century French composer, 26
Chambroux, J., 19th century French composer, 26
Chanel, 19th century publisher in Lyon, 1
Chapelle, Ed., 19th century French composer, 26
Chargnioux, Marie, 19th century French composer, 26
Charigny, J.-A.-L, 19th century French composer, 26
Charles X, 43, 149
Charles, ?, 19th century French composer, 26
Charles, Prince of Baviere, 187
Charlotte de Saxe, Princesse, 170
Charlotte von Preussen, German composer, 152
Chassain, Raoul, 19th century French composer, 26
Chasseigneau, Paul, 19th century French composer, 26
Chassin, A., 19th century French composer, 26
Chaulier, Cyriaque, 19th c. French comp., conductor, Musique au 6md de Ligne, 27
Chausson, Ernest, 1855–1899, French composer, 27
Chavatte, Henri, 19th century French composer, 27
Chelard, Hippolyte, 1789–1861, German composer, arranger, 152, 196
Chemischen Druckerey, 19th century publisher in Vienna, 211, 220, 218, 241, 243
Cherubini, Luigi, 1760–1842, 27

Cherubini, arranged for band, 141, 196, 197, 245
Chevalier, R., 19th century French composer, 27
Chic, Léon, 19th century French composer, conductor 66e de Ligne, 1, 2, 28
Chomel, L., 19th century French composer, 28
Choquard, E., 19th century French composer, 29
Cianchi, Emilio, 19th century Italian composer, 116
Cimarosa, Domenico, 1749–1801, Italian composer, 122
Cimoso, Domenico, 1780–1850, Italian composer, 116
Clapisson, Louis, 1808–1966, French composer, 29 [biographical note]
Clement, J., 19th century English composer, 268
Clendon, Hugh, 19th century English composer, 268
Clodomir, P., 19th century French composer, 29
Coccon, Nicolo, 1826–1903, Venetian composer, , 116
Codivilla, Filippo, b. 1841, Italian composer, , 117
Cohen, Karl, 1851–1938, German composer, , 152
Col. J., 19th century French composer, conductor 66e de Ligne, 1
Coll, Joseph, 19th century French composer, 29
Collardo, ? composer in Schlesinger collection, 141
Collauf, ?, 19th century American composer, 137
Collection, 20 Italian *Märsche* for military band, 115
Collection, anonymous Polish group of 71 works without titles, 1800–1868, 129
Collection, anonymous Polish, ten *Polonoises*, 1800–1868, 130
Collection, US, 11th US Infantry, 1862, for band, 137
Collection, US, 25th Mass. Regiment band books, 70 works for band, 137
Collection, US, 26th Regimental Band, NC, c. 1862–1865, parts for band, 137
Collection, US, 3rd New Hampshire Infantry band books, 50 works for band, 137
Collection, US, *Brass Band Journal*, 1854, 137
Collection, US, of dances, marches, 65 full scores, 137
Collection, US, Stratton *Military Band Journal*, 1866–1871, 150 works, 137
Collet, 19th century publisher in Paris, 36
Colline, Victor, 19th century English composer, 269
Colmier, L., 19th century French composer, 29
Comina, W., 19th century French composer, 29
Commer, Franz, 1813–1887, German composer, 152
Conor, Léon, 19th century French composer, 29
Conradi, A., 19th century English composer, 269
Conradi-Carlshall, W., (1864) German composer, 152
Constant, H., 19th century French composer, 30
Constantini, Francesco, 1789–1854, Italian composer, 117
Conterno, G. E., 19th century English composer, 269
Conti, A., 19th century French composer, 30
Cook, H. J., 19th century English composer, 269
Cooke, Grattan, 19th century English composer, 269
Coote, Charles, Jr., 19th century English composer, 269
Coote, Charles, Sr., 19th century English composer, 269

Coqquelin, G., 19th century French composer, 30
Coqueterre, 19th century French arranger, conductor, 13e Artillerie, 2
Coqulet, O., 19th century French composer, 30
Coquterre, François, 19th century French composer, 30
Corbin, A., 19th century French composer, 30
Cordier, 19th century publisher in Paris, 5
Correvon de Ribaucourt, Marie-Louise, 19th c. Fr. composer, 31
Cortazar, M., 19th century French composer, 31
Cossart, Leland, b. 1877, German composer, 152
Cotischau, 19th century German composer, 180
Cotté, E., 19th century French composer, 31
Couldery, Claudius, 19th century English composer, 269
Couleuvrier, 19th century French composer, 31
Courbet, Admiral [dedication], 28
Courtin, ?, 19th century French composer, 31
Cousin, H., 19th century French composer, conductor, 2nd Rég. Da Génie, 1
Couthier, E., 19th century French composer, 31
Cowen, Sir. Frederic, 19th century English composer, 269
Coyon, Emile, 19th century French composer, 31
Crémont, Pierre, 1784–1846, French composer, 31
Cressonnois, Jules, 19th century French composer, 32
Creste, W., 19th century French composer, 32
Crispin, Eugene, 19th century French composer, 32
Croes, H., 19th century composer, 180
Croft, Frederick, 19th century English composer, 269
Croisez, ?, 19th century English composer, 269
Crowe, Alfred, 19th century English composer, 270
Curschmann, Karl, 1805–1841, German composer, 153
Czibulka, Alphons, 1842–1894, composer, 153, 270

# D

Dagnelies, D., 19th century French composer, 32
Dal Vasco, Agostino, Italian composer, 117
Dalayrac, works arranged for band, 197
Dale, 19th century publisher in London, 263
Dallée, ?, 19th century French composer, 2, 32
Damian, François, 19th century French composer, 32
Dasque, Auguste, 19th century French composer, 32
Dassonville, ?, 19th century French composer, 32
Daunot, Louis, 19th century French composer, 32
Dauprat, Louis, 1781–1868, French composer, 33
Davenne, A., 19th century French composer, 33
Davergne, A., 19th century French composer, 33
David, Édouard, 19th century French composer, 33
David, Félicien, 1810–1876, French composer, 33
David, 19th century publisher in Paris, 4, 11
Dawid, Josef, as arranger, 130
De Wailly, L., b. 1854, French composer, 36
Deacon, Charles, 19th century English composer, 270
Debrière ?, 19th century French composer, 33
Declerck, 19th century French composer, 2
Decq, A., 19th century French composer, 33
Dédé, Eugéne, 19th century French composer, 33
Delabaut, Paul, 19th century French composer, 33
Delarue, J., 19th century French composer, 33
Delâtre, Lucien, 19th century French composer, 33
Delattre, A., 19th century French composer, 33
Delaunay, P.-D., 19th century French composer, 34
Delaundis, Ad., 19th century French composer, 34
Delaye, Georges, 19th century French composer, 34
Delbove, ?, 19th century French composer, 34
Delchavalerie, Henri, 19th century French composer, 34
Dellac, H., 19th century French composer, 34
Delsouc, F., 19th century French composer, 34
Demance, 19th century French composer, 34
Demaré, E., 19th century French composer, 34
Demersseman, Jules, A. E. 19th century French composer, 34
Déo, Louis, 19th century French composer, 34
Deola, Paolo, 19th century Italian composer, 117
Déplace, Claude, 19th century French composer, 35
Deransart, Édouard, 19th century French composer, 35
Dervieux, ?, 19th century French composer, 35
Desailly, L., 19th century French composer, 35
Desblins, A., 19th century English composer, 270
Deschalumeaux, work arranged for band, 197
Descoins, ?., 19th century French composer, 35
Deserbelles, Claude, 19th century French composer, 35
Deshayes, ?, 19th century French composer, 35
Desiro, ?, Italian composer, 117
Dessane, 19th century French composer, 1
Dessane, L. A., 19th century French composer, 1, 2, 35
Destrube, ?, 19th century French composer, 35
Desvignes, Pierre, late 19th century French composer, 36
Dethou, Léon, 19th century French, *Treatise on Instrumentation*, 36
Devasini, Giuseppe, 1822–1878, Italian composer, 117
Devienne, François, 1759–1803, French composer, arranger, 113, 141
Diabelli, Anton, 1781–1858, Austrian composer, publisher, 243, 244, 254
Dias, J.-B., 19th century French composer, 36
Dickhut, ?, 1800–1828, German composer, 153
Dieppo, 19th century French composer, 2
Dierolf, H., 19th century French composer, 36
Dietsch, Pierre, 1808–1865, French composer , 36
Dignam, Walter, 19th century American composer, 137
Divoir, Victor, S., 19th century French composer, 36
Dodwell, Samuel, 19th century English composer, 270
Dodworth, Allen, 19th century American composer, 137
Doering, ?, 19th century French composer, 36
Doinelle, A., 19th century French composer, 36
Dolezálek, Jan, 1780–1858, 210
Domerque, Charles, 19th century French composer, 36

Domerque, F., 19th century French composer, 36
Donderer, Benedick, 19th century German composer, 153
Donizetti, Gaetono, 1797–1848, Italian composer, arranged for band, 28, 43, 62, 117, 118, 174, 253, 255
Donizetti, Giuseppe, 118
Donjon, Johannes, 19th century French composer, 37
Dörffeld, 19th century German composer, 141
Dorfner, Felise, 19th century Austrian composer, 210
Dornaus, Jr., 1800–1828, German composer, 153
Dornheckter, Robert, 1839–1890, German composer, 153
Dornois, ?, 19th century French composer, 37
Douard, A., 19th century French composer, conductor, 51e de Ligne, 1, 2, 37
Doubravsky, Frantisck, 19th century Czech composer, 211
Dozlowski, Józef, 1757–1831, Polish composer, 130
Dreher, Jos, 19th century German composer, 153
Drobisch, Karl, 1803–1854, German composer, 153
Dubez, ?, 19th century Hungarian composer, 211
Dubois, Charles, 19th century French composer, 37
Dubois, Theodore, 1837–1924, 37
Dubreu, F., 19th century French composer, 37
Dubreuil, E., 19th century French composer, 37
Dufant et Dubos, 19th century publisher in Paris, 97, 106, 107, 220
Dufayel, ?, 19th century French composer, 72
Duhamel, ?, 19th century French composer, 38
Dukas, Paul, 1865–1935, 38
Duke of Wellington, 265
Dumaine, A., 19th century French composer, 38
Dumas, 19th century French composer, conductor a bord du Montebello, 2
Dumas, Alexandre, 19th century French composer, conductor Musique a bord du Montebello, 38
Dunkler, Franc, 1816–1878, German composer, 153
Dunkler, Franz, 1779–1861, Dutch composer for band, 125
Dupart, Charles, 19th century French composer, 38
Dupiré, A., 19th century French composer, 38
Dupouy, A., 19th century French composer, 39
Duprato, Jules, 19th century French composer,, 39
Duquat, ?, 19th century French composer, 39
Durand, 19th century publisher in Paris, 86, 96
Dureau, Th., 19th century French composer, 39
Durrieu, Paul, 19th century French composer, 39
Durrieu, R., 19th century French composer, 39
Dusautoy, ?, 19th century French composer, 39
Dussap, Dey., 19th century French composer, 39
Dussek, Jan, 1760–1812, Czech composer, 178, 253
Dust, Charles, 19th century English composer, 270
Dvořák, Antonín, Bohenian composer, 211
Dwurzek, Josef, (1852), Czech composer, 211
Dyke, Robert, 19th century English composer, 270

E

Eaton, E. K., 19th century American composer, 137
Eaton, William, 19th century English composer, 271
Ebend, 19th century publisher in Paris, 7, 46, 59, 62, 109, 148, 155, 156, 158, 162, 163, 164, 168, 170, 178, 183, 188, 240ff, 246
Ebers, Charles, 1770–1836, German composer, 153
Eberwein, Traugott, 1775–1831, German composer, 153
Ebner, 19th century publisher in Stuttgart, 154
Eckard, C., composer, 142
Eckhardt, Josef, 19th century Austrian composer, 211
Eckschlager, R., 19th century Austrian composer, 211
Eder, Philipp, 19th century Austrian composer, 211
Eder, 19th century publisher in Vienna, 241, 246
Egal, J., 19th century French composer, 39
Egger, Franz, as arranger, 255
Egwolf, Joseph (1870), German composer, 153
Eichhorn, A., German composer, march for band, 154
Eilenberg, Richard, 19th century English composer, 271
Eilhardt, Friedrich 19th century German composer, 154
Eitzenberger, Joseph (1845), Austrian composer, 211
Elector of Hesse (1830), 189
Elise von Bayern, Princess, 173
Elliot, Stanislaus, 19th century English composer, 271
Elrington, William, 19th century English composer, 271
Elwart, Antoine, 1808–1877, French composer, 39
Embury, ?, 19th century English composer, 271
Emmerig, Joseph (1827), German composer, 154
Emmert, Adam 19th century, Austrian composer 211
Enckhausen, ?, fl. 1800–1828, German composer, 154
Endres, Franz (1805), German composer, 154
Engelhardt, P., as arranger, 142
Enzinger, Ludwig, 19th century German composer, 154
Eppinger, ?, 19th century Austrian composer, 211
Ercilla, B. de, 19th century English composer, 271
Erkel, Ferenc, 1810–1893, Austrian composer, 212
Ernesti, Titus, 19th century Austrian composer, 212
Ernst, Edouard, 19th century French composer, 39
Ernst, Heinrich, 1814–1865, Austrian composer, 212
Escudié, H., 19th century French composer, 40
Esterl, ?, (1898) German composer, 154
Etchepare, H., 19th century French composer, 40
Eters, 19th century publisher in Leipzig, 183
Ett, Casper, 19th century German composer, 154
Ettling, Emile, 19th century French composer, 2, 40
Eugen zu Bentheim-Bentheim, Fürsten, 161
Eurich, 19th century publisher in Linz, 243
Eustache, Charles, 19th century French composer, 40
Evans, Charles, 19th century English composer, 271
Evette & Schaeffer, 19th century publisher in Paris, 34, 67
Eybert, ?, 19th century French composer, 40
Eybler, Joseph, 1765–1846, Austrian composer, 212

## F

Fabre, Casimir, 19th century French composer, 40
Fackler, M., (1840), German composer, 154
Fahrbach, Anton, 19th century Austrian composer, 212
Fahrbach, J., (1840) Austrian composer, 212
Fahrbach, Philipp, 1815–1885, 197
Fahrbach, Philipp, Jr., 19th century Austrian composer, 212
Fahrbach, Philipp, Sr., 19th century Austrian composer, 196, 212
Fahrbach, arranged for band, 186
Faisst, Immanuel, 1823–1895, German composer, 154
Fajolle, A., 19th century French composer, 40
Falter, 19th century publisher in Munich, 183, 185, 186, 195
Faltis, Josef, 19th century Austrian composer, 213
Fanciulli, Francesco, 19th century American composer, 138
Fanst, Karl, 19th century Austrian composer, 213
Fanucchi, Domenico (ca. 1839), Italian composer, 118
Fare, Florence (pseud., A. W. Rawlings), 19th century English composer, 271
Farigoul, J., 19th century French composer, 41
Farrell, James, 19th century English composer, 271
Farrenc, Jeanne-Louise, 1804–1875, composer, 41
Fasquel, ?, 19th century French composer, 41
Fauconier, B. C., 19th century Belgium composer, 259
Faurel, ?, 19th century French composer, 41
Faust, C., 19th century English composer, 271
Favre, E., 19th century French composer, 41
Favre, Joanny, 19th century French composer, 41
Favre-Danne, E., 19th century French composer, 41
Feautrier, E., 19th century French composer, 41
Feautrier, L., 19th century French composer, 41
Febore, Gustave, 19th century French composer, 42
Febvre, F., (1867), German composer, 154
Fechner, A. M., 19th century English composer, 271
Fedou, A., 19th century French composer, 42
Fendt, A., (1812) Austrian composer, 213
Ferand, Henri, 19th century French composer, 42
Ferranti, L., 19th century French composer, 42
Ferri, Angelo, 19th century Italian composer, 118
Fesca, Alexander, 1820–1849, German composer, 154
Fessy, Alexandre, 19th century French composer, 42
Festival Artistique, 19th century publisher in Paris, 5
Fétis, François, 1784–1871, Belgium composer, 259
Fetras, Oscar, 19th century English composer, 271
Fiala, Alois, 19th century Austrian composer, 213
Fiala, Anton (1867) Austrian composer, 213, 255
Fibiger, Jan, 19th century Austrian composer, , 213
Fichu, J., 19th century French composer, 43
Fiedler, ?, fl. 1800–1828, German composer, 155
Fiehrer, 19th century English composer, 272
Field, Alfred, 19th century English composer, 272
Filiberti, ?, 19th century French composer, 43
Fiquet, ?, 19th century French composer, 43
Fiquet, Gabriel, 19th century French composer, 43
Fiquet, Montididier, 19th century French composer, 43
Fischer, 19th century publisher in Frankfurt, 157
Fischer, ?, as arranger, 113
Fischer, C., fl. 1800–1828, German composer, 155
Fischer, Emile, 19th century French composer, 43
Fischer, G., 19th century French composer, arranger, 34, 43
Fischer, Heinrich, (1815) German composer, 155
Fischer, Hermann, 19th century German composer, 155
Fischer, J. G. C., 1800–1828, German composer, 155
Fischlin, E., 19th century French composer of works, 43
Flad, Anton, 19th century German oboist, 191
Flèche, F., 19th century French composer, 44
Fleury, B., 19th century French composer, 44
Flori, ?, 19th century French composer, 44
Florschutz, Eucharius, b. 1757, German composer, 155
Foare, Charles, 19th century French composer, 44
Fondard, J. T., 19th century French composer, 44
Fontbonne, Leon, principal flute, Garde Républicaine Band, 91
Fontebasso, Pietro, 19th century Italian composer, 118
Fontenelle, Emile, 19th century French composer, 44
Forberg, 19th century publisher in Leipzig, 148, 154
Förster, 19th century publisher in Breslau, 179
Foster, D., 19th century English composer, 272
Fouant, Jolibois, 19th century French composer, 44
Fouque, Octave, 19th century French composer, 44
Fournier, C., 19th century French composer, 44
Française I, 74
François, ?, 19th century French composer, 44
François, Emile, 19th century French composer, 44
François, L., 19th century French composer, 44
Frank, Ernst, 1847–1889, German composer, 155
Franke, F. C., 19th century German composer, 155
Franke, Theodor, 19th century English composer, 272
Franz Josef, Austrian emperor, 80, 209, 211, 226, 240
Fränzel (Frantzl), (1803), German composer, 155
Fraulich, Joseph, 19th century Austrian composer, 214
Fré-d'rick, L., 19th century French composer, 45
Frédéric Guillaume de Prusse, 171
Frédéric of Hesse, 170
Frederick the Great, 141 [as composer], 143
Fredhe, ?, 19th century English composer, 272
Frére, 19th century publisher in Paris, 11
Frese, C., 19th century German composer, 155
Frewin, Edward, 19th century English composer, 272
Frey, 19th century Publisher in Paris, 48, 60, 109
Fricke, C., 19th century English composer, 272
Fried, Gotther, 19th century Austrian composer, 214
Friedemann, F., 19th century German composer, 155
Friedheim, ?, 19th century French composer, 45
Friedrich Franz III, 160
Friedrich Wilhelm von Prussia (1870), 151

Friedrich August von Sachsen, king, 168
Friedrich der Niederlande (and Prinzessin Louise, 1828), 184
Friedrich Franz I, Grossherzog, 145
Friedrich II, King, 19th century German, 148, 155 [as composer], 159
Friedrich Leopold v. Anhalt-Dessau, 188
Friedrich Wilhelm IV, German, 154, 156 [as composer], 195
Friedrich Wilhelm [dedication], 173
Friedrich, Wilh. III, King, German, 155 [as composer], 235
Frier, ?, 19th century French composer, 45
Friesse, 19th century publisher in Dresden, 183
Frion, Eugène, 19th century French composer, 45
Frisnais, 19th century French composer, conductor, 34e de Ligne, 1, 45
Fritsch, E., 19th century French composer, 45
Fröhlich, ?, 19th century German composer, 156
Frohmann, C., 19th century Austrian composer, 214
Fromentin, L., 19th century French composer, 45
Fromont, Célestin, 19th century French composer, 45
Fuchs, Julius (1867) German composer, 156
Fucik, Julius, 19th century Czech composer, 214
Führer, Robert, 19th century Austrian composer, 214
Furgeot, J., 19th century French composer, 45

## G

Gabetti, Giuseppe, 1796–1862, Italian composer, 253
Gabriel, ?, 19th century French composer, 45
Gabrielli, Graf Nicolaus, 1814–91, German composer, 156
Gache, F., 19th century French composer, 45
Gadenne, Henri, 19th century French composer, 45
Gaffet, E., 19th century French composer, 45
Gagne, fils., 19th century French composer, 45
Gaillaguet, E., 19th century French composer, 46
Gaillard, C., 19th century French composer, 46
Gaittet, J. B., 19th century French composer, 46
Galli, Amintore, 1845–1919, Italian composer, 118
Gambaro, 19th century publisher in Paris, 2, 5, 12, 19, 31, 46, 54, 70, 164
Gand, jeune, 19th century French composer, 46
Gandner, Victor, 19th century French composer, 1, 2, 46
Ganne, Louis, 19th century French composer, 47
Gänsbacher, Johann, 1778–1844, Austrian composer, arranger, 214, 257
Gantz, J., 19th century French composer, 47
Garciau, Ernest, 19th century French composer, 47
Garibaldi, Giuseppe, 1807–1882, Italian politician, 10 [dedication]
Gariel, arr., 19th century French arranger, conductor, 2e Carabiniers, 2
Gariel, J. A. V., 19th century French composer, 47
Garnier, Felix, 19th century French composer, 47
Garot, Pierre, 19th century French composer, 47
Garrouste, J., 19th century French composer, 47

Gasparini, Giovanni, 19th century Italian composer, 118
Gasser, Alexandre, 19th century French composer, 47
Gasser, Victor, 19th century French composer, 47
Gassner, G., 19th century English composer, 272
Gattermann, Hubert, 19th century French composer, 47
Gattermann, Philippe, 19th century French composer, 48
Gattermann, Prosper, 19th century French composer, 48
Gaubert, Eugène, professor at the Conservatoire de Lille, 110
Gaudefroy, E., 19th century French composer, 48
Gautier, Léon, 19th century French composer, 48
Gautrol, 19th century publisher in Paris, 145
Gavaldá, José, fl. 1818–1890, Spanish composer, 131
Gaveaux, G., 19th century publisher in Paris, 48
Gaveaux, 19th century publisher in Paris, 15, 59
Gaveaux, Pierre, work arranged for band, 113
Gaveaux, S., 19th century publisher in Paris, 48
Gebauer, François René, 19th century French composer, 48
Gebaur, Franz, 1784–1822, German composer, 156
Gebel, ?, fl. 1800–1828, Austrian composer, 214
Gebel, A. François, fl. ca. 1834, composer, 48
Geisler, Victor, 19th century Austrian composer, 214
Gélin, Charles, 19th century French composer, 48
Gellert, ?, 19th century Austrian composer, 214
Genard, ?., 19th century French composer, 48
General Bertrand, 144
Général Lafayette [dedication], 183
General Walter, 235
Generali, Pietro, 1773–1832, Italian composer, 118
Genin, T., 19th century French composer, 48
Gentil, Victor, 19th century French composer, 49
Gentsch, E., (1863), German composer, 156
Georges, Jules, 19th century French composer, 49
Gérard, Marcelin, 19th century French composer, 49
Gérin, Louis, 19th century French composer, 49
Gerke, Auguste, 19th century French composer, 49, 156
Germain, Emile, 19th century French composer, 49
Gesus, R., 19th century French composer, 49
Gibert, ?, arranger, 113
Gibert, Antoine, 19th century French composer, 49
Gilg., Frz, 19th century German composer, 204
Gillard, F., 19th century French composer, 50
Gillet, F., 19th century French composer, 50
Gilmore, Patrick, 19th century American composer for band, 138
Gilson, Paul, 1865–1942, Belgium composer, 259
Giorza, Paul, 19th century Italian composer, 118
Girard, L., 19th century French composer, 50
Giraud, Adolphe, 19th century French composer, 50
Girerd, Edouard, ?, 19th century French composer, 50
Girolet, ?, 19th century French composer, 50
Givord, ?, 19th century French composer, 50
Gleize, F., 19th century French composer, 50
Gloger, 19th century German composer, 141

Glöggel, 19th century publisher in Vienna, 242, 244
Glover, Charles, 19th century English composer, 272
Gluck, Christoph, 1714–1787, German composer, 141, 248
Gnisson, Emile, 19th century French composer, 48
Godard, Amédée, 19th century French composer, 50
Godard, Charles, 19th century Austrian composer, 214
Godefroid, 19th century French composer, 2
Godfrey, Adolphus, 19th century English composer, 272
Godfrey, Arthur, 19th century English composer, 273
Godfrey, Charles, Jr., 19th century English composer, 273
Godfrey, Charles, Sr., 19th century English composer, 273
Godfrey, Sr. Daniel, 19th century English composer, 273
Goepfert, 19th century German composer, 180
Goethe, German poet, 227
Goguelat, E., 19th century French composer, conductor, 56e de Ligne, 1
Golde, J. (1813–1815), German composer, 156
Goldmark, Carl, 1830–1915, Austrian composer, 215
Gombart, 19th century publisher in Augsburg, 177, 181, 188
Gomez, Carlos, arranged for band, 255
Goodale, Ezekiel, 19th century American composer, 138
Göpfert, Carl, 1800–1828, German composer, 156
Gor, Alph., 19th century French composer, 72
Gostiau, G., 19th century French composer, 50
Gotherot, G., 19th century French composer, 50
Götz, Francesco, 19th century Austrian composer, 215
Goueytes, R., 19th century French composer, arranger, 51
Gouirand, Joseph, 19th century French composer, 51
Gouly, ?, 19th century French composer, 51
Goumas, 19th century publisher in Paris, 6
Gounod, Charles, 1818–1893, French composer, 51
Gounod, arranged for band, 255
Gouvy, Louis, 1819–1898, German composer, 156
Goyer, ?, 19th century French composer, 51
Graffeuil, Charles, 19th century French composer, 51
Grangé, Léon, 19th century French composer, 51
Grange, Théodore, 19th century French composer, 51
Gras, D.-L., 19th century French composer, 51
Grass, 19th century publisher in Breslau, 144
Graves, W. T., 19th century English composer, 274
Grawert, E., 19th century German composer, 157
Grell, Eduard, fl. 1800–1886, German composer, 157
Grétry, André, 1741–1813, Belgium/French composer, arranged for band, 180, 197, 245
Grieg, Edvard, 1843–1907, Norway composer, 127
Grillet, Laurent, 19th century French composer, arranger, 52, 113
Grimm, ?, (ca. 1810), German composer, 157
Grimm, Anton, 19th century Austrian composer, 215
Grimm, Julius, 1827–1903, German composer, 157
Groh, A., 19th century Austrian composer, 215
Groh, Josef, 19th century Austrian composer, 215
Gross, G., 19th century French composer, 52

Grote, A. R., (1886), German composer, 157
Gruber, Felix, (1878), Austrian composer, 215
Gruber, Johann, 19th century Austrian composer, 215
Gruber, Josef, 19th century Austrian composer, 215
Grund, Eduard, 1802–1871, German composer, 157
Guerings, ?, (1818), Austrian composer, 215
Guéroult, Th., 19th century French composer, 52
Guerra, E., (1888), German composer, 157
Gués, A., 19th century French composer, 1, 52
Guespereau, ?, 19th century French composer, 52
Guest, George, 1771–1831, English composer, 274
Guévin, Arthur, 19th century French composer, 52
Guida, Agostino, Banda del L. di Linea, 122
Guidi, 19th century publisher in Firenze, 171
Guilbert, ?, 19th century French composer, 52
Guille, J., 19th century French composer, 52
Guillement, G., 19th century French composer, 52
Guimbal, A., 19th century French composer, 53
Guion, Edmond, 19th century French composer, 53
Gung'l, Jozsef, 1810–1889, Hungarian composer, 215
Günther, Karl, (1802), German composer, 157
Gurtner, ?, 19th century French composer, conductor, Musique 4e de Ligne, 53
Gurtner, Jean, 19th century French composer, 1, 274
Gutenberg, 186, 234
Gyrowetz, Adalbert, 1763–1850, Czech composer, 249

# H

Habert, Johannes, 1833–1896, German composer, 157
Hacker, Benedikt, 1769–1829, German composer, 157
Hafemeister, Richard, 19th century French composer, 53
Hagmann, ?, fl. 1800–1828, German composer, 157
Hainaut, A., 19th century French composer, 53
Hairaud, Hte., 19th century French composer, 53
Hájek, Josef, 19th century Hungarian composer, 216
Halévy, J.-F., 1799–1862, French composer, 54
Hallager, A., 19th century, German composer, 157
Haller, Michael, 19th century Austrian composer, 216
Hallmayr, Victtorin, 19th century Austrian composer, 216
Hamelle, 19th century publisher in Paris, 57
Hamm, Johann Valentin, 1811–1875, German composer, 158
Hammer, 19th century publisher in Vienna, 253
Hammer, August, 19th century German composer, Principal Oboe 'chez le 7 Reg. s. Hollande,' 158
Hammerl, Cornelius, 1769–1839, German composer, 158
Handel, arranged for band, 113
Handl, Johann, 19th century Austrian composer, 216
Hanssens, Charles, 1802–1871, century Belgium composer, 259
Hanzel, A., fl. 1800–1828, German composer, 158
Hare, Edwin, 19th century English composer, 274
Haring, Alfred, 19th century French composer, 54
Harper, ?, 19th century English composer, 275

Hartmann, 19th century publisher in Paris, 26
Hartmann, Emil, 1836–1898, Danish composer, 261
Hartmann, Johann, 1805–1900, Danish composer, 261
Hartner, H., 19th century English composer, 275
Haslinger, ?, 1800–1828, 19th century Austrian composer, 216
Haslinger, J., 19th century French composer, 54
Haslinger, L.-J., 19th century French composer, 54
Haslinger, 19th century publisher in Vienna, 48, 211, 214, 216, 221, 227, 240, 243, 244, 245, 246, 254
Hasse, A. G., German composer, 158
Hassloch, Carl, 1769–1829, German composer, 158
Haunreiter, Peter, (1877), German composer, 158
Hauptmann, Moritz, 1792–1868, German composer, 158
Hause, Carl, 19th century German composer, 158
Hausser, Josef (1867), Austrian composer, 54, 216
Havel, ?, 19th century Austrian composer, arranger, 216, 222ff
Hawkes, W., 19th century English composer, 275
Haydn, Josef, arranged for band, 9, 113, 158, 180, 236, 250, 253
Haydn, Michael, work arranged for band, 236
Heidenreich, 19th century Austrian composer, 216
Heine, Gotthelf, (1805), German composer, member of the court ensemble in Ludwigslust, 159
Heine, Samuel, (1804), German composer, 159
Heinrich, Anthony, 1781–1861, American composer, 138
Heinrich, Carl, 19th century Austrian composer, 216
Heinrichshofen, 19th century publisher in Berlin, 192
Heinsdorff, ?, 19th century English composer, 275
Heitz, Allexis, 19th century French composer, 54
Hejtmanek, ?, 19th century Austrian composer, 216
Hellmuth, ?, 19th century French composer, 54
Hemet, E., 19th century French composer, 1
Hemet, E., 19th century French composer, 54
Hemmerlé, Charles, 19th century French composer, 54
Hemmerlé, J., 19th century French composer, 55
Henchenne, Laurent, 19th century Belgium composer, 259
Henneberg, Johann, 1768–1822, Austrian composer, 216
Henneberg, Richard, 1853–1925, Swedish composer, 133
Hennig, Karl, 1819–1873, German composer, 159
Hennig, T., (1849), German composer, civic music director in Gustrow, marches for band, 159
Henny, H., 19th century French composer, 56
Henrich IV, of Russia, composer, 135
Henry, 19th century publisher in Paris, 113
Hentz, 19th century publisher in Paris, 12
Hepworth George, 19th century German composer, 159
Hérard, Camille, 19th century French composer, 56
Herbeck, Johann, 1831–1877, Austrian composer, 217
Hérbert, Charles, 19th century French composer, 56
Herbert, Victor, 1859–1924, 19th century American composer, 138
Herbuté, E.-N., 19th century French composer, 56
Herfurth, R., (1879), German composer, 159

Herold, A., 19th century German composer, 159
Herold, arranged for band, 255
Herschel, Sir William, as composer, 278
Herweg, Georg, 19th century German composer, 159
Herzog von Gotha [dedication], 191
Herzog, Auguste, 19th century French composer, 56
Herzogenberg, Henrich, 1843–1900, Aust. Composer, 217
Herzogin Amalia, 145
Heugel, 19th century publisher in Paris, 37, 85
Heuschkel, Johann, 1800–1828, German composer, 159
Heyn, Catharina, 19th century German composer, 159
Hiebesch, Johann, 1766–1820, German composer 159
Hiller, Ferdinand, 1811–1885, German composer, 159
Hinchliff, W. S., 19th century English composer, 275
Hinkel, ?, as arranger, 198
Hitchcock, E. A., General, American military band collection ca. 1825, 138
Hitz, Franz, 19th century composer in Paris, 56
Hitzemann, H., 19th century French composer, 56
Hladky, as arranger, 256, 257
Hnojil, J., (1820), 19th century Hungarian composer, 217
Hoby, C., 19th century English composer, 275
Hoch, ?, 19th century Austrian composer, 217
Hôdieir, Romain, 19th century French composer, 56
Hofer, Frédéric, 19th century French composer, 56
Hoffmann, 19th century publisher in Prague, 215
Hoffmann, Ernst, 1776–1822, German comp., important literary person, 160
Hoffmeister & Kühnel, 19th century publishers in Leipzig, 166
Hofmann, Heinrich, 1842–1902 German composer, 160
Hofmeister, 19th century publisher in Leipzig, 148, 153, 168, 172, 173, 187
Hoftheater, 19th century publisher in Vienna, 253
Hol, Richard, b. 1825, Dutch composer, 125
Holden, A., Jr., 19th century English composer, 275
Hollandre, Jean, 1785–1837, 19th century French composer, 56
Honig, ?, as arranger, 227
Höppler, ?, 19th century Austrian composer, 217
Horn, Karl, 1762–1830, German composer, 160
Hortense, Reine, 1783–1837, Queen of Holland, as composer, 56
Hoste, L., 19th century French composer, 56
Hotis, Jan, 19th century Austrian composer, 217
Hottisch, ?, 19th century Austrian composer, 217
Hourenaeghel, L., 19th century French composer, 56
Houziaux, H., 19th century French composer, 57
Howe, Elias, Jr., 19th century American composer, 138
Hradecky, ?, 19th century Hungarian composer, 217
Hubans, Charles, 19th century French composer, 57
Huber, Emile, 19th century French composer, 57
Hübschmann, J., ca. 1803–1816, German composer, 160

Hüe, Georges, 1858–1948, 19th century French composer, 57
Hulbe, Franze, 1867–1876, as arr., 254
Hummel, Johann, 1778–1837, Austrian composer, arranged for band, 143, 180, 189, 197, 217
Hummel, Joseph, (1901), Austrian composer., 218
Hutschenruyter, Wouter, 1859–1943, Dutch composer, founder of the band of the Rotterdam Municipal Guard, 125
Huyts, C., 19th century French composer, 57

## I

Imbault, 19th century publisher in Paris, 15
Imprimerie mus., 19th century publisher in Paris, 7
Indy, Vincent, 1851–1931, French composer, 57
Isouard, Nicolas, 1775–1818, Maltese composer, arranged for band, 197, 180
Istres, H., 19th century French composer, 57
Ithier, Louis, 19th century French composer, 57

## J

Jacob, ?, 19th century French composer, 57
Jacob, E., 19th century French composer, 57
Jacob, Jules, 19th century French composer, 57
Jacotin, L., 19th century French composer, 58
Jacque, E., 19th century French composer, 58
Jacquemet, L., 19th century French composer, 58
Jacquet, Charles, 19th century French composer, 58
Jadassohn, Saloman, 1831–1902, German composer, , 160
Jadin, 19th century French composer, 1
Jaeger, Will., 19th century German composer, 160
Jähn, *Weber Verzeichnis*, 190
Jancières, V., 19th century French composer, 58
Jancourt, E., 19th century French composer, 58
Janet, 19th century publisher in Paris, 2, 11, 22, 25, 31, 59, 62, 73, 90, 101, 107
Janin-Jaubert, ?, 19th century French composer, 58
Jannopulos, Anastas (1847), Greek composer, 160
Janvier, L., 19th century French composer, 58
Jaubert, J., 19th century French composer, 58
Jauffret, ?, 19th century French composer, 58
Jaussaud, C., 19th century French composer, 58
Javault, ?, fl. 1800–1828, French composer, 59
Javelot, Jules, 19th century French composer, 59
Jeandel, F., 19th century French composer, 59
Jeanjean, Camille, 19th century French composer, 59
Jeannin, ?, 19th century French composer, 59
Jeaune d'Arc, 30, 51
Jedlüczka, (1860) Austrian composer, 218
Jell, J., 19th century Austrian composer, 218
Jenette, Adolf, (1870), German composer, 160
Jenny Lind, 19th century singer, 65
Jobin, E., 19th century French composer, 59

Jochum, Otto, 19th century German composer, 160
Joerg, N., 1800–1828, German composer, 160
Johann Albrecht of Mecklenburg-Schwerin, 144
Jolivet, Jules, 19th century French composer, 59
Jonas, Émile, 1827–1905, French composer, professor, Conservatoire Impérial, 1, 59
Jones, J. G., 19th century English composer, 276
Jones, Sidney, 19th century English composer, 276
Jonnet, Henry, 19th century French composer, 59
Jorelle, J., 19th century French composer, 59
Josepha von Menz, of Wasserburg, 145
Josneau, A., 19th century French composer, 1
Josneau, August, 19th century French composer, conductor Musique du 1er de Ligne, 59
Jouve, ?, ca. 1800–1828, French composer, 60
Jouve, J., 19th century English composer, 276
Julien, ?, 19th century French composer, 60
Jullien, ?, 19th century English composer, 276
July, Fortune, 19th century French composer, 60
Junod, Laurent, 19th century French composer, 60

## K

Kakosky, ?, 19th century French composer, 60
Kalkbrenner, 19th century German composer, 178
Kalliwoda, Johann, 1801–1866, German composer, 160
Kanka, Johann, 1772–1865, German composer 160
Kanne, ?, (1810), Austrian composer, 218
Kappey, Jacob, 19th century English composer, 276
Karlowicz, Miscyzslaw, 1876–19090, Polish composer, 130
Karren, Leon, 19th century French composer, conductor, Musique a la Division de Brest, 60
Kaschte, Franz, as arranger, 256, 257
Kastner, Jean-Georges, 1810–1867, French composer, historian, 60
Kathaliery, ?, 19th century Austrian composer, , 218
Katschthaler, Philipp, 19th century Austrian composer, 218
Kattner, Otto, 19th century German composer, 160
Katzer, Ignace, b. 1785, French composer of works Harmoniemusik, 61
Katzer, Ignaz (1820) German composer, 161
Kauffmann, ?, 19th century French composer, 61
Kaulich, Josef, 19th century Austrian composer, 218
Kélér, Béla, 1820–1882, Hungarian composer, 218
Kelsen, ?, 19th century French composer, conductor Musique de l'Ecole d'Artillerie de Bourges, 61
Kempter, Friedrich, b. 1810, German composer, 161
Kempter, Karl, 1819–1871, German composer, 161
Kern, Max, 19th century German composer, 161
Kessels, Joseph, 19th century German composer, 161
Kewitsch, Th., 19th century German composer, 161
Keyser, ?, fl. 1800–1828, French composer, 61
Kinast (1874), as arranger, 255, 256, 257
King of Bavaria (1870), 160

King of Hannover, as 19th century composer, 192
Kistler, Cyrill, 1848–1907, German composer, 161
Kistner, 19th century publisher in Leipzig, 156, 162
Kittl, Jan Bedrich, 1809–1868, 19th c. Czech composer, 218
Klaus, Josef, 19th century Austrian composer, 218
Kleczinsky, Jan, d. 1828, Polish composer, 130
Klee, L., 19th century German composer, 161
Kleiber, Leonhard, b. 1863, German composer, 161
Klein, (Bernhard, 1793–1832?), German composer, 161
Kleinheinz, Franz, 1765–1832, German composer, 161
Kleitz, ?, fl. 1800–1828, French composer, 61
Kling, Henri, 1842–1918, French composer, 61
Klinkicht, 19th century publisher in Meissen, 159
Klopow, 19th century German composer, 141
Klosé, Hiacynthe, 1808–1880, French composer, arranger, 62, 113
Klughardt, August, 1847–1902, German composer, 161
Kniess, Fr., b. ca. 1800, German composer, 161
Knipfer, F., 19th century German composer, 161
Knofl, G., 19th century Austrian composer, 219
Koch, A., 19th century German composer, 161
Kodrin, ?, (1886), Austrian composer, 219
Koehler, Benjamin, b. 1777, French composer, 62
Koenig, H. L., 19th century English composer, 276
Kohler, Ernst, (1831), German composer, 162
Kölb, ?, (1835), Austrian composer, 219
Kollmann, 19th century publisher in Leipzig, 188
Kolovrátek, Tomás, 19th century Czech composer, 219
Komzak, Karl, 19th century Bohemian composer, 219
Kopff, ?, 19th century French composer, 62
Körnlein, Justus, d. 1866, German composer, 162, 198
Kosleck, ?, 19th century German composer, 162
Koslowsky, composer, 141
Kösporer, Johann, 19th century German composer, 162
Koubek, ?, 19th century Austrian composer, 219
Kovacs, Josef, 19th century Austrian composer, 219
Kraknest, Herrmann, (1871), German composer, 162
Kral, Johann, 19th century Austrian composer, 219
Krasa, ?, 19th century Austrian composer, 219
Kraus, Joseph, 19th century German composer, 162
Krause, J. II., 19th century German composer, 162
Krein, Michel, 19th century French composer, 62
Krempel, ?, fl. 1800–1828, French composer, 62
Krempel, Charles, 19th century French composer, 62
Krempel, Em., 19th century French composer, conductor, Musique au 54e de Ligne, 62
Krenn, Franz, 1839–1890, 19th century Austrian composer, 219
Kreutzer, ?, 19th century Austrian composer, 219
Kreutzer, works arranged for band, 180, 198
Kreutzer, Konradin, 1780–1849, German composer, 162
Kreuzer, 19th century composer, 364
Krickel, ?, 19th century Czech composer, 219

Krimpel, ?, 19th century French composer, 63
Kroh, ?, 19th century Austrian composer, 219
Krokowitsch, as arranger, 197
Krommer, Franz, 1759–1831, Czech composer, 220ff
Krug, Diederich, 1821–1880, German composer, 162
Kubicek, V., 19th century Czech composer, 225, 253
Kuecken, F. W., 19th century English composer, 276
Küffner, Joseph, 1776–1856, German composer, arranger, 162ff, 196
Kuhn, F., 19th century French composer, 63
Kühner, ?, 19th century composer, 276
Kunerth, J. Leopold, 19th century Austrian composer, Stadt Kremierer Turnermeister, 225
Kunerth, Johann, German composer, 164
Kunheim, W. L., 19th century German composer, 164
Kunstanstalt, 19th century publisher in Innsbruck, 214
Kuntze, Carl, 19th century German composer, 164
Kunz, Konrad, 1812–1875, German composer, 164
Kupler, ?, 19th century German composer, 165
Kussy, Franz, 19th century Austrian composer, 226
Kwiatkowski, ?, 19th century Austrian composer, 226
Kyle, Alexander, 19th century American composer, 138

## L

La Bretesche, J., 19th century French composer, 64
Laurent, E., 19th century French composer, 66
Labit, Henri, 19th century French composer, conductor, Musique au 84e de Ligne; Directeur de l'Ecole Nationale de Musique de Valenciennes, 63
Labitzki, ?, 19th century French composer, 63
Lábler, Frantisek, 19th century Austrian composer, 226
Labole, P.-N., 19th century French composer, 63
Laborde, E., 19th century French composer, 64
Laborde, Léon, 19th century French composer, 64
Labric, J. B., 19th century French composer, conductor, Musique du 23e de Ligne, 1, 64
Lacaire, Thé., 19th century French composer, 64
Lacher, 19th century French arranger, conductor, 9e Cuirassiere a Andrinople, 2, 64
Lachner, works arranged for band, 174
Lachner, Franz, 1803–1890, German composer, 165
Lacombe, Louis, 1818–1884, French composer, 64
Lafille, Charles, 19th century French composer, 64
Lafitte, Jacques, 19th century French composer, 64
Laforest, Thiard, 19th century Austrian composer, 226
Lagard, A., 19th century French composer, 64
Lagny, A., 19th century French composer, 64
Laigre, Paul, 19th century French composer, 65
Lair, Alfred, as arr. of Beauvqis, 28
Lajarte, as arranger, 113
Lajarte, Théodore, 1826–1890, French composer, 65
Lambert, Auguste, 19th century French composer, 65
Lambert, E., 19th century French composer, 65

Lamiable, 19th century French composer, 1, 2
Lamotte, Antony, 19th century French composer, 65
Lampe, Walther, 19th century German composer, 165
Lamperini, ?, 19th century Italian composer, 118
Landa, W., 19th century Austrian composer, arranger, 226, 257
Langa, Pascal, 19th century French composer, 66
Lange, Gustav, 19th century German composer, 165, 276
Langlane, Geo., 19th century French composer, 65
Langlois, Jules, 19th century French composer, 66
Lanner, works arranged for band, 186
Lanner, Joseph, 1801–1843, Austrian composer, 226
Lanz, Engelbert (1887), Austrian composer, 226
Lapara, ?, 19th century French composer, 66
Laporte, Raymond, 19th century French composer, 66
Lardenois, Arthur, 19th century French composer, 66
Lardeur, Henri, 19th century French composer, conductor, Musique a l'École d'Artillerie de Versailles, 66
Larriu, A., 19th century French composer, 66
Lasalle, E., 19th century German composer, 165
Lasek, ?, fl. 1800–1828, German composer, 166
Latann, C., 19th century German composer, 336
Lattenberg, Felix, 19th century Austrian composer, 226
Laurent, H., 19th century English composer, 276
Lautier, F., 19th century French composer, 66
Lauzun, F., 19th century French composer, 66
Lazennec, I., 19th century French composer, 67
Lazzeri, Sylvio, 1857–1944, French composer, 67
Le Blanc Duvernoy, Paul, 19th century French composer, 67
Le Boulch, Jules, 19th century French composer, 67
Le Bref, A., 19th century French composer, 67
Le Breton, H., 19th century French composer, 67
Le Sueur, Jean-François, arranged for band 113
Lebeau, 19th century publisher in Paris, 51
Lebigre, Auguste, 19th century French composer, 67
Leblan, E., 19th century French composer, 67
Leblanc, L., 19th century French composer, 67
Lechleitner, ?, 19th century French composer, conductor, Musique 14me d'Artillerie, 67
Lecoeur, E., 19th century French composer, 67
Lecomte, A., 19th century French composer, 67
Leduc, 19th century publisher in Paris, 1, 3, 37, 44, 48, 57, 68, 86
Lefabre, A., 19th century French composer, 68
Lefebvre, Charles, 1843–1917, French composer, 68
Lefebvre, Fortuné, 19th century French composer, 68
Lefrancois, F., 19th century French composer, 68
Legendre, Jules, 19th century French composer, 68
Legrand, William, 19th century German composer, 336ff
Lehmann, Friedrich, 19th century German composer, 166
Lehmann, R., as arranger, 196
Lehne, 19th century publisher in Hannover, 178
Leibl, Karl, 1784–1870, German composer, 166

Leidersdorf, Franz (1837) 19th century Austrian composer, 226
Lekeu, Guillaume, 1870–1894, Belgium composer, 259
Lelong, ?, 19th century French composer, 68
Lemaigre, A.-T., 19th century French composer, 68
Lemalle, J., 19th century French composer, 68
Lemarié, A., 19th century French composer, 68
Lemière de Corvey, Jean, 1770–1832, French composer, 68
Lemoine, 19th century publisher in Paris, 22, 51, 75, 80
Lennert, V., 19th century German composer, 166
Lentz, Frédéric, 19th century French composer, 68
Leoncavallo, Ruggero, 1857–1919, arranged for band, 198
Leonhardt, Andreas, 19th century Austrian composer, 226
Leopold I of Belgium, 260
Lépagnole, L., 19th century French composer, 68
Leplat, E., 19th century French composer, 68
Leroux, Charles, 19th century French composer, 69
Leroux, Felix, 19th century French composer, conductor, Musique l'École d'Artillerie de Vincennes, 69
Leroy, 19th century publisher in Lyon, 1
Leslie, Steward, 19th century English composer, 276
Lessel, Franciszek, 1780–1835, Polish composer, 130
Lessing, German poet, 150
Lesueur, L., 19th century French composer, 69
Leuckart, 19th century publisher in Breslau, 148
Leuckart, 19th century publisher in Leipzig, 175, 217
Lévêque, Emile, 19th century French composer, 69
Lévêque, L., 19th century French composer, 69
Liadov, ?, 1855–1914, Russian composer, 135
Lickl, Johann, 1769–1843, Austrian composer, 227
Liddell, John, 19th century English composer, 276
Liechtenstein, Prince Alois of Vienna, 249
Liess, ?, as arranger, 143
Ligner, F., 19th century French composer, 69
Lilman, V., 19th century French composer, 70
Limnander, ?, 19th century French composer, 70
Lincke, P., 19th century English composer, 276
Lindner, ?, (1820), German composer, 166
Lindner, 19th century German composer, 180
Lindner, H., fl. 1800–1828, 19th century German composer, 166
Lindner, Henri, 19th century French composer, 70
Lindpainter, arranged, 196
Lindpaintner, Peter, 1791–1856, German composer, 166
Linek, Yiri, 19th century Czech composer, 227
Linglin, ?, 19th century French composer, 70
Link, Joseph, 1783–1837, German composer, 166
Lipawsky, Giuseppe, 19th century Italian composer, 118
Liszt, Franz, 1811–1886, Hungarian composer, 227
Livorka, ?, 19th century Austrian composer, 228
Llaue, 19th century publisher in Berlin, 173
Lobe, J. C., 19th century German composer, 198
Loetz, Paul de, 19th century English composer, 277

Loewe, Johann, 1796–1869, German composer, 166
Logier, Jean, 1780–1846, French composer, 70
Lointier, Eugene, 19th century French composer, 70
Lortzing, Albert, 1801–1851, German composer, 166
Lortzing, G. A., 19th century composer, 277
Loubet, A., 19th century French composer, 70
Louis XI, 86
Louis XIII, 14
Louis XVIII, 48
Louis, ?, 19th century French composer, 70
Louis, 19th century French composer, 1
Louise, Queen of Prussia (1876), 151
Loustallot, G., 19th century French composer, 1, 70
Löw, Jos., 19th century German composer, 166
Lozes, L., 19th century French composer, 71
Lucas, Charles, 1808–1869, English composer, 277
Luce, 19th century French composer, 1
Luce, E., 19th century French composer, 71
Luce, L., 19th century French composer, 1, 71
Ludwig I, 145, 174, 178, 186
Ludwig IX, as composer, 143
Ludwig, F., 19th century German composer, 167
Luigini, Joseph, 19th century French composer, 71
Luigini, Laurent, 19th century French composer, 71
Luitpold v. Bayern, 161
Luschwitz, H., 19th century English composer, 277
Lutz, Meyer, 19th century English composer, 277

# M

Maanen, J. C., 19th century composer, 277
Mabellini, Teodulo, 1817–1897, Italian composer, 118
Mabille, H., 19th century French composer, 71
Mabire, E., 19th century French composer, 71
Mackenzie, Alexander, 1847–1935, English composer, 277
Magasin de l'imprimerie, 19th century publisher in Vienna, 227, 243
Magasin della Caes. Real priv., 19th century publisher in Vienna, 227
Magnan, G., 19th century French composer, 71
Magnan, Louis, 19th century French composer, 71
Magnard, Lucian, 1865–1914, French composer, 71
Maguet, H. 19th century French composer, 71
Maillart, L. A., 19th century composer, 277
Maillochaud, J. B., 19th century French composer, 71
Mailly, A., 19th century French composer, 72
Mairetet, E., 19th century French composer, 72
Malchow, F., 19th century German composer, 167
Malézieux, L., 19th century French composer, 72
Mancini, A., ?, 19th century French composer, 72
Mandanici, Placido, 1798–1852, Italian composer, 119
Manfrin, Giuseppe, 19th century Italian composer, 118
Mangeant, ?, 19th century French composer, 72
Mangold, Wilhelm, 1796–1875, German composer, 167

Manina, Fortunato, 19th century Italian composer, , 119
Mankels, ?, fl. 1800–1828, German composer, 167
Mansion, Horace, 19th century French composer, 73
Mansion, P., 19th century French composer, 73
Marchal, ?, 19th century French composer, 73
Marchesi, Tommaso, 1773–1852, Italian composer, 119
Marcus, P., 19th century French composer, 73
Margueritat, 19th century publisher in Paris, 5
Marie de Prusse, Princess, 170
Marie of Bayern (1842), 186
Marie, E., 19th century French composer, 73ff
Marie-Louise d'Orléans, Queen of Belgium, 259
Marin, E., 19th century French composer, 74
Marion, Claude, 19th century French composer, 74
Marliani, M. A., 19th century English composer, 277
Maron, A., 19th century French composer, 74
Marra, Vincenzo, 19th century Italian conductor, composer, 119
Marsal, E., 19th century French composer, 74
Marsano, Luigi, 1769–1841, Italian composer, , 119
Marschalk, ?, 19th century French composer, 74
Marschner, Heinrich, 1795–1861, German composer, arranged for band, 143, 255
Marteau, Henri, 1874–1934, German composer, 167
Martin de La Moutte, L., 19th century French composer, 75
Martin, Camille, 19th century French composer, 74
Martin, L., 19th century French composer, 75
Martin, The., 19th century French composer, 74
Marulli, Angelo, 19th century Italian composer, 119
Maschek, Albin, 1804–1878, Czech composer, 228
Maschek, Paul, 1761–1826, Czech composer, 228ff
Maschek, Vincenc, 1755–1931, Czech composer, 229ff
Massak, Franz, 19th century Austrian composer, arranger, 233, 254
Massard, R., 19th century French composer, 75
Massat, F., 19th century French composer, 75
Masson du Breuil, ?, 19th century French composer, 75
Mastio, E., 19th century French composer, 75
Matha, ?, 19th century French composer, 75
Matous, ?, 19th century Austrian composer, 233
Mattiozzi, Rudolphe, 19th century German composer, 167
Mauchen, W., 19th century French composer, 75
Maurer, Ludwig, 1789–1878, German composer, 168
Maximilian I, 187
Maximilian II, 187
Mayer, ?, 19th century German composer, 168
Mayeur, L., 19th century French composer, 75
Mayr, Simone, 1763–1845, Italian composer, 119
Mazzinghi, Joseph, 1765–1844, English composer, 277
Mazzorin, Michele, 19th century Italian composer, 119
Mechetti, 19th century publisher in Paris, 85
Mechetti, 19th century publisher in Vienna, 240
Medau, 19th century publisher in Prag, 245

Mees, Joseph, 1777–1858, Belgium composer, 260
Méhul, work arranged for band, 180
Meier, ?, (1899), German composer, 168
Meinhardt, F., 19th century German composer, 168
Meisaler, J., 19th century English composer, 277
Meissner, F. W., 19th century German composer, 168, 180
Meissonnier, 19th century publisher in Paris, 41
Meister, G., 19th century French composer, 75
Mejo, W., 19th century German composer, 168
Melusin, Rudolf, 19th century Austrian composer, 233
Mendelssohn, Arnold, 1855–1933, German composer, 168
Mendelssohn, Felix, 1809–1847, German composer, 168
Mendelssohn, works arranged for band, 198, 213
Mengal, Martin, 1784–1851, Belgium composer, 260
Mennesson, A., 19th century French composer, 76
Mérat, Léon, 19th century French composer, 76
Mercadane, Saverio, 1795–1870, Italian composer, 119
Mercier, Roger, 19th century French composer, 76
Mercier, V., 19th century French composer, 76
Mérigeault, Désireé, 19th century French composer, 76
Merz, C., composer, 142
Merz, Karl, 1836–1890, German composer, 169
Meser, 19th century publisher in Dresden, 158
Métra, Olivier, 19th century French composer, 76
Mettenleiter, Johann, 1812–1858, German composer, 169
Metzdorff, F. G., 19th century German composer, 169
Metzdorff, Richard, 19th century German composer, 170
Metzner Leblanc, 19th century publisher in Angers, 13
Meunier, Armand, 19th century French composer, 76
Meurer, Maurice, 19th century French composer, 76
Meurgey, L., 19th century French composer, conductor, Musique, 2e Reg. de Zouaues; Chavlier de la Legion d'Honneur, 76
Meyer, ?, 19th century French composer, 77
Meyer, Carl, b. 1772, 19th century German composer, 170
Meyer, J., 19th century French composer, 77
Meyerbeer, Giacomo, 1791–1864, German composer, 170
Meyerbeer, arranged for band, 130, 166, 198, 256
Michael, David, 19th century American composer, 138
Michaëli, Jean, 19th century French composer, 77
Michaelis, ?, 19th century English composer, 277
Michalicka, ?, 19th century Austrian composer, 233
Michel, ?, 19th century French composer, 77
Migette, E., 19th century French composer, 77
Mignon, L., 19th century French composer, 77
Miguel, 19th century composer published in England, 263
Milanscoff, Arman, 19th century French composer, 77
Miller, ?, 19th century French composer, 77
Millescampa, Jules, 19th century French composer, 77ff
Millet, E., 19th century French composer, 78
Millingre, ?, 19th century French composer, 77
Millon, E., 19th century French composer, 78
Millot, Marius, 19th century French composer, 78
Miltitz, ?, 1800–1828, German composer, 171
Mimart, Auguste, 19th century French composer, arranger, 78
Mirambeau, E., 19th century French composer, 78
Mischke, L., 19th century German composer, 171
Missud, Jean, American military band collection c. 1840, 65 works, 138
Mohr, Andreas, 19th century German composer, 172
Mohr, J., 19th century French composer, 78
Möller, M., 19th century German composer, 172
Molloy, J. L., 19th century English composer, 277
Momigny, Lysias, 19th century French composer, organiste de la Cathédrale d'Angouleme, 2, 79
Momigny, 19th century publisher in Paris, 112
Monbarin, E., 19th century French composer, 79
Moncel, A., 19th century French composer, 79
Monge, Fernandez, 19th century French composer, 79
Monicard, G., 19th century French composer, 79
Monier, F., 19th century French composer, 79
Monnereau, J., 19th century French composer, 79
Montalent, R., 19th century French composer, 79
Moornay, A., 19th century French composer, 79
Morand, G., 19th century French composer, 79
Morandi, Giovanni, 1777–1856, Italian composer, 120
Moreau, Charles, 19th century French composer, 80
Moret, Victor, 19th century French composer, 80
Moretti, Niccolo, 19th century Italian composer, 120
Morhange, Emile, 19th century French composer, 80
Morillon, F., 19th century French composer, 80
Morse, Samuel, 19th century American composer, 139
Morten, F., 19th century English composer, 277
Moser, Franz, 1880–1939, 19th century Austrian composer, 233
Mösner, ?, 19th century French composer, 80
Moths, ?., 19th century English composer, 277
Mougeot, C., 19th century French composer, 80
Mouquet, Jules, b. 1867, 19th century French composer, 80
Mourque, F., 19th century French composer, 80
Moussard, A., 19th century French composer, 80
Mozart, arranged for band, 55, 113, 141, 177, 179, 180, 181, 198ff, 245, 246, 249, 256
Mozart, Leopold, 256
Mrkvicka, Josef, Hungarian composer, 233
Muck, Beda, (1833), Austrian composer, 233
Mühling, ?, 1800–1828, German composer, 172
Mulder, ?, 19th century French composer, 81
Müller, ?, 19th century Austrian composer, 233
Müller, ?, 19th century French composer, 81
Müller, C. F., 1800–1828, German composer, 172
Müller, Christian Gottlich 1800–1828, German composer, 172
Müller, F. D., 19th century German composer, 172
Müller, Frederic, 1786–1871, German composer, 172
Müller, J., 19th century French composer, 81

Müller, W., arranged for band, 256
Müller, work arranged for band, 199
Mullot, E., 19th century French composer, 81ff
Münchs, 19th century French composer, 1
Münchs, A., fl. 1800–1828, German composer, 172
Münchs, Conrad, 19th century French composer, 82
Münchs, French composer, 70
Musik-Comptoir, 19th century pulisher in Leipzig, 188
Muth, A., 19th century English composer, 277

## N

Nagiller, Mathäus, 19th century Austrian composer, 233
Nanke, Sr., 19th century Austrian composer, 234
Napoleon III, 11, 56, 79
Napoleon, 187, 228ff, 239, 263
Napravnik, ?, 19th century composer, 277
Naudin, T., 19th century French composer, 82
Naue, J. F., 19th century German composer, 142, 173
Nava, Gaetano, 1802–1875, Italian composer, 120
Navratil, Fran., 19th century Austrian composer, 234
Necke, Herman, 19th century German composer, 173
Nehr, Emile, 19th century French composer, 82
Neithardt, August, 1793–1861, German composer, arranger, conductor, Kaiser Franz Grenadier Regiment, Berlin, 142, 173
Neukäufler, F., ca. 1780–1843, German composer, 173
Neukomm, Sigismund, 1778–1858, Austrian composer, 180, 234ff
Neumann, ?, 19th century English composer, 278
Neumann, H., (1833) German composer, 173
Nevue, Alban, 19th century French composer, 82
Nicaise, E., 19th century French composer, 82
Nicola, Georg, 19th century Austrian composer, 238
Nicolai, Willem, 1829–1896, Dutch composer, 125
Nicolas, ?, 19th century French composer, 82
Nicolas, Grand Duc de Russia, 217
Nicolaus, Grossfürsten, composer, 141
Nicolini, works arranged for band, 166, 196
Nicolo, composer, 141
Nicosias, Charles, 19th century French composer, 82
Nicou, G., 19th century French composer, 82
Niedermeyer, ?, German composer, 149
Niessel, Hte., 19th century student, Gymnase Musical Militaire, 1
Nitzchke, C., 19th century German composer, 173
Niverd, M., 19th century French composer, 82
Niverd, R., 19th century French composer, 82
Niverd, V., 19th century French composer, 83
Nocentino, Domenico, 1848–1924, Italian composer, 120
Noël Le Mire, A., 19th century French composer, 83
Norroy, H., 19th century French composer, 83
Nosvadba, J., 1824–1876, German composer, arranger, 173, 198
Nouvelle France chorale, 19th century publisher in Paris, 6
Nováček, Rudolf, 1860–1929, Austrian composer, 239
Novotni, ?, 19th century Austrian composer, 239
Nowotny, A. (1845–1847), as arr., 256
Nudra, J., 19th century Austrian composer, 239

## O

Obersteiner, Johann, (1827) Aust. comp., 239
Ochernal, ?, 19th century German composer, 174
Oelschlegl, Alfred, 19th century English composer, 278
Oertel, 19th century publisher in Hannover, 158, 161, 166, 172, 173, 175, 181, 182, 183
Oertel, 19th century publisher in Berlin, 192
Offenbach, French composer, arranged for band, 19
Oldenburg, P. G., 19th century English composer, 278
Olsen, Ole, 1850–1927, Norway composer, 127
Omer Fort, ?, 19th century French composer, conductor Musique au 7e Hussards, 83
Onslow, Georges, 1784–1853, French composer, 83
Orelly, J. de, 19th century French composer, 83
Osswald, A., (1827) Austrian composer, arranger, 239, 256
Ostreich, Carl (1831), German composer, 174
Otto I, King of Greece, 160, 186

## P

Pacak, Frantisek, 19th century Austrian comp., 239
Pacini, 19th century publisher in Paris, 21, 22, 46, 82, 89, 94, 149
Pacini, Giovanni, 1796–1867, Italian composer, 120
Pacini, G., arranged for band, 105, 166, 256
Paer, Ferdinand, 1771–1816, French composer, 83
Paer, various works arranged for band, 122, 141, 180, 199, 256
Paganini, work arranged for band, 149
Pagés, Paul, 19th century French composer, 84
Paimparé, ?, 19th century French composer, 84
Paisiello, Giovanni, 1740–1816, 122, 246
Palausi, ?, 19th century French composer, 84
Paliard, Leon, 19th century French composer, 84
Panizza, Giacomo (1822) Austrian composer, 239
Panseron, ?, 19th century German composer, 149
Paoletti, 19th century publisher in Firenze, 118
Parès, Gabriel, 19th century French composer, conductor, Musique de la Garde Républicaine, 84
Paris, Hte., 19th century French composer, 84
Pariser, E., 19th century French composer, 85
Paris-Kerjullou, Charles, 19th century French composer, 84
Parízek, Alexius, 19th century Czech composer, 239
Parlow, Albert, 19th century Austrian composer, 239
Parry, C. H., 1848–1918, English composer, 278
Parry, John, 1776–1851, English composer, 278
Patrie, J., 19th century French composer, 85
Paulis, Johann, as arr., Director, Military Music Club of Prague, 255, 256

Paulmann, S. A., 19th century Austrian composer, 240
Pautrat, Pierre, 19th century French composer, 85
Pawlikowski, Franz, 19th century Austrian composer, 240
Payer, Hieronymus (1819), Austrian composer, 240
Payer, Hyr., 19th century German composer, 174
Payer, Jerome, 1787–1845, French composer, 85
Pearsall, Robert, 1795–1856, Swiss composer, 174
Pechacek, Franz, 1793–1840, Czeck composer, 240
Peirot, J., 19th century French composer, 85
Pejrinovsky, Martin, (1844) Austrian comp., 240
Pellarin, Giuseppe, 1815–1865, Venetian composer, 120
Pennauer, 19th century publisher in Vienna, 165
Peplow, ?, 19th century English composer, 278
Perilhou, Armand, d. 1936, French composer, 85
Perin, L., 19th century French composer, 85
Perlat, Lucien, 19th century French composer, 85
Perron, Ed., 19th century French composer, 85
Pertl, Vincez, 19th century Austrian composer, 240
Pessard, Émile, 19th century French composer, 85
Pessière, Émile, 19th century French composer, 85
Péter, Sylvestre, 19th century French composer, 86
Peters, 19th century publisher in Leipzig, 153, 170, 171, 184
Peters' American *Saxhorn Journal*, ca. 1859, 286
Petit, A., 19th century publisher in Paris, 59, 97, 106, 109
Petit, Alexandre, 19th century French composer, 86
Petit, Fernand, 19th century French composer, 86
Petit, I., 19th century French composer, 86
Petit, Oscar, 19th century French composer, 86
Petrali, Giuliano, 19th century Italian composer, 120
Pfeffel, ?, 19th century German composer, 174
Pfisterer, K. L., 19th century German composer, 174
Phile, ?, 19th century American, 139
Philiberti, ?, 19th century French composer, 86
Philippe, Edouard, 19th century French composer, 86
Pick, Henry, 19th century English composer, 278
Piefke, Gottfried, 19th century German composer, 174
Pierné, Gabriel, 1863–1937, French composer, 86
Pillevestre, J., 19th century French composer, 86
Pilliard, T., 19th century French composer, conductor, 3e Rég. D'Inf. Le Marine, 1
Pinault, V., 19th century French composer, 87
Pipelart, Maurice, 19th century French composer, 87
Pique, Adolphe, 19th century French composer, 87
Pirouelle, ?, 19th century French composer, 87
Pitot, ?, 19th century French composer, 87
Pivet, L., 19th century French composer, 87
Pleyel, 19th century Austrian composer, 180
Pleyel, 19th century publisher in Paris, 17, 93, 97, 113
Plouvier, ?, 19th century French composer, 88
Pluchart, H., 19th century French composer, 88
Poisal, Johann, 1783–1865, German composer, 174
Poli, Giovanni, 19th century Italian composer, 120
Ponchielli, Amilcare, 1834–1886, Italian composer, 120

Pontet, E., 19th century French composer, 88
Posse, ?, 19th century English composer, 278
Potter, Samuel, 19th century English composer 278
Préau, ?, 19th century French composer, 88
Preisser, M. A., 19th century French composer, 88
Prendiville, Hayyr, 19th century American composer, 139
Preston, 19th century publisher in London, 274
Preuss, 19th century publisher in Berlin, 162
Prèvost, Charles, 19th century French composer, 88
Prince Luitold v. Bayern, 161, 182, 185
Prince of Saxe-Meiningen, 170
Prince Wilhelm v. Schaumburg-Lippe, 247
Princiaux, fils, 19th century French composer, 88
Princiaux, J., 19th century French composer, 88
Pritchard, ?, 19th century English composer, 278
Probst, 19th century publisher in Leipzig, 172
Proch, Heinrich, 1809–1878, Austrian composer, 240
Proksch, Robert, 19th century German composer, 175
Prost, Jules, 19th century French composer, 89
Prout, Edwin, 19th century English composer, 278
Provent, C., 19th century French composer, 89
Prudhomme, Marius, 19th century French composer, 89
Prunier, Edoward, 19th century French composer, 89
Puccini, Giacomo, 1858–1924, Italian composer, 121
Puchot, L., 19th century French composer, 89
Purebl, Joseph, 1768–1838, Austrian composer, arranger, 240ff, 256
Pustet, 19th century publisher in Regensburg, 152
Pütz, Pierre, 19th century French composer, 89
Puyau, G., 19th century French composer, 89

## Q

Queen of Bavaria, 1827, 154
Queen Victoria, 263
Quentin, Alfred, 19th century French composer, 89
Quilici, Domenico, 19th century Italian composer, 121
Quirici, Giovanni, 19th century Italian composer, 121

## R

Rafael, Fr., 19th century Austrian composer, 241
Raff, Joachim, as orchestrator, 227
Raff, Joseph, 1822–1882, German composer, 175
Raffara, J., 19th century French composer, 1, 89
Ramin, ?, ca. 1800–1828, French composer, 89
Randhartinger, Benedict, 1802–1893, Austrian composer, 241
Rastrelli, Joseph, 1799–1842, German composer, 175
Ratzenberger, Th., 19th century German composer, 175
Rauchenecker, Georges, 19th century French composer, 89
Rauski, Joseph, 19th century French composer, 90
Raux, Jules, 19th century French composer, 90
Ravizza, F., 19th century French composer, 90
Rawlings, A. W. [see Florence Fare]

Raynaud, ?, 19th century French composer, 90
Reckling, August, 1843–1900, German composer, 175
Recoux, Charles, 19th century French composer, 90
Reeves, D. W., 19th century American composer, 139
Régent, D., 19th century French composer, 90
Regnier Canaux, 19th century publisher in Paris, 36
Reh, Hermann (ca. 1860), German composer, 175
Reicha, Antoine, 1770–1836 composer, 90
Reill, Josef, 1793–1865, German composer, 175
Reinecke, Carl, 1824–1910, German composer, 175
Reinhardt, C., Jr., German composer, 175
Reissigler, G. C., 19th century English composer, 278
Reissinger, Carl, 1798–1859, German composer, 175
Relle, M., 19th century English composer, 278
Renard, Pierre, 19th century French composer, 90
Renault, 19th century French composer, 1
Requin, L., 19th century French composer, 90
Reuland, H., 19th century French composer, 91
Reuss, August, 1871–1935, German composer, 175
Reyloff, Ed., 19th century English composer, 278
Reynaud, J., 19th century French composer, 91
Reynaud, Louis, 19th century French composer, 91
Rheinberger, Josef, 1839–1901, German composer, 175
Ribaute, 19th century publisher in Paris, 4
Richard, Charles, 19th century French composer, 91
Richard, J., 19th century French composer, 91
Richart, Alfred, 19th century French composer, 92
Richault, 19th century publisher in Paris, 7, 61, 88, 109, 163
Riche, J. B., 19th century English composer, 279
Richer, H., 19th century French composer, 92
Richoux, L., 19th century French composer, 92
Richter, Pius, (1880), Austrian composer, 241
Riedel, A., 19th century French composer, 92
Riefenstahl, C., (1858), as arr., 257
Riegel, as arranger, 256
Rieger, Gottfried, 1764–1855, composer, 176, 241
Rièl, Léon, 19th century French composer, 92
Ries, Ferdinand, 1784–1838, German composer, 176
Riess, ?, 19th century German composer, 176
Rieter, 19th century publisher in Leipzig, 178
Riki, Vaclav, 19th century Czech composer, 241
Rillé, Laurent, 19th century French composer, 92
Rinck, Johann, 1770–1846, Ger. composer, 176ff
Ritiez, B., 19th century French composer, 92
Ritz, Jean, 19th century French composer, 92
Rival, L., 19th century French composer, 92
Rivet, H., 19th century French composer, 92
Rivetti, Giovanni, 19th century composer, 92
Riviere, J., 19th century French composer, 92
Robert, A., 19th century French composer, 93
Robert, E., 19th century French composer, 93
Robertson, G. P., 19th century English composer, 279
Roche, Gustave, 19th century French composer, 93

Röder, Georg, 19th century Austrian composer, 242
Rodes, Oscar, 19th century French composer, 93
Rodet, Auguste, 19th century French composer, 93
Roedeberk, ?, 19th century English composer, 279
Roeder, O., 19th century English composer, 279
Rogers, ?, 1800–1828, French composer, 93
Rohde, 19th century publisher in Paris, 5
Rohner, ?, 19th century German composer, 177
Rollé, Emile, 19th century French composer, 93
Romain, F., 19th century French composer, 93
Röntgen, Julius, b. 1829, Dutch composer, 125
Rose, G., 19th century German composer, 177
Rosenkranz, Anton, 19th century Austrian composer, 242
Rosenkranz, Fr., 19th century German composer, conductor, 27th Inf. Regiment, 177
Rosenstein, T., 19th century English composer, 279
Rosiniack, as arranger, 222ff
Rossberg, G., 19th century German composer, 177
Rossini, Gioacchino, 1792–1868, Italian composer, 94
Rossini, arranged for band, 2, 19, 28, 58, 113, 142, 143, 149, 163, 166, 180, 181, 186, 189, 196, 199, 256
Rosulek, Antonin, 19th c. Czech composer, 242
Rothe, ?, 1800–1828, German composer, 177
Rothe, composer, 143
Rouart-Lerolle, 19th century publisher in Paris, 36, 71, 94
Rouquet, Felix, 19th century French composer, 94
Roussel, Albert, 1869–1937, French composer, 94
Roussel, C., 19th century French composer, 94
Routier, L., 19th century French composer, 94
Rouvayre et Leblont, 19th century publisher in Paris, 156
Rouveirol, F., 19th century French composer, 94
Rouveirolis, H., 19th century French composer, 94
Roux, Emile, 19th century French composer, 95
Roux, Jacques, 19th century French composer, 95
Rova, Giovanni, 19th century Italian composer, 121
Roÿ, Charles de, 19th century French composer, 95
Royle, Thomas, 19th century English composer, 279
Rozan, Charles, de, 19th century French composer, 95
Ruhl, Hans, 19th century German composer, 177
Rumler, ?, 1800–1828, German composer, 177
Rumler, Jean, b. 1780, French composer, 95
Rummel, Christian, 1787–1849, German composer, 178
Ruppert, ?, 19th century German composer, 178
Ruscheweyn, E., 19th century German composer, 178
Ruzitska, Georg (1837) Hungarian composer 242
Ruzni, ?, 19th century Austrian composer, 242
Ryembault, ?, 19th century French composer, 95

## S

Sabel, Carl, 19th century German composer, 178
Sachse, C., 19th century German composer, 178
Saint-André, A., 19th century French composer, 95
Saint-Saëns, Charles, 1835–1921, French composer, 95

Salieri, (Overture to *Palmyra*), arr. Schmitt for band, 200
Salis, E., 19th century French composer, 96
Salomez, Charles, 19th century French composer, 96
Sambin, V., 19th century French composer, 96
Samuel, Adolphe, 1824–1898, Belgium composer 260
Sandra, P. A., 19th century French composer, 96
Santner, Karl, 19th century Austrian composer, 242
Santner, Karl, 19th century German composer, 178
Sarrè, François, 19th century French composer, 96
Sarrus, A., 19th century French composer, 96
Sartorius, G., 19th century German composer, 178
Sauer, ?, 19th century German composer, 178
Sauer, Ignaz, (ca. 1825), Austrian composer, 242
Sauvagniac, H., 19th century French composer, 96
Sauvan, F., fils, 19th century French composer, 96
Savari, ?, 19th century French composer, conductor Musique au 34e, 97
Sax, 19th century publisher in Paris, 42, 97
Sax, Adolphe, 42
Sazenhofer, 19th century German composer, 141
Scala, Francis, 19th century American composer, 139
Schaffner, ?, 1800–1828, French composer, 97
Schallehn, ?, 19th century English composer, 279
Schaller, ?, 19th century French composer, 97
Schaller, J., 19th century French composer, 97
Schandl, Franz, 19th century Austrian composer, 242
Scheibl, Johann, 19th century Czech composer, 242
Schepper, L.-J., 19th century French composer, 97
Schenk, Johann, 1753–1836, Austrian composer, 242
Scherrer, H., b. 1865, German composer, 178
Scherzer, ?, 19th century German composer, 178
Scherzer, A. P., 19th century German composer, 178
Schick, F., as arranger, 142
Schiedermayer, arranged for band, 256
Schiedermayr, Johann, 19th century Austrian composer, 243
Schier, 19th century French composer, 101
Schiller, German poet, 168, 177
Schilling, Hans, b. 1869, German composer, 178
Schillings, Max von, 1868–1933, Ger. composer, 178
Schiltz, ?, 19th century French composer, 97
Schindlocker, M., 19th century Austrian composer, 243
Schlesinger, 19th century publisher in Paris, 1, 35
Schlesinger, 19th century publisher in Berlin, 162, 169, 171, 173, 192
Schletterer, Hans, 1824–1893, German composer, 178
Schlier, Johann, 19th century Austrian composer, 243
Schlosser, Augsburg, 162
Schmacht, F., 19th century German composer, hornist, Füsilier-Bataillion de Duke de Braunsweig Inf. Reg. Nr. 92, 179
Schmid, Josef, b. 1868, German composer, 179
Schmidt, A., 19th century publisher in Boston and Leipzig, 160

Schmidt, E., 19th century German composer, 179
Schmidt, G., 19th century English composer, 279
Schmidt, Henri, 19th century French composer, 97
Schmidt, Henri, 97
Schmiedecke, A., 19th century German composer, 179
Schmitt, Alois, 19th century German composer, 179
Schmitt, Geo., as arr., 391
Schnabel, Joseph, 1767–1831, German composer, 179
Schneider, ?, 19th century German composer, arranger, 179, 180, 181
Schneider, Anton, 19th century German composer, and leader, 179, 180
Schneider, Friedrich, 1786–1853, German composer, 181
Schneider, G. A., 19th century German composer, 141
Schneider, Georg, 1770–1839, German composer, 181
Schneider, Harmann, b. 1862, German composer, 181
Schneider, Julius, 19th century German composer, 182
Schneider, Louis, 19th century French composer, 97
Schneklud, Ad., 19th century French composer, 97
Scholl, W., 19th century German composer, 182
Scholz, Bernhard, 1835–1916, German composer, 182
Schönemann, ?, 19th century German composer, 182
Schott, 19th century publisher in Mainz, 90, 148ff, 155, 159, 162, 163, 164, 165, 172, 183, 185, 186, 188, 189, 192, 195, 234
Schrammel, J., 19th century French composer, 97
Schreck, Gustav, 1849–1918, German composer, 182
Schreck, P., 19th century German composer, 182
Schreiner, Adolf, 19th century German composer, 182
Schröder, F., 19th century German composer, 182
Schroll, Ludwig, 19th century German composer, 182
Schubert [arranged], 14
Schubert, Franz, 62
Schubert, F. L. (brother to Franz Schubert, as arr., 198
Schubert, Ferdinand, 1794–1859, Austrian composer, 244
Schubert, Franz, 1797–1828, Austrian composer, 243
Schubert, Raoul, 19th century French composer, 98
Schuberth, 19th century publisher in Hamburg, 227
Schultz, ?, 19th century German composer, 182
Schultz, Th., 19th century French composer, 98
Schulz, Christian, 1773–1827, German composer, 182
Schumann, Robert, 1810–1856, German composer, 55, 182
Schwarer, Ph., 19th century French composer, 98
Schwartz, ?, 19th century French composer, 98
Schwartz, Ad., 19th century French composer, 98
Schwartz, K., 19th century French composer, 98
Schwarz, A., 19th century German composer, 182
Schwarz, M., 19th century Austrian composer, 244
Schwencke, Christian, 1767–1822, German composer, 182
Schweska, H., 19th century French composer, 98
Sciers, Dominique, 19th century French composer, 98
Scontrino, Antonio, 1850–1922, Italian composer, 121
Scrépel, Carlos, 19th century French composer, 98

Seelicke, 19th century German composer, 142
Seeling, 19th century publisher in Dresden, 165
Sega, A., 19th century French composer, 98
Seghers, Frédéric, 19th century French composer, 98
Seidel, ? 19th century Austrian composer, 244
Seidel, Arthur, 19th century German composer, arranger, 183, 198
Seifer, R., 1800–1828, German composer, 183
Seifert, Anton, 19th century English composer, 279
Seiff, J., 19th century German composer, 183
Seiffert, ?, 19th century Austrian composer, 244
Seiller, Franz, 19th century German composer, 183
Sellenik, 19th century French composer, conductor, 2e Régiment de Voltigeurs de la Garde Impériale, 1
Sellenik, Ad., 19th century French composer, conductor Musique 2e Regiment de Voltigeurs de la Garde Imperiale, 98
Sellner, Josef, .19th century Austrian composer, 244
Selmair, Franz, d. 1888, German composer, 183
Selmer, Johan, 1844–1910, Norway composer, 127
Selter, H., 19th century French composer, 99
Selva, as arranger, 254
Senée, Henri, 19th century French composer, 99
Serfert, A., 19th century French composer, 99
Serpette, Gaston, 19th century French composer, 99
Setaccioli, Giacomo, 1868–1925, Italian composer, , 121
Sévérény, H.-A., 19th century French composer, 99
Seydel, Oscar, ?, 19th century English composer, 279
Seyfried, Ignaz, 1776–1841, Austrian composer, arranger, 245, 254
Seyler, Josef, 19th century Austrian composer, 245
Shipman, W. H., 19th century American composer, 139
Sibelius, Jan, b. 1865, Finnish composer, 123
Sibillot, Charles, 19th century French composer, 100
Sieber, 19th century publisher in Paris, 31, 48, 62, 77
Siebert, E., 19th century German composer, 183
Siegbert, S., 19th century German composer, 183
Siégrist, ?, 19th century French composer, 100
Signard, ?, 19th century French composer, 100
Signard, P., 19th century French composer, 100
Simiot, André, 19th century French composer, 100
Simon, 19th century publisher in Paris, 5
Simon, Anton, b. 1851, French composer, 100
Simrock, 19th century publisher in Berlin, 165
Simrock, 19th century publisher in Bonn, 90, 147, 155, 160, 183, 186, 235
Sinoquet, E., 19th century French composer, 100ff
Sinsoilliez, Adolphe, 19th century French composer, 101
Skroup, Jan, 1811–1892, Austrian composer, 245
Snel, Joseph, 1793–1861, Belgium composer, conductor, Société Royale de la Grande-harmonie (1831), 260
Sohier, Henry, 19th century French composer, 101
Soland, 19th century French composer, 2
Soler, Francisco, Spanish composer, 131
Solère, ?, 19th century French composer, 101
Sombrun, Alexis, 19th century French composer, 101
Sonneleiter, Antonius, 19th century Austrian composer, 245
Sor, Joseph Fernando, 1778–1839, Spanish composer, 131
Sousa, John Philip, 19th century American composer, 139
Souyeux, E., 19th century French composer, 101
Sowinski, A., arr. Berr, fl. 1800–1828, German composer, 183
Soyer, Adolphe, 19th century French composer, conductor Musique 109e de Ligne, 101
Späth, André, 1790–1876, German composer, 183
Splichal, Jan, 19th century Czech composer, 245
Spohr, Ludwig, 1784–1859, German composer, 180, 184
Spontini, Gasparo, 1774–1851, Italian composer, 184
Spontini, works arranged for band, 141, 180
Springer, ?, 19th century Austrian composer, 246
St. Leger, W. N., 19th century English composer, 279
Stackelberg, 19th century German composer, 141f
Stadler, J., 1800–1828, Austrian composer, 246
Stadler, Maximilian, 1748–1833, Austrian composer, 246
Stager, 19th century French composer, 72
Standhaft, H. F., 19th century English composer, 279
Stanford, Charles, 1852–1924, English composer, 279
Stappen, A., 19th century French composer, 102
Starke, Friedrich, 1774–1835, Austrian composer, arranger, 196, 246, 254
Stasny, ?, 19th century English composer, 279
Stechi, Antonine, 19th century Austrian composer 247
Steffens, Fr., 19th century German composer, 184
Steibelt, 19th century German composer, 141
Steinacker, 19th century German composer, 180
Steiner, Ernst, 19th century Austrian composer, , 246
Steiner, 19th century publisher in Vienna 209, 211, 218, 219, 220ff, 227, 240, 243, 254
Sténosse, Ed., 19th century French composer, 102
Stich, Josef, 19th century German composer, 185
Stock, Christoph, b. 1862, German composer, 185
Storch, Anton (1838), German composer, 185
Storck, ?, 19th century German composer, 185
Stössel, ?, fl. 1800–1828, German composer, 185
Stoupan, F., 19th century French composer, arranger, 102
Strauss (Johann), (arranged) 186
Strauss, arranged for band, 256
Strauss, E., 19th century Austrian composer, 247
Strauss, J., 253
Strauss, Johann, 1804–1848, 247
Strauss, Johann, arranged for band, 257
Strauss, Josef, 1827–1870, Austrian composer, 247
Strauss, Richard, 1864–1949, German composer, 185
Streck, P., 19th century Austrian composer, 246
Streck, Peter (ca. 1833), 19th century German composer, 186
Streicher, Nanette (née Stein), 1800–1828, German composer, 186

Strepponi, Feliciano, 1767–1832, Italian composer, 121
Strobe, Heinrich, 19th century Austrian composer, 247
Stumpf, Johann, 19th century German composer, 180, 186
Stuntz, Joseph, 1793–1859, Ger. composer, 186
Stupfler, Ph., 19th century French composer, 102
Sudessi, P., 19th century French composer, 102
Sudre, ?, 19th century French composer, 102
Suppé, Franz von, arranged for band, 257
Suppé, Franz, 1819–1895, 19th century Austrian composer, 247
Suzanne, Marius, 19th century French composer, 102
Swoboda, ?, 19th century Austrian composer, 247
Sydow, Herrn v., German composer, 192
Sykora, Franz, arranged for band, 257
Sylvani van, Dutch student of Mozart, composer, 125

## T

Taffnel, French flutist, 67
Tag, Christian, 1777–1839, German composer, 187
Tanejew, Alexander, 1850–1915, Russian composer, 135
Tebaldini, Giovanni, 1864–1952, Italian composer, 121
Teike, Carl, 1864–1922, German composer, 187
Teissier, A., 19th century French composer, 102
Theny, Jan, 19th century Austrian composer, 247
Therese, 19th century Queen of Bavaria, 182
Théret, G., 19th century French composer, 102
Theuss, ?, fl. 1800–1828, German composer, 143, 187
Thiabot, Victor, 19th century French composer, 102
Thiele, Eduard, 19th century Austrian composer, 247
Thomas, C. S., 19th century English composer, 279
Thomas, J., 19th century French composer, 103
Thomas, P. J., 19th century German composer, 188
Thomas, P., 19th century French composer, 103
Tilliard, Geroges, 19th century French composer, 103ff
Tinet, Charles, 19th century French composer, 104
Tinney, F. G., 19th century English composer, 280
Titl, A. E., arranged for band, 257
Titl, Anton, 1809–1882, German composer, 188
Titoff, 19th century German composer, 141
Tollet, A.-E., 19th century French composer, 104
Tollet, Edouard, 19th century French composer, 104
Tomásek, Vaclav, 1774–1850, 19th century Czech composer, 247
Török, Francesco (1858), as arr., 257
Tost, Frantisek, 19th century Czech composer, 247
Tourey, Charles, 19th century French composer, 105
Tourneur, L., 19th century French composer, 105
Tournier, 19th century publisher in Paris, 1
Traut, M., 19th century French composer, 1
Trautwein, 19th century publisher in Berlin, 181
Trautzl, Jacob, 19th century Austrian composer, 247
Trave, D., 19th century French composer, 105
Tréfouel, E., 19th century French composer, 105
Trefz, V., 19th century French composer, 105
Triebensee, Joseph, 19th century Austrian composer, 248
Trottier, A., 19th century French composer, 105
Trousseau, Charles, 19th century French composer, 105
Truelove, J., 19th century French composer, 105
Trusson, A., 19th century French composer, 105
Tschaikowsky, Peter, 1840–1893, Russian composer, 135
Tschirch, Ernst, 19th century German composer, 188
Tschirch, Rudolf, (1868), German composer, 188
Tual, Théophile, 19th century French composer, 105
Tucek, Vincenc, 19th century Czech composer, 250
Tuch, Heinrich, 1766–1821, German composer, 188
Tuerlinckx, Corneille, 1783–1850, Belgium composer, conductor in Mechlin, 260
Tulon, ?, 19th century French composer, 105
Turine, V., 19th century French composer, 105

## U

Ulrich, E., fl. 1800–1828, German composer, 188
Unrath, ?, 19th century French composer, 105

## V

Vaillant, ?, fl. 1800–1828 French composer, 106
Valenta, Bedrich, d. 1934, Hungarian composer, 251
Valenti, A., 19th century French composer, 106
Valentin (1844), as arranger, 255
Valentin, Léon, 19th century French composer, 106
Van Berghe, Carl, 19th century French composer, 106
Van Buggenhout, Ed., 19th century French composer, 106
Van Campenhout, François, 19th century French composer, 106
Van Wedingen, J., 19th century French composer, 106
Vanremoortel, A., 19th century French composer, 106
Vanremoortel, Michel, 19th century French composer, 106
Varlet, A., 19th century French composer, 106
Vasely (Wessely), Thad, 19th century Czech composer, 251
Vasseillière, fils, 19th century French composer, 106
Vasseur, J., 19th century English composer, 280
Verbregge, Auguste, 19th century French composer, 107
Verdi, arranged for band, 28, 257
Verdier, J., 19th century French composer, 107
Verhulst, Johannes, 1816–1891, Dutch composer, 125
Verleye, ?, 19th century French composer, 107
Vern, ?, fl. 1800–1828, century French composer, 107
Vern, Auguste, 19th century German composer, 180, 188
Vernazobres, C. Z., 19th century French composer, 107
Vernet, H., 19th century French composer, 107
Viallon, J., 19th century French composer, professor of composition, Gymnase-musical-militaire, 1
Viallon, Justinien, 19th century French composer, professor of composition at the Gymnasse Musical Militaire and the College de Vaugirard, 107

Victoria, Queen of England, 192
Vidal, H., 19th century French composer, 107
Vidal, Paul, 19th century French composer, 107
Videix, Paul, 19th century French composer, 107
Vié, L., 19th century French composer, 107
Villebichot, P., 19th century French composer, 108
Vincent, Henri, 19th century French composer, 108
Vincent, R., 19th century French composer, 108
Vineux, P.-E., 19th century French composer, 108
Viney, Victor, 19th century French composer, 108
Violetta, Gregorio, 19th century French composer, 108
Violot, Antony, 19th century French composer, 108
Virenque, ?, 19th century French composer, 108
Vitásek (Witasek), Jan, 1770–1839, Czech composer, 251
Vivian, L., 19th century English composer, 280
Vivier, ?, 19th century French composer, 108
Vivier, A., 19th century French composer, 108
Vobaron, ?, 1800–1828, 19th century French composer, 109
Vogel, 19th century German composer, 141
Vogler, C., 19th century English composer, 280
Vogt, Gustave, 1781–1870, French composer, arranger, 109, 180
Voight, 19th century composer published in England, 263
Voigt, Marie, 19th century French composer, 109
Vojacek, H, 19th century Czech composer, arranger, 251, 254, 255, 256
Volke, ?, 19th century German composer, 188
Volkert, Frantisek, 19th century Czech composer, 251
Vollstedt, Robert, 1854–1919, German composer, 188
Vos, Camille, 19th century French composer, 109
Vulder, J. de, 19th century French composer, 109

## W

Wachs, Paul, 19th century Italian composer, 121
Wacker, Charles, 19th century French composer, 109
Waddell, James, 19th century English composer, 280
Waele, Ed., de, 19th century French composer, 109
Wagner [dedication], 161
Wagner, ?, 1800–1828, German composer, 189
Wagner, F. A., 19th century German composer, 189
Wagner, Franz J., 19th century Austrian composer, arranger, 252, 254
Wagner, Richard, 19th century German composer, 189
Wagner, Richard, arranged for band, 39, 94, 113, 122, 200, 258
Walch, Johann, as arr., 189
Waldeck, Karl (1874) Austrian composer, 252
Waldteufel, E., 19th century composer, 280
Waley, Simon, 19th century English composer, 280
Wallerstein, F., 19th century French composer, 109
Walrand, J., 19th century French composer, 109
Walter, ?, 19th century composer, 253
Walter, Albert, d. 1860, French composer, 109
Wangemann, ?, fl. 1800–1828, German composer, 190

Wanisek, Otto, 19th century Austrian composer, 252
Warmuth, C., 19th century German composer, 190
Waterson, James, 19th century French composer, Bandmaster 1er Life Guards, 109
Watier, ?, 19th century French composer, 109
Watson, William, 19th century English composer, 280
Webb, William, 19th century English/ American composer, 139, 280
Weber, Bernhard, 1766–1821, German composer, 190
Weber, Carl, 1786–1826, German composer, 190
Weber, works arranged for band, 55, 114, 149, 163, 177, 178, 180, 186, 189, 196, 201
Weber, Friedrich, 1766–1842, Austrian composer, 252
Weber, Jacob, 1779–1839, German composer, 192
Weber, S. J., as arranger, 197
Weber, Wilhelm. 19th century Austrian composer, 252
Weger, 19th century publisher in Brixen, 169
Weigl, ?, 216
Weigl, J., (1818) Austrian composer, 252
Weigl, Josef, works arr. for band, 201
Weill, Karl, 19th century English composer, 280
Weilland, 19th century English composer, 280
Weinlich (1845), as arranger, 256
Weiss, Heinrich, 19th century German composer, 192
Weller, F., 1800–1828, German composer, 142, 192
Welter, Louis, 19th century French composer, 110
Wenusch, Stanislaus, 19th century Austrian composer, 252
Wenzel, Edovard, 19th century German composer, 192
Werkmeister, Rudolf, (1804) German composer, 192
Weschke, Paul, 19th century German composer, 192
West, Alfred, 19th century English composer, 280
Wettge, Gustave, 19th century French composer, conductor Musique de la Garde Républicaine, 110
Wettge, Léon, 19th century French composer, conductor, Musique du genie en retraite, Chavalier de la legion d'Honneur, 110
Weyr, F. W. (1857), as arranger, 257
Widor, Charles, 1845–1937, French composer, 110
Wiedemann, Josef, 19th century Austrian composer, 252
Wieprecht, Wilhelm, 1802–1872, German composer, 143, 170, 192ff
Wilhelm I, Kaiser, 152 [funeral, 1864], 171, 175
Wilhelm II, Kaiser (1891), 160
Wilhelm von Prussia (and Princess Auguste von Saxe-Weimar, 1829), 184
Wilk von, ?, 19th century German composer, 194
Williams, Warwick, 19th century English composer, 280
Winkelmayer, ?, 1800–1828, German composer, 194
Winkler, Johann, 19th century Austrian composer, 252
Winkler, Martin, 19th century Austrian composer, 252
Winter, Peter, arranged for band, 158, 258
Witt, ?, 1800–1828, German composer, 194
Wittassek, August (1843), Austrian composer, 252

Witte, Johann, 19th century Austrian composer, arranger, 253, 255
Wittmann, ?, 19th century French composer, 111
Wittmann, G., fils, 19th century French composer, 111
Wittmann, J.-B., 19th century French composer, 111
Witzleben von, ?, 19th century German composer, 195
Witzleben, Colonel of a Prussian regiment, 27
Wohlmuth, Andreas, 1809–1884, German composer, 195
Wöhning, S. C., 1800–1828, German composer, , 195
Wolf, Cyrill, 19th century Austrian composer, 253
Wolf, Josef, 19th century Austrian composer, 253
Wölfl, Joseph, 1773–1812, Austrian composer, 253
Wood, James, 19th century English composer, 281
Wormser, Andre, 1851–1926, French composer, 111
Wranitzky, Anton, Jr., 19th century Austrian composer, 253
Wüllner, Franz, 1832–1902, German composer, 195
Wurst, M. L. F., (1824), German composer, 195

# Z

Zaininger, Benedikt, 19th century German composer, 195
Zangl, Josef, 19th century Austrian composer, 253
Zavertal, Josef, 1819–1893, Austrian composer, 253
Zavertal, Ladislao, 1849–1942, Austrian composer, 253
Zavertal, Vaclav, 19th century Austrian composer, 253
Zerezo, Isidore, 19th century Belgium composer 260
Zetter. 19th century publisher in Paris. 90
Zetterquist, L. J., 19th century German composer, 195
Zichy, Graf Geza, 1849–1924, German composer, 195
Ziegler, ?, 19th century French composer, conductor, Musique, 1er Hussards, numerous works for large band, 111ff
Ziehrer, ?, 19th century English composer, 281
Ziehrer, Carl, 19th century Austrian composer, 253
Zierfuss, 19th century publisher in Munich 175
Zifra, Antonio, 19th century Italian composer, 121
Zikoff, ?, 19th century English composer, 281
Zimmermann, 19th century French composer, 112
Zimmermann, Carl, (1847) German composer, 195
Zincaarelli, arranged for band, 258
Zingarelli, 19th century composer, 141
Zitek, ?, 19th century Austrian composer, 253
Zulehner, Georg, 1770–1841, Ger. composer, 195
Zumsteeg, Jan, 19th century Austrian composer, 253
Zweckstetter, Christoph, 1772–1836, German composer, 195

# About the Author

Dr. David Whitwell is a graduate ('with distinction') of the University of Michigan and the Catholic University of America, Washington DC (PhD, Musicology, Distinguished Alumni Award, 2000) and has studied conducting with Eugene Ormandy and at the Akademie fur Musik, Vienna. Prior to coming to Northridge, Dr. Whitwell participated in concerts throughout the United States and Asia as Associate First Horn in the USAF Band and Orchestra in Washington DC, and in recitals throughout South America in cooperation with the United States State Department.

At the California State University, Northridge, which is in Los Angeles, Dr. Whitwell developed the CSUN Wind Ensemble into an ensemble of international reputation, with international tours to Europe in 1981 and 1989 and to Japan in 1984. The CSUN Wind Ensemble has made professional studio recordings for BBC (London), the Koln Westdeutscher Rundfunk (Germany), NOS National Radio (The Netherlands), Zurich Radio (Switzerland), the Television Broadcasting System (Japan) as well as for the United States State Department for broadcast on its 'Voice of America' program. The CSUN Wind Ensemble's recording with the Mirecourt Trio in 1982 was named the 'Record of the Year' by The Village Voice. Composers who have guest conducted Whitwell's ensembles include Aaron Copland, Ernest Krenek, Alan Hovhaness, Morton Gould, Karel Husa, Frank Erickson and Vaclav Nelhybel.

Dr. Whitwell has been a guest professor in 100 different universities and conservatories throughout the United States and in 23 foreign countries (most recently in China, in an elite school housed in the Forbidden City). Guest conducting experiences have included the Philadelphia Orchestra, Seattle Symphony Orchestra, the Czech Radio Orchestras of Brno and Bratislava, The National Youth Orchestra of Israel, as well as resident wind ensembles in Russia, Israel, Austria, Switzerland, Germany, England, Wales, The Netherlands, Portugal, Peru, Korea, Japan, Taiwan, Canada and the United States.

He is a past president of the College Band Directors National Association, a member of the Prasidium of the International Society for the Promotion of Band Music, and was a member of the founding board of directors of the World Association for Symphonic Bands and Ensembles (WASBE). In 1964 he was made an honorary life member of Kappa Kappa Psi, a national professional music fraternity. In September, 2001, he was a delegate to the UNESCO Conference on Global Music in Tokyo. He has been knighted by sovereign organizations in France, Portugal and Scotland and has been awarded the gold medal of Kerkrade, The Netherlands, and the silver medal of Wangen, Germany, the highest honor given wind conductors in the United States, the medal of the Academy of Wind and Percussion Arts (National Band Association) and the highest honor given wind conductors in Austria, the gold medal of the Austrian Band Association. He is a member of the Hall of Fame of the California Music Educators Association.

Dr. Whitwell's publications include more than 127 articles on wind literature including publications in Music and Letters (London), the London Musical Times, the Mozart-Jahrbuch (Salzburg), and 39 books, among which is his 13-volume *History and Literature of the Wind Band and Wind Ensemble* and an 8-volume series on *Aesthetics in Music*. In addition to numerous modern editions of early wind band music his original compositions include 5 symphonies.

David Whitwell was named as one of six men who have determined the course of American bands during the second half of the 20th century, in the definitive history, *The Twentieth Century American Wind Band* (Meredith Music).

A doctoral dissertation by German Gonzales (2007, Arizona State University) is dedicated to the life and conducting career of David Whitwell through the year 1977. David Whitwell is one of nine men described by Paula A. Crider in *The Conductor's Legacy* (Chicago: GIA, 2010) as 'the legendary conductors' of the 20th century.

'I can't imagine the 2nd half of the 20th century—without David Whitwell and what he has given to all of the rest of us.' Frederick Fennell (1993)

www.ingramcontent.com/pod-product-compliance
Lightning Source LLC
Chambersburg PA
CBHW080534300426
44111CB00017B/2723